# The Selected Works of George J. Benston

VOLUME 2

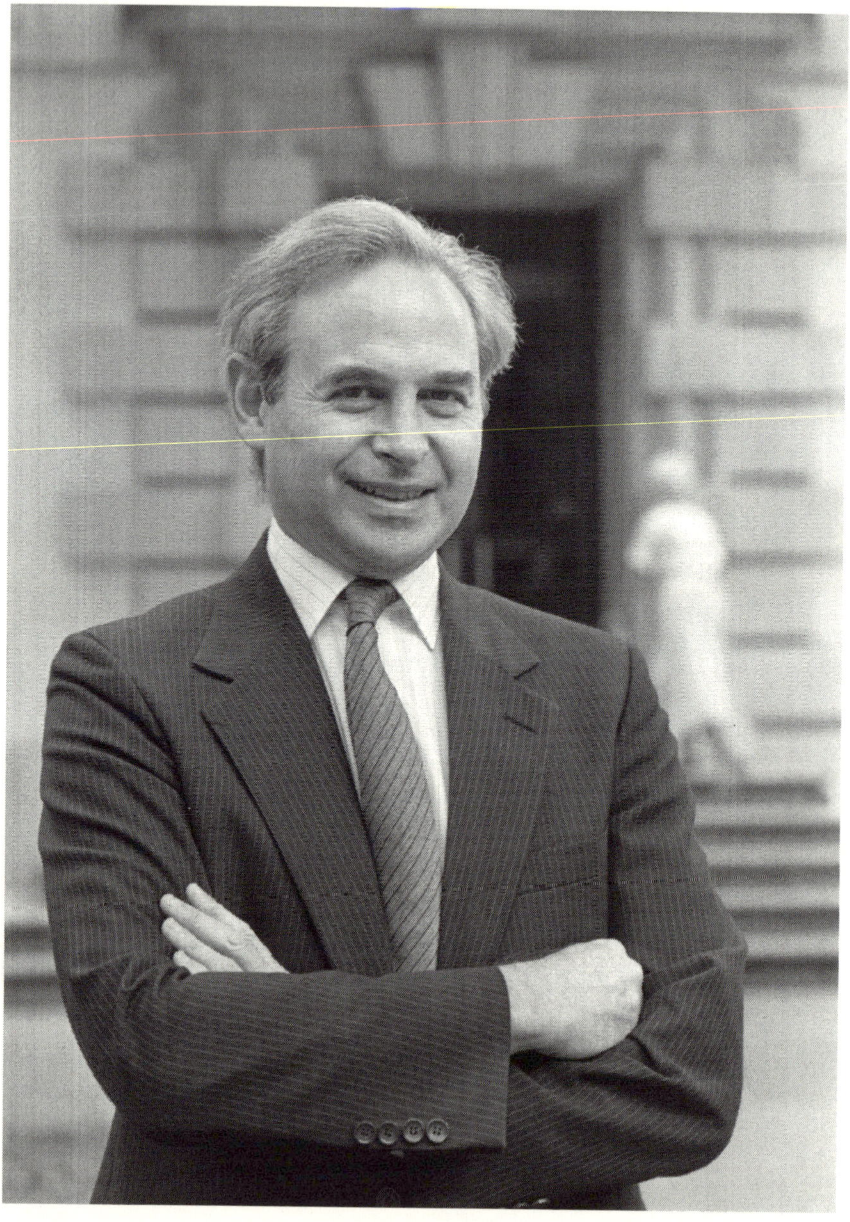

# The Selected Works of George J. Benston

VOLUME 2

Accounting and Finance

*Edited by*
JAMES ROSENFELD

**OXFORD**
UNIVERSITY PRESS
2010

# OXFORD
## UNIVERSITY PRESS

Oxford University Press, Inc., publishes works that further
Oxford University's objective of excellence
in research, scholarship, and education.

Oxford   New York
Auckland   Cape Town   Dar es Salaam   Hong Kong   Karachi
Kuala Lumpur   Madrid   Melbourne   Mexico City   Nairobi
New Delhi   Shanghai   Taipei   Toronto

With offices in
Argentina   Austria   Brazil   Chile   Czech Republic   France   Greece
Guatemala   Hungary   Italy   Japan   Poland   Portugal   Singapore
South Korea   Switzerland   Thailand   Turkey   Ukraine   Vietnam

Copyright © 2010 by Oxford University Press, Inc.

Published by Oxford University Press, Inc.
198 Madison Avenue, New York, New York 10016

www.oup.com

Oxford is a registered trademark of Oxford University Press.

All rights reserved. No part of this publication may be reproduced,
stored in a retrieval system, or transmitted, in any form or by any means,
electronic, mechanical, photocopying, recording, or otherwise,
without the prior permission of Oxford University Press.

Library of Congress Cataloging-in-Publication Data
Benston, George J.
The selected works of George J. Benston / edited by James Rosenfeld.
    p. cm.
Includes bibliographical references and index.
ISBN 978-0-19-538902-9 (v. 2)
1. Banks and banking.   2. Financial services industry.   3. Finance.
I. Rosenfeld, James.   II. Title.
HG1601.B424 2010
332.1—dc22          2009026457

1 3 5 7 9 8 6 4 2
Printed in the United States of America
on acid-free paper

*This collection of Professor Benston's papers is dedicated to his loving wife, Alice Benston; his two sons, Randall and Kimberly; and his many friends and colleagues at Emory University.*

# *Foreword*

GEORGE BENSTON WAS MY FRIEND FOR MUCH OF OUR lives. He was a master of economics, finance, and accounting. No one surpassed him at this combination of disciplines.

George made many contributions. As we think about the use of mark-to-market accounting in the current economic crisis, we recognize how rare his skills were and how valuable his analysis of that issue would be.

George was a skeptic, a very good one. He did not accept popular arguments; he always wanted to evaluate the evidence to see whether it supported popular claims. Often he showed that the facts did not support popular beliefs.

I first met George about 1962 when he was a graduate student at Chicago. I think he came to a job interview at the University of Pittsburgh. He came over to visit and talk. We ended by having dinner. That was the start of our long friendship.

At the time, George was working on two landmark papers. One was his study of the antecedents of the Glass-Steagall Act. He showed that most of the case for the act was based on repeated reference to an unsupported allegation. There was no evidence that the combination of investment and commercial banking contributed to the Great Depression, as the proponents claimed. The second paper was an analysis of the case for banning payment of interest on demand deposits. Again, the proponents supported their charges with unsupported claims that his examination dismissed as incorrect and unfounded.

George's research covered a very large range of issues. Much of it remains highly relevant today. He did careful and valuable work on banking structure, economies of scale, discrimination in lending, deposit insurance, safety and soundness, and much more.

At one point, he was named to the Home Loan Bank Board. His research record frightened key members of Congress, who had to approve his appointment. They did not want a skeptical George Benston looking closely at the regulation of savings and loans or their relation with members of Congress.

One of George's major successes is FDICIA, the Federal Deposit Insurance Corporation Improvement Act. At a conference on banking problems, George Benston and George Kaufman proposed a way to reduce or possibly eliminate the cost to the public of financial failures. They called it "early intervention" and proposed steps that regulators should take to reorganize failing financial firms. The presentation was timely. Lenient Federal Reserve policies allowed banks to function long past the point at which their capital was exhausted. The result was higher claims and payments by the FDIC. To avoid the need for a possible bailout of the FDIC, Congress adopted a weaker version of early intervention.

George's life had three centers of interest: work, art, and family. He was great at each of them. We will miss him.

Allan H. Meltzer

# *Preface*

IT IS AN HONOR TO BE THE EDITOR of a two-volume collection of George Benston's academic work. The selection of these essays was no small task. George was a remarkable scholar in both the range of his interests and the breadth of his accomplishments. Simply put, he was a world-class scholar in the fields of banking, economics, accounting, and finance, with more than 100 articles published in the professional journals. In addition, George authored or coauthored 7 books and 14 monographs. It was therefore necessary to assemble a group of people in each of these areas to assist me in the selection process.

For volume 2, which comprises his major work in accounting and finance, we enlisted the services of Greg Waymire (Emory University) and Rashad Abdel-Khalik (University of Illinois) to select essays from the accounting literature. Similar to volume 1, we do not have a special section on policy matters, since the selected essays incorporate most of these issues. This is best demonstrated in his essay titled "Required Disclosure and the Stock Market: An Evaluation of the Securities Exchange Act of 1934" (*American Economic Review*, 1973). In this essay, George conducted empirical work on major policy issues concerning the Securities Exchange Act of 1934. His essay on "Published Corporate Accounting Data and Stock Prices" (*Journal of Accounting Research*, 1967) was a groundbreaking article that showed the relationship between corporate earnings and stock prices. It was the first major publication in the accounting literature on this important topic, a fact that many accounting scholars are unaware of. George's essay "Multiple Regression Analysis of Cost Behavior" (*Accounting Review*, 1966), which shows how a sophisticated statistical tool can be used to estimate cost functions and evaluate corporate performance, further demonstrates the breadth of his academic interests. George was naturally drawn to controversial issues, so we include his essay "Fair-Value Accounting: A Cautionary Tale from Enron" (*Journal of Account-*

*ing and Public Policy*, 2006). He points out that Enron's use (or misuse) of fair-value accounting rules was primarily responsible for its demise. His essay "DAAM: The Demand for Alternative Accounting Measurements" (*Journal of Accounting Research*, 1978) was chosen because George was adamant about the selection bias in survey data, a view he held his entire academic career. George wrote extensively on issues relating to accounting and financial disclosures. Accordingly, we include "Public (U.S.) Compared to Private (U.K.) Regulation of Corporate Financial Disclosure" (*Accounting Review*, 1976) and another publication titled "The Value of the SEC's Accounting Disclosure Requirements" (*Accounting Review*, 1969). His final essays in this part, "Financial Reporting of Derivatives: An Analysis of the Issues, Evaluation of Proposals, and a Suggested Solution" (*Journal of Financial Engineering*, 1995) and "Principles- versus Rules-Based Accounting Standards: The FASB's Standard Setting Strategy" (*Abacus*, 2006) further demonstrate his research versatility.

The second part of volume 2 is devoted to George's publications in the finance literature. The selectors include Lemma Senbet (University of Maryland) and myself. Similar to his scholarly work in banking and accounting, George's research interests in finance were broad and dealt with issues that were quite controversial. In the area of consumer finance, he published a number of articles that were well cited in the literature. "Risk on Consumer Finance Company Personal Loans" (*Journal of Finance*, 1977) investigates the principal factors responsible for the loan losses experienced by consumer finance companies. He wrote a companion essay titled "Rate Ceiling Implications of the Cost Structure of Consumer Finance Companies" (*Journal of Finance*, 1977), where he shows that the ceiling rates of interest permitted by state small loan laws for consumer cash loans are inversely rated to the loan size. This finding suggests that the size-of-loan method of stating ceiling rates is inappropriate. George's work in the area of security transaction costs was also quite extensive. "Determinants of Bid–Asked Spreads in the Over-the-Counter Market" (*Journal of Financial Economics*, 1974) explored the causal factors impacting on the bid–ask spreads of unlisted common stocks. George's last publication was "Why Effective Spreads on NASDAQ Were Higher Than on the New York Stock Exchange in the 1990s" (*Journal of Empirical Finance*, 2008). In it, he challenged the widespread belief that the wider bid–ask spreads on over-the-counter stocks were primarily due to collusion among the NASDAQ market makers. He shows quite convincingly that the principal cause can instead be attributed to the trading activities of a sophisticated group of traders (known as SOES bandits) and that any collusion that took place was of a secondary cause. In the area of bank regulation, we chose two of his essays: "A Transactions Cost Approach to the Theory of Financial Intermediation" (*Journal of Finance*, 1976) and "The Impact of Maturity Regulation on High Interest Rate Lenders and Borrowers" (*Journal of Financial Economics*, 1977). His essay "The Self-Serving Management Hypothesis: Some Evidence" (*Journal of Accounting and Economics*, 1985) showed that corporate managers of conglomerates in the 1970s appeared to act in the best interests of their shareholders. This conclusion was contrary to the popular belief that managers of highly diversified firms were primarily concerned with benefiting themselves at the expense of their shareholders.

Overall, we think that this collection provides the reader with a fairly complete representation of George's academic work in these areas. It is unfortunate that we will never know which future research projects he would have pursued. However, we do know that the issues would have been timely, important, and, above all, extremely challenging. It is an understatement to say that George will be greatly missed by both the academic profession and everyone who was fortunate to know him.

James Rosenfeld

# Contents

| | |
|---|---|
| *Contributors* | xv |
| *Sources* | xvii |

PART I ACCOUNTING

| | |
|---|---|
| 1. Multiple Regression Analysis of Cost Behavior | 3 |
| 2. Published Corporate Accounting Data and Stock Prices | 24 |
| 3. Required Disclosure and the Stock Market: An Evaluation of the Securities Exchange Act of 1934 | 66 |
| 4. Public (U.S.) Compared to Private (U.K.) Regulation of Corporate Financial Disclosure | 97 |
| 5. DAAM: The Demand for Alternative Accounting Measurements *with Melvin A. Krasney* | 116 |
| 6. Fair-Value Accounting: A Cautionary Tale from Enron | 146 |
| 7. The Value of the SEC's Accounting Disclosure Requirements | 165 |
| 8. Financial Reporting of Derivatives: An Analysis of the Issues, Evaluation of Proposals, and a Suggested Solution *with Shehzad L. Mian* | 189 |
| 9. Principles- versus Rules-Based Accounting Standards: The FASB's Standard Setting Strategy *with Michael Bromwich and Alfred Wagenhofer* | 216 |

## PART II FINANCE

10. Determinants of Bid-Asked Spreads in the Over-the-Counter Market   245
    *with Robert L. Hagerman*

11. A Transactions Cost Approach to the Theory of Financial Intermediation   257
    *with Clifford W. Smith Jr.*

12. The Impact of Maturity Regulation on High Interest Rate Lenders and Borrowers   277

13. Risk on Consumer Finance Company Personal Loans   304

14. Rate Ceiling Implications of the Cost Structure of Consumer Finance Companies   321

15. The Self-Serving Management Hypothesis: Some Evidence   352

16. Why Effective Spreads on NASDAQ Were Higher than on the New York Stock Exchange in the 1990s   370
    *with Robert A. Wood*

*Index*   411

# Contributors

GEORGE J. BENSTON, Professor of Finance, Accounting, and Economics, Goizueta Business School, Emory University, Atlanta, Ga.

MICHAEL BROMWICH, Professor of Accounting and Financial Management, London School of Economics, London, England.

ROBERT L. HAGERMAN, Professor of Finance, School of Management, State University of New York, Buffalo, N.Y.

MELVIN A. KRASNEY, Professor of Business Administration and Accounting, University of Rochester Graduate School of Management, Rochester, N.Y.

SHEHZAD MIAN, Associate Professor of Finance, Goizueta Business School, Emory University, Atlanta, Ga.

CLIFFORD W. SMITH JR., Professor of Business Administration and Finance, University of Rochester Graduate School of Management, Rochester, N.Y.

ALFRED WAGENHOFER, Professor of Accounting and Management, University of Graz, Graz, Austria.

ROBERT A. WOOD, Professor of Finance, Fogelman College of Business and Economics, University of Memphis, Memphis, Tenn.

# Sources

Chapter 1: "Multiple Regression Analysis of Cost Behavior." *Accounting Review*. Reprint with permission from American Accounting Association.

Chapter 2: "Published Corporate Accounting Data and Stock Prices." *Journal of Accounting Research*. Reprint with permission from Blackwell Publishing.

Chapter 3: "Required Disclosure and the Stock Market: An Evaluation of the Securities Exchange Act of 1934." *American Economic Review*. Reprint with permission from American Economic Association.

Chapter 4: "Public (U.S.) Compared to Private (U.K.) Regulation of Corporate Financial Disclosure." *Accounting Review*. Reprint with permission from American Accounting Association.

Chapter 5: "DAAM: The Demand for Alternative Accounting Measurements." *Journal of Accounting Research*. Reprint with permission from Blackwell Publishing.

Chapter 6: "Fair-Value Accounting: A Cautionary Tale from Enron." *Journal of Accounting and Public Policy*. Reprint with permission from Elsevier.

Chapter 7: "The Value of the SEC's Accounting Disclosure Requirements." *Accounting Review*. Reprint with permission from the American Accounting Association.

Chapter 8: "Financial Reporting of Derivatives: An Analysis of the Issues, Evaluation of Proposals, and a Suggested Solution." *Journal of Financial Engineering*. Reprint with permission from the American Association of Financial Engineers.

Chapter 9: "Principles- versus Rules-Based Accounting Standards: The FASB's Standard Setting Strategy." *Abacus*. Reprint with permission from Blackwell Publishing.

Chapter 10: "Determinants of Bid–Asked Spreads in the Over-the-Counter Market." *Journal of Financial Economics*. Reprint with permission from Elsevier.

Chapter 11: "A Transactions Cost Approach to the Theory of Financial Intermediation." *Journal of Finance*. Reprint with permission from Blackwell Publishing.

Chapter 12: "The Impact of Maturity Regulation on High Interest Rate Lenders and Borrowers." *Journal of Financial Economics*. Reprint with permission from Elsevier.

Chapter 13: "Risk on Consumer Finance Company Personal Loans." *Journal of Finance*. Reprint with permission from Blackwell Publishing.

Chapter 14: "Rate Ceiling Implications of the Cost Structure of Consumer Finance Companies." *Journal of Finance*. Reprint with permission from Blackwell Publishing.

Chapter 15: "The Self-Serving Management Hypothesis: Some Evidence." *Journal of Accounting and Economics*. Reprint with permission from Elsevier.

Chapter 16: "Why Effective Spreads on NASDAQ Were Higher Than on the New York Stock Exchange in the 1990s." *Journal of Empirical Finance*. Reprint with permission from Elsevier.

# PART I

## ACCOUNTING

# 1

# Multiple Regression Analysis of Cost Behavior

ACCOUNTANTS PROBABLY HAVE ALWAYS BEEN CONCERNED WITH MEASURING and reporting the relationship between cost and output. The preeminence of financial accounting in this century resulted in directing much of our attention toward attaching costs to inventories. However, the recent emphasis on decision making is causing us to consider ways of measuring the variability of cost with output and other decisions variables. In this essay, the application, use, and limitations of multiple regression analysis, a valuable tool for measuring costs, are discussed.[1]

A valid objection to multiple regression analysis in the past has been that its computational difficulty often rendered it too costly. Today, with high-speed computers and library programs, this objection is no longer valid: most regression problems ought to cost less than $30 to run. Unfortunately, this new ease and low cost of using regression analysis may prove to be its undoing. Analysts may be tempted to use the technique without adequately realizing its technical data requirements and limitations. The GI-GO adage, "garbage in, garbage out," always must be kept in mind. A major purpose of this essay is to state these requirements and limitations explicitly and to indicate how they may be handled.

The general problem of cost measurement is discussed in the first section of this essay. Multiple regression analysis is considered first in relation to other methods of cost analysis. Then its applicability to cost decision problems is delineated.

---

[1]. The use of statistical analysis for auditing and control is outside the scope of this essay. Excellent discussions of these uses of statistics may be found in Richard N. Cyert and H. Justin Davidson, *Statistical Sampling for Accounting Information* (Prentice Hall, 1962), and Herbert Arkin, *Handbook of Sampling for Auditing and Accounting, Volume I: Methods* (McGraw-Hill, 1963).

Second, the method of multiple regression is discussed in nonmathematical terms so that its uses can be understood better. The third section represents the "heart" of the essay. Here the technical requirements of multiple regression are outlined, and the implications of these requirements for the recording of cost data in the firm's accounting records are outlined. The functional form of the regression equation is then considered. In the final section, we discuss some applications for multiple regression analysis.

## The General Problem

In his attempts to determine the factors that cause costs to be incurred and the magnitudes of their effects, the accountant is faced with a formidable task. Engineers, foremen, and others who are familiar with the production process being studied usually can provide a list of cost-causing factors, such as the number of different units produced, the lot sizes in which units were made, and so forth. Other factors that affect costs, such as the season of the year, may be important, though they are more subtle than production factors. The accountant must separate and measure the effects of many different causal factors whose importance may vary in different periods.

### Commonly Used Methods of Cost Analysis

Perhaps the most pervasive method of analyzing cost variability is separation of costs into two or three categories: variable, fixed, and sometimes semivariable. But this method does not provide a solution to the problem of measuring the costs caused by each of many factors operating simultaneously. In this "direct costing" type of procedure, output is considered to be the sole cause of costs. Another objection to this method is that there is no way to determine whether the accountant's subjective separation of costs into variable and fixed is reasonably accurate. Dividing output during a period into variable cost during that period yields a single number (unit variable cost) whose accuracy cannot be assessed. If the procedure is repeated for several periods, it is likely that different unit variable costs will be computed. But the accountant cannot determine whether the average of these numbers (or some other summary statistic) is a useful number. Another important shortcoming of this method is the assumption of linearity between cost and output. While linearity may be found, it should not be assumed automatically.

A variant of the fixed-variable method is one in which cost and output data for many periods are plotted on a two-dimensional graph. A line is then fitted to the data, the slope being taken as variable cost per unit of output. When the least-squares method of fitting the line is used, the procedure is called simple linear regression. Until the recent advent of computers, simple regression was considered to be quite sophisticated.[2] While it was recognized that its use neglects the effects on cost of factors other than output, it was defended on the then reasonable grounds that multiple regression with more than two or three variables is too difficult computationally to be considered economically feasible.

## Multiple Regression

Multiple regression can allow the accountant to estimate the amount by which the various cost-causing factors affect costs. A very rough description is that it measures the cost of a change in one variable, say, output, while holding the effects on cost of other variables, say, the season of the year or the size of batches, constant. For example, consider the problem of analyzing the costs incurred by the shipping department of a department store. The manager of the department believes that his costs are primarily a function of the number of orders processed. However, heavier packages are more costly to handle than are lighter ones. He also considers the weather an important factor; rain or extreme cold slows down delivery time. We might want to eliminate the effect of the weather, since it is not controllable. But we would like to know how much each order costs to process and what the cost of heavier against lighter packages is. If we can make these estimates, we can (1) prepare a flexible budget for the shipping department that takes account of changes in operating conditions, (2) make better pricing decisions, and (3) plan for capital budgeting more effectively. A properly specified multiple regression equation can provide the required estimates.

A criticism of multiple regression analysis is that it is complicated, and so would be difficult to "sell" to lower management and supervisory personnel. However, the method allows for a more complete specification of "reality" than do simple regression or the fixed-variable dichotomy. Studies have shown that supervisors tend to disregard data that they believe are "unrealistic," such as those based on the simplification that costs incurred are a function of units of output only.[3] Therefore, multiple regression analysis should prove more acceptable to supervisors than procedures that require gross simplification of reality.

The regression technique also can allow the accountant to make probability statements concerning the reliability of the estimates made.[4] For example, he may find that the marginal cost of processing a package of average weight is $0.756, when

---

2. National Association of Accountants, *Separating and Using Costs as Fixed and Variable*, June 1960.
3. H. A. Simon, H. Guetzkow, G. Kozmetsky, and G. Tyndall, *Centralization versus Decentralization in Organizing the Controllers Department* (New York: Controllership Foundation, 1954).
4. This and the following statements are made in the context of a Bayesian analysis, in which the decision maker combines sample information with his prior judgment concerning unknown parameters. In the examples given, a jointly diffuse prior distribution is assumed for all parameters.

the effects on cost of different weather conditions and other factors are accounted for. If the properties underlying regression analysis (discussed below) are met, the reliability of this cost estimate may be determined from the standard error of the coefficient (say, $0.032) from which the accountant may assess a probability of .95 that the marginal cost per package is between $0.692 and $0.820 (0.756 ± 0.064).

Multiple regression analysis, then, is a very powerful tool; however, it is not applicable to all cost situations. To decide the situations for which it is best used, let us first consider the problem of cost estimation in general and then consider the subclass of problems for which multiple regression analysis is useful.

## Types of Cost Decision Problems

In general, cost is a function of many variables, including time. For example, the cost of output may be affected by such conditions as whether production is increasing or decreasing, the lot sizes are large or small, the plant is new or old, the White Sox are losing or winning, and so forth. Since there is *some* change in the environment of different time periods or in the circumstances affecting different decisions, it would seem that the accountant must make an individual cost analysis for every decision considered.

However, the maximization rule of economics also applies to information technology: the marginal cost of the information must not exceed the marginal revenue gained from it. The marginal revenue from cost information is the additional revenue that accrues or the losses that are avoided from not making mistakes, such as accepting contracts where the marginal costs exceed the marginal revenue from the work, or rejecting contracts where the reverse situation obtains. The marginal cost of information is the cost of gathering and presenting the information, plus the opportunity cost of delay, since measurement and presentation are not instantaneous.[5] Since these costs can be expected to exceed the marginal revenue from information for many decisions, it usually is not economical to estimate different costs for each different decision. Thus, it is desirable to group decision problems into categories that can be served by the same basic cost information. Two such categories are proposed here: (1) recurring problems and (2) one-time problems.

Recurring decision problems are those for which the data required for analysis are used with some regularity. Examples are determining the prices that will be published in a catalog, preparation of output schedules for expected production, the setting of budgets and production cost standards, and the formulation of forecasts. These decisions require cost data in the form of schedules of expected costs due to various levels of activity over an expected range.

---

5. These two costs are related since delay can be reduced by expending more resources on the information system.

One-time problems are those which occur infrequently, unpredictably, or are of such a magnitude as to require individual cost estimates. Examples of these problems are cost-profit-volume decisions, such as whether the firm should take a one-time special order; make, buy, or lease equipment; develop a new product; or close a plant. These decisions require that cost estimates be made which reflect conditions especially relevant to the problem at hand.

These categories present different requirements for cost estimation. Recurring problems require a schedule of *expected* costs and activity. Since these problems are repetitive, the marginal cost of gathering and presenting data each time usually is expected to be greater than the marginal revenue from the data. Thus, while the marginal cost of additional production, for example, will differ depending on such factors as whether overtime is required or excess capacity is available, in general it is more profitable to estimate the amount that the marginal cost of the additional production may be, on the average, rather than to take account of every special factor that may exist in individual circumstances.

In contrast, one-time problems are characterized by the economic desirability of making individual cost estimates. We do not rely on average marginal costs because the more accurate information is worth its cost. This situation may occur when the problem is unique, and average cost data are therefore not applicable. Or the decision may involve a substantial commitment of resources, making the marginal revenue from avoiding wrong decisions quite high.

## Multiple Regression Analysis

Regression analysis is particularly useful in estimating costs for recurring decisions.[6] The procedure essentially consists of estimating mathematically the *average* relationship between costs (the "dependent" variable) and the factors that cause cost incurrences (the "independent" variables). The analysis provides the accountant with an estimate of the expected marginal cost of a unit change in output, for example, with the effects on total cost of other factors accounted for. These are the data he requires for costing recurring decisions.

The usefulness of multiple regression analysis for recurring decisions of costs can be appreciated best when the essential nature of the technique is understood. It is not necessary that the mathematical proofs of least squares or the methods of inverting matrices be learned since library computer programs do all the work.[7]

---

6. Indeed, its use requires the assumption that the past costs used for a regressions analysis are a sample from a universe of possible costs generated by a continuing, stationary, normal process.

7. The mathematics of multiple regression is described in many statistics and econometrics texts.

However, it is necessary that the assumptions underlying use of multiple regression be fully understood so that this valuable tool is not misused.

Multiple regression analysis presupposes a linear relationship between the contributive factors and costs.[8] The functional relationship between these factors, $x_1, x_2, \ldots, x_n$, and cost, $C$, is assumed in multiple regression analysis to be of the following form:

$$C_t = \beta_0 x_{0,t} + \beta_1 x_{1,t} + \beta_2 x_{2,t} + \cdots + \beta_n x_{n,t} + \mu_t, \tag{1.1}$$

where

$\beta_0$ is a constant term ($x_0 = 1$ for all observations and time periods),

the $\beta$'s are fixed coefficients that express the marginal contribution of each $x_i$ to $C$, and

$\mu$ is the sum of unspecified factors, the disturbances, that are assumed to be randomly distributed with a zero mean and constant variance, and $t = 1, 2, \ldots, m =$ time periods.

The $\beta$ coefficients are estimated from a sample of $C$'s and $x$'s from time periods 1 through $m$. For example, assume that the cost recorded in a week is a function of such specified factors as $x_1 =$ units of output, $x_2 =$ number of units in a batch, and $x_3 =$ the ratio of the number of "deluxe" units to total units produced. Then the right-hand side of equation (1.2) is an estimate of the right-hand side of equation (1.1), obtained from a sample of weekly observations, where the $\beta$'s are estimates of the $\beta$'s and $u$ is the residual, the estimate of $\mu$, the disturbance term:

$$C_t = b_{0,t} + b_1 x_{1,t} + b_2 x_{2,t} + b_3 x_{3,t} + u_t. \tag{1.2}$$

If the values estimated for coefficients of the three independent variables, $x_1$, $x_2$, and $x_3$, are $b_0 = 100$, $b_1 = 30$, $b_2 = -20$, and $b_3 = 500$, the expected cost ($\hat{C}$) for any given week ($t$) is estimated by:

$$\hat{C} = 100 + 30 x_1 - 20 x_2 + 500 x_3.$$

Given estimates of the $\beta$'s, one has, in effect, estimates of the marginal cost associated with each of the determining factors. In the example given above, the marginal cost of producing an additional unit of output, $x_1$, is estimated to be $30, with the effects or costs of the size of batch ($x_2$) and the ratio of the number of deluxe to total units ($x_3$) accounted for. Or, $\beta_2$, the marginal reduction in total cost of increasing the batches by three units, given fixed values of the number of units and the relative proportions of deluxe units produced, is estimated to be −$60 (−$20 times 3).

---

8. A curvilinear or exponential relationship also can be expressed as a linear relationship. This technique is discussed below.

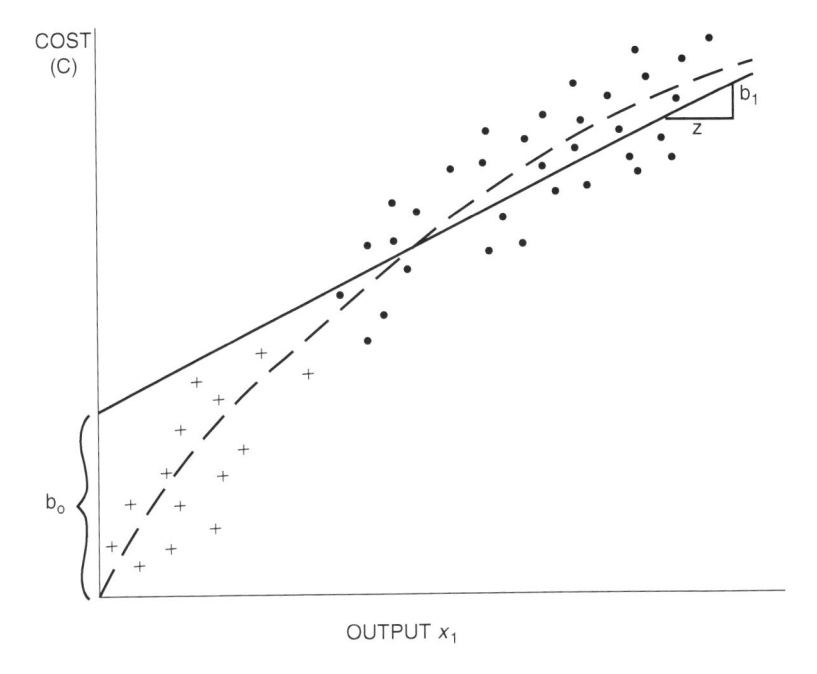

FIGURE 1.1

It is tempting to interpret the constant term, $b_0$, as fixed cost. But this is not correct unless the linear relationship found in the range of observations obtains back to zero output.[9] This can be seen best in the following two-dimensional graph of cost on output (figure 1.1). The line was fitted with the equation $C = b_0 + b_1 x_1$, where the dots are the observed values of cost and output. The slope of the line is the coefficient, $b_1$, an estimate of the marginal change in total cost ($C$) with a unit change ($z$) in output ($x_1$). The intercept on the $C$ axis is $b_0$, the constant term. It would be an estimate of fixed cost if the range of observations included the point where output were zero, and the relationship between total cost and output were linear. However, if more observations of cost and output (the $x$'s) were available, it might be that the dashed curve would be fitted and $b_0$ would be zero. Thus the value of the constant term, $b_0$, is not the costs that would be expected if there were no output; it is only the value that is calculated as a result of the regression line computed from the available data.

9. Fixed cost is defined here as avoidable cost related to time periods and not to output variables.

The data for the calculations are taken from the accounting and production records of past time periods. The coefficients estimated from these data are averages of past experience. Therefore, the $b$'s calculated are best suited for recurring cost decisions. The fact that the $b$'s are averages of past data must be emphasized, because their use for decisions is based on the assumption that the future will be like an average of past experience.

The mathematical method usually used for estimating the $\beta$'s is the least-squares technique. It has the properties of providing best, linear, unbiased estimates of the $\beta$'s. These properties are desirable because they tend "to yield a series of estimates whose average would coincide with the true value being estimated and whose variance about that true value is smaller than that of any other unbiased estimators."[10] While these properties are not always of paramount importance, they are very valuable for making estimates of the expected average costs required for recurring problems.

Another important advantage of the least-squares technique is that when it is combined with the assumptions about the disturbance term ($\mu_t$) that are discussed below, the reliability of the relations between the explanatory variables and costs can be determined. Two types of reliability estimates may be computed. One, the standard error of estimate, shows how well the equation fits the data. The second, the standard error of the regression coefficients, assesses the probability that the $\beta$'s estimated are within a range of values. For example, if a linear cost function is used, the coefficient ($b_1$) of output ($x_1$) is the estimated marginal cost of output. With an estimate of the standard error of the coefficient, $s_{b_1}$, we can say that the true marginal cost, $\beta_1$, is within the range $b_1 \pm s_{b_1}$, with a given probability.[11]

## Requirements of Multiple Regression and Cost Recording Implications

Although multiple regression is an excellent tool for estimating recurring costs, it does have several requirements that make its use hazardous without careful planning.[12] Most of the data requirements of multiple regressions analysis depend on the way cost-accounting records are maintained. If the data are simply taken from the ordinary cost-accounting records of the company, it is unlikely that the output of the regression model will be meaningful. Therefore, careful planning of

---

10. J. Johnston, *Statistical Cost Analysis* (New York: McGraw-Hill, 1960), p. 31.
11. The interpretation of the confidence interval is admittedly Bayesian.
12. Proofs of the requirements described may be found in many econometrics textbooks, such as Arthur S. Goldberger, *Econometric Theory* (Wiley, 1964), and J. Johnston, *Econometric Methods* (McGraw-Hill, 1963).

the extent to which the initial accounting data are coded and recorded is necessary before regression analysis can be used successfully. This section of the essay is organized into four groupings that include several numbered subsections in which the principal technical requirements are described, after which the implications for the cost system are discussed. In the first group, (1) the length and (2) number of time periods, (3) the range of observations, and (4) the specification of cost-related factors are described, following which their implications for cost recording are outlined. In the second group, (5) errors of measurement and their cost recording implication are considered. The third group deals with (6) correlations among the explanatory variables and the important contribution that accounting analysis can make to this problem. Finally, (7) the requirements for the distribution of the nonspecified factors (disturbances) are given. The implications of these requirements for the functional form of the variables are taken up in the last section.

## 1. Length of Time Periods

(a) The time periods (1, 2, 3,..., $m$) chosen should be long enough to allow the bookkeeping procedures to pair output produced in a period with the cost incurred because of that production. For example, if 500 units are produced in a day, but records of supplies used are kept on a weekly basis, an analysis of the cost of supplies used cannot be made with shorter than weekly periods. Lags in recording costs must be corrected or adjusted. Thus, production should not be recorded as occurring in one week while indirect labor is recorded a week later when the paychecks are written.

(b) The time periods chosen should be *short* enough to avoid variations in production within the period. Otherwise, the variations that occur during the period will be averaged out, possibly obscuring the true relationship between cost and output.

## 2. Number of Time Periods (Observations)

For a time series, each observation covers a time period in which data on costs and output and other explanatory variables are collected for analysis. As a minimum, there must be one more observation than there are independent variables to make regression analysis possible. (The excess number is called "degrees of freedom.") Of course, many more observations must be available before one could have any confidence that the relationship estimated from the sample reflects the "true" underlying relationship. The standard errors, from which one may determine the range within which the true coefficients lie (given some probability of error), are reduced by the square root of the number of observations.

## 3. Range of Observations

The observations on cost and output should cover as wide a range as possible. If there is very little variation from period to period in cost and output, the functional relationship between the two cannot be estimated effectively by regression analysis.

## 4. Specification of Cost-Related Factors

All factors that affect cost should be specified and included in the analysis.[13] This is a very important requirement that is often difficult to meet. For example, observations may have been taken over a period when input prices changed. The true relationship between cost and output may be obscured if high output coincided with high input due to price-level effects. If the higher costs related to higher price levels are not accounted for (by inclusion of a price index as an independent variable) or adjusted for (by stating the dependent variable, cost, in constant dollars), the marginal cost of additional output estimated will be meaningful only if changes input prices are proportional to changes in output and are expected to remain so.

## Implications for Cost Recording of 1, 2, 3, and 4

In general, the time period requirements (1a, 1b, and 2) call for the recording of production data for periods no longer than one month and preferably as short as one week in length. If longer periods are chosen, it is unlikely that there will be a sufficient number of observations available for analysis because, as a bare minimum, one more period than the number of explanatory variables is needed. Even if it is believed that only one explanatory variable (such as units of output) is needed to specify the cost function in any one period, requirement 4 (that all cost-related factors be specified) demands consideration of differences among time periods. Thus, such events as changes in factor prices and production methods, whether production is increasing or decreasing, and the seasons of the year might have to be specified as explanatory variables.

The necessity of identifying all relevant explanatory variables such as those just mentioned, can be met by having a journal kept in which the values or the behavior of these variables in specific time periods is noted. If such a record is not kept, it will be difficult (if not impossible) to recall unusual events and to identify them with the relevant time periods, especially when short time periods are used. For example, it is necessary to note whether production increased or decreased substantially in

---

13. Complete specification is not mandatory if requirement 7 (below) is met. However, requirement 7 is not likely to be fulfilled if the specification is seriously incomplete.

each period. Increases in production may be met by overtime. However, decreases may be accompanied by idle time or slower operations. Thus, we would expect the additional costs of increases to be greater than the cost savings from decreases.[14]

Other commonly found factors that affect costs are changes in technology, changes in capacity, periods of adjustment to new processes or types of output, and seasonal differences. The effect of these factors may be accounted for by including variables in the regression equation, by specific adjustment of the data, or by excluding data that are thought to be "contaminated."

The wide range of observations needed for effective analysis also argues against observation periods of longer than one month. With long periods, variations in production would more likely be averaged out than if shorter periods were used (which violates requirement 1b). In addition, if stability of conditions limits the number of explanatory variables other than output that otherwise would reduce the degrees of freedom, this same stability probably would not produce a sufficient range of output to make regression analysis worthwhile. Thus, weekly or monthly data usually are required for multiple regression.

## 5. Errors of Measurement

It is difficult to believe that data from a "real-life" production situation will be reported without error. The nature of the errors is important since some kinds will affect the usefulness of regression analysis more than others will. Errors in the dependent variable, cost, are not fatal since they affect the disturbance term, $\mu$.[15] The predictive value of the equation is lessened, but the estimate of marginal cost ($\beta_1$) is not affected.

But where there are errors in measuring output or the other independent variable ($x$'s), the disturbance term, $\mu$, will be correlated with the independent variables.[16] If this condition exists, the sample coefficient estimated by the least-squares

---

14. A dummy variable can be used to represent qualitative variables, such as $P = 1$ when production increased and $P = 0$ when production decreased. From the coefficient of $P$, we can estimate the cost effect of differences in the direction of output change and also reduce contamination of the coefficient estimated for output.

15. Let $\gamma$ stand for the measurement errors in $C$:

$$C + \gamma = \beta_0 + \beta_1 x_1 + \mu$$
$$C = \beta_0 + \beta_1 x_1 + \mu - \gamma.$$

16. In this event, where $\psi$ stands for the measurement error in $x_1$:

$$C = \beta_0 + \beta_1(x_1 + \psi) + \mu$$
$$C = \beta_0 + \beta_1 x_1 + \beta_1 \psi + \mu.$$

The new disturbance term $\beta_1 \psi + \mu$ is not independent of $x_1$ because of the covariance between these variables.

procedure will be an underestimate of the true marginal cost. Thus, it is very important that the independent variables be measured accurately.

The possibility of measurement errors is intensified by the number of observations requirement. Short reporting periods increase the necessity for careful classification. For example, if a cost caused by production in week 1 is not recorded until week 2, the dependent variable (cost) of both observations will be measured incorrectly. This error is most serious when production fluctuates between observations. However, when production is increasing or decreasing steadily, the measurement error tends to be constant (either in absolute or proportional terms) and hence will affect only the constant term. The regression coefficients estimated, and hence the estimates of average marginal cost, will not be affected.[17]

Another important type of measurement error is the failure to charge the period in which production occurs with future costs caused by that production. For example, overtime pay for production workers may be paid for in the week following their work. This can be adjusted for easily. However, the foreman may not be paid for his overtime directly. Rather, many months after his work he might get a year-end bonus or a raise in pay. These costs cannot easily be associated with the production that caused them but will be charged in another period, thus making both periods' costs incorrect.[18] This type of error is difficult to correct. Usually, all that one can do is eliminate the bonus payment from the data of the period in which it is paid and realize that the estimated coefficient of output will be biased downward. Average marginal costs, then, will be understated.

A somewhat similar situation follows from the high cost of the careful record keeping required to charge such input factors as production supplies to short time periods. In this event, these items of cost should be deducted from the other cost items and not included in the analysis. If these amounts are large enough, specific analysis may be required, or the decision not to account for them carefully may be reevaluated.

This separation of specific cost items also is desirable where the accountant knows that their allocation to time periods bears no relation to production. For example, such costs as insurance or rent may be allocated to departments on a monthly basis. There is no point in including these costs in the dependent variable because it is known that they do not vary with the independent variables. At best, their inclusion will only increase the constant term. However, if by chance they are correlated with an independent variable, they will bias the estimates made (requirement 7a). This type of error may be built into the accounting system if fixed costs are allocated to time periods on the basis of production. For example,

---

17. If the error is proportionally constant (i.e., 10 percent of production), transformation of the variables (such as to logarithms) is necessary.

18. Actually, the present value of the future payment should be included as a current period cost.

depreciation may be charged on a per unit basis. The variance of this cost, then, may be a function of the accounting method and not of the underlying economic relationships.[19]

## 6. Correlations among the Explanatory (Independent) Variables

When the explanatory variables are highly correlated with one another, it is very difficult, and often impossible, to estimate the separate relationships of each to the dependent variable. This condition is called multicollinearity, and it is a severe problem for cost studies. When we compute marginal costs, we usually want to estimate the marginal cost of *each* of the different types of output produced in a multiproduct firm. However, this is not always possible. For example, consider a manufacturer who makes refrigerators, freezers, washing machines, and other major home appliances. If the demand for all home appliances is highly correlated, the number of refrigerators, freezers, and washing machines produced will move together, all being high in one week and low in another. In this situation it will be impossible to disentangle the marginal cost of producing refrigerators from the marginal cost of producing freezers and washing machines by means of multiple regression.[20]

Problems similar to that of our manufacturer can be alleviated by disaggregation of total cost into several subgroups that are independent of each other. Preanalysis and preliminary allocations of cost and output data may accomplish this disaggregation. This is one of the most important contributions the accountant can make to regression analysis.

If the total costs of the entire plant are regressed on outputs of different types, it is likely that the computed coefficients will have very large standard errors and, hence, will not be reliable. This situation may be avoided by first allocating costs to cost centers where a single output is likely to be produced. This allows a set of multiple regressions to be computed, one for each cost center. The procedure (which may be followed anyway for inventory costing) also reduces the number of explanatory variables that need be specified in any one regression.[21] Care must be taken to ensure that the allocation of costs to cost centers is not arbitrary or unrelated to output. For example, allocation of electricity or rent on a square footage basis can serve no useful purpose. However, allocation of the salary of the foremen

---

19. Depreciation is assumed to be time, not user, depreciation.
20. However, the computed regression can provide useful predictions of total costs if the past relationships of production among the different outputs are maintained.
21. The author used this procedure with considerable success in estimating the marginal costs of banking operations. See "Economies of Scale and Marginal Costs in Banking Operations," *National Banking Review*, 1965, pp. 507–49.

on a time basis is necessary when they spend varying amounts of time per period supervising different cost centers.

A further complication arises if several different types of outputs are produced within the cost centers. For example, the assembly department may work on different models of television sets at the same time. In most instances, it is neither feasible nor desirable to allocate the cost center's costs to each type of output. Cost, then, should be regressed on several output variables, one for the quantity of each type of output. If these independent variables are multicollinear, the standard errors of their regression coefficients will be so large relative to the coefficients as to make the estimates useless. In this event, an index of output may be constructed, in which the different types of output are weighted by a factor (such as labor hours) that serves to describe their relationship to cost. Cost then may be regressed on this weighted index. The regression coefficient computed expresses the average relationship between the "bundle" of outputs and cost and cannot be decomposed to give the relationship between one output element and cost. However, since the outputs were collinear in the past, it is likely that they will be collinear in the future, so that knowledge about the cost of the "bundle" of outputs may be sufficient.

A valid objection to the allocation of costs to cost centers is that one can never be sure that the allocations are accurate. Nevertheless, some allocations must be made for multicollinearity to be overcome. Therefore, the statistical method cannot be free from the accountant's subjective judgment; in fact, it depends on it.

A limitation of analysis of costs by cost centers also is that cost externalities among cost centers may be ignored. For example, the directly chargeable costs of the milling department may be a function of the level of operations of other departments. The existence and magnitude of operations outside of a particular cost center may be estimated by including an appropriate independent variable in the cost center regression. An overall index of production, such as total direct labor hours on total sales is one such variable. Or, if a cost element is allocated between two cost centers, the output of one cost center may be included as an independent variable in the other cost center's regressions. The existence and effect of these possible intercost center elements may be determined from the standard error of the coefficient and sign of this variable.

Some types of costs that vary with activity cannot be associated with specific cost centers because it is difficult to make meaningful allocations or because of bookkeeping problems (as discussed above). In this event, individual regression analyses of these costs probably will prove valuable. For example, electricity may be difficult to allocate to cost centers although it varies with machine hours.[22] A regression can be computed such as the following:

---

22. Machine hours may not be recorded by cost center although direct labor hours are. If machine hours ($M$) are believed to be proportional to direct labor hours ($L$), so that $M_i = k_i L_i$, where $k$ is a constant multiplier that may vary among cost centers, $i$, $k_i L_i$ is a perfect substitute for $M_i$.

$$E = b_0 + b_1 M + b_2 S_1 + b_3 S_2 + b_4 S_3 \tag{1.3}$$

where

$E$ = electricity cost
$M$ = total machine hours in the plant
$S$ = seasonal dummy variables
$S_1$ = 1 for summer, 0 for other seasons
$S_2$ = 1 for spring, 0 for other seasons
$S_3$ = 1 for winter, 0 for other seasons
$b_0, b_1, b_2, b_3$, and $b_4$ are the computed constants and coefficients.

If the regression is fully specified, with all factors that cause the use of electricity included (such as the season of the year), the regression coefficient of $M$, $b_1$, is the estimate of the average marginal cost of electricity per machine hour. This cost can be added to the other costs (such as materials and labor) to estimate the marginal cost of specific outputs.

For some activities, physical units, such as labor hours, can be used as the dependent variable instead of costs. This procedure is desirable where most of the activity's costs are a function of such physical units and where factor prices are expected to vary. Thus, in a shipping department, it may be best to regress hours worked on pounds shipped, percentage of units shipped by truck, the average number of pounds per sale, and other explanatory variables. Then, with the coefficients estimated, the number of labor hours can be estimated for various situations. These hours then can be costed at the current labor rate.

## 7. Distribution of the Nonspecified Factors (Disturbances)

(a) *Serial correlation of the disturbances.* A very important requirement of least squares that affects the coefficients and the estimates made about their reliability is that the disturbances not be serially correlated. For a time series (in which the observations are taken at successive periods of time), this means that the disturbances that arose in a period $t$ are independent from the disturbances that arose in previous periods, $t-1, t-2$, and so on. The consequences of serial correlation of the disturbances are that (1) the standard errors of the regression coefficients ($b$'s) will be seriously underestimated, (2) the sampling variances of the coefficients will be very large, and (3) predictions of cost made from the regression equation will be more variable than is ordinarily expected from least-squares estimators. Hence, the tests measuring the probability that the true marginal costs and total costs are within a range around the estimates computed from the regression are not valid.

(b) *Independence from explanatory variables.* The disturbances which reflect the factors affecting cost that cannot be specified must be uncorrelated with the explanatory (independent) variables. $(x_1, x_2, \ldots, x_n)$. If the unspecified factors are correlated with the explanatory variables, the coefficients will be biased and inconsistent estimates of the true values. Such correlation often is the result of bookkeeping procedures. For example, repairs to equipment in a machine shop is a cost-causing activity that often is not specified because of quantification difficulties. However, these repairs may be made when output is low because the machines can be taken out of service at these times. Thus, repair costs will be negatively correlated with output. If these costs are not separated from other costs, the estimated coefficient of output will be biased downward, so that the true extent of variableness of cost with output will be masked.

(c) *Variance of the disturbances.* A basic assumption underlying use of least squares is that the variance of the disturbance term is constant; it should not be a function of the level of the dependent or independent variables.[23] If the variance of the disturbance is nonconstant, the standard errors of the coefficients estimated are not correct, and the reliability of the coefficients cannot be determined.

When the relationship estimated is between only one independent variable (output) and the dependent variable (cost), the presence of nonconstant variance of the disturbances can be detected by plotting the independent against the dependent variable. However, where more than one independent variable is required, such observations cannot be easily made. In this event, the accountant must attempt to estimate the nature of the variance from other information and then transform the data to a form in which constant variance is achieved. At the least, he should decide whether the disturbances are likely to bear a proportional relationship to the other variables (as is commonly the situation with economic data). If they do, it may be desirable to transform the variables to logarithms. The efficacy of the transformations may be tested by plotting the independent variables against the residuals (the estimates of the disturbances).

(d) *Normal distribution of the disturbances.* For the traditional statistical tests of the regression coefficients and equations to be strictly valid, the disturbances should be normally distributed. Tests of normality can be made by plotting the residuals on normal probability paper, an option available in many library regression programs. While requirement 7 does not have implications for the accounting system, it does determine the form in which the variables are specified. These considerations are discussed in the following section.

---

23. Constant variance is known as homoskedasticity. Nonconstant variance is called heteroskedasticity.

## Functional Form of the Regression Equation

Thus far we have been concerned with correct specification of the regression equation rather than with its functional form. However, the form of the variables must fit the underlying data well and be of such a nature that the residuals are distributed according to requirement 7 above.

The form chosen first should follow the underlying relationship that is thought to exist. Consider, for example, an analysis of the costs ($C$) of a shipping department. Costs may be a function of pounds shipped ($P$), percentage of pounds shipped by truck ($T$), and the average number of pounds per sale ($A$). If the accountant believes that the change in cost due to a change of each explanatory variable is unaffected by the levels of the other explanatory variables, a linear form could be used, as follows:

$$C = a + bP + cT + dA. \qquad (1.4)$$

In this form, the estimated marginal cost of a unit change in pounds shipped ($P$) is $\partial C/\partial P$ or $b$.

However, if the marginal cost of each explanatory variable is thought to be a function of the levels of the other explanatory variables, the following form would be better:

$$C = aP^b T^c A^d. \qquad (1.5)$$

In this case, a linear form could be achieved by converting the variable to logarithms:

$$\log C = \log a + b \log P + c \log T + d \log A. \qquad (1.6)$$

Now, an approximation to the expected marginal cost of a unit change in pounds shipped ($P$) is $\partial C/\partial P = baP^{b-1}\bar{T}^c\bar{A}^d$, where the other explanatory variables are held constant at some average values (denoted by bars over the letters). Thus, the estimated marginal cost of $P$ is a function of the levels of the other variables.

The logarithmic form of the variables also allows for estimates of nonlinear relationships between cost and the explanatory variables. The form of the relationships may be approximated by graphing the dependent variable against the independent variable. (The most important independent variable should be chosen where there is more than one, although in this event the simple two-dimensional plotting can only be suggestive.) If the plot indicates that a nonlinear rather than a linear form will fit the data best, the effect of using logarithms may be determined by plotting the data on semi-log and log-log ruled paper.

If the data seem curvilinear even in logarithms, or if an additive rather than a multiplicative form describes the underlying relationships best, polynomial forms of the variables may be used. Thus, for an additive relationship between cost ($C$) and quantity of output ($Q$), the form fitted may be $C = a + bQ + cQ^2 + cQ^3$. If a multiplicative relationship is assumed, the form may be $\log C = \log a + \log Q + (\log Q)^2$. Either form describes a large family of curves with two bends.

When choosing the form of the variables, attention must always be paid to the effect of the form on the residuals, the estimates of the disturbances. Unless the variance of the residuals is constant, not subject to serial correlation, and approximately normally distributed (requirement 5), inferences about the reliability of the coefficients estimated cannot be made. Graphing is a valuable method for determining whether or not these requirements are met. (The graphs mentioned usually can be produced by the computers.) Three graphs are suggested. First, the residuals should be plotted in time sequence. They should appear to be randomly distributed, with no cycles or trends.[24] Second, the residuals can be plotted against the predicted value of the dependent variable. There should be as many positive or negative residuals scattered evenly about a zero line, with the variance of the residuals about the same at any value of the predicted dependent variable. Finally, the residuals should be plotted on normal probability paper to test for normality.

If the graphs show that the residuals do not meet the requirements of least squares, the data must be transformed. If serial correlation of the residuals is a problem, transformation of the variables may help. A commonly used method is to compute first differences, in which the observation from period $t$, $t - 1$, $t - 2$, $t - 3$, and so on, are replaced with $t - (t - 1)$, $(t - 1) - (t - 2)$, $(t - 2) - (t - 3)$, and so forth. With first difference data, one is regressing the change in cost on the change in output, and so on, a procedure which in many instances may be descriptively superior to other methods of stating the data. However, the residuals from first difference data also must be subjected to serial correlation tests, since taking first differences often results in negative serial correlations.[25]

Where nonconstant variance of the residuals is a problem, the residuals may increase proportionally to the predicted dependent variables. In this event transformation of the dependent variable to logarithms will be effective in achieving constant variance. If the residuals increase more than proportionately, the square root of the dependent variable may be a better transformation.

---

24. A more formal test for serial correlation is provided by the Durbin-Watson statistic, which is built into many library regression computer programs. (J. Durbin, and G. J. Watson, "Testing for Serial Correlation in Least-Squares Regression," Parts I and II, *Biometrica*, 1950 and 1951.)

25. If there are random measurement errors in the data, observations from period $t - 1$ might be increased by a positive error. Then $t - (t - 1)$ will be lower and $(t - 1) - (t - 2)$ will be higher than if the error were not present. Consequently, $t - (t - 1)$ and $(t - 1) - (t - 2)$ will be negatively serially correlated.

## An Illustration

Assume that a firm manufactures a widget and several other products, in which the services of several departments are used. Analysis of the costs of the assembly department will provide us with an illustration. In this department, widgets and another product, digits, are produced. The widgets are assembled in batches while the larger digits are assembled singly. Weekly observations on cost and output are taken and punched on cards. A graph is prepared, from which it appears that a linear relationship is present. Further, the cost of producing widgets is not believed to be a function of the production of digits or other explanatory variables. Therefore, the following regression is computed:

$$\hat{C} = 110.3 + 8.21N - 7.83B + 12.32D$$
$$\phantom{\hat{C} = }(40.8)\ (.53)\ \ (1.69)\ \ \ (2.10)$$
$$\phantom{\hat{C} = } + 235S + 523W - 136A$$
$$\phantom{\hat{C} = }\ (100)\ \ (204)\ \ \ (154) \tag{1.7}$$

where

$\hat{C}$ = expected cost
$N$ = number of widgets
$B$ = average number of widgets in a batch
$D$ = number of digits
$S$ = summer dummy variable, where $S = 1$ for summer, 0 for other seasons
$W$ = winter dummy variable, where $W = 1$ for winter, 0 for other seasons
$A$ = autumn dummy variable, where $A = 1$ for autumn, 0 for other seasons
$R^2$ = .892 (the coefficient of multiple determination)
Standard error of estimate = 420.83, which is 5% of the dependent variable, cost.
Number of observations = 156.

The numbers in parentheses beneath the coefficients are the standard errors of the coefficients. These results may be used for such purposes as price and output decisions, analysis of efficiency, and capital budgeting.

For price and output decisions, we would want to estimate the average marginal cost expected if an additional widget is produced. From the regression we see that the estimated average marginal cost, $\partial C/\partial N$ is 8.21, with the other factors affecting costs accounted for. The standard error of the coefficient, 0.53, allows us to assess a probability of .67 that the "true" marginal cost is between 7.68 and 8.74 (8.21 ± 0.53) and .95 that it is between 7.15 and 9.27 (8.21 ± 1.06).[26]

---

26. The statements about probability are based on a Bayesian approach, with normality and diffuse prior distributions assumed.

The regression also can be used for flexible budgeting and analysis of performance. For example, assume that the following production is reported for a given week:

$W = 532$
$B = 20$
$D = 321$
$S = \text{summer} = 1$

Then we expect that, if this week is like an average of the experience for past weeks, total costs would be:

$$100.3 + 8.21(532) - 7.83(20) + 12.32(321) + 235.3(1) = 8511.14.$$

The actual costs incurred can be compared to this expected amount. Of course, we do not expect the actual amount to equal the predicted amount, if only because we could not specify all of the cost-causing variables in the regression equation. However, we can calculate the probability that the actual cost is within some range around the expected cost. This range can be computed from the standard error of estimate and a rather complicated set of relationships that reflect uncertainty about the height and tilt of the regression plane. These calculations also reflect the difference between the production reported for a given week and the means of the production data from which the regression was computed. The greater the difference between given output and the mean output, the less confidence we have in the prediction of the regression equation. For this example, the adjusted standard error of estimate for the values of the independent variables given is 592.61. Thus, we assess a probability of .67 that the actual costs incurred will be between 2,918.53 and 9,103.75 (8,511.14 ± 592.61) and probability .95 that they will be between 9,696.36 and 7,325.92 (8,511.14 ± 2,592.61). With these figures, management can decide how unusual the actual production costs are in the light of past experience.

The regression results may be useful for capital budgeting, if the company is considering replacing the present widget assembly procedure with a new machine. While the cash flow expected from using the new machine must be estimated from engineering analyses, they are compared with the cash flows that would otherwise take place if the present machines were kept. These future expected flows may be estimated by "plugging" the expected output into the regression equation and calculating the expected costs. While these estimates may be statistically unreliable for data beyond the range of those used to calculate the regression, the estimates may still be the best that can be obtained.

## Conclusion

The assertion has been made throughout this essay that regression analysis is not only a valuable tool but a method made available, inexpensive, and easy to use by computers. The reader may be inclined to accept all but the last point, having read through the list of technical and bookkeeping problems. Actually it is the case of computation that the library computer programs afford which makes it necessary to stress precautions and care: it is all too easy to "crank out" numbers that seem useful but actually render the whole program, if not deceptive, worthless.

But when one considers that costs often are caused by many different factors whose effects are not obvious, one recognizes the great possibilities of regression analysis, limited as it may be. Nevertheless, it is necessary to remember that it is a tool, not a cure-all. The method must not be used in cost situations where there is not an ongoing stationary relationship between cost and the variables upon which cost depend. Where the desired conditions prevail, multiple regression can provide valuable information for solving necessary decision problems, information that can put "life" into the economic models that accountants are now embracing.

# 2

# Published Corporate Accounting Data and Stock Prices

## The Problem

Published accounting reports—the balance sheet, income statement, and funds statement—are prepared for the use of investors, creditors, and others with whom the accountant is not in direct contact. It is therefore difficult for him to determine which data they find useful. Consequently, several arguments have arisen as to which data are the "best." Examples of these competing theories are the current operating performance concept versus clean surplus, price level versus historical cost depreciation, and sales versus cash flow versus net income.

Even if accountants knew which constructs were best, other questions would remain. For example, are the annual data published in corporate reports used by investors to make decisions? Do quarterly reports add useful information? Most corporations publish comparative data that date back many years. Do stockholders use these past data?

This essay seeks to answer some of these questions by determining, empirically, which published data are used by investors, as reflected by changes in the market price of common stocks. To provide a meaningful test, the relationship between common stock prices, published accounting information, and other factors is specified first. Then models are developed that describe how investors may use published accounting data. Finally the model is tested with relevant data, and conclusions are drawn.

## The Method of Investigation

Several methods can be used to determine how accounting data are used by readers of financial statements. The interview or questionnaire approach was used by

Horngren (1957), Cerf (1961), and Roper (1948). This method can provide valuable insights, but it is limited because one cannot know whether the persons interviewed are "representative," in some sense, whether they tell interviewers what they really want or whether their actions have a measurable effect on stock prices or some other variable.

Simulation was used by Bruns (1965) and Dyckman (1964a, b) to construct the earnings and other data for "firms" using alternative inventory and depreciation rules. Samples of students were given the data and asked to make management and investment decisions. Jensen (1966) simulated similar data and asked security analysts by mail to make investment decisions based on these data. Bonini (1963) constructed the data for a hypothetical firm and contrasted the results determined by alternative accounting procedures with a set of managerial decision rules derived from interviews and "the literature." Greenball (1965) developed a somewhat similar simulation and compared the data with investment rules. These simulations can be valuable in assessing the sensitivity of net income to different accounting methods and the effect on some price determination models of different concepts of income. Their great advantage is that "laboratory" conditions can be specified. However, this also is their weakness, for one does not know whether the simulation models are valid representations of reality.

The method of this essay is empirical.[1] The published accounting data for companies are related to market prices for the companies' common stock to assess which accounting data are used by investors (present and potential). If investors use the accounting statements of a corporation, it is to evaluate their expectations of the corporation. The change in their expectations caused by the data, ceteris paribus, should be reflected in a change in the price of corporation's stock. For example, investors may use the data contained in the financial reports to evaluate management's performance. In most instances, if they gather from the reports that the management is better or worse than they previously believed, the investors' only alternatives are to buy or sell the corporation's stock. If investors use the accounting reports to predict the future economic course of the corporation, again they can react to a change in their expectations by buying, selling, or holding the stock. In these and other situations, investors' reactions to published accounting reports should be reflected in changes in the market price of the stock.

---

1. The only other empirical studies of accounting data and stock prices of which I am aware, other than studies that seek to test whether retained earnings or dividends are superior determinants of stock prices, are O'Donnell (1965), Staubus (1965), and Ashley (1962). O'Donnell's study (1965) examines the price earnings ratios of 37 electric utilities—grouped according to their method of reporting depreciation. Staubus's paper (1965) relates net earnings, fund and cash flow, dividends, and book value at the beginning of a period to the discounted market value and dividends at the end of and throughout the period of several years. These studies differ from the present study both in method and basic approach. Ashley's (1962) method is somewhat similar to the method adopted in this essay: he associates changes in stock prices with preceding changes in earnings.

Some doubts concerning the effectiveness of the procedure must be admitted. First, a "significant" correlation between accounting data and stock prices may not be found for many reasons other than that investors disregard published accounting statements. The model by which the accounting data are related to stock prices may be incorrect. Or, it may not be aggregative or stable for investors at the margin. The accounting information may be used in combinations not tested. Or, the information may affect stock prices, but its effects may be "swamped" by the effects of other factors or inadequately measured by the available data. Additionally, the effect of the information contained in the published statements may predate the time of their publication. The data, when published, simply may confirm the knowledge gained by investors some other way. Many other limitations could be cited. Consequently, it should be clear that this procedure, like the interview and simulation approaches described above, suffers from serious inadequacies. Perhaps all three can make contributions which, together, will enable us to understand how accounting statements are used.

## The Model

It is not necessary to specify a complete model of stock valuation to analyze the use made of accounting data. It is only necessary to consider the change in the investors' expectations due to receipt of accounting information. These changed expectations presumably are discounted by investors and, hence, are measured by changes in the market price of the corporations' stock in the time period when the information became known.

Other variables also affect the change in stock prices during the period when accounting data are published. Prominent among these, in terms of current controversy, is cash dividends declared. The distribution of dividends decreases the ownership of assets by stockholders. In addition, changes in dividends are thought to convey information about the corporation's prospects (Fama et al., 1969). Since these changes often occur at the same time that the accounting statements are published, their effects on stock prices should be accounted for. Other factors are changes in general market conditions that affect all stocks. Examples of such events are changes in the structure of interest rates, expectations about inflation, an illness of the president, and the prospect of war or peace. This information may affect individual companies differently, and so must be accounted for company by company. However, some information, such as a change in the demand for steel or automobiles, may affect all companies in an industry. These variables also must be accounted for. Finally, the economic income generated by a company during a period increases the value of its shares by that amount. The effect of this variable could be important for periods as long as a year, but probably is not very important for short periods such as a month.

The variables mentioned above must be specified so that their effects can be measured. The model that has been described can be summarized as follows:

$$P_{jt} - P_{jt-1} = \Delta P_{jt} = f(A_{jt}, D_{jt}, \Delta D_{jt}, \Delta M_t, I_{kt}, Y_{jt}, U_{jt}), \tag{2.1}$$

where

- $P_{jt}$ = stock prices of the common shares of company $j$ in period $t$,
- $A_{jt}$ = published accounting data of company $j$ in period $t$, when the data became "known" (as discussed further below),
- $D_{jt}$ = distributions to stockholders of company $j$ of assets or claims over assets (such as cash dividends) during period $t$,
- $\Delta D_{jt}$ = changes in dividends of company $j$ in period $t$, that affect investors' expectations,
- $\Delta M_t$ = changes in general market conditions in period $t$, that affect the market valuations of companies during this period,
- $I_{kt}$ = information that affects the market valuations of all firms in a given industry, $k$, that becomes "known" in period $t$,
- $Y_{jt}$ = economic income generated by the assets of the company $j$ during period $t$, that change the present value of the company,
- $U_{jt}$ = other information about company $j$ that becomes "known" in period $t$, that affects investors' expectations.

The variables given in equation (2.1) are stated in terms of levels. A regression computed from these variables would most likely be dominated by scale (corporations with large absolute price changes are likely to have large changes in accounting data), giving rise to an unfounded conclusion that "significant" relationships were measured.[2] Therefore, it is desirable that the data be deflated.

A form of the market price change variable, $\Delta P_{jt}$, that accomplishes the required deflation and that has been found useful in a variety of studies,[3] is rates of return. In effect, the variable is measured as $PR_{jt} = \log_e (P_{jt}/P_{jt-1})$, the rate of return with continuous compounding provided by a security held during time $t$. A measurement advantage of the logarithmic, rate of change, form is that the distribution of monthly values (which are used for this study) of the variable has been found to be fairly symmetric (Fama et al., 1969). Models that use symmetrically distributed data present fewer estimation problems than those that must use skewed distributions.

Some of the variables on the right-hand side of equation (2.1) also must be deflated. One reason is to maintain consistency. Another reason for transforming

---

2. Staubus's study (1965) is particularly subject to this criticism.
3. Some examples are the studies published in Cootner (1964) and Fama (1965).

the independent variables to their rates of change is that their joint relationship with respect to the dependent variable is more likely to be multiplicative than additive. The residuals from the regressions are also likely to be proportionally homoskedastic. Therefore, the following variables in equation (2.1) are converted to their rates of change, and are symbolically represented, as follows:

price of common stock (dependent variable): $PR_{jt} = \log_a (P_{jt}/P_{jt-1})$

accounting data (principal independent variable): $AR_{jt} = \log_a (A_{jt}/A_{jt-1})$

change in dividends (other information variable): $\Delta DR_{jt} = \log_e (\Delta D_{jt})$.

The economic income generated by the $j$th firm's assets during period $t(Y_{jt})$ can be disregarded, because it is likely either to be relatively small (the price change period that is used in the study is one month) or is accounted for by the $AR_{jt}$ variable. However, several studies (cited below) have shown that $D_{jt}$, $\Delta M_t$, $I_{kt}$, and $\Delta DR_{jt}$ are likely to be important. In the next section, a procedure for eliminating the effects of $D_{jt}$ and $\Delta M_t$ is described. Following this is a discussion of specification of the $AR_{jt}$ variables. Finally, variables that may account for $I_{kt}$ and $\Delta DR_{jt}$ will be described and included in the estimation equations.

## Adjustment for Cash Dividends and for General Market Conditions

The nominal effect on price of cash dividends, $D_{jt}$, is adjusted by adding the amount of the dividend back to the price of the stock at the end of the period during which the stock was sold ex-dividend,[4] yielding

$$P'_{jt} = P_{jt} + D_{it}.$$

This method was used and tested by Moore (1964) who found that it was effective in removing the reduction in price that follows when a security goes ex-dividend. (The "information" effect on security prices of a change in dividends, which is discussed below, is not adjusted for at this time.) Next the price of the stock at the end of a month is adjusted for capital changes in the following month, $t + 1$, by a method developed by Fisher (1966), yielding

$P''_{jt} = P'_{jt}$, adjusted for capital changes in month $t + 1$.

---

4. This section follows the description given in Fama et al. (1969).

The rate of change of security prices for the $j$th security in time period $t$ now is measured as[5]

$$\log_e R_{jt} = \log_e (P'_{jt}/P''_{j,t-1}). \tag{2.2}$$

The change in general market conditions during period $t$, $\Delta M_t$, can now be accounted for by a method used and tested by Fama, Fisher, Jensen, and Roll (1969). They used the following model to express the relationship between an individual security and general market conditions:

$$\log_e R_{jt} = \alpha_j + \beta_j \log_e L_t + P^a_{jt} \tag{2.3}$$

where

$L_t$ = the measure of general market conditions. It is the link relative developed by Fisher (1965) ("$L_t$ is a complicated average of the $R_{jt}$ for all securities that were on the N.Y.S.E. at the end of months $t$ and $t-1$"),[6]

$\alpha_j$ and $\beta_j$ = parameters that can vary from security to security, and

$P^a_{jt}$ = a disturbance term which estimates the rate of change of security prices adjusted for the average effect of changes in general market conditions during period $t$. $P^a_{jt}$ is uncorrelated with $L_t$, its variance is uncorrelated with $t$, and $E(P^a_{jt}) = 0$. However, $E(P^a_{jt} | AR_{jt})$ may be different from 0. This is what is tested in this chapter.

They found that, for their sample of 940 securities covering the period 1926 through 1960, the disturbance terms, $P^a_{jt}$, met all of the requirements for linear regression, except that they were not normally distributed.[7]

Since the individual security and market index variables are measured as rates of return for a given month, the model (2.3) represents the monthly rate of return of a security as a linear function of the corresponding rate of return for the market. As such, it provides a means by which the change resulting from changed general market conditions in the return of an individual security can be accounted for and removed from the data. Fama et al. (1969) present tests and conclude: "In sum we find that regressions of security returns on market returns over time are a satisfactory method for abstracting from the effects of general market conditions on the monthly rates of return on individual securities."[8] The residuals ($P^a_{jt}$) from

---

5. The symbol $R_{jt}$ is used in the literature cited above to refer to the "price relative" of securities.
6. Fama et al. (1969), p. 5.
7. Fama et al. (1969) point out that least squares estimating procedures may be used even though the distribution of the residuals may be stable non-Gaussian. They state that least squares estimates are unbiased and consistent, even though they are not "efficient."
8. Fama et al. (1969), p. 9.

the regressions encompass the effects on security prices of other factors, such as published accounting data.[9] Thus, equation (2.1) can be restated as:

$$P_{jt}^a = f(AR_{jt}, \Delta DR_{jt}, I_{kt}, U_{jt}) \tag{2.4}$$

(The symbols are measured as natural logarithms of ratios, as discussed above with the exception of $I_{kt}$, which is discussed below.)

## Specifications of $AR_{jt}$: Accounting Data and Expectations

The accounting data made available to the public should affect the market price of stock only to the extent they lead to changes in expectations. If stockholders (present or potential) discover that earnings per share, for example, are $10.32 for the present year, and they expected these earnings to be $9.00 per share, it is reasonable to predict that this unexpected increase will be reflected in an increase in the market price of the stock. Conversely, if actual and expected earnings are the same, there is no reason to predict that the market price of the stock will change. Therefore, some specification of expected accounting information is required before relating the published accounting data to stock price changes.

The questions of how individual stockholders form their expectations and whether the individual expectations of stockholders can be aggregated into a general expectations model have not been solved. At this stage, one can only try various plausible expectations models to see if they will be consistent with the data and hope that a general model will serve to describe adequately the expectations of stockholders at the margin. However, it should be noted that the general class of expectations models that are described and tested have been used successfully in a variety of economic investigations (Cagan, 1956; Friedman, 1957; Koyck, 1954; Nerlove, 1958; Palda, 1965).

To forecast the use of the expectations models developed below, equation (2.5) shows how the data are used in the estimating equations. For simplicity, only the effects of annual accounting data on adjusted price changes are shown.

$$P_{jt}^a = \alpha + \delta(AR_{jt} - AR_{jt}^*) \tag{2.5}$$

---

9. The $\alpha_j$ and $\beta_j$ coefficients should be computed only from the observations that do not include the periods in which accounting data may have affected stock prices. The coefficients then are used to compute the residuals. However, Fama et al. (1969), n. 8 report that for their study they compared the residuals computed from all observations with those computed from observations with stock-split months omitted and found that there was little measurable difference in the distribution of the residuals.

where

$P_{jt}^a$ = the rate of change of market prices of the securities of the *j*th firm in period *t*,

$AR_{jt}$ = the published accounting data of firm *j* made known in time period *t*, measured as a rate of change (for the present, the accounting data refer to the firms' operations for a year ended just prior to period *t*. Quarterly data are discussed later),

$AR_{jt}^*$ = AR expected for firm *j* in time *t*.

This model may be interpreted as specifying that market price changes in period *t* by a constant ($\alpha$), plus a multiple ($\delta$) of the unexpected change in published accounting data.

In constructing an expectations model to estimate $AR_{jt}^*$, it is reasonable to assume that the accounting data that people expect to see in a published report is a function, in large part, of the data that were published in previous reports.[10] (An empirical test of this assumption is made.) Some support for this assumption can be cited in the publication by some firms of balance sheets and income statements that present the figures for several years (often 10 to 20), the AICPA requirement that comparative figures be given and the often repeated admonition that a single year's accounting data can be interpreted meaningfully only by comparison with those of previous years.

It is reasonable, then, to assume that investors' expectations of published accounting data are a function of past data:

$$AR_t^* = f(AR_{t-1}, AR_{t-2}, AR_{t-3}, \ldots) \tag{2.6}$$

where

$AR_t^*$ = expected accounting data at time *t*,

*t* = 1, 2, 3, ..., *T* fiscal years for which data are available (the *j* subscripts are dropped in this section for convenience, since the models refer to all companies individually).

A linear form usually is assumed:[11]

$$\begin{aligned}AR_t^* &= b_1 AR_{t-1} + b_2 AR_{t-2} + b_3 AR_{t-3} \cdots \\ &= \sum_{i=1}^{T} b_i AR_{t-i}.\end{aligned} \tag{2.7}$$

---

10. The effect of information that becomes available between published accounting statement dates is considered below.

11. Nonlinear forms can be approximated by the use of transformations. Such is the situation in this study where logarithms of the variables are used. Since the data are in logarithmic form, the constant term equals zero and, therefore, is not shown in equation (2.7).

The $b$'s may be estimated in several ways. Among these, the following cases are tried:

1. Previous year forecast: this year's rate of change of accounting data is the same as last year's. In this event, $b_1 = 1$ and $b_2 = b_3 \ldots = b_T = 0$.[12]
2. Average of several past years: simple averages of the past three and five years' rates of change are computed. For this version $b_1 = b_2 = b_3 = 1/3$ and $b_1 = b_2 = b_3 = b_4 = b_5 = 1/5$.
3. Declining distributed lags: the most recent rates of change are weighted most heavily, with the weights ($b$'s) declining geometrically. This version has been used successfully in several economic studies, as noted above, and is consistent with theoretical constructs of rational behavior (Muth, 1961). It allows for a drastic reduction in the number of parameters that have to be estimated or assumed.

The expectation form for this version becomes:

$$AR^*_{jt} = b_0 \sum_{i=1}^{\infty} \omega^i AR_{t-i} \qquad (2.8)$$

where

$b_0$ = the general coefficient,
$\omega$ = the weights, $0 \leq \omega < 1$, and $\sum_{i=1}^{\infty} \omega^i = 1$,
$i = 1,\ldots, \infty$ (time periods are assumed to run to $\infty$).

By specifying $\omega \leqq 0$, it is asserted that a period's data cannot have a negative effect and that the coefficient will not alternate in sign. For the present problem, these are reasonable assumptions. (If $\omega = 0$, the weight for the first period is 1 and that for the preceding periods is 0, in which case the model is equivalent to case 1.)

The geometrically declining distributed lag equation (2.8) still requires estimation of a very large number of parameters. But by assuming that the number of periods is infinite, or very large, some simplifying substitutions may be made that result in the following equation:[13]

$$P^a_t = \alpha(1-\omega) + \delta AR_t - \delta\omega(b_0 + 1) AR_{t-1} + \omega P^a_{t-1}. \qquad (2.9)$$

Thus the reduced form, equation (2.9), requires specification only of the current period's accounting data, $(AR_t)$, and the previous period's accounting data $(AR_{t-1})$ and price change $(P^a_{t-1})$.

---

12. It should be recalled that $AR_t$ is $\log_a (A_t/A_{t-1})$, and so is a function of the accounting data of year $t$ and the previous year. Thus, the previous year's forecast really uses two years' data.
13. The derivation of equation (2.9) is given in note 16.

The models described above specify that prior accounting data forms the basis for the formation of expectations. This need not be true. The following model may serve to test this assumption:

$$P_t^a = \alpha + \delta AR_t, \tag{2.10}$$

Thus, the accounting data is specified only as the current rate of change. If this model is "best," one might conclude either that investors formed their expectations about rates of change of the accounting data from sources other than previous reports or that they held no expectations at all.

## Specification of Other Factors

A serious complication affecting the analysis is the presence of information made available to the public between the dates of annual reports. This information may alter the public's expectations of the annual published data such that a model constructed with annual data only is seriously misspecified. Unfortunately, information in the form of rumors, speeches by the company officers, reports made by security analysts and others, and so on, cannot be adequately determined. This limitation may prove troublesome.

However, one important source of information that intervenes between the annual reports can be specified: interim reports. For this study, only the third quarter report has to be considered since it includes all the information made available in the first two quarter reports.[14] The third quarter interim report accounting data, $Q_3$, are specified in expectational form, as are the annual accounting data, $AR$, and for the same reasons. The models used to estimate the expected annual accounting data, $AR_t^*$, are used to estimate the expected third quarter data, $QR_{3t}^*$.[15] The inclusion of third quarter information changes equations (2.5) and (2.9). However, before these equations are rewritten, the effect of other independent variables is discussed. The effect on stock market prices caused by changes in dividends ($\Delta DR$) that occur within the stock price change period $t$ and industry effects ($I_k$) must also be considered.

An important finding of Fama et al. (1969) is that dividend changes have a large effect on stock prices. Most of these effects take place prior to the time the dividend change is announced, but some effect is measured in the period to the change. Hence, a variable that measures a dividend change (as described below) should be specified.

---

14. The change in third quarter reports between years is accounted for by measuring the variable as rates of change. However, the information content of the differences in the rate at which third quarter data were accumulated is not accounted for. Some model that used first and second quarter data might provide better specification, if this information were meaningful.

15. The $3t$ subscript refers to third quarter before time $t$ and after time $t-1$. $QR$ refers to $\log_e(Q_{3t}/Q_{2t-1})$.

King (1966) found that the rate of change of prices ($\log_e R_{jt}$) of stocks move together according to familiar industry groupings. Thus, a source of variation of the prices of individual securities may be due to industry effects. The industry effect could be allowed for in a manner similar to that employed for the general market effects. However, computer programming problems make it desirable, at this time, to adjust for this factor by including dummy variables in the regressions which account for industry differences. The symbol $I_k$ is used, where $k$ refers to 1, 2, ··· 24 industries.

To summarize, the following models are estimated. (For simplicity, the $j$'s are left out and $a$'s are used for the coefficients. The $u_t$'s are random disturbance terms, assumed to be uncorrelated serially or with the independent variables, having mean = 0 and constant variance.)

No Forecast Model (from equation 2.10):

$$P_t^a = a_1 + a_2 AR_t - a_3 QR_{3t} + a_4 \Delta DR_t + a_5 I_1 + \cdots a_{28} I_{24} + u_t \tag{2.11}$$

Previous Ratio Forecase Model:

$$P_t^a = a_1 + a_2(AR_t - AR_{t-1}) + a_3(QR_{3t} - QR_{3t-1}) \\ + a_4 \Delta DR_t + a_5 I_1 + \cdots a_{28} I_{24} + u_t. \tag{2.12}$$

Three-Year Forecast Model:

$$P_t^a = a_1 + a_2(AR_t - [AR_{t-1} + AR_{t-2} + AR_{t-3}]/3) \\ + a_3(QR_{3t} - [QR_{3t-1} + QR_{3t-2} + QR_{3t-3}]/3) + a_4 \Delta DR_t \\ + a_5 I_1 + \cdots + a_{28} I_{24} + u_t. \tag{2.13}$$

Five-Year Forecast Model:

$$P_t^a = a_1 + a_2(AR_t - [AR_{t-1} + \cdots + AR_{t-5}]/5) \\ + a_3(QR_{3t} - [QR_{3t-1} + \cdots + QR_{3t-3}]/5) + a_4 \Delta DR_t \\ + a_5 I_1 + \cdots + a_{28} I_{24} + u_t. \tag{2.14}$$

Geometrically Distributed Lags Model:[16]

$$P_t^a = a_1 + a_2 AR_t - a_3 AR_{t-1} - a_4 QR_{3t} + a_5 QR_{3t-1} \\ + a_6 \Delta DR_t - a_7 \Delta DR_{t-1} + a_8 I_1 + \cdots + a_{31} I_{24} + a_{32} P_{t-1}^a + u_t. \tag{2.15}$$

---

16. The reduced form of the geometrically distributed declining weights model is derived as follows:
   1. equation (2.5) expanded to include third quarter data, change in dividends, and industry variables:

$$P_t^a = \alpha + \delta(AR_t - AR_t^*) - \alpha(QR_{3t} - QR_{3t}^*) + \Delta DR_t + I_t \tag{a}$$

To test the question whether quarterly data are used by investors, the models also are tested with the quarterly accounting ratios, $QR_{3t}$, omitted.

## The Data

The data used for this study came from three sources. Market price data ($P_{jt}$) were gathered by the Center for Research in Security Prices (CRSP) of the University of Chicago. Beginning and end of month prices of all the common stocks on the New York Stock Exchange for the period January 1926 through December 1964 were gathered and carefully checked. The data were adjusted for capital changes such as stock splits, mergers, and so on, as discussed in (Fama et al., 1969). While data for shorter periods than a month would have been desirable, it is doubtful if such data could be gathered with anything like the accuracy of the CRSP data.

The accounting data ($A_{jt}$) were recorded by the Standard Securities Corporation, a subsidiary of Standard and Poor's.[17] They organize the data into categories, which makes a comparison among companies possible. The sample used for this

---

2. substitute formulation of equation (2.8) for expected accounting data:

$$P_t^a = \alpha + \delta(AR_t - b_0 \sum_{i=1}^{\infty} \omega^i AR_{t-i})$$
$$- \alpha(QR_{3t} - c_0 \sum_{i=1}^{\infty} \omega^i QR_{3t-i}) + \Delta DR_t + I_t \quad \text{(b)}$$

3. lag (b) one period and multiply by $w$:

$$\omega P_{t-1}^a = \omega\alpha + \delta(\omega AR_{t-1} - b_0 \sum_{i=1}^{\infty} \omega_i AR_{t-i})$$
$$- \alpha(\omega QR_{3t} - c_0 \sum_{i=1}^{\infty} \omega^i QR_{3t-i}) + \omega\Delta DR_{t-1} + \omega I_{t-1} \quad \text{(c)}$$

4. subtract (c) from (b):

$$P_t^a - \omega P_{t-1}^a = \alpha - \omega\alpha + \delta(AR_t - b_0 \omega AR_{t-1} - \omega AR_{t-1}) - \alpha(QR_{3t} - c_0 \omega QR_{3t-1} - \omega QR_{3t-1}) + \Delta DR_t - \omega\Delta DR_{t-1} + I_s - \omega I_{t-1} \quad \text{(d)}$$

5. solve for $P_t^a$ and consolidate:

$$P_t^a = \alpha(1-\omega) + \delta AR_t - \delta\omega(b_0+1)AR_{t-1} - \alpha QR_{3t} + \alpha\omega(c_0+1)QR_{3t-1}$$
$$+ \Delta DR_t - \omega\Delta DR_{t-1} + I_t - \omega I_{t-1} + \omega P_{t-1}^a \quad \text{(e)}$$

Since the industry variables, $I_t$, are measured in dummy variable form, both the current period and lagged form are the same. Therefore only one of the two is used in the model. It should be noted that estimation of the coefficients of the lagged annual and quarterly accounting variables will not serve to measure the lag operator, $w$. However, the coefficient of the lagged price change variable, $P_{t-1}^a$, should provide an estimate of the extent by which previous data are used: the larger is $w$, the greater the importance of previous data in current price formation.

17. The data were generously made available without charge by the Standard Statistics Corp.

study consists of almost all companies (483 for 1964) that are on the CRSP and the Standard and Poor computer tapes.[18] Data from 1964 were used because these are the latest available from both sources.

One purpose of the study is to discover which specific accounting data investors use. The test by which this is determined is the computing of regressions (as specified by the models described above) in which alternative accounting data, in rate of change form, are used as the $AR_{jt}$ and $QR_{j,2t}$ variables. The data that provide the best fit, as discussed below, are considered the data found most useful by investors.

The following alternative constructs of accounting data are tested:[19]

1. Sales, net (Compustat item 12);
2. Net income, before deduction of depreciation and amortization, income taxes, and nonrecurring items (Compustat item 13);
3. Net income, before deduction or addition of nonrecurring expense or income (Compustat item 18 less item 17);
4. Net income, before deduction or addition of nonrecurring expense or income that is stated in the published reports as being "net of tax" (Compustat item 18);
5. Net income, after all deduction and additions (Compustat item 18 less item 48).

Table 2.1 shows the correlation between the annual accounting data variables, in rate of change form ($AR$), for each of four models.[20] In general, all the variables are positively correlated: if a random, multivariate normal distribution could be assumed, almost all are "significantly" correlated at the .01 level ($R \geq .12$). This correlation is not unexpected, because it is unlikely that many companies would have, say, a declining rate of sales and an increasing rate of net profit.

The net income before nonrecurring items and before and after extraordinary items variables (3, 4, and 5) are quite highly correlated. Indeed, net income before nonrecurring items and before extraordinary items (3 and 4) are almost perfectly correlated. It appears, then, that the companies sampled experienced similar high or low rates of change in the three constructs of net income. Therefore, it is unlikely that much difference between these alternative constructs can be found (especially 3 and 4), although such a difference might exist in another, more extreme sample of companies.

---

18. A few companies had to be omitted because of a programming error.
19. The Compustat term numbers given below in parenthesis refer to the categories used by Compustat. Detailed descriptions of the data are given in Standard Statistics (1966).
20. The Geometrically Distributed Lags model is excluded because the variables are $AR_{62}$ and $AR_{63}$: $AR_{62}$ is the same variable used in the No Forecast Model and there seemed to be no point in showing the correlation of $AR_{62}$ with the other variables. The time period symbols, 63 and 62, refer to years where $AR_{63} = \log_e (A_{63}/A_{62})$.

TABLE 2.1 Correlation of Annual Accounting Data Variables within Models

|  | Annual Accounting Variables ||||
| Models | Sales (1) | Net Income before Depreciation (2) | Net Income before Nonrecurring Items (3) | Net Income before Extraordinary Items (4) |
| --- | --- | --- | --- | --- |
| a. No Forecast | | | | |
| 2 | 0.36 | | | |
| 3 | 0.26 | 0.44 | | |
| 4 | 0.25 | 0.44 | 0.99 | |
| 5 | 0.25 | 0.40 | 0.81 | 0.80 |
| b. Previous Year | | | | |
| 2 | 0.40 | | | |
| 3 | 0.06 | 0.23 | | |
| 4 | 0.06 | 0.24 | 0.98 | |
| 5 | 0.09 | 0.32 | 0.73 | 0.72 |
| c. Three-Year Average | | | | |
| 2 | 0.40 | | | |
| 3 | 0.25 | 0.40 | | |
| 4 | 0.20 | 0.40 | 0.96 | |
| 5 | 0.22 | 0.35 | 0.78 | 0.75 |
| d. Five-Year Average | | | | |
| 2 | 0.53 | | | |
| 3 | 0.47 | 0.56 | | |
| 4 | 0.46 | 0.56 | 0.99 | |
| 5 | 0.40 | 0.50 | 0.83 | 0.81 |

Table 2.2 shows the correlation of the accounting data variables (*AR*) among the models. As in table 2.1, the correlations are all positive and fairly high. These correlations indicate that, while the models used are different, they do not result in radically different independent variables.[21] This finding may indicate that additional alternative forms of expectations models would not give results that are much different from those presented below.

Quarterly data are available only for sales (1) and net income before nonrecurring items or net income before extraordinary items (3 and 4). The distinction between nonrecurring and ordinary income and expense was not consistently followed. Therefore, the quarterly variable used for the net income before nonrecurring items and before extraordinary items is the same. However, since these constructs are highly correlated (table 2.1), this procedure probably does not make much difference.

---

21. Again, note that the Geometrically Distributed Lags model is excluded.

TABLE 2.2 Correlation of Annual Accounting Data Variables among Models

|  | Models | | |
| --- | --- | --- | --- |
| Accounting Variables and Models | No Forecast (a) | Previous Years (b) | Three-Year Average (c) |
| 1. Sales | | | |
| Previous year (b) | 0.65 | | |
| Three-year average (c) | 0.30 | 0.70 | |
| Five-year average (d) | 0.37 | 0.30 | 0.37 |
| 2. Net income before depreciation | | | |
| Previous year (b) | 0.80 | | |
| Three-year average (c) | 0.40 | 0.80 | |
| Five-year average (d) | 0.86 | 0.72 | 0.84 |
| 3. Net income before nonrecurring item | | | |
| Previous year (b) | 0.70 | | |
| Three-year average (c) | 0.94 | 0.73 | |
| Five-year average (d) | 0.88 | 0.64 | 0.84 |
| 4. Net income before extraordinary items | | | |
| Previous year (b) | 0.72 | | |
| Three-year average (c) | 0.92 | 0.75 | |
| Five-year average (d) | 0.88 | 0.66 | 0.86 |
| 5. Net income including all items | | | |
| Previous year (b) | 0.79 | | |
| Three-year average (c) | 0.96 | 0.82 | |
| Five-year average (d) | 0.92 | 0.76 | 0.90 |

(a) No forecast = $AR_{63}$.
(b) Previous year = $AR_{63} - AR_{62}$.
(c) Three-year average = $AR_{63} - [(AR_{62} + AR_{61} + AR_{60})/3]$.
(d) Five-year average = $AR_{62} - [(AR_{62} + AR_{61} + AR_{60} + AR_{59} + AR_{58})/5]$.

Quarterly data are not available for years as early as 1959. Therefore, the Three-Year Average and Five-Year Average models cannot be tested with quarterly data.

The dating of the periods (months) in which the accounting data became available to the public represents the greatest data collection problem. The months in which earnings were announced in the *Wall Street Journal* are used for this purpose. The dates of the final and preliminary reports are recorded to identify the month of the rate of change of stock price ($P_{jt}^a$) that is used as the dependent variable. To test for the presence of "leakage" of information, the price changes ($P_{jt}^a$) one month, two months, and the sum of the three months (preliminary through two months previous) prior to the release of preliminary data are used as alternative dependent variables.

The information to quantify the dividend change variable ($\Delta D_{jt}$) also is taken from the *Wall Street Journal*. The variable used in the regressions, $\Delta DR_{jt}$, is measured as $\log_e (D_{jt}/D_{jt-1})$ where $D_{jt}$ is the dividend per share declared for firm $j$ in the period when the accounting data are thought to have become available, and $D_{jt-1}$ is the previous dividend declared. Thus, if there is no change in the dividend, or no dividend ordinarily declared, $\Delta DR_{jt} = 0$. Where the dividend declined ($D_{jt}/$

$D_{jt-1}$ = negative), the logarithm of the absolute value was taken and the resulting number was multiplied by −1. The announcement date, not the ex-dividend date, is used. Care is taken to measure the present and the previous dividend on the same basis. For example, if the dividend announced when the annual reports were made public includes an "extra" that was declared in the previous year, but not in the previous quarter, the "previous" dividend is measured as the previous annual amount, including the extra. In the regressions, dividend changes in a given time period are regressed on the price changes in that same time period.

The companies are identified as belonging to industries according to the industry classifications used by Compustat. However, several Compustat industries are grouped to provide at least 10 companies for each industry. Basically, the first two digits of the four-digit Compustat industry code are used to identify industries. Twenty-four such industries are identified. Dummy variables are used that equal $\log_e 2.718\ldots = 1$ when a company is in a given industry, and $\log_e 1 = 0$ when it is not in that industry.

## The Findings

Tables 2.3 through 2.10 present the estimates derived from the regressions computed for each of the models. The coefficients of the change in dividends ($\Delta DR_t$) and industry dummy ($I_1, \cdots, I_{24}$) variables and the constant term are not shown. Generally, about a fifth of the industry dummy variables have partial regression coefficients that are larger than the standard errors of the coefficients. The dividend change similarly is "significant" in somewhat less than half the regressions.

Some overall observations on the regressions are made first, followed by a more detailed analysis. First, note that since the variables are measured as natural logarithms, the coefficients are estimates of elasticities of the relative (rate of change) accounting data with respect to the rate of change in stock prices. The largest of these elasticities is 0.18, for the "sales" construct (No Forecast model, sales construct—table 2.4). Most of the elasticities measured for the "net income" constructs are around 0.02. Thus, a 100 percent change in the rate of change of accounting data is associated with a 2 percent or at most an 18 percent change in the monthly rate of change of stock prices. The findings indicate that the effects (as measured here) of published accounting data on stock prices are not very great, especially when one considers that the market is capitalizing the future expected changes in net income.

Second, the tables show some differences among the models and alternative accounting constructs—but these are not striking or consistent. Some constructs fit one model "better" than others, but not for all time periods. Some models are "better" than others, but not for all constructs or time periods. Analyses of the differences among the constructs, models, and time periods are presented below. However, the conclusions of the analyses are tentative, due to the lack of large differences.

TABLE 2.3 No Forecast Model (Annual Accounting Data Only) [$AR_{62}$]

| Accounting Data Variable (AR) | Partial Regression Coefficient | Standard Error | t Statistic | $R^3$ of Regression | F Statistic |
|---|---|---|---|---|---|
| A. *Month in which final data are announced* | | | | | |
| 1. Sales, net | 0.0422 | 0.0349 | 1.21 | 0.1064 | 2.09* |
| 2. Net operating income before depreciation | 0.0138 | 0.0076 | 1.83* | 0.1101 | 2.17** |
| 3. Net operating income before nonrecurring items | 0.0191 | 0.0069 | 2.76** | 0.1183 | 2.35** |
| 4. Net operating income before extraordinary items | 0.0173 | 0.0071 | 2.42** | 0.1150 | 2.28** |
| 5. Net operating income including all income and expense | 0.0100 | 0.0058 | 1.73* | 0.1094 | 2.15** |
| B. *Month in which preliminary data are announced* | | | | | |
| 1. Sales, net | 0.0112 | 0.0346 | 0.32 | 0.0562 | 1.05 |
| 2. Net operating income before depreciation | 0.0017 | 0.0075 | 0.23 | 0.0561 | 1.04 |
| 3. Net operating income before nonrecurring items | 0.0093 | 0.0069 | 1.35 | 0.0598 | 1.12 |
| 4. Net operating income before extraordinary items | 0.0090 | 0.0071 | 1.27 | 0.0594 | 1.11 |
| 5. Net operating income including all income and expense | 0.0017 | 0.0055 | 0.30 | 0.0562 | 1.04 |
| C. *Month before preliminary data month* | | | | | |
| 1. Sales, net | 0.0445 | 0.0304 | 1.46 | 0.1457 | 2.99** |
| 2. Net operating income before depreciation | −0.0114 | 0.0066 | 1.72* | 0.1473 | 3.03** |
| 3. Net operating income before nonrecurring items | −0.0005 | 0.0061 | 0.08 | 0.1417 | 2.90** |
| 4. Net operating income before extraordinary items | −0.0003 | 0.0063 | 0.05 | 0.1417 | 2.90** |
| 5. Net operating income including all income and expense | 0.0015 | 0.0049 | 0.30 | 0.1419 | 2.90** |
| D. *Two months before preliminary data month* | | | | | |
| 1. Sales, net | 0.0192 | 0.0313 | 0.61 | 0.0858 | 1.65 |
| 2. Net operating income before depreciation | −0.0158 | 0.0068 | 2.34** | 0.0960 | 1.86* |
| 3. Net operating income before nonrecurring items | 0.0024 | 0.0063 | 0.38 | 0.0854 | 1.64 |
| 4. Net operating income before extraordinary items | −0.0003 | 0.0064 | 0.05 | 0.0851 | 1.63 |
| 5. Net operating income including all income and expense | 0.0005 | 0.0050 | 0.10 | 0.0851 | 1.63 |

| | | | | | |
|---|---|---|---|---|---|
| E. *Cumulative, two months before through preliminary data month* | | | | | |
| 1. Sales, net | 0.0729 | 0.0550 | 1.33 | 0.1555 | 3.23** |
| 2. Net operating income before depreciation | −0.0257 | 0.0119 | 2.16* | 0.1608 | 3.36** |
| 3. Net operating income before nonrecurring items | 0.0112 | 0.0110 | 1.01 | 0.1541 | 3.20** |
| 4. Net operating income before extraordinary items | 0.0083 | 0.0113 | 0.74 | 0.1532 | 3.17** |
| 5. Net operating income including all income and expense | 0.0034 | 0.0088 | 0.39 | 0.1525 | 3.16** |

All dependent variables are the relative change of stock prices ($P_j^a$) in months as stated (A, B, C, D, and E) below.

Coefficients and standard errors are not reported for the change in dividends ($DR_j$) and the industry dummy ($I_{jk}$) variables and the constant term, which are included in the regressions.

Number of observations = 483
Degrees of freedom = 456

\* = "Significant" at .05 level (one tail $t \geq 1.65$, $F \geq 1.68$).
\*\* = "Significant" at .01 level (one tail $t \geq 2.34$, $F \geq 2.12$).

TABLE 2.4 No Forecast Model (Annual and Third Quarter Accounting Data) [$AR_{62}$, $QR_{63}$]

| Accounting Data Variable (AR) | Partial Regression Coefficient | Standard Error | t Statistic | $R^2$ of Regression | F Statistic |
|---|---|---|---|---|---|
| A. *Month in which final data are announced* | | | | | |
| 1. Sales, net | | | | | |
|    Annual $AR_{62}$ | 0.1042 | 0.0488 | 2.13** ⎫ | 0.1128 | |
|    Third quarter $QR_{63}$ | −0.0624 | 0.0345 | 1.81* ⎭ | | 2.14** |
| 3. Net operating income before nonrecurring items | | | | | |
|    Annual | 0.0192 | 0.0069 | 2.76** ⎫ | 0.1183 | |
|    Third quarter | −0.0005 | 0.0033 | 0.16 ⎭ | | 2.26** |
| 4. Net operating income including nonrecurring items | | | | | |
|    Annual | 0.0173 | 0.0071 | 2.43** | 0.1150 | |
|    Third quarter | −0.0005 | 0.0033 | 0.16 | | 2.19** |
| B. *Month in which preliminary data are announced* | | | | | |
| 1. Sales, net | | | | | |
|    Annual | 0.1288 | 0.0478 | 2.69** ⎫ | 0.0811 | |
|    Third quarter | −0.1184 | 0.0338 | 3.51** ⎭ | | 1.49 |
| 3. Net operating income before nonrecurring items | | | | | |
|    Annual | 0.0088 | 0.0069 | 1.27 ⎫ | 0.0683 | |
|    Third quarter | 0.0067 | 0.0033 | 2.04* ⎭ | | 1.24 |
| 4. Net operating income including nonrecurring items | | | | | |
|    Annual | 0.0084 | 0.0071 | 1.19 | 0.0679 | |
|    Third quarter | 0.0067 | 0.0033 | 2.04* | | 1.23 |

(*continued*)

TABLE 2.4 Continued

| Accounting Data Variable (AR) | Partial Regression Coefficient | Standard Error | t Statistic | $R^2$ of Regression | F Statistic |
|---|---|---|---|---|---|
| C. Month before preliminary data month | | | | | |
| 1. Sales, net | | | | | |
|    Annual | 0.0289 | 0.0426 | 0.68 | 0.1462 | |
|    Third quarter | 0.0157 | 0.0301 | 0.52 | | 2.89** |
| 3. Net operating income before nonrecurring items | | | | | |
|    Annual | −0.0005 | 0.0061 | 0.09 | 0.1419 | |
|    Third quarter | 0.0008 | 0.0029 | 0.29 | | 2.79** |
| 4. Net operating income including nonrecurring items | | | | | |
|    Annual | −0.0004 | 0.0063 | 0.06 | 0.1419 | |
|    Third quarter | 0.0008 | 0.0029 | 0.29 | | 2.79** |
| D. Two months before preliminary data month | | | | | |
| 1. Sales, net | | | | | |
|    Annual | 0.0226 | 0.0439 | 0.52 | 0.0859 | |
|    Third quarter | 0.0035 | 0.0310 | 0.11 | | 1.58 |
| 3. Net operating income before nonrecurring items | | | | | |
|    Annual | −0.0018 | 0.0062 | 0.29 | 0.0975 | |
|    Third quarter | 0.0073 | 0.0030 | 2.47** | | 1.82* |
| 4. Net operating income including nonrecurring items | | | | | |
|    Annual | −0.0010 | 0.0064 | 0.15 | 0.0974 | |
|    Third quarter | 0.0074 | 0.0030 | 2.49** | | 1.82* |
| E. Cumulative, two months before through preliminary data month | | | | | |
| 1. Sales, net | | | | | |
|    Annual | 0.1798 | 0.0769 | 2.34** | 0.1627 | |
|    Third quarter | −0.1077 | 0.0543 | 1.99* | | 3.28** |
| 3. Net operating income before nonrecurring items | | | | | |
|    Annual | 0.0099 | 0.0109 | 0.91 | 0.1689 | |
|    Third quarter | 0.0148 | 0.0052 | 2.84** | | 3.42** |
| 4. Net operating income including nonrecurring items | | | | | |
|    Annual | 0.0070 | 0.0112 | 0.62 | 0.1681 | |
|    Third quarter | 0.0148 | 0.0052 | 2.84** | | 3.40** |

All dependent variables are the relative change of stock prices $\left(P_j^a\right)$ in months as stated (A, B, C, D and E) below.

Coefficients and standard errors are not reported for the change in dividends ($DR_j$) and the industry dummy ($I_{jk}$) variables and the constant term, which are included in the regressions.

Number of observations = 483
Degrees of freedom = 455

\* = "Significant" at .05 level (one tail $t \geq 1.65$, $F \geq 1.67$).
\*\* = "Significant" at .01 level (one tail $t \geq 2.34$, $F \geq 2.09$).

TABLE 2.5 Previous Ratio Forecast Model (Annual Accounting Data Only) $[AR^*_{63} = AR_{62}]$

| Accounting Data Variable (AR) | Partial Regression Coefficient | Standard Error | $t$ Statistic | $R^2$ of Regression | $F$ Statistic |
|---|---|---|---|---|---|
| A. *Month in which final data are announced* | | | | | |
| 1. Sales, net | 0.0285 | 0.0249 | 1.15 | 0.1061 | 2.08* |
| 2. Net operating income before depreciation | 0.0107 | 0.0054 | 1.99* | 0.1113 | 2.20** |
| 3. Net operating income before nonrecurring items | 0.0070 | 0.0036 | 1.97* | 0.1112 | 2.19** |
| 4. Net operating income before extraordinary items | 0.0058 | 0.0036 | 1.63 | 0.1087 | 2.14** |
| 5. Net operating income including all income and expense | 0.0021 | 0.0033 | 0.64 | 0.1044 | 2.04* |
| B. *Month in which preliminary data are announced* | | | | | |
| 1. Sales, net | −0.0050 | 0.0246 | 0.20 | 0.0561 | 1.04 |
| 2. Net operating income before depreciation | 0.0022 | 0.0053 | 0.42 | 0.0564 | 1.05 |
| 3. Net operating income before nonrecurring items | 0.0080 | 0.0035 | 2.26* | 0.0665 | 1.25 |
| 4. Net operating income before extraordinary items | 0.0073 | 0.0035 | 2.07* | 0.0648 | 1.22 |
| 5. Net operating income including all income and expense | 0.0022 | 0.0032 | 0.69 | 0.0570 | 1.06 |
| C. *Month before preliminary data month* | | | | | |
| 1. Sales, net | −0.0227 | 0.0217 | 1.05 | 0.1438 | 2.94** |
| 2. Net operating income before depreciation | −0.0162 | 0.0046 | 3.49** | 0.1641 | 3.44** |
| 3. Net operating income before nonrecurring items | −0.0043 | 0.0031 | 1.39 | 0.1453 | 2.98** |
| 4. Net operating income before extraordinary items | −0.0041 | 0.0031 | 1.30 | 0.1449 | 2.97** |
| 5. Net operating income including all income and expense | −0.0050 | 0.0028 | 1.76* | 0.1475 | 3.04** |
| D. *Two months before preliminary data month* | | | | | |
| 1. Sales, net | −0.0187 | 0.0223 | 0.84 | 0.0865 | 1.66 |
| 2. Net operating income before depreciation | −0.0171 | 0.0048 | 3.59** | 0.1102 | 2.17** |
| 3. Net operating income before nonrecurring items | 0.0008 | 0.0032 | 0.23 | 0.0852 | 1.63 |
| 4. Net operating income before extraordinary items | 0.0003 | 0.0032 | 0.08 | 0.0851 | 1.63 |
| 5. Net operating income including all income and expense | −0.0013 | 0.0029 | 0.45 | 0.0855 | 1.64 |
| E. *Cumulative, two months before through preliminary data month* | | | | | |
| 1. Sales, net | −0.0478 | 0.0392 | 1.22 | 0.1550 | 3.22** |
| 2. Net operating income before depreciation | −0.0312 | 0.0084 | 3.72** | 0.1772 | 3.78** |

(*continued*)

TABLE 2.5 Continued

| Accounting Data Variable (AR) | Partial Regression Coefficient | Standard Error | t Statistic | $R^2$ of Regression | F Statistic |
|---|---|---|---|---|---|
| 3. Net operating income before nonrecurring items | 0.0044 | 0.0056 | 0.78 | 0.1533 | 3.18** |
| 4. Net operating income before extraordinary items | 0.0030 | 0.0057 | 0.53 | 0.1527 | 3.16** |
| 5. Net operating income including all income and expense | −0.0041 | 0.0051 | 0.80 | 0.1534 | 3.18** |

All dependent variables are the relative change of stock prices $(P_j^a)$ in months as stated (A, B, C, D, and E) below.

Coefficients and standard errors are not reported for the change in dividends $(DR_j)$ and the industry dummy $(I_{jk})$ variables and the constant term, which are included in the regressions.

Number of observations = 483
Degrees of freedom = 456

\* = "Significant" at .05 level (one tail $t \geq 1.65$, $F \geq 1.68$).
\*\* = "Significant" at .01 level (one tail $t \geq 2.34$, $F \geq 2.12$).

TABLE 2.6 Previous Ratio Forecast Model (Annual and Third Quarter Accounting Data) $[AR_{63}^* = AR_{62}, \quad QR_{63}^* = QR_{62}]$

| Accounting Data Variable (AR) | Partial Regression Coefficient | Standard Error | t Statistic | $R^2$ of Regression | F Statistic |
|---|---|---|---|---|---|
| A. *Month in which final data are announced* | | | | | |
| 1. Sales, net | | | | | |
| Annual | 0.0422 | 0.0330 | 1.28 | 0.1069 | |
| Third quarter | −0.0128 | 0.0204 | 0.63 | | 2.02* |
| 3. Net income before nonrecurring items | | | | | |
| Annual | 0.0058 | 0.0036 | 1.62 | 0.1088 | |
| Third quarter | 0.0004 | 0.0019 | 0.19 | | 2.06* |
| 4. Net income before extraordinary items | | | | | |
| Annual | 0.0070 | 0.0036 | 1.97* | 0.1112 | |
| Third quarter | 0.0003 | 0.0019 | 0.18 | | 2.11** |
| B. *Month in which preliminary data are announced* | | | | | |
| 1. Sales, net | | | | | |
| Annual | 0.0534 | 0.0324 | 1.65* | 0.0714 | |
| Third quarter | −0.0548 | 0.0200 | 2.74** | | 1.30 |
| 3. Net income before nonrecurring items | | | | | |
| Annual | 0.0073 | 0.0035 | 2.07* | 0.0681 | |
| Third quarter | 0.0024 | 0.0019 | 1.27 | | 1.23 |
| 4. Net income before extraordinary items | | | | | |
| Annual | 0.0079 | 0.0035 | 2.25* | 0.0697 | |
| Third quarter | 0.0024 | 0.0019 | 1.26 | | 1.26 |

C. Month before preliminary data
   month
   1. Sales, net
      Annual            −0.0314   0.0288   1.09   0.1442
      Third quarter      0.0082   0.0178   0.46                2.84**
   3. Net income before nonrecurring
      items
      Annual            −0.0041   0.0031   1.30   0.1452
      Third quarter      0.0007   0.0017   0.42                2.86**
   4. Net income before extraordinary
      items
      Annual            −0.0043   0.0031   1.39   0.1457
      Third quarter      0.0007   0.0017   0.43                2.87**

D. Two months before preliminary data
   month
   1. Sales, net
      Annual            −0.0384   0.0296   1.30   0.0886
      Third quarter      0.0185   0.0182   1.01                1.64
   3. Net income before nonrecurring
      items
      Annual            −0.0003   0.0032   0.09   0.0995
      Third quarter      0.0046   0.0017   2.70**              1.86*
   4. Net income before extraordinary
      items
      Annual             0.0007   0.0032   0.21   0.0996
      Third quarter      0.0046   0.0017   2.69**              1.86*

E. Cumulative, two months before
   through preliminary data month
   1. Sales, net
      Annual            −0.0173   0.0520   0.33   0.1564
      Third quarter     −0.0286   0.0321   0.89                3.13**
   3. Net income before nonrecurring
      items
      Annual             0.0029   0.0056   0.52   0.1646
      Third quarter      0.0077   0.0030   2.54                3.32**
   4. Net income before extraordinary
      items
      Annual             0.0042   0.0056   0.75   0.1651
      Third quarter      0.0077   0.0030   2.54*               3.33*

All dependent variables are the relative change of stock prices $(P_j^a)$ in months as stated (A, B, C, D, and E) below.

Coefficients and standard errors are not reported for the change in dividends $(DR_j)$ and the industry dummy $(I_{jb})$ variables and the constant term, which are included in the regressions.

Number of observations = 483
Degrees of freedom = 455

\* = "Significant" at .05 level (one tail $t \geq 1.65, F \geq 1.67$).
\*\* = "Significant" at .01 level (one tail $t \geq 2.34, F \geq 2.09$).

TABLE 2.7 Average of Past Three-Year Forecast Model (Annual Data Only)
$[AR_{63}^{*} = (AR_{62} + AR_{61} + AR_{60})/3]$

| Accounting Data Variable (AR) | Partial Regression Coefficient | Standard Error | $t$ Statistic | $R^2$ of Regression | $F$ Statistic |
|---|---|---|---|---|---|
| **A. Month in which final data are announced** | | | | | |
| 1. Sales, net | 0.0380 | 0.0285 | 1.33 | 0.1070 | 2.10* |
| 2. Net operating income before depreciation | 0.0092 | 0.0063 | 1.45 | 0.1077 | 2.12** |
| 3. Net operating income before nonrecurring items | 0.0148 | 0.0059 | 2.50** | 0.1157 | 2.30** |
| 4. Net operating income before extraordinary items | 0.0153 | 0.0061 | 2.52** | 0.1159 | 2.30** |
| 5. Net operating income including all income and expense | 0.0083 | 0.0050 | 1.64 | 0.1088 | 2.14** |
| **B. Month in which preliminary data are announced** | | | | | |
| 1. Sales, net | 0.0095 | 0.0283 | 0.34 | 0.0562 | 1.05 |
| 2. Net operating income before depreciation | −0.0002 | 0.0063 | 0.03 | 0.0560 | 1.04 |
| 3. Net operating income before nonrecurring items | 0.0051 | 0.0059 | 0.87 | 0.0576 | 1.07 |
| 4. Net operating income before extraordinary items | 0.0069 | 0.0060 | 1.15 | 0.0588 | 1.09 |
| 5. Net operating income including all income and expense | −0.0004 | 0.0049 | 0.08 | 0.0560 | 1.04 |
| **C. Month before preliminary data month** | | | | | |
| 1. Sales, net | 0.0485 | 0.0248 | 1.95* | 0.1488 | 3.07** |
| 2. Net operating income before depreciation | −0.0066 | 0.0055 | 1.19 | 0.1444 | 2.96** |
| 3. Net operating income before nonrecurring items | 0.0023 | 0.0052 | 0.44 | 0.1421 | 2.90** |
| 4. Net operating income before extraordinary items | 0.0009 | 0.0053 | 0.17 | 0.1418 | 2.90** |
| 5. Net operating income including all income and expense | 0.0026 | 0.0043 | 0.61 | 0.1424 | 2.91** |
| **D. Two months before preliminary data month** | | | | | |
| 1. Sales, net | 0.0184 | 0.0256 | 0.72 | 0.0861 | 1.65 |
| 2. Net operating income before depreciation | −0.0128 | 0.0057 | 2.26* | 0.0952 | 1.85* |
| 3. Net operating income before nonrecurring items | 0.0045 | 0.0053 | 0.85 | 0.0865 | 1.66 |
| 4. Net operating income before extraordinary items | 0.0023 | 0.0055 | 0.43 | 0.0855 | 1.64 |
| 5. Net operating income including all income and expense | 0.0007 | 0.0044 | 0.16 | 0.0851 | 1.63 |

E. *Cumulative, two months before through preliminary data month*

| | | | | | |
|---|---|---|---|---|---|
| 1. Sales, net | 0.0750 | 0.0449 | 1.67* | 0.1574 | 3.28** |
| 2. Net operating income before depreciation | −0.0197 | 0.0100 | 1.98* | 0.1594 | 3.33** |
| 3. Net operating income before nonrecurring items | 0.0119 | 0.0094 | 1.28 | 0.1552 | 3.22** |
| 4. Net operating income before extraordinary items | 0.0102 | 0.0096 | 1.06 | 0.1543 | 3.20** |
| 5. Net operating income including all income and expense | 0.0028 | 0.0078 | 0.36 | 0.1525 | 3.15** |

All dependent variables are the relative change of stock prices $(P_j^a)$ in months as stated (A, B, C, D, and E) below.

Coefficients and standard errors are not reported for the change in dividends $(DR_j)$ and the industry dummy $(I_{jk})$ variables and the constant term, which are included in the regressions.

Number of observations = 483
Degrees of freedom = 456

\* = "Significant" at .05 level (one tail $t \geq 1.65$, $F \geq 1.68$).
\*\* = "Significant" at .01 level (one tail $t \geq 2.34$, $F \geq 2.12$).

TABLE 2.8 Average of Past Five Years Forecast Model (Annual Data Only)
$[AR^*_{63} = (AR_{62} + AR_{61} + \cdots AR_{53})/5]$

| Accounting Data Variable (AR) | Partial Regression Coefficient | Standard Error | t Statistic | $R^2$ of Regression | F Statistic |
|---|---|---|---|---|---|
| A. *Month in which final data are announced* | | | | | |
| 1. Sales, net | −0.0043 | 0.0116 | 0.37 | 0.1038 | 2.03* |
| 2. Net operating income before depreciation | 0.0082 | 0.0057 | 1.45 | 0.1077 | 2.12** |
| 3. Net operating income before nonrecurring items | 0.0123 | 0.0057 | 2.15* | 0.1126 | 2.22** |
| 4. Net operating income before extraordinary items | 0.0106 | 0.0059 | 1.80* | 0.1099 | 2.17** |
| 5. Net operating income including all income and expense | 0.0056 | 0.0049 | 1.13 | 0.1061 | 2.08* |
| B. *Month in which preliminary data are announced* | | | | | |
| 1. Sales, net | −0.0131 | 0.0114 | 1.15 | 0.0587 | 1.09 |
| 2. Net operating income before depreciation | −0.0008 | 0.0056 | 0.14 | 0.0561 | 1.04 |
| 3. Net operating income before nonrecurring items | 0.0037 | 0.0057 | 0.66 | 0.0569 | 1.06 |
| 4. Net operating income before extraordinary items | 0.0034 | 0.0058 | 0.58 | 0.0567 | 1.05 |
| 5. Net operating income including all income and expense | −0.0017 | 0.0047 | 0.35 | 0.0563 | 1.05 |

(*continued*)

TABLE 2.8 Continued

| Accounting Data Variable (AR) | Partial Regression Coefficient | Standard Error | t Statistic | $R^2$ of Regression | F Statistic |
|---|---|---|---|---|---|
| **C. Month before preliminary data month** | | | | | |
| 1. Sales, net | 0.0043 | 0.0101 | 0.43 | 0.1421 | 2.90** |
| 2. Net operating income before depreciation | −0.0075 | 0.0049 | 1.53 | 0.1461 | 3.00** |
| 3. Net operating income before nonrecurring items | −0.0019 | 0.0050 | 0.38 | 0.1420 | 2.90** |
| 4. Net operating income before extraordinary items | −0.0017 | 0.0051 | 0.34 | 0.1419 | 2.90** |
| 5. Net operating income including all income and expense | 0.0004 | 0.0042 | 0.09 | 0.1417 | 2.90** |
| **D. Two months before preliminary data month** | | | | | |
| 1. Sales, net | 0.0016 | 0.0104 | 0.15 | 0.0851 | 1.63 |
| 2. Net operating income before depreciation | −0.0100 | 0.0051 | 1.97* | 0.0928 | 1.79* |
| 3. Net operating income before nonrecurring items | 0.0032 | 0.0052 | 0.61 | 0.0858 | 1.65 |
| 4. Net operating income before extraordinary items | 0.0009 | 0.0053 | 0.17 | 0.0851 | 1.63 |
| 5. Net operating income including all income and expense | 0.0002 | 0.0043 | 0.06 | 0.0851 | 1.63 |
| **E. Cumulative, two months before through preliminary data month** | | | | | |
| 1. Sales, net | −0.0074 | 0.0183 | 0.40 | 0.1525 | 3.16** |
| 2. Net operating income before depreciation | −0.0183 | 0.0089 | 2.06* | 0.1600 | 3.34** |
| 3. Net operating income before nonrecurring items | 0.0050 | 0.0091 | 0.55 | 0.1528 | 3.16** |
| 4. Net operating income before extraordinary items | 0.0025 | 0.0093 | 0.27 | 0.1523 | 3.15** |
| 5. Net operating income including all income and expense | −0.0012 | 0.0076 | 0.15 | 0.1523 | 3.15** |

All dependent variables are the relative change of stock prices ($P_j^a$) in months as stated (A, B, C, D, and E) below.

Coefficients and standard errors are not reported for the change in dividends ($DR_j$) and the industry dummy ($I_{jk}$) variables and the constant term, which are included in the regressions.

Number of observations = 483
Degrees of Freedom = 456

\* = "Significant" at .05 level (one tail $t \geq 1.65$, $F \geq 1.68$).
\*\* = "Significant" at .01 level (one tail $t \geq 2.34$, $F \geq 2.12$).

TABLE 2.9 Geometrically Declining Distributed Lags Model (Annual Data Only) [$AR_{63}, AR_{62}, P_{62}^a$]

| Accounting Data Variable (AR) | Partial Regression Coefficient | Standard Error | $t$ Statistic | $R^2$ of Regression | $F$ Statistic |
|---|---|---|---|---|---|
| **A. Month in which final data are announced** | | | | | |
| 1. Sales, net, $AR_{63}$ | 0.0413 | 0.0353 | 1.17 | 0.1073 | |
| Sales, net, $AR_{62}$ | −0.0143 | 0.0341 | 0.42 | | 1.88* |
| Relative stock price change previous year, $P_{t-1}^a$ | 0.0215 | 0.0522 | 0.42 | | |
| 2. Net operating income before depreciation, $AR_{62}$ | 0.0124 | 0.0078 | 1.60 | | |
| Net operating income before depreciation, $AR_{62}$ | −0.0080 | 0.0091 | 0.89 | 0.1120 | 1.97* |
| Relative stock price change previous year, $P_{62}^a$ | 0.0188 | 0.0523 | 0.36 | | |
| 3. Net operating income before nonrecurring items, $AR_{63}$ | 0.0189 | 0.0074 | 2.56** | | |
| Net operating income before nonrecurring items, $AR_{62}$ | −0.0002 | 0.0052 | 0.03 | 0.1185 | 2.10** |
| Relative stock price change previous year, $P_{62}^a$ | 0.0100 | 0.0525 | 0.19 | | |
| 4. Net operating income before extraordinary items, $AR_{63}$ | 0.0172 | 0.0075 | 2.28* | | |
| Net operating income before extraordinary items, $AR_{62}$ | 0.0003 | 0.0051 | 0.07 | 0.1153 | 2.03** |
| Relative stock price change previous year, $P_{62}^a$ | 0.0113 | 0.0525 | 0.21 | | |
| 5. Net operating income including all income and expense, $AR_{62}$ | 0.0123 | 0.0062 | 1.97* | 0.1124 | |
| Net operating income including all income and expense, $AR_{62}$ | 0.0061 | 0.0054 | 1.14 | | 1.98* |
| Relative stock price change previous year, $P_{62}^a$ | 0.0102 | 0.0526 | 0.19 | | |
| **B. Month in which preliminary data are announced** | | | | | |
| 1. Sales, net, $AR_{63}$ | −0.0016 | 0.0351 | 0.04 | 0.0685 | |
| Sales, net, $AR_{62}$ | 0.0219 | 0.0337 | 0.65 | | 1.15 |
| Relative stock price change previous year, $P_{t-1}^a$ | 0.0738 | 0.0541 | 1.36 | | |
| 2. Net operating income before depreciation, $AR_{62}$ | −0.0006 | 0.0076 | 0.08 | | |
| Net operating income before depreciation, $AR_{62}$ | −0.0070 | 0.0092 | 0.76 | 0.0689 | |
| Relative stock price change previous year, $P_{62}^a$ | 0.0851 | 0.0548 | 1.55 | | 1.16 |
| 3. Net operating income before nonrecurring items, $AR_{62}$ | 0.0048 | 0.0072 | 0.67 | 0.0786 | |
| Net operating income before nonrecurring items, $AR_{62}$ | −0.0097 | 0.0050 | 1.93* | | 1.33 |
| Relative stock price change previous year, $P_{62}^a$ | 0.0799 | 0.0530 | 1.51 | | |

(*continued*)

TABLE 2.9 Continued

| Accounting Data Variable (AR) | Partial Regression Coefficient | Standard Error | t Statistic | $R^2$ of Regression | F Statistic |
|---|---|---|---|---|---|
| 4. Net operating income before extraordinary items, $AR_{62}$ | 0.0052 | 0.0073 | 0.71 | 0.0767 | |
| Net operating income before extraordinary items, $AR_{62}$ | −0.0085 | 0.0049 | 1.72* | | 1.50 |
| Relative stock price change previous year, $P_{62}^a$ | 0.0786 | 0.0530 | 1.48 | | |
| 5. Net operating income including all income and expense, $AR_{62}$ | 0.0000 | 0.0058 | 0.01 | | |
| Net operating income including all income and expense, $AR_{62}$ | −0.0048 | 0.0053 | 0.91 | 0.0696 | |
| Relative stock price change previous year, $P_{62}^a$ | 0.0822 | 0.0535 | 1.54 | | 1.17 |
| C. *Month before preliminary data month* | | | | | |
| 1. Sales, net, $AR_{63}$ | 0.0346 | 0.0303 | 1.14 | 0.1695 | |
| Sales, net, $AR_{62}$ | 0.0842 | 0.0293 | 2.87** | | 3.19** |
| Relative stock price change previous year, $P_{t-1}^a$ | 0.0099 | 0.0455 | 0.22 | | |
| 2. Net operating income before depreciation, $AR_{63}$ | −0.0096 | 0.0066 | 1.45 | 0.1812 | |
| Net operating income before depreciation, $AR_{62}$ | 0.0273 | 0.0078 | 3.52** | | 3.46** |
| Relative stock price change previous year, $P_{62}^a$ | 0.0138 | 0.0451 | 0.31 | | |
| 3. Net operating income before non-recurring items, $AR_{63}$ | 0.0027 | 0.0063 | 0.42 | 0.1586 | |
| Net operating income before non-recurring items, $AR_{62}$ | 0.0087 | 0.0044 | 1.95* | | 2.94** |
| Relative stock price change previous year, $P_{62}^a$ | 0.0196 | 0.0457 | 0.43 | | |
| 4. Net operating income before extraordinary items, $AR_{63}$ | 0.0024 | 0.0065 | 0.38 | 0.1575 | |
| Net operating income before extraordinary items, $AR_{62}$ | 0.0079 | 0.0044 | 1.80* | | 2.92** |
| Relative stock price change previous year, $P_{62}^a$ | 0.0181 | 0.0457 | 0.40 | | |
| 5. Net operating income including all income and expense, $AR_{62}$ | 0.0067 | 0.0051 | 1.32 | 0.1721 | |
| Net operating income including all income and expense, $AR_{62}$ | 0.0152 | 0.0046 | 3.35** | | 3.25** |
| Relative stock price change previous year, $P_{62}^a$ | 0.0178 | 0.0454 | 0.39 | | |
| D. *Two months before preliminary data month* | | | | | |
| 1. Sales, net, $AR_{63}$ | 0.0192 | 0.0310 | .062 | 0.1117 | |
| Sales, net, $AR_{62}$ | 0.0576 | 0.0302 | 1.91* | | 1.97* |
| Relative stock price change previous year, $P_{t-1}^a$ | 0.1320 | 0.0436 | 3.03** | | |
| 2. Net operating income before depreciation, $AR_{63}$ | −0.0152 | 0.0068 | 2.24* | 0.1356 | |
| Net operating income before depreciation, $AR_{62}$ | 0.0241 | 0.0080 | 3.03** | | 2.45** |
| Relative stock price change previous year, $P_{62}^a$ | 0.1428 | 0.0431 | 3.32** | | |

| | | | | | |
|---|---|---|---|---|---|
| 3. Net operating income before nonrecurring items, $AR_{63}$ | 0.0013 | 0.0065 | 0.20 | 0.1038 | |
| Net operating income before nonrecurring items, $AR_{62}$ | 0.0007 | 0.0046 | 0.15 | | 1.81* |
| Relative stock price change previous year, $P_{62}^a$ | 0.1234 | 0.0438 | 2.87** | | |
| 4. Net operating income before extraordinary items, $AR_{63}$ | −0.0010 | 0.0066 | 0.15 | 0.1038 | 1.81* |
| Net operating income before extraordinary items, $AR_{62}$ | 0.0009 | 0.0045 | 0.20 | | |
| Relative stock price change previous year, $P_{62}^a$ | 0.1264 | 0.0437 | 2.89** | | |
| 5. Net operating income including all income and expense, $AR_{63}$ | 0.0008 | 0.0053 | 0.15 | 0.1057 | 1.85* |
| Net operating income including all income and expense, $AR_{62}$ | 0.0047 | 0.0047 | 1.00 | | |
| Relative stock price change previous year, $P_{62}^a$ | 0.1294 | 0.0438 | 2.95** | | |
| E. *Cumulative, two months before through preliminary data month* | | | | | |
| 1. Sales, net, $AR_{63}$ | 0.0569 | 0.0557 | 1.02 | 0.1732 | |
| Sales, net, $AR_{62}$ | 0.1568 | 0.0535 | 2.93** | | 3.27** |
| Relative stock price change previous year, $P_{t-1}^a$ | 0.0355 | 0.0628 | 0.57 | | |
| 2. Net operating income before depreciation, $AR_{63}$ | −0.0211 | 0.0120 | 1.75* | 0.1826 | |
| Net operating income before depreciation, $AR_{62}$ | 0.0449 | 0.0144 | 3.12** | | 3.49** |
| Relative stock price change previous year, $P_{62}^a$ | 0.0347 | 0.0628 | 0.55 | | |
| 3. Net operating income before nonrecurring items, $AR_{63}$ | 0.0099 | 0.0115 | 0.86 | 0.1569 | 2.91** |
| Net operating income before nonrecurring items, $AR_{62}$ | −0.0010 | 0.0081 | 0.12 | | |
| Relative stock price change previous year, $P_{62}^a$ | 0.0597 | 0.0625 | 0.96 | | |
| 4. Net operating income before extraordinary items, $AR_{63}$ | 0.0072 | 0.0118 | 0.61 | 0.1561 | 2.89** |
| Net operating income before extraordinary items, $AR_{62}$ | −0.0006 | 0.0080 | 0.08 | | |
| Relative stock price change previous year $P_{62}^a$ | 0.0610 | 0.0625 | 0.98 | | |
| 5. Net operating income including all income and expense, $AR_{62}$ | 0.0084 | 0.0093 | 0.90 | 0.1611 | |
| Net operating income including all income and expense, $AR_{62}$ | 0.0146 | 0.0084 | 1.74* | | 3.00** |
| Relative stock price change previous year, $P_{62}^a$ | 0.0509 | 0.0624 | 0.82 | | |

All dependent variables are the relative change of stock prices ($P_j^a$) in months as stated (A, B, C, D, and E) below.

Coefficients and standard errors are not reported for the change in dividends ($DR_j$) and the industry dummy ($I_{jk}$) variables and the constant term, which are included in the regressions.

Number of observations = 483<br>
Degrees of freedom = 453

\* = "Significant" at .05 level (one tail $t \geq 1.65$, $F \geq 1.64$).
\*\* = "Significant" at .01 level (one tail $t \geq 2.34$, $F \geq 2.03$).

TABLE 2.10 Geometrically Distributed Lags Model (Annual and Third Quarter Data)
[$AR_{62}, AR_{62}, P^a_{62}, QR_{62}, QR_{62}$]

| Accounting Data Variable (AR) | Partial Regression Coefficient | Standard Error | t Statistic | $R^2$ of Regression | F Statistic |
|---|---|---|---|---|---|
| **A. Month in which final data are announced** | | | | | |
| 1. Sales, net | | | | | |
| Annual ($AR_{63}$) | 0.1293 | 0.0514 | 2.52** | | |
| Annual lagged ($AR_{62}$) | 0.0334 | 0.0480 | 0.69 | 0.1196 | 1.98** |
| Third quarter ($QR_{62}$) | −0.0883 | 0.0375 | 2.36** | | |
| Third quarter lagged ($QR_{62}$) | −0.0594 | 0.0353 | 1.68* | | |
| Relative price change lagged ($P^a_{62}$) | 0.0261 | 0.0522 | 0.50 | | |
| 3. Net operating income before nonrecurring items | | | | | |
| Annual ($AR_{63}$) | 0.0198 | 0.0075 | 2.65** | | |
| Annual lagged ($AR_{62}$) | 0.0009 | 0.0053 | 0.17 | 0.1198 | 1.98** |
| Third quarter ($QR_{62}$) | −0.0022 | 0.0040 | 0.56 | | |
| Third quarter lagged ($QR_{62}$) | 0.0032 | 0.0041 | 0.79 | | |
| Relative price change lagged ($P^a_{62}$) | 0.0129 | 0.0527 | 0.25 | | |
| 4. Net operating income before extraordinary items | | | | | |
| Annual ($AR_{62}$) | 0.0183 | 0.0077 | 2.39** | | |
| Annual lagged ($AR_{62}$) | 0.0014 | 0.0052 | 0.26 | 0.1167 | 1.92* |
| Third quarter ($QR_{62}$) | −0.0023 | 0.0040 | 0.59 | | |
| Third quarter lagged ($QR_{62}$) | −0.0034 | 0.0041 | 0.83 | | |
| Relative price change lagged ($P^a_{62}$) | 0.0145 | 0.0528 | 0.28 | | |
| **B. Month in which preliminary data are announced** | | | | | |
| 1. Sales, net | | | | | |
| Annual ($AR_{62}$) | 0.1164 | 0.0505 | 2.30* | | |
| Annual lagged ($AR_{62}$) | 0.0152 | 0.0469 | 0.32 | 0.0912 | 1.46 |
| Third quarter ($QR_{63}$) | −0.1185 | 0.0369 | 3.21** | | |
| Third quarter lagged ($QR_{62}$) | −0.0104 | 0.0346 | 0.30 | | |
| Relative price change lagged ($P^a_{62}$) | 0.0810 | 0.0538 | 1.50 | | |
| 3. Net operating income before nonrecurring items | | | | | |
| Annual ($AR_{63}$) | 0.0020 | 0.0072 | 0.28 | | |
| Annual lagged ($AR_{62}$) | −0.0128 | 0.0052 | 2.47** | 0.0930 | 1.49 |
| Third quarter ($QR_{62}$) | 0.0103 | 0.0039 | 2.68** | | |
| Third quarter lagged ($QR_{62}$) | 0.0060 | 0.0041 | 1.47 | | |
| Relative price change lagged ($P^a_{62}$) | 0.0754 | 0.0531 | 1.42 | | |
| 4. Net operating income before extraordinary items | | | | | |
| Annual ($AR_{63}$) | 0.0024 | 0.0074 | 0.32 | | |
| Annual lagged ($AR_{62}$) | −0.0111 | 0.0051 | 2.19* | 0.0901 | 1.44 |
| Third quarter ($QR_{63}$) | 0.0099 | 0.0039 | 2.57** | | |
| Third quarter lagged ($QR_{62}$) | 0.0054 | 0.0041 | 1.34 | | |
| Relative price change lagged ($P^a_{62}$) | 0.0741 | 0.0531 | 1.40 | | |

C. Month before preliminary data month

1. Sales, net
  Annual ($AR_{63}$)                0.0064   0.0443   0.15    0.1710
  Annual lagged ($AR_{62}$)         0.0848   0.0413   2.05*           3.00**
  Third quarter ($QR_{63}$)         0.0282   0.0324   0.87
  Third quarter lagged ($QR_{62}$)  0.0032   0.0305   0.10
  Relative price change
    lagged ($P_{62}^a$)             0.0111   0.0457   0.24

3. Net operating income before nonrecurring items
  Annual ($AR_{63}$)                0.0034   0.0064   0.53    0.1596
  Annual lagged ($AR_{62}$)         0.0095   0.0046   2.06*           2.76**
  Third quarter ($QR_{63}$)        −0.0012   0.0034   0.35
  Third quarter lagged ($QR_{62}$) −0.0026   0.0035   0.74
  Relative price change
    lagged ($P_{62}^a$)             0.0169   0.0459   0.37

4. Net operating income before extraordinary items
  Annual ($AR_{63}$)                0.0032   0.0066   0.48    0.1583
  Annual lagged ($AR_{62}$)         0.0085   0.0045   1.88*           2.74**
  Third quarter ($QR_{63}$)        −0.0010   0.0034   0.28
  Third quarter lagged ($QR_{62}$) −0.0023   0.0035   0.66
  Relative price change
    lagged ($P_{62}^a$)             0.0155   0.0460   0.34

D. Two months before preliminary data month

1. Sales, net
  Annual ($AR_{63}$)                0.0328   0.0455   0.72    0.1160
  Annual lagged ($AR_{62}$)         0.1015   0.0425   2.39**          1.91*
  Third quarter ($QR_{62}$)        −0.0137   0.0333   0.41
  Third quarter lagged ($QR_{62}$) −0.0461   0.0315   1.46
  Relative price change
    lagged ($P_{62}^a$)             0.1243   0.0439   2.83**

3. Net operating income before nonrecurring items
  Annual ($AR_{62}$)                0.0014   0.0065   0.22    0.1206
  Annual lagged ($AR_{62}$)         0.0009   0.0047   0.20            2.00**
  Third quarter ($QR_{63}$)         0.0054   0.0035   1.54
  Third quarter lagged ($QR_{62}$) −0.0047   0.0036   1.32
  Relative price change
    lagged ($P_{62}^a$)             0.1333   0.0436   3.06**

4. Net operating income before extraordinary items
  Annual ($AR_{62}$)               −0.0008   0.0067   0.11    0.1207
  Annual lagged ($AR_{62}$)         0.0011   0.0046   0.24            2.00**
  Third quarter ($QR_{63}$)         0.0054   0.0035   1.57
  Third quarter lagged ($QR_{62}$) −0.0046   0.0035   1.29
  Relative price change
    lagged ($P_{62}^a$)             0.1343   0.0435   3.08**

(*continued*)

TABLE 2.10 Continued

| Accounting Data Variable (AR) | Partial Regression Coefficient | Standard Error | t Statistic | $R^2$ of Regression | F Statistic |
|---|---|---|---|---|---|
| E. *Cumulative two months before through preliminary data month* | | | | | |
| 1. Sales, net | | | | | |
|    Annual ($AR_{62}$) | 0.1645 | 0.0809 | 2.03* | 0.1797 | |
|    Annual lagged ($AR_{62}$) | 0.2021 | 0.0750 | 2.70** | | 3.19** |
|    Third quarter ($QR_{62}$) | −0.1081 | 0.0588 | 1.84* | | |
|    Third quarter lagged ($QR_{62}$) | −0.0609 | 0.0555 | 1.10 | | |
|    Relative price change lagged ($P^a_{62}$) | 0.0430 | 0.0631 | 0.68 | | |
| 3. Net operating income before nonrecurring items | | | | | |
|    Annual ($AR_{62}$) | 0.0078 | 0.0116 | 0.67 | 0.1718 | |
|    Annual lagged ($AR_{62}$) | −0.0033 | 0.0084 | 0.39 | | 3.02** |
|    Third quarter ($QR_{62}$) | 0.0146 | 0.0062 | 2.36** | | |
|    Third quarter lagged ($QR_{62}$) | −0.0006 | 0.0064 | 0.10 | | |
|    Relative price change lagged ($P^a_{62}$) | 0.0630 | 0.0621 | 1.01 | | |
| 4. Net operating income before extraordinary items | | | | | |
|    Annual ($AR_{62}$) | 0.0052 | 0.0119 | 0.44 | 0.1710 | |
|    Annual lagged ($AR_{62}$) | −0.0027 | 0.0082 | 0.33 | | 3.00** |
|    Third quarter ($QR_{62}$) | 0.0145 | 0.0062 | 2.36** | | |
|    Third quarter lagged ($QR_{62}$) | −0.0007 | 0.0064 | 0.11 | | |
|    Relative price change lagged ($P^a_{62}$) | 0.0643 | 0.0621 | 1.03 | | |

All dependent variables are the relative change of stock prices ($P^a_j$) in months as stated (A, B, C, D, and E) below.

Coefficients and standard errors are not reported for the change in dividends ($DR_j$) and the industry dummy ($I_{jk}$) variables and the constant term, which are included in the regressions.

                Number of observations = 483
                Degrees of freedom    = 451

\* = "Significant" at .05 level (one tail $t \geq 1.65$, $F \geq 1.59$).
\*\* = "Significant" at .01 level (one tail $t \geq 2.34$, $F \geq 1.94$).

The conclusions are based upon an evaluation of the relative size of the partial regression coefficients, *t* statistics, and *F* ratios given in tables 2.3 through 2.10, as summarized in tables 2.11, 2.12, and 2.13.

The partial regression coefficients (table 2.11) are elasticities, and as such provide a measure of the percentage change in the rate of change of stock prices related to a doubling of the rate of change of the accounting data. The larger the elasticities, the greater the magnitude of the relationship. The *t* statistic (table 2.12) indicates the degree of confidence one might have that a coefficient is not simply the result

TABLE 2.11 Summary of Partial Regression Coefficients of the Annual Accounting Data Variable Shown in Tables 2.3 through 2.10

|  | Models |  |  |  |  |  |  |  |
|---|---|---|---|---|---|---|---|---|
|  | No Forecast |  | Previous Forecast |  | Three-Year Average, AR | Five-Year Average, AR | Geometrically Dist. Lags |  |
|  | AR | AR + QR | AR | AR + QR |  |  | AR | AR + QR |
| **1. Sales** | | | | | | | | |
| A | 0.042 | 0.104** | 0.029 | 0.042 | 0.038 | −0.004 | 0.041 | 0.129** |
| B | 0.011 | 0.129** | −0.005 | 0.053* | 0.010 | −0.013 | −0.003 | 0.115* |
| C | 0.045 | 0.029 | −0.023 | −0.031 | 0.049* | −0.004 | 0.035 | 0.006 |
| D | 0.019 | 0.023 | −0.019 | −0.038 | 0.018 | 0.002 | 0.019 | 0.033 |
| E | 0.073 | 0.180** | −0.048 | −0.017 | 0.075* | −0.007 | 0.057 | 0.165* |
| **2. Net income before depreciation** | | | | | | | | |
| A | 0.014* |  | 0.011* |  | 0.009 | 0.008 | 0.012 |  |
| B | 0.002 |  | 0.002 |  | −0.000 | −0.001 | −0.001 |  |
| C | −0.011* |  | −0.016** |  | −0.007 | −0.008 | −0.001 |  |
| D | −0.016** |  | −0.171** |  | −0.013* | −0.010* | −0.015* |  |
| E | −0.026* |  | −0.031** |  | −0.020* | −0.018* | −0.021* |  |
| **3. Net income before nonrecurring items** | | | | | | | | |
| A | 0.019** | 0.019** | 0.007* | 0.006 | 0.015** | 0.012* | 0.019** | 0.020** |
| B | 0.009 | 0.009 | 0.008* | 0.007* | 0.005 | 0.004 | 0.005 | 0.002 |
| C | −0.001 | −0.001 | −0.004 | −0.004 | 0.002 | −0.002 | 0.003 | 0.003 |
| D | 0.002 | −0.002 | 0.001 | −0.000 | 0.005 | 0.003 | 0.001 | 0.001 |
| E | 0.011 | 0.010 | 0.004 | 0.003 | 0.012 | 0.005 | 0.001 | 0.008 |
| **4. Net income before extraordinary items** | | | | | | | | |
| A | 0.017** | 0.017** | 0.008 | 0.007* | 0.015** | 0.011* | 0.017* | 0.018** |
| B | 0.009 | 0.008 | 0.007* | 0.008* | 0.007 | 0.003 | 0.005 | 0.002 |
| C | −0.000 | −0.000 | −0.004 | −0.004 | 0.001 | −0.002 | 0.002 | 0.003 |
| D | −0.000 | −0.001 | 0.000 | −0.001 | 0.002 | 0.001 | −0.001 | −0.001 |
| E | 0.008 | 0.007 | 0.008 | 0.004 | 0.010 | 0.003 | 0.007 | 0.005 |
| **5. Net income including all items** | | | | | | | | |
| A | 0.010* |  | 0.002 |  | 0.008 | 0.006 | 0.012* |  |
| B | 0.002 |  | 0.002 |  | −0.000 | −0.002 | 0.000 |  |
| C | 0.002 |  | −0.005* |  | 0.003 | 0.000 | 0.007 |  |
| D | 0.001 |  | −0.001 |  | 0.001 | 0.000 | 0.007 |  |
| E | 0.003 |  | −0.004 |  | 0.002 | −0.001 | 0.008 |  |

A = Month in which final data are announced; B = Month in which preliminary data are announced; C = Month before preliminary data month; D = Two months before preliminary data month; E = Cumulative, two months before through preliminary; AR = annual accounting data only regression; AR + QR = annual and third quarter data regression.
\* = "Significant" at .05 level.
\*\* = "Significant" at .01 level.

TABLE 2.12 Summary of t Statistics Shown in Tables 2.3 through 2.10

|  | \multicolumn{2}{c}{No Forecast} | \multicolumn{2}{c}{Previous Forecast} | Three-Year Average, AR | Five-Year Average, AR | \multicolumn{2}{c}{Geometrically Dist. Lags} |
|---|---|---|---|---|---|---|---|---|
|  | AR | AR + QR | AR | AR + QR |  |  | AR | AR + QR |
| **1. Sales** |  |  |  |  |  |  |  |  |
| A | 1.2 | 2.1** | 1.2 | 1.3 | 1.3 | 0.4 | 1.2 | 2.5** |
| B | 0.3 | 2.7** | 0.2 | 1.7* | 0.3 | 1.2 | 0.0 | 2.3* |
| C | 1.5 | 0.7 | 1.1 | 1.1 | 2.0* | 0.4 | 1.1 | 0.2 |
| D | 0.6 | 0.5 | 0.8 | 1.3 | 0.7 | 0.2 | 0.6 | 0.7 |
| E | 1.3 | 2.3** | 1.2 | 0.3 | 1.7* | 0.4 | 1.0 | 2.0* |
| **2. Net income before depreciation** |  |  |  |  |  |  |  |  |
| A | 1.8* |  | 2.0* |  | 1.5 | 1.5 | 1.6 |  |
| B | 0.2 |  | 0.4 |  | 0.0 | 0.1 | 0.1 |  |
| C | 1.7* |  | 3.5** |  | 1.2 | 1.5 | 1.5 |  |
| D | 2.3** |  | 3.6** |  | 2.3* | 2.0* | 2.2* |  |
| E | 2.2* |  | 3.7** |  | 2.0* | 2.1* | 1.8* |  |
| **3. Net income before nonrecurring items** |  |  |  |  |  |  |  |  |
| A | 2.8** | 2.8** | 2.0* | 1.6 | 2.5** | 2.2* | 2.6** | 2.7** |
| B | 1.4 | 1.3 | 2.3* | 2.1* | 0.9 | 0.7 | 0.7 | 0.3 |
| C | 0.1 | 0.1 | 1.4 | 0.4 | 0.4 | 0.4 | 0.4 | 0.5 |
| D | 0.4 | 0.3 | 0.2 | 0.1 | 0.9 | 0.6 | 0.2 | 0.2 |
| E | 1.0 | 0.9 | 0.8 | 0.5 | 1.3 | 0.6 | 0.9 | 0.4 |
| **4. Net income before extraordinary items** |  |  |  |  |  |  |  |  |
| A | 2.4** | 2.4** | 1.6 | 2.0* | 2.5** | 1.8* | 2.3* | 2.4** |
| B | 1.3 | 1.2 | 2.1* | 2.3* | 1.2 | 0.6 | 0.7 | 0.3 |
| C | 0.1 | 0.1 | 1.3 | 0.4 | 0.2 | 0.3 | 0.4 | 0.5 |
| D | 0.1 | 0.2 | 0.1 | 0.2 | 0.4 | 0.2 | 0.2 | 0.2 |
| E | 0.7 | 0.6 | 0.5 | 0.8 | 1.1 | 0.3 | 0.6 | 0.4 |
| **5. Net income including all items** |  |  |  |  |  |  |  |  |
| A | 1.7* |  | 0.6 |  | 1.6 | 1.1 | 2.0* |  |
| B | 0.3 |  | 0.7 |  | 0.1 | 0.4 | 0.0 |  |
| C | 0.3 |  | 1.8* |  | 0.6 | 0.1 | 1.3 |  |
| D | 0.1 |  | 0.5 |  | 0.2 | 0.1 | 0.2 |  |
| E | 0.4 |  | 0.8 |  | 0.4 | 0.2 | 0.9 |  |

A = Month in which final data are announced; B = Month in which preliminary data are announced; C = Month before preliminary data month; D = Two months before preliminary data month; E = Cumulative, two months before through preliminary; AR = annual accounting data only regression; AR + QR = annual and third quarter data regression.
\* = "Significant" at .05 level.
\*\* = "Significant" at .01 level.

TABLE 2.13 Summary of F Statistics Shown in Tables 2.3 through 2.10

|  | \multicolumn{7}{c}{Models} |
| --- | --- | --- | --- | --- | --- | --- | --- |
|  | \multicolumn{2}{c}{No Forecast} | \multicolumn{2}{c}{Previous Forecast} | Three-Year Average, | Five-Year Average, | \multicolumn{2}{c}{Geometrically Dist. Lags} |
|  | AR | AR + QR | AR | AR + QR | AR | AR | AR | AR + QR |
| 1. Sales |  |  |  |  |  |  |  |  |
| A | 2.1** | 2.1** | 2.1* | 2.0* | 2.1* | 2.0* | 1.9* | 2.0** |
| B | 1.1 | 1.5 | 1.0 | 1.3 | 1.1 | 1.1 | 1.2 | 1.5 |
| C | 3.0** | 2.9** | 2.9** | 2.8** | 3.1** | 2.9** | 3.2** | 3.0** |
| D | 1.7* | 1.6 | 1.7* | 1.6 | 1.7 | 1.6 | 2.0* | 1.9* |
| E | 3.2** | 3.3** | 3.2** | 3.1** | 3.3** | 3.2** | 3.3** | 3.2** |
| 2. Net income before depreciation |  |  |  |  |  |  |  |  |
| A | 2.2** |  | 2.2** |  | 2.1** | 2.1** | 2.0* |  |
| B | 1.0 |  | 1.1 |  | 1.0 | 1.0 | 1.2 |  |
| C | 3.0** |  | 3.4** |  | 3.0** | 3.0** | 3.5** |  |
| D | 1.9* |  | 2.2** |  | 1.9* | 1.8* | 2.5** |  |
| E | 3.4** |  | 3.8** |  | 3.3** | 3.3** | 3.5** |  |
| 3. Net income before nonrecurring items |  |  |  |  |  |  |  |  |
| A | 2.4** | 2.3** | 2.2** | 2.1* | 2.3** | 2.2** | 2.1** | 2.0** |
| B | 1.1 | 1.5 | 1.3 | 1.2 | 1.1 | 1.1 | 1.3 | 1.5 |
| C | 2.9** | 2.8** | 3.0** | 2.9** | 2.9** | 2.9** | 2.9** | 2.8** |
| D | 1.6 | 1.8* | 1.6 | 1.9* | 1.7 | 1.7 | 1.8* | 2.0** |
| E | 3.2** | 3.4** | 3.2** | 3.3** | 3.2** | 3.2** | 2.9** | 3.0** |
| 4. Net income before extraordinary items |  |  |  |  |  |  |  |  |
| A | 2.3** | 2.2** | 2.1** | 2.1** | 2.3** | 2.2** | 2.0** | 1.9* |
| B | 1.1 | 1.2 | 1.2 | 1.3 | 1.1 | 1.1 | 1.5 | 1.4 |
| C | 2.9** | 2.8** | 3.0** | 2.9** | 2.9** | 2.9** | 2.9** | 2.8** |
| D | 1.6 | 1.8* | 1.6 | 1.9* | 1.6 | 1.6 | 1.8* | 2.0** |
| E | 3.2** | 3.4** | 3.2** | 3.3** | 3.2** | 3.2** | 2.9** | 3.0** |
| 5. Net income including all items |  |  |  |  |  |  |  |  |
| A | 2.2** |  | 2.0* |  | 2.1* | 2.1* | 2.0* |  |
| B | 1.0 |  | 1.1 |  | 1.0 | 1.1 | 1.2 |  |
| C | 2.9** |  | 3.0** |  | 2.9** | 2.9** | 3.3** |  |
| D | 1.6 |  | 1.6 |  | 1.6 | 1.6 | 1.9* |  |
| E | 3.2** |  | 3.2** |  | 3.2** | 3.2** | 3.0** |  |

A = Month in which final data are announced; B = Month in which preliminary data are announced; C = Month before preliminary data month; D = Two months before preliminary data month; E = Cumulative, two months before through preliminary; AR = annual accounting data only regression; AR + QR = annual and third quarter data regression.

\* = "Significant" at .05 level.
\*\* = "Significant" at .01 level.

of a chance deviation from a "true" value of zero.[22] The $F$ statistic (table 2.13) is a measure of the "goodness of fit" of the model to the data, that is, $F$ expresses the degree of confidence one might have in the fit. The levels of "significance" denoted in the tables by asterisks indicate the probabilities that the coefficients and goodness of fit of the regressions are the result of chance alone. Rigorous tests were not made to determine whether the data meet the requirements of these significance tests. Although it is believed that the sample does not seriously violate their requirements, the significance levels indicated by asterisks should be taken as suggestive only.

## The Period in Which Accounting Data Are "Known"

The month in which accounting reports are made public, either in preliminary or final form, may not be the time at which the information they contain is acted upon by investors. A month may be too long a period to measure the effect of the data on investors' expectations. Alternatively, the information content of the data may have been known and acted upon by astute investors as a result of leakage of inside information or analysis of other sources of information. To test for information leakage, the accounting data were related to price changes in earlier months (assuming, again, that a month is not too long a period). The independent variables were regressed on the rate of stock price change in the month in which final data are announced $(A)$, the month in which preliminary data are announced $(B)$, one month prior to the preliminary data month $(C)$, two months prior to the preliminary data month $(D)$, and the sum of the month prior to the preliminary data month and the two months previous $(E)$. (To save space, the letters A through E are used here and in the tables to identify these periods.)

The dependent variables are not completely independent as table 2.14 shows. Often, preliminary data are announced in the same month as is the final data, or no preliminary data are announced at all. The sum of three months $(E)$ is not independent of $(B)$, $(C)$, or $(D)$, since it is composed of them. The other variables are essentially uncorrelated.

One generalization can be made about which period is most highly related to the independent variables. Table 2.13, which summarizes the $F$ statistics, shows that the cumulative period $(E)$ has the highest $F$ statistics for all models and all accounting constructs. The month before the preliminary month $(C)$ consistently shows the next highest $F$ statistics; this indicates that the relatively high $F$'s for E

---

22. The following descriptions of the statistics are brief and nonrigorous and therefore are somewhat inaccurate. A statistics text should be consulted for complete descriptions.

TABLE 2.14 Correlation of the Dependent Variables, $P_t^a$

|  | B | C | D | E |
|---|---|---|---|---|
| A. Month in which final data are announced | 0.372 | −0.035 | −0.060 | 0.169 |
| B. Month in which preliminary data are announced | 1.000 | 0.011 | 0.004 | 0.603 |
| C. Month before preliminary data month | 0.011 | 1.000 | 0.060 | 0.589 |
| D. Two months before preliminary data month | 0.004 | 0.060 | 1.000 | 0.583 |
| E. Cumulative, two months before through preliminary data month | 0.603 | 0.589 | 0.582 | 1.000 |

are due to large measure to C. These findings could be due either to the accounting variables or to the other independent variables. Analysis of the simple correlation coefficients of the industry dummy variables with the dependent variables and of the coefficients of the dummy variables in the regressions indicates that, for some reason, a few industries are strongly related to the cumulative (E) and month prior to the preliminary month (C) dependent variables. The principal industries so related are the air transport industry (positively correlated), and the electronics, textile apparel manufacturers, and office and business equipment industries (negatively correlated). The change in dividend variable ($\Delta DR$) is much more highly (positively) correlated to the dependent variable in period C.[23] The industry and dividend change variables, then, probably account for most of the higher F statistics in periods C and E. However, the differences in the magnitude and significance of the accounting variables for different periods warrant analysis. Since these differences are not the same for all of the accounting data constructs, a discussion of each follows. (The Five-Year Average model is discarded below: therefore the discussion excludes consideration of data from this model.)

The coefficients of the "sales" construct is highest in magnitude and in statistical significance for the cumulative period, E, for all of the models except one. However, the preliminary data month, B, generally is the only important one of the three months that comprise period E. This is especially true for the models which include third quarter data. For the models using only annual data the month before the preliminary data are released, C, is more important. The final data period, A, is of next greatest importance. Therefore, it appears that the sales data have their greatest impact in the month in which they are formally made public, although there is some evidence of leakage in the previous month, and to a

---

23. The means of $\Delta DR$ in periods A, B, C, and D are 0.024, 0.016, 0.020, and 0.002. But the simple correlation coefficient of $\Delta DR$ and $P^a$ in period C is 0.10 as against 0.04 or less in the other periods. The relatively high correlation coefficient in period C may be evidence of the information effect of dividend changes that precede, and possibly forecast, the information content of the preliminary accounting data published in the following month.

much lesser extent over the period between the close of the year and the publication of the annual report.

The "net income before depreciation" construct also has its greatest effect in the cumulative period, $E$, for most of the models. This finding is curious, because one would expect much less knowledge of this information prior to the month in which the final reports are published. Further, the coefficients in period $E$ are negative; this indicates that an increase in the rate of net income before depreciation is associated with a decrease in the rate of change of stock prices. (This is considered further below.) The only significant positive coefficients are in the final report period, $A$, a finding that is consistent with expectations.

The most significant coefficients of the income constructs, "net income before nonrecurring items," "before extraordinary items," and "after extraordinary items" are almost all in period $A$. This result conforms to expectations since these data usually are not made public except in the final reports.

In summary, the month when the final data are announced ($A$) appears to be most important, with some exceptions for the "sales" and "net income before depreciation" constructs.

## The Information Content of Third Quarter Data

Third quarter accounting data are included in the No Forecast, Previous Ratio, and Geometrically Distributed Lags models for the "sales," and "net income before nonrecurring items" and "net income before extraordinary items" constructs. A comparison of the regressions with and without the third quarter data reveals the following. First, in all three models "sales" show predominantly larger coefficients for the annual accounting variable when the third quarter variable is included. The $t$ statistics of the coefficients also are predominantly higher when the third quarter variables are included. Second, "net income before nonrecurring items" and "before extraordinary items" show almost no difference in the magnitude of partial regression coefficients or $t$ statistics of the annual accounting data variable, whether the third quarter data are included or not.

Hence, it is concluded that the third quarter data are useful only for the "sales" construct of income. This is a somewhat unexpected finding, since sales data often are available from sources other than published accounting reports while income data are not as readily available. As discussed above, the final ($A$) and preliminary ($B$) data months are the most important for the "sales" construct regressions that include the third quarter data. A further analysis of the Geometrically Distributed Lags model (tables 2.9 and 2.10) reveals that for periods $A$ and $B$ the coefficients of the lagged values of the annual variable are insignificant and relatively small. The No Forecast model, then, would seem to fit the sales data better. In this model, the investor's expectations are presumed to be derived from sources other than past years' accounting data. (Recall that the "current" year's data are logarithms of the ratios of the current and prior years' published data.)

Therefore it appears that quarterly published sales figures are used by investors, along with other sources of data, to evaluate the annual data, but that prior year's data are not so used. A shortcoming of the present study may be that insufficient attention was given to the specification of quarterly data. A comparison of results of the final quarter's data with those of the previous three quarters may have proved more fruitful than the comparison made between the third quarter and annual results of succeeding years.

## Evaluation of the Models: Implications for Determining How Much Data Investors Use

No one model is "best" for all of the accounting data constructs or all of the time periods. Further, the $F$ statistics summarized in table 2.13 are almost the same for a given time period, regardless of the model. Hence, it appears that the choice of model is not very important in explaining the rate of change of stock prices. However, differences do exist among the models in estimating the relationship between the accounting data variables and stock prices. The Five-Year Average model can be rejected immediately. All except one of the coefficients for all of the accounting data variables round to 0.01 and the standard errors of most coefficients are as large or larger. The other models appear to be inconsistently better for some accounting data constructs than for others.

The "sales" construct has the largest and most statistically significant coefficients when used in the No Forecast and Geometrically Distributed Lags models that include third quarter data (as is discussed above). There is evidence that investors do not use prior years' sales data in forming their expectations as shown by the fact that the coefficients are lowest for the Five-Year Forecast and small and insignificant for the lagged variables in the Geometrically Distributed Lags model.

The "net income before depreciation" construct also appears to do best in the No Forecast model, although the differences between the models are small. Nevertheless, it is interesting to note that for the final data month, $A$ (the only period with positive and significant coefficients), the Three- and Five-Year Average models are least significant and the coefficients of the lagged variables in the Geometrically Distributed Lags model are small and insignificant. Hence, it appears that investors do not use past years' ratios, if they use the "net income before depreciation" construct of income at all.

The "net income before nonrecurring items" and "net income before extraordinary items" constructs show the largest and most significant coefficients in the No Forecast and Geometrically Distributed Lags models. However, the advantage over the other models is not striking. As with the "sales" and "net income before depreciation" constructs, the coefficients of the lagged variables in the Geometrically Distributed Lags model are small and quite insignificant. If it were not for the fact that the coefficients in the Three- and Five-Year Average models are almost as great and significant as those in the No Forecast models, one could conclude that investors do not seem to use past years' ratios at all in forming their expectations.

The No Forecast and Geometrically Distributed Lags models are the most important models for the "net income after extraordinary items" construct. For the important final data month, $A$, the coefficients of the lag variables are small and insignificant. Interestingly, the coefficients of the lagged variables are important in the preliminary data month, $B$. This may signify that investors use past years' information when they do not have access to the current data.

To summarize, the No Forecast model, which uses the least prior data, appears to be generally the most useful in explaining the relationship between accounting data and stock prices. There is evidence that investors do not use past changes in rates of change of accounting data in forming their expectations, except for the months prior to those in which the preliminary and final data are made public. If this finding is verified in future research, it may be concluded that the tables of past data presented in many annual reports are not used by investors.

## The Accounting Construct Used by Investors

From the relative size of the coefficients, it appears that the "sales" construct is used more by investors than are the other constructs tested. The highest value of the "sales" coefficients is 0.18 while the highest of the other constructs is 0.019.

The coefficients of "net income before depreciation" construct are positive in all of the models only for the final data month, $A$. In two models positive, though relatively small, coefficients are found for the preliminary data month, $B$. That the coefficients otherwise are negative and largely statistically significant is evidence that this construct is not used by investors in periods other than the month in which final data are published, or if used, is used in some perverse manner. It also may be evidence that the significant positive coefficients found for period $A$ are spurious.

The least important of the "net income" constructs, by the size of coefficient test, is "net income after extraordinary items." Its highest coefficient is 0.012. The coefficients of the "net income before nonrecurring items" and "net income before extraordinary items" are the highest of the group and so alike that the two constructs cannot be distinguished. But the coefficients of the four "net income" constructs are not so different that one can conclude that investors use one rather than another.

## Conclusions and Suggestions for Future Research

The conclusions offered in this section must be taken as tentative, because the differences among the time periods, models, and accounting constraints are not great. In addition, although many of the coefficients and regressions are statistically significant, they cannot be accepted with great confidence until the experiment has been replicated.

However, one finding is striking. Only a relatively small, though significant, relationship was found between the rates of change of data found in corporate published reports and rates of change of stock prices. At most, the positive elasticities are 0.18 for sales data and 0.02 for one of the net income constructs. Thus, as measured in this study, the information contained in published accounting reports is a relatively small portion of the information used by investors.

Within this limited use, it appears that (1) the information is used primarily in the period in which it is made public; (2) third quarter data are used only for the "sales" construct, except that the third quarter data are important for the "net income constructs" in the months before the preliminary and final data are made public; (3) the importance of the No Forecast model and the small size and nonsignificance of the coefficients of the lagged variables indicate that past annual ratios are not used by investors; and (4) "sales" is the construct most highly related to the rate of change in stock prices.

The finding that it does not make a great deal of difference which accounting construct of net income or model is used may be interpreted to mean that the accounting data are used only to confirm information otherwise gathered from news sources, interviews, inside information, and so on, and that the arguments within the accounting profession of which concept of income is "best" are beside the point. Alternatively, the findings may indicate that the data and/or models used are not adequate for the purpose of the research. Therefore, before the disputes within the profession can be dismissed as "much ado about nothing," some improvement in the methods described should be undertaken.

First, the procedure used above can be replicated as soon as the Center for Research on Security Prices makes available data more current than 1964. Second, it may be that a period of a month is too long for the effect of accounting data on stock prices to be measured. Weekly or even daily stock price data could be substituted for the monthly dependent variable. However, it is interesting to note that Ashley (1962) used daily price changes in his study, which utilized a model that is similar to the No Forecast model. He measured the effect on daily stock prices of large changes in net earnings that followed publication of the accounting information. His findings are very similar to those reported above. Third, a better specification of the quarterly data could be made. A shortcoming of the present study may be that insufficient attention was given to the specification of quarterly data. A comparison of final quarter's data with those of the previous three quarters may have proved more fruitful than the comparison made between the third quarter and annual results of succeeding years. Fourth, the aggregative models used may not be correct. An alternative procedure is to use the stock price and accounting data for individual companies over a period of years. Companies that experienced large changes in their sales and income would be preferable. Finally, some detailed studies could be made to determine how investors use published accounting data. Interviews could be taken from which hypotheses may be developed that could be tested further in laboratory studies. These studies may give rise to better models than those used in the present study.

**REFERENCES**

John W. Ashley, "Stock Prices and Changes in Earnings and Dividends: Some Empirical Results," *Journal of Political Economy*, 70 (February 1962), 82–85.

Charles P. Bonini, *Simulation of Information and Decision Systems in the Firm* (Englewood Cliffs N.J.: Prentice Hall, 1963).

William J. Bruns Jr., "Inventory Valuation and Management Decisions," *Accounting Review*, 40 (April 1965), 345–57.

Phillip D. Cagan, "The Monetary Dynamics of Hyperinflation," in Milton Friedman, ed., *Studies on the Quantity Theory of Money* (Chicago: University of Chicago Press, 1956), pp. 25–117.

Alan R. Cerf, *Corporate Reporting and Investment Decisions* (Berkeley, Calif.: Institute of Business and Economic Research, 1961).

Paul Cootner, ed., *The Random Character of Stock Market Prices* (Cambridge: MIT Press, 1964).

Thomas R. Dyckman, "The Effects of Alternative Accounting Techniques on Certain Management Decisions," *Journal of Accounting Research*, 2 (Spring 1964a), pp. 91–107.

Thomas R. Dyckman, "On the Investment Decision," *Accounting Review*, 39 (April 1964b), 285–95.

Eugene F. Fama, "The Behavior of Stock-Market Prices," *Journal of Business*, 38 (January 1965), 34–105.

Eugene F. Fama, Lawrence Fisher, Michael Jensen, and Richard Roll, "The Adjustment of Stock Prices to New Information," *International Economic Review* (1969).

Lawrence Fisher, "Outcomes for 'Random' Investments in Common Stocks Listed on the New York Stock Exchange," *Journal of Business*, 38 (April 1965), 149–61.

Lawrence Fisher, "Some New Stock Market Indexes," *Journal of Business*, 39 (Supplement, January 1966), 191–225, Table A1, "Combination Investment Performance Indexes."

Milton Friedman, *A Theory of the Consumption Function* (Princeton: Princeton University Press for the National Bureau of Economic Research, 1957).

Melvin N. Greenball, "The Concept, Relevance and Estimation of the Permanent Earnings of the Firm" (unpublished Ph.D. dissertation, University of Chicago, 1965).

Charles T. Horngren, "Disclosure: 1957," *Accounting Review*, 32 (October 1957), 598–604.

Robert E. Jensen, "An Experimental Design for Study of Effects of Accounting Variations in Decision Making," *Journal of Accounting Research*, 4 (Autumn 1966), 224–38.

Benjamin F. King, "Market and Industry Factors in Stock Price Behavior," *Journal of Business*, 39 (January 1966), 139–90.

L. M. Koyck, *Distributed Lags and Investment Analysis* (Contributions to Economic Analysis No. 4) (Amsterdam: North Holland, 1954).

Arnold Moore, "Some Characteristics of Changes in Common Stock Prices," in Paul Cootner, ed., *The Random Character of Stock Market Prices* (Cambridge: MIT Press, 1964), pp. 139–61.

John F. Muth, "Rational Expectations and the Theory of Price Movements," *Econometrica*, 29 (July 1961), 315–35.

Marc Nerlove, "Distributed Lags and Estimation of Long-Run Supply and Demand Elasticities: Theoretical Considerations," *Journal of Farm Economics*, 40, No. 2 (May 1958), 301–11.

John L. O'Donnell, "Relationships between Reported Earnings and Stock Prices in the Electric Utility Industry," *Accounting Review*, 40 (January 1965), 135–43.

Kristian S. Palda, "The Measurement of Cumulative Advertising Effects," *Journal of Business*, 38 (April 1965), 162–79.

Elmo Roper, *A Report on What Information People Want about Policies and Financial Conditions of Corporations*, Vols. I and II (New York: Controllers Institute Foundation, 1948).

Standard Statistics Company, *Compustat Information Manual* (New York: 1966).

George J. Staubus, "The Association of Financial Accounting Variables with Common Stock Values," *Accounting Review*, 40 (January 1965), 119–34.

# 3

# Required Disclosure and the Stock Market: An Evaluation of the Securities Exchange Act of 1934

THE SECURITIES EXCHANGE ACT OF 1934 WAS ONE of the earliest and, some believe, one of the most successful laws enacted by the New Deal. The stock market crash in 1929 and the Great Depression provided the impetus for reform of the stock markets in the belief that weaknesses of the institutions and ineptitude and/or chicanery among brokers and bankers were partially responsible for the losses incurred by stockholders. Although many critics, reformers, and Congressmen wanted Congress to enact "blue skies" legislation that would require all securities sold and traded to be approved by the federal government, President Franklin Roosevelt preferred the concept of "disclosure" (see Wheat, 1967). Rather than having the government approve or disapprove securities, corporations whose securities are publicly sold and traded are required to disclose a large amount of predominantly financial information to the Securities and Exchange Commission (SEC) who make these data available to the public. Indeed, the Securities Exchange Act is described in its title and usually referred to as a "disclosure statute."

Although the financial community generally opposed this legislation and the preceding Securities Act of 1933,[1] most brokers, investors, and government officials probably would find it difficult to conceive of the successful operation of the stock markets without the Securities Acts. Yet the economic rationale for the regulation of the securities markets was not examined carefully before the legislation was passed (which is not surprising, given turbulent times) nor has it been since,[2]

---

Thanks are due to Robert Hagerman and Stanley Engerman for their criticisms, some of which I agree with.

1. A recent history by Ralph DeBedts (1964) reviews these events uncritically.
2. George Stigler (1964a,b) and Irwin Friend and Edward Herman (1964) provide the first quantitative analysis of the Securities Act of 1933 of which I am aware. The only other analyses are in two papers which I published in 1969.

even though the Securities Act of 1934 was extended in 1964 to include most corporations whose stock is publicly owned. Such an examination of one important part of the law—the financial disclosure requirements—is presented here. This analysis is particularly timely because the SEC appears to be shifting its emphasis toward increasing the disclosure requirements of almost all corporations whose stock is traded in the markets.[3]

## I. The Disclosure Requirements of the Securities Exchange Act of 1934

The 1934 act requires that a corporation whose stock is traded on a registered stock exchange or who registered a stock issue:

a. file detailed balance sheets, income statements, and supporting substatements (form 10K) within 120 days after the close of its fiscal year;
b. file a much less detailed semiannual report (form 9K) within 45 days after the first half of the fiscal year;
c. file a "current report" (form 8K) 10 days after the end of any month in which certain "significant" events occurred (such as a change of control of the corporation, material legal proceedings undertaken, material change of securities outstanding, and revaluation of assets).

In 1964, the disclosure requirements were extended to almost all corporations with at least 500 stockholders or $1 million in assets. (Exceptions are regulated companies whose statements were prescribed, such as banks and insurance companies). Thus, all but the smallest corporations now are covered by the act.

Section 13(b) of the 1934 act (and section 19(a) of the 1933 act) gives the SEC the power to prescribe the form and content of the financial statements filed under the act. In general, the SEC has followed generally accepted accounting procedures, although it has influenced these procedures by insisting that assets not be revalued upward, goodwill be amortized rapidly, and other "conservative" biases be reinforced. In this regard, the SEC has not followed the "disclosure rather than approval" philosophy of the Securities Exchange Act. This policy was established by Accounting Series Release No. 4 in 1938, which states that

---

3. A rather detailed "Report and Recommendations to the Securities and Exchange Commission" from the Disclosure Policy Study headed by Wheat recommends "that for the future, greater attention be paid to those continuing disclosures which benefit the trading markets in securities. Prior to 1964 the continuing disclosure reached only those issues whose securities were listed on exchanges and those which had voluntarily registered securities under the '33 Act. Full exercise of that authority might have deterred listing. This is no longer the case, and a serious impediment to progress in disclosure policy has been removed" (Wheat Report, 1969, p. 11).

where financial statements filed...are prepared in accordance with accounting principles for which there is no substantial authoritative support, such financial statements will be presumed to be misleading or inaccurate *despite disclosures* contained in the certificate of the accountant or in footnotes to the statements provided the matters involved are material. (emphasis added)

Whether disclosure, as defined and required by the SEC, has been meaningful and beneficial, is the question asked here—not whether disclosure, as such, is good or bad.[4]

## II. The Rationale Underlying the Legislation

It would seem that any argument against disclosure is equivalent to an argument for secrecy. But such is not the case. Prior to the passage of the Securities Exchange Act, corporations could disclose what they wished to their current and potential stockholders and, if they were listed on the New York Stock Exchange (NYSE), American, Chicago (Midwest), or other regional exchanges, had to submit balance sheets and income statements to the exchange. For the year ended December 31, 1933, all NYSE corporations were audited by CPA firms, all listed current assets and liabilities in their balance sheets, 62 percent gave their sales, 54 percent the cost of goods sold, and 93 percent disclosed the amount of depreciation expense. These percentages had been increasing fairly steadily prior to 1933, although there was little change after 1928. (See Benston, 1969b, p. 519.) One could argue (as did the NYSE) that the legislation was not needed.

One could also argue that the disclosure policy followed by corporations in the absence of legislation is in the best interests of their stockholders. If management believed that the marginal revenue to the stockholders as a group from disclosure would exceed the marginal cost of preparing and supplying the information, they would disclose their financial and other data. The marginal revenue might include the savings to stockholders of not having to gather the data privately, the reduced cost of capital to the firm if prospective stockholders' uncertainty about the firm were reduced, improvement in the marketability of the firms' shares if investors desired financial information, and so on. The marginal costs of disclosure might include the cost of preparing and distributing the statements; the costs incurred in informing competitors, suppliers, customers, and government officials; and the cost of misinforming stockholders when accounting statements report economic

---

4. The possible detrimental effect of the SEC's definition of disclosure on the development of improved and innovative accounting procedure has been argued elsewhere (Benston, 1969b). While the issue is important to the question of the efficient operation of securities market, it is not emphasized in this essay.

events incorrectly or inadequately (as when all research and development and advertising expenditures are charged to expense currently).

However, management might not issue financial statements (or might issue incomplete statements) if they underestimate the value of these statements to their current or potential investors, mismanage the corporation, intend to defraud investors, or if there are positive externalities in the efficient allocation of resources when all (or most) companies disclose financial data. Thus, one cannot immediately dismiss the argument that there is need for required disclosure solely by reference to the invisible hand of the market. Rather the question must be examined with respect to the rationale upon which the Securities Exchange Act of 1934 is based.

Underlying the disclosure requirements of the 1934 act is the belief that required disclosure of financial data is necessary for the fair and efficient operation of capital markets. The SEC's 1969 Wheat Report (and most other writings on the subject) views disclosure as necessary to (1) prevent financial manipulation and (2) provide investors and speculators with enough information to enable them to arrive at their own rational decisions (Wheat Report, p. 10).[5] Perhaps even more important is the concept of "fairness," the belief that all investors, big and small, insiders and outsiders, should have equal access to relevant information. Whether these objectives can be achieved, a priori, by disclosure of financial data, and if they can, whether or not the evidence supports or rejects the hypothesis that they were, is considered in the balance of the chapter. To facilitate the presentation of the material, fraud and manipulation are discussed first in section III, followed by an empirical analysis of information and investors' decisions in section IV, and the effects of the 1934 act on traded securities in section V, on losses by stockholders in section VI, and on investors' confidence in the market in section VII.

## III. Fraud and Manipulation

Fraud and manipulation may be of two different types with respect to disclosure. Published statements may contain false or misleading data or desired data may not be published at all but may be released in the form of news stories, rumors, and so on, to manipulate the public's expectations and so affect stock prices. These are discussed in turn.

It is very difficult to determine whether the 1934 act prevented the publication of fraudulent or misleading financial statements or even whether much fraud

---

5. Also mentioned is "the belief that appropriate publicity tends to deter questionable practices and to elevate standards of business conduct" (p. 10). These goals are inherently nonoperational, except as they refer to the prevention of fraud and manipulation, which is discussed below, or perhaps to insider stock dealings, which is not affected by the disclosure of financial data and hence is outside the scope of this essay. However, see Henry Manne (1966) for one view contrary to the SEC's position.

existed to any greater extent before or after the passage of the act. In a situation of personal fraud by self-dealing or simple defalcation, required disclosure is of little value. Certified public accountants insist that they do not audit explicitly for fraud nor does the SEC ask them to do this, although I believe a good case could be made for this requirement. With respect to fraudulently prepared financial statements, I have reviewed such evidence as exists in another article (Benston, 1969a, pp. 51–55). A search of the available literature, including the Senate and House hearings on the proposed securities legislation, fails to reveal much evidence of fraud in the preparation or dissemination of financial statements prior to 1934. For example, Wiley Rich, the author of a comprehensive survey of the legal responsibilities of accountants (1935), states that "an extensive search has revealed not a single American case in which a public accountant has been held liable in a crime for fraud" (p. 100). It appears that the feeling in the early 1930s that published accounting statements were fraudulent or misleading was based on the "exposés" of William Ripley (1916, 1927) and others of the behavior of some large corporations at the turn of the century. Further, the recent BarChris, Yale Transport, Green Department Store, Continental Vending, and other cases show that fraud in financial statements, while relatively rare, has not been banished from the land.

The lack of evidence on fraudulent financial statements does not imply that published financial statements were or were not misleading. Prior to the passage of the Securities Act, it was very difficult for third parties, such as prospective stockholders, to sue accounting firms for negligently prepared financial statements. The courts held, under the rule of privity, that these reports were prepared for management only (see *Landell v. Lybrand*).

However, accountants were (and still are) liable for fraud "if their audit has been so negligent as to justify a finding that they had no genuine belief in its adequacy for this again is fraud" (see *Ultramares Corp. v. Touche, Niven and Co.*, p. 488). The Securities Act changed accountants' liability dramatically, and now an investor may sue an accountant if, having relied on false or misleading statements, he "shall have purchased or sold a security at a price which was affected by such statement" (section 18). It is important to note that the accountant must prove that the investor's loss was not a consequence of the financial statements rather than that the investor prove that he actually was misled by or even saw the statements.

In contrast to the lawmakers' expectations, an important consequence of this change in the law and of the SEC's administration of the acts appears to be that financial statements are more misleading than they were. The considerable liability of accountants under section 18 has contributed to accountants following conservative, often worthless practice, since it is difficult to sue them successfully for preparing misleading statements if they follow traditional procedures. In addition, the SEC has insisted on historically based accounting, discouraging price level and other revaluation of assets and liabilities, refusing to permit publication of sales and income projections and other valuable economic data, and so on. Thus published financial statements are more misleading than they otherwise might have been. Although accountants might not have made much progress in reporting the economic position and progress of corporations had there been no Securities Act, there is no empirical or a priori basis for an assertion that the 1934 act has had a net positive effect on the publication of fraudulent or misleading financial statements.

While there is little direct evidence that corporate managers issued fraudulent financial statements, they may have refused to disclose information to create a climate in which they could manipulate stock prices by means of "pools" and "bear raids." At least such is the opinion of the SEC. In their booklet, *A 25 Year Summary of the Activities of the Securities and Exchange Commission, 1934–1959* (1959), they say these practices

> resulted in a situation in which no one could be sure that market prices for securities bore any reasonable relation to intrinsic values or reflected the

TABLE 3.1 Disclosure of Financial Data by Corporations Whose Securities were Subject to Pools

| Pool Year | Statement Year | Percentage Disclosing[a] Sales | Percentage Disclosing[a] Cost of Goods Sold |
|---|---|---|---|
| 1929 pools | 1927 | 58 | 47 |
| (103 corporations)[b] | 1928 | 58 | 48 |
|  | 1929 | 61 | 50 |
|  | 1930 | 60 | 52 |
| 1930 pools | 1928 | 70 | 50 |
| (30 companies)[c] | 1929 | 70 | 53 |
|  | 1930 | 70 | 60 |
|  | 1931 | 63 | 70 |
| 1931 pools | 1929 | 67 | 50 |
| (6 companies) | 1930 | 67 | 50 |
|  | 1931 | 67 | 50 |
|  | 1932 | 33 | 50 |
| 1932 pools | 1930 | 100 | 100 |
| (2 companies) | 1931 | 100 | 100 |
|  | 1932 | 50 | 100 |
|  | 1933 | 50 | 100 |
| 1933 pools | 1931 | 67 | 42 |
| (12 companies)[d] | 1932 | 67 | 42 |
|  | 1933 | 67 | 42 |

*Source*: Pools: U.S. Senate Committee on Banking and Currency, part 17, pp. 7948–50, Financial Data: Moody's Investors Service, various years.
[a] Corporations whose statements were not in Moody's (four of the 1929 pools and two of the 1930 pools) are included as "nondisclosure."
[b] Number of securities = 105; 2 securities of two corporations were listed.
[c] Number of securities = 31; 2 securities of one corporation were listed.
[d] Number of securities = 13; 2 securities of one corporation were listed.

impersonal forces of supply and demand. In fact, the investigation record demonstrated that during 1929 the prices of over 100 stocks on the New York Stock Exchange were subject to manipulation by massive pool operations. One of the principal contributing factors to the success of the manipulator was the inability of investors and their advisers to obtain reliable financial and other information upon which to evaluate securities. (pp. xv–xvi)

To test this assertion, the financial statements (as published in Moody's Investors Services, various years) of those over 100 corporations whose securities were subject to pools, as revealed by the Senate Committee on Banking and Currency, were examined for years before, during, and after the pools. Table 3.1 gives the percentage that disclosed such important information as sales and cost of goods sold. (All except four corporations included in the 1929 pools and two included in the 1930 pools had otherwise complete balance sheets and income statements published in Moody's.) The percentages with respect to sales were almost the same as those found for all companies listed on the NYSE and a little lower with respect to cost of goods sold. Thus, while "pools" and "bear raids" may or may not have been unfair to investors, it is clear that their operations (successful or not) owed little to the nondisclosure of accounting data.

## IV. Information and Rational Decisions of Investors and Speculators

The second rationale for the disclosure requirements is to allow "investors [to] make a realistic appraisal of the merits of securities and thus exercise an informed judgment in determining whether to purchase them" (Securities Exchange Commission, 1967, p. 1). This rationale is based on a belief that the data required by the SEC are "information." That is, the financial statements must provide data about a corporation that affect investors' expectations about its future prospects and relative riskiness and that were not previously known, such that the information was completely discounted and impounded in the market price of the securities before the time of disclosure.

There is serious question whether the financial data approved by the SEC can provide the investor with information. The SEC does not allow current market valuation of assets, estimates of future sales, or projection of the effects of discoveries, favorable regulatory rulings, public acceptance of new products, and other economic events. Additionally, the present value of many important occurrences such as management changes, styling, advertising campaigns and other marketing strategies, changes in the competitive environment, and the like cannot be estimated very well even if the SEC allowed accountants or others to publish their efforts. While this information need not come to the public through the financial statements, the SEC's requirement that these statements be prepared in a specified form implies that they include some relevant quantitative financial information.

But even if financial statements do contain information that is of value to investors, the data may not be made available to the public before insiders (including bookkeepers, secretaries, accountants, typists, and printers) see and take advantage of them. In requiring the filing of financial statements, the SEC is caught in a choice between speed and accuracy (in the sense of reporting to the letter of the formal and informal regulations), a choice which is resolved in favor of accuracy. As is noted above, the annual reports (10K) need not be filed with the SEC until 120 days after the close of a corporation's fiscal year. Whether the statements that have been filed are meaningful to investors and sufficiently timely to be of value is, of course, an empirical question, to which I now turn.

## A. The Information Content of Published Financial Data: Financial Statements and Stock Prices

If the SEC's disclosure requirements are meaningful, the statements they require should contain information, and thus investors' expectations about a corporation's earnings and prospects, riskiness, relationship to other firms, and so on, should be affected by the information. Since numerous studies show that the market adjusts rapidly to new information,[6] the effect, if any, of previously unexpected data published in the financial reports of a corporation ($j$) should be reflected in changes in its stock prices ($\Delta P_{jt}$) in the period $t$ when these unexpected financial data ($F_{jt}^*$) become publicly available. Other factors also may occur during the same period and must be accounted for. Principal among these are changes in general market conditions ($\Delta M_t$), changes in expected dividend payments (which often are announced at the same time that earnings data are announced) ($\Delta D_{jt}$), and changes specific to the corporation's industry ($\Delta I_{kt}$). In summary,

$$\Delta P_{jt} = f(F_{jt}^*, \Delta M_t, \Delta D_{jt}, \Delta I_{kt}, U_{jt}), \tag{3.1}$$

where $U_{jt}$ are other unspecified factors. This model was specified and tested, and the results were reported in a paper I published in 1967. They are summarized very briefly here. The specified model whose description follows was used for these tests, used in another study reviewed below (Ball and Brown, 1968) and in further tests described below in section V.

A two-stage estimating procedure was used that is based on a "market model" originally suggested by Markowitz and first applied in a context similar to the present study by Eugene Fama et al. (1969):

$$\hat{r}_{jt} = \alpha_j + \beta_j r_{Mt} + \tilde{u}_{jt}, \tag{3.2}$$

---

6. See Eugene Fama (1970) for a summary and review.

where $r_{jt}$ is the rate of return for security $j$ for month $t$ (defined as $ln((P_{jt}+D_{jt})/P_{jt-1})$ where $P_{jt}$ is adjusted for stock dividends and splits and $D_{jt}$ is dividend payments declared); $r_{Mt}$ is a similarly measured rate of return on a market index $M$; $\alpha_j$ and $\beta_j$ are parameters that can vary from security to security; and $\tilde{u}_{jt}$ is a random disturbance.[7] Tests applied by Fama et al. (1969) and Marshall Blume (1968, 1970) indicate that equation (3.2) "is well specified as a linear regression model in that (i) the estimated parameters $\alpha_j$ and $\beta_j$ remain fairly constant over long periods of time [e.g., the entire post–World War II period in the case of Blume], (ii) $r_{Mt}$ and the estimated $\hat{u}_{jt}$ are close to serially independent, and (iii) the $\hat{u}_{jt}$ seem to be independent of $r_{Mt}$" (Fama, 1970, p. 403). The $E(\hat{u}_{jt}|F^*_{jt})$ may not $= 0$. This is what was tested.

Equation (3.2) was applied in my 1967 paper to a sample of 483 companies traded on the NYSE in 1964 (the latest year data were available at the time of the study). These included almost all NYSE traded companies from whom annual and quarterly financial data were available on the Compustat tapes. The statistics $\tilde{\alpha}_j$ and $\hat{\beta}_j$ were computed from data that excluded months when the financial statements were made public. These statistics were then "plugged" into equation (3.2a) to compute the residuals, $\hat{u}_{jt}$, for the months when the financial data were published:

$$\hat{r}_{jt} - \hat{\alpha}_j - \hat{\beta}_j r_{Mt} = \hat{u}_{jt}. \tag{3.2a}$$

The $\hat{u}_{jt}$ computed with equation (3.2a) were regressed on estimated unexpected financial data, unexpected dividends, and variables that accounted for industry effects.

An expectation model had to be specified in order to estimate the unexpected financial data ($F^*_{jt}$). Since the SEC's regulations require disclosure of accounting statements for prior periods as well as the present period,[8] expected financial data were taken to be a function of previously published data. Three averages of past data (a weighted average with geometrically declining weights determined by a variant of the Koyck transformation, and simple averages of three and five years' data) and a naive model (previous year's data) were used. Unexpected financial data $F^*_{jt}$, then, is measured by the difference between the reported and the expected data. Although the SEC did not require companies to report their quarterly data until recently, such data were required by the NYSE. Since investors' expectations would be affected by these reports, their effect is estimated by including third quarter financial data in the regressions in forms analogous to those used for the annual data.[9]

---

7. Fama shows that this model is consistent with the Sharpe-Markowitz expected return model.

8. The SEC requires that companies who float a stock issue under the provisions of the Securities Act of 1933 publish at least five years of comparative data, three of which must be certified by an independent CPA.

9. There is some possibility that these third quarter data could be collinear with the annual data, which might reduce the significance of the measured coefficients. I am indebted to Ross Watts for pointing out this possible error.

Since it is not clear which specific financial data investors use, the financial variables were defined alternatively as sales, cash flow net income, current operating income, and net income after extraordinary gains and losses. Thus 16 regressions were computed for the month when the financial data were sent to the SEC and stockholders (four expectations models and four definitions of income).

The regressions reveal that, except for the sales definition of financial data, none of the financial data variables in any of the expectations forms has a greater than minimal economic relationship to changes in stock prices, although the coefficients estimated are statistically significant. On the average, a 100 percent unexpected increase (or decrease) in the rate of change of income is associated with a 2 percent increase (or decrease) in the rate of change of stock prices in the month of announcement. Similar regressions were computed for the month when earnings were announced (which usually is a month before the SEC receives them), and similar results were found. The findings are not very dependent on the form of the expectations model used, although the naive model, where last year's rate of change is expected this year (a sort of "no expectations" model), performed the best. This finding is contrary to the SEC's requirement that companies provide comparative data for several past years. Thus, I conclude that this evidence is not consistent with the underlying assumption of the legislation, that the financial data made public are timely or relevant, on average.

Corroborative findings are reported by Ball and Brown (1968), whose study used a variant of the model described above in equation (3.2). Their sample consists of 261 firms who reported on an annual basis. For most of these firms, data were available in the period 1946 through 1968 on the Compustat tapes. Ball and Brown considered each firm's year as an independent observation. They separated the data into two samples, one consisting of years in which income increased and the other of years in which income decreased unexpectedly, as determined from an expectation model in which a firm's expected income is a function of the income reported by the other firms. However, they did not account for dividend changes or for the information content of quarterly reports. Ball and Brown found that cumulatively, over a year, firms that show greater (or lesser) than expected income changes averaged greater (or lesser) than normal stock price returns. However, they calculate that "of the value of information contained in reported income no more than 10 to 15 percent...has not been anticipated by the month of the [preliminary] report" and compute that the marginal monthly rate of return of buying or selling short a portfolio of stock based on the information contained in the preliminary report is less than 1 percent (pp. 175–76). By the time of the final (SEC-required) report, there is almost no information that has not already been impounded in the price of the stock.

Another study of interest was made by William Beaver (1968), who measured the volume of trading in the weeks before and after the announcement of preliminary earnings. He analyzed weekly price and volume for a sample of 143 firms (those included on the Compustat tape, traded on the NYSE, with other than December 31 fiscal years, with no dividends announced in the same week as the announcement, no stock splits in the quarters around that date, and with relatively few other "announcements"). A model similar to that given in equation (3.2) was used to abstract from market effects. Beaver found that the variance, average volume, and residual positive or negative return are much greater in the week that the preliminary reports are announced (without regard to the sign or magnitude of the earnings) than in the previous or following eight weeks. Further, the greater than normal activity appears to continue for about two to three weeks after the announcement date, but with a considerably smaller magnitude. Contrary to the other studies, Beaver's results seem to indicate that financial statements do contain information or are at least used in some way. One interpretation is that investors use the announcements of preliminary earnings to switch their portfolios. Another is that brokers use the earnings reports as an excuse for "churning." A third explanation, one consistent with the findings of Robert Hagerman (1972) on the effect of requiring commercial banks to report earnings to the public in forms specified by regulatory agencies, is that while financial statements, as such, provide information, required reporting adds nothing. (Recall that all NYSE companies published some form of statement before passage of the 1934 act.)

One other study has been published that considers directly the usefulness of published annual financial statements in purchasing securities. Richard McEnally (1970) tested the value of using low price/earnings (P/E) ratios to choose portfolios of stocks. He used a randomly selected sample of 100 calendar-year stocks from which five portfolios of 20 stocks each were chosen for each of five years, 1961–65. High or low P/E ratios were the basis for forming portfolios. The stocks are assumed to be purchased on April 1 and held for a year. When the earnings used in the P/E ratio were those of the previous year ($E_{t-1}$), the portfolio with the lowest $P/E_{t-1}$ outperformed the others slightly in terms of mean return, there being little difference among the other four portfolios.[10] McEnally then used the ratio of price to earnings of the year in which stocks were purchased, $P/E_t$ (which assumes perfect forecast of the year's earnings in April), to choose portfolios. Except for the little difference between the third and fourth groups, the portfolios so chosen provided consistently higher holding period returns according to the P/E criterion. Since market participants do not have perfect knowledge of the year's earnings, McEnally used the earnings forecasts of the three most popular advisory services of the P/E ratios. The results were almost the same as those reported for published earnings. Thus the research is consistent with Ball and Brown's (1968) study in

---

10. The geometric mean return for the lowest $P/E_{t-1}$ portfolio is 1.20 compared to the average of all portfolios of 1.15. No significance tests were made. However, McEnally reports that "Simple correlation coefficients between $P_t/E_{t-1}$ and the next year's holding period return for these five holding periods…cast doubt on the validity of any relationship" (p. 30).

that financial statement data seems to reflect the economic situation of corporations but either are completely discounted by the market before they are published or do not predict the economic future. In either case, the data are not useful to investors at the time the SEC requires disclosure.

## B. Returns to Sophisticated Users of Financial Data

It may be that the studies cited above approach a complicated problem in too simple a way. It often is claimed that the detailed reports required by the SEC are more useful to trained analysts than to the ordinary stockholder. The analyst then passes on his information to his clients or, in any event, trades on the information, thereby bringing its effects to the market. No doubt information about firms does get to the market. But does it get there by means of the financial reports required by the SEC?

One way to answer these questions is to examine whether well-trained analysts outperform the market. I am aware of two studies that test directly the ability of security analysts to use published financial data. John G. Cragg and Burton Malkiel (1968) recorded predictions made by five investment firms of the earnings of 185 corporations whose stock is widely held. In particular, they compared the earnings' growth rate forecast by the analysts with the actual growth rates. They report that "the remarkable conclusion of the present study is that the careful estimates of security analysts participating in our survey, the bases of which are not limited to public information, perform little better than the past growth rates" [the naive predictor, that the future will be like the past] (p. 83). The second study, by Lyn Pankoff and Robert Virgil (1970), was a controlled, laboratory study. They allowed security analysts to "buy" financial statements of companies in whose stock they can invest. The data are actual data and the stock prices are those that actually prevailed for the stocks whose identity they disguised. While their study is not yet complete, Pankoff and Virgil found that analysts who use financial data (or any other data) do not do as well as they could have had they followed a "naive" buy and hold strategy.

Several indirect tests of the ability of trained analysts to use financial data publicly can be derived from studies of the performance of mutual funds and research departments of brokerage houses. F. E. Brown and Douglas Vickers (1962), William Sharpe (1964), and Michael Jensen (1968) studied the performance of mutual funds compared to that of random selections of securities with similar risk characteristics. They used different techniques and all came to the same conclusion. Mutual funds do not earn for their investors a higher rate of return than would have been earned had the investors held a similarly diversified market portfolio, gross of research costs. Nor is the record of the research departments of brokerage houses any better. A study by R. E. Diefenbach (1972) of the market performance of stocks whose purchase or sale was recommended by 24 institutional research services found that their recommendations, if followed, would have yielded returns equivalent to those earned by investments in the Standard and Poor's (S & P) 425 Index. Thus, even mutual fund and brokerage house research department analysts do not benefit from detailed analysis of SEC reports, among other data.

Even though the evidence reviewed does indicate that the financial reports required by the SEC, when made available, have almost no information content, this does not prove that the required disclosure is not valuable to investors. One might argue that the statements provide a confirmation of data previously released. Because investors know that a corporation's sales, operating expenses, extraordinary gains and losses, assets, and liabilities will be reported, they may have some assurance that the preliminary reports, press releases, and so on, are not prevarications. Thus when the financial statements are made public the data they contain are fully anticipated. But had it not been for the SEC's disclosure requirements, such a state of affairs might not exist. It is to this consideration that I turn next.

## V. An Empirical Analysis of the Effect of the 1934 Act on NYSE Securities

When the Securities Exchange Act was enacted in June 1934, the United States was in the midst of the Great Depression. Hence, it is difficult to separate the effect of the legislation on the stock market from other economic events, and the effect of the disclosure requirements of the act from its other provisions. In addition, it is necessary to determine when the legislation affected the stock market, since it might have been anticipated such that, when passed, its impact already had been discounted.

Fortunately, the data and the particular legislative history of the 1934 act allow an unusual opportunity to test the effect of legislation. Hearings on the 1934 act did not begin until February 1934, nor was there much belief before this date by most observers that such legislation would be enacted (see Sobel, 1965). Prior to this time, it was not considered part of the president's legislative "package." Nevertheless, the bill was signed by President Roosevelt in June 1934 and took effect that year, although full compliance did not occur within the year. Therefore, I have considered the period of adjustment to include February 1934 through June 1935. Thus there is a relatively short and distinct period over which the effect of the legislation may be measured.

The effect of the disclosure provisions of the act may be tested by examining its differential effect on the securities of corporations that were and were not affected by the legislation. At the time of the passage of the Securities Exchange Act of 1934, about 70 percent of stock exchange transactions were made on the NYSE, 13 percent on the American (Curb) Exchange, 1.6 percent on the Chicago (Midwest) Stock Exchange, and the balance on 19 other regional exchanges. The three principal exchanges, at least (the others didn't reply to my inquiries), had similar rules that required listed companies to send certified income statements and balance sheets to stockholders in advance of the annual meeting. The principal reporting requirement imposed by the 1934 act, in addition to the filing of detailed forms, was the required disclosure of sales. Of the 508 corporations whose stock was traded on the NYSE in 1934, 193 (38 percent) did not disclose their sales.[11] Since sales are considered very important information by analysts, and the study reported above (Benston, 1968) found sales the only relatively important accounting number, these corporations are considered as those most likely to be affected by the disclosure requirements of the 1934 act.[12]

Thus two samples of NYSE corporations can be distinguished: the 314 (62 percent) "disclosure" corporations and 193 (38 percent) "nondisclosure" corporations (with respect to sales). These data allow a fairly comprehensive test of the law, since the 1934 act applied (until 1965) only to corporations whose stock is traded on registered exchanges, and most of these corporations were listed on the NYSE in 1934. If disclosure of the sales data required by the 1934 act were meaningful to investors, these effects should be observed in the market returns of the securities affected in the period after the law was effective. As was discussed above in greater detail, if the data disclosed are information, investors would alter their previous estimates of the relative value and/or riskiness of the firms.

The model given by equation (3.2) above can be used to measure these effects. The $\hat{u}_{jt}$ measure the returns on a security after the effect of changes in the return for the market as a whole is accounted for. A change in the $\hat{u}_{jt}$ represents a revaluation of the present value of future returns from a security. As such, it provides a valuable measure of the information content of mandated disclosure.

The $\hat{\beta}_j$ provide a measure of the relative systematic portfolio risk of a security, its covariance with the market relative to the market's variance.[13] As such the $\hat{\beta}_j$ might be affected if the data disclosed in the financial statements provide information about the risk class of a company and the relationship of its economic value to changes in the economy (as reflected by the market).

The variance of returns from a stock may be stated as:[14]

$$\sigma^2(r_j) = \beta_j^2 \sigma^2(r_M) + \sigma^2(u_j), \tag{3.3}$$

where the variables are as defined for equation (3.2) above. The variance of returns on a security, $j$, can be reduced by reducing the variance of the market, $\sigma^2(r_M)$, the

---

11. Fifty-four percent did not report "cost of goods sold," almost all of whom also did not report sales (see table I in Benston, 1969b).
12. The analysis also was carried out for the corporations that did and did not disclose cost of goods sold, with similar results to those reported.
13. See Fama (1970), pp. 401–404, for a more complete exposition of this concept.
14. I am indebted to Michael Jensen for clarifying my thinking on this issue and for the equations presented.

sensitivity of the security to the market, $\beta_j$, and/or the residual variance, $\sigma^2(u_j)$. Fisher and Dorie's (1970) study shows that the dispersion of the market index is higher for the immediate post–1934 act period than it was in the years before 1932. It is not until 1945 that it is of a lower magnitude than the late 1920s. A reduction in the $\beta_j$, though, would reduce the variance in stock's returns. While a reduction in the variance of the residuals of a stock, $\sigma^2(u_j)$, also reduces the variance, it should be noted that investors can reduce or eliminate this "risk" by holding a portfolio of securities. Let

$$r_p = \sum_{j=1}^{n} \frac{1}{n} r_j$$

be the returns on a portfolio of securities with an equal dollar investment in each security. The variance of the returns on such a portfolio is given by

$$\sigma^2(r_p) = \left(\sum_{j=1}^{n} \frac{1}{n}\beta_j\right)^2 \sigma^2(r_M)$$
$$+ \sum_{j=1}^{n} \frac{1}{n^2} \sigma^2(u_j) \qquad (3.4)$$
$$= \overline{\beta}^2 \sigma^2(r_M) + \frac{1}{n}\overline{\sigma^2(u)},$$

assuming that $\text{cov}(u_i, u_j) = 0$ for $i \neq j$. As $n$, the number of stocks in the portfolio increases, the residual variance of the portfolio goes to zero (as long as the $\sigma^2(u_j)$ are bounded from above). Nevertheless, the legislators and many economists believe it desirable to reduce the riskiness of individual stocks, since "small investors" cannot purchase enough different securities for efficient diversification.[15]

Thus, three statistics derived from equation (3.2) are of interest: $\hat{u}_{jt}$, $\hat{\beta}_j$, and $\hat{\sigma}^2(\hat{u}_{jt})$. Equation (3.2) was computed for each NYSE traded security on monthly data for the period January 1926 through January 1934 (pre-SEC period) and July 1935 through November 1941 inclusive (post-SEC period). January 1926 was taken as the initial month because this is the first month for which data are available on the Center for Research on Security Prices (CRSP) tape of NYSE monthly security prices.[16] November 1941 was taken as the last month because it allowed for the longest post-SEC period that did not include the next major dislocation—World War II. There are 98 months in the pre-SEC period and 90 in the post-SEC period. To allow for a sufficient number of observations for the regressions, securities that

---

15. While small investors can purchase mutual funds to obtain diversification, this alternative may not be considered sufficient or even desirable by legislators.
16. The center is at the University of Chicago. The tape presently is administered by the Standard Statistics Corporation.

were traded for less than 10 months in each time period were excluded.[17] This left 466 companies, of which 290 are disclosure corporations (62 percent) and 176 nondisclosure corporations (38 percent).[18]

Five hypotheses about the effectiveness of required disclosure can be tested with observations of the $\hat{\beta}_j$ and $\sigma^2(\hat{u}_{jt})$ for the periods before and after disclosure and of the $\hat{u}_{jt}$ for the adjustment period following immediately after required disclosure.

1. Managers avoided disclosure to hide their poor performance. If the managers did not publish financial data because they wanted to hide their poor performance from their stockholders, the $\hat{u}_{jt}$ of the nondisclosure companies compared to the disclosure companies would be negative since investors would revalue downward the returns to the securities. Similarly, such managers might not disclose financial data to mislead investors about the relative riskiness of the firm, in the hope that stockholders might be willing to hold stock having a lower rate of return if they believed the firm to be less risky than it really was. In this event, disclosure would result in higher $\hat{\beta}_j$ if the market (portfolio) risk of the nondisclosure firms was underestimated and greater $s^2(\hat{u}_{jt})$ if the individual, diversifiable security risk was underestimated and not diversified away.

2. Managers did not disclose because they did not realize the value of the information to investors. If required disclosure provided investors with valuable information, the $\hat{u}_{jt}$ would change, and the $\hat{\beta}_j$ and $\sigma^2(\hat{u}_{jt})$ might change. However, the direction of the changes cannot be predicted.

3. Required disclosure imposes a cost on corporations without compensating benefits to stockholders. If managers were disclosing adequately before the legislation was passed (the marginal cost of disclosure equaled its marginal benefits), investors might view disclosure as a net cost imposed on the firm. (Included in this cost is the value of the information to competitors). In this event, the $\hat{u}_{jt}$ would decrease (as in hypothesis 1), but there is no reason to believe that the $\hat{\beta}_j$ and $\sigma^2(\hat{u}_{jt})$ would be affected.

4. Required disclosure results in benefits to the market as a whole because investors would prefer stocks on registered exchanges to alternative investments, such as over-the-counter stocks or real estate. However, some costs are imposed on those firms that would not otherwise have disclosed. If this hypothesis holds, the $\hat{\beta}_j$ and $\sigma^2(\hat{u}_{jt})$ should not be affected, the $\hat{u}_{jt}$ of the firms that were required to disclose might decrease, and the $\hat{u}_{jt}$ of firms

---

17. A study of the disclosure practices of corporations who left the NYSE before February 1934, and hence were excluded from the analysis, is presented below.

18. Since the percentages of disclosure and nondisclosure corporations are the same, this procedure does not appear to have introduced any obvious bias.

that were not so affected might increase, as investment in equities traded on the stock exchanges became relatively more attractive to investors. Thus the difference in the $\hat{u}_{jt}$ between disclosure and nondisclosure firms should be positive.

5. Required disclosure did not impose sufficient costs or benefits to be measured. Should the "null" hypothesis obtain, there would be little change in the $\hat{u}_{jt}$, $\hat{\beta}_{jt}$, or $\sigma^2(\hat{u}_{jt})$. Of course there could be costs to firms not traded at the time (such as the cost of newly registering with the SEC) or costs or benefits too small to be measured by the model.

Tests on the $\hat{\beta}_j$ are discussed first because, if the $\hat{\beta}_j$ are stable between periods, the $\hat{u}_{jt}$ can be computed more efficiently by using data from the entire data set, excluding the adjustment periods.

Table 3.2 gives the mean differences of the $\hat{\beta}_j$ computed for the pre- and post-SEC periods, in both algebraic and absolute terms.[19] Distributions of the $\hat{\beta}_j$ show them to be approximately normally distributed, so the standard errors of the means

TABLE 3.2 Estimate of Portfolio Risk $\hat{\beta}_j$: Differences and Correlations Post-SEC Period less Pre-SEC Period[a]

|  | Disclosure Corporations (290 observations) | Nondisclosure Corporations (170 observations) |
|---|---|---|
| Algebraic differences |  |  |
| Mean | 0.0320 | 0.0264 |
| SEM | 0.0218 | 0.0227 |
| Absolute differences |  |  |
| Mean | 0.2722 | 0.2133 |
| SEM | 0.0149 | 0.0159 |
| Correlation of pre- and post-periods | 0.5725 | 0.7326 |
| Data underlying $\beta_j$ statistics |  |  |
| Average number of observations (months) |  |  |
| Pre-SEC period | 79.0 | 80.6 |
| Post-SEC period | 75.3 | 76.9 |
| Standard deviation of observations (months) |  |  |
| Pre-SEC period | 20.9 | 22.3 |
| Post-SEC period | 10.1 | 6.9 |

[a]Pre-SEC period: Jan. 1926 through Feb. 1934; Post-SEC period: July 1935 through Nov. 1941.

19. The means (and standard errors of the means) of the $\hat{\beta}_j$ in the pre-SEC period is 0.9968 (0.0202) for the disclosure corporations and 0.9854 (0.0312) for the nondisclosure group. In the post-SEC period, these statistics are 1.0115 (0.0248) for the disclosure corporations and 1.0006 (0.0328) for the nondisclosure companies. The $\hat{\beta}_j$ are lower in both periods for the disclosure group, but insignificantly so.

given in table 3.2 can serve as valid summary statistics.[20] Since the stability of the $\hat{\beta}_j$ are dependent, in part, on the number of observations used to compute them, the average number and standard deviations of the underlying observations also are given in table 3.2. These data do not indicate any bias between the groups from this source. The algebraic differences between periods for both groups are positive, but hardly greater than zero and almost of the same magnitude and dispersion for the disclosure and nondisclosure groups. The absolute differences are presented because several of the hypotheses do not specify a change in the $\hat{\beta}_j$ of any particular sign, and the algebraic means could mask significant changes. Of course, the absolute means are larger than their algebraic counterparts. Most important, the absolute mean change of the disclosure group is somewhat greater than that of the nondisclosure group, which indicates a smaller change in perceived portfolio riskiness for those corporations affected by the 1934 act. An additional test of this conclusion was made by correlating the $\hat{\beta}_j$ from the pre-SEC period with the $\hat{\beta}_j$ from the post-SEC period for each group. The correlation coefficient of the pre- and post-SEC $\hat{\beta}_j$ (reported in table 3.2) is higher for the nondisclosure group, which again indicates a lesser change in the $\hat{\beta}_j$ between periods.

In summary, the tests indicate that the disclosure requirements of the 1934 act had a somewhat lesser effect on the securities of corporations that did not previously disclose sales as compared with those that did. This finding is inconsistent with hypothesis 1 and casts doubt on hypothesis 2.

The stability of the $\hat{\beta}_j$ between periods (or, at the least, a small differential change between the groups) provides support for estimating the $\hat{u}_{jt}$ with the following procedure.[21] Equation (3.2) was computed for each security that was traded on the NYSE for at least five months prior to February 1934 and five months after July 1935, allowing at least 10 observations. A total of 487 securities were included under this rule, of which 306 (63 percent) had disclosed their sales and 180 (37 percent) had not prior to the 1934 act. While the number of observations is slightly higher than those used for the $\hat{\beta}_j$ tests, the percentages in the disclosure and nondisclosure groups are almost identical. The $\hat{u}_{jt}$ were computed by running the following "market model" regression for each security:

$$r_{jt} = \alpha_j + \beta_j r_{Mt}, \tag{3.5}$$

---

20. The standard errors of the means (SEM) are relatively small, in part because the sample size ($n$) is large (SEM = standard derivation/$\sqrt{n-1}$).

21. The correlation coefficients between the $\hat{\beta}_j$ in the pre- and post-SEC periods reported above may not be sufficiently high for some readers to accept this procedure. The alternative procedure would have been to use fewer observations to calculate the statistics, which, I believe, introduces more severe possible biases. In any event, the $\hat{u}_{jt}$ were calculated with $\hat{\beta}_j$'s from the pre-SEC period for the adjustment period and the results were little different from those reported below.

where $t$ excludes February 1934 through June 1935. The computed $\hat{\alpha}_j$ and $\hat{\beta}_j$ then are used to compute the $\hat{u}_{jt}$ for each month during the "adjustment period," February 1934 through June 1935:

$$\hat{u}_{jt} = \hat{\alpha}_j + \hat{\beta}_j r_{mt} - r_{jt}, \tag{3.5a}$$

where $t$ runs from February 1934 through June 1935. The expected value of the $\hat{u}_{jt}$ is zero in the absence of an unanticipated change in the economic environment, such as the disclosure of previously undisclosed information.

The average (algebraic mean) residuals for each month of the $j$ securities $([\sum_1^n \hat{u}_{jt}]/n)$, $n$ = number of securities in each month) were computed for the disclosure and nondisclosure groups. Since several of the hypotheses do not predict a sign of the $\hat{u}_{jt}$, the average absolute residuals for each month $([\sum_1^n |\hat{u}_{jt}|]/n)$ also were computed for each group. Plots of these data were made and summary statistics are given in table 3.3 for several subperiods before and after the adjustment period to contrast the behavior of the residuals during that period.

Two basic conclusions can be derived from these data. First, there appears to be somewhat less variance of the residuals of both groups during the months of the adjustment period of February 1934 through June 1935 compared to the following and preceding months. These data indicate that by the time the initial hearings on the Securities Act of 1934 were begun, the impact of the Great Depression on the revaluation of individual shares was largely spent. Second, there is little difference in the behavior of the average residuals of the nondisclosure compared with the disclosure groups. The plots (not presented) show that their residuals behaved almost the same over time, with differences between the two groups being far overshadowed by differences between time periods.

Table 3.3 is not quite adequate to test the hypothesis that the 1934 act affected each group differently, since the algebraic or absolute mean monthly values and standard deviations over months may not describe the underlying distribution of the individual $\hat{u}_{jt}$. Therefore, figures 3.1 and 3.2 were prepared in which the fractiles (.05 and .95, .10 and .90, .75 and .25, and the median) are plotted for each group over time. If the plot of residuals for one group could have been printed as a transparency and placed over the plot of the other, the reader could see that there is almost no difference in the distribution of residuals between the groups.

The data presented thus far are based on monthly averages of the $\hat{u}_{jt}$. However, it also is necessary to consider the effect of the disclosure statute on individual securities. The possible revaluation of the present value of returns on individual securities need not have taken place entirely in any given month. In addition, it is not clear exactly when corporations made their financial data available as required by the 1934 act. Therefore, the $\hat{u}_{jt}$ were cumulated algebraically for the adjustment period ($\sum_{t=1}^{17} \hat{u}_{jt}$ where t = 2/34 through 6/35). As a further check, the $\hat{u}_{jt}$ were cumulated for an additional year ($\sum_{t=1}^{29} \hat{u}_{jt}$ where t = 2/34 through 6/36).

TABLE 3-3 Average Monthly Residuals in Subperiods[a]

| | Algebraic Means ÷ 0.001 | | | Absolute Means ÷ 0.001 | | |
|---|---|---|---|---|---|---|
| Subperiod | Disclosure | Nondisclosure | Disclosure-Nondisclosure | Disclosure | Nondisclosure | Disclosure-Nondisclosure |
| 2/26 thru 1/28 | 0.074 (0.742) | 0.206 (0.986) | −0.132 (1.429) | 6.653 (0.919) | 6.459 (0.919) | 0.194 (0.774) |
| 2/28 thru 1/30 | 0.020 (0.924) | 0.075 (1.086) | −0.056 (1.634) | 8.028 (1.604) | 7.647 (1.460) | 0.381 (0.748) |
| 2/30 thru 1/32 | 0.026 (1.181) | −0.002 (1.525) | −0.024 (1.742) | 10.475 (2.214) | 9.795 (1.913) | 0.680 (1.007) |
| 2/32 thru 1/34 | −0.349 (1.638) | −0.325 (1.892) | −0.024 (2.328) | 14.452 (3.707) | 12.884 (2.875) | 1.568 (1.375) |
| 2/34 thru 6/35 (adjustment period) | 0.125 (0.865) | 0.728 (0.968) | −0.603 (1.124) | 8.435 (1.115) | 7.802 (1.250) | 0.633 (0.812) |
| 7/35 thru 6/37 | 0.227 (0.941) | −0.263 (1.624) | 0.491 (1.676) | 8.221 (1.813) | 7.332 (1.592) | 0.888 (0.728) |
| 7/37 thru 6/39 | 0.017 (0.773) | 0.203 (1.226) | −0.186 (1.314) | 6.972 (1.185) | 6.225 (1.299) | 0.747 (0.609) |
| 7/39 thru 6/41 | 0.077 (0.910) | 0.085 (1.093) | −0.008 (1.175) | 7.151 (2.961) | 6.196 (2.378) | 0.955 (0.743) |

[a] Standard deviations shown in parentheses.

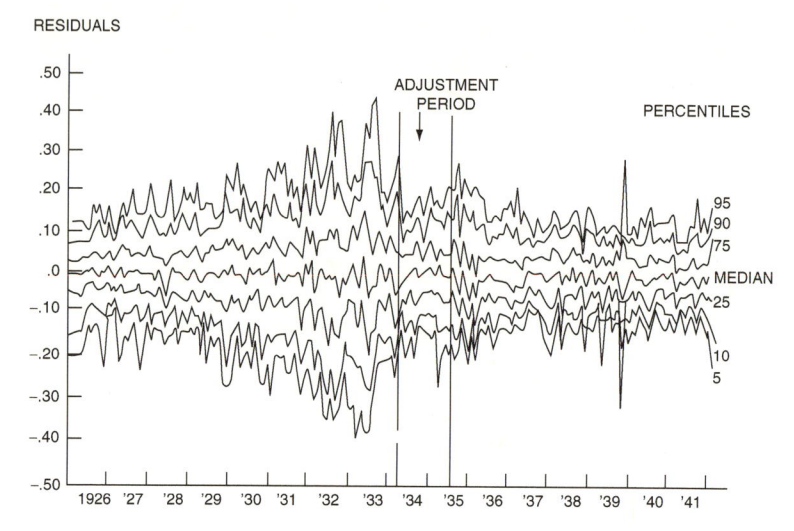

FIGURE 3.1 Nondisclosure Corporations Distributions of Residuals ($\hat{u}_{jt}$)

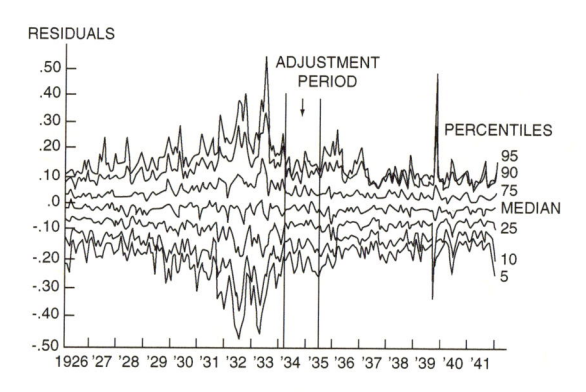

FIGURE 3.2 Disclosure Corporations Distribution of Residuals ($\hat{u}_{jt}$)

Figure 3.3 presents the data in the form of histograms, in which the distribution of the cumulative residuals for the corporations in the disclosure and nondisclosure group are plotted together. It is clear from these histograms and from the summary statistics (not presented)[22] that there is little difference between the two groups and that neither group experienced a revaluation of its rates of return that is significantly different from the expected value of zero.

---

22. The algebraic means (and standard deviations) of the cumulative residuals in the February 1934 through June 1935 adjustment period are 0.0010 (0.0307) for the disclosure corporation and 0.0072 (0.0290) for the nondisclosure corporations. In the February 1934 through June 1936 adjustment period, the statistics are −0.0004 (0.0228) and 0.0022 (0.0206).

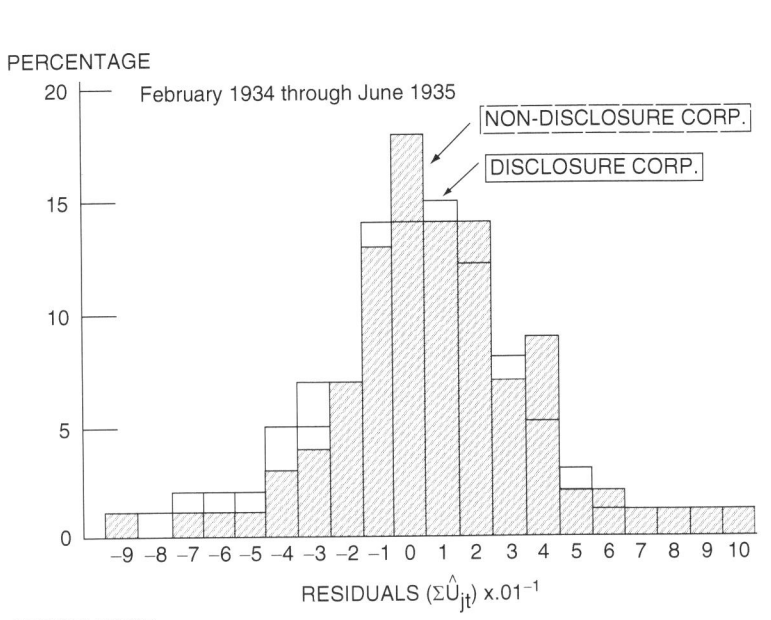

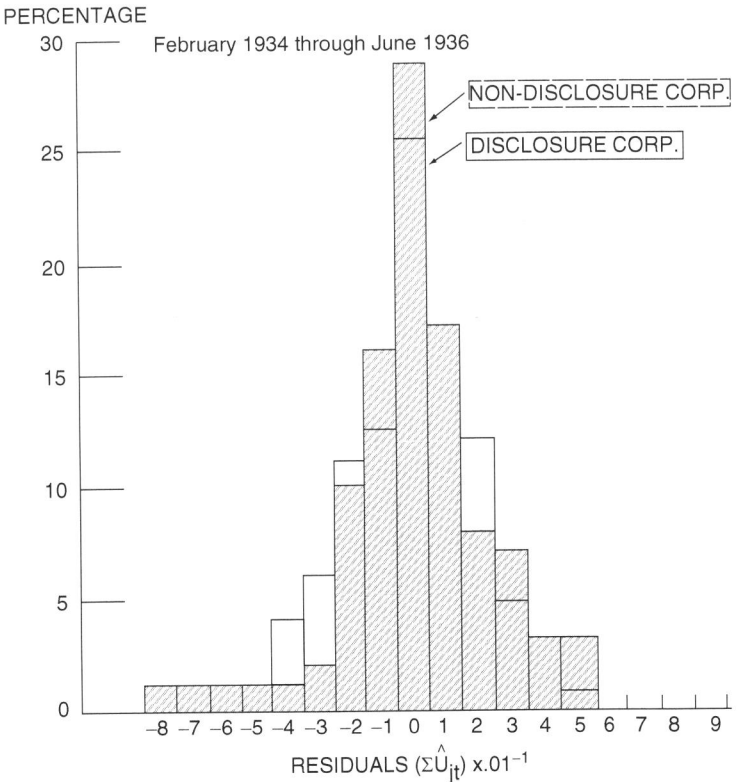

FIGURE 3.3 Histograms of Cumulative Residuals Disclosure and Nondisclosure Corporations

TABLE 3.4 Variance of Residuals ($\hat{u}_{jt}$) of Individual Companies Pre- and Post-SEC Periods

|  | Disclosure | Nondisclosure |
|---|---|---|
| A. Means |  |  |
| Pre-SEC Period (1/26–2/34) |  |  |
|   Mean of standard deviations | 0.1496 | 0.1351 |
|   Standard deviation of mean | 0.0623 | 0.0507 |
|   Outliers |  |  |
|     >mean ± 1σ | 29.1[a] | 30.9[a] |
|     >mean ± 2σ | 4.2[a] | 3.1[a] |
|   Number of observations | 309 | 191 |
| Post-SEC Period (7/35–11/41) |  |  |
|   Mean of standard deviations | 0.1033 | 0.0885 |
|   Standard deviation of mean | 0.0535 | 0.0363 |
|   Outliers |  |  |
|     >mean ± 1σ | 14.9[a] | 20.3[a] |
|     >mean ± 2σ | 5.1[a] | 2.8[a] |
|   Number of Observations | 296 | 177 |
| B. Change in variances: post-SEC less pre-SEC period |  |  |
|   Mean algebraic differences | −0.0433 | −0.0435 |
|   Standard deviation of mean | 0.0534 | 0.0385 |
|   Mean absolute differences | −0.0540 | −0.0469 |
|   Standard deviation of mean | 0.0435 | 0.0343 |
|   Number of observations | 290 | 176 |

[a]Shown in percent.

The variance of the residuals of each company, $\sigma^2(\hat{u}_{jt})$ provides an estimate of the volatility of the individual security. A comparison of the mean and distribution of the standard deviations of the residuals of the disclosure and nondisclosure corporations are given in part A of table 3.4. The disclosure corporations show a slightly higher mean standard deviation of residuals in the pre-SEC period and, surprisingly, an even greater mean standard deviation in the post-SEC period. It is possible, however, that the means of the standard deviations of the $\hat{u}_{jt}$ of each group in the pre- and post-SEC periods obscure changes in the variance of individual securities. To test for this possibility, the differences between the standard deviations of the residuals of each company in each period was computed. The mean and distribution of these changes is presented in part B of table 3.4. The mean change is negative for each group, consistent with part A of the table. Most important, the change in variance of individual stock prices (after accounting for the variance of the stock market as a whole) once the Securities Act of 1934 was effective, is almost the same for those corporations that were and were not affected by the act.

From these data and the data reported above, I conclude that the 1934 act did not contribute to a reduction in the variance of returns from securities traded on the NYSE, as measured by the $\hat{\beta}_j$ (the covariance-variance ratio of security $j$ to the market as a whole) and the standard deviations of the residual returns on securities, $\sigma^2(\hat{u}_{jt})$.[23]

Considering the evidence presented above, I must conclude that the data are consistent only with the hypothesis 5, that the disclosure provisions of the 1934 act were of no apparent value to investors.

## VI. Losses by Stockholders

The data used in the tests presented above are of NYSE corporations that survived the depression, at least until December 1935 (five months of postadjustment period data were required for the regressions). A question that should be raised is whether stockholders of corporations that disclosed their sales fared better than those who held stock in nondisclosing corporations. Should this be the case, the findings presented above could be biased because the worst offenders, with respect to disclosure, would have been delisted from the NYSE.

To determine whether such was the case, the listing of NYSE corporations was traced. The base year chosen was 1929, because this is the last year before the Depression and because I could use a study made by Standard Statistics Company, reported by Lawrence Sloan (1931, pp. 66–74). This study of the income statements of 484 corporations listed on the NYSE revealed that 266 (55 percent) reported gross income in 1929 and 218 (45 percent) did not. Table 3.5 presents the listing history of these securities, showing whether the security was delisted because it went over the counter (OTC) or the corporation was merged. Either event is taken to mean a greater than normal loss for stockholders. If this assumption is correct, it is clear that stockholders of corporations that did not disclose gross income in 1929 fared better than those who held stock in the disclosure corporations.

This conclusion is interesting, because it implies that companies that did not disclose their sales were, in fact, better investments than those that did. Such investigations as I could make did not reveal the reasons that some companies disclosed their sales and others did not. A reason consistent with the data would be that those who disclosed had a greater real need to assure their stockholders of their worth than those who did not.

---

23. The smaller mean values of the standard deviations of the residuals of securities in both groups in the post-SEC compared to the pre-SEC period is due primarily to the period of May 1932 through June 1933.

TABLE 3.5 NYSE Delisting of Corporations that Did and Did Not Disclose Gross Income in 1929

| Number | Disclosure Corp. OTC | Disclosure Corp. Merged | Disclosure Corp. Total | Nondisclosure Corp. OTC | Nondisclosure Corp. Merged | Nondisclosure Corp. Total |
|---|---|---|---|---|---|---|
| Delisted in: | | | | | | |
| 1929 | 1 | 1 | 2 | | | |
| 1930 | 1 | 4 | 5 | 1 | | 1 |
| 1931 | 4 | 2 | 6 | 3 | | 3 |
| 1932 | 6 | 5 | 11 | 6 | | 6 |
| 1933 | 5 | | 5 | 5 | | 5 |
| 1934 | 3 | | 3 | 1 | | 1 |
| Subtotal: Pre-SEC | 20 | 12 | 32 | 16 | | 16 |
| 1935 | 4 | | 4 | 3 | 1 | 4 |
| 1936 | 2 | 1 | 3 | | | |
| 1937 | 2 | 1 | 3 | | | |
| Subtotal: 1935–37 | 8 | 2 | 10 | 3 | 1 | 4 |
| 1938 | 5 | 1 | 6 | 2 | | 2 |
| 1939 | 4 | 1 | 5 | | | |
| 1940 | 2 | 1 | 3 | 1 | | 1 |
| Subtotal: 1938–40 | 11 | 3 | 14 | 3 | | 3 |
| Total 1929–40 | 39 | 17 | 56 | 22 | 1 | 23 |
| On NYSE in 1941 | | | 210 | | | 195 |
| Total | | | 266 | | | 218 |
| Percentages | | | | | | |
| Delisted 1929–34 | 7.5 | 4.5 | 12.0 | 7.3 | | 7.3 |
| Delisted 1934–37 | 3.0 | 0.8 | 3.8 | 1.4 | 0.4 | 1.8 |
| Delisted 1938–40 | 4.1 | 1.2 | 5.3 | 1.4 | | 1.4 |
| Subtotal | 14.6 | 6.5 | 21.1 | 10.1 | 0.4 | 10.5 |
| Not delisted as of 1941 | | | 78.9 | | | 89.5 |
| Total | | | 100.0 | | | 100.0 |

## VII. Investor's Confidence in the Market: Risk and Fairness

A major reason for enactment (and continuance) of the disclosure provisions of the 1934 act was the belief that disclosure was necessary to restore the confidence of investors in the stock market. It is obvious that depressions and the reduction of stock values (either with a "crash" or gradually over a relatively short period) reduce investor confidence and that such events have occurred before and since the passage of the 1934 act and were little affected by it. Therefore, a more meaningful (and charitable) definition of "investor confidence" might be related to the riskiness of returns from securities and to the concept of fairness, that all investors should have equal access to financial information about a company whose shares they own or contemplate buying. Each of these somewhat related concepts is considered in turn.

A reduction of the riskiness of returns, ceteris paribus, is considered a benefit because this would reduce the cost of capital to firms and increase investors' confidence in the market. Both assertions are based on the belief that investors are risk averse. (Speculators may prefer risk, but they are considered by legislators to be a nonpreferred group.) Of course, disclosure, as such, cannot reduce the inherent riskiness of corporations except where disclosure reduces or prevents the risk of fraud. However, disclosure might reduce the risk to the investor of not knowing about significant events (such as a large loss, lawsuit, discovery, etc.) and/or diversifiable risk by reducing the residual variance of security returns (as is discussed above in section V).

The evidence presented above indicates that disclosure as required by the 1934 act did not reduce fraud, nor did corporations who disclosed their sales fare better in the depression than those who didn't. The data on the variance of the securities of disclosure firms compared to that of nondisclosure firms (tables 3.2 and 3.4), discussed above, indicate that the 1934 act did not have the desired effect on risk (as measured herein). The percentages of large residuals (outliers) reported in table 3.4 also provide evidence on the effectiveness of the 1934 act in reducing the risk of large, presumably unanticipated stock movements. The percentage of outlyers in the pre-SEC period was about the same for the disclosure and the nondisclosure firms. However, in the post-SEC period, there were relatively fewer mean $\pm 1\sigma$ outliers for the disclosure group but more mean $\sigma \pm 2$ outliers for the nondisclosure group.

Some additional evidence on the effect of the 1934 act on the stock market is provided by a study of corporate total capital formation met by stock market issues and publicly sold debt issues compared to private placements in the pre- and post-SEC years (through 1954). As I reported in 1969 (see Benston, 1969b), the percentage of new issues (net of redemptions) to expenditures on plant and equipment gross and net of price-level adjusted depreciation was the following:[24]

| 1900–24 | 30.9 (gross) | 58.3 (net) |
| 1919–29 | 36.8 (gross) | 354.3 (net) |
| 1932–38 | — (gross) | — (net) |
| 1938–46 | 6.5 (gross) | 51.2 (net) |
| 1946–49 | 23.1 (gross) | 50.2 (net) |
| 1949–54 | 20.6 (gross) | 68.6 (net) |

I also found that a ranking of industries by the percentage of private placements to total debt issues was almost exactly the same as a ranking of the extent of bias

---

24. Stock redemptions exceeded new issues in the 1932–38 period.

of the SEC's conservative accounting rules against a fuller reporting of economic events (such as the extent of mining claims, the value of airline routes, etc.). Thus it appears that, contrary to the expectations of its supporters, the 1934 act may have reduced the value of stock markets to corporations and, therefore, to investors.

The concept of fairness is difficult to define operationally. The belief that all investors should have equal access to financial information about a company whose shares they own or contemplate purchasing is perhaps the most important concept, politically, that supports the federal disclosure requirements. While some writers, such as Henry Manne, have argued that investors and the economy are served better when insiders are allowed to profit from information before it is disclosed, legislators argue that all current and potential owners of a corporation have an equal right to information without regard to cost. But since any information must be available to someone before it is known to all, this is a nonoperational concept in its extreme form. And, insofar as the SEC's disclosure requirements require the publication of useless or untimely data (as seems to be the case), the 1934 act has not served its purpose.

Nevertheless, the stock market could be considered "fair" if the prices of securities at any point in time are unbiased estimators of their intrinsic values, at least with respect to the financial data which corporations must disclose under the 1934 act. Then whenever an investor decides to buy or sell or hold a security, he can be assured that the market price has discounted completely the financial information. The average investor need not worry about discovering some important financial information about which he is unaware. He will just as often find himself buying or selling a security that is "overvalued" as "undervalued." In this event, the market would be "efficient" in what Fama calls the semi-strong form of the martingale hypothesis.

Fama (1970) reviews the theory and evidence on efficient capital markets and concludes that "for the purposes of most investors the efficient markets model seems a good first (and second) approximation to reality. In short, the evidence in support of the efficient markets model is extensive, and (somewhat uniquely in economics) contradictory evidence is sparse" (p. 416). But this evidence is based on data from years after enactment of the 1934 act. The act may have altered the way in which information gets to the market and the speed with which it is dispersed such that a previously inefficient market became efficient.

The data presented above, that the disclosure required by the 1934 act had no measurable effect on the residual market prices of companies that did and did not disclose their sales, are consistent with the hypothesis that the market was efficient before the legislation was enacted, at least with respect to the financial data.[25] In addition, runs tests on the signs of price changes before 1934 of the securities of

---

25. These data also are consistent with the hypothesis that published financial data have no information content.

the disclosure and nondisclosure corporations revealed that the price changes of both groups confirmed to a random walk.[26] The results of this weaker test of the efficient markets hypothesis is consistent with the belief that the 1934 act did not make the stock market a "fairer game" for investors.

## VIII. Summary and Conclusions

The Securities Exchange Act of 1934 is called a "disclosure statute" because its purpose is to force corporations to provide the public with financial data as prescribed by the SEC. The act was passed and extended because of the belief that such disclosure was required to correct the abuses of the pre–Great Depression period, provide information necessary for investors to allocate their resources wisely and efficiently, and make the stock market a "fair game" for the average investor.

A review of the evidence on fraudulently or misleadingly prepared financial statements prior to enactment of the 1934 act revealed very little evidence of abuses in reporting. The assertion by the SEC that "pools" and other presumably manipulative devices were made possible by inadequately disclosed financial information is not supported by the data. Proportionately, there was little difference between the reporting practices of corporations whose securities were subject to pools as those who were not.

The value of reported financial data for investors' decisions is based on the assumption that the data the SEC requires be made public is useful and timely. The SEC's adherence to historically based, "conservative" accounting procedures reduces the value of the numbers. Nevertheless, the question is an empirical one for which an empirical answer is sought. The extant statistical studies that relate published accounting statement data with stock prices all lead to the conclusion that the data either are not useful or have been fully impounded into stock prices before they are published.[27] Since these studies use relatively simple decision models, evidence on the ability of professional analysts to use financial data for stock choices was reviewed. This evidence supports the conclusion that the accounting statements either are not useful, timely, or both.

---

26. The mean percentage deviations between actual and expected (assuming a random distribution) total runs in the pre-SEC and post-SEC periods are −1.2 and 4.9 percent for the disclosure corporations and −1.5 and 7.5 percent for the nondisclosure corporations. On a probability basis, the percentage of individual stocks whose runs were significantly different at the 5 percent level from expected are 4.3 and 7.8 for the pre- and post-SEC disclosure corporations and 2.3 and 12.2 for the pre- and post-SEC nondisclosure corporations. It appears that the security prices of both groups more nearly conformed to a random walk in the pre-SEC period than in the post-SEC period. Most interesting for present purposes, prices of the securities of corporations that did disclose appear to reflect a less efficient market after the 1934 act became effective than did those of corporations that did not disclose their sales.

27. An exception may be Beaver's (1968) study of preliminary reports.

However, these findings are based on data from the post-SEC period. It may be that the SEC has created a climate of confidence in financial data such that the public can accept information as it becomes available during the year. In this event, the annual financial statements, when published, simply confirm that which was previously released, and therefore do not affect stock prices. Investors could believe the information because they know that a reputable government agency, the SEC, is concerned about the veracity of financial statements.

The hypothesis was tested by examining statistically the change in riskiness and returns in the stock prices on the NYSE before, after, and as a result of the Securities Exchange Act of 1934. Financial statements were available for almost all NYSE corporations, but only 62 percent reported their sales or other similarly important information. These corporations are a control sample against which the effects of the 1934 act can be measured. The Sharpe (1964)-Markowitz (1959) "market model" was used to account for general stock market changes and to provide estimates of the market risk of stocks for each of the samples (disclosure and nondisclosure corporations) in the periods before and after the regulations became effective. Revaluations of securities as a result of the required disclosure of information also were measured with the model. All of the many measurements and analyses show that the 1934 act's financial disclosure requirements had no measurable effect on the securities of the corporation presumedly affected.

The effect of the 1934 act on investors' confidence and on the fairness of the market also was analyzed. Riskiness of securities, as measured by the variance of market prices net of covariance with the market, does not seem to have been reduced by the act. Nor were the relative percentage of large price movements reduced. Also, the effect of the 1934 act on the capital market may have been perverse, since the percentage of corporate expenditures on plant and equipment financed with new public stock and debt issues was lower in the post- than in the pre-SEC decades. With respect to fairness, the evidence that the disclosure requirements did not result in a revaluation of the securities of the affected firms and the conformity of price changes before 1934 to a random walk indicates that the pre-SEC stock market was a fair game for investors.

The conclusion of this study, then, must be that the disclosure requirements of the Securities Exchange Act of 1934 had no measurable positive effect on the securities traded on the NYSE. There appears to have been little basis for the legislation and no evidence that it was needed or desirable. Certainly there is doubt that more required disclosure is warranted.

### REFERENCES

R. Ball and P. Brown, "An Empirical Evaluation of Accounting Income Numbers," *J. Accounting Res.*, Autumn 1968, 6, 159–78.

W. H. Beaver, "The Information Content of Annual Earnings Announcements," *J. Accounting Res., Empirical Research in Accounting: Selected Studies 1968*, 67–92.

G. J. Benston, "Published Corporate Accounting Data and Stock Prices," *J. Accounting Res., Empirical Research in Accounting: Selected Studies 1967*, 1–54.

G. J. Benston, "The Effectiveness and Effects of the SEC's Accounting Disclosure Requirements," in H. G. Manne, ed., *Economic Policy and the Regulation of Corporate Securities*, Washington 1969a.

G. J. Benston, "The Value of the SEC's Accounting Disclosure Requirements," *Accounting Rev.*, July 1969b, *44*, 515–32.

M. Blume, "The Assessment of Portfolio Performance," unpublished doctoral dissertation, Univ. Chicago, 1968.

M. Blume, "Portfolio Theory: A Step Towards its Practical Application," *J. Bus. Univ. Chicago*, Apr. 1970, *43*, 152–73.

F. E. Brown and D. Vickers, in I. Friend et al., *A Study of Mutual Funds*, Washington, 1962, ch. 5, 289–358.

J. G. Cragg and B. G. Malkiel, "The Consensus and Accuracy of Some Predictions of the Growth of Corporate Earnings," *J. Finance*, Mar. 1968, *22*, 67–84.

R. F. DeBedts, *The New Deal's SEC*, New York, 1964.

R. E. Diefenbach, "How Good Is Institutional Research?" *Financial Analysis J.*, Jan./Feb. 1972, *28*, 54–60.

E. Fama, "Efficient Capital Markets; A Review of Theory and Empirical Work," *J. Finance*, May 1970, *25*, 383–417.

E. Fama, L. Fisher, M. Jensen, and R. Roll, "The Adjustment of Stock Prices to New Information," *Int. Econ. Rev.*, Feb. 1969, *10*, 1–21.

L. Fisher and J. H. Dorie, "Some Studies of Variability of Returns on Investments in Common Stocks," *J. Bus. Univ. Chicago*, Apr. 1970, *43*, 99–134.

I. Friend and E. Herman, "The SEC through a Glass Darkly," *J. Bus. Univ. Chicago*, Oct. 1964, *37*, 382–405.

R. Hagerman, "An Investigation of Effects of Disclosure and Audits on the Efficiency of the Market for Bank Stock," unpublished doctoral dissertation, Univ. Rochester, 1972.

M. C. Jensen, "The Performance of Mutual Funds in the Period 1954–64," *J. Finance*, May 1968, *23*, 389–416.

*Landell vs. Lybrand*, 264, Pa. 496, 107 Atl. 783, 1919.

H. G. Manne, *Insider Trading and the Stock Market*, New York, 1966.

H. M. Markowitz, *Portfolio Selection: Efficient Diversification of Investments*, New York, 1959.

R. McEnally. "Information Effect and P/E Ratios," *Miss. Vall. J. Bus. Econ.*, Spring 1970, *5*, 24–38.

Moody's Investors Services, *Manual of Investments, American and Foreign*, Industrial Securities, New York, various years.

L. D. Pankoff and R. Virgil, "Some Preliminary Findings from a Laboratory Experiment on the Usefulness of Financial Accounting Information to Security Analysts," *J. Accounting Res., Empirical Research in Accounting: Selected Studies 1970*.

W. D. Rich, *Legal Responsibility and Rights of Public Accountants*, New York, 1935.

W. Z. Ripley, *Trusts, Pools and Corporations*, rev. ed., New York, 1916.

W. Z. Ripley, *Main Street and Wall Street*, Boston, 1927.

Securities and Exchange Commission, *A 25 Year Summary of the Activities of the Securities and Exchange Commission*, Washington, 1959.

Securities and Exchange Commission, *The Work of the Securities and Exchange Commission*, Washington, May 1967.

W. F. Sharpe, "Capital Asset Prices: A Theory of Market Equilibrium under Conditions of Risk," *Journal of Finance*, Sept. 1964, *19*, 425–42.

L. H. Sloan, *Everyman and His Common Stocks*, New York, 1931.

R. Sobel, *The Big Board: A History of the New York Stock Market*, New York, 1965.

Standard and Poors, Industrial 425 Index, New York, various years.

G. J. Stigler, "Public Regulation of the Securities Markets," *J. Bus. Univ. Chicago*, Apr. 1964a, *37*, 117–42.

G. J. Stigler, "Comment," *J. Bus. Univ. Chicago*, Oct. 1964b, *37*, 414–22.

*Ultramares Corp. v. Touche, Niven & Co.*, 229 App. Div. 581, 243 N.Y. Supp. (1st Dept. 1930), rev., 225 N.Y. 170, 174 N.E. 441, 1931.

U.S. Congress, Senate Committee on Banking & Currency, Stock Exchange Practices, *Hearings*, on S. Res. 84 and S. Res. 56, 73 Cong., Part 17, Washington, 1934.

F. M. Wheat, "Truth in Securities Three Decades Later," *Howard Law Review*, Winter 1967, *13*, 100–107.

F. M. Wheat, Wheat Report, *Disclosure to Investors, A Reappraisal of Administrative Policies Under the '33 and '34 Securities Acts*, Report and Recommendations to the Securities and Exchange Commission from the Disclosure Policy Committee, Mar. 1969.

# 4

# Public (U.S.) Compared to Private (U.K.) Regulation of Corporate Financial Disclosure

THOUGH THE UNITED STATES AND THE UNITED KINGDOM are dissimilar in many important respects, their security markets are rather alike. In both countries, almost instantaneous sales and purchases can be made of securities representing claims on thousands of companies. The securities are owned and traded by a large number of individuals and institutions at prices that are made public. The companies whose securities are traded are required to publish financial statements that conform to legally required minimum standards of disclosure, and the accounting on which these statements are based is surprisingly similar. However, the United States relies on public regulation of financial disclosure (SEC), whereas the United Kingdom relies on private regulation (The Stock Exchange). This essay explores the differences, costs, and benefits of the two systems and concludes that, in many important respects, private regulation is preferable.

Though the U.S. Federal Securities Acts were modeled after the U.K. Companies Acts (which predated them by almost a century), they are administered quite differently. In 1934, the United States established the Securities and Exchange Commission (SEC), giving it the authority to prepare and administer regulations governing the financial disclosure mandated by the Securities Act of 1933 and the Securities Exchange Act of 1934. In contrast, the U.K. Companies Acts (1948 and 1967) stand on their own in the sense that the specific disclosure required is

---

An earlier version of this essay was presented at the annual meeting of the American Accounting Association, New Orleans, Louisiana, August 1974. My discussants, John (Sandy) Burton and James Mandel, and my colleagues, particularly Jerold Zimmerman, provided me with many useful comments. Of course, they are not responsible for any remaining errors or misstatements nor should their aid be construed as approval. I also thank the anonymous reviewers whose criticisms led me to revise the paper considerably.

given in the acts rather than in regulations promulgated by the Department of Trade (DT). Although the DT has the power to investigate failures of directors to conform to the requirements of the acts, particularly when such an investigation is requested by security holders, it serves primarily as a repository for the statements filed persuant to the acts. However, in the United States, the SEC actively investigates situations that its staff believes may mislead investors and obtains stop orders preventing trading in or issuance of securities. It also reviews the financial statements filed in accordance with the Securities Acts and rejects those which, in its opinion, do not conform to its regulations. This "screening" is particularly extensive with respect to prospectuses. In the United Kingdom, a somewhat similar function is performed by private regulatory agencies, that is, by the Quotations Department of The (London) Stock Exchange[1] and the issuing houses (investment bankers and underwriters).[2] Before considering the costs and benefits of these regulatory systems, the scope of legally required corporate disclosure in each country is sketched.

## The Scope of Regulation of Corporate Financial Disclosure in the United States and the United Kingdom

Unlike the U.K. Companies Acts, the U.S. Securities Acts do not apply to all incorporated (limited liability) companies. Since 1966, the Securities Exchange Act of 1934 requires periodic reporting by all corporations that have more than $1 million in assets and a single class of equity securities that has more than 500 holders. In 1975, some 10,500 companies filed financial statements with the SEC (a number that has grown steadily over time). Of these, about 3,500 were listed on registered stock exchanges. Additionally, the SEC registers prospectuses of all corporations who wish to offer securities to the public (except when the offering is entirely intrastate). In 1974, 2,890 registration statements were declared effective (down from the high of 3,712 in 1972).

The U.K. Companies Acts apply to all limited liability companies, whether widely held or not. In 1974, 598,000 companies not in liquidation were registered.[3] Of these, 15,500 were public companies, about 27 percent of which were listed on The (London) Stock Exchange. The prospectus requirements of the Companies Act of 1948 apply to all new securities offered to the public. However, unlike the United States, which has a large over-the-counter market, such an offering usually

---

1. There is only one stock exchange in the United Kingdom.
2. See Benston (1976, section 2.2.2) for a more detailed description.
3. See Benston (1976, chapter 2) for a more extensive discussion.

is made in conjunction with obtaining a stock exchange listing. Also unlike the situation in the United States, prospectuses are not required for rights offerings or other issues that are in all respects similar to securities already listed. Furthermore, many instruments, such as interests in petroleum wells, limited partnership interests and investment plans, are considered securities in the United States but not in the United Kingdom. Consequently, only about 120 prospectuses per year are issued in the United Kingdom (though the number varies widely).

The extensiveness of the regulations, and hence the cost of complying with them, reflects the regulatory structures adopted by the countries. The SEC, having been given the authority and responsibility of drawing up and enforcing disclosure regulations by section 19(a) of the 1933 act and section 13(b) of the 1934 act, at first delegated much of this task to the public accounting profession. In part because of this delegation, the accounting profession, primarily through the American Institute of Certified Accountants (AICPA) and the Financial Accounting Standards Board (FASB) and its predecessor committees, has adopted a large number of rules and suggestions for recording specific situations. On the other hand, the stock exchanges have adopted few additional rules governing financial statements, though before enactment of the Securities Acts they had established some reporting standards.

However, the SEC has become increasingly more active in assuming its regulatory responsibilities. Regulation S-X, supplemented by Accounting Series Releases (ASRs), which codifies the specific disclosure required of corporations subject to the Securities Acts, increasingly is more detailed. Additional requirements are added and few, if any, are removed. As instances of poor or apparently fraudulent reporting by individual companies come to public attention, the SEC has assumed more control over public reporting by all subject corporations. For example, in 1967 the SEC extended its authority over annual reports to shareholders (Rule 14a–3), in part because of the revelation in 1962 that the Atlantic Research Corporation of America did not report a large loss in its annual report to shareholders, though it disclosed this information in its 10K report, which is available to the public. The SEC now requires that financial statements in annual reports must conform to those filed with the SEC or must contain a reconciliation or explanation of all such differences. Another example is the near failure of Penn-Central and the subsequent belief that more information about its short-term borrowings might have been useful. This led to the requirement that all corporations must report their compensating balance arrangements. Most recently, the Watergate revelations apparently have led the SEC into requiring disclosure of illegal campaign contributions and into "suggesting" disclosure of legal, though perhaps immoral, payments to foreign government officials.

In contrast, the U.K. Companies Acts simply list the specific items that must be disclosed. Additionally, the statutes provide that financial statements shall "give a true and fair view" of the company's state of affairs and profit and loss (Companies

Act 1948, sec. 149(1) ). This important phrase is not further defined nor is there recent case law that provides a definition. However, U.K. accountants generally understand it to require accounts that present a layman's definition of "a true and fair view" of specific circumstances, within the constraint that financial statements are not expected to report completely current realizable or other definitions of economic value.[4]

The DT is given the power to adapt the disclosure provisions of the Companies Acts to the circumstances of individual companies (Companies Act 1948, sec. 149). Though the DT also has the power to alter the acts' financial disclosure requirements, it cannot render them more onerous (Companies Act 1948, sec. 454(1) ). Hence, the U.K. counterpart to the SEC has not extended or rarely has even interpreted the specific disclosure mandated by the Companies Acts.

The U.K. professional accountancy bodies have not been as active as their U.S. confreres in promulgating disclosure rules.[5] Regulation differences, in part, explain this relative lack of activity.[6] The U.K. statutes do not give anyone the authority to promulgate financial disclosure rules and procedures. Hence, unlike the SEC, the DT could not delegate this authority to the official accounting profession.

However, The (London) Stock Exchange has authority over companies whose securities are listed thereon. It has exercised this authority to promulgate disclosure rules, primarily for prospectuses. Since virtually all U.K. companies whose shares are traded publicly must be listed on The Exchange, its rules dominate. Its Quotations Bureau operates rather like the SEC in accepting or rejecting prospectuses before they can be issued to the public. In addition, the issuing houses (investment bankers and underwriters) exercise control over the contents of prospectuses, since public acceptance of a security issue depends importantly on the reputation of its sponsor. Consequently, most prospectuses include a statement by a generally well-known firm of chartered accountants (called reporting accountants) in addition to the statement of the company's auditor. The role of U.S. investment bankers and underwriters (with respect to financial disclosure) is negligible relative to that of their U.K. counterparts, since the SEC's regulations and prospectus registration procedures are so extensive and the Securities Act of 1933's provisions so encompassing that they dominate all others. Consequently,

---

4. Based on interviews and a review of the literature.
5. As of December 1975, there are 51 Accounting Research Bulletins, 31 Accounting Principal Board Opinions and 4 statements, and 12 statements and 6 interpretations of the FASB in the United States. In contrast, the U.K. Institute of Chartered Accountants in England and Wales issued 15 Recommendations on Accounting Principles and the Accounting Standards Steering Committee has issued 11 Statements of Standard Accounting Practice, one of which is an amendment to another statement.
6. Professional, economic and legal environment differences between the United States and the United Kingdom also explain this phenomenon. These are analyzed in Benston (1975).

strict conformance with the law and regulations is required, leaving little room for deviations or extensions.

## The Costs of Regulation in the United States and the United Kingdom

The cost of financial disclosure regulation reflects, in large measure, the structures adopted by each country. The U.S. disclosure regulations, codified in Regulation S-X and supplemented by ASRs, are much more detailed and explicit than those which face a U.K. company and accountant. An indication of this difference may be gathered from a comparison of the number of specific items required to be disclosed in each country. With respect to the balance sheet, Regulation S-X (as extended and amended) calls for more than 65 items compared to the 39 required in the United Kingdom by the Companies Acts and The Stock Exchange.[7] In the income statement, the United States requires about 53 items compared to 37 required in the United Kingdom. Regulation S-X and the instructions to the forms also specify rules for consolidating statements of a company and its subsidiaries, for disclosing contingent liabilities, and so on. In addition, quarterly statements and monthly reports are required in the United States but not in the United Kingdom.[8] The recent adoption of ASR 177, which requires inclusion of quarterly data in annual reports certified by public accountants, probably will increase costs to clients considerably.

One important aspect of cost is the necessity of learning and following the disclosure regulations. Though comparative figures are not available, it is obvious that these direct costs are greater for U.S. than for U.K. companies. This is particularly true for periodic reporting, which is much simpler in the United Kingdom.

Prospectuses also are more detailed and extensive in the United States; for example, a prospectus in the United States (which must be printed at considerable cost because even a small error can be the basis of an expensive lawsuit) usually runs to 50 or more 7.5" by 9" pages. In the United Kingdom, a legally required prospectus is, and must be, printed on one to two pages of two daily London newspapers. The prospectus provided to the public, though, may be longer at the option of the issuer.

---

7. The count of items is taken from Benston (1976, chapter 3), which lists the specific items required in each country. The counts reported are likely to be inexact because this listing was made for purposes of reference rather than for the present purpose.

8. See Kellogg and Poloway (1971) and Rappaport (1972) for annotated manuals of the SEC's disclosure requirements.

A corollary is the indirect cost of delay and inconvenience in fulfilling the more complex, more highly structured U.S. administrative rules, particularly with respect to prospectuses. In the United Kingdom, an auditor can call the manager of the Quotations Department of The Stock Exchange, discuss a question about whether a requirement is met by a particular procedure or can be modified to meet a special circumstance, and get an answer often within the day or with a delay of no more than about three days if a decision is required of a panel of members. Generally, no more than a few days will elapse between the day a prospectus proof goes to the Quotations Department and the time of its acceptance for further proofing. Completion of the work necessary to comply with the comments of the department usually is achieved within one week.

The more complex and formal U.S. rules and procedures do not permit as much flexibility or speed. The SEC staff attempts to answer telephoned questions. However, often conferences involving top officers of the company, senior auditors and legal counsel with SEC officials are needed. The time required for clearance also is longer—a median of 36 days in 1974 (down from 45 in 1973, possibly because of the greatly decreased number of filings).

In part, the greater U.S. costs of preparing acceptable prospectuses is due to the greater number of prospectuses that the SEC must process—some 3,000 compared to about 120 processed by The Stock Exchange's Quotations Department. The greater number in the United States is not only a function of its considerably greater size, but also it is a function of the SEC's regulations. In the United States *all* issues of securities by companies, except private placements and intrastate offerings, must be registered. Unlike the prevailing rule in the United Kingdom, it matters not whether the security issued is in all respects similar to securities currently being traded and quoted on a stock exchange. In addition, U.K. law applies only to security issues by a company and by underwriters who are acting in a professional capacity. However, in the United States, secondary offerings are subject to the SEC's regulations. As a consequence of these differences, it is estimated that from one-half to two-thirds of all registration statements filed in the United States would not be required in the United Kingdom (Krauss, 1971, p. 64).

The larger number of activities regulated by the SEC, the greater complexity of its disclosure regulations, and the greater formality of its administrative procedures necessarily require a more extensive and expensive bureaucracy. For fiscal year 1975, the SEC expects to employ 2,219 people and expend $43 million. It is difficult to compare these figures with those of the U.K. authorities, since both they and the SEC do more than process financial statements. Nevertheless, it does appear that the Quotations Department's (1972) complement of 15 professionals and 25 assistants, typists, and so on, is proportionately smaller than the number employed by the SEC. Thus, both the costs to companies and to society appears relatively lower under the U.K. system than under the U.S. system.

Proponents of the U.S. system, though, claim that its benefits more than offset its greater costs. These benefits are listed, described, and evaluated next.

## Delineation and Evaluation of the Presumed Benefits from Administration by an Active Public Regulatory Agency

Several benefits may be achieved by having an administrative agency, such as the SEC, actively regulate financial disclosure. The seven benefits outlined are not mutually exclusive nor are they exhaustive. However, they do give something of the "flavor" of the arguments for an agency such as the SEC. While they are not "authoritative," they appear to be more complete than the rationale generally found in the SEC's publications and in most textbooks and articles.

The following advantages are thought to flow from a continuing professional administrative agency such as the SEC: (1) adaptability, (2) professional implementation of the securities statutes and regulations, (3) less discriminatory application of the securities statutes, (4) an expert and public interest source of information for legislative changes, (5) uniformity with respect to the type and format of data disclosed, (6) improvement of the quality of information disclosed, and (7) protection of the small investor and prevention of fraud. Each "benefit" is described and analyzed in turn. In the analysis that follows, all of the evidence of which this author is aware is applied to the evaluation of the SEC's administration of the Securities Acts.[9] Unfortunately, except for studies of the reaction of security prices to published financial data and of the behavior of share prices, few "hard" empirical studies have been published. Consequently, this study is based more on reasoning and "hearsay" evidence than desired. Nevertheless, this evidence is, in general, sufficient for most of the questions considered.

First, an agency like the SEC is claimed to be *adaptive* in determining the specific disclosure presumably needed to meet the public's "legitimate" demand for information. The agency can propose new rules, receive the opinions of interested parties, interpret these opinions in the light of its experience, and draft new

---

9. Evidence on the extent to which many of these benefits are achieved by administration of the U.S. Securities Acts is reviewed in Benston (1976, ch. 4). This evidence does not support the contention that the Securities Acts have increased significantly the reliability or usefulness of published financial statements. There is little evidence that financial statements published before passage of the acts were more fraudulent or misleading than they are today or that, as a consequence of required disclosure, they are more useful to investors. But since one cannot ever be certain that some unmeasurable (or unmeasured) benefit does not flow from the SEC's administration of the acts, it is necessary to analyze the arguments for an SEC type of agency.

disclosure rules and revise old rules to meet the present needs of investors. In contrast, disclosure required of U.K. companies is specified in the Companies Acts by Parliament. If a given requirement appears unneeded, ineffective, or inadequate, it generally is not changed except by the passage of a new or amended act.[10] Since passage of new legislation rarely occurs more often than each decade (in the past in the United Kingdom, at about 20-year intervals), it appears that the Companies Acts lack the currency that can be achieved by the SEC.

However, the SEC's power to promulgate disclosure requirements also serves to reduce the adaptability of the Securities Acts. Because the SEC is given broad power to implement the disclosure provisions of the Securities Acts, it has been forced to specify detailed rules and regulations that necessarily apply to a wide variety of circumstances. At first, the addition of a rule or regulation or publication of an opinion may serve to adapt the law to specific circumstances. But later, circumstances change and the regulations remain. Even though the regulations no longer may be meaningful to a changed environment or to the circumstances of specific corporations, the commission appears reluctant to eliminate or even to change them: at least, that is an inference one can draw from the fact that the SEC's regulations are almost never withdrawn or even changed except to increase their specificity or coverage. Once a regulation is adopted or a rule formally interpreted, the commission's staff understandably is reluctant to waive a requirement to meet particular circumstances. If they do, they risk being accused later of favoritism or even bribery, should it occur that the petitioner misled them or proved, or appeared, guilty of fraudulent acts. Thus as time passes, the SEC's administration of the Securities Acts' disclosure requirements tends to become less adaptive to changed environments and individual situations.

A private regulatory agency, such as The (London) Stock Exchange, can in practice be more adaptive than the SEC since it need not, and in general does not, promulgate a detailed set of rules and regulations. It has the power to adapt reporting standards to the circumstances of individual corporations, since it is not prevented by law or established precedent from waiving or adding requirements. The Quotations Department also can answer questions and resolve problems more quickly than can the SEC's staff because it need not be as concerned with uninformed ex post criticism.

It should be noted, though, that the considerably greater number of prospectuses processed by the SEC compared to The Quotations Department necessitates more formal, and hence less flexible, procedures. It may be that were the U.K. financial market as great as is the U.S. market, the United Kingdom would tend to adopt similarly formal written rules and regulations.

---

10. Statutory instruments are issued occasionally by the DT which clarify or extend (to a small degree) the Companies Acts.

Second, an active administrative agency can provide *professional implementation of the securities statutes and regulations*. The SEC is staffed with accountants, lawyers, and financial experts who specialize in administering the Securities Acts. Consequently, they are presumed to be much more competent to determine investors' needs and the costs of compliance by companies than are legislators. Few legislators are expert or even very knowledgeable about the securities markets, accounting principles, and procedures, financial institutions, and the like. Nor do they come into regular contact with market participants and the day-to-day problems of investors, brokers, accountants, comptrollers, and others who are concerned with financial statements. In contrast, the staff and administrators of an agency such as the SEC are in daily contact with the parties who are affected by the securities legislation. Further, since the agency is charged with enforcing the law, it is assumed to be the best judge of how the regulations should be most effectively written. In particular, an SEC type of agency can "plug" a loophole in the regulations which allows an unscrupulous issuer of financial statements to mislead the public.

It does seem correct to conclude that the SEC provides professional implementation of the law. The agency is well staffed with lawyers and accountants. However, while many (if not most) of these professionals administer the law, they also serve an apprenticeship for private practice in which they will earn fees from clients for steering them through and around the law. For lawyers, in particular, a profession that deals entirely with the regulation of the securities industry has developed in the United States. The securities bar, as it is called, is perhaps unaware of the inherent self-interest of its position as drafters and interpreters of the securities laws whose complexity is the primary source of the bar's marketable expertise. This conflict and confusion of interest is intensified by the apprenticeship served in and constant dealings with a regulatory agency. As Manne (1974, pp. 94–95) describes it:

> To be a leader of the securities bar, one must be on extremely friendly terms with important SEC staff members and even commissioners. Such a "social" position is not reached automatically by studying law-books. Rather, typically, it requires an apprenticeship at the Commission and then practice in one of the important corporate law firms. Then begins the gradual ascendancy through the committee structure of the American Bar Association or related organizations to the exalted position of "leading securities lawyer."
>
> If at any point along the way an individual begins to wonder out loud whether the whole system of regulation is actually in the public's interest, he will not appear to other leaders to have the stuff from which leadership is made. He may also find that he is less able to serve his clients well, since a continuing friendly relationship with the SEC staff is essential to that

function. The circle will then be complete, for certainly one cannot be a leading securities lawyer without numerous or important clients.

I believe that the extant empirical evidence (reviewed in Benston, 1976, chapter 4) is consistent with the hypothesis that the multitude of rules and regulations, court cases, releases, journal articles, and conferences generated by the SEC and the securities bar has benefited investors only slightly, if at all. The bar, though, does appear to have benefited.

Third, an agency such as the SEC is thought to be less *discriminatory in its application of the securities statutes*, because it makes its rules, regulations, and rulings public and minimizes its informal dealings with registrants. An extensively detailed set of regulations and publication of opinions and rulings permits all companies and accountants to file the required documents without benefit of an "inside connection." In contrast, critics of the U.K. system (Stamp and Marky, 1970) charge that the more informal regulation by The Stock Exchange gives rise to an "old boy network" in which established public accounting firms and issuing houses have a decided advantage over others who are not acquainted personally with Stock Exchange officials. In addition, they claim that less information is available to the ordinary investor and poor performance by "members of the club" is covered up. While few, if any, such instances are cited by the critics, they claim that the limited disclosure required by The Exchange does not permit revelations that otherwise would occur.

A related advantage claimed for the U.S. system is that, because it is funded by Congress, it serves the general public rather than private persons or groups. A private agency, such as The (London) Stock Exchange, critics claim, rather will serve The Exchange members and related parties. Aside from possibly covering up these insiders' wrongdoings, a private agency may prevent outsiders from competing with its constituency.

Though there is little evidence of cover-ups or similar scandals in the United Kingdom, it does seem clear that Stock Exchange rules restrict the establishment of new companies. The Stock Exchange rarely permits a company to apply for listing unless it can show at least five years of successful operations. The Stock Exchange also is the only market in which shares can be traded publicly. In contrast, a new company in the United States is not restricted by the SEC from offering its shares to the public, regardless of its "track record." Indeed, the shorter its financial history, the less onerous are the SEC's prospectus requirements. This difference between the United States and the United Kingdom may be a consequence of the fact that the SEC's constituency is more diverse than is The Stock Exchange's, since several stock exchanges and over-the-counter stock brokers and dealers vie for the public's business in the United States compared to the monopoly situation in the United Kingdom.

The Stock Exchange's limitation of new companies also may reflect the desire of all regulators, indeed, most persons, to reduce risks as well as costs to themselves and their constituency, ceteris paribus. Should a newly listed company fail, The Stock Exchange, established issuing houses and accountants and listed companies will be damaged if the public loses investments in ventures that, in retrospect, appear to be fraudulent or to have been more risky than was expected. While the public and economy might benefit from investments in risky enterprises, established firms generally only lose. If the new ventures are successful, the newcomers provide unwanted competition to established firms and few gains to The Stock Exchange. If they are unsuccessful, investors may blame their losses on poor administration by Exchange officials.

However, the situation in the United States, while better for new companies, presents considerable difficulties to them as well. First, though the SEC's regulations and rulings are available to anyone who subscribes to a good reporting service, considerable professional expertise is required to interpret them and file properly the required statements.[11] This professional help necessarily is expensive, so much so that many smaller companies cannot afford to sell shares to the public unless they can qualify for the private placement or intrastate exemptions. Second, the SEC tends to reduce the risk of registrants' failing, as does The Stock Exchange, since it is criticized should companies fail but is not rewarded should they succeed. Consequently, it has interpreted the permitted exemptions of securities from registration to limit them severely; has extended its authority to require registration of ventures such as franchises and condominium apartments; has accepted only conservative and easily administered accounting procedures (such as requiring write-offs of goodwill and not permitting upward revaluations of assets); has tended to restrict diversity of permissible accounting procedures; has refused to accept for registration statements of corporations which appear to have inadequate working capital to operate successfully,[12] and so on. Though many of these actions may benefit the public, they also tend to complicate the disclosure requirements which makes access to securities markets more costly, particularly for small companies, and limits accounting for registrants to auditors (generally the large firms) who are expert in SEC practice. Thus the public regulatory agency may, in fact, be as discriminatory as a private monopoly.

Third, the *expertise and public interest orientation of the SEC may be an invaluable source of information to legislators* in evaluating proposals to change the law. The agency can carry out studies requested by the legislature. Examples in the United States are the 1963 Special Study of Securities Market and the 1972 Study of Institutional Investors requested by the Congress, and the 1969 SEC-initiated

---

11. The standard SEC accounting practice manuals contain 1,217 (Rappaport, 1972) and 929 (Kellogg and Poloway, 1971) pages of outlined requirements and commentary. In addition, most large CPA firms maintain their own manuals to keep up with the changes (proposed and adopted) issued by the SEC in increasing numbers and complexity. Similar manuals do not exist in the United Kingdom, apparently because they are not necessary.

12. See Shefsky and Schwartz (1973) for an analysis of ASR 115.

study of Disclosure to Stockholders (Wheat Report) prepared by the commission. Since the agency is not supported directly by accountants (as are the AICPA and the Institute of Chartered Accountants in England and Wales), lawyers (as are the bar associations), brokers (as are the stock exchanges), or others, it presumably acts in the public interest. In effect, then, the agency may be thought of as a continuous Royal Commission.

This benefit, though, is of limited value because of the inherent self-interest of the securities bar and of the SEC as a regulatory agency. The more complex a law, the more work for lawyers and regulators. Though simplification and/or elimination of many disclosure requirements may result in a net benefit to investors, the SEC rarely conducts rigorous benefit-cost analyses. The commission employs few professional economists and sponsors almost no economic research, despite the fact that the Securities Acts are based on presumed economic problems. Consequently, the economic effect of its regulations are measured rarely and economic analyses are not undertaken to determine whether the present regulations are beneficial, in some sense, or even effective.

Nor is the SEC necessarily concerned with the interests of the general public when their interests conflict with those of the analysts, public accountants, investment bankers, brokers, stock exchange officials, and others who constitute perhaps its most influential constituency. The general public might not want (in the sense of be willing to pay for) additional detailed disclosure, as evidenced by the relatively few requests by shareholders of 10-K Reports.[13] Since the public has no means of telling the SEC that less information is wanted (there being no market mechanism), the SEC tends to interpret the vocal demand by security analysts for "more" as the voice of the public. As a consequence, perhaps, the commission tends to add disclosure requirements and rarely removes them, though it has this power.

In addition, the commission tends to suggest legislative changes that only increase regulation on the assumption that additional regulation almost always is in the public interest. Thus, despite good intentions, the SEC cannot serve the legislature as an unbiased expert source of information as to what changes in the Securities Acts will best serve the public interest.

Fifth, the SEC can impose a *uniformity with respect to the type and format of data disclosed* by companies. Ambiguities in the interpretation of law and regulations

---

13. A survey of 50 companies that included a notice in their 1973 annual reports advising shareholders that they could obtain a copy of Form 10-K on request revealed the following: (1) 0.16 percent of the companies' total number of investors requested the material; (2) in most cases, inclusion of the notice of availability of Form 10-K did not appear to have elicited favorable comment from shareholders or others: (3) there was no correlation between the percentage of shareholder requests and the size of the company or number of shareholders of a particular company ("Shareholders Exhibit Lack of Interest in 10-K data," 1974).

can be reduced by means of published decisions and opinions on accounting practices. This uniformity may reduce the cost of gathering and analyzing financial data.

It is questionable, though, that the benefits from detailed regulations exceed the costs thereof.[14] Nonadministered legislation, such as the Companies Acts, can provide analysts and other company data users with specified data which can be processed as readily by a nonregulatory agency, such as the DT, as by an SEC.

Sixth, proponents of the U.S. system (such as Kripke, 1970) believe that the SEC also can *improve the quality of the financial data available to investors* by enforcing the maintenance of minimum standards with the threat of sanctions should the data be misleading. In addition to the extreme threat of criminal charges, these sanctions include court orders stopping the sale or trading of a security, injunctions against corporate officers and directors, and temporary suspension of, or barring from practice, public accountants who prepare misleading statements, are not independent, or conduct grossly inadequate audits.

Assuming that the "quality of information" is an operationally meaningful term, there is little evidence to support the belief that the SEC has improved the quality of information disclosed. Regulatory agencies, in general, tend to remove ambiguity and judgment to reduce their risk. As a consequence, the data reported necessarily are less useful to investors. As SEC Commissioner A. A. Sommer Jr. put it (before he became a commissioner) after reciting specific examples: "You could often predict with precision what a prospectus would say about various problems. There was always a consensus that conservatism was the safest course" (1973, p. 507). Schneider agrees, saying, "Historically, certain types of highly relevant information—which I will call 'soft' information—have been largely excluded from filings by the SEC" (1973, p. 506). He goes on to say: "Generally, filings are treated as insurance policies against liability, and all of the juicy soft information is disseminated through oral selling" (1973, p. 507). As Schneider says, the potential legal liability of accountants and others results in rigid conservatism and following the letter (though not the spirit) of the regulations and law. Accountants and managers appear concerned primarily with following the rules and regulations in a manner that will avoid lawsuits and problems with the SEC. Unfortunately, this approach also limits presentation of judgments that could be valuable to investors.

Last, because a public regulatory agency receives its support primarily from the government, many believe it will be particularly concerned with *protecting the small investor and preventing fraud*. In addition, an agency that specializes in securities laws, such as the SEC, should be able to prosecute criminals and other wrongdoers more efficiently than ordinary police and legal officers. Security law specialists also should be better equipped to promulgate and enforce regulations

---

14. See Benston (1976, chapter 4) for a review of evidence that supports this assertion.

and propose disclosure and other laws to counter new methods devised by swindlers to cheat the public.

This "service" of the SEC is considered by many to be the most important benefit derived from a public regulatory agency. Many, perhaps most, small investors see the SEC as their "ombudsman." Should they have a dispute with their brokers, not be able to get information from a company, think they were misinformed by a security salesman, and so on, the SEC is there to help. The SEC assures them that their brokers execute their order at the best price, that insiders do not profit at their expense, and so forth. While many of these expectations no doubt are met, recent and past history indicates a considerable failure by the SEC to meet this obligation to the public.[15] However, these considerations are beyond the scope of this study, which is limited to financial disclosure of corporations.

Considering fraud related to financial statements, it is difficult to determine whether the SEC has been a more effective "policeman" than a police fraud squad would have been. It is not useful to compare the record of the U.S. Justice Department (which works with the SEC, since the SEC can only recommend criminal prosecution) with that of the U.K. police fraud squad, since the commission of frauds is not known, only arrests for fraud. Nor can one even know the extent to which fraud was prevented because wrongdoers fear the SEC or the police fraud squad.

Nevertheless, it is clear that securities fraud is still a problem in the United States and does not appear to be nearly as much a problem in the United Kingdom. The SEC's Annual Report gives a very brief summary of the actions taken. Each year, several hundred companies and persons are investigated; stop orders are issued preventing securities from being sold or traded when the financial statements of the companies involved appear materially misleading; and some 30 to 50 cases are referred to the Justice Department for criminal prosecution. While very few of these cases involve certified public accountants and financial statements, the impact of an SEC action of any kind upon an accountant, even a temporary suspension from practice, is great. Even the threat of such an action is powerful. Therefore, one cannot measure the SEC's effectiveness in preventing fraudulently prepared financial statements simply by counting the number of cases filed.

However, there were very few cases of fraudulently prepared financial statements before the Securities Acts were enacted.[16] Most security specialists believe that SEC prosecution has little effect on anyone who really is dishonest. In particular, a lawyer who worked for the SEC and the Justice Department said (in personal

---

15. Among the important instances that could be described are the failure of the SEC to prevent brokers from mishandling transfers and from maintaining inadequate capital and the SEC's past support of the stock exchanges' minimum commission schedules.

16. The evidence is reviewed in Benston (1969).

conversation, after recounting the cases he had worked on and the need for an agency like the SEC):

> I must admit, the principal difference between now and the 1920's is that you need the help of a lawyer to commit a successful fraud. But it's still a good business. These people are almost never caught. If caught, they're almost never indicted. If indicted, they rarely are found guilty. If found guilty, they almost never are fined much or sent to jail. If sent to jail, they get out on parole in a few months or years at most and then are welcomed back to their country club in Westchester.

While the SEC may reduce the amount of fraud, it may be that an individual investor's best defense still is caveat emptor. It is possible that the SEC had made the small investor too complacent about purchasing securities by giving him or her the impression that the "bad old days" no longer are with us. For as former SEC chairman Ray Garrett Jr. stated: "We have had cases of fraud and of mismanagement and disregard of investor interests that rival anything known to the men of 1933 who set about to construct a system that would make the world safe for small investors" (1974, p. 9).

One other dysfunctional aspect of the SEC's role in preventing fraud should be mentioned. Law enforcement officers, in general, often tend to see prevention of crime and punishment of wrongdoers as more important than the presumption of innocence and protection of civil liberties. The courts and even the prosecuting attorneys act as a balance against the understandable bias of the police who, coming into direct contact with the consequences of crime, may become rather zealous concerning the need to punish criminals. Unfortunately, a public regulatory agency, such as the SEC, has the power of policeman, prosecutor, and judge over an accountant, lawyer, or other professional who represents clients before it. When the client (company) wishes to offer a security to the public, the SEC also has almost total power over it, by delaying registration.

One prominent accountant, H. Kapnick, chairman and chief executive of Arthur Andersen and Co., commented after members of his firm were found innocent of criminal fraud charges brought by the SEC:

> Too often today, it appears that the SEC staff is wielding power to attempt to discipline and control accountants with utter disregard for the effect on the public interest at large. The SEC, more so perhaps than other government agencies, should understand that allegations made by it, even though unsubstantiated, are accepted as fact by a large portion of the public. The mere allegation carries more impact than the ultimate resolution of the allegation. In fact, even though certain accountants recently were found innocent of charges alleged by the SEC [Four Seasons trial], a senior officer of the SEC recently stated publicly that such accountants were not

vindicated by the jury but that the jury found that there was reasonable doubt as to their "criminal conduct." If this attitude is right, how does a professional ever eliminate the unproven charges? No longer, it seems, is one deemed innocent until proven guilty! (Kapnick, 1974).

Lawyers apparently have been even more subject to possible abuses of power by the SEC. In a well-documented paper, M. H. Freedman, dean of Hofstra University Law School, concluded:

> In sum...securities regulation is characterized by denial of the right to counsel, corruption of the independence of the Bar and of the traditional professional standards of lawyers' obligations to their clients, a police state system of investigations, and denial of a variety of other basic due process rights. (Friedman, 1974, p. 288)[17]

## Conclusions

I believe that the U.S. regulatory system, with all its benefits and costs, evolved and will continue to evolve as a consequence of the establishment in 1934 of an active regulatory agency, the SEC. It is no criticism of the SEC (which most observers acknowledge to be as honest and efficient an agency as exists in Washington) to say that it strives to extend its authority beyond the statutes under which it was created; that it avoids risks, even though it imposes costs on others; and that it tends to serve those who support or are likely to support it rather than the general public. Similar behavior is expected of any agency, public or private.

However, a public agency, unlike a private company or agency, cannot benefit from risks assumed—it can only lose. For example, consider a company that undertakes a risky research project. It may lose its investment, but if the project proves successful, it gains the benefits. However, if the SEC allows the company to publish subjective estimates of the value of the research, it risks public criticism if the estimates prove over-optimistic, but gains nothing should the estimates prove correct. Similarly, if a new company turns out to be a failure, in retrospect its prospectus may appear misleading, even fraudulent. Even though the prospectus states (in block letters), "these securities have not been approved or disapproved by the Securities and Exchange Commission nor has the Commission passed on the accuracy or adequacy of this prospectus," purchasers of the company's securities may blame the SEC for "passing" the registration. Therefore, it is not surprising that the SEC prohibits appraisals of assets, since these later may prove vastly

---

17. Also see Guzzardi (1974) for additional material.

incorrect; forbids estimates since these cannot be "objectively" determined; and requires reporting of very detailed data and analyses by all companies, despite the relevance of these numbers to relatively few companies and situations. If even one fraud or scandal is prevented thereby, or if it occurs and the SEC is not blamed, to the agency the benefits exceed the costs since it does not assume the costs imposed on the general public, including the cost of not getting possibly useful information (such as valid appraisals and estimates).

It also is not surprising that the SEC attempts to expand its activities. Thus when specific items are added to the list of requirements by the SEC in response to specific situations, they rarely are removed since they may serve some purpose or group. In a particular case, analysis of depreciation accounts might be helpful to an analyst. In another case, knowledge of the amount of specific intangible assets not yet written off may be valuable. An analyst might want to know the amount of the provision for doubtful accounts, or royalties, or advertising expenses or maintenance and repairs, and so on. Addition of each requirement seems to place but a small burden on corporations and may yield some benefits. But even after it is clear that the amount of the benefit is nonexistent or very small, the requirement for disclosure remains and is imposed on all registrants. Aside from the natural aversion of public regulatory agencies toward contracting their activities, the SEC must be concerned that it will drop a reporting requirement that someone later claims would have been useful in a specific case.

In seeking to expand its activities, the SEC must be cognizant of the fact that its budget is approved by the president and voted on by Congress. Hence it must be concerned to serve those who approve the budget and to obtain a "good press." Therefore, it is not surprising that it has extended its authority over annual reports (most recently by requiring in 1974 that the reports contain five-year summaries of earnings, information about the business, disclosure of its principal occupation and employer of each director and executive officer, etc.), has ruled that a complete 10-K report must be provided to shareholders free of charge upon request and has been concerned publicly about corporate contributions to politicians and payments to overseas officials and persons. These actions apparently are popular with analysts and the general public, whose support the SEC needs, even though they might harm shareholders, whom the SEC is charged with protecting.

A private regulatory body, such as The (London) Stock Exchange, also acts to maximize its welfare. Thus, it serves *its* constituency—the companies listed on The Exchange, issuing houses, brokers, bankers, and the major public accounting firms. Consequently, it is unlikely to require disclosure of superfluous or embarrassing information. And, as is discussed above, it tends to reduce its risk by excluding new, untried companies from listing. With respect to growth, since The Stock Exchange derives its budget from its members rather than from the government, its incentive to expand its activities is restricted by the unwillingness of its constituents to pay for this expansion.

The issuing houses also serve as private regulatory agencies, as do the reporting accountants. In conjunction with The Stock Exchange's Quotations Department, they determine the content of prospectuses and the investigations of company data that underlie them. The issuing houses and reporting accountants have a very great incentive for ascertaining that the prospectuses they issue and sign are not fraudulent or misleading—protection of their reputations. The issuing house's reputation is a direct function of the after-issue performance of the companies it sponsors. Should subsequent events show that the prospectuses issued misstated the companies' economic position and prospects, the issuing house's reputation is a direct function of the after-issue performance. Reporting accountants are valued in prospectuses because they are known to be independent, careful auditors. Should the public's faith turn out to have been misplaced, the auditors' perhaps most valuable asset, their reputations may be lost or damaged seriously. Thus, though these private regulators may wish to protect their client from bad publicity, they may do so at the peril of their own fortunes.

In conclusion, the evidence reviewed provides little reason to believe that the U.S. system gives the public greater benefits, on the whole, than does the U.K. system. The cost of the U.S. system, though, appears considerably greater. On balance then, there is little (if any) evidence that the disclosure regulations promulgated by the SEC provides a benefit, net of costs, to the public. Rather, the U.S. experience shows that once powers are granted to an active, regulatory agency, they almost never contract and almost always expand, regardless of their demonstrated lack of efficacy for solving problems or propensity to create new problems. Perhaps, though, the more formal, more explicitly codified, more regulated U.S. system is politically necessary for a large, diverse country where there are relatively few restrictions (though considerable costs) on a company that wishes to sell its shares to the public.

Consequently, were I asked, I would recommend that the United States move toward the U.K. system by reducing the authority and power of the SEC. The concept of "disclosure" should be restated to make it clear that the SEC is primarily an agency to which corporations report what they have disclosed to shareholders and how they determined the numbers rather than an agency that determines what and how corporations must report to the public.

## REFERENCES

Benston, G. J., "The Effectiveness and Effects of the SEC's Accounting Disclosure Requirements," in Henry G. Manne, ed. *Economic Policy and the Regulation of Corporate Securities* (American Enterprise Institute for Public Policy Research, 1969), pp. 23–79.

Benston, G. J., "Accounting Standards in the U.S. and the U.K.: Their Nature, Causes and Consequences." *Vanderbilt Law Review.* Vol. 28 (January 1975), pp. 235–68.

Benston, G. J., *Corporate Financial Disclosure in the U.K. and the U.S.: A Comparison and Analysis* (Institute of Chartered Accountants in England and Wales; D. C. Heath, 1976).

Freedman, M. H., "A Civil Libertarian Looks at Securities Regulation," *Ohio State Law Journal*, Vol. 35 (November 1974), pp. 280–89.

Garrett, R. Jr., "New Directions in Professional Responsibility," *Business Lawyer*, Vol. 29 (March 1974), pp. 7–13.

Guzzardi, W. Jr., "Those Zealous Cops on the Securities Beat," *Fortune*, Vol. 90 (December 1974), pp. 144–47, 192ff.

Kapnick, H., "Concern or Crisis? The Deteriorating Relationship between the SEC and the Accounting Profession Is Not in the Public Interest," *Executive New Briefs,* Vol. 2 (Arthur Andersen and Co., April 1974).

Kellogg, H. L., and M. Poloway, *Accountants SEC Practice Manual* (Commerce Clearing House, 1971).

Krauss, R. L., "Securities Regulation in the United Kingdom: A Comparison with the United States," *Vanderbilt Journal of Transnational Law*, Vol. 5 (Winter 1971), pp. 49–132.

Kripke, H., "The SEC, The Accountants, Some Myths and Some Realities," *New York University Law Review*, Vol. 45 (December 1970), pp. 1151–205.

Manne, H. G., "Economic Aspects of Required Disclosure under Federal Securities Laws," in M. G. Manne, E. Solomon, K. J. Cohen, and W. J. Baumol, eds., *Wall Street in Transmission: The Emerging System and Its Impact on the Economy* (New York University Press, 1974), Charles C. Moskowitz Lectures, pp. 21–110.

Rappaport, L. H., *SEC Accounting Practice and Procedures*, 3rd ed. (Ronald Press, 1972).

Schneider, C. W., "Nits, Grits, and Soft Information in SEC Filings," *University of Pennsylvania Law Review*, Vol. 121 (1972), pp. 254–305.

"Shareholders Exhibit Lack of Interest in 10-K Data," *Journal of Accountancy*, Vol. 138 (November 1974), pp. 20, 22, 24.

Shefsky, L. E., and E. J. Schwartz, "Disclosure and Reporting under SEC's ASR No. 115," *Journal of Accountancy*, Vol. 136 (September 1973), pp. 53–61.

Sommer, A. A. Jr., "New Approaches to Disclosure in Registered Security Offerings: A Panel Discussion," *Business Lawyer*, Vol. 28 (January 1973), pp. 505–35.

Stamp, E., and C. Marley, *Accounting Principles and the City Code: The Case for Reform* (Butterworth, 1970).

# 5

# DAAM: The Demand for Alternative Accounting Measurements

WITH MELVIN A. KRASNEY

## I. Introduction

"The literature indicates a substantial acceptance of current value accounting in accounting theory, but an impressive lack of implementation in accounting practice. The promotion of practical application obviously needs executive direction; why else would a quality product remain on the shelf" (Edwards, 1975, p. 235). The financial accounting literature is replete with exhortations on the "need" for or mechanics of publicly reporting some variant of current value or price-level-adjusted financial information in lieu of or as a supplement to conventional historical cost-based statements.[1] The advocates of such innovations typically argue that the information provided would be more relevant or useful to investors, though they rarely explicitly consider the costs of the proposed change. If the benefits of the prescribed information are greater than the costs, why don't we

---

We are indebted to the American Council of Life Insurance and Kenneth Wright for their generous support, financial and otherwise, and to our colleagues, Ken Gaver, Gregg Jarrell, Ross Watts, and Jerold Zimmerman, and the members of the University of Rochester's Graduate School of Management finance accounting workshop for their helpful comments.

1. To cite just a few examples: Edwards and Bell (1961), Sprouse and Moonitz (1962), American Institute of Certified Public Accountants (1963), American Accounting Association (1966), Ross (1966), Chambers (1966), Staubus (1971), Vancil and Weil (1976), and Davidson, Stickney, and Weil (1976).

observe widespread reporting of these measurements? The most frequent explanations of this apparent anomaly allude to the "public good" nature of accounting information—the inability of corporations to charge users for the data, imperfections, or failures in the financial and/or political markets for accounting information, or other similar restrictions.

This essay reports the results of an empirical study designed to avoid (to the extent possible) these kinds of constraints. We surveyed a sample of "sophisticated" investors who comprise a large portion of the supply side of U.S. capital markets. These investors can request and legally obtain firm-specific financial information other than publicly reported accounting statements. Furthermore, the costs of and benefits from this information are internalized by these investors and firms. We find that these parties generally do not believe that the benefits of current value or price-level-adjusted financial information outweigh the costs of providing, obtaining, and using it. For a few financial statement items, however, many of the respondents do show a preference for these alternative valuations.

In section II we discuss the shortcomings of most surveys of the demand for alternative financial accounting data. In section III we justify our sample of "sophisticated" investors—life insurance company direct (private) placement and common stock investment officers. The development of the study, description of the questionnaires, and the empirical results are provided in section IV. Section V considers possible limitations of the study and presents our conclusions.

## II. Shortcomings of Surveys of the Demand for Alternative Financial Accounting Data

Though surveys of and public statements by investment analysts, brokers, and so on,[2] show that they would like to have additional financial measurements and details on corporate activities, several shortcomings limit the conclusions which can be drawn from this information. First, their expressed desires necessarily are speculative because they have had little or no firsthand experience with the alternative measurements. Second, those sampled typically do not value some attributes of financial accounting data. Financial accounting data have other uses besides aiding individuals in making capital market investment decisions. For instance, accounting terminology, constructs, and numbers are used to formulate many types of financial contracts (e.g., leases and bond covenants); accounting numbers are used by various agents[3] of a corporation to monitor the performance of other agents (often corporate management). There exists a vast body of efficient market

---

2. See, for example, Estes (1968) and Brenner (1970).
3. See Jensen and Meckling (1976) for a thorough discussion of the theory of agency.

research which indicates that by the time annual or quarterly financial statements are released, most of their information content has already been impounded into security prices.[4] The essence of this information, therefore, must have been available to market participants on a more timely basis from alternative sources, such as the financial press, investment services, and so on. Consequently, it is quite possible that the benefits from financial accounting stem from its other uses. Third, since investment analysts and others do not pay the costs of producing financial data,[5] they have no incentive to temper their requests for additional numbers.

These criticisms could be mitigated if the group consisted of people who (1) have practical experience with the alternative financial data, (2) have uses for financial accounting information beyond supporting a recommendation to buy or sell a share of stock at a given market price, and (3) bear (at least in the short run) some of the associated information production, dissemination, and processing costs. This research examines the uses of and attitudes toward alternative financial accounting measurement methods by two groups of sophisticated investors—life insurance company common stock and direct placement investment officers. As we discuss below, the latter subject group seems particularly appropriate.

## III. Reasons for Studying Life Insurance Company Investment Officers

### Size and Sophistication

Sophisticated and/or large institutional investors certainly are important users of financial information. The Financial Accounting Standards Board (FASB) (1976, pp. 3–4) has even proposed that financial accounting issues be resolved under the assumption that sophisticated investors are the primary users of financial statements.

The life insurance industry, in particular, is a major participant in the market for corporate investments. At the end of 1976, for example, U.S. life insurance companies held $321.6 billion in assets, including $120.7 billion in corporate bonds (at amortized cost) and $34.3 billion in corporate stocks (at market value).[6] At year-end 1976, these holdings were about one-third of the total corporate bonds outstanding and 3.5 percent of the market value of all corporate stocks.[7]

---

4. See Benston (1976, chap. 4) for a survey and references and Foster (1977).
5. We do not consider the increased product costs that these individuals might bear in their roles as consumers if and when the higher information production and dissemination costs a company incurs are reflected in higher prices for its products.
6. American Council of Life Insurance (1977, p. 68).
7. Estimates of year-end outstanding made by the Federal Reserve Board, "Flow of Funds Section," *Federal Reserve Bulletin* 63 (1977).

The corporate stock figures, however, are deceivingly low. Because of legal restrictions, life insurance companies' investments in stocks were very small until the 1950s. Not until the late 1960s did they become a major investor in common stocks, primarily to meet the competition of commercial bank trust departments for pension funds. Over the years 1970–76, life insurance companies have averaged $3.1 billion per year of net corporate stock purchases, or about one-fourth of the net purchases of institutional investors.[8]

The economy-wide importance of this industry is evidenced by the fact that by the end of 1976, close to 150 million individuals (two-thirds of the population) owned $2.3 trillion of life insurance issued by legal reserve life insurance companies.[9] The life insurance industry also writes many pension and other annuity contracts. Thus, most people in this country delegate to life insurance companies the decision on how to invest at least a portion of their savings. We expect that competition within the industry itself and between different financial intermediaries and the existence of statutory investment regulations, with attendant legal and other costs of noncompliance, furnish strong incentives for life insurance companies to make very thorough and purposeful analyses before making specific investment decisions. Therefore, life insurance company investment officers who are responsible for making investment recommendations and decisions which affect many people, decisions which involve huge amounts of funds, satisfy virtually anyone's definition of sophisticated investors or users of accounting information.

## Availability, Use, and Cost of Nonpublic Information

Perhaps our strongest justification for choosing life insurance company investment officers as a subject group pertains to life insurance company specialization in directly placed bonds.[10] A corporation that wants to raise cash with a new bond issue can either (1) sell the issue to investment bankers who then resell it to the public or (2) sell the issue directly to one or a small group of investors. The first procedure is known as a public offering, while the second is called a direct (or private) placement. The Securities Act of 1933 requires that a company planning to issue (interstate) securities (debt or equity) to more than a few prospects must file a prospectus with the SEC containing specific, audited financial data. The buying public is entitled only to this prospectus data; issuing companies are prohibited from providing anything else. The 1933 act legally acknowledged the different distribution processes employed in the direct placement market by exempting

---

8. Based on data provided by the Federal Reserve Board, "Flow of Funds Section" (n. 7).
9. American Council of Life Insurance (1977, p. 17).
10. See Shapiro and Wolf (1972) for a thorough discussion and history of direct placement markets.

directly placed issues from its registration requirement. Presumably, the institutional investors who comprise the supply side of this market possess the resources and the sophistication to acquire and evaluate financial information relating to a particular security and company before they make a lending decision.

The life insurance industry is the primary supplier of funds in the direct placement bond market, since it acquires roughly 80 percent of all directly placed corporate bonds. The borrowers in this market tend to be smaller, less financially secure companies. They are attracted to this form of debt financing because they can avoid the time delays and monetary expenses associated with underwriting and Securities and Exchange Commission (SEC) registration. In addition, relative to floating an issue publicly, they have much greater flexibility to determine, and later modify, details of the bond according to their particular requirements. As a result, life insurance company direct placement officers' jobs involve more than merely deciding whether to accept or reject standard loan contracts at going market prices.

Furthermore, direct placement investors, unlike common stock investors, do not have at their disposal market prices that reflect all publicly available information (if, as most evidence suggests, the market is efficient in the semi-strong form). In fact, when the two parties come to terms, the interest rate they agree on is, by definition, the market price. In a typical year, more than 50 percent of the bonds directly placed with the life insurance industry are from companies with the equivalent of Moody's Baa credit rating. It is not uncommon for a life insurance company to buy bonds of different companies with yields varying by more than two percentage points. Hence, the determination of an appropriate interest rate (market price) for these long-term[11] loans requires a thorough analysis of the specific borrower—by no means a trivial task. Financial information also may be used to determine specific covenants to be written in the bond contract. Therefore, we expect the direct placement officers to request information which they find useful for these purposes. Since they appear to have a greater dependence on financial information than do common stock investment officers, we expect that they desire a broader spectrum of financial accounting data.[12]

Potential lenders in the direct placement market can request any type of financial information from prospective borrowers, regardless of whether it is publicly available. Of course, the prospective borrowers always have the option of refusing to supply the information, in which event the lenders can adjust their information

---

11. The only evidence on term to maturity that we are aware of is in Cohan (1967, pp. 145–48). For the years 1956–61, he indicates the average term to maturity was about 16 years for directly placed industrial bonds and about 25 years for directly placed public utility bonds.

12. They also can obtain nonfinancial information which may be more useful for analyzing the condition and prospects of a company (e.g., technical information on capital spending plans may dominate dollar estimates of replacement costs).

demands, adjust the terms of the loans, or refuse to make the loans. Prospective borrowers may comply with the modified information requests or terms, or may search for alternative sources of funds instead. In either case, borrowers and (in the short run) lenders bear increased negotiation costs or the cost of lost investment opportunities. Therefore, one may view the amount and type of information provided as the outcome of a market process in which the supply and demand functions are relatively unconstrained, unlike the public market for financial accounting information. Consequently, evidence that suppliers of funds to direct placement borrowers do not generally request and receive a specific class of supplementary financial information is consistent with the hypothesis that sophisticated investors and the companies in which they invest do not find it cost-beneficial.

## Existence of a Comparison Group

Finally, life insurance companies employ direct placement and common stock investment officers. Since both types of investment officers face the same set of organizational constraints and very similar institutional constraints (e.g., statutory investment regulations), such factors need not be accounted for when comparing these investors' uses of and/or attitudes toward financial accounting information. Furthermore, common stock investment officers in life insurance companies differ from investment analysts generally, since they recommend security transactions for their own firms; in effect, they are direct investors. It is important to remember, however, that in contrast with the direct placement officers, they can use only publicly available information for their decisions.

For the reasons just discussed, life insurance company investment officers are a very attractive group to study. In particular, an examination of the unregulated financial information negotiation behavior of participants in the direct placement market should yield insights into many current accounting issues.

# IV. The Study

## Development of the Study

The empirical results of this study are based on analysis of responses to questionnaires mailed to life insurance company direct placement and common stock investment officers.[13] The questionnaires were carefully developed and systematically tested before being sent to the complete subject group. In order to gain

---

13. Two very similar questionnaires were developed and used, one for each type of investment officer. The differences in the questionnaires relate to the information set that legally may be acquired and used to make investment decisions.

insights into this industry, a series of interviews were conducted with the investment officers and comptrollers of five, very large, mutual and stock life insurance companies.[14] The questionnaires were designed, modified, and pretested with the help of the people at these companies. By the end of the fifth company visit, we felt reasonably confident that the questionnaires were meaningful, understandable, and would not consume too much of a respondent's time. Nonetheless, we continued to test these forms, sending them to the American Council of Life Insurance (ACLI), the five companies we had already interviewed, and several additional companies for further suggestions. The responses were encouraging. Several relatively minor alterations to remedy some apparent ambiguities put the questionnaires in their final form.

We next selected the companies to be included in the study. As of year-end 1975, there were 1,603 stock and 143 mutual life insurance companies in the United States. Many of these are small organizations with little or no direct placement or common stock investment activities. Hence, a random sample was not desirable. Instead, we relied on the ACLI (whose membership includes larger companies) to select industry representatives thought to be active participants in these markets. The 62 companies that were chosen include the largest 20 stock and 20 mutual companies (measured by assets) as of December 31, 1976, according to Best's *Insurance News Digest*. The full sample contained 29 mutual and 33 stock companies, holding 59.7 and 21.8 percent, respectively, of the assets of all U.S. life insurance companies, a total of 81.5 percent of industry assets as of year-end 1976.

The chief investment officer of each company was sent a common stock and a direct placement questionnaire to distribute to the appropriate decision makers in his firm. To provide incentives for serious consideration and rapid completion of the questionnaires, a title page on ACLI letterhead was attached to each form and a cover letter from Dr. Kenneth M. Wright, vice president and chief economist of the ACLI, asked for the investment officer's cooperation. In conjunction with telephone follow-ups to those who did not reply promptly, this resulted in usable questionnaires from 58 companies for a response rate of 94 percent. We called the respondents when their answers to questions were incomplete or unclear. From these calls, we also learned that most of the people who completed the forms supervised their company's activity for that specific type of investment. The stock versus mutual and common stock investment versus direct placement investment breakdown of respondents is detailed in table 5.1.

---

14. We considered the possibility of bias that might result from the fact that a number of life insurance companies oppose revaluing their bond portfolio to market values, primarily because they would have to restructure similarly their liabilities for insurance contracts. We were convinced during our interviews and subsequent telephone conversations, however, that this aspect was not an issue to the companies' investment officers. Rather, they seemed concerned only with the value of price-level-adjusted or current value financial information of other companies as an aid to making investment decisions.

THE DEMAND FOR ALTERNATIVE ACCOUNTING MEASUREMENTS    123

TABLE 5.1 Sample Summary Statistics

|  | Companies ||| Questionnaires |||
| --- | --- | --- | --- | --- | --- | --- |
|  | Stock | Mutual | Total | Common Stock | Direct Placement | Total |
| Responses: | | | | | | |
| Companies making both types of investments | 27 | 25 | 52 | 52 | 52 | 104 |
| Companies making direct placement investments only | 2 | 3 | 5 |  | 5 | 5 |
| Companies making common stock investments only | 1 |  | 1 | 1 |  | 1 |
| Total responses | 30 | 28 | 58 | 53 | 57 | 110 |
| Nonresponses | 3 | 1 | 4 | 4[a] | 4[a] | 8[a] |
| Total sample | 33 | 29 | 62 | 57 | 61 | 118 |
| Response percentage = $100 \left(\frac{\text{Total response}}{\text{Total sample}}\right)$ | 90.91 | 96.55 | 93.55 | 92.98 | 93.44 | 93.22 |

[a] The four companies that did not respond are assumed to have both common stock and direct placement investment operations.

## Questionnaire

The questionnaire listed 17 balance sheet and income statement items. The life insurance company direct placement investment officers were told: "We want to learn whether you regularly request corporations to provide any of these [listed] alternatives as supplementary data for use in lending decisions." The common stock investment officers were presented with an identical list of items, but were instructed: "Assume that for each item *only one* alternative measurement will be presented in the financial statements provided by corporations. For each of the listed financial statement items indicate which *one* alternative you would like to see defined as GAAP." In another section of the questionnaire the common stock investment officers were asked: "As a supplement to financial statements as *presently produced*, for each of the listed items which *one* measurement basis would you *require* and *rely* on for making investment decisions? ('Rely' means that you would use the number in your analysis, not that you would use the number without further analysis.)" All respondents also were asked:[15] "Assume that financial statements would be based, as consistently as possible, on only one of the [listed] measurement alternatives, which one would you choose?"

---

15. Additional questions not reported herein concerned the respondents' (1) opinions about the usefulness of changes instituted by and proposed in recent FASB statements and exposure drafts, (2) rankings of the importance of nine qualitative characteristics of accounting numbers upon which a choice among valuation alternatives might be based, and (3) assessments of the usefulness of additional items (specified and unspecified) of financial information requested of or desired from corporate management. These findings (except for 1) are presented in our paper (Benston and Krasney, 1978) prepared for the American Council of Life Insurance for submission to the FASB.

TABLE 5.2 Sample Summary Statistics: Descriptive Data

|  | Common Stock | Direct Placement |
|---|---|---|
| Portfolio size ($ millions) | | |
|   Median | $ 99 | $ 350 |
|   Mean | 500 | 1400 |
|   Standard deviation | 1100 | 3000 |
| Total assets ($ millions) | | |
|   Median | 1538 | 1665 |
|   Mean | 5100 | 4800 |
|   Standard deviation | 8600 | 8400 |
| Years of professional experience | | |
|   Median | 11 | 11 |
|   Mean | 14 | 14 |
|   Standard deviation | 9 | 9 |

Factors other than the type of investment decision (direct placement or common stock) could be responsible for the responses. One is the scale of the respondents' investment operations, as measured by the total dollar amount of their companies' portfolios as of year-end 1976. Total company assets as of year-end 1976 also is used as an alternative measure. Another factor is the extent of the respondents' experience with financial data and investment analysis. The number of years of professional experience is used as the variable; information on the respondents' education or other professional qualifications was not available.[16] (See table 5.2.)

We analyze first the relationship between the investment activity (direct placement and common stock) and type of alternative measurements of financial data requested and used, or preferred. Then, within each group, we analyze the relationship of the valuation alternatives to the size of a company's operations and to the respondent's years of professional experience. Finally, we use multivariate analysis to consider the joint effect of these variables on the type of measurements demanded.

## Direct Placement Compared to Common Stock Investment Officers' Demand for Alternative Accounting Measurement

As the preferred *single* valuation basis for all financial statements accounting data, the direct placement officers overwhelmingly choose generally accepted

---

16. See table 5.2 for descriptive statistics of the variables. We also considered the form of company organization (mutual versus stock) in the event that mutual companies tend to be more risk-averse, which might affect the company's investment objectives, and, hence, the accounting information that investment officers (desire to) use. This variable was rarely statistically significantly related to the questions investigated. Therefore, we do not report on it here.

accounting principles (GAAP), as presently defined (*GA*); 89 percent prefer *GA*, 9 percent prefer replacement cost (*RC*), and the balance of 2 percent prefer general price-level-adjusted statements (*GP*) (see table 5.3). The common stock investment officers also prefer *GA*, but in relatively fewer numbers: 66 percent want *GA*, 25 percent *RC*, 6 percent current values (*CV*), and 2 percent *GP*. None of the

TABLE 5.3 Alternative Valuations for Financial Accounting Statements by Type of Investment Officer Percentage Distribution of Responses[a]

| Item | Question[b] | Prob[c] $X^2$ | Investment Officer[d] | GA | PV | RC | CV | GP |
|---|---|---|---|---|---|---|---|---|
| Complete financial statements[f] | DG | .003 | CS | 66 | 0 | 25 | 6 | 2 |
|  |  |  | DP | 89 | 0 | 9 | 0 | 2 |
| *Assets* |  |  |  |  |  |  |  |  |
| Receivables | DG | .019 | CS | 83 | 4 | 8 | 4 | 2 |
|  | SG | .0001 | DP | 96 | 0 | 0 | 4 | 0 |
|  |  |  | CS | 62 | 8 | 9 | 15 | 6 |
| Inventories | DG | .413 | CS | 60 | 0 | 26 | 13 | 0 |
|  | SG | .001 | DP | 53 | 2 | 21 | 25 | 0 |
|  |  |  | CS | 23 | 0 | 51 | 23 | 4 |
| Other current assets | DG | .112 | CS | 72 | 0 | 11 | 15 | 2 |
|  | SG | .0004 | DP | 84 | 3 | 2 | 11 | 0 |
|  |  |  | CS | 53 | 2 | 17 | 25 | 4 |
| Deferred charges | DG | .021 | CS | 87 | 6 | 6 | 2 | 0 |
|  | SG | .0001 | DP | 98 | 2 | 0 | 0 | 0 |
|  |  |  | CS | 72 | 13 | 8 | 6 | 2 |
| Long-term leases | DG | .838 | CS | 47 | 45 | 8 | 0 | 0 |
|  | SG | .069 | DP | 49 | 51 | 0 | 0 | 0 |
|  |  |  | CS | 32 | 57 | 8 | 2 | 2 |
| Fixed assets | DG | .557 | CS | 55 | 0 | 38 | 8 | 0 |
|  | SG | .002 | DP | 49 | 2 | 30 | 19 | 0 |
|  |  |  | CS | 21 | 0 | 68 | 9 | 2 |
| Intangible assets | DG | .175 | CS | 85 | 2 | 4 | 9 | 0 |
|  | SG | .011 | DP | 93 | 0 | 2 | 5 | 0 |
|  |  |  | CS | 75 | 2 | 6 | 13 | 4 |
| *Liabilities* |  |  |  |  |  |  |  |  |
| Long-term debt | DG | .669 | CS | 83 | 8 | 4 | 0 | 6 |
|  | SG | .024 | DP | 86 | 12 | 0 | 2 | 0 |
|  |  |  | CS | 68 | 15 | 9 | 0 | 8 |
| Lease obligations | DG | .061 | CS | 47 | 45 | 4 | 2 | 2 |
|  | SG | .861 | DP | 30 | 70 | 0 | 0 | 0 |
|  |  |  | CS | 28 | 62 | 6 | 0 | 4 |

(*continued*)

TABLE 5.3 Continued

| Item | Question[b] | Prob[c] $X^2$ | Investment Officer[d] | GA | PV | RC | CV | GP |
|---|---|---|---|---|---|---|---|---|
| Unfunded pensions | DG | .340 | CS | 55 | 36 | 4 | 4 | 2 |
|  | SG | .061 | DP | 46 | 49 | 0 | 4 | 2 |
|  |  |  | CS | 28 | 58 | 4 | 4 | 6 |
| Deferred credits | DG | .115 | CS | 89 | 2 | 4 | 2 | 4 |
|  | SG | .0001 | DP | 96 | 4 | 0 | 0 | 0 |
|  |  |  | CS | 66 | 17 | 8 | 4 | 6 |
| Contingent liabilities | DG | .058 | CS | 91 | 4 | 4 | 0 | 2 |
|  | SG | .660 | DP | 77 | 19 | 0 | 4 | 0 |
|  |  |  | CS | 74 | 17 | 6 | 0 | 4 |
| *Income & expenses* |  |  |  |  |  |  |  |  |
| Cost of sales | DG | .504 | CS | 77 | 2 | 19 | 2 | 0 |
|  | SG | .0001 | DP | 82 | 2 | 7 | 7 | 2 |
|  |  |  | CS | 45 | 0 | 42 | 6 | 8 |
| Depreciation | DG | .027 | CS | 66 |  | 28 | 2 | 4 |
|  | SG | .0001 | DP | 84 | 0 | 14 | 0 | 2 |
|  |  |  | CS | 28 | 0 | 60 | 6 | 6 |
| Other expenses | DG | .021 | CS | 87 | 2 | 9 | 2 | 0 |
|  | SG | .0001 | DP | 98 | 2 | 0 | 0 | 0 |
|  |  |  | CS | 70 | 0 | 17 | 4 | 9 |
| Net profits | DG | .036 | CS | 79 | 2 | 15 | 2 | 2 |
|  | SG | .0001 | DP | 93 | 4 | 4 | 0 | 0 |
|  |  |  | CS | 47 | 2 | 30 | 6 | 15 |
| Unrealized gains & losses | DG | .352 | CS | 94 | 0 | 4 | 0 | 2 |
|  | SG | .215 | DP | 89 | 2 | 2 | 7 | 0 |
|  |  |  | CS | 81 | 0 | 8 | 8 | 4 |

[a] Due to rounding, the percentages may sum to slightly more or less than 100.
[b] DG = Define GAAP: Common stock investment officers were instructed: "For each of the listed financial statement items...indicate which *one* alternative (see e) you would like to see defined as GAAP." Direct placement officers were not asked this question. SG = Supplement GAAP: Common stock investment officers were asked: "As a supplement to financial statements *as presently produced*, for each of the listed (financial statement) items, which *one* measurement basis (see e) would you *require* and *rely* on for making investment decisions?" Direct placement investment officers were asked to indicate "whether you regularly request corporations to provide any of these alternatives (see e) as supplementary data for use in lending decisions."
[c] *Prob* $X^2$ is interpreted as the probability of observing the sample responses from the two groups of investment officers, given that they both belong to populations with identical attitudes about accounting information. For statistical validity, responses were dichotomized into "prefer GAAP as presently defined" or "prefer some other measurement" before running the test.
[d] CS refers to the common stock investment questionnaires. DP refers to the direct placement investment questionnaires.
[e] The response code is: GA = GAAP as presently defined.
  PV = present values (capitalization) or future (undiscounted) cash flows.
  RC = replacement cost.
  CV = current market selling (exit) values.
  GP = general price-level-adjusted.
[f] Respondents were asked: "Assume that financial statements would be based, as consistently as possible, on only one of the measurement alternatives. Which one (see e) would you choose?"

investment officers opts for present value $(PV)$[17] as an overall measurement basis. The differences between the two groups of investment officers is statistically significant at the .003 level (chi-square test).[18] This difference is more clearly reflected in the specific financial statement items that they request and use (direct placement officers) or want (common stock investment officers).

Two comparisons are made between the responses of the common stock and the direct placement investment officers with respect to each of the 17 financial statement items specified in the questionnaires (see table 5.3). The common stock investment officers were asked to choose the valuation alternative on which they want to base generally accepted accounting principles and, hence, the numbers reported in financial statements. Their responses, in percentage terms, are summarized as *DG*, for "define GAAP." These respondents also were asked to indicate the measurement alternative they would require and rely on (if any) for data that would supplement financial statements as currently produced. Their responses, in percentage terms, are given as *SG*, for "supplement GAAP." These responses are compared to those of the direct placement officers who were asked to indicate supplementary measurements that they actually request and use. The "*Prob X²*" provides a nonparametric estimate of the probability that the common stock investment officers' responses ("define GAAP" or "supplement GAAP") are drawn from the same population as the direct placement officers' responses. Although we believe the direct placement officers' responses are more appropriately compared to the "supplement GAAP" responses of the common stock investment officers, comparisons with the "define GAAP" responses are also provided.

The individual item responses indicate that the direct placement investment officers are generally satisfied with GAAP as presently defined (*GA*). Over 76 percent of the direct placement investment officers request no valuations other than *GA* for 12 of the 17 financial statement items. (For 6 of the 12, over 92 percent of the responses were *GA*.) From 47 to 54 percent of these respondents do request and use alternative bases for inventories, long-term leases, fixed assets, and unfunded pensions. *PV* is used by 70 percent of the direct placement officers for lease obligation liabilities;[19] it also is the preferred measurement for unfunded pensions and long-term leases. *RC* measurements are used by substantial minorities of the direct placement officers for inventories (21 percent), fixed assets (30 percent),

---

17. *PV* refers to discounted or undiscounted future cash flows.
18. The number of observations required for statistical validity of the chi-square test dictated a comparison between *GA* and the other alternatives as a group. For the same reason, all of the subsequent chi-square tests are based on the same comparison. See, for example, Siegel (1956) for a discussion of the chi-square test for independence and its statistical requirements.
19. Note that GAAP does not require that all leases be capitalized. Therefore, we interpret the *PV* responses to the lease asset and liability items to refer to data that otherwise would not be provided in financial statements.

and depreciation (14 percent). *CV* measurements are used by substantial minorities for inventories (25 percent), other current assets (11 percent), and fixed assets (19 percent). *GP* data are used by almost no direct placement investment officers.

With reference to the "define GAAP" questions, the common stock investment officers generally prefer the individual statement items to be measured as they are now, but to a lesser extent than is indicated by the direct placement respondents. For 5 of the 17 items (receivables, deferred charges, depreciation, other expenses, and net profits), the percentage of these respondents who prefer *GA* is statistically significantly less (at the .05 level or below) than the percentage for the direct placement group. *RC*, although it has little support compared to *GA*, is the principal measurement alternative desired by the common stock group for these items. For lease obligations and contingent liabilities, however, the percentage of this group that prefers *GA* is statistically significantly greater (at the .06 level) than the corresponding percentage of the direct placement group.

The principal differences between the two investment officer groups are reflected in the supplementary measurements desired by common stock investment officers versus those requested and used by direct placement officers. Supplementary measurements are desired by significantly higher (at the .07 level or below) percentages of common stock investment officers than are requested and used by the direct placement officers for 14 of the 17 items. (Ten of these are significantly different at the .01 level or below.) The only items for which the two groups essentially agree are lease obligations, contingent liabilities, and unrealized gains and losses. In comparison with the direct placement officers, the major alternatives desired by the common stock investment officers (i.e., where over a 10-percentage-point-higher preference is displayed) are *PV* for deferred charges and deferred credits; *RC* for inventories, other current assets, fixed assets, cost of sales, depreciation, other expenses, and net profits; *CV* for receivables, other current assets, and intangible assets; and *GP* for net profits.

Thus, the questionnaires reveal a marked tendency toward GAAP as presently defined by the direct placement officers who can request and legally obtain nonpublished financial data with few constraints; their common stock investment officer counterparts indicate that (at a near zero price)[20] they prefer alternative measurements somewhat more, but primarily as supplementary data. For further insight, we turn to an analysis of the responses in relation to the magnitude of the life insurance company's investment operations and the investment officer's number of years of professional experience.

---

20. The price of alternative valuations may be perceived as being positive by the common stock investment officers only in so far as greater demands for such numbers increase the information production and dissemination costs to corporations whose shares of common stock are owned by the life insurance companies.

## The Relationship of Scale of Investment Operations to the Demand for Alternative Accounting Measurements

The dollar size of the portfolios as of December 31, 1976 (at market value for common stock and amortized cost for direct placements), is one measure of the scale of the investment operations. For each group of investment officers, we analyzed the proportion of respondents who request and use (direct placement officers) or prefer (common stock investment officers) the various measurement alternatives for each of the 17 financial statement items specified and for the statements as a whole. Within each group, the responses were dichotomized at the median portfolio amount. Chi-square statistics were computed to estimate the probability that the choice of *GA* rather than an alternative differs significantly according to whether the respondent's affiliation is with a smaller (less than or equal to the median) or larger (greater than the median) portfolio. The responses differ significantly at the .05 level or below for only one question—"supplement GAAP" for fixed assets (see table 5.4, section A). Relatively more of the common stock investment officers associated with larger (as opposed to smaller) portfolios prefer supplementary data on fixed assets to be valued at *RC* or *CV*. Differences significant between the .05 and .10 levels are found for four additional questions. Relatively more of the common stock investment officers associated with larger portfolios want GAAP for long-term debt defined as *PV* (15 percent compared to 0 percent for common stock investment officers working with smaller portfolios). However, those employed by companies with smaller portfolios prefer *PV* for supplementary measurement of contingent liabilities (26 percent compared to 8 percent for respondents involved with larger portfolios). Direct placement officers affiliated with larger portfolios request replacement cost depreciation data more often than do those working with smaller portfolios (24 percent compared to 4 percent), but for the overall financial statements they exhibit a greater preference for *GA* (97 percent compared to 82 percent).

For each group of investment officers, the responses also were dichotomized at the median amount of total assets of the companies, another measure of the scale of operations (see table 5.4, section *B*). No differences statistically significant at the .05 level or below are found. But precisely the same results are found for three of the five questions mentioned above. (The exceptions are fixed assets and long-term debt.)

On the whole, then, there are few statistically significant differences in the responses of either group of investment officers that are related to the size of the investment portfolio or to the total asset size of the insurance company. No differences significant at the .05 level or below are found for the 18 questions asked the direct placement investment officers; 2 questions, though, show differences at the .08 level. Of the 35 questions asked the common stock investment officers, portfolio size is associated with statistically different responses for one question at the .02 level and two questions at about the .07 level. It appears, therefore, that the size

TABLE 5.4 Alternative Valuations for Financial Accounting Statements by Type of Investment Officer and Size of Operations; Percentage Distribution of Responses for Questions Showing Significant (10%) Differences[a]

| Item | Question[b] | Investment Officer[c] | Prob[d] $X^2$ | Size of Operation[e] | GA | PV | RC | CV | GP |
|---|---|---|---|---|---|---|---|---|---|
| **A. Size of portfolio** | | | | | | | | | |
| Fixed assets | SG | CS | .021 | S | 33 | 0 | 56 | 7 | 4 |
| | | | | L | 8 | 0 | 81 | 12 | 0 |
| Long-term debt | DG | CS | .059 | S | 93 | 0 | 4 | 0 | 4 |
| | | | | L | 73 | 15 | 4 | 0 | 8 |
| Contingent liabilities | SG | CS | .074 | S | 63 | 26 | 7 | 0 | 4 |
| | | | | L | 85 | 8 | 4 | 0 | 4 |
| Depreciation | SG | DP | .079 | S | 93 | 0 | 4 | 0 | 4 |
| | | | | L | 76 | 0 | 24 | 0 | 0 |
| Complete financial statements[g] | DG | DP | .076 | S | 82 | 0 | 14 | 0 | 4 |
| | | | | L | 97 | 0 | 3 | 0 | 0 |
| **B. Total asset size of insurance company** | | | | | | | | | |
| Contingent liabilities | SG | CS | .074 | S | 63 | 26 | 7 | 0 | 4 |
| | | | | L | 85 | 8 | 4 | 0 | 4 |
| Depreciation | SG | DP | .079 | S | 93 | 0 | 4 | 0 | 4 |
| | | | | L | 76 | 0 | 24 | 0 | 0 |
| Complete financial statements[g] | DG | DP | .076 | S | 82 | 0 | 14 | 0 | 4 |
| | | | | L | 97 | 0 | 3 | 0 | 0 |

[a] Due to rounding, the percentages may sum to slightly more or less than 100.
[b] DG = Define GAAP: Common stock investment officers were instructed: "For each of the listed financial statement items...indicate which *one* alternative (see f) you would like to see defined as GAAP." Direct placement officers were not asked this question. SG = Supplement GAAP: Common stock investment officers were asked: "As a supplement to financial statements as *presently produced*, for each of the listed (financial statement) items, which one measurement basis (see f) would you *require* and *rely* on for making investment decisions?" Direct placement officers were asked to indicate "whether you regularly request corporations to provide any of these alternatives (see f) as supplementary data for use in lending decisions."
[c] CS refers to the common stock investment questionnaires. DP refers to the direct placement investment questionnaires.
[d] *Prob* $X^2$ is interpreted as the probability of observing the sample responses from the large versus the small (see e) components of the indicated (CS or DP) class of investment officers, given that they both belong to populations with identical attitudes about accounting information. For statistical validity, responses were dichotomized into "prefer GAAP as presently defined" or "prefer some other measurement" before running the test.
[e] S = smaller than or equal to and L = larger than the median sample portfolio size or total asset size of the life insurance companies employing the indicated (CS or DP) class of investment officers (see table 5.2).
[f] The response code is: GA = GAAP as presently defined.
   PV = present values (capitalization) or future (undiscounted) cash flows.
   RC = replacement cost.
   CV = current market selling (exit) values.
   GP = general price-level-adjusted.
[g] Respondents were asked: "Assume that financial statements would be based, as consistently as possible, on only one of the measurement alternatives. Which one (see f) would you choose?"

of operations is not a significant determinant of the demand for alternative financial accounting measurements.

## The Relationship of Years of Professional Experience to the Demand for Alternative Measurements

Within each group of investment officers, the responses were divided at the median number of years (11) of the respondents' professional experience (hereafter referred to as "experience"). The results are given in table 5.5, where LE11 refers to the subgroup with less than or equal to 11 years of experience, and G11 refers to those with greater than 11 years of experience. Several generalizations can be drawn from the table.

(1) The direct placement officers do not differ significantly (at the .25 level or below) in their responses with respect to experience, except for the "complete financial statements" question, for which 17 percent of the less experienced respondents request and use replacement cost valuations, compared to 0 percent for their more experienced cohorts. (2) In no instance do a higher percentage of the less experienced compared to the more experienced common stock investment officers prefer *GA*.[21] For the complete financial statements, *GA* is preferred by 81 percent of the more experienced respondents compared to 50 percent of their less experienced cohorts. The less experienced common stock investment officers prefer *RC* 35 percent compared to 15 percent, and *CV* 12 percent compared to 0 percent. For the "define GAAP" questions, significant differences are found for seven financial statement items at the .05 level or below, and for four additional items at the .05 to .10 level. With respect to the "supplement GAAP" questions, for 14 of 17 items, the responses of the high- and low-experience subgroups differ significantly at the .05 level or below. (3) *PV* is preferred by the less experienced common stock investment officers by more than a 10-percentage-point difference over their more experienced cohorts for supplementary data on long-term leases and lease obligations. The less experienced direct placement respondents also request and use *PV* measurements for lease obligations more often than those officers with greater experience; this is the only item for which the percentage responses of the direct placement experienced subgroups of *PV* differ by more than 10 percentage points. (4) *RC* is preferred by the less experienced common stock investment officers by more than a 10-percentage-point difference over their more experienced

---

21. The common stock investment officers' responses also were separated into quartiles by years of experience. For only 3 of the 35 questions ("define GAAP" for 17 financial statement items plus the complete financial statements, and "supplement GAAP" for 17 financial statement items) were the percentages for *GA* in a more-experience quartile lower than the percentages in the less-experience quartiles. Therefore, the dichotomy used does not appear seriously to obscure offsetting variations within the groups.

TABLE 5.5 Alternative Valuations for Financial Accounting Statements by Type of Investment Officer and Years of Professional Experience: Percentage Distribution of Responses[a]

| Item | Question[b] | Investment Officer[c] | Prob[d] $X^2$ | Experience[e] | GA | PV | RC | CV | GP |
|---|---|---|---|---|---|---|---|---|---|
| Complete financial statements[g] | DG | CS | .016 | LE11 | 50 | 0 | 35 | 12 | 4 |
| | | | | G11 | 81 | 0 | 15 | 0 | 4 |
| | DG | DP | .093 | LE11 | 83 | 0 | 17 | 0 | 0 |
| | | | | G11 | 96 | 0 | 0 | 0 | 4 |
| *Assets* | | | | | | | | | |
| Receivables | DG | CS | .009 | LE11 | 69 | 4 | 15 | 8 | 4 |
| | | | | G11 | 96 | | 0 | 0 | 0 |
| | | | | | | 4 | | | |
| | | DP | .980 | LE11 | 97 | 0 | 0 | 3 | 0 |
| | | | | G11 | 96 | 0 | 0 | 4 | 0 |
| | SG | CS | .0005 | LE11 | 38 | 8 | 19 | 23 | 12 |
| | | | | G11 | 85 | 7 | 0 | 7 | 0 |
| Inventories | DG | CS | .340 | LE11 | 54 | 0 | 31 | 15 | 0 |
| | | | | G11 | 67 | 0 | 22 | 11 | 0 |
| | | DP | .230 | LE11 | 45 | 0 | 17 | 38 | 0 |
| | | | | G11 | 61 | 4 | 25 | 11 | 0 |
| | SG | CS | .011 | LE11 | 8 | 0 | 65 | 19 | 8 |
| | | | | G11 | 37 | 0 | 37 | 26 | 0 |
| Other current assets | | | | LE11 | 58 | 0 | 19 | 19 | 4 |
| | DG | CS | .026 | G11 | 85 | 0 | 4 | 11 | 0 |
| | | DP | .674 | LE11 | 86 | 0 | 0 | 14 | 0 |
| | | | | G11 | 82 | 7 | 4 | 7 | 0 |
| | SG | CS | .009 | LE11 | 35 | 0 | 23 | 35 | 8 |
| | | | | G11 | 70 | 4 | 11 | 15 | 0 |
| Deferred charges | DG | CS | .037 | LE11 | 77 | 8 | 12 | 4 | 0 |
| | | | | G11 | 96 | 4 | 0 | 0 | 0 |
| | | DP | .305 | LE11 | 100 | 0 | 0 | 0 | 0 |
| | | | | G11 | 96 | 4 | 0 | 0 | 0 |
| | SG | CS | .005 | LE11 | 54 | 15 | 15 | 12 | 4 |
| | | | | G11 | 89 | 11 | 0 | 0 | 0 |
| Long-term leases | DG | CS | .072 | LE11 | 35 | 50 | 15 | 0 | 0 |
| | | | | G11 | 59 | 41 | 0 | 0 | 0 |
| | | DP | .509 | LE11 | 45 | 55 | 0 | 0 | 0 |
| | | | | G11 | 54 | 46 | 0 | 0 | 0 |
| | SG | CS | .049 | LE11 | 19 | 65 | 12 | 0 | 4 |
| | | | | G11 | 44 | 48 | 4 | 4 | 0 |
| Fixed assets | DG | CS | .075 | LE11 | 42 | 0 | 46 | 12 | 0 |
| | | | | G11 | 67 | 0 | 30 | 4 | 0 |
| | | DP | .509 | LE11 | 45 | 0 | 38 | 17 | 0 |
| | | | | G11 | 54 | 4 | 21 | 21 | 0 |
| | SG | CS | .021 | LE11 | 8 | 0 | 73 | 15 | 4 |
| | | | | G11 | 33 | 0 | 63 | 4 | 0 |

| | | | | | | | | | |
|---|---|---|---|---|---|---|---|---|---|
| Intangible assets | DG | CS | .954 | LE11 | 85 | 0 | 8 | 8 | 0 |
| | | | | G11 | 85 | 4 | 0 | 11 | 0 |
| | | DP | .971 | LE11 | 93 | 0 | 0 | 7 | 0 |
| | | | | G11 | 93 | 0 | 4 | 4 | 0 |
| | SG | CS | .691 | LE11 | 73 | 0 | 8 | 12 | 8 |
| | | | | G11 | 78 | 4 | 4 | 15 | 0 |
| *Liabilities* | | | | | | | | | |
| Long-term debt | DG | CS | .246 | LE11 | 77 | 0 | 8 | 8 | 8 |
| | | | | G11 | 89 | 7 | 0 | 0 | 4 |
| | | DP | .957 | LE11 | 86 | 14 | 0 | 0 | 0 |
| | | | | G11 | 86 | 11 | 0 | 4 | 0 |
| | SG | CS | .031 | LE11 | 54 | 19 | 15 | 0 | 12 |
| | | | | G11 | 81 | 11 | 4 | 0 | 4 |
| Lease obligations | DG | CS | .072 | LE11 | 35 | 50 | 8 | 4 | 4 |
| | | | | G11 | 59 | 41 | 0 | 0 | 0 |
| | | DP | .340 | LE11 | 24 | 76 | 0 | 0 | 0 |
| | | | | G11 | 36 | 64 | 0 | 0 | 0 |
| | SG | CS | .040 | LE11 | 15 | 73 | 8 | 0 | 4 |
| | | | | G11 | 41 | 52 | 4 | 0 | 4 |
| Unfunded pensions | DG | CS | .219 | LE11 | 46 | 35 | 8 | 8 | 4 |
| | | | | G11 | 63 | 37 | 0 | 0 | 0 |
| | | DP | .681 | LE11 | 48 | 52 | 0 | 0 | 0 |
| | | | | G11 | 43 | 46 | 0 | 7 | 4 |
| | SG | CS | .150 | LE11 | 19 | 58 | 8 | 8 | 8 |
| | | | | G11 | 37 | 59 | 0 | 0 | 4 |
| Deferred credits | DG | CS | .008 | LE11 | 77 | 4 | 8 | 4 | 8 |
| | | | | G11 | 100 | 0 | 0 | 0 | 0 |
| | | DP | .980 | LE11 | 97 | 3 | 0 | 0 | 0 |
| | | | | G11 | 96 | 4 | 0 | 0 | 0 |
| | SG | CS | .066 | LE11 | 54 | 19 | 12 | 8 | 8 |
| | | | | G11 | 78 | 15 | 4 | 0 | 4 |
| Contingent liabilities | DG | CS | .146 | LE11 | 85 | 4 | 8 | 0 | 4 |
| | | | | G11 | 96 | 4 | 0 | 0 | 0 |
| | | DP | .808 | LE11 | 76 | 17 | 0 | 7 | 0 |
| | | | | G11 | 79 | 21 | 0 | 0 | 0 |
| | SG | CS | .184 | LE11 | 65 | 15 | 12 | 0 | 8 |
| | | | | G11 | 81 | 19 | 0 | 0 | 0 |
| *Income & expenses* | | | | | | | | | |
| Cost of sales | DG | CS | .007 | LE11 | 62 | 4 | 31 | 4 | 0 |
| | | | | G11 | 93 | 0 | 7 | 0 | 0 |
| | | DP | .951 | LE11 | 83 | 0 | 7 | 10 | 0 |
| | | | | G11 | 82 | 4 | 7 | 4 | 4 |
| | SG | CS | .037 | LE11 | 31 | 0 | 54 | 8 | 8 |
| | | | | G11 | 59 | 0 | 30 | 4 | 7 |
| Depreciation | DG | CS | .208 | LE11 | 58 | 0 | 35 | 4 | 4 |
| | | | | G11 | 74 | 0 | 22 | 0 | 4 |
| | | DP | .251 | LE11 | 90 | 0 | 10 | 0 | 0 |
| | | | | G11 | 79 | 0 | 18 | 0 | 4 |
| | SG | CS | .008 | LE11 | 12 | 0 | 69 | 12 | 8 |
| | | | | G11 | 44 | 0 | 52 | 0 | 4 |
| Other expenses | DG | CS | .004 | LE11 | 73 | 4 | 19 | 4 | 0 |

(*continued*)

## TABLE 5.5 Continued

| Item | Question[b] | Investment Officer[c] | Prob[d] $X^2$ | Experience[e] | Alternative Responses[f] ||||| 
|---|---|---|---|---|---|---|---|---|---|
| | | | | | GA | PV | RC | CV | GP |
| Other expenses | | | | G11 | 96 | 4 | 0 | 0 | 0 |
| | | DP | .305 | LE11 | 100 | 0 | 0 | 0 | 0 |
| | | | | G11 | 96 | 4 | 0 | 0 | 0 |
| | SG | CS | .013 | LE11 | 54 | 0 | 27 | 8 | 12 |
| | | | | G11 | 85 | 0 | 7 | 0 | 7 |
| Net profits | DG | CS | .002 | LE11 | 62 | 4 | 27 | 4 | 4 |
| | | | | G11 | 96 | 0 | 4 | 0 | 0 |
| | | DP | .971 | LE11 | 93 | 3 | 3 | 0 | 0 |
| | | | | G11 | 93 | 4 | 4 | 0 | 0 |
| | SG | CS | .004 | LE11 | 27 | 4 | 42 | 12 | 15 |
| | | | | G11 | 67 | 0 | 19 | 0 | 15 |
| Unrealized gains & losses | DG | DP | .069 | LE11 | 88 | 0 | 8 | 0 | 4 |
| | | | | G11 | 100 | 0 | 0 | 0 | 0 |
| | | CS | .964 | LE11 | 90 | 0 | 0 | 10 | 0 |
| | | | | G11 | 89 | 4 | 4 | 4 | 0 |
| | SG | DP | .004 | LE11 | 65 | 0 | 12 | 15 | 8 |
| | | | | G11 | 96 | 0 | 4 | 0 | 0 |

[a] Due to rounding, the percentages may sum to slightly more or less than 100.

[b] DG = Define GAAP: Common stock investment officers were instructed: "For each of the listed financial statement items...indicate which *one* alternative (see f) you would like to see defined as GAAP." Direct placement officers were not asked this question. SG = Supplement GAAP: Common stock investment officers were asked: "As a supplement to financial statements *as presently produced*, for each of the listed (financial statement) items, which *one* measurement basis (see f) would you *require* and *rely* on for making investment decisions?" Direct placement investment officers were asked to indicate "whether you regularly request corporations to provide any of these alternatives (see f) as supplementary data for use in lending decisions."

[c] CS refers to the common stock investment questionnaires. DP refers to the direct placement investment questionnaires.

[d] Prob $X^2$ is interpreted as the probability of observing the sample responses from the more versus the less experienced (see e) components of the indicated (CS or DP) class of investment officers, given that they both belong to populations with identical attitudes about accounting information. For statistical validity, responses were dichotomized into "prefer GAAP as presently defined" or "prefer some other measurement" before running the test.

[e] LE11 = less than or equal to and G11 = greater than eleven years of professional experience. Eleven years of experience is the median of the complete sample and also of each of the two component classes (CS and DP) of investment officers (see table 5.2).

[f] The response code is: GA = GAAP is presently defined.
PV = present values (capitalization) or future (undiscounted) cash flows.
RC = replacement cost.
CV = current market selling (exit) values.
GP = general price-level-adjusted.

[g] Respondents were asked: "Assume that financial statements would be based, as consistently as possible, on only one of the measurement alternatives. Which one (see f) would you choose?"

cohorts for 12 of the 17 items: both "define GAAP" and "supplement GAAP" questions—receivables, other current assets, deferred charges, fixed assets, cost of sales, depreciation, other expenses, and net profits; "define GAAP" question only—long-term leases; and "supplement GAAP" question only—inventories, long-term debt, and contingent liabilities. The less experienced direct placement investment officers also request and use *RC* measurements for fixed assets more often than those officers with greater experience; this is the only item for which the percentage responses of the direct placement experience subgroups for *RC* differ by more than 10 percentage points. (5) *CV* is preferred as supplementary information by the less experienced common stock investment officers by more than a 10-percentage-point difference over their more experienced cohorts for receivables, other current assets, deferred charges, fixed assets, depreciation, net profits, and unrealized gains and losses. The less experienced direct placement officers also request and use *CV* measurements for inventories more often than those officers with greater experience; this is the only item for which the percentage responses of the direct placement subgroups for *CV* differ by more than 10 percentage points. (6) *GP* is preferred by more than a 10-percentage-point difference only by the less experienced common stock investment officers for supplementary information on receivables.

Thus, the questionnaire responses reveal that years of professional experience has a strong association with the common stock investment officers' preferences for alternative measurement bases, but a very weak association (if any) with the direct placement officers' actual requests for and uses of valuations other than GAAP as presently defined. These results are consistent with the hypothesis that the real world (as compared to classroom) exposure to alternative valuations afforded private placement officers rapidly tempers any inexperience-related naïveté they may have concerning the quality or usefulness of such numbers; it apparently takes common stock investment officers longer to comprehend the full extent of the practical problems and costs associated with these kinds of measurements.[22]

---

22. The common stock investment officers' responses also are consistent with the hypothesis that less experienced investment officers, since they are on average younger, have more recently completed a formal (i.e., college) education likely to emphasize the (normative) theoretical limitations of historical cost accounting data and the merits of some form of current value or price-level-adjusted financial information as a basis for making investment decisions. We reject this hypothesis because the distribution of years of professional experience of the sample of direct placement officers is similar to that of the sample of common stock investment officers, yet their responses (as a function of experience) are dramatically different (as we report above). We cannot, however, dismiss the possibility that direct placement officers' jobs are more difficult and/or important to life insurance companies than are the jobs of common stock investment officers, and consequently, that the two populations differ in terms of intelligence, type of training, and so on.

## Multivariate Analysis

A multivariate procedure was employed to determine the joint associations between the respondents' preference for alternative financial accounting measurements and the type of investment decision (direct placement versus common stock) they are responsible for, the relative size of the corresponding investment portfolio, and their years of professional experience. Since the dependent variable, preference for a valuation basis, is discrete and purely categorical in nature (i.e., GA, PV, RC, CV, GP), the assumptions underlying ordinary least squares (OLS) regression analysis are not satisfied. Consequently, we coded the dependent variable 1 if GA was preferred and 0 otherwise, *and used a multivariate probit regression procedure*.[23]

The investment-type independent variable was coded 1 for a direct placement officer respondent and 0 for a common stock investment officer. A respondent's number of years of professional experience was coded 1 if greater than the median value of 11 years and 0 if less than or equal to the median.[24] Relative portfolio size was measured as the ratio of each company's direct placement or common stock amounts at year-end 1976 to the respective sample means. This transformation was used because direct placement portfolios are, on average, almost three times larger than common stock portfolios (see table 5.2); we were concerned that an unscaled measure would be collinear with the investment-type variable. We rejected the year-end 1976 total asset size of the respondent's company as the variable because it is strongly positively correlated with portfolio size, and our priors were that portfolio size is the more relevant of the two. (A constant term also was included in the regressions, but is not reported herein.)

We ran the probit regressions on the complete financial statements question and on each of the 17 specified financial statement items. For these latter regressions, the common stock investment officers' responses to the supplement GAAP questions were used because the direct placement officers were explicitly asked about supplementary valuations for these items. Analogous to the *F*-test for OLS regressions, a likelihood ratio test is used to test the null hypothesis that all of the coefficients (except the constant term) are zero. For large values of −2 times the

---

23. See Maddalla (1977, chap. 9) for a description and discussion of the probit model. We would rather have used a multinomial logit routine that permitted multiple categories for the dependent variable; unfortunately, we were unable to find a reliable computer program for this analysis.

24. We considered using the reported number of years of experience as the variable, but decided instead to use a dummy variable formulation for two reasons: (1) we doubt that the number of years was recorded accurately to the year, and (2) we have no theory to justify the assumption of the purely linear relationship that this would imply. (It also is consistent with the formulation used in the univariate analysis.)

log of the likelihood ratio[25] (which is asymptotically $X^2$ distributed with degrees of freedom equal to the number of independent variables excluding the constant) the null hypothesis can be rejected. Similarly, the null hypothesis that a specific coefficient is zero can be tested with the equivalent of the *t*-test for OLS regressions. The *t*-statistic from the probit regressions is calculated in a similar fashion as in OLS (i.e., the estimated coefficient divided by its asymptotic standard error) and is asymptotically distributed as a standard normal random variable. The null hypothesis is rejected for large absolute values of this asymptotic *t*. In order to understand the importance of the independent variables better, partial derivatives of the estimated probit probabilities (with respect to a unit change in each independent variable) are calculated and evaluated at the sample means.

The results of the probit regressions are very consistent with the univariate findings (see table 5.6). For the complete financial statements question, the regression as a whole and both investment type and experience are statistically significant at the .01 level; portfolio size, however, does not appear to be important. In our sample, a direct placement investment officer has, on average, a .24 higher probability of choosing *GA* than does a common stock investment officer. Similarly, a more experienced respondent has, on average, a .23 higher probability of selecting *GA* than does a less experienced respondent.

The 17 probit regressions for the specific financial statement items indicate that investment type is statistically significantly related to the respondents' use of or preference for supplementary valuations. As evidenced by the sign of the asymptotic *t*-statistics (and, hence, the coefficients themselves) for each item, the direct placement officers are more content with *GA* valuations alone than are the common stock investment officers. Investment type is statistically significant at the .01 level for 10 items, at the .05 level for 2 items, at the .10 level for 2 items, and relatively insignificant for 3 items. The univariate analysis of this variable (see table 5.3) shows a *Prob $X^2$* at the same level of statistical significance for each item (and also for the complete financial statements question). It is interesting to note that the derivatives with respect to investment type of the estimated probit probabilities for three income statement items–cost of sales, depreciation, and net profits—are quite large (0.399, 0.682, and 0.487, respectively).

Portfolio size, although measured differently than in the univariate analysis (where it is dichotomized above or below the median), continues to be unimportant. Of the 17 items, this variable is statistically significant at the .05 level for long-term debt and depreciation, and at the .10 level for receivables and cost of sales. Depreciation is the only item for which this variable is also statistically significant in the univariate analysis (see table 5.4, section *A*, *SG* questions). For 14 of the 17

---

25. See Maddalla (1977, chap. 9) for a discussion of this test.

TABLE 5.6 Preference for GAAP as Presently Defined vs. All Other Alternatives (dependent variable) as a Function of Investment Type, Experience, and Portfolio Size (independent variables); Complete Financial Statements and Supplement GAAP Questions, All Respondents (110 observations); PROBIT Analysis[a]: Likelihood Ratios, Derivative (evaluated at means), and Asymptotic t-Statistics

| Item | −2 Log Likelihood Ratio[b] | Investment Type[c] Derivative[f] | Investment Type[c] Asymptotic t[g] | Experience[d] Derivative[f] | Experience[d] Asymptotic t[g] | Portfolio Size[e] Derivative[f] | Portfolio Size[e] Asymptotic t[g] |
|---|---|---|---|---|---|---|---|
| Complete financial statements | 19.30** | 0.239 | 3.08** | 0.226 | 2.90** | 0.023 | 0.94 |
| *Assets* | | | | | | | |
| Receivables | 35.84** | 0.313 | 4.27** | 0.194 | 3.05** | −0.023 | −1.86† |
| Inventories | 18.62** | 0.333 | 3.37** | 0.253 | 2.59** | −0.024 | −0.99 |
| Other current assets | 17.26** | 0.325 | 3.56** | 0.154 | 1.70† | −0.024 | −1.15 |
| Deferred charges | 24.10** | 0.221 | 3.57** | 0.112 | 2.21* | −0.012 | −1.17 |
| Long-term leases | 9.78* | 0.181 | 1.88† | 0.171 | 1.78† | −0.046 | −1.58 |
| Fixed assets | 17.71** | 0.312 | 3.25** | 0.183 | 1.94† | −0.054 | −1.61 |
| Intangible assets | 7.38† | 0.171 | 2.50* | 0.022 | 0.33 | −0.011 | −0.78 |
| *Liabilities* | | | | | | | |
| Long-term debt | 13.65** | 0.185 | 2.31† | 0.135 | 1.69† | −0.039 | −2.40* |
| Lease obligations | 5.52 | 0.020 | 0.23 | 0.183 | 2.09* | −0.023 | −0.94 |
| Unfunded pensions | 5.96 | 0.178 | 1.90† | 0.058 | 0.62 | −0.035 | −1.29 |
| Deferred credits | 23.87** | 0.274 | 3.89** | 0.099 | 1.60 | 0.033 | 1.18 |
| Contingent liabilities | 2.16 | 0.040 | 0.49 | 0.092 | 1.12 | −0.015 | −0.86 |
| *Income & expenses* | | | | | | | |
| Cost of sales | 22.41** | 0.399 | 4.12** | 0.151 | 1.57 | −0.037 | −1.66† |
| Depreciation | 49.18** | 0.682 | 5.94** | 0.116 | 1.04 | −0.101 | −2.55* |
| Other expenses | 23.52** | 0.246 | 3.67** | 0.096 | 1.82† | 0.008 | 0.55 |
| Net profits | 36.97** | 0.487 | 5.14** | 0.209 | 2.36* | −0.017 | −0.94 |
| Unrealized gains & losses | 6.37† | 0.073 | 1.13 | 0.140 | 2.10* | 0.008 | 0.41 |

† Significant at .10 level.
* Significant at .05 level.
** Significant at .01 level.
[a] GA responses are coded 1 and all other responses are coded 0.
[b] −2 times the log of the likelihood ratio is asymptotically $X^2$ distributed.
[c] Investment type is coded 1 for a direct placement officer and 0 for a common stock investment officer.
[d] Experience is coded 1 for a respondent having greater than, and 0 for a respondent having less than or equal to, the median of 11 years of professional experience.
[e] Portfolio size is coded as the ratio of the year-end 1976 direct placement or common stock portfolio amount to the corresponding sample mean.
[f] Partial derivatives of the estimated probit probabilities with respect to a unit change in the particular independent variable.
[g] The t-statistic derived from a probit regression is asymptotically distributed as a standard normal random variable.

items, however, the signs of the coefficients are negative, suggesting that there may be a slight tendency for investment officers associated with relatively large portfolios to use or desire alternatives to GA valuations more than those respondents associated with relatively small portfolios.

Experience is statistically significant for receivables and inventories at the .01 level, four additional items at the .05 level, and five other items at the .10 level. In all cases, the signs of the coefficients (even if not statistically significant at the .10 or lower level) and derivatives are positive, indicating that more experienced investment officers use or prefer fewer alternative valuations than less experienced investment officers. In the univariate analysis (see table 5.5), we observe that while experience appears to be quite important in explaining the common stock investment officers' preferences for alternative measurement bases, it is not helpful in differentiating among direct placement officers' actual use of supplementary valuations. We became concerned, therefore, that the results in table 5.6 understate the statistical significance of this variable for common stock investment officers and overstate its statistical significance for direct placement officers. Hence, we ran the probit regressions with two independent variables (experience and portfolio size) on each group of investment officer responses.

As expected, experience again proves unimportant in explaining the responses of direct placement officers. While it is statistically significant at the .10 level (with derivative of only .01) for the complete financial statements question, it is not important for any of the 17 specific financial statement item questions. Furthermore, the signs of the coefficients and derivatives are negative for 11 of the items, while in table 5.6 they are uniformly positive. The results for portfolio size are very similar to those reported in table 5.6. The only differences we could detect are the following: for deferred charges and intangible assets the signs of the coefficients (and derivatives) are now positive, and for contingent liabilities and net profits the coefficients are now statistically significant at the .05 and .10 levels, respectively.

The results of the probit regressions for the common stock investment officers are reported in table 5.7 for all 35 questions asked. The signs of the experience coefficients and derivatives are positive for every question; more experienced common stock investment officers are consistently more satisfied with the current definitions of GAAP and want fewer supplementary valuations than the less experienced common stock investment officers. The coefficients for the complete financial statements question and for each of the supplement GAAP questions are statistically significant at the same levels (i.e., .01, .05, .10, or insignificant) as are found in the univariate analysis reported in table 5.5. With regard to the define GAAP questions, the same observation holds, except for five items—receivables, deferred charges, deferred credits, other expenses, and unrealized gains and losses—where experience appears now to be less significant or insignificant. Portfolio size is only statistically significant for 1 of the 35 questions asked the common stock investment officers—the define GAAP question for deferred charges (at the .05 level). For the complete financial statements question and the supplement GAAP questions, except for contingent liabilities, the signs of the coefficients of the portfolio size variable are the same in table 5.7 as they are in table 5.6. The signs for the define GAAP questions also are quite similar. Thus, the multivariate probit results confirm the univariate findings.

## V. Conclusions

### Possible Limitations of the Study

The response rate to our questionnaire survey was extremely high (94 percent). Therefore, any nonrespondent bias, if it exists, would have an immaterial effect on the results and, hence, on our conclusions. As with all studies of this type, the results technically represent only the views and experiences of the actual respondents. Nonetheless, we are reasonably confident that the responses are indicative of the preferences of a broader population of "sophisticated investors."

It is possible that the direct placement and common stock investment officers' responses vary because of their experience with different types of financial instruments (debt versus equity). This factor may explain the direct placement officers' relatively greater preference for present value data for lease obligations. However, since they do not use supplementary valuations of other liabilities as often as the common stock investment officers report that they would, we do not believe that experience with debt or equity obligations, as such, is a principal determining factor of the investment officers' responses.

It is also possible that decisions on common stocks and direct placement loans, which are different financial instruments, benefit from different financial data as inputs to the investment decision process. However, we contend above that the direct placement loan decision requires more, not less, "economically relevant" (e.g., current value or price-level-adjusted) information, because a market price is not exogenously provided as with common stocks, but must be endogenously determined by the lender and borrower. Were this the case, we should have found the direct placement officers to be more, not less, in favor of alternative valuations than the common stock investment officers.[26] Consequently, we are not too concerned with this objection.

Some readers familiar with the internal workings of life insurance company investment operations may point out that investment officers tend to specialize in a relatively small number of companies (typically those in one or two specific industries) in which the insurance company is currently or has previously

---

26. Recall, however, that direct placement officers' employers internalize the costs associated with their requests for and subsequent use of nonpublic financial information, while common stock investment officers probably ignore these costs since their employers are affected only partially and indirectly.

TABLE 5.7 Preference for GAAP as Presently Defined versus All Other Alternatives (dependent variable) as a Function of Experience and Portfolio Size (independent variables); Complete Financial Statements, Define GAAP, and Supplement GAAP Questions, Common Stock Investment Officers (53 observations); PROBIT Analysis[a]: Likelihood Ratios, Derivatives (evaluated at means), and Asymptotic $t$-Statistics

| | Supplement GAPP | | | | | | Define GAAP | | | | | |
|---|---|---|---|---|---|---|---|---|---|---|---|---|
| | | Experience[c] | | Portfolio Size[d] | | | | Experience[c] | | Portfolio Size[d] | |
| Item | $-2$ Log Likelihood Ratio[b] | Derivative[c] | Asymptotic $t$[c] | Derivative[c] | Asymptotic $t$[d] | | $-2$ Log Likelihood Ratio[b] | Derivative[c] | Asymptotic $t$[c] | Derivative[c] | Asymptotic $t$[d] |
| Complete financial statements | | | | | | | 6.09* | 0.319 | 2.38* | 0.010 | 0.28 |
| Assets | | | | | | | | | | | |
| Receivables | 14.54** | 0.520 | 3.54** | −0.038 | −1.23 | | 7.75* | 0.265 | 2.49* | −0.008 | −0.34 |
| Inventories | 7.03* | 0.301 | 2.50* | −0.004 | −0.17 | | 1.50 | 0.124 | 0.91 | 0.027 | 0.72 |
| Other current assets | 8.33* | 0.390 | 2.69** | −0.039 | −1.13 | | 5.23† | 0.276 | 2.19* | 0.013 | 0.38 |
| Deferred charges | 11.17** | 0.390 | 2.93** | −0.042 | −1.60 | | 11.98** | 0.179 | 1.74† | −0.024 | −2.20* |
| Long-term leases | 4.55 | 0.262 | 1.99* | −0.024 | −0.73 | | 3.31 | 0.253 | 1.81† | −0.007 | −0.21 |
| Fixed assets | 9.71** | 0.198 | 2.35* | −0.108 | −1.28 | | 4.09 | 0.261 | 1.86† | −0.030 | −0.92 |
| Intangible assets | 1.12 | 0.061 | 0.51 | −0.025 | −0.97 | | 1.51 | 0.025 | 0.25 | −0.023 | −1.21 |
| Liabilities | | | | | | | | | | | |
| Long-term debt | 5.93† | 0.298 | 2.24* | −0.031 | −1.11 | | 1.37 | 0.119 | 1.16 | −0.001 | −0.05 |
| Lease obligations | 4.65† | 0.262 | 2.06* | −0.016 | −0.54 | | 3.31 | 0.253 | 1.81† | −0.007 | −0.21 |
| Unfunded pensions | 2.44 | 0.182 | 1.45 | −0.017 | −0.56 | | 1.56 | 0.167 | 1.20 | 0.006 | 0.21 |
| Deferred credits | 6.01* | 0.239 | 1.82† | 0.081 | 1.22 | | 11.02** | 0.045 | 0.84 | 0.006 | 0.83 |
| Contingent liabilities | 4.91† | 0.156 | 1.37 | 0.097 | 1.24 | | 4.42 | 0.052 | 1.46 | 0.049 | 0.88 |

(*continued*)

TABLE 5-7 Continued

| | Supplement GAPP | | | | | | Define GAAP | | | | | |
|---|---|---|---|---|---|---|---|---|---|---|---|---|
| | | Experience[e] | | Portfolio Size[d] | | | | Experience[e] | | Portfolio Size[d] | | |
| Item | −2 Log Likelihood Ratio[b] | Derivative[e] | Asymptotic t[f] | Derivative[e] | Asymptotic t[f] | | −2 Log Likelihood Ratio[b] | Derivative[e] | Asymptotic t[f] | Derivative[e] | Asymptotic t[f] |
| *Income & expenses* | | | | | | | | | | | | |
| Cost of sales | 4.80† | 0.300 | 2.12* | −0.020 | −0.62 | | 7.80* | 0.312 | 2.63** | 0.001 | 0.04 |
| Depreciation | 12.17** | 0.308 | 2.72** | −0.131 | −1.23 | | 3.11 | 0.183 | 1.37 | −0.036 | −1.20 |
| Other expenses | 6.51* | 0.317 | 2.45* | 0.012 | 0.34 | | 12.50** | 0.020 | 0.82 | −0.001 | −1.16 |
| Net profits | 8.64* | 0.416 | 2.88** | −0.001 | −0.04 | | 10.97** | 0.344 | 2.91** | −0.005 | −0.21 |
| Unrealized gains & losses | 9.31** | 0.299 | 2.68** | 0.008 | 0.25 | | 5.10† | 0.023 | 0.58 | 0.003 | 0.56 |

† Significant at .10 level.
* Significant at .05 level.
** Significant at .01 level.
[a] GA responses are coded 1 and all other responses are coded 0.
[b] −2 times the log of the likelihood ratio is asymptotically $X^2$ distributed.
[c] Experience is coded 1 for a respondent having greater than, and 0 for a respondent having less than or equal to, the median of 11 years of professional experience.
[d] Portfolio size is coded as the ratio of the year-end 1976 direct placement or common stock portfolio amount to the corresponding sample mean.
[e] Partial derivatives of the estimated probit probabilities with respect to a unit change in the particular independent variable.
[f] The t-statistic derived from probit regression is asymptotically distributed as a standard normal random variable.

invested. As a result of following a particular company or industry for many years, an investment officer may be cognizant of its "true" financial status and future prospects without current value or price-level-adjusted accounting data. We contend, however, that this in-depth knowledge and analysis of a firm or industry is one of the prime characteristics that distinguish a "sophisticated" from a "naive" investor. Furthermore, the argument fails to consider that life insurance company investments are not restricted to companies in which they have previously invested. If the evaluation of a potential "new" investment would benefit from current value or price-level-adjusted accounting numbers, then this benefit should be reflected in the questionnaire responses. Furthermore, those investment officers who are relatively new to their jobs most likely do not possess the knowledge that may come from following a particular company or industry over an extended period of time. Thus, we believe that this criticism does not significantly limit our conclusions.

Finally, because GAAP as presently defined includes other than historical-cost valuations for some financial statement items, it is possible that the respondents checked a use or preference for an alternative even though they meant to check "GA." Or, they may have meant to indicate their use of, or preference for, the alternative in those instances where it is not so reported in publicly available statements. If the latter is generally the case, our conclusions are not affected. If the former obtains, we have overstated the respondents' use of, or preference for, alternatives to GAAP.

## Summary

We surveyed the practices and opinions of investment officers employed by 62 life insurance companies that represent 82 percent of the industry's assets. The response rate was 94 percent. Two types of officers were surveyed. Direct placement officers can request any financial data they desire from the firms with whom they negotiate loans. Common stock investment officers in these companies differ from investment analysts generally, since they recommend security transactions for their own firms: in effect, they are direct investors. In contrast with the direct placement officers, however, they can use only publicly available information for their decisions.

The following major conclusions are drawn from this study. (1) The direct placement officers were asked for valuations (presently defined GAAP, present value, replacement cost, current value, or general price-level-adjusted) of 17 specific financial statement items that they regularly request as supplementary data for use in lending decisions. Their single preferred valuation basis for financial statements also was requested. The common stock investment officers were asked to indicate the valuation bases that they prefer defined as GAAP for the same

17 specific financial statement items and for the statements as a whole. In addition, they were asked to indicate the measurements they prefer as supplements to presently defined GAAP. Their answers are reported and compared to those given by the direct placement officers. (1a) When the respondents were asked their preference for a uniform valuation basis for financial statements, GAAP as presently defined was preferred by 89 percent of the direct placement and 66 percent of the common stock investment officers. (1b) We found that GAAP as presently defined is used overwhelmingly (and almost exclusively) by the direct placement officers who can request and legally obtain alternative valuations (and other types of information), the costs and benefits of which are internalized. At least 74 percent of the respondents do not request valuations other than GAAP for receivables, other current assets, deferred charges, intangible assets, contingent liabilities, long-term debt, deferred credits, cost of sales, depreciation, other expenses, unrealized gains and losses, and net profits. About one-half or fewer request and use other measures for inventories, long-term leases, fixed assets, and unfunded pensions. For lease obligations, however, 70 percent of the direct placement officers request and use present value measures. (1c) The common stock investment officers' preferences for definitions of GAAP generally concur with those of the direct placement officers. However, when they assume the data will be supplemental to that presently reported in financial statements, they exhibit a stronger preference for additional valuations of more items. (2) The scale of investment operations of the life insurance companies, measured either by portfolio size or total assets, is not a statistically significant determinant of the demand for alternative financial accounting measurements. (3) The years of professional experience of the direct placement officers is not significantly related to their responses to the valuation questions. The more experienced common stock investment officers, however, are much more GAAP oriented than are their less experienced cohorts.

In conclusion, many have argued that reliance on historical cost accounting data, or more specifically "generally accepted accounting principles" (GAAP) as presently defined, has induced a misallocation of resources in the economy. Our study has considered this question only with respect to private costs and benefits. Therefore, we cannot conclude that the social benefits of current value or price-level-adjusted numbers are less than their social costs. It is conceivable that economies of scale in the production and dissemination of this information could only be effected were its public disclosure mandated. It also is conceivable that positive externalities are associated with this information. These possible benefits may exceed the cost to society of administering and complying with a mandatory change in the measurement basis of GAAP. We suggest, especially in light of the evidence we report, that it is the responsibility of those who would impose a change in GAAP to demonstrate the existence of these net social benefits, rather than merely to assert their existence.

## REFERENCES

American Accounting Association. *A Statement of Basic Accounting Theory*. Evanston, Ill.: AAA, 1966.

American Council of Life Insurance. *Life Insurance Fact Book 1977*. New York: ACLI, 1977.

American Institute of Certified Public Accountants. *Reporting the Financial Effects of Price-Level Changes*. Accounting Research Study no. 6. New York: AICPA, 1963.

Benston, G. J. *Corporate Financial Disclosure in the U.K. and the U.S.A.* Lexington, Mass.: Lexington Books, D. C. Heath, 1976.

Benston, G. J. and M. A. Krasney. "The Economic Consequence of Financial Accounting Statements." In *Economic Consequences of Financial Accounting Standards: Selected Papers*. Stamford, Conn.: Financial Accounting Standards Board, 1978.

Brenner, V. C. "Financial Statement Users' Views of the Desirability of Reporting Current Cost Information." *Journal of Accounting Research* 8 (Autumn 1970): 159–66.

Chambers, R. J. *Accounting, Evaluation and Economic Behavior*. Englewood Cliffs, N.J.: Prentice Hall, 1966.

Cohan, A. B. *Yields on Corporate Debt Directly Placed*. National Bureau of Economic Research, General Series, no. 84. New York: Columbia University Press, 1967.

Davidson, S., C. P. Stickney, and R. L. Weil. *Inflation Accounting: A Guide for the Accountant and the Financial Analyst*. New York: McGraw-Hill, 1976.

Edwards, E. O. "The State of Current Value Accounting." *Accounting Review* 50 (April 1975): 235–45.

Edwards, E. O., and P. W. Bell. *The Theory and Measurement of Business Income*. Berkeley and Los Angeles: University of California Press, 1961.

Estes, R. W. "An Assessment of the Usefulness of Current Cost and Price-Level Information by Financial Statement Users." *Journal of Accounting Research* 6 (Autumn 1968): 200–207.

Financial Accounting Standards Board. *Tentative Conclusions of Objectives of Financial Statements of Business Enterprises*. Stamford, Conn.: FASB, 1976.

Foster, G. "Quarterly Accounting Data: Time Series Properties and Predictive Ability Results." *Accounting Review* 52 (January 1977): 1–21.

Jensen, M. L., and W. H. Meckling. "Theory of the Firm: Managerial Behavior, Agency Costs and Ownership Structure." *Journal of Financial Economics* 3 (October 1976): 305–60.

Maddalla, G. S. *Econometrics*. New York: McGraw-Hill, 1977.

Ross, H. *The Elusive Art of Accounting*. New York: Ronald Press, 1966.

Shapiro, E., and C. Wolf. *The Role of Private Placements in Corporate Finance*. Boston, Mass.: Harvard University Business School, 1972.

Siegel, S. *Nonparametric Statistics for the Behavioral Sciences*. New York: McGraw-Hill, 1956.

Sprouse, R. T. and M. Moonitz. *A Tentative Set of Broad Accounting Principles for Business Enterprises*. Accounting Research Study no. 3. New York: AICPA, 1962.

Staubus, G. J. "The Relevance of Evidence of Cash Flows." In *Asset Valuation*, edited by R. Sterling, pp. 42–69. Lawrence, Kans.: Scholars Book, 1971.

Vancil, R. F. and R. L. Weil. *Replacement Cost Accounting: Readings on Concepts, Uses and Methods*. Glen Ridge, N.J.: Thomas Horton & Daughters, 1976.

# 6

# Fair-Value Accounting: A Cautionary Tale from Enron

## Introduction

The U.S. and International Financial Accounting Standards Boards (FASB and IASB) have been moving toward replacing historical-cost with fair-value accounting. In general, fair values have been limited to financial assets and liabilities, at least in the financial statements proper.[1] A Proposed Statement of Financial Accounting Standards (SFAS), *Fair-Value Measurements* (FASB, 2005, p. 5), specifies a "fair-value hierarchy." Level 1 bases fair values on "quoted prices for identical assets and liabilities in active reference markets whenever that information is available." If such prices are not available, level 2 would prevail, for which "quoted prices on similar assets and liabilities in active markets, adjusted as appropriate for differences" would be used (FASB, 2005, p. 6). Level 3 estimates "require judgment in the selection and application of valuation techniques and relevant inputs." The exposure draft discusses measurement problems that complicate application of all three levels. For example, with respect to levels 1 and 2, how should prices that vary by quantity purchased or sold be applied and, where transactions costs are significant, should entry or exit prices be used? As difficult as are these problems, at least many independent public accountants and auditors have dealt with them extensively and are aware of measurement and verification pitfalls. However, company accountants and external auditors have had less experience with the third level (at least for external reporting), which uses estimates based on discounted cash flows and other valuation techniques produced by company managers rather than by reference to market prices.

---

1. The exceptions include goodwill impairment and, in Europe, appraisals of other assets under specified conditions.

Indeed, there are few situations that have revealed the problems encountered when companies use third-level estimates for their public financial reports. Instances in which transaction-based historical-based numbers have been misleadingly and/or fraudulently reported abound, such as companies reporting revenue before it is earned (and sometimes not ever earned), inventories misreported and mispriced, and expenditures capitalized rather than expensed. Mulford and Comiskey (2002) and Schilit (2002) provide many illustrations of such "shenanigans" (as Schilit characterizes them). But they (and to my knowledge, few, if any, others) do not describe how fair-value numbers not grounded on actual market prices have been misused and abused. Enron's bankruptcy and the subsequent investigations and public revelations of how their managers used level 3 fair-value estimates for both internal and external accounting and the effect of those measurements on their operations and performance should provide some useful insights into the problems that auditors are likely to face should the proposed SFAS *Fair-Value Measurements* be adopted.

Although Enron's failure in December 2001 had many causes,[2] both immediate (admissions of massive accounting misstatements) and proximate (more complicated, as described below), there is strong reason to believe that Enron's early and continuing use of level 3 fair-value accounting played an important role in its demise. It appears that Enron initially used level 3 fair-value estimates (predominantly present value estimates) without any intent to mislead investors, but rather to motivate and reward managers for the economic benefits they achieved for shareholders. Enron first revalued energy contracts, reflecting an innovation in how these contracts were structured, with the increase in value reported as current period earnings. Then level 3 revaluations were applied to other assets, particularly what Enron termed "merchant" investments. Increasingly, as Enron's operations were not as profitable as its managers predicted to the stock market, these upward revaluations were used opportunistically to inflate reported net income. This tendency was exacerbated by Enron's basing managers' compensation on the estimated fair values of their merchant investment projects. This gave those managers strong incentives to overinvest resources in often costly, poorly devised, and poorly implemented projects that could garner a high "fair" valuation. Initially, some contracts and merchant investments may have had value beyond their costs. But contrary to the way fair-value accounting should be used, reductions in value rarely were recognized and recorded because they either were ignored or were assumed to be temporary. Market prices, specified as level 2 estimates in *Fair-Value Measurements* (FASB, 2005), were used by Enron to value restricted stock, although in most instances they were not adjusted to account for differences in value between Enron's holdings and publicly traded stock, as specified by the FASB. Market prices were also used by Enron's traders in models to value their

---

2. See Partnoy (2002), who blames Enron's use of derivatives, and Coffee (2002), who points to inadequate "gatekeepers," particularly external auditors and attorneys.

positions. In almost all of these applications, the numbers used tended to overstate the value of Enron's assets and reported net income.

As the following largely chronological description of Enron's adoption of level 3 fair-value accounting shows, its abuse by Enron's managers occurred gradually until it dominated their decisions, reports to the public, and accounting procedures. Although, technically, fair-value accounting under generally accepted accounting principles was limited to financial assets, Enron's accountants were able to get around this restriction and record present-value estimates of other assets using procedures that were accepted and possibly designed by its external auditor, Arthur Andersen.

In the following section, I describe Enron's initial and then widespread use and abuse of level 3 fair-value in its accounting for energy and other commodity-trading contracts, energy production facilities, "merchant" investments, its major international projects and energy management contracts, investments in broadband (including particularly egregious accounting for its Braveheart project with Blockbuster), and derivatives trading.[3] This is followed by a description of the incentives from basing management compensation on fair-value estimates. I then show how Enron, by structuring transactions so as to report cash flows from operations, "validated" the profits it reported. Finally, I consider why Enron's internal control system and its external auditor, Arthur Andersen, did not prevent Enron's using fair-value estimates to produce misleading financial statements.

## Enron's Adoption and Use of Fair-Value Accounting

Enron's initial substantial success and later failure was the result of a succession of decisions.[4] Fair-value accounting played an important role in these decisions because it affected indicators of success and managerial incentives. These led to accounting cover-ups and, I believe, to Enron's subsequent bankruptcy. I present these developments essentially in chronological order, which shows how Enron's initial "reasonable" use of fair-value accounting evolved and eventually dominated its accounting and corrupted its operations and reporting to shareholders.

### Energy Contracts

Enron developed from the merger of several pipeline companies that made it the largest natural gas distribution system in the United States. In 1990, Jeffrey Skilling

---

3. Although Enron used the term "mark-to-market" accounting, it rarely based the valuations on actual market prices. Hereafter, "fair value" refers to level 3 valuations, those based on present value and other estimates that are not taken from market prices.

4. This description is largely derived from and documented in McLean and Elkind (2003) and (to a much less extent) Bryce (2002) and Eichenwald (2005), as well as other sources, as noted.

joined Enron after having been a McKinsey consultant to the company. He had developed a method of trading natural gas contracts called the Gas Bank. Enron's CEO, Kenneth Lay, persuaded him to join the company. Skilling became chairman and CEO of a new division, Enron Finance, with the mandate to make the Gas Bank work, for which he would be richly compensated with "phantom" equity (wherein he received additional pay in proportion to increases in the market price of Enron stock). Enron Finance sold long-term contracts for gas to utilities and manufacturers. Skilling's innovation was to give natural gas producers upfront cash payments, which induced them to sign long-term supply contracts. He insisted on use of "mark-to-market" (actually "fair value," as there was no market for the contracts) accounting to measure his division's net profit. In 1991 Enron's board of directors, audit committee, and its external auditor, Arthur Andersen, approved the use of this "mark-to-market" accounting. In January 1992 the Securities and Exchange Commission (SEC) approved it for gas contracts beginning that year. Enron, though, used mark-to-market accounting for its not-as-yet-filed 1991 statements (without objection by the SEC) and booked $242 million in earnings. Thereafter, Enron recorded gains (earnings) when gas contracts were signed, based on its estimates of gas prices projected over many (e.g., 10 and 20) years.

In 1991, Enron created a new division that merged Enron Finance with Enron Gas Marketing (which sold natural gas to wholesale customers) and Houston Pipeline to form Enron Capital and Trade Resources (ECT), all of which were managed by Skilling. He adopted fair-value accounting for ECT and he compensated the division's managers with percentages of internally generated estimates of the fair values of contracts they developed. An early (1992) example was a 20-year contract to supply natural gas to the developer of a large electric generating plant under construction, Sithe Energies. ECT immediately recorded the estimated net present value of that contract as current earnings. During the 1990s, as changes in energy prices indicated that the contract was more valuable, additional gains resulting from revaluations to fair value were recorded, which allowed Enron to meet its internal and external quarterly net income projections. By the late 1990s, Sithe owed Enron $1.5 billion. However, even though Enron's internal Risk Assessment and Control (RAC) group estimated that Sithe's only asset (worth just over $400 million) was inadequate to pay its obligation, the fair value of the contract was not reduced and, consequently, a loss was not recorded. In fact, the loss was not recorded until after Enron declared bankruptcy.

## Energy Production Facilities

Enron International (EI), another major division of Enron, developed and constructed natural gas power plants and other projects around the world. Enron's developer, John Wing, had previously (in 1987) developed a gas-fired electricity plant in Texas City, Texas. It was financed almost entirely with high-yield, high-return (junk) bonds and was very profitable as measured by historical cost accounting. In 1990, Wing completed a deal for a giant plant in Teesside (U.K.) that could produce 4 percent of the United Kingdom's entire energy demands. Enron put up almost no cash and still owned half the plant valued at $1.6 billion in exchange for its role in conceiving and constructing the plant. In the early 1990s, Enron booked more than $100 million in profits from development and construction fees. Wing received at least $18 million in Enron stock plus several million dollars in salary and bonuses for his work on the project, establishing performance-based compensation. Such rewards were later aggressively demanded by and used to reward Enron's senior managers, but with one major difference—unlike Wing's compensation that was based on his project's profitable completion and operation as measured by historical cost numbers, their rewards were based on the projected future benefits from (or fair values of) projects.

To provide gas for the Teesside plant, Enron signed a long-term "take-or-pay" contract in 1993 for North Sea J-Block gas. After gas prices decreased instead of increasing as Enron had expected, the contract became increasingly costly. Nevertheless, the contract was not marked down to fair value to reflect the losses until 1997. That year, Enron was able to change the contract to one where the price of gas floated with the market, at which point it had to record a $675 million pretax loss.

## "Merchant" Investments

Enron also used fair-value accounting for its "merchant" investments–partnership interests and stock in untraded or thinly traded companies it started or in which it invested. As was the situation for the energy contracts, the fair values were not based on actual market prices, because no market prices existed for the merchant investments. Although the SEC and FASB require fair-value accounting for energy contracts, FAS 115 limits revaluations of securities to those traded on a recognized exchange and for which there were reliable share prices, and valuation increases in nonfinancial assets are not permitted. Enron (and possibly other corporations) used the following procedure to avoid these limitations. Enron incorporated major projects into subsidiaries, the stock of which it designated as "merchant" investments, and declared that it was in the investment company business, for which the American Institute of Certified Public Accountants Investment Company Guide applies. This guide requires these companies to revalue financial assets held (presumably) for trading to fair values, even when these values are not determined from arm's-length market transactions. In such instances, the values may be determined by discounted expected cash flow models, as are level 3 fair values.[5] The models allowed Enron's managers to manipulate

---

5. "Real" investment companies, which often are limited partnerships, tend to value investments conservatively and values are not changed until a material event occurs to change the value (National Venture Capital Association, undated, under valuation), apparently to limit the amount that would be paid out to investors who take out their investments.

net income by making "reasonable" assumptions that would give them the gains they wanted to record. (Some notable examples are provided below.)

Enron chief accounting officer, Rick Causey, used revaluations of these investments to meet the earnings goals announced by Skilling and Enron's CEO and chairman of the board, Kenneth Lay. "By the end of the decade," McLean and Elkind (2003, p. 127) report, "some 35 percent of Enron's assets were being given mark-to-market treatment." When additional earnings were required, contracts were revisited and reinterpreted, if increases in their fair values could be recorded. However, recording of losses was delayed if *any* possibility existed that the investment might turn around.

An example is Mariner Energy, a privately owned Houston oil and gas company that did deep water exploration in which Enron invested and which it bought out for $185 million in 1996. Enron's accountants periodically marked up its investment as needed to report increases in earnings until, by the second quarter 2001, it was on the books for $367.4 million. Analyses in the second and third quarters of 2001 by Enron's RAC department that valued the investment at between $47 and $196 million did not result in accounting revaluations. After Enron's bankruptcy, Mariner Energy was written down to $110.5 million.

Enron's investment in Rhythms Net Connections (Rhythms) is another example, except that the valuation was based on an actual market price. Enron's April 1999 investment of $10 million before Rhythms went public in April 1999 had an estimated market value of $90 million following its initial public offering (IPO). However, Enron could not realize this gain because it had signed a lock-up agreement that precluded sale of the stock until November. Not surprisingly, Enron could not purchase a reasonably priced hedge. With the approval of Enron's board of directors, a special purpose entity (SPE), LJM1, controlled by Enron's chief financial officer, Andrew Fastow, was created to provide the hedge through an SPE it created, LJM Swap Sub.[6] LJM1 was almost entirely funded with Enron's own stock purchased with a promissory note at a 39 percent discount (because it was restricted). LJM Swap Sub was funded with half the stock and a promissory note from LJM1. In effect, Enron was writing the option on itself, for a substantial fee paid to Fastow. It was not really hedging against a possible economic loss on the Rhythms stock, but against having to recognize the loss in its accounts. Thus, Enron's accounting "shenanigans" were not limited to booking income from increasing estimated fair values.

## Dabhol, Other Enron International Projects, and Azurix

In 1996 Rebecca Mark became CEO of Enron International, having previously been head of Enron Development. She developed projects around the world at a frenetic

---

6. The transaction is very complicated. See Benston and Hartgraves (2002, pp. 109–10) for a much more complete description.

pace. She and her managers were given bonuses for each project they developed of about 9 percent of the present value of its expected net cash flows, one half paid at the financial close and the other half when the project became operational. The costs of projects that did not come on line but were not officially declared to be dead were recorded as assets, if the amounts were under $200 million. Mark's largest project, begun in 1992 when she managed Enron Development, was a giant electricity power plant in Dabhol, India. To be economically viable, the government of the Indian state of Maharashtra would have to purchase a fixed amount of electricity at a high price, despite the fact that it was unable to collect for electricity sold at lower prices. The project was severely criticized in India, and the contract was renegotiated several times. Eventually, Enron invested and lost about $900 million in the project, which now stands idle. Nevertheless, Mark and her team received $20 million in bonuses for the project, based on their estimates of its present value.

Relatively few of Enron International projects actually became operational and few were profitable according to traditional accounting standards after they became operational. Some prebankruptcy evidence is available as a result of a dispute between Skilling and Mark. In 1998, Skilling had an in-house accountant value Enron International's projects. He calculated that the division returned only a 2 percent return on equity, excluding Enron's substantial contingent liability for project debts it guaranteed. Mark's accountant, though, estimated that her division returned an average of 12 percent on equity. After Enron declared bankruptcy, few of the division's projects were found to have any value.

In May 1998 Skilling forced Mark out of her post as CEO of Enron International. (In December 1996, Lay had appointed Skilling, rather than Mark, as Enron's president and chief operating officer.) Perhaps as a consolation prize, in July 1998 the board of directors (with Skilling's blessing) allowed Mark to establish a new Enron subsidiary, Azurix, which would develop water supply projects around the world. The business began with a $2.4 billion purchase of a British water utility, Wessex Water Services, for a 28 percent premium.[7] The purchase was largely financed with debt sold by an off-balance-sheet partnership, Marlin, which itself was financed with debt that Enron guaranteed. Enron's obligation on that debt was not reported on its financial statements. Most of the balance came from public sales of Azurix shares for $700 million. Azurix then successfully bid for a Buenos Aires, Argentina, water utility that was privatized, paying three times more than the next highest bidder. Azurix later learned that the deal did not include the utility's headquarters and records, making it difficult (often impossible) to collect past-due and present account balances.[8] By year-end 2000, $402 million had to be written off on the project. Other disastrous projects were undertaken, Azurix stock

---

7. Eichenwald (2005, p. 191) reports the purchase as costing $2.25 billion.

8. Eichenwald (2005, p. 231) reports that Azurix paid twice the next bid and that computers and records were trashed by the former employees.

declined to $3.50 a share, and Enron had to repurchase the publicly held shares for $8.375. Mark resigned, receiving the balance of her $710,000 Azurix contract, based on the projected (mark to fair value) benefits to Enron of the enterprise.

## Energy Management Contracts

In December 2000, after Skilling became president of Enron, he created a separate business, Enron Energy Services (EES), with Lou Pai as its CEO. EES expected to sell power to retail customers, based on assumptions that the market would be deregulated and that the existing utilities could be undersold. Enron sold 7 percent of EES to institutional investors for $130 million. Based on this sale (which might have qualified as a level 2 estimate), Enron valued the company at $1.9 billion, which allowed it to record a $61 million profit. However, EES's efforts were unsuccessful, in part because retail energy was generally not deregulated. Losses on the retail operations were not reported separately, but were combined with the wholesale operations.

Pai then concentrated on selling contracts to companies and institutions to provide them with energy over long periods with guaranteed savings over their present costs. Customers often were given up-front cash payments in advance of the promised savings. These contracts were accounted for on a mark-to-fair-value basis as of the date the contracts were signed. Sales personnel and managers (especially Pai) were paid bonuses based on those values. Not surprisingly, this compensation scheme generated a lot of bad contracts. A particularly costly (to Enron) contract was signed in February 2001 with Eli Lilly to make improvements in its energy supply and use over 15 years. Discounting these amounts by 8.25–8.50 percent, Enron valued the contract at $1.3 billion and recorded a $38 million gain.[9] Within two years, this contract was considered to be worthless.

In 2001, after Pai left EES and Enron, a longtime in-house Enron accountant, Wanda Curry, was asked to evaluate the EES contracts. Her group examined 13 (of 90) contracts that comprised 80 percent of the business. Each of them had been recorded as profitable. Nevertheless, Curry found that the 13 contracts had a total negative value of at least $500 million. For example, a deal for which the company had booked $20 million in profits actually was $70 million under water. Although, according to mark-to-fair-value accounting the decrease in value documented by Curry should have been recorded, no such entry was made and Curry was reassigned.

## Enron Broadband Services

Enron Broadband Services (EBS) was another major portion of Enron's business. Skilling established it in April 1999 to develop a fiber-optic network and trade capacity in its and other firms' networks. Skilling announced the new venture

---

9. See Batson (2003a, pp. 32–33) for details.

to stock analysts on January 20, 2000, together with Scott McNealy, CEO of Sun Microsystems, who said that Enron would purchase 18,000 of Sun's best servers for use in its network. By day end, Enron's stock increased by 26 percent. Enron, though, did not then or ever have software that could provide bandwidth on demand by and for alternative networks. Rather, Enron's business involved swapping the right to use surplus (dark) fiber on its own network for the right to use surplus on other networks. Overall, Enron invested more than $1 billion on broadband and reported revenue of $408 million in 2000, much of it from sales to Fastow-controlled SPEs. For example, in the first quarter 2000, EBS recorded a mark-to-fair-value-determined gain of $58 million from revaluing and then swapping dark fiber, which was designated a "sale." In the second quarter 2000 EBS revalued and "sold" that asset to LJM2, an SPE controlled by Fastow, and recorded another $53 million pretax gain. Based on mark-to-fair-value accounting, EBS booked a $110.9 million profit in the fourth quarter 2000 and first quarter 2001.

In the third quarter 2000 EBS recorded a $150 million fair-value gain on its $15 million investment in a tech start-up (Avici Systems) that went public, using the public IPO price as the basis for the transaction even though Enron's stock could not be sold for 180 days. Enron "locked in" the gain with a hedge provided by another SPE (Talon), even though Talon would not have been able to meet its obligation if the stock price declined. Before year-end, the stock price declined by 90 percent. Talon and other similar SPEs (collectively called "Project Raptor") could not cover this loss and other losses amounting to $500 million. Nevertheless, the losses were not recorded, based on Enron's (invalid) assertion that the SPEs' obligations could be cross-collateralized with other SPEs that were claimed (incorrectly) to have sufficient assets. Those assets were Enron shares and rights to shares obtained from Enron for which the Raptors had not paid. Consequently, for Enron the assets did not exist, because if the SPEs had to pay Enron their obligations for the hedges by selling the shares, they would be unable to pay their other debt to Enron. Andersen's partner-in-charge, David Duncan, agreed to this procedure despite an objection from Carl Bass, a member of the firm's Professional Standards Group who previously was on the audit team. At Enron's request, Bass was excluded from commenting on issues related to Enron. Andersen was paid $1.3 million for its Raptor-related work. When the Raptors were terminated in 2001 a $710 million pretax loss was booked.

## Braveheart Partnership with Blockbuster

In the fourth quarter 2000 EBS announced a 20-year project (Braveheart) with Blockbuster to broadcast movies on demand to television viewers. However, Enron did not have the technology to deliver the movies and Blockbuster did not have the rights to the movies to be broadcast. Nevertheless, as of December 31, 2000, Enron assigned a fair value of $125 million to its Braveheart investment and a profit of $53 million from increasing the investment to its fair value, even though no sales had been made. Enron recorded additional revenue of $53 million from the venture in the first quarter of 2001, although Blockbuster did not record any income from the venture and dissolved the partnership in March 2001. In October 2001 Enron had to announce publicly that it reversed the $110.9 million in profit it had earlier claimed, which contributed to its loss of public trust and subsequent bankruptcy.

How could Enron have so massively misestimated the fair value of its Braveheart investment, and how could Andersen have allowed Enron to report these values and their increases as profits? Indeed, the examiner in bankruptcy (Batson, 2003a, pp. 30–31) finds that Andersen prepared the appraisal of the project's value. Andersen assumed the following: (1) the business would be established in 10 major metro areas within 12 months; (2) 8 new areas would be added per year until 2010 and these would each grow at 1 percent a year; (3) digital subscriber lines would be used by 5 percent of the households, increasing to 32 percent by 2010, and these would increase in speed sufficient to accept the broadcasts; and (4) Braveheart would garner 50 percent of this market. After determining (somehow) a net cash flow from each of these households and discounting by 31–34 percent, the project was assigned a fair value. I suggest that this calculation illustrates an essential weakness of level 3 fair-value calculations that necessarily are not grounded on actual market transactions. How can one determine whether or not such assumptions about a "first-time" project are "reasonable"?

## Derivatives Trading

Enron's (derivatives) trading activities expanded beyond natural gas and power contracts to contracts in metals, paper, credit derivatives, and commodities. Much of this trading was done over an Internet system it developed, Enron On Line (EOL), which enabled Enron to dominate several markets. Enron often established the prices on those markets, prices that were used to mark its trades to fair values. Thus, Enron's traders could establish the prices at which positions would be valued and, as described below, their compensation was determined.[10]

Trading may have been the only really profitable portion of Enron's business. Partnoy (2002) analyzed Enron's 1998, 1999, and 2000 financial statements. He determined that "other revenue" meant income (loss) from derivatives trading, and produced table 6.1.

Table 6.1 shows that the other aspects of Enron's business, described earlier, were operated at a net loss or small gain, even considering that the reported numbers were inflated by mark-to-fair-value accounting and other accounting procedures.

---

10. As the dominant player, Enron took large positions, which made maintaining market participants' perception that its credit standing was solid absolutely necessary, which is a major reason that Enron's accountants went to great lengths to hide its debt obligations, as documented by Batson (2003a, appendix Q).

TABLE 6.1 Enron Corp. and Subsidiaries 2000 Consolidated Income Statement (in $millions)

|  | 2000 | 1999 | 1998 |
|---|---|---|---|
| Nonderivatives revenues | 93,557 | 34,774 | 27,215 |
| Nonderivatives expenses | 94,517 | 34,761 | 26,381 |
| Nonderivatives gross margin | (960) | 13 | 834 |
| Other revenue (income from derivatives) | 7,232 | 5,338 | 4,045 |
| Other expenses | (4,319) | (4,549) | (3,501) |
| Operating income | 1,953 | 802 | 1,378 |

However, Partnoy (2002) found that the reported gains from trading derivatives were not reported accurately. Note, though, that these reported gains and losses were based on the traders' estimated present (fair) values of the derivatives contracts, which often covered many years. Most of these contracts were not actively traded, or traded at all. The traders, therefore, valued them with models and estimates of forward price curves, both of which could be easily manipulated. As Partnoy (2002, p. 327) puts it:

> because Enron's natural-gas traders were compensated based on their profits, traders had an incentive to hide losses by mismarking forward curves....In some instances, a trader would simply manually input a forward curve that was different from the market....For more complex trades, a trader would tweak the assumptions in the computer model used to value the trades, in order to make them appear more valuable.

Traders also understated their profits or deferred reporting the profits with "prudency reserves." This practice allowed them to shift income to future periods when they had already attained their maximum bonuses and to offset losses. Partnoy (2002, p. 327) concludes: "The extent of mismarking at Enron remains unclear, although several traders said the inaccuracies were more than a billion dollars." Thus, the extent to which Enron's traders actually benefited Enron's shareholders is unclear. Indeed, Bryce (2002, p. 336) reports that, in 2001, when Enron was negotiating a merger with Dynergy, whose personnel examined Enron's operations, "it became increasingly obvious to them [Dynergy] that despite the enormous volumes that were being generated on the [EOL] web site, Enron actually was losing money on its trading business."

## Management Compensation, Expenses, and Fair-Value Accounting

Enron promised investors that its earnings would grow by 15 percent a year, a goal that Enron employees could meet with mark-to-fair-value valuations and revaluations of their projects. In addition, in granting options to its senior executives, Enron specified that a third would vest each year if Enron's earnings grew by at least 15 percent (McLean and Elkind, 2003, pp. 92–93). Senior executives additionally were motivated to inflate the values of projects with bonuses and stock options based on a percentage of the mark-to-fair-values of the projects and deals they developed, as determined by their present-value calculations. Furthermore, Enron used a "rank and yank" system of evaluating employees, whereby those who did not meet their targets had reason to believe they would be dismissed.[11]

Enron's senior managers exercised little control over costs, in large part because their compensation was based substantially on estimates of the present value of the projects they generated, rather than on the profitability of the projects as substantiated by actual performance measured with historical costs and actual market prices, with the cost of developing the projects matched to the revenue generated therefrom. Enron's managers and traders were given a percentage (generally 9 percent) of the estimated present value of their deals and trades, which imparted a strong incentive for them to expend whatever resources were necessary to develop and close a deal or trade. The deal makers were paid substantial amounts for projects when the financing was complete, even before construction began. But, as McLean and Elkind (2003, p. 76) put it: "no one felt responsible for managing the projects once they were up and running." McLean and Elkind offer many examples of uncontrolled expenditures. They report (McLean and Elkind, 2003, p. 119):

> people began spending as if every day were Christmas. Expenses soared, for items large and small.... There was no requirement to use a particular vendor; if you didn't want to wait for something, you could just pick up a phone and order it yourself. Anyone with a half-baked idea to launch a business in Europe could hop a plane and fly to London. Hundreds of deal makers made a habit of flying first class and staying in deluxe hotels; no one seemed to care.... The corporate administrative types gave up trying to keep a lid on things.

The expenditures were not limited to the deal makers, but extended throughout Enron. With respect to trading, McLean and Elkind (2003, p. 226) say: "Overhead was obscene; one executive estimated that the North American trading operation alone spent between $650 and $700 million a year just in overhead. Expense accounts were over the top, but nobody dared rein them in." But the largest expense was compensation. McLean and Elkind (2003, p. 241) citing a study by the Joint Committee on Taxation, report:

> In 1998, Enron's 200 most highly compensated employees took home a total of $193 million in salaries, bonuses, and various forms of stock. In

---

11. See Bryce (2002, pp. 126–31) for a description.

1999, that leaped to $402 million; in 2000, they took home $1.4 billion.... [In that year] each of the top 200 employees made over $1 million; 26 executives made over $10 million. In 2001, the year Enron went bankrupt, at least 15 employees made over $10 million.

## Cash Flow and Fair-Value-Determined Net Income

Although mark-to-fair-value accounting allowed Enron to record substantial profits, it did not provide cash flow. Enron had to deal with analysts who were suspicious of accounting net income and looked to cash flow as a superior measure of performance. ("Net profit is what accountants want it to be, cash is real.") Enron attempted to bring these alternative performance measures into balance, as well as obtain cash for its operations and projects without having to sell stock or report debt, primarily with four schemes: prepays, "sales" to SPEs, share trusts, and investment subsidiaries.[12] These represented "real" rather than only accounting manipulations, as they required the development of legal structures for which Enron paid very substantial fees to investment and commercial bankers, lawyers, and accountants.

*Prepays* are arrangements that allowed Enron to record what actually were loans as cash inflows from operations. Enron agreed to deliver oil or gas to an offshore entity established by a bank (Citigroup or Chase-Morgan). The offshore entity (Delta or Mahonia) paid Enron in advance with funds obtained from the bank for the same amount of oil or gas, but for future delivery. The bank, in turn, agreed to deliver the same amount of the oil or gas to Enron in exchange for a fixed price plus an additional amount equal to what interest on a loan would be. The bank did not actually take a price risk, as an Enron subsidiary wrote the bank a guarantee. The bank's only risk was similar to the risk of a loan, that Enron could not meet its obligation (which, when Enron declared bankruptcy, turned out to be the case). At the due date, the bank "delivered" the oil or gas to Enron and received payment, Enron "delivered" the oil or gas to the offshore entity, and the entity "delivered" the oil or gas to the bank. Thus, Enron really just borrowed funds from the bank, but recorded the cash inflow as coming from operations rather than from financing. The debt was recorded as "price risk liability," which to the unaware financial statement reader appeared to offset or explain some marked-to-fair-value "price risk" assets and the related "earnings from price-risk activities." Batson (2003a, appendix Q) calculates that in its year 2000 financial statements, Enron overstated cash flow from operations and understated cash flow from financing (and debt) by $1.53 billion. Indeed, 32 percent of Enron's reported cash flow from operations in 2000 and almost all in 1999 were due to prepays (Batson, 2003a, appendix E, p. 6).

---

12. The schemes were complex. See Batson (2003a, pp. 58–66 and appendix E) for descriptions.

Over the years 1997–2001, when prepays were used, Batson estimates that Enron overstated its reported cash flow from operations by at least $8.6 billion.

*"Sales" to SPEs* allowed Enron to "validate" profits derived from mark-to-fair-value increases in its subsidiaries' stock (and the assets represented by that stock). The procedures used are complicated (see Benston and Hartgraves, 2002, Batson, 2002, 2003a, appendix M, pp. 1–23, for descriptions of these "FAS 140" transactions).[13] One example, in simplified form, provides a good illustration. Enron created a subsidiary to hold a major asset it was developing, receiving in return Class A voting and Class B nonvoting stock that was entitled to almost all of the subsidiary's economic interests. At the same time Enron created an SPE in which it held no equity interest. The SPE was financed with funds borrowed from a bank, a subsidiary of which held the equity, which was equal to 3 percent of the assets (the other 97 percent was the bank loan). Enron then "sold" its subsidiary's Class B common stock to the SPE in exchange for all its assets (cash), but kept the Class A voting-rights stock. If Enron had not already written up the stock (a financial asset held as a "merchant" investment) to fair value, thereby recording gains as current income, it now recorded a gain from the "sale" of the Class B stock to the SPEs. At the same time Enron entered into a "total return swap," wherein it assumed the SPE's obligation to pay the bank debt for all the cash flow from the Class B stock less amounts necessary to repay the 3-percent-equity holder's investment plus a specified (usually 15 percent per annum) return. The swap was accounted for as a derivative and, pursuant to FAS 133, marked to fair value, which enabled Enron to record the change in the present value of expected cash flows from the underlying asset as additional current profit (or loss).

Thus, Enron continued to control and operate the asset, recorded as a gain (and, later, a loss) its calculated increase in the present value of expected net cash flows, and did not report as a liability its obligation to repay the bank debt incurred by the SPE. This procedure allowed Enron to keep $1.4 billion of debt off its December 31, 2000, balance sheet and report over $541 million of additional net income before taxes ($352 million after taxes) on its 2000 income statement (Batson, 2003a, appendix Q, p. 1) by recording the transaction as a sale and the cash received as cash flow from operations rather than cash flow from financing (loans).

*Share trusts* (Marlin and Whitewing) allowed Enron to refinance its purchase of water systems for Azurix without reporting the debt on its financial statements (Marlin), and to "sell" assets to SPEs through Whitewing. These share trusts obtained the necessary funds from banks and other creditors that Enron indirectly guaranteed. The trusts were not consolidated with Enron's financial statements as a result of Andersen's accepting Enron's contention that it did not control the trusts

---

13. Enron's accounting for SPEs, as such, was not the problem, as explained by Benston and Hartgraves (2002). Rather, Enron failed to follow FAS 5 and report its contingent liability for the SPEs' debt and reported "sales" to the SPEs that were not valid, as explained and concluded by Batson (2002).

because outside parties had the right to appoint half the directors (a right that was never exercised, because the outside parties relied on Enron for repayment of their investments).[14] Batson (2003a, appendix Q) calculates that this scheme allowed Enron in its year 2000 financial statement to overstate cash flow from operations by $0.42 billion and understate cash flow from financing (and debt) by $1.67 billion.

*Investment subsidiaries* (also called minority-interest transactions) also were used to provide "cash flow from operations." In simplified form, this is how it worked. (See Batson, 2003a, appendix I, particularly annex 3 for detailed descriptions.) In 1999, for example, Enron created an SPE with outside equity of $15 million, which borrowed $485 million from a bank; the equity usually was provided by the bank's subsidiary. Because Enron had no equity in the SPE and the SPE had equity held by independent investors equal to 3 percent of its assets, it was not consolidated with Enron. The SPE purchased $500 million in Treasury notes and used them to purchase a minority interest in an Enron-controlled subsidiary whose business included buying and selling Treasury notes. Shortly thereafter, in December, the subsidiary sold the notes, recording a cash inflow from operations. When the subsidiary was consolidated, Enron's financial statements reported a minority equity interest (rather than debt) of $500 million and cash flow from operations (rather than cash flow from financing) of $500 million.

## Auditors' Validation of Enron's Fair-Value Accounting

It is or should be obvious that managers' whose career success and compensation are based on and derived from estimated fair-value amounts have strong incentives to inflate those amounts, either because of a tendency toward overoptimism, opportunism, or both. This bias could be constrained by internal controls and reviews and at least should be revealed and criticized by internal or external auditors. In fact, at Enron it was not.

Skilling established and publicized a RAC department that was charged with reviewing and, presumably, changing, approving, or disapproving the numbers submitted by managers for deals they were promoting and on which they were compensated. Proposals involving more than $500,000 had to be supported by a deal-approval sheet (known as DASH) that included an approval or disapproval by RAC. McLean and Elkind (2003, p. 115) report that Skilling "made RAC a centerpiece of management presentations to Wall Street analysts, investors, and credit-rating agencies." It had a $30 million budget and a staff of 150 professionals. It was headed by Rick Buy, who McLean and Elkind describe (McLean and Elkind, 2003, p. 116) as "uncomfortable with confrontation. When his analysts raised

---

14. Batson's (2003a, section IV) analysis shows that Enron actually had more than a 50 percent equity interest of Whitewing through subsidiaries that it owned or controlled.

issues with a deal, Buy would dutifully take them up the chain of command. But in a head-to-head with the company's senior traders and originators, it was no contest, as those on both sides of the table recognized." Another factor that apparently blunted Buy's unwillingness to allow his group to challenge deal makers' "absurdly optimistic assumptions for the complex models that spat out the likelihood of various outcomes for a transaction" (McLean and Elkind, 2003, p. 117) was fear that he would lose his compensation, including stock options that had not yet vested. McLean and Elkind (2003, p. 118) report that he was paid $400,000 in 1999 and sold Enron shares for $4.3 million in 2001. Other RAC employees also were reluctant to resist pressures to approve deals, because this could hurt their careers within Enron as well as affect their compensation. Bryce (2002, p. 131) reports that "people who questioned deals 'would get attacked by the business units because they weren't as cooperative on a deal as the developers wanted,'" which would have strong negative effect on their evaluation by Enron's Personal Review Committee. In addition, Bryce (2002, p. 131) quotes an Enron employee as saying: "You'd have a hard time finding another rotation if you were too hard on certain deals."

Internal auditors might have questioned the validity of fair-value assessments. However, as noted earlier, when in-house accountant Wanda Curry reviewed and questioned the validity of presumed profitability of EES contracts, she was reassigned and no changes were made. I am not aware of any other form of or results from internal audits.

Considering Enron's compensation structure, Enron's external auditor, Arthur Andersen, had reason to be skeptical of management's fair-values estimates, as is required by generally accepted auditing standards of fieldwork 2 and 3. In particular, SAS 57 ("Performance and Reporting Guidelines Related to Fair Value Disclosures," February 1993), AU.9342.01–10, states that "the auditor should collect sufficient competent evidential matter to reasonably assure that (1) valuation methods are acceptable and (2) estimation methods and significant assumptions are disclosed." Other than Batson's (2003a, pp. 30–31) description of Andersen's appraisal of the fair value of the ill-fated Braveheart project, I am not aware of a publicly available analysis (or privately conducted examination) of the procedures Andersen employed to audit Enron's fair-value estimates.

It seems clear that Andersen had strong monetary incentives to keep its client, Enron, happy. Indeed, Zeff (2003) and Wyatt (2004), among many others, ascribe Andersen's bad behavior to the corrosive influence of consulting fees and consulting partners.[15] The evidence (documented in Benston, 2004, pp. 309–11), though,

---

15. Wyatt (2004) also blames consulting for having introduced into CPA firms a disregard or insufficient regard for "accounting professionalism," since consultants do not have the benefits of auditing courses that "focused on professional responsibilities and the importance of ethical behavior." However, it should be noted that Andersen not only was controlled by CPAs, rather than by consultants, but took a very strong public stand on the importance of professional ethics, including preparing cases and training materials.

does not support their conclusion with respect to consulting fees. Nevertheless, prescriptions against CPA firms providing many consulting services to audit clients have been instituted in the Sarbanes-Oxley Act of 2002, although consulting on tax matters, for which CPA firms necessarily adopt a promanagement advocacy position, is still permitted. Furthermore, the fees paid by companies for audit services and the importance of those fees to the individual partner in charge of the audit, often are sufficiently substantial to give the auditor reason to be nice to clients. Thus, if current and prospective monetary rewards were the force driving Andersen to compromise its integrity, there still should be concern for future Enrons, particularly considering the inherent difficulty of auditors challenging managers' fair-value estimates.[16]

## Conclusions

The Enron experience should give the FASB, IASB, and others who would permit (indeed, mandate) level 3 fair-value accounting, wherein the numbers reported are not well grounded in relevant market prices, reason to be cautious. Once Enron was permitted to use fair values for energy contracts, it extended revaluations to a wide and increasing range of assets, both for external reporting and internal personnel evaluations and compensation. As documented above, the result was overstatement of revenue and net income, and structuring transactions to present cash flows from operations rather than from financing. Basing compensation on fair values gave employees strong incentives to develop and overvalue projects, resulting in high operating expenses and rarely successful projects. The losses incurred gave rise to additional accounting subterfuges, until the entire enterprise collapsed.

Enron's internal control system was incapable of controlling the misstatements. Enron's auditors, Arthur Andersen, did not appear to have criticized the fair-value estimates, either to Enron's accountants or to Enron's Board of Directors (U.S. Senate, 2002, pp. 14–24). Nor did the board's Audit Committee ask Andersen's auditors to review and comment on the fair-value calculations, despite their having been told by the auditors that this was a "high-risk" accounting procedure (Batson, 2003b, appendix B, section IV-I).

---

16. Andersen's organizational structure and culture also appear to have played an important role. Andersen vested power in the partner-in-charge of an audit, discouraged more junior auditors from questioning decisions by their seniors, and emphasized increasing revenues to the firm, as described by Toffler (2003). Thus, although the firm would have to (and did) pay a heavy price for compromises and other derelictions of individual senior auditors, those individuals had strong incentives to do what was necessary to keep from losing the account. See Benston (2003) for data on past failures by the SEC and other authorities to discipline individual independent public accountants who attested to seriously misleading and fraudulent financial statements.

Of course, overoptimistic, opportunistic, and dishonest managers have misused historical-cost-based accounting to overstate revenue and assets and understate liabilities and expenses. Fair-value numbers derived from company created present value models and other necessarily not readily verified estimates provide such people with additional opportunities to misinform and mislead investors and other users of financial statements. The Enron example provides some evidence that this concern may not be misplaced or overstated.

REFERENCES

Batson, N., 2002. First interim report of Neal Batson, court-appointed examiner. United States Bankruptcy Court, Southern District of New York. In: re: Chapter 11 Enron Corp., et al., Debtors, Case No. 01-16034 (AJG), Jointly Administered, September 22.

Batson, N., 2003a. Second interim report of Neal Batson, court-appointed examiner. United States Bankruptcy Court, Southern District of New York. In: re: Chapter 11 Enron Corp., et al., Debtors, Case No. 01-16034 (AJG), Jointly Administered, January 21.

Batson, N., 2003b. Final report of Neal Batson, court-appointed examiner, United States Bankruptcy Court, Southern District of New York. In: re: Chapter 11 Enron Corp., et al., Debtors, Case No. 01-16034 (AJG), Jointly Administered, November 21.

Benston, G.J., 2003. The regulation of accountants and public accounting before and after Enron. *Emory Law Journal* 52 (Summer), 1325–51.

Benston, G.J., 2004. The role and limitations of financial accounting and auditing for financial market discipline. In: Curt Hunter, W. (Ed.), *Market Discipline: The Evidence across Countries and Industries*. MIT Press, Cambridge, Mass., pp. 303–21.

Benston, G.J., Hartgraves, A.L., 2002. Enron: What happened and what we can learn from it. *Journal of Accounting and Public Policy* 21, 105–27.

Bryce, R., 2002. *Pipe Dreams: Greed, Ego, and the Death of Enron*. Public Affairs (Perseus Books Group), New York.

Coffee, J.C. Jr., 2002. Understanding Enron: "It's about the Gatekeepers, Stupid." *Business Law Journal* 57, 1403–10.

Eichenwald, K., 2005. *Conspiracy of Fools: A True Story*. Broadway Books, New York.

Financial Accounting Standards Board, 2005. Project Updates, Fair Value Measurements. May 2. Available from http://www.fasb.org/project/fv_measurement.shtml.

McLean, B., Elkind, P., 2003. *The Smartest Guys in the Room: The Amazing Rise and Scandalous Fall of Enron*. Penguin Group, New York.

Mulford, C.W., Comiskey, E.E., 2002. *The Financial Numbers Game: Detecting Creating Accounting Practices*. Wiley, New York.

National Venture Capital Association, undated. The Venture Capital Industry—An Overview. Downloaded on May 18, 2005. Available from http://www.nvca.org/def.html.

Partnoy, F., 2002. Testimony of Frank Partnoy Professor of Law, University of San Diego School of Law. Hearings before the United States Senate Committee on Governmental Affairs, January 24.

Schilit, H., 2002. *Financial Shenanigans: How to Detect Accounting Gimics Fraud in Financial Reports*, 2nd ed. McGraw-Hill, New York.

Toffler, B.L., Reingold, J., 2003. *Final Accounting: Ambition, Greed, and the Fall of Arthur Andersen*. Broadway Books, New York.

U.S. Senate, 2002. The role of the board of directors in Enron's collapse. Report Prepared by the Permanent Subcommittee on Investigations of the Committee on Governmental Affairs, United States Senate, 107th Congress 2nd Session, Report 107–70, July 8.

Wyatt, A.R., 2004. Accounting professionalism—They just don't get it. *Accounting Horizons* 18 (March), 45–54.

Zeff, S., 2003. How the US accounting profession got where it is today: Parts I and II. *Accounting Horizons* 17 (September/December), 189–205, 267–301.

# 7

# The Value of the SEC's Accounting Disclosure Requirements

## Introduction

THE Securities Act of 1933 and the Securities Exchange Act of 1934 are aptly referred to as "disclosure" statutes. This early, major New Deal legislation was enacted in the aftermath of the stock market "crash" of 1929 and in the depths of the Great Depression, as a remedy to the faults that many believed characterized the stock markets.[1] Considering the current possibility that the Securities and Exchange Commission (SEC) will require more disclosure from conglomerates and the 35 years that have elapsed since the acts were enacted, we should examine whether or not the legislation was, in fact, justified and what its impact has been.

This examination is limited to the accounting disclosure requirements of the Securities Acts. While the acts include provisions for regulating the operation of stock exchanges, registration of brokers, and so on, the required disclosure of financial accounting information by corporations is of primary importance. Indeed, a typical description of the goals of the acts is that given by Robert Mundheim, in his foreword to a recent Symposium on Securities Regulation:

> The theory of the Securities Act is that if investors are provided with sufficient information to permit them to make a reasoned decision concerning the investment merits of securities offered to them, investor interests can

---

In the interests of full disclosure, thanks are due to Henry Manne, Robert Hagerman, Philip Meyers, Myron Gordon, and Richard Fortner. They neither fully agree nor disagree with what is presented here. This essay was presented at the 52nd Annual Meeting of the American Accounting Association, San Diego, California.

1. Ralph F. DeBedts, *The New Deal's SEC* (Columbia University Press, 1964).

be adequately protected without unduly restricting the ability of business ventures to raise capital.[2]

But how much is "sufficient information"? If the question is asked, "would you not prefer more disclosure to less?" most people might say, "why more, of course!" Certainly surveys made of financial analysts reveal their desire for more information. But then we ask (or should ask), "more disclosure at what price?" for disclosure is not a free good. Like most other goods, its production entails costs. These costs include the direct cost of preparing detailed financial statements, the cost to the corporation of revealing information to competitors, the cost of delay in selling securities, and the cost of misinformation should investors believe that most elements of financial statements reflect the economic affairs of companies.

Nevertheless, the value of information disclosed in financial statements may exceed its cost. In this event, if corporate managers were acting in the best interests of stockholders (i.e., maximizing the present value of the stockholders' wealth, with a given degree of risk), they would provide information to them and to other investors according to their best estimates of how the marginal costs and benefits accrue.

Should the managers not provide the information, a stockholder or potential investor who believes that financial information is valuable to him is free to purchase it in the market place much as other goods are purchased. Several means are available. Large shareholders generally have the right and small shareholders have some right to examine the books of corporations in which they own stock.[3] Or one would expect information-gathering services to spring up, if the economies of scale in gathering financial information result in savings that exceed the value to individual investors from not sharing information with others. Indeed, this is supposed to be one of the important functions of stockbrokers and of the many investment services. An interesting development of this sort is the formation of investment analyst firms in Europe (where there is generally inadequate accounting disclosure and no SEC). One of these, Eurofinance, set up six years ago by 12 European and American banks, has a staff of 95 who have compiled files on 20,000 European companies.[4]

If these arguments are correct, the imposition of a requirement by a public authority could only be detrimental to stockholders, although such action might benefit other groups (competitors, other investors, academicians, curiosity seekers, etc.).

However, three circumstances could alter this conclusion. First, corporate officers could be dishonest—they might be misappropriating the resources of the

---

2. Robert H. Mundheim, "Foreword, Symposium on Securities Regulation," *Law and Contemporary Problems* (Summer 1964), p. 648.
3. Arthur S. Dewing, *The Financial Policy of Corporations*, 5th ed. (Ronald Press, 1953), p. 88.
4. Robert Ball, "The Declining Art of Concealing Figures," *Fortune* (September 1967), p. 138.

corporation and covering up their dishonesty by not disclosing the firm's financial affairs. Or, they could be disseminating false or biased information about the corporation's assets, liabilities, income and expense, and so on, to mislead and cheat current and potential investors. Second, corporate officers could be mistaken about the value of disclosure. They might not realize that the marginal value of financial statements is greater to stockholders than is its marginal cost to the enterprise. Third, there may be economies of scale in the production of information or other advantages that a government agency might have over private services.

To determine whether a government agency, the SEC in this instance, can or has improved the lot of investors, net of costs, this study considers four major questions. First, were the accounting disclosure requirements justified? This question is answered by examining (1) the evidence of fraudulent and misleading financial statements, (2) investors' legal actions against public accountants, and (3) the degree of corporate financial disclosure, in the period prior to 1933. Second, what evidence is there to support or deny the underlying assumption of the Securities Acts that disclosure of financial accounting information is of value to investors? To answer this question, (1) the relationship between reported accounting data and stock prices is examined empirically, and (2) the value of detailed analysis of financial data and other information by mutual funds, as examples of sophisticated analysts, also is examined empirically. Third, what is the impact of the SEC's accounting disclosure requirements on the securities markets? Answers are found (1) in the use by corporations of the new securities market, relative to their needs, and (2) in the effect of the SEC's accounting regulations on direct placements of debt securities. Finally, the impact of the acts on accounting is discussed briefly.

## The Justification for the Securities Acts

### Misrepresentation and Fraud in Corporate Financial Statements

One of the two stated goals of the Securities Act of 1933 is "to prevent frauds in the sale" of securities. The SEC was given the power to institute accounting rules and review financial statements, in part to prevent the deliberate misstatements of accounting data that people believed existed. But were such practices so widespread as to constitute a serious problem?

It is difficult to believe that there was no deliberate misrepresentation in financial statements prepared by public accountants, given the existence of larceny among other (though lesser) men. However, a search of the available literature in several libraries revealed only anecdotal reports of fraudulent or misrepresentative accounting. For example, in *Main Street and Wall Street*, William Z. Ripley severely chastises a number of prominent corporations for failing to disclose any information or for presenting stockholders with confusing reports.[5] In an earlier study he criticizes the practices of some corporations of paying dividends out of capital when stockholders were led to believe that income had been earned.[6] Most of the practices he describes date from before 1910.

Overcapitalization and watered stock also are mentioned. Henry Clews (in 1908) claims that "on the average, the railroads of the country were capitalized at probably 50 per cent in excess of their cost."[7] Most of the litigation appears to have been concerned with the "true" value of property exchanged by promoters for stock. A thorough review of the U.S. court records to about 1929 by David L. Dodd lists almost 300 cases that are in some way related to watered stock.[8] But most of the cases deal with nonfraudulent differences of opinion about the value of property.

Moreover, fraudulent financial statements do not appear to have been proximate determinants of the Securities Acts. A careful examination of the Senate hearings that preceded passage of the Securities Act of 1933[9] and the voluminous Pecora hearings that preceded the Securities Exchange Act of 1934[10] turned up only one citation of fraudulently prepared financial statements. And even in this case (the Guardian Group of Banks), Ferdinand Pecora states that:

> The beautiful annual financial statements which had aroused so much enthusiasm and congratulations among their banking colleagues did not arrest the debacle.... The public was apparently harder to fool than the bankers. They kept drawing their money out by the millions.[11]

Thus, the need for the financial disclosure requirements that are the "heart" of the Securities Act of 1933 appear to have had their genesis in the general folklore of turn-of-the-century finance rather than in the events of the 1920s that preceded the legislation, insofar as fraud and misrepresentation are concerned.

---

5. William Z. Ripley, *Main Street and Wall Street* (Little Brown, 1927), especially chapter 6.

6. William Z. Ripley (ed.), *Trusts, Pools and Corporations*, rev. ed. (Ginn, 1916), pp. xxiv–xxv.

7. Henry Clews, *Fifty Years on Wall Street* (Irving Publishing, 1908), p. 250. The most often cited case is that of U.S. Steel, in which it is computed that the J. P. Morgan syndicate extracted a profit of $62,500,000 (Ripley, op. cit. pp. 204–5). Whether this promoter's profit was excessive or not is not clear, for George Stigler has shown that the stockholders of U.S. Steel did twice as well as the stockholders of its competitors over a period of 18 years, per dollar of original investment. George J. Stigler, "The Dominant Form and the Inverted Umbrella," *Journal of Law and Economics* (October 1965), pp. 117–27.

8. David L. Dodd, *Stock Watering* (Columbia University Press, 1930).

9. United States Senate, Committee on Banking and Currency, *Hearings on S. 875* (73d Congress, 1st Session, 1933).

10. United States Senate, Committee on Banking and Currency, *Stock Exchange Practices*, Report No. 1455 (73d Congress, 2d Session, 1934).

11. Ferdinand Pecora, *Wall Street under Oath* (Simon and Schuster, 1939), p. 251.

## Investors' Legal Actions against Public Accountants

In a comprehensive study of the legal responsibilities of accountants, published in 1935, Wiley D. Rich states that "an extensive search has revealed not a single American case in which a public accountant has been held liable in a criminal suit for fraud."[12] Recently (November 1967) Edward Daus, a member of the bar of the state of New York, writes that "since the turn of the century, there have been less than a dozen reported decisions in the State of New York adjudicating issues with respect to claimed fraud or negligence of accountants in the performance of their services. Indeed, most of the decisions date back to the aftermath of the depression years."[13] These post-Depression decisions are important, however, especially for understanding the changed nature of the accountant's liability for fraud under the Securities Acts.

Prior to the Securities Acts, it was very difficult for a stockholder to bring suit against public accountants for fraudulently or negligently prepared financial statements. Stockholders and potential investors were considered third parties to the contract between the corporation and its public accountants. Hence, under the rule of privity, the courts ruled that an investor had no claim against a firm of certified public accountants who audited and certified financial statements that were alleged to be untrue.[14]

The Securities Act of 1933 changed radically the ability of the stockholder to sue a public accountant (and others who prepared a registration statement). Section 11 provides that any person who acquires registered securities may sue the accountant, regardless of the fact that he is not the accountant's client. His claim may be based on an alleged false statement or misleading omission in the financial statements. He does not have to prove that the accountant was negligent or fraudulent in certifying to the financial statements. Nor does the investor have to prove that he relied on the statements or that the loss he suffered was the proximate result of its falsity or misleading character. Rather the accountant has the burden of establishing that he was free from negligence or fraud by proving that after reasonable investigation he could believe that the financial statements he certified were true as of the time the registration statement became effective. The loss suffered by the investor is deemed to be the

---

12. Wiley D. Rich, *Legal Responsibility and Rights of Public Accountants* (American Institute Publishing, 1935), p. 100.

13. Edward J. Daus, "Accountants' Liability Today," *New York Certified Public Accountant* (November 1967), p. 835.

14. *Landell v. Lybrand*, 264, Pa., 406, 107 Atl., 783 (1919); *Ultramers Corp. v. Touche, Niven & Co.*, 229 App. Div. 581, 243 N. Y. Supp. (1st Dep't, 1930), rev'd, 225 N.Y. 170, 174, N.E. 441 (1931); *State Street Trust v. Ernst*, 278 N.Y., 104, N.E. 2d 416 (1938); *O'Connor v. Ludlam*, 92 F. 2d 50 (sd Cir), 5B, Cert. denied, 302 U.S. 758 (1937).

drop in the market price of his shares, unless the accountant can prove the loss resulted from causes other than false statements or misleading omissions in the financial statements.[15]

Section 18 of the Securities Exchange Act of 1934 differs from section 11 of the 1933 act in that the investor may sue if, in reliance on false or misleading statements, he "shall have purchased or sold a security at a price which was affected by such statement." Thus, under the 1934 act, the accountant may be liable for both under- and overreported income, while under the 1933 act he appears liable only if he overestimates.[16] Other sections of the acts (section 17 (a) of the 1933 act and Rule 10b–5 under the 1934 act) also could be used against accountants for misstatements.[17]

It is now very easy to sue public accountants, as a review of the current court dockets could readily attest.[18] The ultimate in accountants' liability appears to have been reached in a recent decision.[19] If upheld, public accountants will be liable not only for misstatements in the registration statement, but for later material changes that occurred through the registration date.

From this brief review of the past and current status of misrepresentation and fraud in published financial statements, two conclusions can be drawn. First, no evidence was found to substantiate the hypothesis that misrepresentation or fraud was widespread in the period before passage of the Securities Acts of 1933 and 1934. Second, the Securities Acts increased the liability of accountants enormously, shifting the weight of the law substantially to the side of the investor. Therefore, it appears that the investor now seems quite able to protect himself through the courts, should he be misled by fraudulent or misleading financial statements.[20]

## Corporate Financial Disclosure Prior to the SEC

That stockholders need, deserve, and were not receiving financial accounting information is the other justification for the disclosure requirements. As was the situation for fraud, a valid question is whether there was a sufficiently widespread lack of disclosure, as such, to warrant the imposition of a federal statute.

---

15. Saul Levy, *Accountants' Legal Responsibility* (American Institute of Accountants, 1954), pp. 46–47.

16. The advantages of conservatism (which is discussed further below), are evident, since investors who gain, even if insufficiently, are not as likely to sue as those who lose, and those who are discouraged from buying cannot sue.

17. See *H. L. Green Co. v. Childree*, 185 F. Supp. 95 (S.D.N.Y. 1960), in which a possible right against accountants under Rule 10b–5 was recognized for false financial statements prepared for the acquired company in a merger.

18. Daus, op. cit., pp. 835–43.

19. *Esscott et. al. v. Bar Chris Construction Corporation et al.*, F. Supp. 643 (S.D.N.Y. 1968).

20. Although the court costs of the plaintiffs probably would be high, the cost to public accountants of both defending and possibly losing a case would be relatively much higher.

TABLE 7.1 Financial Accounting Information Disclosed by Companies Traded on the New York Stock Exchange before 1935

|  | Year | Total Number of Companies | Percentage that Reported | Percentage that Did Not Report |
|---|---|---|---|---|
| Balance sheet | 1926 | 333 | 100 | 0 |
|  | 1934 | 508 | 100 | 0 |
| Current assets and liabilities | 1926 | 333 | 100 | 0 |
|  | 1934 | 508 | 100 | 0 |
| Sales | 1926 | 333 | 55 | 45 |
|  | 1927 | 360 | 57 | 43 |
|  | 1928 | 396 | 60 | 40 |
|  | 1929 | 460 | 61 | 39 |
|  | 1930 | 486 | 62 | 38 |
|  | 1931 | 498 | 61 | 39 |
|  | 1932 | 501 | 61 | 39 |
|  | 1933 | 508 | 62 | 38 |
|  | 1934 | 508 | 62 | 38 |
| Cost of goods sold | 1926 | 333 | 45 | 55 |
|  | 1934 | 508 | 54 | 46 |
| Depreciation | 1926 | 333 | 71 | 29 |
|  | 1934 | 508 | 93 | 7 |
| Net income | 1926 | 333 | 100 | 0 |
|  | 1934 | 508 | 99.6 | 0.4 |
| Audited by CPA | 1926 | 333 | 82 | 18 |
|  | 1934 | 508 | 94 | 6 |

Source: *Moody's Manuals*, 1927 through 1935.

To answer this question, the statements of all the companies traded on the New York Stock Exchange (NYSE) in June 1935 (the month before filing was required under the Securities and Exchange Act of 1934) were examined. At this time, sales on the NYSE constituted 70 percent of stock sales on all registered exchanges.[21] The source of the financial statements is *Moody's Manuals*.

The statements were examined for disclosure of the following data: (1) balance sheet, (2) current assets and liabilities, (3) sales, (4) cost of goods sold, (5) depreciation, and (6) net income. Table 7.1 gives a summary of the findings. All corporations reported their balance sheets, current assets and liabilities, and net income. Reporting of sales is examined for each year from 1926 through 1934. The percentage of companies reporting sales rose over this period from 55 to 62 percent. The disclosure of cost of goods sold also rose, from 45 to 54 percent. By 1934, 93 percent of the companies reported depreciation.

21. Securities and Exchange Commission, *First Annual Report*, Fiscal Year Ended June 30, 1935, p. 87.

In 1932, the NYSE and the American Institute of Accountants (AICPA) began the correspondence that led to the codification of "generally accepted accounting principles." In the same year, all corporations applying for a listing on the NYSE were required to have their annual statements audited by independent public accountants. As table 7.1 shows, most companies traded were audited by CPAs. Thus, there was a considerable amount of disclosure prior to the passage of the Securities Acts.

## The Relevance to Investors of Financial Statements Required by the SEC

The other stated goal of the Securities Acts (besides fraud prevention) is to ensure that investors "make a realistic appraisal of the merits of securities and thus exercise an informed judgment whether to purchase them."[22] It is assumed that the financial accounting information disclosed is relevant for this purpose.

But for the information to be relevant to an investor, it must be timely. "Stale" information is of no value, since those who receive the information first will find it profitable to buy or sell securities until its economic value is exhausted. If the SEC is to serve the public, its procedures should provide for the timely dissemination of accounting data equally to all investors.

The 1934 act, as amended in 1964, requires that most corporations with over $1 million in assets and 500 stockholders file prescribed annual and semiannual financial reports. Form 10K, the annual report, must be filed within 120 days after the close of the corporation's fiscal year. Form 9K, the semiannual report, is much less detailed. It is filed within 45 days after the end of the first half of the fiscal year. Form 8K, the "current report," must be filed within 10 days after the end of any month during which certain "significant" events occur (such as change of control of the registrant, material legal proceedings undertaken, material changes in securities outstanding, and revaluation of assets). These forms are made available to the public very shortly after they are filed with the commission in Washington, D.C.

The delay in reporting the period's financial data after the close of the period is due, of course, to the fact that the companies need time to record the considerable detail required of them. The conflicting needs of accuracy—in the sense of reporting according to the letter of the formal (and informal) regulations—and dispatch are resolved in favor of accuracy.

---

22. Securities and Exchange Commission, *The Work of the Securities and Exchange Commission* (May 1967), p. 13.

Given the time required for corporations to report information that conforms to the SEC's regulations, are the financial statements relevant (in the sense that they contain primarily unanticipated information) when they become available to the public? This is a question for which an empirical answer is required.

## Reported Financial Accounting Data and Stock Prices

The empirical test is based on the assumption that the expectations of investors about the present value of a corporation would change if they received previously unexpected relevant information. Hence, if the financial reports filed with the SEC contain this type of information, a change of investors' expectations would be reflected in (and correlated with) a change in the market price of the corporation's shares. However, if the information was previously known and discounted, or if investors do not find accounting reports useful, the publication of the reports would not cause a change in stock prices.

A valid test of the hypothesis that investors find the data reported to the SEC relevant requires that (1) the effect on stock prices of factors other than reported accounting data be isolated; (2) the particular accounting data investors find useful be determined; and (3) the expected accounting data be distinguished from the reported data.[23]

A variety of statistical techniques are used to account for the effect on changes in stock prices of such factors as cash dividends distributed, announced changes in dividend amounts, changes in capitalization, fluctuations in general market and economic conditions, and changes related to specific industries. Third quarter accounting data are also included to account for information that becomes available between annual reports.

Since it is not clear which reported accounting data are used by investors, four alternative constructs are tested: (1) net sales, (2) cash flow (net income before depreciation), (3) net operating income (net income before nonrecurring and extraordinary income and expense) and (4) all-inclusive net income.[24]

It is assumed that stockholders use previously reported accounting data to form their expectations about forthcoming data. Four assumptions about the use of past data are tested: (1) last year's rate of change of accounting data is expected this year; (2) a simple average of the past three years' rates of change is expected this year; (3) a simple average of the past five years' rates of change is

---

23. A complete description of the theory and statistical procedures described very briefly here may be found in George J. Benston, "Published Corporate Accounting Data and Stock Prices," *Journal of Accounting Research*, Selected Studies—Empirical Research in Accounting, 1967, pp. 1–54.

24. The accounting and stock price data are expressed as "rates of change per share" to allow for possible effects due to differences in the size of companies.

expected this year; and (4) a weighted average of all available past rates of change, with the most recent data weighted most heavily and the weights declining geometrically, is expected this year.

The unexpected accounting data is the difference between the data reported and the amounts calculated as just described. In the event that investors either formed their expectations about rates of change of accounting data from sources other than previous reports or held no expectations about change, the relationship also is tested with the current year's data used alone.

A sample of 483 corporations whose stock is listed on the NYSE is used for the test. These are almost all NYSE corporations traded in 1964 for which accounting data are available on the Compustat tapes. The test consists of regressing the change in the market price of shares (expressed as yields) for the month in which the financial reports were available to the public on the unexpected financial accounting data reported, with other factors mentioned above accounted for.

The following conclusions can be drawn from the test, assuming that the model is a valid representation of reality. There is a statistically "significant" but quite small relationship between the unexpected accounting data and stock prices for some of the expectations models. The three income constructs show (at best) but slight relationships to stock prices: a 100 percent increase in income (defined as cash flow, net operating income, or all-inclusive net income) is associated with at most a 2 percent increase in relative stock prices (on the average) for all of the expectations models tested. Hence, it must be concluded that the reported accounting income data is of very limited relevance to investors.

Sales are of greater importance. For the "best" model, in which investors are assumed to hold no previous expectations, a 100 percent increase in sales is associated with a 10 percent increase in relative stock prices (on the average). But when third quarter sales are not included in the regression, the relationship becomes insignificant. Thus it appears that the sales of the previous year are stale information unless quarterly sales are available. Considering that sales information often is reported in trade papers and other sources before the SEC reports are released, the specific source of the small statistical relationship found between reported sales and stock prices may not be the accounting reports.

The conclusion that income, when reported to the SEC, is not relevant to investors must be tempered by the fact that only four rather gross measures of the financial status of corporations are tested. However, the reports required by the SEC are characterized by the wealth of detail they call for. It may be that careful analysis of this detailed data does give investors insight into the affairs of corporations that are of economic value to them. It is not feasible to make a statistical test of this hypothesis because of the unknown interrelationships that may be computed and evaluated by sophisticated analysts of financial statements. But one way that the hypothesis may be examined empirically is to look at the success in the

## Detailed Analysis of Financial Statements: The Performance of Mutual Funds

Mutual funds are such a group, since they generally have large staffs of "experts" who spend all of their time making such analyses and therefore are able to obtain and dissect the reports before most individuals can.

The test is biased in favor of the usefulness of the SEC reports, because it is not possible to determine whether the good performance of mutual funds is due to their use of the reports or to other information that they gathered about corporations. But if it is found that the mutuals do not perform better than the market, on the average, then there must be some doubt that the reports are economically useful.

The three published studies on the performance of mutual funds are reviewed briefly. One of the earliest studies of mutual fund performances is by F. E. Brown and Douglas Vickers.[25] They analyze the performance of 152 funds over the 5.75-year period 1953 through the first nine months of 1958. The performance of each fund is compared to a similarly constructed index of general market performance. The funds also are grouped by size and types to reveal any possible systematic differences among them. Brown and Vickers conclude that:

> When adjustments are made for [differences in the composition of portfolios], the average performance by the funds did not differ appreciably from what would have been achieved by an unmanaged portfolio with the same division among asset types.[26]

William F. Sharpe examines the performance of 34 mutual funds (all for whom data were available in Weisenberger's *Investment Companies*) for the 20 years 1943–63.[27] He finds differences among funds in their return to variability (R/V) ratio. Return (R) includes dividends and capital gains (realized and unrealized) less the expenses of operating the fund. Variability (V) measures the riskiness of the fund. Differences in performance (R/V ratio) among the funds could be due either to differences in the ability of management to find incorrectly priced securities (by analyzing the SEC required accounting reports, among other data) or to

---

25. Irwin Friend, F. E. Brown, Edward S. Herman, and Douglas Vickers, *A Study of Mutual Funds*, prepared for the Securities and Exchange Commission by the Securities Research Unit, Wharton School of Finance and Commerce, University of Pennsylvania (Government Printing Office, 1962), chap. V, pp. 289–358.

26. Ibid., pp. 17–18.

27. William F. Sharpe, "Mutual Fund Performance," *Journal of Business* (January 1966), pp. 119–38.

differences in expenses, since Sharpe accounts for differences in risk and size of the funds. The correlation between the R/V ratios and the ratios of expenses (other than brokerage fees and loading and selling charges) to net assets shows that good performance is associated with low expense ratios.

Sharpe also compares the performance of the funds with a portfolio consisting of Dow Jones Industrials. He finds that

> the average fund manager selects a portfolio at least as good as the Dow-Jones Industrials, but that the results actually obtained by the holder of mutual fund shares (after the costs associated with the operation of the funds have been deducted) fall somewhat short of those from the Dow-Jones portfolio.[28]

The most recent (and best) study of the ability of mutual funds is by Michael C. Jensen.[29] He examines the performance of 115 mutual funds for the 10-year period, 1954–64. Jensen provides a rigorous theoretical formulation derived from a general model of the determination of capital asset prices.[30] The unique value of his approach is that his model allows an evaluation of the absolute performance of mutual funds, with the effects of risk explicitly accounted for. Thus, a direct estimate of the fund manager's ability to use the SEC data, as well as other sources of information is obtained.

Jensen concludes that:

> the evidence on mutual fund performance discussed above indicates not only that these 115 mutual funds were *on average* not able to predict security prices well enough to outperform a buy-the-market-and-hold policy, but also that there is very little evidence that any *individual* fund was able to do significantly better than that which we expected from mere random chance. It is also important to note that these conclusions hold *even* when we measure the fund returns gross of management expenses (that is assume their bookkeeping, research, and other expenses except brokerage commissions were obtained free). Thus on average the funds apparently were not quite successful enough in their trading activities to recoup even their brokerage expenses.[31]

---

28. Ibid., p. 137.
29. Michael C. Jensen, "The Performance of Mutual Funds in the Period 1954–64." Presented at the 1967 Annual Meetings of the American Finance Association, Washington, D.C., *Journal of Finance* (May 1968), pp. 389–416.
30. See William F. Sharpe, "Capital Asset Prices: A Theory of Market Equilibrium Under Conditions of Risk," *Journal of Finance* (September 1964), pp. 425–42 and John Litner, "Security Prices, Risk, and Maximal Gains from Diversification," *Journal of Finance* (December 1965), pp. 547–616.
31. Jensen, op. cit., p. 24.

The studies reported above all show that the resources spent by mutual fund managers for analysis of financial statements and the like have largely been to no avail. It would appear, then, that even very sophisticated users of the accounting reports required by the SEC are not able to profit from them. However, several points must be admitted that weaken this conclusion. The managers of the mutual funds may garner useful information from the statements but use these insights for their personal benefit rather than for the fund. Or, other analysts might be better or faster than the fund managers and use the information content of the statements first. But if either of these possibilities obtain, the "average" investor, for whom the regulations presumably are designed, certainly gets the information too late for it to be relevant.

The general conclusion of this section must be that the data examined do not support the hypothesis that the financial reports filed under the Securities Act of 1934 are sufficiently timely to be of value to investors. This is not to say that such data are useless: indeed, it would be virtually impossible to demonstrate this possibility, since no statistical test can fully encompass the complicated ways in which people might use information. Nevertheless, it is incumbent upon the regulators to provide some evidence to support their belief that investors can, and do, use the 9K and 10K reports that are filed with the SEC.

## The Impact of Disclosure on the Securities Markets

The "crash" in 1929 and the Depression were supposed to have damaged severely investors' confidence in the stock market. The belief that required disclosure of financial information would restore this confidence is based, in part, on an assumption that the public's willingness to invest depends on a study of, and confidence in, accounting reports. While the studies reported above give us reason to doubt the validity of this belief, the issue still is worthy of additional examination, especially considering the SEC's more recent extensions of reporting requirements to companies whose stock is traded over the counter.

### Use by Corporations of the New Securities Market

One cannot know whether the amount of new corporate stock issues purchased by the public would have been greater or smaller had it not been for the SEC, except by replaying (as in a football telecast) the last 35 years without the SEC. Since this technique is not available, the alternative is to look at data before and after the SEC, with the possible effect of events other than the existence of the SEC at least acknowledged, if not accounted for.

Among the factors that should be accounted for, before one can judge whether the public increased its purchases of new securities after the SEC's creation, are the needs of corporations for financing, general economic conditions, and institutional constraints (other than the SEC). An approach to this problem is made in table 7.2, where new security issues, net of redemptions, are presented as percentages of gross expenditures on plant and equipment and as percentages of net adjusted expansion of plant and equipment. New security issues are taken net of redemptions to account for issues that are floated merely for refinancing purposes. Gross expenditures on plant and equipment measures the amount corporations spend to replace and expand their fixed assets. Net adjusted expansion measures the amount that they spend to increase their fixed assets, less depreciation adjusted for changes in replacement costs. Both amounts measure the need of corporations for additional funds. The percentage of net new issues to each of these amounts indicates the degree to which corporate needs for financing were satisfied by the stock markets.

TABLE 7.2 New Security Issues Net of Redemption as Percent of Expenditures on Plant and Equipment Manufacturing and Mining Corporations Averages over Business Cycles Measured Trough-to-Trough

| Period | Gross Expenditures[a] | Net Adjusted Expansion[b] | Personal Income Tax Rates Dividends—Capital Gains[g] |
|---|---|---|---|
| *Pre-SEC* | | | |
| 1900–1904 | 51.3% | 81.9 | — |
| 1904–8 | 25.5 | 45.2 | — |
| 1908–11 | 29.7 | 63.8 | — |
| 1911–14 | 22.8 | 48.9 | — |
| 1914–19 | 23.9 | 72.3 | 0 |
| 1919–21 | 45.9 | 284.9[e] | 0 |
| 1921–24 | 31.9 | —[d] | 0 |
| 1924–27 | 34.1 | 350.6[f] | 0 |
| 1927–32 | 25.7 | —[d] | 0 |
| 1900–24 | 30.9 | 58.3 | 0 |
| 1919–29 | 36.8 | 354.3 | 0 |
| *Post-SEC* | | | |
| 1932–38 | —[c] | —[c] | 0 |
| 1938–46 | 6.5 | 51.2 | 33 |
| 1946–49 | 23.1 | 50.2 | 42 |
| 1949–54 | 20.6 | 68.6 | 44 |
| 1936–40 | 6.4 | 28.8 | 0 |
| 1946–53 | 21.9 | 59.9 | 42 |

[a] Gross expenditures source: Daniel Creamer, et al., op. cit., table 40, p. 12.
[b] Net expansion = gross expenditures—depreciation adjusted for changes in replacement costs. *Source*: Ibid., table 42, p. 137.
[c] Not computed because redemptions exceeded new issues.
[d] Not computed because adjusted depreciation exceeded gross expenditures.
[e] The percentage is very large because net security issues were large.
[f] The percentage is very large because net adjusted expansion was very small.
[g] Based on personal tax rates for $25,000 taxable income, centered at approximate midpoint of business cycle.

Differences in general economic conditions are controlled by computing the percentages as averages over successive business cycles, measured trough to trough (National Bureau of Economic Research dating). The data used are for manufacturing and mining corporations.[32] Excluding public utilities, railroads, and financial institutions reduces variations due to the effects of regulation on these industries. One other important institutional change—income taxes—is given in the right-hand column of table 7.2. The differential individual tax rates on dividend and capital gains income probably reduced the flow of new issues in the post-SEC period.

Table 7.2 and figure 7.1 show that the SEC had a somewhat perverse effect on the use of securities markets for new financing by corporations, if all other factors really are equal. When a subjective adjustment for the income tax effects is made, the difference between the pre- and post-SEC periods probably is not significant. Hence, it appears that the SEC has not had a positive effect on the use of stock markets by corporations.

That the Securities Acts had little demonstrable positive effect on the relative amount of new issues floated does not mean that the legislation does not affect the stock markets. The manner in which the SEC has administered the accounting disclosure requirements has affected the content of corporate financial statements and these in turn, may have affected the securities market.

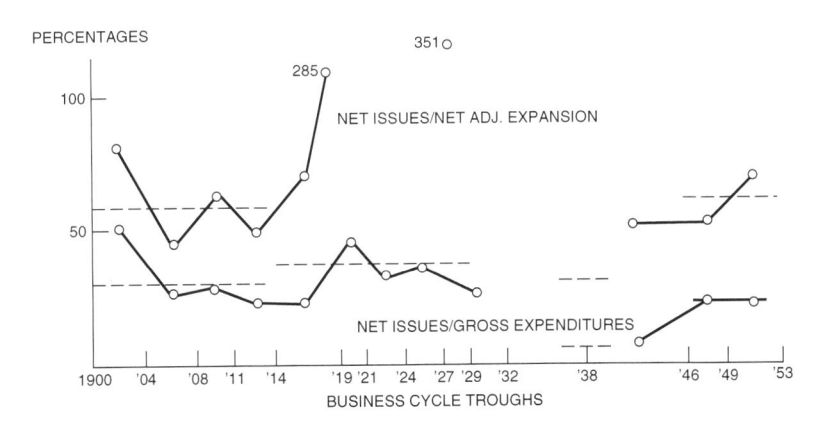

*Source*: Table ll

FIGURE 7.1 Net Security Issues as Percentage of Expenditures on Plant and Equipment—Manufacturing and Mining Corporations (averages over business cycles)

---

32. Daniel Creamer, Sergei P. Dobrovolsky, and Israel Borenstein, *Capital in Manufacturing and Mining, Its Formation and Financing* (National Bureau of Economic Research, 1960).

## The Effect of the SEC's Accounting Regulations on Direct Placements

Section 19(a) of the 1933 act and 13(b) of the 1934 act give the SEC the powers to prescribe

> the items or details to be shown in the balance sheet and the earnings statement, and the methods to be followed in the preparation of reports, in the appraisal or valuation of assets and liabilities, in the determination of depreciation and depletion, in the differentiation of recurring and nonrecurring income, in the differentiation of investment and operating income, and in the preparation, where the Commission deems it necessary or desirable of separate and/or consolidated balance sheets or income accounts.

In general, the SEC has not used this power, a forebearance that has won it much praise from the accounting profession.[33] Rather, it chose to accept generally practiced accounting procedures, and to encourage and even enforce the conservative bias generally followed by public accountants. Most prominently, the commission has a very strong force in banishing from accepted accounting practice the writing up of assets above their original cost.[34] And Rappaport observes that "there was a period...when the SEC was conducting something in the nature of a campaign to eliminate goodwill from all balance sheets filed with it."[35]

Perhaps because of the SEC's position, most accountants today would applaud the conservative bias. But the result is that the financial accounting information presented to investors often is not accurate. If the present market values (or present value) of land, buildings, equipment, patents, or other assets are greater than their original cost, less depreciation, the investor will undervalue the stock of a corporation if he takes the financial reports at face value. If there has been an inflation, depreciation based on non–price-level-adjusted assets may result in understated expenses. Additional examples of the misleading effects of the conservative bias on financial accounts could be added, but they have been well cataloged in texts and articles.

---

33. Carmen Blough, the SEC's first chief accountant, argued successfully for this forebearance, over the objections of two of the commissioners who were lawyers. Carmen G. Blough, "Development of Accounting Principles," *Papers at the Berkeley Symposium on the Foundations of Financial Accounting* (University of California, 1967), p. 5.

34. Philip L. Defliese, "Influence of SEC on Accounting Principles and Procedures and the Practice of Accounting," *Accounting Papers of the Twelfth Annual Conference of Accountants* (University of Tulsa, 1958), p. 71.

35. Louis H. Rappaport, *SEC Accounting Practice and Procedure*, 2d ed. (Ronald Press, 1963), p. 5.3.

The commission also has not allowed registrants to give investors estimates of future earnings,[36] statement of assets at fair market value,[37] appraisals of almost any sort,[38] and the like.[39] Thus the SEC has prevented the disclosure of relevant information by corporations to investors.

The restriction of information that corporations can provide in their financial statements and the conservative accounting bias enforced by the SEC may have had an impact on the ability of some firms to sell their securities to the public. If a firm that wants to raise capital is prevented by the SEC from providing relevant information to the public (that would allow investors to make a correct, superior assessment of its future, and hence, its present value), the firm has but two alternatives (other than violating the law). It can underprice its new securities, to the detriment of its present stockholders, or it can turn to the private placement market, which generally is not regulated by the SEC's accounting disclosure regulation.

The private placement market (of almost entirely debt securities) was virtually unknown prior to 1934. In the 34 years from 1900 to 1934, only about 3 percent of corporate debt was privately placed. However, in the next 31 years, from 1935 to 1966, privately placed debt rose to 46 percent of the total.[40] Of course, the coincident use of private placements with the creation of the SEC need not be causally related. Corey[41] and Cohan,[42] the two principal writers on the subject, claim other factors are more responsible. Therefore, an additional test of the hypothesis is required.

If it were true that the SEC's accounting regulations force some corporations to use private placements rather than public sales, those corporations for whom conservative accounting is misleading should use this exemption more than others. Data on private placements are available only for fairly broad industry groups, so the empirical test can be only suggestive. Nevertheless, some valid generalizations can be made about the impact of the SEC's accounting regulations on private placements.

Industries for which data on private and public placements are available are ranked according to the degree of negative bias imposed by the SEC's accounting and reporting regulations. The order of listing is necessarily subjective, but it was made *before* the rankings of ratios of private placements to total debt flotations

---

36. Harry Heller, "Disclosure Requirements under Federal Securities Regulation," *Business Lawyer* (1961), p. 307.

37. Andrew Barr and Elmer C. Kock, "Accounting and the SEC," *George Washington Law Review* (1959), pp. 181–82.

38. Defliese, op. cit., p. 71.

39. An exception is the required reporting of the market value of marketable securities.

40. Avery B. Cohan, *Yields on Corporate Debt Directly Placed* (National Bureau of Economic Research, 1967), p. 1.

41. Robert E. Corey, *Direct Placements of Corporate Securities* (Harvard University Press, 1951).

42. Cohan, op. cit.

were made. The reasons for choosing the order are given for each industry. The reader is invited to challenge this ranking, but only if he also does not prejudge the issue by looking at table 7.3.

1. Extractive (mining and oil wells, not including re-refining). This industry is listed first because the value of a mine or oil well to an investor depends on estimates of the ore, oil, or gas in the ground. Appraisals, therefore, are needed but not allowed by the SEC. The historical cost of the property and the past history of the company are less meaningful for this industry than for any other. Unfortunately for the test, the speculative nature of the extractive industry mitigates against private placement of securities, because insurance companies, and so on, generally do not invest in these types of issues. Nevertheless, if the hypothesis tested is correct, the extractive industry should have the highest proportion of private placements to total debt issues.
2. Other transportation (airlines, trucking, shipping). Other transportation is ranked second, because it is dominated by companies whose primary asset is the franchise awarded them by the regulating authorities. The value of the routes assigned airline and trucking companies is a function of the expected future flow of passengers and freight. Historical accounting is but of limited value in making this assessment. Further for airlines, the nature of the equipment used, its acceptance by the public and the delivery dates from the manufacturers also are very important factors not disclosed well by traditional accounting statements.
3. Commercial and other. Commercial enterprises, such as department stores, have their assets understated because goodwill cannot be shown. This intangible asset is of great value to a retail or wholesale establishment.
4. Finance and real estate. The prohibition against appraisals is most biased against real estate ventures. Meaningful accounting for finance companies also is very difficult to communicate, but this is not the fault of the SEC. Nevertheless, since the data do not allow separation of the industry, it is ranked fourth.
5. Manufacturing. This is such a broad category that it is difficult to know how to evaluate it. Manufacturing firms that are set up to exploit a new invention or patent, and those engaging in a great amount of research and development would be harmed by the conservative bias of the SEC's rules. Others would not be greatly affected. Since the former group are likely to be a relatively small proportion of the industry, manufacturing is ranked fifth.
6. Communications (telephone, telegraph, and broadcasting). This industry is dominated by AT&T, the Bell System, and other telephone and

TABLE 7.3 Private Debt Placements as Percent of Total Debt Offered for Cash Ordered with Highest Average Percentages to the Left—Annual Ranks in Parentheses

| Year | Total | Other Transportation | Extractive | Commercial and Other | Financial and Real Estate | Manufacturing | Electric, Gas, & Water | Communication | Railroad |
|---|---|---|---|---|---|---|---|---|---|
| 1953 | 45.6 | 90.0 (1) | 80.0 (2) | 77.8 (3) | 64.2 (4) | 52.2 (5) | 34.7 (6) | 7.9 (7) | 2.0 (8) |
| 1954 | 46.5 | 98.3 (1) | 97.4 (2) | 60.3 (5) | 73.8 (3) | 65.4 (4) | 27.8 (6) | 13.8 (7) | 8.1 (8) |
| 1955 | 44.5 | 98.4 (1) | 93.0 (2) | 67.4 (3) | 54.7 (5) | 57.0 (4) | 33.5 (6) | 10.4 (7) | 2.8 (8) |
| 1956 | 47.2 | 74.6 (1) | 44.1 (5) | 72.3 (3) | 74.1 (2) | 53.8 (4) | 32.9 (6) | 11.6 (7) | 3.2 (8) |
| 1957 | 38.6 | 92.7 (1) | 70.1 (2) | 67.1 (3) | 51.3 (5) | 56.0 (4) | 20.9 (6) | 10.3 (7) | 0 (8) |
| 1958 | 34.4 | 90.5 (1) | 74.6 (2) | 31.1 (5) | 63.3 (3) | 42.6 (4) | 18.3 (6) | 12.3 (7) | 0 (8) |
| 1959 | 50.5 | 87.8 (1) | 64.4 (3) | 61.8 (5) | 72.1 (2) | 61.9 (4) | 27.6 (6) | 15.2 (7) | 12.6 (8) |
| 1960 | 40.5 | 77.9 (1) | 67.1 (3) | 72.5 (2) | 52.6 (5) | 60.7 (4) | 17.0 (6) | 9.4 (7) | 8.5 (8) |
| 1961 | 50.1 | 75.9 (2) | 95.8 (1) | 65.0 (4) | 72.1 (3) | 52.5 (5) | 26.7 (7) | 2.7 (8) | 28.9 (6) |
| 1962 | 50.5 | 75.8 (3) | 84.2 (1) | 75.6 (4) | 81.3 (2) | 72.9 (5) | 18.3 (6) | 11.6 (7) | 4.0 (8) |
| 1963 | 56.6 | 85.7 (2) | 55.2 (5) | 89.4 (1) | 73.2 (3) | 69.7 (4) | 26.9 (6) | 19.5 (7) | 11.4 (8) |
| 1964 | 52.8 | 86.3 (3) | 91.4 (2) | 96.1 (1) | 77.8 (5) | 85.2 (4) | 21.2 (7) | 47.9 (6) | 14.1 (8) |
| 1965 | 59.4 | 81.3 (2) | 90.9 (1) | 64.0 (4) | 62.7 (5) | 74.8 (3) | 24.0 (7) | 41.8 (6) | 7.8 (8) |
| 1966 | 48.5 | 58.0 (4) | 97.7 (1) | 84.1 (3) | 85.0 (2) | 57.9 (5) | 15.2 (7) | 17.8 (6) | 2.4 (8) |
| Average | 47.5 | 83.8 | 79.0 | 70.3 | 68.4 | 61.6 | 24.8 | 17.3 | 7.6 |
| Average of annual rankings | | 1.7 | 2.3 | 3.3 | 3.5 | 4.2 | 6.3 | 6.9 | 7.9 |
| Rank according to accounting bias against industry | | 2 | 1 | 3 | 4 | 5 | 7 | 6 | 8 |

Source: Securities and Exchange Commission, Office of Policy Research, Corporate Securities Offered for Cash, 1934–66.

telegraph companies. Because it is a regulated industry, its earnings can be measured well by its statements. If the broadcasting part of the industry could have been separated, it would rank near the top since the value of a broadcasting network depends on its franchise and on the acceptance of its programming by the public. These factors cannot be quantified adequately within the historical accounting framework.

7. Electric, gas, and water.[43] The earnings of utilities are fairly well stated by financial statements because it is a regulated industry. However, it is a growing industry. As a result, the accounting statements undervalue its assets and do not correctly reflect the present value of increased demands. This consideration causes its rank to be above that of railroads.

8. Railroads. As both a declining and regulated industry, railroads are likely to present relatively unbiased traditional financial statements. It is predicted that its private placements are low despite the fact that railroad securities are a conservative and favorite investment of the financial institutions.

Table 7.3 presents the percentages of direct debt placements to total debt securities issued for cash for the industry groups given by the SEC. Comparable data are available only for the years 1953–66. It is clear from the table that the data are consistent with the hypothesis—the degree of accounting bias against the industry is almost consistently associated with use of private placements as opposed to public issues.

## The Impact of the SEC on the Accounting Profession

The SEC has affected the accounting profession in many ways. Among these are widening the scope of audits, development of a clear and operational definition of independence, reinforcement of the conservative bias in accounting, and improvement in accountants' income due to an increased demand for certified statements and the imposition of complex regulations. While the salutary effects of the SEC on accountants' income needs no explication,[44] the first three influences should be discussed.

---

43. Other regulatory agencies have primary jurisdiction over the accounting used by public utilities and railroads. The SEC, however, does control the amount and nature of additional information disclosed in registration statements.

44. Kenneth MacNeal's observation is instructive: "Any qualms the profession may have had about the New Deal prying were soon allayed, and the SEC became God's gift to accounting." "What's Wrong with Accounting?" reprinted in W. T. Baxter, ed., *Studies in Accounting* (Sweet & Maxwell, 1950), p. 214.

## Auditing

With respect to auditing, it is true that the unfavorable publicity that the SEC can bring to bear on individual accounting firms and on the profession have been a powerful weapon in changing some practices. While the landmark cases—*McKesson & Robbins* and *Interstate Hosiery Mills*—were not brought to light by the SEC, the agency did have an important influence on changing auditing practices. The requirement that inventories be physically verified, accounts receivable confirmed, and the improvements in supervision by the accounting firms of their employees that followed both cases probably were due to the SEC's authority.

## Independence

The requirement that public accountants be independent of those audited was imposed by credit and investment bankers, state legislation, and the NYSE before the drafting of the Securities Acts.[45] This is not at all surprising since, as many writers have pointed out, it is in the self-interest of public accountants that they be considered independent: integrity is the public accountant's stock-in-trade. Until January 1964 the AICPA's definition of independence (rule 13) allowed member firms to invest in companies they audit, provided their interest was disclosed and not material, and to serve as directors or officers of the firms audited.

However, the AIPCA's rule was changed to conform to the SEC's rules 2–01(b) and (c) of Regulation S-X, which declares that any relationship between client and accountant evidenced by direct or indirect financial interest or position as promoter, employee, underwriter, trustee, and so on is prima facie evidence of nonindependence. At the present time, the only difference between the AIPCA and SEC rules is that the SEC will not accept statements prepared by a public accountant who did much of the original bookkeeping for his client.

The SEC's definition of independence is an improvement in the appearance of independence, and possibly even in the fact of independence. But this benefit to the image of the profession may have been detrimental to the smaller practitioners. Smaller firms often acquire new clients who are just beginning business, from whom they accept stock in lieu of fees. They also may serve these clients as members of the board or part-time financial officers, or they may supervise bookkeepers or even write up the record themselves. But should these companies decide to go public, the SEC will not accept the statements prepared by the accountant for the previous three years. Data do not exist to determine just how much business small firms have lost

---

45. Rappaport, op. cit., p. 22.2.

as a consequence of the SEC's definition of independence.[46] It is possible that the smaller public accountants can make the necessary arrangements to sell their stock and disassociate themselves (in the formal SEC sense) from their clients. But the extension of the Securities Exchange Act in 1967 to corporations with as few as 500 stockholders probably will not make the existence of smaller CPA firms any easier.

## Accounting Practices and Principles

Most accountants would assert that the SEC has shown admirable restraint, given the powers to prescribe accounting rules granted it by Congress. But as was discussed above (under The Effect of the SEC's Accounting Regulations on Direct Placements), the commission has not restrained itself completely. Rather it insists on historical cost based accounting. I believe that the SEC adopted a conservative bias, because it was created as a consequence of the Great Depression at a time when many people believed that investors were misled during the 1920s by "inflated" accounting statements. Their emphasis on historical cost and disapprovals of appraisals probably was strongly affected by the administrative burden they encountered in dealing with registrations that included appraised asset values.[47] Hence, given their charge by Congress not to allow investors to be misled, they seem to have adopted the administratively easy technique of insisting on the rigid, simple, verifiable historical cost basis of accounting for assets.

This same need for operational efficiency (the hallmark of regulatory agencies generally) pervades the commission's accounting regulations, which in turn have shaped considerably the present state of accounting. The influence of the SEC on accounting and of accounting on the SEC is so intertwined that a much more detailed study than is possible here is required.[48] While it is probable that the SEC eliminated appraisals and goodwill from most balance sheets, it is not clear whether the lack of innovation in financial accounting since the 1920s is due to its influence or to the "natural" conservatism of accountants.

Whether the SEC has followed or led the accounting profession, there is little doubt that it can exercise a very powerful influence.[49] The influence has been, on

---

46. It is interesting to note that the AICPA's rule 13 (now rule 1.01) was not changed until 1964, after several rather tumultuous sessions at the annual membership meetings.

47. A review by MacChesney and O'Brien (Brunson MacChesney and Robert H. O'Brien. "Full Disclosure under the Securities Act," *Law and Contemporary Problems* (1957), pp. 133–53) of many of the early cases reveals the difficulty faced by the SEC in deciding whether an appraisal was accurate.

48. Such a study is being made by Harold E. Singer, who is writing a dissertation titled *A Study of the Extent of the Influence of the Securities and Exchange Commission on the Development of Specific Accounting Principles from 1950–1967* at the University of Washington under the direction of Professors Kenneth B. Berg, Sumner Marcus, and Loyd C. Heath.

49. A recent example is the position taken by the SEC on the investment credit. The refusal of the SEC to back the recommendations of the AICPA Accounting Principles Board effectively destroyed the position of the board.

the whole, an important factor in making accounting more uniform. Few accountants or clients can use or fail to use a procedure once the SEC has rejected or approved it. This influence of the SEC on annual reports recently was extended by Reg. 241.14A-3, which requires that differences between the reports filed with the SEC and those sent to stockholders be reported and reconciled.

One advantage, for CPAs, of the tendency toward uniform accounting is less criticism of the accounting profession (such as that given in a recent article in *Fortune*[50]) for being "unclear" as to which accounting procedures are "correct." This state of affairs probably is beneficial to the larger CPA firms, especially, for it saves them the time and effort of arguing with clients over whether one arbitrary procedure is preferable to another. The other side of this coin is the tendency for innovations in financial accounting methods (such as current dollar accounting, probabilistically stated values, and multibasis statements) to be stifled.

## Conclusions

This study sought to answer several questions related to the impact of the SEC's accounting disclosure requirements. I found that there was little evidence of fraud related to financial statements in the period prior to the enactment of the Securities Acts. Nor was there a widespread lack of disclosure. A considerable number of corporations traded on the NYSE disclosed at least sales, gross profit, and depreciation and almost all reported net income and detailed balance sheets with current assets and current liabilities given. Investors who wanted accounting data had many investment opportunities available. Hence, I conclude that there was little justification for the accounting disclosure required by the acts.

Returning to the present, a statistical association between accounting data reported to the SEC and stock prices indicates that investors probably do not find the data timely. Examinations of the performance of mutual funds reveals that, despite their expenditures on close analysis of accounting reports (and other sources of data), they do not perform better than a randomly selected portfolio of stocks. These findings indicate that the data required by the SEC do not seem to be useful to investors.

Therefore, the finding that the SEC contributed little of positive value to the use of stock markets by corporations, indicated by new stock issues (relative to their needs) before and after the SEC's creation, should not be surprising. However, the restriction by the SEC of information that can be provided by corporations and the SEC's conservatively biased accounting regulations do appear to

---

50. Arthur M. Louis, "The Accountants Are Changing the Rules," *Fortune* (June 1968), p. 177 ff.

have had an important influence on the shift of many corporations away from the public markets to the direct placement of their debt securities.

The impact of the SEC on the accounting profession has been more salutary than their impact on the securities market. Auditing standards, the appearance of the independence of public accountants, and accountants' income all have improved. Whether accounting practices have improved or not is a matter of taste. But it does seem clear that the SEC has extended or at least supported the conservative bias in accounting.

This essay began with the statement that the Securities Acts are disclosure statutes. Or, at least, they were so intended by Congress and President Franklin Roosevelt, who rejected the alternative of "blue sky" legislation, under which a federal commission would pass on the merits of securities.[51] Unfortunately, perhaps because of the administrative problems inherent in regulation, the full disclosure concept has not been applied to financial accounting statements. *Accounting Series Release No. 4* (1938), which has been implemented rigorously, states that:

> where financial statements filed... are prepared in accordance with accounting principles for which there is no substantial authoritative support, such financial statements will be presumed to be misleading or inaccurate *despite disclosures* contained in the certificate of the accountant or in footnotes to the statements provided the matters involved are material. (emphasis added)

Considering the findings reported above, should the SEC continue to insist that it knows better than the public which data are "misleading or inaccurate"? The law now gives investors considerable power to sue accountants if there are errors, intentional or otherwise, in published financial statements. Perhaps the authorities should allow corporations to decide the type and form of information they will publish, so long as they disclose their standard of disclosure to investors.

What role then should the SEC play with respect to accounting? I would hope that it would lead the profession in developing (but not requiring) methods that would make accounting statements relevant to investors. The authority and resources of the SEC could be used to research and demonstrate relatively objective methods of reporting data that reflect economic realities. In this way the SEC might help the public make informed investment decisions.

---

51. Francis M. Wheat, "Truth in Securities Three Decades Later," *Harvard Law Review* (Winter 1967), pp. 100–107.

# 8

# Financial Reporting of Derivatives: An Analysis of the Issues, Evaluation of Proposals, and a Suggested Solution

WITH SHEHZAD L. MIAN

## I. Introduction

Derivatives have recently received considerable attention in the popular press, in Congress, and at the Securities and Exchange Commission (SEC), particularly since the derivative-related losses experienced by firms such as Dell Computers, Procter & Gamble, Gibson Greetings, Mead Corporation, Metallgesellschaft, and Baring Brothers.[1] The impression created by reports of these incidents is that firms are using derivatives speculatively rather than as hedges against risks and that financial reporting requirements have failed to keep pace with the multifold increase in corporate use of derivatives. Congress has expressed concern over the perceived danger posed by derivatives, and the Securities and Exchange Commission is currently investigating this issue as well.

---

The authors benefited from comments and suggestions made by participants in the Goizueta Business School Accounting/Finance Workshop, especially from Greg Waymire and Kumar Sivakumar.

1. Dell Computers' risk management practices were reported to be unorthodox and potentially speculative in nature (*Wall Street Journal*, November 23, 1992). Gibson Greetings reported a loss of $3 million (first quarter, 1994) on interest rate derivatives (*Wall Street Journal*, April 21, 1994). Mead Corporation reported a loss of $7.4 million (first quarter, 1994) on interest rate swaps (*Wall Street Journal*, April 21, 1994). Procter & Gamble reported a loss of $157 million on interest rate derivatives (*Wall Street Journal*, April 13, 1994). Metallgesellschaft's losses are estimated to be in excess of $1.3 billion (Edwards and Canter, 1995, note 1).

These events have placed increased pressure on the Financial Accounting Standards Board (FASB) to reconsider its present financial reporting requirements for derivatives. The current debate has focused on two related issues: (1) the accounting adequacy of current derivatives-related financial statement reporting (about which much has been written), and (2) the economic consequences of reporting requirements for derivatives (about which little actually is known).

Prior to the well-publicized losses mentioned above, the FASB had addressed the issue of derivatives disclosure in several Statements of Financial Accounting Standards (SFAS), beginning with SFAS 52 (effective 1983), which deals with foreign currency, through SFAS 119 (effective for fiscal years ending December 1994), which specifies rules for disclosing the fair value of and other information on derivatives. These statements were adopted to deal with specific problems as they occurred. The ad hoc nature of their adoption has resulted in reporting requirements that are incomplete and inconsistent. The various SFASs permit firms to defer gains and losses on some, but not on all, derivatives and in some, but not all, economically similar circumstances. FASB Staff Project Manager Jane Adams reports that, after "three years of deliberation and the consideration of a variety of alternatives, the FASB tentatively adopted an approach that would alter current accounting for derivative instruments" (Adams, 1995a, p. 1). The FASB approach would simplify accounting for derivatives by requiring realized gains and losses on derivatives held as hedges (as well as those for which the firm acts as an investor, dealer, or trader) to be recorded as income or expense, and unrealized changes in the market values of derivatives classified as "other than trading" to be shown as changes to equity on the firms' balance sheets. Alternatively, the FASB might require firms to mark all financial assets and liabilities to market (or fair) values. If adopted, either of these procedures would substantially change currently acceptable practices.

The FASB's current mandated reporting requirements allow firms to defer income statement recognition of some derivative gains and losses. These "hedge accounting" rules have been criticized, because they allow firms with similar economic characteristics to look different on their financial statements and firms with different economic characteristics to look similar. For example, consider three firms, Hegaccount, Hegreport, and Noheg, that are identical except with respect to their use of derivatives. Hegaccount hedges and receives hedge accounting treatment for its derivative gains and losses. Hegreport must report derivatives gains and losses, as they occur, on its income statement, because it hedges with instruments that do not qualify for hedge accounting. Noheg does not hedge its risks. Hegaccount and Hegreport are similar in that they both hedge, yet their financial statements make them appear different. On the other hand, Hegaccount and Noheg are different (hedger versus nonhedger), yet their financial statements make them appear similar, since neither one reports derivative gains and losses on their respective income statements.

These accounting anomalies would be of interest primarily to accountants, if it were not for the possibility that the current hedge accounting rules have real economic consequences for individual firms. In particular, the restrictive nature of current hedge accounting rules as they apply to currency derivatives are said to severely limit firms' ability to engage in cost-effective hedging of their exposures.[2] A recent Wharton/Chase survey of 183 firms reports that required accounting is the issue which most concerns them with respect to their use of derivatives.[3] The FASB's proposed solution to this situation was opposed by Moody's Investors' Services on the grounds that firms would forgo risk-reducing hedging rather than report current gains and losses on derivatives, and by several major public accounting firms, among others.[4] Contrary to expectations, the FASB did not adopt the proposal and is reconsidering the issue, including the possibility of requiring firms to mark all financial assets and liabilities to market.

To provide evidence on whether the present accounting rules for derivatives affect firms' behavior, we report the findings of a survey conducted by Chase/Wharton of firms' reasons for not using derivatives and present our analysis of the financial reporting by 440 currency-price hedgers in their 1992 financial statements. In particular, we examine the types of derivatives used and the nature of exposures hedged. Our analysis indicates that many firms either are not hedging their currency risks effectively or that they are violating the accounting rules, perhaps by mislabeling or hiding the derivatives used. In either event, the current accounting rules appear to be dysfunctional.

We next review and find wanting the FASB's approaches to the problem of financial accounting for derivatives. Our proposed solution to the derivatives accounting problem is based on our understanding of the essential functions of accounting. We review these functions briefly and point out that traditional accounting has already developed generalized rules to deal with situations such as those posed by derivatives. Consistent with these general rules, we propose that accountants use their professional judgment in matching income and expenses, as was the practice before attempts (such as those made by the FASB and other authoritative bodies) to promulgate specific rules to cover all or most situations. Our suggested alternative accounting procedure is consistent with traditional

---

2. In late 1994, RJR Nabisco announced that it was discontinuing its use of derivatives that are now or may be required to be marked to market. At about the same time, Kodak announced that it had unwound derivatives with total notional value of $6 billion. According to Kodak's treasurer: "We don't want to get into a situation where we have volatility in earnings because of derivatives." Kodak's decision to unwind its derivatives portfolio was accompanied by a deleveraging of its balance sheet (*Derivatives Week*, October 10, 1994).

3. Other concerns of lesser importance were credit risk, liquidity risk, transaction costs, lack of knowledge about derivatives within the firm, and difficulty in understanding the firm's exposures (Wharton/Chase, 1995).

4. *Wall Street Journal*, March 15, 1995.

accounting and also does not constrain firms from using derivatives effectively and from reporting adequately.

The balance of the paper is organized as follows. In section II we outline current financial-statement reporting requirements for derivatives and point out their inconsistencies. In section III we examine firms' financial reporting of foreign currency derivatives, which provides evidence that the accounting rules are likely to have been dysfunctional. In section IV we outline the FASB's proposed solutions and their shortcomings. In section V, as a prelude to our suggested solution, we delineate the basic functions of accounting and the general rules that have been devised to deal with difficult situations, such as derivatives accounting. Our proposal is given in section VI. Section VII summarizes the paper.

## II. Mandated Disclosure and Hedge Accounting Issues

Table 8.1 describes the key features of the FASB's and the American Institute of Certified Public Accountants' (AICPA) statements, pronouncements, and advisories. These reporting requirements have been criticized on four grounds. First, they are internally inconsistent. SFAS 52 (adopted in 1981, effective in 1983) mandates specific rules for the financial reporting of hedging activities relating to currency-price risk. It allows hedge accounting for firm commitments, but not for anticipated or forecasted transactions. However, SFAS 80 (issued in 1984) allows hedge accounting for probable transactions, but it applies only to interest rate and commodity-price hedging, while SFAS 52 applies only to foreign exchange activities. SFAS 52 and SFAS 80 also differ in terms of their risk assessment method. SFAS 52 employs a transaction-level approach, which can lead to inconsistent results as compared to SFAS 80, which uses an enterprise-wide approach. Thus, the application of hedge accounting rules is ambiguous and inconsistent.

Second, the hedge accounting requirements are not uniform across various types of derivatives. For example, neither SFAS 52 nor SFAS 80 specify how to account for options. The AICPA's Issue Paper 86-2 offers nonauthoritative accounting guidance for recording options and the FASB's Emerging Issues Task Force (EITF) has addressed specific issues that fall within the gaps of their two pronouncements. However, as noted earlier, the accounting treatment specified in these various statements often is inconsistent. The EITF allows hedge accounting for simple purchased options that hedge anticipated foreign currency transactions. However, with regard to forwards and futures as hedges of anticipated transactions, the FASB does not allow the use of hedge accounting.

Third, accounting for derivatives is further complicated by the fact that derivatives can be either bought (or sold) directly from a market participant or synthetically created. Furthermore, derivatives can be hidden if they are embedded in

TABLE 8.1 Hedge Accounting Criteria as Described in FASB Statements and AICPA Papers[a]

| | SFAS 52[b] | SFAS 80[c] | EITF 90–17[d] | EITF 91–1[e] | EITF 91–4[f] | AICPA Paper 86–2[g] |
|---|---|---|---|---|---|---|
| Exposure covered | Foreign currency | Interest rates & commodities | Purchased currency options | Intercompany foreign currency | Foreign currency | Foreign currency |
| Instruments covered | Forwards, swaps futures and forward-type | Futures | Purchased currency options (out-of-the-money) | Forwards purchased options | Option combinations (complex options) | All options |
| **Hedge accounting criteria** | | | | | | |
| Designate as a hedge | Yes | Yes | Yes | Yes | Yes | Yes |
| Risk assessment basis | Transaction | Enterprise | Enterprise | Enterprise | Enterprise | Transaction |
| Correlation | Not explicit | High | High | High | High | High |
| Ongoing assessment | Not explicit | Yes | Yes | Yes | Yes | Yes |
| Allow anticipated transaction | No | Yes[h] | Yes[i] | Yes[i] | No consensus[j] | Yes |
| Allow cross hedges | Usually not | Yes | Yes | Yes | No consensus[j] | Yes |
| Accounting if hedge criteria not met | Formula value | Market | Market | Market | Market | Market |

[a] Data source: Information on SFAS 52, SFAS 80, and AICPA paper 86–2 is from "The Challenges of Hedge Accounting," *Journal of Accountancy*, November 1989. Information on FASB EITF issued consensus statements EITF 90–17, EITF 90–1, and EITF 91–4 is from EITF updates in *Journal of Accountancy*, February 1992 and July 1992.
[b] SFAS 52 is Statement of Financial Accounting Standard 52 *Foreign Currency Translation*.
[c] SFAS 80 is *Accounting for Futures Contracts*.
[d] EITF 90–17 is *Hedging Foreign Currency Risks with Purchased Options*.
[e] EITF 91–1 is *Hedging Inter-company Foreign Currency Risks*.
[f] EITF 91–4 is *Hedging Foreign Currency Risks with Complex Options and Similar Transactions*.
[g] AICPA issues paper AICPA 86–2, *Accounting for Options*.
[h] Expected terms are identified and it is probable transaction will occur.
[i] Linked third-party commitments or firm commitments.
[j] Footnote disclosure required. SFAS 52 applies to most complex options.

other financial instruments. For example, a firm can buy a put option on United Kingdom pounds (UKP) to hedge its UKP receivables. Alternatively, the firm can embed this put option in another U.S. dollar–denominated financial instrument. This financial instrument would be denominated in U.S. dollars, with interest payments in U.S. dollars as well, with the level of interest payments linked to the UKP/U.S. dollar exchange rate. In effect, the firm can create the same set of cash flows offered through the use of derivatives. But since the derivative is "hidden" (embedded), the firm bypasses the current derivatives-related reporting requirements. Thus, the current rules result in inconsistent reporting of "natural" and direct derivatives in comparison with the financial reporting of synthetic and embedded derivatives, even though the risks and costs of both may be the same.

Fourth, hedge accounting is not consistent with several important accounting practices. Income and expense that result from the same or a related transaction are not reported in the same reporting period when hedge accounting is not permitted. When hedge accounting is used, the inclusion of realized gains and losses in balance sheet equity but not in the income statement is inconsistent with the "all-inclusive income" concept, which holds that all changes in equity other than changes in capital (e.g., dividends and stock issues) should flow through the income statement.

## III. Evidence on Financial Reporting of Currency Derivatives

### Survey of Firms

Some evidence on the effect of accounting on a firm's willingness to use derivatives to hedge risks may be gleaned from a survey of 183 firms conducted by Wharton for and in conjunction with the Chase Manhattan Bank in February 1995 (Wharton/Chase, 1995).[5] The firms were asked: "What concerns you about using derivatives?" Responses were requested for six concerns. Table 8.2 shows the percentages of firms that indicated varying degrees of concern (Wharton/Chase, 1995, p. 3). The respondents that used derivatives gave "accounting treatment" as their most important concern, with 26 percent indicating high and 38 percent moderate concern.

The survey respondents' concerns about accounting might result in these firms deciding to forgo using derivatives to hedge risks (e.g., RJR Nabisco and Kodak[6]), or to use less efficient and more costly derivatives when these allowed the firms to

---

5. The survey was sent to 2,000 firms, randomly selected from Compustat. Of the 530 firms that responded, 183 use derivatives. Given the low response rate (27 percent) and the possibility of nonresponse bias, the results should be viewed with caution.
6. See note 2.

TABLE 8.2 Concern Expressed by 183 Firms That Used Derivatives in Wharton/Chase Survey

| Issue | Level of Concern[a] | | | | |
|---|---|---|---|---|---|
| | High + Moderate | High | Moderate | Low | No |
| Accounting treatment | 64% | 26% | 38% | 25% | 11% |
| Credit risk | 52% | 18% | 34% | 34% | 13% |
| Liquidity risk | 50% | 14% | 36% | 38% | 11% |
| Transactions cost | 45% | 13% | 32% | 49% | 5% |
| Lack of knowledge about derivatives within my firm | 43% | 10% | 33% | 39% | 17% |
| Firm's exposures | 32% | 7% | 25% | 42% | 25% |

*Source*: "A Survey of Derivative Use by Non-Financial Corporations in the U.S." (1995, p. 3). Sponsored by the Weiss Center for International Financial Research of the Wharton School, University of Pennsylvania and The Chase Manhattan Bank.
[a] Some percentages do not sum to 100 because of rounding.

use accounting methods they preferred. The expressed concern about accounting also might be responsible for many firms using derivatives in ways that do not have to be reported. Or, firms that use or want to use derivatives to increase risk in ways that are contrary to the interests of their shareholders, creditors, or other stakeholders may be concerned that the accounting rules do not allow them to hide their actions. Thus, the present accounting rules could have a significant effect on firms' behavior and, hence, on shareholders' returns and risk. However, given the biases inherent in the survey and the difficulty of interpreting its findings, the results should be viewed only as indicating that accounting rules do affect a firm's behavior toward using derivative instruments.

## Study of Annual Reports

We examine the possibility that accounting problems affected a firm's behavior with respect to foreign currency transactions, as this is the major area in which a firm's preferred solutions may conflict with accounting requirements. In particular, firms that hedge anticipated exposures with forwards must classify these contracts as speculation, and hence report gains and losses (realized or not) currently as income and expense.

We obtained information provided in financial statement footnotes to examine two aspects of currency-price hedging: (1) how currency-price hedgers report their use of financial instruments on the financial statements, and (2) the types of instruments they use to hedge their currency exposures. Our analysis also provides insight into the relative frequency with which firms hedge anticipated exposures and the types of instruments they use in exposure management. We employ these data to examine the interaction between the hedge accounting rules and the hedging decision.

We use data from Compustat and the NAARS file available on the LexisNexis database. Financial entities (SIC codes 60 to 69) are excluded, because they are both users and providers of risk management products. Of the remaining 3,022 firms, 440 (15 percent) are classified as currency-price hedgers if they explicitly state that they manage currency-price risk and/or state that they use currency derivatives such as forwards, futures, swaps, or options. The balance of 2,582 (85 percent) are classified as nonhedgers. Table 8.3 reports the distribution by industry of currency-price hedgers and nonhedgers for the sample firms. Currency-price hedging appears to vary both across and within industries.

For each of the 440 currency-price hedgers, we examined the footnote disclosures and obtained three pieces of information: (1) whether they hedge firm commitments, net investments, or anticipated exposures; (2) whether they currently recognize gains or losses in income; and (3) the type of derivative used. Most firms did not give all three pieces of information in a fashion that allowed us to match each type of derivative with the type of exposure hedged or to determine whether gains or losses were recognized currently as income or expense. For example, some

TABLE 8.3 Cross-Tabulation of Hedging Policy by Industrial Classification for 3,022 Firms

| Industry | SIC | Currency-Price Risk Nonhedgers | Hedgers | Total Number of Firms |
|---|---|---|---|---|
| Agriculture & forestry | 1–8 | 9 | 4 | 13 |
| Mining | 10–14 | 168 | 17 | 185 |
| Construction | 15–19 | 32 | 4 | 36 |
| Food & tobacco | 20–21 | 59 | 20 | 79 |
| Textiles & apparel | 22–23 | 62 | 6 | 68 |
| Lumber & furniture | 24–25 | 41 | 3 | 44 |
| Paper & printing | 26–27 | 91 | 18 | 109 |
| Chemicals | 28 | 163 | 61 | 224 |
| Petroleum, rubber, & plastics | 29–30 | 55 | 24 | 79 |
| Leather, stone, clay, concrete, & glass | 31–32 | 35 | 5 | 40 |
| Primary & fabricated metals | 33–34 | 120 | 19 | 139 |
| Machinery & electrical machinery | 35–36 | 386 | 116 | 502 |
| Transportation equipment | 37 | 68 | 23 | 91 |
| Measurement instruments & miscellaneous machinery | 38–39 | 191 | 49 | 240 |
| Transportation and utilities | 40–49 | 344 | 28 | 372 |
| Wholesale trade | 50–52 | 159 | 9 | 168 |
| Retail trade | 53–59 | 232 | 7 | 239 |
| Hotels | 70 | 6 | 1 | 7 |
| Services | 72–89 | 361 | 26 | 387 |
| Total | 1–89 | 2,582 | 440 | 3,022 |

Data on hedging are obtained from 1992 annual reports. Currency-price hedgers are firms which state that they hedge currency-price risk and/or firms which mention use of currency derivatives such as options, swaps, forwards, futures, caps, collars, or floors.

firms stated that they hedged firm commitments and anticipated exposures, and that they used currency forwards and futures. However, these firms did not state which instrument was used to manage which type of exposure (anticipated or firm commitment). Nevertheless, we can draw inferences based on SFAS 52. If a firm states that it hedges anticipated exposures and defers gains and losses, we can conclude that the derivative could not have been a currency forward or futures contract, as these do not qualify for hedge accounting.

The evidence, as shown in table 8.4, indicates that, out of the 440 currency hedgers in the sample, only 51 firms (12 percent) reported some gains and losses in current income. Of these, 10 firms (2 percent) gave "anticipated exposures" as the reason for not using hedge accounting. However, an additional 20 firms (5 percent) both hedged anticipated transactions and deferred gains and losses.

In all, hedge accounting was used, in whole or in part, by 323 firms (73 percent of the 440). Forty-seven of these firms (11 percent) used hedge accounting for their net investments in foreign subsidiaries. The justification given by 4 firms (1 percent of the total) is "probable transactions," and 112 firms (25 percent) specified "firm commitments." The largest number of firms, 243 (55 percent), said they used hedge accounting because the financial instruments qualified as hedges for financial reporting purposes.

To provide an alternative analysis on the relative importance of anticipated exposures versus firm commitments, we examined descriptions of the instrument used to hedge currency risk. Out of 440 firms, 37 firms (8 percent) used forwards, 281 (64 percent) used futures, and 74 (17 percent) used swaps. Overall (considering that some firms use multiple financial instruments), 337 firms (77 percent) reported use of forwards, futures, and/or swaps. Since hedge accounting treatment is allowed for these instruments under SFAS 52 only for firm commitments, and considering that the data presented in table 8.4 indicate that only 30 firms reported that they hedged anticipated transactions, it appears that firms use forwards, futures, and/or swaps predominantly to hedge firm commitments.

Next, we investigated financial reporting of currency options. Firms that want to use hedge accounting have incentives to use options over forwards and futures, particularly with respect to anticipated exposures. However, hedge accounting rules limit the substitutability of options for forwards or futures. First, only purchased options which are out-of-the-money get hedge accounting treatment for anticipated transactions. Second, the Securities and Exchange Commission's chief accountant sent a letter to the FASB in March 1992 disallowing hedge accounting treatment for certain complex option strategies, such as those which essentially created synthetic forwards. In our sample of 440 currency-price hedgers, 92 (21 percent) use currency options. However, only 10 firms which report use of options also report that they hedge anticipated exposures. Based on the relative infrequency with which options appear to have been used for hedging anticipated exposures, we conclude that the flexibility associated with financial reporting of options appears to be limited.

TABLE 8.4 Frequency Distribution of Disclosures Made by 440 Currency Hedgers as Reported in 1992 Financial Statements by Instruments Used to Hedge Currency-Price Risk and by Hedge Accounting versus Income Recognition (entries are number of firms using a specific financial instrument versus frequency of firms with a specific reporting method).[a]

| Reasons Given for Financial Reporting of Hedging Transactions | Type of Financial Instrument Used ||||| Number of Currency-Hedgers with Financial Instrument Specified[b] | Number of Currency-Hedgers with Financial Instrument *not* Specified[b] | All Currency Hedgers[b] |
|---|---|---|---|---|---|---|---|---|
| | Forwards | Futures | Swaps | Options | | | | |
| A. Gains and losses included in income (no hedge accounting) | | | | | | | | |
| Anticipated exposures | 0 | 7 | 2 | 5 | | 10 | 0 | 10 |
| Gains and losses recognized in income | 8 | 28 | 5 | 17 | | 33 | 8 | 41 |
| Total included in income[b] | 8 | 35 | 7 | 22 | | 43 | 8 | 51 |
| B. Gains and losses deferred (hedge accounting) | | | | | | | | |
| Anticipated exposures | 4 | 15 | 1 | 10 | | 18 | 2 | 20 |
| Net investments in foreign subsidiaries | 2 | 35 | 15 | 10 | | 38 | 9 | 47 |
| Probable transactions | 0 | 3 | 0 | 4 | | 4 | 0 | 4 |
| Firm commitments | 8 | 90 | 11 | 26 | | 101 | 11 | 112 |
| Financial instruments qualify as hedges | 18 | 169 | 27 | 56 | | 180 | 63 | 243 |
| Total deferred[b] | 25 | 222 | 39 | 71 | | 244 | 79 | 323 |
| Total included in income + Total deferred (A + B)[c] | 27 | 233 | 39 | 77 | | 258 | 82 | 340 |
| C. Not classified above[b,d] | 10 | 48 | 35 | 15 | | 88 | 12 | 100 |
| D. Currency hedgers reporting use of financial instrument (A + B + C)[b] | 37 | 281 | 74 | 92 | | 346 | 94 | 440 |

[a] For example, eight firms reported use of forwards and also reported that gains and losses were recognized in income. However, the gains and losses were not necessarily due to forwards.
[b] Column (row) totals will not add up to sum of entries in the column (row) if firms have multiple references.
[c] Column totals for A + B will not add up to sum of A and B if firms have multiple references.
[d] Insufficient information to determine whether gains and losses were included in income or deferred.

We draw the following conclusions from the evidence on currency-price hedging. First, it suggests that derivatives have been used predominantly to hedge firm commitments. Second, use (or reporting) of derivatives to hedge anticipated exposures is relatively infrequent. Finally, we find infrequent use of options to hedge anticipated exposures despite the greater possibilities for deferring gains and losses (with hedge accounting) for options as compared to forwards and futures. Obviously, our evidence does not rule out the explanation that firms do engage in hedging anticipated exposures but simply misrepresent the facts to the auditors, or that the firms have chosen to imbed the derivatives in other financial contracts that do not have to be marked to market.

## IV. The FASB's Proposed Solutions

The FASB has considered three approaches to dealing with accounting for derivatives: (1) footnote disclosure of the range of probable values for derivative instruments; (2) mark hedge instruments to current values and largely eliminate hedge accounting; and (3) mark the hedged assets and liabilities (and possibly others) as well as the hedge instruments to market, with gains and losses included in the income statement. The first two possibilities were "shot down"; the third is (at the moment) under consideration.

### Footnote or Other Supplementary Disclosure of "Fair Values"

The FASB issued SFAS 119, "Disclosure about Derivative Financial Instruments and Fair Value of Financial Instruments," in October 1994 (effective for financial statements issued after December 15, 1994).[7] The FASB felt that the nature of required disclosures should depend on an entity's purpose for holding or issuing derivatives. For derivatives held or issued for trading purposes, SFAS 119 requires firms to disclose fair values of those derivatives either in the body of the financial statements or in the footnotes. For these derivatives, firms also have to report information on the net trading revenues, disaggregated by class, business activity, risk, and so on.

For derivatives held or issued for purposes other than trading, entities have to describe their objectives and strategy with respect to the use of derivative instruments and indicate how each class of derivative is reported on the financial

---

7. Fair value includes market values but also refers to estimates of the amounts at which assets could be exchanged or liabilities settled by knowledgeable parties in an arm's-length transaction. It can be approximated by calculations of the present value of expected net cash flows. However, for a restructured loan, SFAS 114 prescribes discounting the promised cash flows by the *original* loan interest rate rather than the current rate charged for similar loans.

statements, including information on policies for recognizing and measuring the derivative financial instruments. For derivatives designated as hedges of anticipated transactions, entities have to provide information on the amount and timing with respect to the anticipated transaction, the amount of hedging gains and losses explicitly deferred (when this is permitted), and a description of events that result in recognition of gains or losses.[8]

The required disclosures, though, do not solve the problems of accounting for derivatives described here. Hence, the FASB's staff generated two proposals, which we now outline and analyze.

## Largely Eliminate Hedge Accounting

Following three years of deliberations, the FASB announced in November 1994 that it had tentatively adopted an approach to revise the current financial reporting requirements for derivatives. Then, in June 1995, the board decided that there was insufficient support for the approach to adopt it. However, it has not been dismissed and may be accepted after "further study."

The proposal is essentially a three-step approach. As a first step, all free-standing derivatives (forwards, futures, options, and swaps) will be recognized either as assets or liabilities and will be reported on the balance sheet at their "fair values."[9] Second, all derivatives will be classified into one of two categories: derivatives held for trading purposes, and others. The third step deals with the rules for reporting gains and losses on derivatives. If the derivative is held for trading purposes, gains (and losses) are recognized as income (and expenses) for the period in which they occur. If the derivative is held for reasons other than trading, *unrealized* gains (and losses) bypass the income statement and are reported as changes in equity, and realized gains (and losses) are recognized in the income statement.

This FASB proposal offers several advantages. As outlined by Project Director Adams (1995b), these include enhanced visibility, simplicity, comparable accounting

---

8. The International Accounting Standards Committee adopted a similar statement (IAS 32) in June 1995 (operative for financial statement periods beginning on or after January 1, 1996). This statement requires disclosure of the fair values of all financial assets and liabilities, including derivatives. In addition, a large amount of detailed information must be given about the extent to which the financial instruments are subject to price risk, credit risk, liquidity risk, and cash flow risk. This information includes data on contractual repricing dates, effective interest rates, the extent to which the instruments might be affected by each kind of risk, and concentration of risks. IAS 32 does not require or forbid inclusion of fair values and unrealized changes in these values in a firm's balance sheets and income statements. (A partial exception is when book values of assets exceed fair values; in this event, the reasons for not reducing the book values must be disclosed in the financial statements.) Nor does the statement specify how changes in the values of hedges should be accounted for, except to state that the transactions hedged and the hedges should be described, with (¶ 91) "the amount of any deferred or unrecognized gain or loss and the expected timing of recognition as income or expense" disclosed.

9. Non-freestanding derivative products, such as structured notes, are beyond the scope of the proposal.

with respect to balance sheets, and the same treatment as cash instruments. She also gives as limitations different income statement results, recognition of some related gains (losses) in different periods, a meaningless (from the economic viewpoint) distinction between realized and unrealized gains and losses, and greater equity volatility. She (and some members of the FASB) believes that the advantages outweigh the limitations.

However, the evidence presented in section III, which finds that relatively few firms report hedging forecasted (or anticipated) transactions, implies that the proposed rules are likely to impose additional costs on firms for which such hedges are economically desirable. Since firms with more growth opportunities relative to assets in place are more likely to have unrecorded exposures, the impact of the proposed current-period reporting of gains and losses from hedges, with the losses and gains on the hedged situations deferred, will be greater as growth opportunities become relatively more important. In addition, Mian (1995) provides evidence that firms with more growth opportunities are ones which are more likely to consider hedging as a method of controlling contracting costs.[10] Hence, this FASB proposal is likely to further restrict the hedging of forecasted transactions, as these mandated changes will impose higher costs on firms for whom the option to hedge is likely to be more valuable. In addition, it will give firms greater incentives to imbed (and, hence, not disclose) derivatives in assets and liabilities that do not have to be marked to market.

Furthermore, this FASB proposal does not address the important problems of measurement of market values of embedded derivatives. Market prices are not available for many derivatives. Users have to approximate market values using pricing models, which often are proprietary. In addition, the fair values calculated with the models often are sensitive to specific required assumptions. Consequently, although the FASB's proposal may seem to offer visibility, simplicity, and comparability, such is not the case for many derivatives.

A further complication is the fact that derivatives can be embedded in other financial instruments (for example, structured notes). If mandated disclosures do not include these "hidden" derivatives as well, they will provide firms with incentives to substitute away from direct use of derivatives and toward financial instruments with imbedded derivatives.[11]

---

10. In the classic descriptions of stockholder–bondholder conflict described by Jensen and Meckling (1976), bondholders forecast the set of possible actions stockholders can undertake once bonds have been issued. Hence, bondholders have incentives to discount the expected value of such discretionary actions in the price of the bond at the time of issuance. Stockholders can reduce this discounting with covenants that restrict managerial discretion and by using convertible or secured debt instead of straight debt. Since hedging limits the extent to which managerial action can reduce the value of the bondholders' claims, bondholders should pay a higher price for bonds issued by hedgers as compared to bonds issued by nonhedgers, ceteris paribus.

11. For example, Walt Disney Co. issued medium-term notes with embedded currency options in response to an SEC decision to tighten hedge accounting rules with respect to currency options (*Investment Dealers' Digest*, September 14, 1992).

Perhaps most important, this FASB proposal constrains firms from reporting in a single period the economic effect for which they purchased derivatives—offsetting gains and losses from transactions (e.g., assets, liabilities, and contracts) with losses and gains from derivatives. Accounting reporting requirements based on realization of gains and losses can alter a firm's incentives to use exchange-traded versus over-the-counter (OTC) products. For example, exchange-traded products, such as futures contracts, have daily settlement, while OTC products, such as forward contracts, are not settled daily. Consequently, firms will have incentives to use derivatives for which gains and losses are not realized daily, thus avoiding the obligation of reporting these gains and losses prior to the expiration of the derivative contract.

For the above reasons, we believe that the FASB's proposal, if adopted, would do more harm than good. While it might simplify the tasks facing accountants, it is likely to constrain firms from using derivatives effectively. Furthermore, it will not even yield financial reports that are more informative to managers and investors.

## Mark All Financial Assets and Liabilities to Market

A third alternative considered by the FASB is having all financial assets and liabilities recorded at fair (e.g., market) values at the end of accounting periods.[12] If adopted, the "mark all financial obligations to market" solution would be a radical change in financial accounting as we now know it; it would go well beyond dealing with the problem of accounting for derivatives.

One version (of two) would follow the three-stage procedure described in the previous subsection, with realized gains and losses recorded only in the income statement, and unrealized gains and losses recorded only in the equity section of the balance sheet. As a result, the income statement and balance sheet will not agree. As noted, firms will still be able to manipulate their income statements by purchasing hedges on which realization can be delayed. Consequently, otherwise identical firms that do and do not hedge could appear to be similar with respect to their income statements.

The second version would have all gains and losses, realized or not, recorded in the income statement, which would answer the objections just discussed. However, it would put even greater burdens on firms and their external accountants to value derivatives that are not regularly traded.

We believe that both versions of the alternative suffer from three important problems. First, because revaluation to fair values are limited to financial assets, this proposal would not solve aspects of derivatives accounting that affect firms' behavior. As discussed earlier, firms still could not report gains and losses from

---

12. We understand that the International Accounting Standards Committee and the U.K. Accounting Standards Committee also are looking (with favor) on this procedure.

anticipated transactions in the same reporting period. Second, derivatives embedded in nonfinancial assets and liabilities would not be revalued. Again, this would result in reporting mismatching.

Third, the costs of obtaining fair values and having external accountants attest to the accuracy of these numbers is likely to exceed the benefits from this reporting. In our opinion, this problem is so severe as to render this alternative nonoperative. Our belief is founded on accountants' experience with two earlier experiments in fair value accounting. One is the SEC's order given in Accounting Series Release (ASR) 190 that firms report the replacement value of their assets.[13] Several empirical studies found no measurable stock market reaction to the release of the data, indicating either that investors had already impounded the information content of the disclosures into share prices or they believed, at the margin, that these data did not provide useful information.[14] The second is the order by the SEC that oil and gas producers use present values to account for their reserves rather than "successful efforts costing" (which was adopted by the FASB in SFAS 19) or "full costing" (which opponents of successful efforts accounting wanted to use).[15] Neither method reflects the market value of the oil that is found. Hence, the SEC required oil and gas producers to calculate the present values of expected cash flows from their reserves. After two years, this procedure was abandoned because it was too costly and imprecise. We believe that this will be the fate of the proposal to estimate the fair values of all financial assets and liabilities.

Therefore, we turn next to our proposal, which is based on an appreciation of the basic functions of accounting and the general rules that accountants have adopted to deal with difficult situations, such as that posed by derivatives.

## V. The Basic Functions and Rules of Accounting

### Control and Valuation

Financial accounting generally serves two functions. One is control, a means by which owners and creditors obtain information that allows them to determine how the resources of the firm in which they have invested have been and are being

---

13. ASR 190 was released by U.S. Securities and Exchange Commission in March 1976.
14. See Beaver, Christie, and Griffin (1980), Gheyara and Boatsman (1980), Ro (1980), and Lustgarten (1982).
15. Under "successful efforts accounting," oil and gas producers report as assets only the costs of drilling and equipping wells that are commercially viable. The cost of unsuccessful wells is charged against income as expenses. Under "full costing," the cost of all wells drilled is shown as an asset. See Collins, Rozeff, and Salatka (1982) and Deakin (1985) for descriptions of the changes in accounting regulations.

employed. Accounting reports and the numbers included therein can help managers, active owners, and boards of directors determine how well various aspects of the firm's activities have been carried out and whether the resources entrusted to employees and managers have not been misappropriated. In part for this reason, events are accounted for when they give rise to market transactions that result in the exchange of resources or claims over resources. These changes in values are considered to have been *realized*. Accounting for these exchanges is necessary so that managers and owners may determine who has responsibility for the firm's resources. This is an important reason for accountants' distinction between events that are "realized," which affect the financial accounting numbers, and those that are "unrealized," which, with some exceptions (e.g., depreciation and "permanent" decreases in value), are not directly included in the financial accounting reports.

For the purpose of control, the original cost of assets and the amount of liabilities at the time they were accepted, adjusted over time with prestructured rules (e.g., depreciation), can be useful. Indeed, the use of historical-cost accounting data and specified rules for changing these numbers offers the advantage of numbers that cannot be manipulated readily and that can be audited objectively. Furthermore, events that have not yet given rise to an exchange of assets or claims to assets, such as contracts for or expectations of sales or purchases, are not recognized as accounting events, in large measure because usually they do not cause control problems.

The second function is valuation. The market transactions that give rise to accounting entries also provide objective information about the value of the assets and liabilities exchanged. However, as market parameters change, these values often change. Decisions by managers and directors should be based on current numbers that reflect the opportunity costs of assets and liabilities. Historical costs are sunk costs; except for tax computations, control, and as proxies for economic market values, historical costs are irrelevant. For example, the amount a firm paid for a security several months ago does not tell the managers its current value (how much the firm currently has invested in it) and what the gain or loss to the firm has been from holding the security. Nor does much of the historical cost–based data reported in financial statements provide useful information about the current values of firms. Unfortunately, the more useful market values of assets and liabilities often are unreliable and costly to obtain and audit. Furthermore, by the time the financial statements are published, many of these numbers no longer reflect current values well.

Indeed, financial reporting has not been (and probably cannot be) designed to measure all aspects of control and valuation. Accounting necessarily is ex post. For example, an employee could obligate the firm to assume a liability for a derivative trade before the action is reported to her manager or shows up in a financial report. Furthermore, the costs of close control may exceed the benefits. Nevertheless, the fact that an employee or manager knows that the consequences of her actions will be reported to supervisors or directors generally serves as an effective means of limiting unauthorized acts.

Valuation of assets and liabilities at economic market values is similarly limited by the costs of the process. Values-in-exchange often cannot be obtained for assets that are not regularly traded. Measurement of values-in-use is complicated by the difficulty of estimating expected cash flows and the appropriate discount rate. For many assets, such as plant and equipment, the cost of obtaining numbers that can meet reasonable verification standards exceeds the value of the numbers to managers and investors. Furthermore, CPAs are not willing to attest to numbers that they cannot readily replicate and verify, numbers that the accountants could justify should they be criticized or sued. Consequently, accounting reports do not even give estimates of the market values of many assets and liabilities, and assets tend to be understated.[16]

## Income and Expense Recognition: The Critical Event and Matching

If assets and liabilities could be valued at their value in use at the end of an accounting period, net income for that period could be easily determined. It would simply be the change in the equity, adjusted for additional investments and distributions. However, as just noted, it is costly to determine these values, and the numbers often are not verifiable. Hence, reasonably effective general accounting rules have been developed for providing a useful estimate of periodic net income. (Other rules that result in distortions of this estimate—conservatism and realization—are discussed shortly.)

Accounting reports of income and expense are brought into rough conformity with economic reality by accruals and the matching concept. Accruals adjust the numbers resulting from transactions to estimates of the values of assets and liabilities as of the date of the financial report. Most accruals recognize changes in claims over the firm's resources. For example, wages owed to employees at the end of an accounting period are recorded as liabilities and the amount of the wages is recorded as an expense of the period. Other accruals allocate the original cost of assets that are expected to decline in value to the periods over which this decline

---

16. Fixed assets generally are stated at cost less amounts written off to expense in accordance with predetermined rules (depreciation or amortization). The numbers are not adjusted to reflect the effects of inflation. Inventory is stated at the lower of cost or market, first-in first-out, or last-in first-out, none of which measure the opportunity cost of the inventory (which, if the inventory used or sold is replaced, is next-in, next-out, with the difference between cost and replacement cost reported as a holding gain or loss). Premiums or discounts on long-term liabilities are amortized, but the liability amount is not restated to account for changes in interest rates. Expenditures on intangible assets created by the firm (such as research and development and advertising) are implicitly assumed to have no future value (in large measure because these values cannot be estimated objectively and with much precision), and are treated as expenses. Many other examples abound. (See Benston, 1982.)

takes place. For example, an expense for depreciation is recorded and the amount of the asset machinery is decreased.

The matching concept generally specifies that income (an increase in equity) is recognized first to the extent that the wealth embodied in the firm has increased as a result of the firm's operations, and the amount of that increase can be verified objectively both in amount and certainty. This is termed the *critical event*. For example, sales income is recognized when title to goods has passed to the purchaser and the amount that the purchaser paid or will pay can be determined. If a customer takes goods on consignment, a sale would not be recorded. Nor is income recorded when goods are manufactured but not sold, even though it is clear that the finished goods are worth more than the sum of the costs of labor, materials, and overhead charged to this asset. Income would not be recorded when the goods were sold when collecting the amount owed from the purchasers is so uncertain that collection becomes the critical event. In that situation, income would be recognized as cash was collected.[17] Similarly, income from long-term contracts often is recognized before the contract is completed, when there is a high probability that the firm has or can establish valid claims to payments for the work.[18]

Once income has been recognized and recorded, the matching concept comes into play. Expenses that are incurred to earn the income are then matched to that income and are recognized as reductions in the wealth of the shareholders. For example, cash might be exchanged or liabilities incurred for labor services and materials that are used to produce inventory for sale. The costs of this labor and materials are carried as assets until the inventory is sold. Then, the assets (which, by then, would be called *finished goods*) are written off to an expense account, "cost of goods sold." Similarly, a three-year insurance policy might be purchased. After a year, one third would be recorded as an expense on the assumption that the insurance protection supported activities that generated income or saved other expenses during the one-year period. Two-thirds would be recorded as an asset, both because income generation or expense reduction would occur in the future and because it is assumed to have future value of approximately this amount. Thus, if income recognition is delayed, the costs are carried as assets, with one exception—costs that are not expected to generate income or save other expenses that are at least as great as the costs are considered to be expenses, since they have no future value.

## Conservatism and Realization

Another basic, or at least long-standing, accounting concept is *conservatism*. Accountants tend to write down assets to their market values, net of disposal costs,

---

[17]. This is called the *installment method* of income recognition.
[18]. This is called the *percentage of completion* method of income recognition.

when these amounts are less than the amounts recorded on the firm's books. The difference is considered to be an expense. However, assets are not written up to their market values when these exceed book values. This procedure is called "conservative" because it shifts income recognition to future periods, while showing expenses in earlier periods.

Another aspect of conservatism is the practice of charging to expense the cost of assets with uncertain future values. Intangible assets generally are treated in this manner. For example, costs incurred for advertising and research and development are not capitalized (carried as assets) because of uncertainty about the amount of income they will generate or expenses they will save in future periods.

Thus, conservatism is inconsistent with the matching concept. It also is not applied consistently or expeditiously with respect to tangible assets and liabilities. Assets often are not written down until it is obvious that their market values are substantially less than their book values. This occurs even when the assets' market values are readily available and easily verified. In particular, until SFAS 115 was adopted in 1993 (effective January 1, 1994), accountants tended not to write down even regularly traded financial assets held as investments that had declined in market value. Even under SFAS 115, financial assets designated as "held to maturity" are carried at historical cost (although their market values are reported in footnotes to the financial statements). Furthermore, the amounts of fixed interest rate liabilities generally are not increased when market rates of interest on similar obligations have decreased.

The realization concept holds that income is not recognized until it is realized in a market transaction—that is, until resources or claims to resources have been exchanged. This concept has been used by accountants in large measure because of the uncertainty about future events. Until a market transaction has occurred, one cannot know whether the amounts expected to be received for assets actually will be forthcoming. A cogent example of the application of this concept is a firm (such as Metallgesellschaft) that holds fixed-price, long-term contracts to deliver a product that has declined in price. The increase in the economic value of these contracts would not be recorded until the goods actually were sold. However, under conservatism, if the firm held other assets (such as derivatives) that decreased in value equivalently, the decrease would be recorded, whether or not it was realized. Under German accounting requirements, that is what was done at Metallgesellschaft, resulting in a massive recorded loss and reduction in equity (Edwards and Canter, 1995, §VIII C).

The *realization* concept is not applied consistently. In particular, financial assets that are regularly traded are marked to market, with gains and losses recorded, whether or not they have been realized. However, nonfinancial assets, such as goods inventories, are not marked to market, even when these numbers are readily available and can be determined reliably. Under SFAS 115, financial assets that are held for sale are recorded at their market values, but the difference between these values and their historical values is not recorded as income or expense until the assets are sold. The recorded values of identical financial assets that are designated as "held to maturity" are maintained at historical costs.

We believe that the accounting concepts of income recognition and matching expenses to that income should be applied to derivatives. The concept of conservatism, while long standing, has been abandoned or not followed (except for intangible assets), particularly as financial statements have been seen as sources of information about firms' economic values. Similarly, the realization concept has been violated or abandoned in many situations where reliable market values were readily available. We also would abandon conservatism and realization for derivatives accounting.

## VI. Application to Accounting for Derivatives

### Derivatives Held for Trading and Investment

Derivatives that are held as inventory for trading purposes generally do not pose serious accounting problems. Both the control and valuation accounting functions are met when the derivatives are marked to market at least daily. Without such current-value accounting, the activities of managers responsible for trading cannot be monitored effectively. Furthermore, market prices are required so that the managers can make informed pricing decisions. Hence, financial reporting of derivatives on a mark-to-market basis does not impose an information burden on firms; indeed, the absence of such information is an indication that the firm is not fully controlling its derivatives operations. This procedure is followed currently under generally accepted accounting principles (GAAP).

Derivatives that are held as investments from which the firm hopes to obtain gains should be accounted for at market prices or fair values as of the ends of accounting periods. As is the situation for derivatives that are regularly traded, this information is necessary for managers and directors to evaluate past decisions and make effective future decisions. The information also should be useful to investors in the firm.

However, under GAAP (specifically, SFAS 115), financial investments that are not regularly traded are recorded at current values only if they are not expected to be held to maturity (held for sale), and then only for balance sheet purposes. The gain or loss from the previous balance sheet valuations are not counted as income or expenses, but are recorded directly as an equity holding account. Profit or loss is recorded in the income statement when the securities are sold and the gain or loss is realized. We accept this accounting treatment as a given, to which accounting for derivatives should concur.

## Derivatives Held as Hedges

Accounting for derivatives that are held to hedge future events and changes in prices should match the accounting for those events and changes. For example, a firm may have a contract to deliver widgets in Japan at a fixed yen price. It may purchase a dollar/yen futures option that will hold the dollar value of the contract constant. The profit on the sale will not be recognized until the critical event, the exchange of title to the goods, occurs. Consequently, even though the futures option may reprice daily, no gain or loss would be recognized until the sale of the widgets was recorded. If the goods contract were canceled, the gain or loss on the futures contract would be recognized, as it has no future value as a hedge.

The matching procedure applies regardless of the form of the hedge. It does not matter if the hedge is repriced periodically or only at its expiration date, or if it is valued according to market prices or by means of a model, or is in the form of an option, future, swap, or is embedded in a financial instrument. Nor does it matter if the hedge is complex, as when a firm hedges a yen-denominated goods contract with a dollar/mark hedge and a mark/yen hedge. Nor is it necessary for the price movements of the item being hedged and any specific hedge to be correlated at some prespecified or vaguely assumed number, as is required by SFAS 52, because the hedging relationship may be complex and not meaningfully measured by a simple correlation of two numbers. The only relevant concerns are the time at which income or expense on the assets, liabilities, or future events will be recognized for financial-reporting purposes, designation of the price movements that are hedged, and identification of the instruments used to hedge those changes.

When, in accordance with GAAP, income or expense on the underlying event is recognized, the offsetting loss or gain on the hedge instrument would then be recorded, whether or not the instrument was terminated. Until that time, realized gains and losses on the associated derivatives would be recorded as either deferred income (a liability account) or deferred expense (an asset account).[19] Neither the income statement nor the equity section of the firm's balance sheet would be affected until the underlying critical event occurred, at which time the economic effect of both the underlying event and the related hedges would be recorded and reflected in the firm's financial statements.

In addition, the financial statements would disclose, in a footnote, descriptions of the hedges, their market values, and the extent to which these values have been realized. The description should be sufficient for readers of the financial statement to adjust the firm's equity and net income to reflect the fair value of the hedges,

---

19. A reader of an earlier draft objected to showing a realized loss on a derivatives instrument as an asset. To those who are similarly concerned, we point out that this asset is the exact equivalent of writing up the underlying asset to at least the amount by which its value increased (or writing down the underlying liability). Thus, it yields the same results as recording all hedged assets and liabilities to market values by amounts limited to the gains on the hedges, with no effect on net income. Furthermore, recording deferred expenses as assets is a generally accepted accounting practice.

much as they now can make these adjustments for investments that are designated as "held to maturity."

## Advantages and Disadvantages of the Proposed Procedure

### Income Statement and Balance Sheet Numbers

The proposed procedure offers the advantages of consistency with traditional accounting, reporting of the economic effects of linked events in the same reporting period, and neutrality with respect to the kinds of instruments used for hedging. It also does not have to be changed when new hedging instruments are designed. The income statements would be consistent with the matching concept. It also is consistent with all-inclusive income convention, wherein changes in equity resulting from the operations of the firm are included contemporaneously in the income statement.

Balance sheets (including the equities section) would report related assets and liabilities on a similar basis. Furthermore, complex positions, in which a large number of transactions are hedged with a number of hedges, which now do not usually qualify for hedge accounting treatment, would be given this treatment if the firm's managers, with the concurrence of their outside auditors, determined that the hedges reduced the firm's exposure to risk.

### Footnote Disclosure

Disclosure of the market or fair values of hedges permits those financial statement users who are uncomfortable with permitting firms to defer realized gains and losses to adjust the numbers to fit their preferences. This would be an improvement over the present situation and the FASB's proposals, as firms that otherwise would be willing to disclose information about their holdings of derivatives no longer would have an incentive to embed (and, hence, not disclose) derivatives as a means of deferring gains and losses.

However, firms should not be required to report details about derivatives that are believed to be harmful to shareholders. As Gasteneau (1995) points out, some disclosures can give competitors and derivatives dealers valuable information that can be used against the firm (such as when and to what extent it must roll over its derivatives position). SFAS 119 now gives firms much latitude in determining how much information should be disclosed. We agree with this position.

Although required footnote disclosure is preferable to requiring firms to report gains and losses on hedging instruments before the associated losses and gains are reported, we should point out that even footnote disclosure might be misleading to some financial statement users. Some users might realize that the footnote-reported gains and losses are not real, as they are expected to be netted out when the transactions are completed. Consequently, we recommend inclusion of such a statement in the footnote.

## Professional Judgment of External Accountants and Manipulation by Managers

In general, accounting rules established by the FASB and its predecessors have benefited external accountants by providing them with the "safe harbor" of accepted practices. As long as CPAs attested to financial statements that were produced in accordance with these rules and with generally accepted auditing standards (GAAS), they usually avoided criticism and lawsuits with negative outcomes. In addition, there are economies of scale in having accepted accounting practices promulgated by a central body rather than by accounting firms and accountants individually.

However, we believe that the FASB's present and proposed rules for derivatives accounting have been and are likely to be dysfunctional. As we discussed and illustrated, the rule makers have been unable to deal with the rapidly changing nature of derivative instruments and situations. We believe that external accountants, who are in direct contact with firms that use derivatives, are likely to develop procedures that are effective in matching related income and expense events, much as they have done for similarly complex transactions.

Furthermore, contrary to an intended advantage, the existence of the current and FASB-proposed rules may enhance management's ability to manipulate financial numbers. In contrast, by substituting professional judgment for specific rules, our proposed procedure takes away a means by which a firm's management might gain the acquiescence of its CPAs and thus can mislead financial statement readers. For example, the FASB's current hedge accounting rules require that all components of a hedge must be designated as part of a hedge to qualify for hedge accounting. Consequently, managers who do not want to use hedge accounting can design hedges that are not qualified, and thus can report gains on hedges that, according to the matching concept, should be deferred until losses on the related hedged positions are reported.

Because the firm met the FASB's rules, its CPAs might be hard pressed to deny its financial statements an unqualified opinion. Of course, the CPA could resign from the engagement or refuse to give the firm's financial statements an unqualified opinion. In these events, though, the firm might sue or threaten to sue the accountant for bringing its financial statements under suspicion, even though the firm meets the requirements set forth by the FASB.

## Possible Disadvantages

The main possible disadvantage of our proposal is that, because it substitutes the judgment of the firm's financial officers and external accountants for externally determined rules, the reporting firm might deliberately mislead investors. For example, the firm might keep losses on derivatives from being included in net income by claiming that the gains from the hedged event have yet to be recorded. Even though the information would not be hidden, since it would be reported in a footnote, investors who do not read or understand financial statement footnotes might be misled. Alternatively, firms could hold assets or liabilities that include embedded options which are not explicitly disclosed.

We believe that there is little merit to these objections. The efficient markets concept posits that market participants have incentives to use all available information to value firms whose shares are traded in markets. Information on the market value of derivative positions is disclosed. The fact that some investors do not read financial statements carefully is not relevant, as those who do would have made trades that result in the stock prices that reflect the information, if it is important, to the benefit of all investors.

Nevertheless, managers may attempt to hide speculative involvement with derivatives or losses on derivatives. Because managers have incentives to manipulate the information (particularly if that information would show that they have done their jobs poorly) or might misperceive the value of assets and liabilities (perhaps because they tend to be overly optimistic), the financial statements prepared by managers usually are attested to by independent experts of acknowledged probity—CPAs. These external accountants, who are professionally and legally accountable, would have exercised their professional judgment in approving the use of hedge accounting and disclosure of the fair value of hedges by firms whose financial statements they attest.

## The Role of CPAs

CPAs have at least two strong incentives to audit the firm's accounts effectively and to report numbers that are not considered to be misleading by investors and other users of the firm's financial statements. First, their services are more highly valued if they are trusted by financial statement users. Second, they can be sued for not doing their jobs adequately. They also might be sued when they permit managers to be overly optimistic and events turn out badly. As partnerships, they offer an attractive target for lawsuits. As a result, the partners individually can suffer severe direct monetary losses and indirect losses from damage to their professional reputations (see Benston, 1985, for an extensive discussion). Consequently, external CPAs have considerable incentives to ensure that managers do not hide poor performance or especially risky investments.

In its attempts to deal with almost all situations by promulgating rules, the FASB and the SEC have been neglecting the historic role of CPAs. It is extremely rare for CPAs to be parties to schemes to mislead investors. However, at times they have conducted poor and sloppy audits. Although the cost to them and their clients has been considerable, it may not be as great as the amount they would have to charge for always conducting excellent audits.

As a cost-effective means of ensuring that CPAs have fulfilled their roles as monitors, we would require CPAs to keep clearly stated and documented working papers that show the basis for their decisions to accept their clients' hedge accounting procedures. These working papers should describe the models used to value hedges, the sources of the information used for the models, the evidence supporting the relationship between the hedges and the hedged transactions, and the steps taken to audit past hedging decisions. We would have these requirements established as a formal part of GAAS.

## Accounting for Derivatives' Risk

Financial accounting generally has not been designed to measure and report on risks. Accounting numbers present, at best, point estimates of the value of assets and liabilities and their change over past time periods. Information about how these values might change often can be gleaned from past valuations. In this regard, there is nothing special about accounting for derivatives. For example, present accounting statements do not inform investors about the probability that a new product will be successful, that competitors will erode the firm's market position, that costs will increase substantially, that the firm's research will result in new successful innovations or products, that a new advertising program will increase demand for the firm's products, and so forth. For many (perhaps most) firms, the potential cost of these risks far exceeds the losses that might be taken on derivatives that are held for investment or speculative purposes and almost always exceed losses on derivatives used as hedges.[20]

We believe that reporting the risks associated only with derivatives would be misleading, as readers might form the impression that these are all or even the most important risks to which the firm is exposed.[21] If the procedure we suggest were followed, changes in derivative values would be negatively associated with changes in the values of the hedged transactions. For this reason, reporting the extent to which derivative values alone might change would be misleading.[22]

---

20. See Smith and Hentschel (1995) for an illuminating discussion and analysis. They point out that "because derivatives are equivalent to combinations of existing securities, they cannot introduce any new, fundamentally different risks into the financial system. What derivatives can and do accomplish, is to isolate and concentrate existing risks, thereby permitting their efficient transfer" (p. 3).

21. Although, in an efficient market, stock prices should reflect an unbiased estimate of firm value, including an unbiased assessment of firm risk, emphasis on the risk of derivatives may impose costs on managers who have to explain to the press and to analysts about the risks posed by derivatives. These costs might cause managers to underuse derivatives.

22. These conclusions do not apply to financial institutions whose deposits are insured by the Federal Deposit Insurance Corporation (FDIC) and, hence, by taxpayers. The public has a right to information about the risks taken by these insured depositories and, from past experience, cannot rely on government supervisory agencies to obtain and act effectively on information that indicates risk taking by depositories that might result in costs being imposed on the FDIC.

## VII. Conclusions

Derivatives accounting is necessarily constrained by the general rules and limitations of financial accounting. From the discussion presented here, we delineate three important concerns that affect inclusion of derivatives in financial accounting reports: (1) measurement of the economic market value of derivatives, (2) matching changes in the values of derivatives that could be reported with offsetting changes in the values of hedged assets and liabilities that are not reported in accordance with financial accounting practice, and (3) reporting the risk that changes in the values of derivatives might result in substantial changes in the value of the firm. A review of current FASB rules shows that derivatives accounting is inconsistent and incomplete, primarily because the rules were adopted in an ad hoc manner. Our empirical study of derivatives reporting with respect to currency hedges (the most important of the affected transactions) indicates that the accounting rules constrain many firms from using or properly reporting hedges.

We find that one FASB-proposed response to this situation—recording the market or "fair" values of hedges and the resulting losses and gains—is likely to make things worse for firms, although possibly easier for accountants. Furthermore, requiring firms to record losses and gains on hedges in one reporting period and the gains and losses on associated transactions in a later period violates basic accounting concepts. Another proposed response—marking all financial assets and liabilities to fair values and recording realized gains and losses in current income—probably would not be operational or would be costly. Furthermore, the problem of reconciling realized gains and losses on hedges with unrealized losses and gains on the hedged assets and liabilities and with unrecognized changes in the values of nonfinancial assets and liabilities still remains.

We suggest an alternative procedure based on traditional accounting practices and concepts. Our review of the basic functions of accounting (control and, to a lesser extent, valuation) leads us to conclude that accountants should follow the matching concept and defer recording changes in the values of derivatives used for hedging until the accounting effects of the hedged transactions are recorded. The market or "fair" values of the derivatives and gains and losses thereon, whether realized or not, should be disclosed in footnotes. CPAs would attest to the financial reports and would be required under GAAS to maintain working papers showing the basis for their judgments. Thus, we recommend returning to reliance on the professional judgment of public accountants rather than on attempts by the FASB to craft rules that might (but probably cannot) fit all relevant situations.

Finally, we see no special reason to have the risks embodied in derivatives reported in firms' financial statements. Other, often much more important, risks are not reported. Furthermore, derivatives used as hedges should reduce risk.

## REFERENCES

Adams, J., "Simplifying Accounting for Derivative Instruments, Including Those Used for Hedging," *Highlights of Financial Reporting Issues*, Norwalk, Conn.: Financial Accounting Standards Board, January 1995a.

Adams, J., "Accounting for Derivatives, Including Derivatives Used in Hedging and Risk Management Activities: The Need for the Hedging Project," presentation to a conference sponsored by Virginia Tech, The Chase Manhattan Bank, and Arthur Andersen, LLP, *Accounting for Hedges: Current Developments and Market Impacts*, Washington, D.C., March 8, 1995b.

Beaver, W. H., A. A. Christie, and P. A. Griffin, "The Information Content of SEC Accounting Series Release No. 190," *Journal of Accounting Research*, Spring 1980, pp. 127–58.

Benston, G. J., "Accounting Numbers and Economic Values," *Antitrust Bulletin*, 27, Spring 1982, pp. 161–215.

Benston, G. J., "The Market for Public Accounting Services: Demand, Supply, and Regulation," *Journal of Accounting and Public Policy*, 4, Spring 1985, pp. 33–79.

Collins, D. W. M. S. Rozeff, and W. K. Salatka, "The SEC's Rejection of SFAS No. 19: Tests of Market Price Reversal," *Accounting Review*, 57, 1982, pp. 1–17.

Deakin, E. B., "Rational Economic Behavior and Lobbying on Accounting Issues: Evidence from the Oil and Gas Industry," *Accounting Review*, 64, 1985, pp. 748–57.

Edwards, F. R., and M. S. Canter, "The Collapse of Metallgesellschaft: Unhedgeable Risks, Poor Hedging Strategy or Just Bad Luck," *Journal of Futures Markets*, 15, 1995, pp. 211–64.

GAO (General Accounting Office), Financial Derivatives: Actions Needed to Protect the Financial System, Report GAO/GDD-94-133, May 1994.

Gastineau, G. I., "Some Derivatives Accounting Issues," *Journal of Derivatives*, Spring 1995, pp. 73–78.

Gheyara, K., and J. Boatsman, "Market Reaction to the 1976 Replacement Cost Disclosures," *Journal of Accounting & Economics*, August 1980, pp. 107–26.

Jensen, M. C., and W. H. Meckling, "Theory of the Firm: Managerial Behavior, Agency Costs, and Ownership Structure," *Journal of Financial Economics*, 3, 1976, pp. 305–60.

Lustgarten, S., "The Impact of Replacement Cost Disclosure on Security Prices," *Journal of Accounting & Economics*, October 1982, pp. 121–41.

Mian, S. L., "Evidence on Corporate Hedging Policy," Working Paper, Goizueta Business School, Emory University, 1995.

Nance, D. R., C. W. Smith Jr., and C. W. Smithson, "On the Determinants of Corporate Hedging," *Journal of Finance*, 48, 1993, pp. 267–84.

Ro, B. T., "The Adjustment of Security Returns to the Disclosure of Replacement Cost Accounting Information," *Journal of Accounting & Economics*, August 1980, pp. 159–89.

Smith, C. W. Jr., and L. Hentschel, "Controlling Risks in Derivatives Markets," Working Paper, William E. Simon Graduate School of Business Administration, University of Rochester, 1995.

Wharton/Chase, *Survey of Derivative Usage among U.S. Non-Financial Firms*, Weiss Center for International Finance, Conducted for The Chase Manhattan Bank, NA, The Wharton School, Philadelphia, February 1995.

# 9

# Principles- versus Rules-Based Accounting Standards: The FASB's Standard Setting Strategy

WITH MICHAEL BROMWICH AND
ALFRED WAGENHOFER

ACCORDING TO A WIDELY HELD VIEW, U.S. accounting standards are more rules-based than principles-based.[1] This observation stems in large part from the emphasis put on two aspects of the wording of the typical attestation statement: "the financial statements *present fairly*, in all material respects, the financial position of X Company as of Date, and the results of its operations and its cash flows for the year then ended *in conformity with generally accepted accounting principles* [GAAP]" (emphasis added).[2] "Present fairly," which indicates a principles-based approach, is essentially converted to a rules-based approach when it is "defined" in SAS 69 (.05 a) by reference to Rule 203 of the AICPA Code of Professional Conduct. This rule states that "present fairly" "implies that the application of officially established accounting principles almost always results in the fair presentation of

---

We appreciate and benefited from comments by Sudipta Basu, David Cairns, Graeme Dean, Thomas Schildbach, and Greg Waymire.

1. The papers in this forum adopt varying positions regarding this view.

2. The FASB's proposed Statement of Financial Accounting Standards, *The Hierarchy of Generally Accepted Accounting Principles* (FASB, 2005a), would more explicitly codify the rules. It says in para. A5 it expects to reduce the number of levels of accounting literature under the GAAP hierarchy to just two ("authoritative and non-authoritative ... [and] integrate GAAP into a single authoritative codification"). The standards adopted by the FASB would be the first level.

financial position, results of operations, and cash flows."[3] GAAP is specified by SAS 69, paragraph AU 411, as a hierarchy of conventions, rules, and procedures promulgated by specified authoritative bodies, particularly the Financial Accounting Standards Board (FASB) and predecessor organizations (e.g., the Accounting Principles Board).[4] Thus, if the enumerated and codified GAAP have been followed as specified, presumably the attesting CPAs have done their jobs correctly and adequately in the eyes of the Securities and Exchange Commission (SEC) and (probably) the Public Company Accounting Oversight Board.

Largely because of the Enron Corporation failure, wherein Arthur Andersen was seen as designing or accepting client-originated financial instruments that met the technical requirements of GAAP while violating the intent,[5] the rules-based approach has come under fire.[6] As a direct result of the misleading accounting procedures revealed in the investigations of Enron's failure, the Sarbanes-Oxley Act of 2002 included a provision, Section 108(d), instructing the SEC to conduct an investigation into "the Adoption by the United States Financial Reporting System of a Principles-Based Accounting System." The SEC's Office of the Chief Accountant, Office of Economic Analysis, issued a 68-page report (the "Report") in July 2003 (SEC, 2003).[7] In July 2004, the FASB (2004) responded and in almost all respects agreed with the SEC Report (in part, no doubt, because the Report agreed with an earlier FASB [2002] statement and recommended that the FASB be the

---

3. The AICPA's Auditing Standards Board proposed amendment to SAS 69 (AICPA Auditing Standards Board, 2005) includes this language. Although the statement includes an "almost always" qualifier, it has not been interpreted to allow for an override.

4. If adopted, SAS 69 applied to nongovernmental entities would delete the GAAP hierarchy specified, particularly the statement in paragraph .05 a that gives as the first source—"Accounting principles promulgated by a body designated by the AICPA Council to establish such principles"—and .05 b which includes: "Pronouncements of bodies composed of expert accountants, that deliberate accounting issues in public forums for the purpose of establishing accounting principles or describing existing accounting practices that are generally accepted." These and other sources would be replaced by the FASB, which "is responsible for identifying the sources of accounting principles and the framework for selecting the principles used in the preparation of financial statements that are presented in conformity with generally accepted accounting principles in the United States" (AICPA Auditing Standards Board, 2005, .08).

5. Andersen actually was charged by the Department of Justice with destroying evidence and was found guilty in a jury trial in June 2002 of "witness tampering" because one of its lawyers had "corruptly" persuaded Andersen employees to destroy documents in advance of an SEC investigation. In May 2005 the Supreme Court reversed that conviction, ruling "that the jury instructions failed to convey properly the elements of a 'corrup[t] persuas[ion]' conviction" (*Arthur Andersen LLP, Petitioner v. United States*, No. 04-368, 31 May 2005, Renquist, J., p. 1). The U.S. Department of Justice then chose not to pursue the case.

6. Following a detailed description and analysis of Enron transactions audited or participated in by Andersen, the Examiner in Bankruptcy for Enron (Batson, 2004, appendix B, p. 167) concludes: "The evidence reviewed by the Examiner, and the reasonable inferences that may be drawn from that evidence, are sufficient for a fact-finder to conclude that Andersen was negligent in the provision of its professional services to Enron. In addition, the evidence is sufficient for a fact-finder to conclude that Andersen aided and abetted certain Enron officers in breaching their fiduciary duties to Enron."

7. Printed in what the Web document describes as the "smaller" text size.

sole U.S. standard setter).[8] Therefore, the Report, which summarizes much of the writing on this subject (including submissions by the FASB), provides a point of departure for an analysis of the "rules versus principles" debate. Given this degree of unanimity and the reasonable presumption that the commission approved the Report, its analyses and recommendations should be taken very seriously.

We begin our analysis by reviewing the SEC's (2003) Report that suggests a principles-based (or, as it calls it, an objectives-oriented) approach and the subsequent strategy of the FASB with respect to principles-based standard setting. Two major shortcomings are discussed in subsequent sections. First, the format of standards cannot be discussed and decided on without considering the contents of what the standard should prescribe. Observing that the FASB follows the asset/liability approach and increasingly adopts fair-value measurements, we argue that the combination of this measurement concept with principles-based standards is inconsistent. A major reason is that fair values require many rules to provide sufficient guidance, they invite manipulation, and they often cannot be assured by auditors.[9] We propose to move back from an asset/liability approach with fair values to the traditional revenue/expense model, which is better able to produce trustworthy and auditable numbers.

The second shortcoming is the dismissal of a true-and-fair override that we argue is a necessary requirement for any standard setting approach. The more rules the standards include, the more an override provision is necessary to avoid allowing or even requiring accountants to follow rules by letter but not by intention. The override gives accountants more professional responsibility for financial statement content, and its disclosure gives sufficient transparency for users to understand and, perhaps, challenge its application. We present evidence on the use of a true-and-fair override from the United Kingdom's experience and discuss how International Financial Reporting Standards (IFRSs) cope with the issue.

The format of accounting standards is not exclusively a U.S. issue, although the current debate has emerged there in the aftermath of accounting scandals, but is of international interest because the FASB and International Accounting Standards Board (IASB) have agreed to converge their standards as much as possible. Recent evidence of convergence is their June 2005 joint exposure draft on business combinations (FASB, 2005b; IASB, 2005a), which has even the same numbering of paragraphs.[10] Thus, the U.S. debate on principles versus rules should not be viewed solely from a U.S. perspective but, rather, from an international one.

---

8. Furthermore, the AICPA Auditing Standards Board (2005, p. 5), states that the FASB's (2005a) proposed statement, *The Hierarchy of Generally Accepted Accounting Principles*, is "in response to recommendations in the [SEC's Report]."

9. It is interesting to note that when accounting standards (or principles) were controlled by accounting practitioners who served on AICPA committees, proposals for fair- and present-value restatements of assets were not taken seriously.

10. However, the IASB draft includes less content, so that some paragraphs are "not used" to preserve the consecutive numbering with the FASB draft.

## The Reasons for Rules-Based Standards

In October 2002 the FASB issued a proposal, *Principles-Based Approach to U.S. Standard Setting*. The proposal's introduction (FASB, 2002, pp. 2–3) explains: "in the Board's view, much of the detail and complexity in accounting standards has been demand-driven, resulting from (1) exceptions to the principles in the standards and (2) the amount of interpretive and implementation guidance provided by the FASB and others for applying the standards." According to the FASB, the exceptions resulted from the board having to make compromises with presumably powerful interest groups that prevented it from implementing its desired principles. The proposal makes particular mention of FAS 133, *Accounting for Derivative Instruments and Hedging Activities*, the complexities of which resulted from the board having to make numerous exceptions from the general principles promulgated in FAS 133, para. 3. The extensive guidance, it says, results from having to fulfill the objectives of comparability and verifiability. The proposal rejects "principles-only" standards, because these "could lead to situations in which professional judgments, made in good faith, result in different interpretations for similar transactions and events, raising concerns about comparability" (p. 9). Comparability may be seen as especially important in an international environment, as there is the danger that local accountants and regulators arrive at differing views on the interpretation of contentious accounting issues.

In addition, the FASB (and its predecessors) have developed rules-based standards to meet the demand of major constituents, particularly management and auditors, who want a clear answer to each and every perceivable accounting issue. The litigious situation in the United States (and increasingly in other countries) means that the risk of lawsuits based on alleged wrong accounting is high and gives accountants a strong incentive to ask for rules they can adhere to in case of a costly law suit. As Schipper (2003) points out, rules are likely to proliferate as accountants ask for guidance that, they hope, will protect them from criticism and lawsuits.

Detailed rules and authoritative guidance also serve standard setters' and regulators' objective of reducing the opportunities of managers to use judgments to manage earnings (and of auditors to have to accept that practice). Standard setters can be and must show that they are active standard setters. Thus, they may tend to overproduce standards and to write detailed rules covering almost any conceivable situation.

## The Case for Principles-Based Standards

Despite the demand for rules-based standards, the FASB (2002, 2004) and the SEC (2003) reject them and have turned to proponents of principles-based standards, presumably because in the light of the accounting scandals they consider the costs of rules-based standards to outweigh their benefits. The SEC Report states:

> Unfortunately, experience demonstrates that rules-based standards often provide a roadmap to avoidance of the accounting objectives inherent in the standards. Internal inconsistencies, exceptions and bright-line tests reward those willing to engineer their way around the intent of the standards. This can result in financial reporting that is not representationally faithful to the underlying economic substance of transactions and events. In a rules-based system, financial reporting may well come to be seen as an act of compliance rather than an act of communication. Moreover, it can create a cycle of ever-increasing complexity, as financial engineering and implementation guidance vie to keep up with one another. (SEC, 2003, at note 13)[11]

For these reasons, and based on an example of how corporations (mis)used the "bright lines" given in APB Opinion No. 16 that specify when a business combination could be accounted for with the pooling of interests method rather than the purchase method, the Report concludes that a rules-based system is not desirable.

Other critics of rules-based standards have pointed out that rules can become useless and, worse yet, dysfunctional when the economic environment changes or as managers create innovative transactions around them (Kershaw, 2005, pp. 596–97). Moreover, such standards need not reduce earnings management and increase the value relevance of financial reports insofar as the rules increase managers' ability to structure transactions that meet these rules while violating the intent (e.g., Nelson, Elliott, and Tarpley, 2002) and real earnings management may overcompensate for judgmental discretion (see Ewert and Wagenhofer, 2005).

The Report therefore examines what it terms "principles-only" standards, which it defines as "high-level standards with little if any operational guidance" (at note 13). It then dismisses this alternative, since "principles-only standards typically require preparers and auditors to exercise judgment in accounting for transactions and events without providing a sufficient structure to frame that judgment. The result of principles-only standards can be a significant loss of comparability among reporting entities" (at note 14).[12] The Report does not

---

11. The Report's page numbers differ depending on the format in which the electronic version is printed. Hence, we locate quoted material by the nearest footnote.

12. The SEC Report (2003, at note 15) gives two numbered additional concerns that could be ascribed to principles-only standards: "(2) a greater difficulty in seeking remedies against 'bad' actors either through enforcement or litigation, and (3) a concern by preparers and auditors that regulatory agencies might not accept 'good faith' judgments." These are not further discussed. However, in a section titled "The Role of Judgment in Applying Accounting Standards," the Report appears to dismiss (3), as it states: "it is simply impossible to fully eliminate professional judgment in the application of accounting standards" (p. 15 at note 21). Nor would we wish to, as we discuss later.

further consider whether or to what extent the financial statements of different entities can be more or less meaningfully compared even when based on common rules or principles.[13] Rather, it offers only two related examples to explain its rejection of principles-only standards, impairment of long-lived assets and recording depreciable assets at their historical "time of acquisition" cost. The Report criticizes the lack of implementation guidance, which leads to a loss of comparability. However, it does not recognize that, no matter how a long-lived asset is initially recorded, comparability is lost as soon as the asset is purchased, as its value in use differs among users. Over time, both value in use and value in exchange or replacement value also change and the alterations will differ among companies; furthermore, the changes often cannot be determined objectively. Consequently, comparability would only be possible if strict rules for revaluing assets at unambiguously specified values were used. It is not "principles-only" that is at fault here, but the inevitable and, indeed, desirable lack of comparability due to different economic environments. Further, the Report does not recognize that a company's choice of accounting measurement or presentation can convey information that is valuable to investors about the managers' operational and investment approach and decisions.

The Report proposes, rather than "principles-only," what it calls "objectives-oriented" standards, which are said to be optimal as between principles-only and rules-based standards, apparently because they offer a much narrower framework that would limit the scope of professional judgment but allow more flexibility than rules-based standards. "Objectives-oriented" standards are similar to what the FASB (2004) calls principles-based standards. They appear to be those where the accounting reflects the economic substance of the accounting problem and is consistent with and derived from a coherent conceptual framework, from which there are few exceptions. These standards, the Report asserts, should

- be based on an improved and consistently applied conceptual framework;
- clearly state the accounting objective of the standard;
- provide sufficient detail and structure so that the standard can be operationalized and applied on a consistent basis ("Note 1 of the Report says: 'In doing so, however, standard setters must avoid the temptation to provide too much detail (that is, avoid trying to answer virtually every possible questions within the standard itself) such that the detail obscures or overrides the objective underlying the standard.'");
- minimize exceptions from the standard;

---

13. See Dye and Sunder (2001, p. 266) for cogent arguments pointing out the shortcomings of uniformity (the same rule, e.g., expense research and development, yields different results when one firm's activities are successful and another's efforts are a failure) and the benefits (reporting choice reveals strategies) from allowing financial statement preparers to choose among alternatives.

- avoid use of percentage tests that allow financial engineers to achieve technical compliance with the standard while evading the intent of the standard. (SEC, 2003, p. 5 at note 1)

This is a sensible and desirable list of characteristics and admonitions. Indeed, it is a wish list to which all standard setters would subscribe. But it begs the question as to how much detail should be included in objectives-oriented standards. Indeed, the Report gives no indication of how such an "objectives-oriented" standard should or can be derived.

The AAA Financial Accounting Standards Committee (2003) also uses the term "concept-based" standards and attaches the following characteristics to them: an emphasis on the economic substance rather than the form of a transaction, a description of the particular transaction that is the subject of the standard, disclosure requirements, and some implementation guidance in the form of examples. The committee says (p. 76): "Concept-based standards have the potential to promote the financial goals of the FASB in ways that rules-based standards cannot ... Concept-based standards reflect a more consistent application of the FASB's Conceptual Framework and enhance individuals' understanding of the framework."[14]

We agree with the view that "optimal" standards are somewhere in the continuum of "principles-only" and "rules-only." In search of a universal, if not an optimal approach to standards, the FASB has been including more principles in their recent standards and exposure drafts (some examples are given below), while the IFRS has added significantly more guidance to their principles-based format in their recent standards (as shown from the increase from year to year in the number of pages of the printed version). In the following, we hypothesize two avenues to correct flaws in this search for improvement to U.S. standard setting: (a) recognizing that the format of standards is related to their contents, and (b) a true-and-fair override in the standards.

## Contents and Format of Standards

An assessment of the format of standards, or their underlying philosophical bases, crucially depends on their regulatory content, that is, on the underlying accounting principles they are intended to observe. A major driver of complexity in accounting standards is the number of exceptions to a basic standard (FASB, 2002); another is the amount of judgment necessary to apply a standard, which then necessitates rules and guidance. To understand the SEC Report's objectives-oriented standards, it is important to consider its underlying accounting measurement or valuation model. We note that although the SEC has not sought to define or develop an accounting model, the close interdependence between the type of standard and its contents implies the need

---

14. The committee also reviews a substantial body of academic research and finds it inconclusive.

to outline such a model when it provides recommendations regarding the format for standards. While a standard seeks to implement a particular principle for an accounting problem, its drafters also should consider and try to avoid potential gaming by opportunistic company managers and accountants. Gaming specifically results from too much leeway given to management and accountants. In general, some principles provide more gaming opportunities than others. The more decision "relevant" and the less "reliable" a standard, the more difficult it is to provide a standard that does not need significant guidance and rules.[15]

## The Asset/Liability Accounting Model

The Report adopts the asset/liability model as the fundamental building block of accounting standards, and emphatically rejects the traditional revenue/expense model.[16] "In the asset/liability view the standard setter, in establishing the accounting standard for a class of transactions would, first, attempt to define and specify the measurement for the assets and liabilities that arise from a class of transactions. The determination of income would then be based on changes in the assets and liabilities so defined." In contrast, when describing the revenue/expense model, the Report states that it gives "primacy to the direct measurement and recognition of the revenue and expenses related to the class of transactions. *Under this approach, the balance sheet becomes residual to the income statement, and contains assets, liabilities, and other accruals/deferrals needed to maintain a 'balance sheet.'*" The Report rejects this approach: "We believe that the revenue/expense view is inappropriate for use in standard-setting—particularly in an objectives-oriented regime." One reason for this conclusion is that there "are a variety of specific revenue recognition standards...for narrowly defined transactions or industries." The other reason given for rejection of the revenue/expense approach is that it is necessary to measure wealth at the beginning and end of periods "as a conceptual anchor to determining revenues and expenses that result from the flow of wealth during the period. Historical experience suggests that without this conceptual anchor the revenue/expense approach can become ad hoc and incoherent."[17] The revenue/expense approach is blamed for the inclusion of deferred revenues and expenses that are incorrectly described as assets and liabilities. The Report concludes: "Not surprisingly, an examination of these standards shows that various inconsistencies exist among the revenue recognition models."[18]

---

15. Bennett, Bradbury, and Prangnell (2005) provide a comparative analysis of the standards on research and development in the U.S., New Zealand and in IFRS.
16. The quotations in this paragraph are taken from the SEC (2003) between notes 72 and 78, emphasis in original.
17. No examples of or references to such historical experience are provided.
18. This statement is supported only by reference to FASB Project Updates, "Revenue Recognition." In fact, this document does not show or even mention inconsistencies.

However, similar, if not greater, problems arise with the asset/liability approach under principles-based standards. The reason is that the asset/liability approach cannot be applied consistently by accountants and managers without such extensive guidance that it would degenerate into providing rules-based standards. Although the Report does not clearly specify how assets and liabilities should be measured, since the economic definition of income is emphasized, it would appear that fair values should be used.[19] Indeed, the FASB (and the IASB) give priority to fair value measurements.[20] The FASB Exposure Draft on *Fair Value Measurements* (2005c, issued 2004 and revised 2005) is part of "the Board's initiatives to simplify and codify the accounting literature, eliminating differences that have added to the complexity in GAAP" (p. ii). A review of the FASB draft statement shows that extensive guidance is necessary to reduce the enormous room for judgment in determining fair values—and provides evidence for our conclusions.

Schipper (2003) additionally shows how, for example, application of a principle governing the fair value of financial instruments presents several difficulties. She lists and examines the definition of the term "financial instruments," the value attribute (exit or settlement amount, entry value, net realizable value, value in use, deprival value), measurement of the value (e.g., bid, ask or midpoint, block discount, model or present value calculation), and the problem of how sparse trades and block trades should be handled. Exceptions to the standards can be dealt with, she says, only by means of rules, which "add to the length and complexity of the standard, and lead to requests for explanations of the breadth of the exceptions" (p. 67). Except for assets and liabilities for which relevant and reliable market prices (on the "relevant market") can be obtained, the values assigned must be determined from appraisals, present value calculations, or by reference presumably to similar assets.[21] It is likely that these numbers often are both costly to determine and subject to possible opportunistic manipulation by managers, if they can be calculated at all, considering the difficulty or impossibility of determining and measuring intrafirm externalities. Thus, if trustworthy numbers are useful to investors, very detailed rules for calculating them would have to be written by the standard setters. This clearly is contrary to the characteristics of the coherent conceptual framework specified

---

19. See also the Report's observation that it is likely that the FASB will issue more standards with fair-value measurements (SEC, 2003, at note 100).

20. Evidence of the movement to fair value are the recent drafts with a full fair value approach for business combinations (FASB, 2005b; IASB, 2005a) and the fair value option for financial instruments (FASB, 2006; IAS 39, as revised June 2005), which is only the first part of a fair value project of the FASB (see Notice for Recipients of the FASB [2006] Exposure Draft). See also the discussion paper on measurement at initial recognition (IASB, 2005b).

21. Some of the complexities of deriving values from models and other measurement issues are described, rather naively and uncritically, in the FASB exposure draft. For a critical assessment see Benston (2006).

by the Report, particularly its admonition against excessive detail (SEC, 2003, at note 1).

A cogent example, discussed by Schipper, is changes that impair the value of recorded goodwill. The necessity of revaluing the assets gives rise to a series of questions that complicate application of the standards and require a significant amount of rules and guidance. Schipper (2003, pp. 64–65) asks:

> at what level in the organization should goodwill be tested for impairment, and how often? Since goodwill cannot be separately measured, how should the impairment test be carried out? If goodwill is found to be impaired, how should it be remeasured? The standard setting issue: How many of these questions should be answered in the standard and at what level of detail?

Besides the difficulties of measuring fair values, the measurement principle covers (at least currently) only a subset of balance sheet assets and liabilities. The SEC Report talks about specifying the measurement for a "class of transactions" (2003, at note 72). This appears to be those that involve assets and liabilities that are economically similar, which, thus, defines the "scope" covered by a standard. The Report would have the standard setter identify the assets and liabilities that are created, eliminated, or changed by a transaction or event such that it is not too narrow or too broad—deemed "optimal scope theory." This implies a need for detailed rules that define "narrow" and "broad" and how recognizable classes of transactions that can be distinguished from other classes. The Report gives an example to illustrate this "theory." The FAS 141 definition of business combinations is described as "near the optimum point on the [objectives-oriented] continuum." "A business combination occurs when an entity acquires net assets that constitute a business or acquires equity interests in one or more other entities and obtains control over that entity or entities" (SEC, 2003, at note 86). Thus, there must be control for there to be consolidation; hence, it is not necessary for the standard explicitly to exclude equity-method investments. We find it difficult to see how this illustration helps one understand what the Report means by "optimal scope theory." The Report does not address whether an objectives-oriented standard could avoid a bright-line definition of control (e.g., one share more than 50 percent, as specified in note 5 to FAS 141), even though the Report keeps saying it wants to do away with bright lines. Perhaps, an objectives-oriented standard would give considerably more weight to the final phrase of note 5, "although control may exist in other circumstances." Here, a bright line would serve only as an indicator to judge the existence of control.

A further implication of measurement for a class of transactions is that it generates the problem of adding the estimated market values of the acquired assets and liabilities with the historical book values of the acquirer's assets and liabilities. What does the sum of these numbers mean in terms of a general principle of "representational faithfulness to economic substance?"[22] Although this concern with economic substance would seem to imply measuring assets and liabilities at their fair values and (presuming zero inflation) net income as the difference between fair values of net assets at the beginning and end of a period, adjusted for distributions and additional equity investments, the Report does not explicitly call for revaluation of *all* assets and liabilities at the end of an accounting period.

## Revenue/Expense Approach

Although the asset/liability approach is consistent with the FASB's relatively recent pronouncements, it is inconsistent with its December 1984 Concept Statement No. 5 (*Recognition and Measurement in Financial Statements of Business Enterprises*), which describes well the traditional accounting model and declares (pp. 5–6):

- A statement of financial position does not purport to show the value of a business enterprise but, together with other financial statements and information, should provide information that is useful to those who desire to make their own estimates of the enterprise's value....
- Earnings is a measure of entity performance during a period. It measures the extent to which assets inflows (revenue and gains) associated with cash-to-cash cycles substantially completed during the period exceed asset outflows (expenses and losses) associated, directly or indirectly, with the same cycles.

We believe financial statements should be based on that traditional revenue/expense model and not the asset/liability model, for several reasons that we discuss at length elsewhere (Benston, Bromwich, Litan, and Wagenhofer, 2006, ch. 2). In our view, the debate about accounting models is unlikely to be solved by analytical methods and that empirical evidence, if available, is unlikely to resolve the issue.

In brief, the revenue/expense model offers several essential benefits. One is that it has developed over many years on the basis of market experience, long before accounting standards were appropriated and became the responsibility and virtual monopoly of well-funded, professionally staffed (rather than practitioner-dominated) quasi-governmental bodies, particularly the FASB. In fact, historically, at times when financial statement preparers reported assets and liabilities at estimated "fair" values, scandals ensued as the following examples show. In the 1870s, Germany experienced many scandals involving overvaluing of assets and the distribution of booked gains; as a reaction, in 1884 the law introduced a lower-of-cost-or-market rule to the earlier common

---

22. Indeed, the former G4+1 (a group of standard setters comprising representatives of the International Accounting Standards Committee, Australia, Canada, New Zealand, the United Kingdom, and the United States; now disbanded) pondered the application of a fresh-start method that would require valuation of the acquiree's and acquirer's assets and liabilities at fair value (although only for a uniting of interest transaction).

current value measurement (see Schröer, 1993) and the balance sheet–oriented asset/liability approach was (partially) replaced by the revenue/expense approach. In the United States, before accounting reporting was regulated, some corporations included the estimated values of intangibles as assets. As shown by Ely and Waymire (1999) using data from 1927, the price of the shares of corporations that reported high values for intangibles were discounted relative to corporations that did not capitalize intangibles. The SEC's early refusal to allow any reporting other than numbers based on historical cost, particularly write-ups of assets and goodwill, apparently as a result of perceived inflation of assets by companies in the 1920s is another example (Rappaport, 1972, pp. 3–27, 7–10; Walker, 1992). Enron's use of fair value accounting, based on present value and other "mark to model" estimates rather than on actual relevant and verifiable market prices, to inflate its asset values and income derived from the revaluation of assets to fair value provides a more recent example (Benston, 2006).

The model also utilizes the great benefit of double-entry bookkeeping, by tying the numbers reported essentially to the results of actual market transactions (Ijiri, 1971). Although accruals that are necessary to assign and match revenue and expense to time periods require judgment and rules, errors and misestimates are quickly self-correcting or are otherwise limited. In addition, the revenue/expense approach avoids the exogenous volatility of market values that have no bearing on the financial performance or position of a going concern, which holds and uses assets for a longer term and consequently cannot avail itself of an opportunity to sell the assets at fair value.

Another benefit offered by the revenue/expense model is that, unlike the asset/liability model, it does not depend on periodic measurements of the fair values of assets and liabilities, particularly those that must be estimated because there are no reliable and verifiable market prices on which to base the values. Such estimates necessarily increase managers' discretion to choose amounts that fulfill their own objectives, such as inflating reported earnings and hiding poor operating performance. Because these essentially subjective judgments rarely can be audited effectively, the audit as a reliable procedure will be devalued. We are concerned that the possibilities for error and opportunistic manipulation of fair values by managers under the asset/liability approach may be so great that many important numbers reported in financial statements will become so untrustworthy as to make the statements of limited value to shareholders and potential investors. Furthermore, as standard setters seek to constrain misuse of fair value estimation, they will be forced to enact more and more detailed constraints and rules, thereby rendering nugatory principles-based or objectives-oriented standards.

To sum up, the Report's proposed objectives-oriented standards that would implement the asset/liability approach, which, particularly when combined with fair values, are inconsistent with its rejection of rules-based standards as they would require extensive and detailed rules. Although, as Schipper (2003, pp. 67–68) points out, it will be difficult to show empirically whether the benefits are greater than the costs, we believe that both past and recent experience and simple logic make it likely that the costs of the asset/liability approach are likely to exceed its benefits, both to accountants and investors. In contrast, the revenue/expense approach is based on procedures that arise from long and tested experience; it has survived and flourished for a long time and should not be lightly abandoned.

## True-and-Fair Override

Regardless of the model adopted, the SEC Report's rejection of the true-and-fair override is an important shortcoming, considering its strong condemnation of rules-based standards and rejection of a principles-only based standard. The override would allow—indeed, require—companies and attesting auditors to not follow a standard or rule if its application would result in the financial statements not presenting a true and fair view of the company's financial position, results of operations, and cash flows. The Report says (SEC, 2003, after note 95), "we believe that when the standard setter establishes standards under an objectives-oriented regime, the accounting should, in virtually all cases, be consistent with the standard setter's view of the nature of the economic arrangement."[23]

Currently, there exists an override in AICPA's Rule 203, which allows members to state that financial statements that contain a departure from GAAP are in conformity with GAAP if, due to unusual circumstances, the statements otherwise would be misleading. However, it is not embodied in the accounting standards and has virtually never been used in practice (see Zeff, 1995). The FASB recently issued an exposure draft (FASB, 2005a), which if adopted would explicitly eliminate an override to codified GAAP because it believes

> that the selection of accounting principles in accordance with the GAAP hierarchy results in relevant and reliable financial information. Therefore, an enterprise cannot represent that its financial statements are presented in accordance with GAAP if its selection of accounting principles departs from the GAAP hierarchy set forth in the Statement and that departure has a material impact on its financial statements. (FASB 2005a, para. A10)

The SEC Report implies that objectives-oriented standards can portray economic arrangements in a way that omits nothing of relevance to investors, creditors, and other users, and can specify and effectively deal with how these should be accounted for. However, the history of rules-based standards suggests that this is an "impossible dream." When companies and auditors seek guidance about how they are to account for a transaction that was not considered by the standard

---

23. The Report makes no attempt to justify this assertion.

setter, new rules will be established. This then gives opportunistic managers a means of producing misleading financial statements that conform to the guidance and, hence, to GAAP. As Weil (2002) puts it, managers would continue to say to auditors, "Show me where it says I can't." A good example is Enron's misuse of the commonly understood definition of a "business" to declare that its acquisition of two different assets (an airplane lease and a security) from a single seller constituted a "business," so that it could record and use negative goodwill, pursuant to APB 16. Until EITF (Emerging Issues Task Force) 98-3, para. 6, specifically defined a "business" as "a self-sustaining integrated set of activities and assets conducted and managed for the purpose of providing a return to investors," Enron could claim and Andersen concurred that calling the simultaneous purchase of two very different assets was a "business" because there was no rule to say that it wasn't.

The need for a true-and-fair override results from the fact that principles in principles-based standards are principles on a number of very different levels and standards cannot be crafted so that they can exclude contradictions among them.[24] In such a case the hierarchy of principles must be clear as to which principles are stronger than others. Indeed, we can imagine that only the following principles-only standard would not need an override provision: "Financial statements should give a true and fair view." Of course, such a standard would not be implementable, if only because true and fair cannot be defined in a sufficiently operational way. An override would seem necessary to allow firms to follow those standards which reflect their economic situation where such conflicts arise. It is also necessary where following a specific standard which otherwise would be binding on the business does not reflect the economics of the situation. Finally, it is required where GAAP does not allow firms to show their economic position. Therefore, a true-and-fair override is necessary in any format of standards, but it is particularly important for a rules-dominated system, such as that currently adopted by the United States. The more rules, the more an override is required to allow for special adaptation. This is because rules-based standards deal with specific settings and are defined in detail, the need for recourse to an override to reflect the underlying economic structure of the business is more likely to be needed than with principles-based standards that allow the use of a variety of methods providing that they produce results consistent with the principle(s) of the standard. Moreover, with rules-based standards, a true-and-fair-view requirement may be a better way to stop management from exploiting rules than trying to write further rules that seek to prohibit such conduct.

A necessary requirement for an override is disclosure of its reasons and effects. Its use, we believe, would improve the quality of financial statements by indicating

---

24. Nobes (2005) argues that a major problem has been inadequate application of or failure to use "appropriate" principles by the FASB and IASB, and provides a discussion of six topics to illustrate his contention; see also Bromwich (1980).

the economic situation of the business and help to return to auditors both the opportunity and responsibility to use their professional judgments as to whether the financial reports of a company they audited actually fairly represent its financial condition, operations, and cash flows.[25] They could refuse the override, if they did not believe this was the case. Were a true-and-fair override both permitted and acceptable, CEOs and CFOs would be unable to claim that they were not required to follow the intent as well as the letter of GAAP or, indeed, that they had to follow the rules specified by GAAP because neither they nor their auditors had the authority to override those rules to give a true and fair view. In a sense, the possibility for an override shifts the burden of proof of what is a true and fair view from the user or regulator to the accountant.

In a recent exposure draft, *Proposed Statement of Financial Accounting Standards "Business Combinations,"* the FASB (2005b) adopted the IASB's "bold print" identification of principles (versus guidance) in standards. This identification reveals that "principles" can be relatively specific and, thus, low in the hierarchy, and even include exceptions from *the* "principle." For example, the exposure draft (FASB, 2005b, para. 28) reads:

> The acquirer shall measure and recognize as of the acquisition date the assets acquired and liabilities assumed as part of the business combination. Except as provided in paragraphs 42–51, the identifiable assets acquired and liabilities assumed shall be measured at fair value and recognized separately from goodwill.

Then, there follow pages of guidance. Without a true-and-fair override it is hard to believe that such "principles" can always result in relevant and reliable financial information. According to Bush (2005) the United States has had difficulty allowing for a true-and-fair override because it has no clear clause, embodied in the law, that could serve as a basis for an override of GAAP. A partial alternative to a true-and-fair override is a differentiation of guidance according to its authoritativeness, although this seems to be something which FASB is turning away from (FASB, 2005a). For example, U.S. GAAP currently includes authoritative guidance that addresses many specific issues that may arise when applying a standard in practice and it includes nonauthoritative literature on various levels of the GAAP hierarchy. Deviation from nonauthoritative guidance is possible, although it is unclear to what extent it must be made transparent in the financial statements. IFRSs distinguish between boldface printed "principles," application guidance, and International Financial Reporting Interpretations Committee interpretations, although all of them are equally mandatory. Much guidance could

---

25. In an equilibrium model, Ewert (1999) shows that (vague) principles-based standards result in a preferable quality of financial statements relative to rules-based standards precisely because they place some risk on the part of the auditor.

be relegated to nonauthoritative literature. For example, in Germany the accounting law is really based on principles and provides no guidance, and the standard setter's output has only the presumption of GAAP; additionally, a substantial commentary literature that fills in the gap of insufficient guidance has developed. In the United Kingdom, as more rules have been adopted, an override has become more necessary, if for no other reason than to operationally resolve conflicts between existing laws and some rules.

## U.K. Experience with a True-and-Fair Override

Some might argue that allowing for a true-and-fair override is fraught with danger because some degree of comparability will be lost when accountants can choose when to depart from standards. The result, the fear, is that there could be chaos. The experience of the United Kingdom, which has had a true-and-fair override for a long time,[26] and the IASB, whose override is much younger and more restrictive than that of the United Kingdom, should be instructive.[27]

In the United Kingdom the dominant duty of management with respect to the financial reports is that "the balance sheet shall give a true and fair view of the affairs of the company as at the end of the financial year; and the profit and loss account shall give a true and fair view of the profit and loss of the company for the financial year" (Sec. 226(2) of the Companies Act, 1985). Failure to comply with that requirement would give grounds for accusations of negligence, thereby subjecting accountants and auditors to charges of professional misconduct, and the necessity of rewriting accounting reports. "True and fair" is deliberately not defined as it is perceived to be a dynamic concept having a technical meaning distinct from its natural meaning (see Hoffman and Arden, 1983).[28] In the end it is a court's responsibility to decide what is necessary to give a true and fair view, but it is the management's responsibility to provide a true and fair view and for the auditors to agree or disagree. The act provides that giving additional information might be sufficient to remedy any defect in the giving of a true and fair view, but in special circumstances the override must be invoked with full information about the departure, the reasons for it, and its effect.[29] U.K. Financial Reporting Standard (FRS) 18, *Accounting Policies* (ASB, 2000), specifies that these remedies should be used sequentially.

---

26. Its occurrence dates back to the U.K. Joint Stock Companies Act, 1844. Chambers and Wolnizer (1991) provide evidence for its use in practice even before that time.
27. Other countries, including Australia, New Zealand, Spain, and the Netherlands, also have a true-and-fair override, based largely on the U.K. provision.
28. Some commentators (e.g., Walton, 1993, p. 49) opine that "no one knows what it [the true and fair view] means." See also other articles in the *European Accounting Review* 1993 (Vol. 2, No. 1) and 1997 (Vol. 6, No. 4). Others, such as Chambers and Wolnizer (1991), dispute that view.
29. Kershaw (2005, pp. 611–14) argues that the U.K. situation is very similar to that of the United States.

U.K. accounting standards have been strongly principles-based but do, of course, have to incorporate rules to provide a structure to the standards, although some recent standards are more rules-based, especially those involving financial instruments, reflecting a wish of the U.K. Accounting Standards Board, the U.K. independent standard setter, to converge their standards with those of IASB and the FASB. An indication of the effect of the principles-based approach of U.K. GAAP is the fact that at the end of 1999 all extant U.K. accounting standards were printed on 900 pages. The increased detail of recent standards is clear. The output of the Accounting Standards Committee (the predecessor of the ASB, 1970–90) accounted for only 239 pages, whereas FRS 13 on derivatives and other instruments (issued by the ASB in 1998) on its own comprised 91 pages. A more telling contrast is with the FASB's Statements of Financial Accounting Standards through No. 140 (September 2000, the last year for which FASB statements were printed) which took up 2,240 pages (FASB, 2003/2004). It also is useful to compare the current FASB-drafted statements of accounting standards with the bulletins issued by its predecessor, AICPA Committee on Accounting Procedures (CAP) from September 1939 through January 1953, compiled in the 56-page *Accounting Research Bulletin* 43. In addition, although the U.K. Urgent Issues Task Force issues interpretations, unlike those issued by the U.S. EITF, they are small in scope, generally address detailed items and do not seek to be comprehensive.

The Accounting Standards Board's conceptual framework is titled *Statement of Principles for Financial Reporting* (ASB, 1999). One of the objectives of the Statement is "to help preparers and auditors faced with new or emerging issues to carry out an initial analysis of the issues involved in the absence of applicable accounting standards" (para. 4). The Statement makes it clear that professional judgment should be exercised. Such judgment is meant to respect the spirit of accounting standards, rather than just follow their form. Under U.K. law, such uses of judgment are also reinforced by the requirement to give a true and fair view of the company's affairs.

Use of the override will be limited under IFRS to those countries where the use of the override is permitted by domestic law. This generated a strong statement from the U.K. Financial Reporting Council (FRC, the umbrella body for accounting and audit regulators) saying that the giving of a true and fair view "remains a cornerstone of financial reporting and auditing in the UK and professional judgment will continue to be central to the preparation and audit of financial statements" (FRC, 2005, p. 1). The FRC also believes that the U.K. requirements and those under IFRS are substantively the same, and stresses that the nontechnical use of the override is small (FRC, 2005, p. 4).

Professional and legal opinion agrees that following accounting standards is necessary to give a true and fair view (see Hoffman and Arden, 1983, and Arden, 1997, for the EU context), but this opinion has not been tested in the courts. The freedom to override is restricted by a number of constraints, including the need to receive external-auditor approval for any override, the wish of those contracting with the company to lay down the accounting methods used by the firm (at least for contracting purposes), the likelihood that the court and the regulators would generally find the Companies Act and accounting standards persuasive and would appeal to current professional practice and that of the relevant industry in considering the application of the override, and concern that the use of the override might cause adverse publicity.[30] Overcoming these restrictions could be burdensome for the company seeking to use the override. Moreover, given the flexibility provided in the United Kingdom's essentially principles-based standards for the proper exercise of professional judgment, the need for recourse to the override is substantially limited. Consequently, true-and-fair overrides have been used rarely in the past. Their use has increased recently, mainly to allow companies to use accounting procedures laid down in standards that otherwise would be inconsistent with the Companies Act. The general picture is given by Livne and McNichols (2004) for the period 1998 to 2002 and by studies in a regular commentary called Company Reporting that give figures for 1997, 2000, and 2002.[31] These studies consider not only explicit use of overrides but also accountings that "look like" overrides. Company Reporting indicates that the frequency of overrides by listed companies was 15 percent in 1997 (536 companies), 20 percent in 2000 (427 companies), and 25 percent in 2002 (337 companies). The vast majority of the overrides (73 percent of those found by Livne and McNichols) are "mechanical," in the sense they were necessary to allow specific U.K. accounting standards to be followed even though they conflict with the requirements of the Companies Act.[32] Thus, use of the true-and-fair override is generally the U.K. method for overcoming the problem where outdated law would otherwise restrict the development of accounting standards.[33] The need for this use of the override will be substantially reduced in the future as the Companies Act has been amended by regulation (effective for the financial year commencing on or

---

30. This view has been confirmed by a legal opinion sought by the FRC (the U.K. accounting and auditing regulator) from the solicitors Freshfields Bruckhaus Deringer, who also make the point that in adopting international accounting standards the EU Commission must ensure that the annual accounts and the consolidated accounts give a true and fair view (see http://www.frc.org.uk/frrp/press/pub0826.html from June 24, 2005).

31. For example, Company Reporting, May 2005, *Issue of the Month*, "True and Fair Override" (see http://www.companyreporting.com). More details are provided in an area restricted to members only.

32. There were two major reasons for these overrides. One is nondepreciation of investment properties, which is required to follow the relevant U.K. accounting standard (SSAP 19, *Accounting for Investment Properties*) issued by the predecessor body to the ASB. This is in contradiction to the Companies Act requirement for all fixed assets to be depreciated/amortized. The other is necessary to allow firms to take up the option offered by the standard on goodwill. FRS 10, *Goodwill and Intangible Assets*, to not amortize purchased goodwill in the face of the Company Act's depreciation/amortization requirement (although strictly the override is available only to companies).

33. See Evans (2003) for a review of the literature that takes a legal perspective on the true-and-fair override.

after January 1, 2005) to remove inconsistencies between the act and IFRS, which also removes inconsistencies between the act and U.K. standards. Thus, the use of the override for other purposes is relatively small (well under 10 percent of U.K. listed companies with the above data) as we would expect with a principles-based regime but does involve a significant number of companies. U.S. data are, of course, not available to test the remaining part of our hypothesis—that the need for an override increases as accounting regimes become more rule intensive.

The Financial Reporting Review Panel (FRRP, established 1990) plays an important role in policing the use of the true and fair view in the United Kingdom. Inspection of its findings in the 81 cases up to and including 2002 yields a number of impressions.[34] First, about 20–30 percent of the companies coming before the panel relied on the true-and-fair override in their defense. Second, the panel seems very concerned to rely on only the requirements of the Companies Act and relevant accounting standard(s) in determining its findings. This approach may be sensible for a relatively new body now also charged with carrying out an annual survey of accounting reports. It is also fair to say that the cases for using the override are often not compelling. However, these cases were prompted by complaints to the FRRP and may not indicate the strength of the other cases. Almost universally, the panel has not accepted arguments based on the true-and-fair override. This suggests that the panel so far has not encouraged innovative accounting going beyond the rules of GAAP. The one case where this defense was allowed involved the rather arcane subject of negative goodwill.[35]

Thus, if we consider only the cases coming before the FRRP, the true-and-fair override does not seem to have generated a large number of innovative treatments that seek to override the Companies Act or the accounting standards. The FRRP's recent more proactive searches for defective accounting reports may bring to light more examples where compelling evidence requires allowing resort to the true-and-fair override. Further evidence of the real extent of the use of the override may be generated as firms switch from U.K. accounting standards to IFRSs.

Livne and McNichols (2004) find that U.K. firms that override a GAAP rule (some 19 percent of their sample), the strongest type of override, report poorer economic performance than control firms that do not use an override and suggest that this is consistent with an opportunistic use of the override, as most overrides tend to increase reported performance. They also find that the capital market appears to

---

34. See http://frc.org.uk/frrp/press.
35. This is the Liberty International case (see http://www.frc.org.uk/frrp/press/pub0267.html from February 26, 2002), which has been followed by a few other firms. As the assets involved were deemed to have an infinite life, the usual treatment of writing negative equity off to the income statement would have meant that negative goodwill would have been retained indefinitely in the balance sheet.

adjust the book-to-market and price-earnings ratios for the effect of an override in some cases, but that the financial reports of override firms are not less informative than those of the control group. On the other hand, use of the true-and-fair override has allowed accounting to respond to current conditions and has not led to anarchy in accounting, as many fear. An example of this is where using the override allowed companies to anticipate later requirements of FASB and IASB not to amortize goodwill.

Other concerns expressed in the SEC Report are that a principles-based approach would result in a loss of comparability and that regulators might not accept "good faith" professional judgments (SEC, 2003, p. 14, at note 15). In the United Kingdom these problems do not appear to have occurred in any substantial way. Few complaints have been made about the U.K. accounting regime, at least under the ASB. Although the professional press does report some incorrectly applied standards or dubious judgments, these have amounted to only about 10 important problems per year among the approximately 1,200 listed companies (excluding technical issues). All this evidence suggests that the principles-based system in the United Kingdom has worked fairly well, partly because even when rules in the form of statements produced by the ASB were instituted, the true and fair view still remained the overriding principle.

## International Financial Reporting Standards

IFRS are purportedly more principles-based than is U.S. GAAP and less permissive with respect to a true-and-fair override than is U.K. GAAP. This less specified GAAP-dominated approach results in less verbose standards than with rules-based standards.[36] An example is accounting for leases, wherein under both IFRS and U.S. GAAP a distinction is made between finance (capital) leases (which give rise to an asset and a liability) and an operating lease, which is not included in the balance sheet of the lessee. IAS 17 (22 pages) defines a finance lease (all others are operating leases) as "a lease that transfers substantially all the risk of rewards incident to ownership of an asset" (IAS 17, para. 3). A lease is a finance lease when its term is for the "major part" of an asset's economic life or the present value of the minimum lease payments are "substantially all" of the fair value of the leased asset. In contrast, FAS 13 (48 pages) specifies bright-line rules. Under the broader more principles-based IAS, accountants might account for the same leases differently, depending on how they interpret "a major part" and "substantially all."[37] Under the more specific FAS, a manager who wants to have a lease recorded as operating

---

36. A notable exception is FAS 5 on loss contingencies, which is extremely thin relative to IAS 37. Ironically, FAS 5 was once voted as one of the best U.S. GAAP standards (Reither, 1998).

37. In practice, there seems to be a tendency to appeal to the bright-line guidance in U.S. GAAP in interpreting IAS 17.

rather than financing can structure it to violate some prescribed requirement. Thus, both approaches might result in differences or be abused.

The IASB (and its predecessor, the IASC) has been struggling with the true-and-fair override, as it was torn between the U.K. and the U.S. approaches. Before 1997, it did not allow for a true-and-fair override and the IASB Framework still states:

> Financial statements are frequently described as showing a true and fair view of, or as presenting fairly, the financial position, performance and changes in financial position of an entity. Although this Framework does not deal directly with such concepts, the application of the principal qualitative characteristics and of appropriate accounting standards normally results in financial statements that convey what is generally understood as a true and fair view of, or as presenting fairly such information. (Framework, para. 46)

In 1997, a highly restrictive true-and-fair override was introduced by an amendment of IAS 1. Presumably, it was at the behest of the European Commission (which had an observer seat in the then IASC) to avoid conceptual differences with the accounting directives, which include a true-and-fair override. In its current version, IAS 1, *Presentation of Financial Statements*, states:

> Financial statements shall present fairly the financial position, financial performance and cash flows of an entity. Fair presentation requires the faithful representation of the effects of transactions, other events and conditions in accordance with the definitions and recognition criteria for assets, liabilities, income and expenses set out in the Framework. The application of IFRSs, with additional disclosure when necessary, is presumed to result in financial statements that achieve a fair presentation. (IAS 1 [rev. 2003], para. 13)

But it also requires an entity to depart from a standard or interpretation if compliance "would be so misleading that it would conflict with the objective of financial statements set out in the Framework" (IAS 1, para. 16). In that case it must make extensive disclosures in the notes. This is very much in line with the U.K. situation, and with the European accounting directives,[38] but caused controversy as the IASC did not want to include an override initially.

Recognizing that the override may conflict with the regulatory framework in some jurisdictions, in the 2003 revision of IAS 1, the IASB qualified the overriding principle and restricts it to cases in which the relevant national regulatory framework requires or permits a departure from a standard. Otherwise the company is required to make extensive disclosures. This appeal to country-specific jurisdiction

---

38. Its introduction into the Fourth Directive reflected again the United Kingdom's demands. It caused controversy in European countries, and there are countries that still have not incorporated it into national law (which presumably should be in conformity with the Directive).

is unprecedented in other IFRSs and is in contrast to the IASB's strategy to avoid a country differentiation in its standards.[39]

We are not aware of any studies that provide statistics on the use of the override in IFRSs, but casual observation suggests it is used only rarely, if ever.[40] This is not surprising, as in the past relatively few companies used IASB standards voluntarily and compliance was patchy and not enforced. In summary, the ability to use the override with IFRS is highly restricted. But the ability to use it where allowed nationally will allow comparisons to be made and provide some evidence as to the importance of an override for a well-functioning accounting standard setting system. New demands for the use of an override with IFRSs may be generated as the substantial majority of first-time adopters gain experience with IFRS and discover problems in conveying the economic substance of the company under in this regime.

## Conclusions and Suggestions

The SEC (2003) Report states that the rules-based nature of U.S. GAAP has generated a mass of detailed rules and guidance and bright-line specifications in the standards encouraging financial engineering to meet the letter but not the intent of GAAP, resulting in less informative or misleading financial statements. We agree with this analysis and support the move toward principles-based standards suggested by the SEC and subsequently followed by the FASB's standard setting strategy. Due to the United States's status as lead example for international standard setting, this change in the format of U.S. GAAP has a significant impact also on other countries.

We are concerned, however, that standard setters do not seem to take into sufficient account that the format of standards and their contents are interdependent. In particular, the more judgment an accounting principle requires, the more difficult is it to cast it into a standard without plenty of guidance and, perhaps, exceptions. The FASB continues to permit and may well extend the fair measurement of assets and liabilities even though those valuations are often not based on relevant (applicable) and reliable (objectively determined) market prices. In our view the FASB will have to promulgate very detailed rules governing the permissible inputs

---

39. However, country-specific IFRS may also result if a country does not adopt full IFRSs but introduces modifications.

40. Research by Company Reporting found only one example of an IFRS override. The European Aeronautic Defense and Space Company (EADS) in its 2001 and 2002 financial reports did not capitalize development as required by IAS 38, but now follows IAS 38 (Company Reporting, May 2005, see http://www.companyreporting.com). Although EADS justified this deviation as providing a better view of the firm, it did not formally invoke the override (nor did the auditor when it gave an exception to the audit opinion).

to and applications of pricing alternatives even when ostensibly using a principles-based regime. Otherwise, on what basis could auditors challenge managers' assertions about appraisals, comparable prices and valuation-model inputs such as expected cash flows, probabilities, and relevant discount rates? The result, we believe, will be a continuation and extension of the present rules-based accounting standards model, with all its attendant faults. This is an important reason for our preference for the traditional revenue/expense model, which provides more trustworthy and auditable procedures than the asset/liability approach in combination with fair value measurement.

We also advocate the inclusion of a true-and-fair override into GAAP standards, especially when these are rules-based. The more rules a standard includes the more conceivable it is that the rules contradict principles (and most likely that lower level principles contradict higher level principles). And thus, the more essential is an override with clear factual disclosure to sustain the main objectives of financial statements. This necessity is reinforced by noting that in a given regime rules develop over time with often inconsistent conclusions by the same or different standard setters. U.K. evidence does suggest that an override is not often needed in what is generally regarded as a principles-based regime. It is impossible to test our hypothesis of the need for such an override in a rules-based system. A true-and-fair override puts the responsibility for accounting judgments where it ultimately belongs—with managements and independent auditors. There is reason, though, for concern that some auditors would cave in to demands by opportunistic, overoptimistic, or dishonest managers. These auditors might claim that, at the time that they accepted management-demanded exceptions, in their professional judgment those exceptions to GAAP that mislead investors were justified.

However, managers' use of and auditors' acceptance of (or, possibly, insistence on) a true-and-fair override would have to be disclosed and explained, which would allow users of financial statements and regulators to form their own opinion on the validity of the exceptions. Allowing companies some leeway to choose accounting, as long as the choices are accepted by their independent public accountants and are clearly disclosed, can offer investors useful insights on the way the managers view their enterprise. Indeed, U.K. experience is contrary to the assumption that auditors and regulators would give in easily. In contrast, opportunistic behavior by U.S. corporations that have used strict adherence to GAAP rules to produce misleading financial reports has been a much worse outcome. Nevertheless, we recognize that the usefulness of a true-and-fair override relies on effective disciplinary measures against managers and auditors.[41] We would also

---

41. Recent evidence by Webster and Thornton (2004) shows that the more principles-based Canadian GAAP result in a higher earnings quality measure than U.S. GAAP; it is only the stronger enforcement in the United States that reinstates earnings quality.

add transparency to actions taken or not taken by bodies such as the U.S. Public Companies Accounting Oversight Board to discipline rogue and incompetent auditors as well as recalcitrant firms. In the end, we agree with the FASB's (2004, p. 6) view that "a move toward more objectives-oriented standards will require shifts in attitude, behavior, and expertise of preparers and auditors." Unfortunately, FASB has not suggested measures to bring about such a shift.

REFERENCES

Accounting Standards Board, *Statement of Principles for Financial Reporting*, ASB, December 1999.

Accounting Standards Board, Financial Reporting Standard 18, *Accounting Policies*, ASB, 2000.

American Accounting Association, Financial Accounting Standards Committee (Laureen A. Maines, Chair; Eli Bartov; Patricia Fairfield; D. Eric Hirst; Teresa E. Iaanaconi; Russell Mallett; Catherine M. Schrand; Douglas J. Skinner; Linda Vincent [principal author]), "Evaluating Concepts-Based vs. Rules-Based Approaches to Standard Setting," *Accounting Horizons*, March 2003.

American Institute of Certified Public Accountants Auditing Standards Board, Exposure Draft, *Amendment to Statement on Auditing Standards No. 69: The Meaning of Present Fairly in Conformity with Generally Accepted Accounting Principles for Nongovernmental Entities*, May 2005.

Arden, Hon. Mrs. Justice, "True and Fair View: A European Perspective," *European Accounting Review*, Vol. 6, No. 4, 1997.

Batson, N. *Final Report of Neal Batson, Court-Appointed Examiner, In Re: Enron Corp., et al., Debtors, United States Bankruptcy Court, Southern District of New York*, appendix B (Role of Andersen), 2004.

Bennett, B., M. Bradbury and H. Prangnell, *Rules, Principles and Judgments in Accounting Standards*, Working Paper, Unitec New Zealand, February 2005.

Benston, G. J., "Fair-Value Accounting: A Cautionary Tale from Enron," *Journal of Accounting and Public Policy*, 2006.

Benston, G. J., M. Bromwich, R. E. Litan and A. Wagenhofer, *Worldwide Financial Reporting: The Development and Future of Accounting Standards*, Oxford University Press, 2006.

Bromwich, M., "The Possibility of Partial Accounting Standards," *Accounting Review*, April 1980.

Bush, T., *Divided by Common Language*, Institute of Chartered Accountants in England and Wales, 2005.

Chambers, R. J., and P. W. Wolnizer, "A True and Fair View of Position and Results: The Historical Background," *Accounting, Business and Financial History*, April 1991.

Dye, R. A., and S. Sunder, "Why Not Allow FASB and IASB Standards to Compete in the U.S.?" *Accounting Horizons*, May 2001.

Ely, K., and G. Waymire, "Intangible Assets and Stock Prices in the Pre-SEC Era," *Journal of Accounting Research*, April 1999.

Evans, L., "The True and Fair View and the 'Fair Presentation' Override of IAS 1," *Accounting and Business Research*, Vol. 3, No. 4, 2003.

Ewert, R., "Auditor Liability and the Precision of Auditing Standards," *Journal of Institutional and Theoretical Economics*, Vol. 155, No. 1, 1999.

Ewert, R., and A. Wagenhofer, "Economic Effects of Tightening Accounting Standards to Restrict Earnings Management," *Accounting Review*, October 2005.

Financial Accounting Standards Board (FASB) Concepts Statement No. 5, *Recognition and Measurement in Financial Statements of Business Enterprises*, FASB, December 1984.

FASB, Proposal, *Principles-Based Approach to U.S. Standard Setting*, FASB, October 2002.

FASB, *Original Pronouncements 2003/2004: Accounting Standards as of June 1, 2003*, Volumes I and II FASB Statements of Standards 1–100 and 101–150, John Wiley & Sons, 2003/2004.

FASB, *Response to SEC Study on the Adoption of a Principles-Based Accounting System*, FASB, July 2004.

FASB, Exposure Draft Proposed Statement of Financial Accounting Standards, *The Hierarchy of Generally Accepted Accounting Principles*, FASB, 28 April 2005a.

FASB, *Proposed Statement of Financial Accounting Standards: A Replacement of FASB Statement No. 141*, FASB, June 2005b.

FASB, Statement of Financial Accounting Standards No. 15X, *Fair Value Measurements*, Working Draft, FASB, October 2005c.

FASB, *Proposed Statement of Financial Accounting Standards, The Fair Value Option for Financial Assets and Financial Liabilities—Including an Amendment of FASB Statement No. 115*, FASB, January 25, 2006.

Financial Reporting Council, Statement PN119, *The Implications of New Accounting and Auditing Standards for the "True and Fair View" and Auditors' Responsibilities*, August 9, 2005.

Hoffman, L., and M. Arden, *Counsel's Opinion on "True and Fair,"* Accounting Standards Committee. See also their 1984, *Supplementary Joint Opinion*, Accounting Standards Committee, 1983.

IASB, Discussion Paper, *Measurement Bases for Financial Accounting—Measurement on Initial Recognition*, prepared by staff of the Canadian Accounting Standards Board, IASB, November 2005b.

Ijiri, Y., "A Defense for Historical Cost Accounting," in R. R. Sterling (ed.), *Asset Valuation and Income Determination*, Scholars Book, 1971.

International Accounting Standards Board (IASB), Exposure Draft of Proposed Amendments to IFRS 3, *Business Combinations*, IASB, June 2005a.

Kershaw, D., "Evading Enron: Taking Principles Too Seriously in Accounting Regulation," *Modern Law Review*, Vol. 68, No. 4, 2005.

Livne, G., and M. F. McNichols, *An Empirical Investigation of the True and Fair Override*, Working Paper, London Business School, January 2004.

Nelson, M. W., J. A. Elliott and R. L. Tarpley, "Evidence from Auditors about Managers' and Auditors' Earnings Management Decisions," *Accounting Review* (Supplement), December 2002.

Nobes, C. W., "Rules-Based Standards and the Lack of Principles in Accounting," *Accounting Horizons*, Vol. 19, No. 1, 2005.

Rappaport, L., *S.E.C. Accounting Practice and Procedure*, 3rd ed., Ronald Press, 1972.

Reither, C. L., "What Are the Best and the Worst Accounting Standards," *Accounting Horizons*, Vol. 12, No. 3, 1998.

Schipper, K., "Principles-Based Accounting Standards," *Accounting Horizons*, Vol. 17, No. 1, 2003.

Schröer, T., "Germany," *European Accounting Review*, Vol. 2, No. 2, 1993.

Securities and Exchange Commission, *Study Pursuant to Section 108(d) of the Sarbanes-Oxley Act of 2002 on the Adoption by the United States Financial Reporting System of a Principles-Based Accounting System*, SEC, July 2003.

Walker, R. G., "The SEC's Ban on Upward Asset Revaluations and the Disclosure of Current Values," *Abacus*, Vol. 28, No. 1, 1992.

Walton, P., "Introduction: The True and Fair View in British Accounting," *European Accounting Review*, Vol. 2, No. 1, 1993.

Webster, E., and D. B. Thornton, *Earnings Quality under Rules- vs. Principles-Based Accounting Standards: A Test of the Skinner Hypothesis*, Working Paper, Queen's University, June 2004.

Weil, R., "Fundamental Causes of the Accounting Debacle at Enron: Show Me Where It Says I Can't," Summary of Testimony for Presentation 06-Feb-2002, The Committee on Energy and Commerce, U.S. Congress, 2002.

Zeff, S., "A Perspective on the U.S. Public/Private-Sector Approach to the Regulation of Financial Reporting," *Accounting Horizons*, Vol. 9, No. 1, 1995.

# PART II

## FINANCE

# 10

# Determinants of Bid-Asked Spreads in the Over-the-Counter Market

WITH ROBERT L. HAGERMAN

## Introduction

The mark-up charged by dealers to consumers in the securities market, as in any other market, is a function of the operational efficiency of the dealers and the nature of the product. Because the security markets are regulated, the specific determinants of this mark-up need to be estimated to answer public policy questions as well as to satisfy intellectual and managerial interest in the dealers' production functions. The importance of these determinants is illustrated by the recent debate over whether or not specialists are natural monopolists, a question central to the furor over the relationship between the New York Stock Exchange (NYSE) and the third market. These questions make it essential that the nature of transactions costs in these markets be understood. The purpose of this essay is to analyze the determinants of spread in the over-the-counter market (OTC), to determine if the dealership function is a natural monopoly and to test other hypotheses.[1]

---

We wish to acknowledge the helpful suggestions made by Michael Canes, Michael Jensen, and an anonymous referee.

1. Several other studies analyze the determinants of the spread between bid and asked per share prices. Demsetz (1968) developed a theory of transactions costs in the securities markets (on which we rely, in large measure) and provides some empirical verification of the theory by analyzing the specialists' spread on NYSE stocks. Tinic and West (1972) used Demsetz's analysis to study the spreads on OTC stocks. These studies made important contributions to the theory and measurement of transactions costs but, as the authors pointed out, the data used are not sufficient to allow more than tentative support for Demsetz's theory. In addition, the treatment of risk in both studies is inadequate (Demsetz does not discuss risk; Tinic and West use a poor measure).

The analysis is based on standard demand theory. The product offered by security dealers (as Demsetz [1968] points out) is an immediate exchange of titles to securities instead of a delayed exchange. Dealers provide this immediate exchange by matching buy and sell orders and by holding an inventory of securities which is used to fill unmatched orders. The price charged for this product is the spread, the difference between the buying (bid) and selling (asked) price per share. The spread is a function of the market demand curve (the amount of immediacy demanded by investors), the competitiveness of the market, and the dealers' cost curves. In this study we take investors' demand for immediacy as given, and analyze per share spreads as a function of dealers' costs and market structure. This analysis allows testing of hypotheses about whether natural monopoly characterizes the share-trading market, whether the market is competitive, and the prevalence and effects of insiders.

## Determinants of the Bid-Asked Price per Share

An important factor affecting the dealers' costs is the amount of inventory required to provide the immediate transfer of shares they offer to investors. The amount of inventory a dealer must carry of a particular stock is a function of the volume of that stock's transactions. As volume increases so does the number of limit orders, which facilitate immediate exchange. These limit orders are a substitute for inventory; the greater the number of transactions, the lower the amount of inventory that must be held per transaction. Even without considering limit orders, standard inventory theory suggests that the inventory a dealer must hold to effect trading immediacy is less than a proportionate function of the number of transactions he expects to make. Thus the per unit cost of immediacy, that is, the spread, should decline as the transactions rate for the security increases. The elasticity of the spread with respect to the number of transactions provides a measure of economies of scale from dealing in a particular stock, ceteris paribus.

Inventory carrying costs per unit are a positive function of the riskiness of holding the inventory, if dealers are risk averse and are unable to eliminate the risk by portfolio diversification. (Since the concept of risk is not discussed extensively in previous studies,[2] an elaboration is provided in the following section.) Unlike

---

2. Demsetz doesn't discuss risk. Tinic and West's (1972) basic discussion is the following: "Our initial notion was to hypothesize a positive relationship between spreads and price volatility on the grounds that the greater the variability in price, the greater the risk associated with performance of the dealership function. On further reflection, however, we concluded that we should not try to predict the sign of this coefficient since it might be possible for the influence of price volatility to be negligible if a dealer could diversify his operations sufficiently." Tinic's study (1970) of spreads on the NYSE reported in Tinic (1972) uses the standard deviation of the price of a security, presumably as a measure of risk (although no explicit rationale for inclusion of the statistic is given in the brief review of his analysis).

most commodities, however, the cost of maintaining an inventory of securities does not include losses in value due to deterioration (although pilferage can be a problem). The cost of capital is also not a relevant cost of carrying the inventory, since the returns from holding the securities normally reflect the opportunity cost of the capital invested. Thus, the inventory carrying costs are primarily due to the risks incurred in holding the inventory.

Dealers also incur costs in matching buy and sell orders. If economies of scale characterize these transactions, per share spreads should be a function of the volume of trades in a specific stock. Transactions costs also may be related to the dollar amount traded. While transactions are stated in terms of the number of shares traded, market participants trade basically in dollar-denominated claims. Were all factors other than price per share equal, traders would use limit orders to equalize the spread per dollar regardless of the price per share traded.[3] Consequently, spreads would be proportional to the per share price. This strict proportionality might be eliminated by disportionate broker costs since, if it is costly per dollar traded to enter the market for low-priced securities, the arbitrage mechanism could not equalize the spread per dollar. Thus spread should be positively, though not necessarily proportionally, related to the price of a stock.

Trading with insiders increases the dealers' costs and hence affects the per share spreads as Bagehot (1974) has pointed out. Insiders (by definition) have information which dealers do not. If they cannot identify the traders who are insiders, dealers must increase spreads on those shares which they believe are traded by insiders.

Finally, the extent of competition, measured by the number of dealers who compete in making a market for a stock, should be reflected by the spread. A large number of dealers should keep the spread down to the competitive level. It is also possible that smaller spreads are associated with a larger number of dealers because the presence of other dealers allows any one dealer to offset a temporary inventory imbalance with interdealer trading. The two factors suggest that spread should be negatively related to the number of dealers making a market in the stock.

It should be noted that the number of dealers and the number of shareholders are likely to be correlated with each other since larger companies have more stockholders and more dealers who are interested in making a market in the stock. To the extent that these variables are correlated with company size, their coefficients may measure the relation between the size of the firm and the spread changed by dealers. This proxy relationship should be remembered when the coefficients are interpreted.[4]

---

3. There is some belief that lower priced shares, as such, have greater variation in price than do higher priced shares. However, Heins and Allison (1966) show that this belief is groundless. Also, as is discussed below, it is irrelevant as a determinant of spreads.

4. There is also some reason to believe that residual variance, which is our measure of holding risk, is negatively related to company size.

In summary, standard economic theory applied to the market for immediate transfer of titles to shares, indicates that

$$SP = f(NT, PS, HR, IR, ND), \qquad (10.1)$$

where

SP = spread per share, the price of an immediate transfer of title;
NT = number of transactions in a stock;
PS = price per share;
HR = holding risk due to holding a stock in inventory whose price might change (up or down);
IR = insider losses due to trading with insiders in a stock which, if purchased, is likely to go down in price or, if sold, is likely to go up in price more than expected;
ND = number of competing dealers making a market in a stock.

The relationship between SP and NT provides an estimate of economies of scale that results from savings in inventory and transactions costs, ceteris paribus. The number of transactions in a particular stock by a given dealer and the spread charged by him would be most appropriate for this estimate. Though market spreads are analyzed, appropriate inclusion of the number of dealers in the analysis allows making an estimate of the elasticity of spreads with respect to the total number of transactions, given the number of dealers. (Some additional evidence is brought in below to delineate market from individual dealer economics of scale.) The relationship of SP and IR, ceteris paribus, also provides a measurement of the extent to which dealers can diversify risk and are risk averse. The relationship of SP and IR, ceteris paribus, provides a measure of the extent and cost to dealers of trading with insiders. The relationship of SP and ND provides an indication of the effect of degrees of competition on the price of immediate stock title transfers. PS serves as a "homogeneity" variable with respect to the transactions costs of transferring titles.

## Specification of the Variables and Sources of Data

Data for a five-year period, January 31, 1963, through December 31, 1967, were collected (laboriously) and checked (carefully) on a randomly selected sample of 314 OTC firms which had at least 500 stockholders and $1 million in assets and for which the information required to specify the variables was available.[5]

---

5. Initially, 326 securities were included in the sample, 12 of which had negative betas. Since we ran regressions in the logarithms, these 12 were dropped from the sample.

Spreads (SP) were computed as the difference between the bid and asked prices for each security. These prices, as of the last trading day in each month, were taken from the National Stock Summary.[6]

When several dealers quoted different prices for the security, the price quoted by the dealer who made a market for the most months in each six-month interval was used, unless two-thirds or more of the other dealers quoted a different price, in which case their price was recorded.[7] The month-end spreads then were averaged for each security over the entire 60-month sample period to reduce potentially spurious correlations due to random fluctuations. The bid price was taken as the price per share of the security (PS), and averaged in the same way as the spreads.

The number of transactions (NT) is not available for OTC shares. Following Demsetz (1968) we approximated NT with the number of shareholders (NS). As he points out, the number of people holding the security is positively related to the number of potential buyers and sellers of the stock. The number of stockholders (NS) at the end of each year was taken from various *Moody's Manuals*. NS equals a simple average of the five yearly numbers.[8]

Specification of holding risk (HR) and insider risk (IR) requires some discussion, since risk either was not considered or ill-defined in previous studies. Demsetz (1968) does not mention risk. Tinic and West (1972) tested the relationship between risk and spread by using the high minus the low price divided by the average price for the period as a proxy for risk. This measure of risk can be criticized on two grounds. First, Pinches and Kinney (1971) have shown that it is not stable over time. Second, it is an ad hoc measure that has no theoretical basis. Consequently, one cannot accept or reject Tinic and West's (1972, p. 1716) conclusion that OTC market makers are able to eliminate risk by diversification based on their empirical finding that spreads are not significantly related to their measure of

---

6. Demsetz's (1968) data are an average of spreads quoted on a randomly selected sample of 192 NYSE securities for two trading days, January 5 and February 28, 1965. Tinic and West (1972) derive their findings from two sets of data: 68 stock issues traded on January 18, 1962, and 300 issues traded during the first five trading days in November 1971. The authors state: "Due to the significant differences in the size of the samples for 1962 and 1971 and the variations in statistical methodology employed, it is not possible to make direct comparisons of the coefficients of the models estimated for those two periods" (p. 1720).

7. Tinic and West (1972) describe their dependent variable as "average representative bid-ask spread."

8. Tinic and West (1972) use total sales and purchases during the day(s) for which they recorded spreads. As they state in analyzing their findings for their January 18, 1962, sample: "The relatively poor 'fit' no doubt reflects the use of only one day's trading data, i.e., the presence of considerable spurious variability in volume" (p. 1712). Their 1971 sample used average of five days' volume. The $t$-ratio for this variable is 3.9 compared to $-1.3$ for the 1968 sample. Demsetz (1968) uses the number of separately recorded transactions ($T$) per day (apparently on each of the two days for which he gathered data) and the number of shareholders ($N$) recorded in Moody's. He finds that $N$ is a slightly better regressor than $T$, though $N$ and $T$ are highly correlated.

risk. However, a well-defined model exists that can provide theoretically defensible and meanfully specified measures of risk.

The "market" model developed by Sharpe (1963) postulates that the relationship between the rate of return on a security and the market may be described by:

$$\tilde{R}_{jt} = a_j + b_j \tilde{R}_{mt} + \tilde{e}_{jt}, \tag{10.2}$$

where ~ designates a random variable, and

$\tilde{R}_{jt} = \ln[(\tilde{P}_{jt} + \tilde{D}_{jt})/P_{jt-1}]$,
$\tilde{P}_{jt}$ = price of the $j$th security at time $t$,
$\tilde{D}_{jt}$ = the dividend paid on the $j$th stock during $t$,
$P_{jt-1}$ = the price of the $j$th stock at $t-1$ adjusted for capital changes during $t$,
$\tilde{R}_{mt} = \ln[\tilde{M}_t/M_{t-1}]$,
$\tilde{M}_t$ = a general market index at $t$,
$\tilde{e}_{jt}$ = a random error term that is serially independent and contemporaneously independent of $\tilde{R}_{mt}$.

The relationship between the return on the stock and the market is measured by $b_j$ which is often called the beta coefficient. If equation (10.2) holds[9] then the variance of $\tilde{R}_j$ is equal to

$$\text{Var}(\tilde{R}_j) = b_j^2 \sigma^2(R_m) + \sigma^2(e_j). \tag{10.3}$$

The term $b_j$ measures the risk of the stock that is due to its correlation with the market; it usually is called the stock's systematic risk. The unsystematic risk, $\sigma^2(e_j)$, is the risk that is unique to the $j$th firm.

The capital asset pricing model, developed by Lintner (1965) and Sharpe (1964), implies that the expected return from holding an asset will fully compensate the owner for bearing the systematic risk associated with it. Thus the spread should not be affected by the systematic risk component of the holding risk (HR) since the dealer will already be compensated for it.[10]

Markowitz (1959) has shown that the unsystematic risk, $\sigma^2(e_j)$, can be eliminated as the number of securities held approaches infinity. However, dealers may not hold a perfectly diversified portfolio of securities because of diseconomies associated with increasing the number of markets they make. Since the number of securities required to reduce a portfolio's unsystematic risk is a positive function of the degree of the individual securities' unsystematic risks, spread and unsystematic risk may be positively associated.

---

9. This model was tested by Fama, Fisher, Jensen, and Roll (1969) and others who found it valid empirically.

10. Jensen (1972) provides a thorough discussion of this model and its empirical validity.

As mentioned before, dealers face the risk of buying from or selling to insiders who, on average, know something positive or negative about a firm's economic position before other market participants. We hypothesize that this insider risk (IR) is related to the security's unsystematic risk; since unsystematic risk (residual variance) results from the market's adjustment to firm-specific information. The more frequent is the occurrence of firm-specific events the larger the residual variance and hence the greater is the insiders' opportunity to trade against dealers, since dealers cannot readily determine if a stock price change is a consequence of inside activity or not.[11] A dealer's reaction to this situation will be to increase the spread on those stocks that present him with this risk and expend resources on discovering "inside" information about the companies whose securities he trades.[12] Consequently, we expect a positive relationship between spreads and unsystematic risk. Because a significant positive relationship between SP and unsystematic risk (UR) is consistent with two hypotheses—insufficient diversification and inside trading—we conduct additional tests.

Thus two measures of risk are identified—systematic risk (SR) which measures the risk of holding a stock whose price changes relatively more or less with respect to market changes, and unsystematic risk (UR) which measures risk specific to a stock with general market risk accounted for. Systematic risk provides one measure of the cost of holding risk (HR). Unsystematic risk provides a measure of HR and insider risk (IR). The measures of risk (SR and UR) were calculated by estimating equation (10.2) for each of the 314 securities in our sample using 60 monthly prices for each stock to calculate the stock's return and the Standard & Poor's 500 Index as a measure of general market conditions (M). As discussed before, the $b_j$'s are the proxies used for systematic risk (SR), and the residual variances from each regression, $\hat{\sigma}^2(e_j)$, are the estimates of unsystematic risk (UR).

The number of dealers making a market in each security (ND) during each half year in the sample period, as indicated by their having offered to buy and sell the security, was taken from the National Stock Summary and averaged.[13]

---

11. The hypothesis that follows is due to Bagehot (1974) and Michael Jensen (in conversation).

12. As with all allocations of resources, the dealer can maximize his gains (or minimize his losses) by using a mix of strategies according to the related marginal costs and revenues associated with each and with various combinations.

13. In their study on OTC spreads, Tinic and West (1972) use a similar measure, although the number of dealers are only those giving quotes on the one day (1962 sample) or the five days (1971 sample) studied. Demsetz (1968) uses the number of markets in which an NYSE security was traded as his measure of competition. In his study of NYSE spreads, Tinic (1970, p. 16) criticizes Demsetz's measure because it "need not indicate the degree of effective competitive pressure on the NYSE specialists," and calculates instead an "index of trading concentration". The index of trading concentration is a Herfindahl concentration index, the sum of the squared ratio of trading in each market, where the sum of the ratios = 1.

## Empirical Findings

Table 10.1 gives the mean, median, standard error, and interquartile range for each of the variables used in the analysis. The data in this table are the values of the variables for each security tabulated over all the securities in the sample.

Since there is no a priori functional relationship between the spread and the explanatory variables, various functional forms were estimated. The log-linear relationship satisfies best the assumptions required for least squares, primarily because this transformation eliminated the obvious skewness in the original variables. The results of the regression when $b_j$ was used as the risk variable are shown in table 10.2. The coefficients associated with price per share (PS), number of dealers (ND), and number of stockholders (NS) are all of the hypothesized sign and are significant at the 1 percent level. The coefficient associated with systematic risk (SR) is insignificant, consistent with our a priori reasoning that the expected return on the stock should compensate the dealer for this risk.

Table 10.3 contains the regression results when unsystematic risk (UR) is used as the risk variable. All of the coefficients, including that of UR, have the expected

TABLE 10.1 Summary Statistics Describing How the Dependent and Independent Variables Are Distributed over the Securities in the Sample, before Transformation to Logarithms (314 securities)

|  | Mean | Median | Standard Error | Interquartile Range |
|---|---|---|---|---|
| Dollar spread (SP), average | 0.88 | 0.68 | 0.67 | 0.51 |
| Bid price (PS), average | 31.85 | 24.50 | 31.34 | 31.06 |
| Number of shareholders (NS), average | 3,883.39 | 2,304.08 | 4,321.51 | 3,279.96 |
| Number dealers (ND), average | 12.48 | 10.10 | 9.22 | 8.67 |
| Systematic risk (SR) | 0.82 | 0.63 | 0.68 | 0.68 |
| Unsystematic risk (UR) × 10 | 0.10 | 0.03 | 0.17 | 0.09 |

*Note:* Variables which are averages were averaged over five years for each security.

TABLE 10.2 Results of Regression Using Market Risk (314 observations)

| Independent Variable | Coefficient | Standard Deviation | t-Ratio |
|---|---|---|---|
| Constant | 0.63 | 0.01 | 46.84[a] |
| ln PS | 0.471 | 0.018 | 26.16[a] |
| ln NS | −0.266 | 0.024 | −11.00[a] |
| ln ND | −0.124 | 0.032 | −3.87[a] |
| ln SR | −0.011 | 0.022 | −0.500 |

$R^2 = .75$,    $F = 232.26$

[a] Statistically significant at 0.1 percent.

TABLE 10.3 Results of Regression Using Unsystematic Risk (314 observations)

| Independent Variable | Coefficient | Standard Deviation | t-Ratio |
|---|---|---|---|
| Constant | 0.59 | 0.01 | 53.90[a] |
| ln PS | 0.594 | 0.023 | 25.82[a] |
| ln NS | −0.165 | 0.026 | −6.35[a] |
| ln ND | −0.268 | 0.032 | −8.38[a] |
| ln UR | 0.137 | 0.019 | 7.21[a] |
| $R^2 = .78$, | $F = 286.4$ | | |

[a] Statistically significant at 0.1 percent.

sign and are statistically significant at the 0.1 percent level. The discussion that follows refers to this table.[14]

Not surprisingly, the price per share (PS) is the most important explanatory variable (in terms of the *t*-ratio). Since all the variables are logarithms, the coefficients provide direct estimates of elasticities. The coefficient of PS, 0.594, indicates that higher priced shares have higher spreads per share but the relationship is less than proportional, since a doubling of share price is associated with only a 59 percent increase in spread, ceteris paribus. This finding is consistent with both the Demsetz (1968) and Tinic and West (1972) studies which found a positive relationship between spread and share price. Demsetz's (1968, p. 53) results also indicate a lack of proportionality in this relationship, although he does not emphasize this finding. The fact that spread does not increase equally with share price is consistent with the hypothesis that brokerage costs may prevent arbitrage from ensuring an equal price of immediacy per dollar traded. This result suggests that simple linear models may be inappropriately specified when used to examine the determinants of spread.

The significant negative coefficient associated with the number of stockholders (NS), the proxy for scale (number of transactions, NT) suggests that as scale increases the per share price of immediacy declines. This result is consistent with Tinic and West (1972) and Demsetz (1968) in terms of sign. The estimated elasticity of −0.165 also indicates that the saving from increased scale (trading volume) is less than proportional to the increase in scale, which is again consistent with Demsetz's (1968, p. 49) results for the NYSE. If the cause of this decline was at the dealer level, then immediacy for any security would be provided by only one dealer who would be a natural monopolist. However, Tinic and West (1972) present evidence which shows that the number of dealers increases with volume, a finding which is not consistent with the hypothesis that the dealer cost curves decline as volume increases.[15]

---

14. The regression results do not suffer from severe multicollinearity based on Haitovsky's (1969) test using a significance level of 0.001 percent.

15. The correlation between the number of dealers and the number of stockholders in our sample is 0.47 when the untransformed data are used. The correlation between the natural logs of these variables is 0.41. As noted above, this correlation might also be due to size.

This conflict can be reconciled by considering each dealer who makes a market in a particular stock as being a member of an industry comprised of all dealers who maintain an inventory of the stock. The spread is the industry supply price of immediacy and it can decline as volume increases because of industry economies which are external to the firm but internal to the industry. Thus, dealers may face positively sloped marginal cost curves which shift down as industry output increases.[16] This reasoning, which is consistent with the data, indicates that dealer firms need not be considered as natural monopolists for public policy purposes, since decreasing cost industries are consistent with pure competition.

Finally, the significant coefficient of unsystematic risk (UR) indicates either that the costs of diversifying make it uneconomical for dealers to eliminate this unsystematic risk and/or that unsystematic risk is a proxy for the average losses due to trading with insiders. Some evidence on the extent of dealer diversification is provided by a survey of dealers in the Special Study (1962, part III, p. 679) which indicates that 57 percent of the dealers made a market in 10 or fewer stocks. Since Fisher and Lorie (1970) have shown that a portfolio of 16 stocks is required to eliminate 90 percent of the unsystematic risk,[17] the survey results suggest that the majority of dealers are not adequately diversified. Since the dealers could, in principle, become more fully diversified by increasing their product line, this lack of diversification suggests that there are costs associated with diversifying.

The hypothesis that dealers increase the spread when faced with the risk of dealing with insiders also is supported by the significant coefficient of the unsystematic risk variable, on the assumption that unsystematic risk is related to insider trading. A crude test of this assumption was made by collecting the percentage of stock held by the top 20 stockholders who were officers and/or directors, that is, insiders, of 59 banks in our sample.[18] We correlated these percentages, which are rough estimates of the potential for insider trading, with the unsystematic risk (UR) of the same 59 banks. The resulting Spearman rank order correlation coefficient was +0.28 which is significant at the 5 percent level. Although much more research needs to be done on the relationship between insiders and unsystematic risk, this evidence leads us to accept tentatively the hypothesis that exposure to insider trading is one of the determinants of spread in the OTC market.

---

16. This idea was first suggested to us by James Hamilton. Industry economies of scale could result from the ability of dealers to offset inventory imbalances by trading with other dealers, although additional research is needed to isolate these economies.

17. See also Evans and Archer (1968) on this point.

18. These data were collected from the U.S. House of Representatives, Subcommittee on Domestic Finance, Committee on Banking and Currency. Twenty Largest Stockholders of Record in Member Banks of the Federal Reserve System, 88th Congress, 2nd Session, October 15, 1964.

## Summary and Conclusion

Traditional economic analysis, first applied by Demsetz (1968) to the price for effecting immediate transfers of title to shares (bid-asked spreads), is used to analyze the determinants of spreads in the OTC market. The sample collected allowed more theoretically and empirically valid tests of hypotheses than are presented in previously published studies. The present study found statistically significant (0.1 percent level) relationships of the sign postulated between spreads per share and price per share, number of stockholders (a proxy for the scale of transactions), number of dealers, and unsystematic risk. None of these relationships appear linear, which suggests that the linear models used in earlier studies were not appropriate, though the findings of these studies generally are consistent with ours.

The estimates provide evidence on the hypotheses presented in the first section of the essay. Economics of scale in trading are found—trading scale (measured by the number of shareholders) is negatively related to spreads (a doubling in the number of shareholders is associated with a 16.5 percent decrease in spread). While this might be taken to mean that dealers are natural monopolists, additional data suggest that the results may be more consistent with security dealing being a decreasing cost industry with economies external to the individual dealer. The coefficients estimated also indicate that competition (measured by the number of dealers) is associated with lower per share spreads (a doubling of the number of dealers is associated with a 26.8 percent decrease in spreads).

The risk (inventory holding and insider) measurements used are derived from the capital-asset pricing model. As was expected, systematic risk (beta) is not associated with spreads. Unsystematic risk (residual variance), which is associated with spreads, measures the dealers' cost of portfolio diversification and their cost of trading with insiders. Additional evidence suggests that both explanations are relevant.

### REFERENCES

Bagehot, W., 1974, The only game in town, *Financial Analysts Journal* 27, 12–14, 22.

Demsetz, H., 1968, The costs of transacting, *Quarterly Journal of Economics* 82, 33–53.

Evans, J.H. and S.H. Archer, 1968, Diversification and the reduction of dispersion, *Journal of Finance* 23, 761–67.

Fama, E., L. Fisher, M. Jensen, and R. Roll, 1969, The adjustment of stock prices to new information, *International Economic Review* 10, 1–21.

Fisher, L. and J.H. Lorie, 1970, Some studies of variability of returns of investments in common stocks, *Journal of Business* 43, 99–134.

Haitovsky, Y., 1969, Multicollinearity in regression analysis: Comment, *Review of Economics and Statistics* 51, 486–89.

Heins, A.J. and S.L. Allison, 1966, Some factors affecting stock price variability, *Journal of Business* 39, 19–23.

Jensen, M.C., 1972, Capital markets: Theory and evidence, *Bell Journal of Economics and Management Science* 3, 357–98.

Lintner, J., 1965, The valuation of risk assets and the selection of risky investments in stock portfolios and capital budgets, *Review of Economics and Statistics* 47, 13–37.

Markowitz, H., 1959, *Portfolio selection: Efficient diversification of investment* (Wiley, New York).

National Quotation Service, Monthly Stock Summary (New York), monthly.

Pinches, G. and W. Kinney Jr., 1971, The measurement of the volatility of common stock prices, *Journal of Finance* 26, 119–26.

Report of the special study of the securities markets of the Securities and Exchange Commission, 1962, 88th Congress, 1st Session, House Document 95, 1963 (Government Printing Office, Washington, D.C.).

Sharpe, W.F., 1963, Simplified model for portfolio analysis, *Management Science* 9, 277–93.

Sharpe, W.F., 1964, Capital asset prices: A theory of market equilibrium under conditions of risk, *Journal of Finance* 19, 425–42.

Tinic, S.M.E., 1970, The value of time preference and the behavior of liquidity costs in the New York Stock Exchange, unpublished Ph.D. dissertation (Graduate School of Business and Public Administration, Cornell University, Ithaca, N.Y.).

Tinic, S.M.E., 1972, The economics of liquidity services, *Quarterly Journal of Economics* 86, 79–93.

Tinic, S.M.E. and R.R. West, 1972, Competition and the pricing of dealer services in the over-the-counter stock market, *Journal of Financial and Quantitative Analysis* 7, 1707–28.

# 11

# A Transactions Cost Approach to the Theory of Financial Intermediation

WITH CLIFFORD W. SMITH JR.

## I. Introduction

In our opinion, a proper framework has yet to be developed for the analysis of financial intermediation. The traditional macroeconomic analysis views financial intermediaries as passive conduits through which monetary policy is effected.[1] Even when a more micro view is taken, though, the analyses often are restricted to studying the effect on the rate of change and allocation of money and credit of required and desired reserve ratios, ceiling rates imposed on loans and deposits, and so on.[2]

Recent (and some past) writers criticize this approach.[3] These authors point out that since financial intermediaries are firms, they should be analyzed with the microeconomic tools that have been employed to analyze other industries. Yet in this implementation, considerable divergence in approach can be found. For example, while Pesek (1970) and Towey (1974) describe

---

1. For example, neither Friedman and Schwartz (1963) nor Cagan (1965) mention bank resource costs.
2. Admittedly, if the costs of production for this industry showed little variability over the period studied, these omissions may cause little difficulty. However, with the technological advancement in such areas as electronic funds transfer, this omission may pose serious problems for subsequent research.
3. See Pyle (1972) for a comprehensive review of this literature.

one financial intermediary, banks, as producing money by employing loans as inputs, Hyman (1972) and Melitz and Pardue (1973) describe them as producing credit with deposits as inputs. Furthermore, although most authors suggest that the intermediaries maximize something, it is sometimes profits, sometimes growth, and sometimes (rather anthropomorphically) utility (e.g., Klein, 1971). We believe that these approaches are not the most productive way to analyze financial intermediaries.

Essentially, we view the role of the financial intermediary as creating specialized financial commodities. These commodities are created whenever an intermediary finds that it can sell them for prices which are expected to cover all costs of their production, both direct costs and opportunity costs.

We see the demand for these financial commodities as a derived demand. Individuals derive utility from consumption, consumption today and consumption in the future. By acquiring financial commodities, intertemporal and intratemporal transfers of consumption may be achieved. Of course, there are many financial commodities other than those produced by financial intermediaries. The raison d'être for this industry is the existence of transactions costs.

Several forms of financial intermediation have arisen to reduce these costs. The most basic form of financial intermediary is the market maker. He simply provides a marketplace where potential buyers and sellers come together, thus lowering relevant information costs. An example of this form of intermediary is the New York Stock Exchange. It does not create assets, it only furnishes a physical location for buyers and sellers to transact. Without this intermediary, the task of locating a potential seller (much less the potential seller with the lowest reservation price) would be much more expensive. A somewhat more sophisticated form of financial intermediation is provided by a dealer who also takes a position at his own risk in the asset transacted. A market specialist on a securities exchange exemplifies this form of intermediation. A more complex form of financial intermediation is one in which new financial commodities are produced. This form of financial intermediary is exemplified by mutual funds, banks, and consumer finance companies. Thus, mutual funds allow individuals to purchase shares in diversified portfolios of securities, in odd amounts, for indefinite lengths of time, generally at a much lower transaction cost than could be achieved through the direct purchase of the underlying securities. This intermediary has a comparative advantage over a stock exchange in serving a particular group. Therefore, it exploits the returns to scale implicit in the structure of the transactions costs of a stock exchange by purchasing large blocks of securities, packaging those securities in a form that is demanded by some individuals, and selling the package at a price which covers all its costs. These examples illustrate the essential feature of financial intermediation—reduction of the transactions costs of effecting inter- and intratemporal consumption decisions.[4]

## II. Demand

A basic problem in the analysis of financial intermediaries may be the lack of an appropriate analytical framework within which to analyze the demand for the financial commodities produced by intermediaries. In the general analysis of consumer demand, individuals are assumed to possess an endowment and act according to the dictates of a utility function. The endowment is expended to purchase consumption goods in such a way as to maximize utility. We assume that individuals derive utility only from consumption, where by consumption we mean consuming different goods at many points in time, allowing for different states of the world. (Note that if this restriction were not imposed, any observed activity could be trivially deduced by an appropriate insertion of that phenomenon into the utility function, thus rendering the analytical apparatus empty.)

The individual's endowment may consist of securities plus his human wealth, the present value of his earnings. If the individual's preferred intertemporal consumption pattern differs from his time profile of earnings, he may rearrange his consumption pattern to achieve a more desired pattern. He does so by directly or indirectly acquiring a long or short position in assets (e.g., by purchasing equities or the financial commodities issued by financial intermediaries). Therefore, an individual's asset holdings do not yield utility in themselves. Assets are held for the inter- and intratemporal rearrangement of consumption possibilities afforded by their holding.[5]

The foregoing explains, in part, why assets are held. We now turn to the question of which assets are held, or what the motivation is for holding the financial commodities created by financial intermediaries. It should be obvious that in a *perfect* market, a market with no frictions such as transactions costs, information costs, or indivisibilities, financial intermediaries would not exist. This argument

---

4. One point about the aggregate supply of the financial commodities created by financial intermediaries should be noted: it is always identically zero. The total long position in mutual fund shares held by the public is exactly offset by the short position in those shares taken by the fund itself. Similarly, the total long position in the installment loan market held by the customers of a consumer finance company is exactly offset by the short position in that market assumed by the finance company itself. This general proposition, that the supply of financial commodities created by financial intermediaries is identically zero, should highlight the fact that the increase in social welfare engendered by this industry comes about only through a reduction in the relevant transactions cost.

5. We include here contingent consumption possibilities as, for example, are afforded by insurance.

focuses explicitly on the rationale for the existence of financial intermediaries—market imperfections.

## Transactions Cost and Intertemporal Consumption

First we consider the consumer's demand for intertemporal consumption. The well-known Sharpe-Lintner-Treynor-Mossin capital asset pricing model (CAPM) describes how the consumer can hold a portfolio of riskless and risky assets to achieve consumption patterns that maximize his utility. This model includes the essential elements appropriate to an analytical framework: consumption is the argument in the individual's preference function, at least two time periods are considered, the range of substitution involved in the portfolio decision is recognized, and risk is explicitly recognized. However, transactions costs are not incorporated.

In an earlier version of this essay, we demonstrate formally how general transactions costs can be included in Hamada's (1971) explication of the CAPM.[6] We draw the following conclusions. First, transactions costs reduce the amount of the consumer's present and future consumption should he want to consume other than his current period income. As a consequence, consumption only of current income and next period income may dominate borrowing and lending and investing in risk-free and risky assets. This conclusion is reinforced where transactions result in differing borrowing and lending rates. Both fixed and differential transactions costs result in a tendency of the individual's consumption patterns to follow his income pattern. Second, although in a perfect market it is never optimal to hold a portfolio with no risky assets, the existence of transactions costs may result in the optimal portfolio containing only riskless assets. Third, where a consumer can achieve a higher level of utility by purchasing risky assets even though he must incur transactions costs, the nature of these costs affect his choice of portfolio. If transactions costs are proportional for all risky assets, the market portfolio is still the optimal portfolio of risky assets,[7] though the amount that can be invested is reduced by the future value of the costs. However, the two fund property of the CAPM is lost virtually all other forms of transactions costs. If transactions costs are associated differentially with individual securities, the market portfolio will not be chosen. Essentially, the individual will add risky securities to his portfolio until the marginal net benefit of increased diversification is zero. The addition of more general increasing returns to scale in transactions costs will generate

---

6. This section of the essay was omitted because of space constraints.
7. Note, however, that if the individual begins with an endowment of risky securities, this property does not hold. See Zabel (1973).

nonlinearities in the model. Both the homogeneity properties associated with the map of the efficient frontier and the linearity of the capital market line will be lost. In particular, the consumer with a relatively small endowment and/or income may find the reduction in expected utility from paying transactions costs greater than the increase in expected utility from purchasing, borrowing, or lending risky or risk-free assets.

The demand for the commodities produced by financial intermediaries, in general, is derived from the consumer's ability to achieve a higher level of utility by incurring lower levels of these transactions costs. In addition, individual specific transactions costs, such as the cost of transportation and inconvenience, also serve to reduce the consumer's consumption possibilities. These costs, we believe, are important for explaining the distribution of the consumer's demands among individual financial intermediaries. When several financial commodities can be obtained in a single location, the marginal transportation and inconvenience cost for services in addition to the first are virtually zero.[8] However, the continuing existence of thrift institutions, unit banks, and other limited service financial institutions suggest either that these costs are not overwhelmingly large or that government regulations prevent transactions cost saving changes. (These alternatives are considered further below.)

The addition of these costs would suggest that individuals' efficient opportunity sets would differ not only with the size of their portfolios, but also with physical location and the opportunity cost of their time. Thus the demands faced by financial intermediaries are also a function of the distribution of wealth among consumers.[9]

## Transactions Costs and Intratemporal Consumption

The demand for financial commodities, such as demand deposits, is derived from the consumer's demand to effect intratemporal consumption decisions across commodities. Demand deposits are acquired because of transactions costs, namely, costs associated with barter and with the use of government-supplied money.[10] Since it is costly to exchange assets for consumption goods, given some

---

8. Consequently, time deposit balances are positive in full-service commercial banks, even though thrift institutions are allowed to pay one-quarter percent more interest on their time deposits (see Kardouche, 1969). This argument may also partially explain the observation that banks with extensive branching tend to dominate in states which permit branch banking.

9. In general, we expect that as the opportunity cost of the consumer's time increases, the value of full-service financial intermediaries to the consumer is likely to increase.

10. See Savings (1971), Feige and Parkin (1971), Brunner and Meltzer (1971), and Karni (1974) for recent analyses of the demand for money that consider explicitly the role of transactions costs.

stochastic expenditure patterns, individuals will choose to hold assets which have low transactions costs associated with conversion to consumption goods. This property of assets, the ability to be transformed into consumption goods at minimal transactions costs, is referred to as liquidity.[11] Given the continuum of liquidity and noting the generally negative correlation between liquidity and expected return, individuals will hold a portfolio of assets in which the marginal benefit of increased liquidity and the accompanying expected reduction in transactions costs is just equal to the marginal cost of the reduction in expected return.

Among these assets, demand deposits and loans provide liquidity at a relatively low transactions cost because they provide consumers with complete divisibility and permit him to monitor his activities at a relatively low cost. A demand deposit permits the consumer to purchase an asset or repay a debt with the exact amount required by writing a check. The cleared check provides him with a legally acceptable, validated record of the transaction. A Treasury bill, on the other hand, usually must be converted to currency or a demand deposit before it can be used to effect transactions.

Loans made for the amounts and periods demanded similarly provide consumers with liquidity that obviates the need to incur the additional transactions costs of investing amounts not wanted. A debenture, on the other hand, involves a relatively large amount of funds for a relatively long period. Neither the amount nor the period may coincide with the consumption preferred by the consumer.

## Transactions Costs and the Demand for Financial Commodities

To summarize, financial intermediaries meet consumers' demands for time-dated consumption by supplying units of generalized purchasing power that can be converted into goods or services at minimal transactions costs in the amounts and at the times demanded.[12] Included in the price of these financial commodities are

---

11. Pierce (1966) following Tobin demonstrates that liquidity may be measured as the amount that can be acquired (either through the sale of an asset or through borrowing) over a given time period and state of the economy relative to the maximum amount that could be realized from the sale of the asset were time not a factor. Therefore, currency, being legal tender, is perfectly liquid. However mortgage loans, which require large information costs for a prospective buyer to ascertain valuation, are generally illiquid.

12. Thus, a consumer who wishes to acquire the services of an automobile now (and over time) in exchange for reduced consumption of other goods and services at specified amounts in the future may borrow $3,800.00 and pay a bank $183.67 a month for 24 months. A manufacturer may acquire the productive services of a machine that costs $10,800, for which he contracts to return $11,880 one year hence.

amounts that compensate the financial institution for the costs of processing the paperwork required to record the transaction, to determine the likelihood that the borrower will repay his debt, to monitor his repayment of the debt and to acquire the funds borrowed. Also included are amounts (interest) that compensate other consumers for deferring present consumption.

Similarly, consumers who wish to consume in the future may invest their funds (currently owned claims over resources) with a financial intermediary. The intermediary provides them with an expected real return for the period over which they choose to invest. Furthermore, consumers generally can invest whatever amounts they wish for whatever period they wish.

Financial intermediaries are organized to meet these consumers' demands at relatively low transactions costs by producing financial commodities and services. The conditions that govern this production are considered in the next section.

## III. Production

### General Considerations for the Production of Financial Commodities

The market price of a financial commodity is a function of the total cost of producing the financial commodity. We begin to examine the price charged by the firm by considering the behavior of an unregulated firm. (The impact of government regulation is considered in section V.) The price of any financial commodity in an efficient, competitive market can be conceptually separated into three parts: one part depends only on the pure riskless rate (what in a two-period world would correspond to the marginal rate of substitution between current and future consumption), one represents a premium for risk, and one is a compensation for the administration, monitoring, and processing costs imposed on the producer. To examine the first two parts, it is convenient to employ the analogy suggested by Black and Scholes (1973) between the valuation of a call option and the valuation of equity.[13] Black and Scholes demonstrate that in a frictionless world without taxes and bankruptcy costs that the value of equity ($E$) and debt ($D$) (defined as pure discount bonds) are functions of the value of the underlying assets ($V$), the

---

13. See Smith (1976) for a review of the option pricing literature and the applications of the option pricing model to value other contingent claim assets.

face value of the debt ($D^*$), the time to maturity of the debt ($T$), the riskless rate of interest ($r$), and the variance rate on the assets ($\sigma^2$):[14]

$$V = E(V, D^*, T, r, \sigma^2) + D(V, D^*, T, r, \sigma^2), \tag{11.1}$$

where

$$\frac{\partial E}{\partial V} \frac{\partial E}{\partial T} \frac{\partial E}{\partial r} \frac{\partial E}{\partial \sigma^2} > 0, \quad \frac{\partial E}{\partial D^*} < 0,$$

$$\frac{\partial D}{\partial V} \frac{\partial D}{\partial D^*} > 0, \quad \frac{\partial D}{\partial T} \frac{\partial D}{\partial r} \frac{\partial D}{\partial \sigma^2} < 0.$$

Even in the absence of transactions costs, any economic agent who purchases or sells a financial commodity must ascertain the values of these variables. The cost of assessing the riskless rate is very low, for it is exogenous to the process and readily observable. However, assessment of the other relevant variables may entail high information costs. This task may be trivial in the case of an investment where repayment is guaranteed by a secure insuror (such as the FDIC, FSLIC, VA, FHA, or NCUA). But for other investments, the assessment of the magnitudes of the variables is costly and the agents incurring these costs must be compensated.

In providing funds to a borrower, lenders are faced with the possibility that honesty on the part of the borrower may not be his best policy. For example, if a borrower obtains a loan based on his stated intention to purchase low-risk assets with the proceeds, he can increase his equity by actually using the proceeds to purchase high-risk assets. If the lender does not perceive that this action is possible (and therefore charges an interest rate which assumes that this action will in fact be taken), he will suffer a capital loss: the market value of the loan will fall because the agreed rate of interest is insufficient compensation for the risk of bankruptcy. Consequently, the lender must charge a price (interest rate) sufficient to compensate him for the riskiest choice of assets that the borrower might acquire. Furthermore, if the lender sets the interest rate at that level, the borrower

---

14. These partial effects have intuitive interpretations: an increase in the value of the underlying assets directly increases the value of the equity and increases the coverage on the debt, thereby lowering the probability of default. An increase in the face value of the debt increases the claim on the assets by the creditors thereby increasing the current value of the debt and, since equity is a residual claim, reduces its current value. An increase in the time to maturity of the debt or an increase in the riskless rate decreases the present value of the debt obligation. Finally, an increase in the variance rate on the assets increases the likelihood of the value of the assets being less than the face value of the debt at maturity, thereby lowering the current value of the debt and increasing the current value of the equity. Furthermore, in the presence of taxes, bankruptcy costs, and other agency costs, the debt–equity ratio would be an argument in the equity and debt functions. As pointed out by Long (1974) the Black-Scholes model cannot be directly applied in the presence of tax effects or agency costs which would make the value of the firm dependent upon the debt–equity ratio. However, it seems unlikely that qualitative results in (11.1) will be affected.

must acquire assets at least as risky as those the lender implicitly expects him to purchase or he will overcompensate the lender.

As pointed out by Jensen and Meckling (1975), the cost of this conflict of interests between the borrower and the lender can be reduced by placing a restrictive covenant into the credit agreement. This covenant contractually limits the activities of the borrower and therefore allows the lender to offer a lower rate of interest on the loan. However, there are other methods which can be used to minimize this problem, specifically the pledging of collateral. If collateral is included in a credit agreement, then the information costs imposed on the lender may be significantly lowered. Instead of calculating the appropriate rate of interest based on the least favorable available action to the borrower, given the covenants in the instruments, the lender can base the rate on his estimate of the risks associated with the collateral. This procedure may be much less expensive to administer and monitor than the procedure of employing general, restrictive covenants.

Of course, in the case of financial commodities such as loans, trade-offs exist between these various ways of protecting one's self as a lender. Increasing the down payment required, pledging collateral, and inserting restrictive covenants into the credit agreements imply different combinations of information and monitoring costs over the life of the loan. It is expected that the combination of these instruments chosen would be such that the marginal reduction in expected costs would be equal for all instruments employed.

It also appears that, for certain types of loans, the information costs associated with ascertaining the magnitudes of the arguments in (11.1) are so high that it is preferable to employ instrumental variables instead. Consequently, financial intermediaries generally gather, check, and update information about borrowers, for frequently the historical record of past obligations is a good source of information about the likelihood of repayment. This information also may be quantified and summarized with the aid of credit scoring techniques and financial statement analysis.

The considerations discussed above are not specific to financial intermediaries—they are relevant to all financial commodities produced by economic agents. Now we turn to the question of why financial intermediaries usually perform these services rather than other services.

## The Costs of Producing Financial Commodities

The production of financial commodities, like the production of any other good, requires the use of various forms of labor and capital goods. In the production of financial commodities, these inputs are more extensively employed in tasks of documentation, information, and monitoring. Extensive documentation is necessary because financial commodities are claims that can be easily converted into generalized purchasing power or consumption goods by the holder with small transactions costs. Therefore, there must be little question that these claims are legally enforceable—so little question that the high legal costs associated with government enforcement of these contracts will be rarely employed.[15]

As suggested above, information costs are often relatively large for the production of financial commodities, especially for those that entail a promise to repay funds at a later date (e.g., loans). Where collateral is required to secure a loan, its value must be ascertained and kept current. This task is not difficult for assets that are continuously traded, such as listed securities; however, determination of the value of other assets may require specialized expertise. Though information and monitoring may be most useful for such financial commodities as loans; deposits and other commodities require these aspects of production to reduce frauds, litigation, and misunderstandings which are expected to be more costly. Financial intermediaries create financial commodities which require the performance of these tasks because they have a comparative advantage in processing documents, in acquiring information about borrowers' ability to repay debts, and in monitoring instruments that can be easily converted into generalized purchasing power.

Three sources of this comparative advantage may be delineated. First, the intermediary is able to achieve economies of scale as a consequence of specialization. Thus, routines designed for and information received about a consumer or types of consumers can be used to process other consumers;[16] further, specialized machinery and forms may be developed and designed.[17] Economies of specialization may make it cost-effective for some institutions to specialize in providing a single type of financial commodity to a specific group of customers (e.g., consumer finance companies), while others carry a limited line of related financial commodities (e.g., wholesale commercial banks, thrift institutions, and investment companies), and others are virtually financial department stores (e.g., full-service commercial banks).[18] Second, some important information, such as details about a borrower's financial condition, can be obtained by a financial institution

---

15. To reduce these enforcement costs and to minimize monitoring costs for the intermediary financial commodities are sometimes negotiable: a holder of a financial claim need prove only that he is a holder in due course, having not obtained the claim through fraud or theft. Consequently, negotiable commodities require extensive control and monitoring by the holder, since it is very difficult to prove that the bearer of such an instrument is not a holder in due course. Therefore, these transactions costs can be shifted directly from the issuer to the bearer.

16. Credit scoring for screening consumer loans and lending by bank officers who specialize in specific industries or types of real estate are examples.

17. Check sorting machines and loan forms and routines are examples.

18. Available evidence indicates that many financial institutions (such as thrift institutions) have achieved virtually all economies of scale available through specialization and consequently might benefit from economies of diversification were they not prohibited by law from producing additional financial commodities (see Benston, 1972). These issues are considered further, below.

at much lower cost than by others because the financial institution is expected to exhibit, and therefore can more easily acquire a reputation for exhibiting, discretion with that type of information.[19] Third, financial institutions can reduce the transactions costs associated with search. An individual who wishes to lend can search for another person who wishes to borrow, but this process is generally more expensive than having a market through which these transactions can be accomplished. (Note, however, that the process does not require a matching of borrower and lender, even within the same institution.)

## Specialization and Diversification in the Production of Financial Commodities

It is generally the case (for reasons that are discussed below) that financial intermediaries tend to produce more than one kind of financial commodity. They tend to have many sources and uses of funds. They can obtain funds through equity, borrowing, accepting deposits of various kinds, and so on. They can employ these funds by making loans, purchasing securities, building offices, buying equipment, and so on. In equilibrium, the total cost of obtaining another dollar from any of these sources should be equal. In equilibrium, the total return from employing another dollar in any of these uses also should be equal. Consequently, financial intermediaries should not necessarily associate sources and uses of funds.

That financial intermediaries should not associate sources and uses of funds does not imply that the two sides of the balance sheet involve independent and separable decisions. As long as bankruptcy costs are positive, the structure of the two are related. For instance, real estate investment trust companies generally borrowed in the short-term credit market and loaned in the intermediate or long-term credit market. This practice exposed these trusts to interest rate risk which could have been hedged by matching the maturity structure of the assets and liabilities. When interest rates rose, the value of their assets fell by a much greater amount than did the value of their liabilities. This resulted in great financial difficulty for many of the trusts. Similarly, government regulations that essentially restrict thrift institutions to mortgage loans and savings deposits expose them to a higher probability of bankruptcy. Thus, a hedging of risks appears desirable. But it need not be achieved (and may not be achievable) by matching deposits from and loans to individuals (or any other group or type of consumers). What, then, determines whether and how financial institutions offer a specialized or diversified array of financial commodities and services?

---

19. Private individuals may be denied access to this information for fear that it may be made available to competitors or others.

Financial intermediaries, as they presently are organized, offer a wide variety and combination of financial commodities and services. Aside from laws and government regulations (which, as we discuss in section V, are a principal determinant), several factors may account for this diversity. Among these are economies of scale from specialization, economies from diversification, economies to customers from purchasing financial commodities and services at a single location or from a single institution, and reduction of the probability of incurring bankruptcy costs. The available empirical evidence suggest that there exist economies of scale in the production of financial commodities. However, the financial intermediaries studied are sufficiently large to have achieved most of these economies with respect to the production of relatively homogeneous financial commodities.[20] Additionally, there appear to be some economies of scale from diversification.[21] Diversification also may be valued because it lowers the probability (and hence the expected cost) of bankruptcy. This occurs because the returns from investments in different types of loans, customer services, locations, and so on, over different states of the world (such as general and local economic depressions, inflation, changes in consumers' tastes and preferences, changes in laws, and changes in the enforcement of regulations) are likely to be imperfectly correlated. Of course, it is expected that institutions will equate the marginal advantage from diversification with the marginal cost of less specialization.

A combination of economies from joint production and lower consumer-borne transactions costs, may explain why specific commodities and services generally are produced by financial intermediaries.[22] Reduced customer transactions costs also explains the offering of these services by many financial institutions. However, specialized financial intermediaries may have some comparative advantages over department store types of institutions.[23] But as we discuss in section V, outdated laws and regulations may prevent change from occurring. First we consider the pricing of financial commodities and services.

---

20. See Benston (1965, 1970, 1974), Bell and Murphy (1968), Longbrake and Haslem (1975), and Halpern and Mathewson (1975).
21. See Benston (1972, 1974, 1975), Halpern and Mathewson (1975), and Bell and Murphy (1968).
22. Safe deposit boxes, for example, require investments in vaults, alarm systems and guards. These also are required for safeguarding the currency and negotiable instruments used for fund transfers, deposits and loans.
23. For example, given the laws and consumers' tastes, specialized small loan companies may be able to supply high-risk consumer cash loans at a lower transactions cost than can commercial banks. Changed conditions (such as changes in consumers' tastes and effective reductions in graduated legal ceiling rates on small loans as a consequence of inflation) may reduce the advantage of specialization to the point where the advantages from diversification dominate.

## IV. Pricing of Financial Commodities and Services

Several studies have suggested that, in the absence of government regulation and in the presence of efficient markets, financial institutions would unbundle charges for their products.[24] In equilibrium, given competitive markets, financial institutions would charge consumers the marginal cost of producing the commodities and services demanded. Similarly, consumers would be rewarded according to the marginal value of the resources they made available to the intermediary. Thus charges would be levied for each check processed, each deposit made, each statement prepared and mailed, each note collected, each installment payment rendered, and so on.

However, this analysis neglects the transactions cost of accounting for transactions. It is clear that, were it not for the prohibition of interest on demand deposits, we would observe direct interest payments rather than "free" checking or lower rates charged on loans to depositors, and so on. But the cost of accounting for each service demanded by consumers might prevent complete unbundling from being cost-effective. Rather it seems likely that for some financial commodities financial institutions would estimate the average cost of processing a given type of account and pay (or charge) an interest rate and/or overall service charge that covers expected costs. This procedure would permit dispensing with the monitoring and accounting system required for the explicit charge system.[25] The issue, of course, is essentially an empirical one—which charging system (or combination of systems) requires the smallest costs net of benefits. However, government regulations impinge on the choice of method and on the ability of financial institutions to repackage and alter their commodities as technology and consumers' tastes change. We turn, next, to this question.

## V. Government Regulation

It is clear that any government regulation presents a constraint on those regulated that reduces aggregate welfare, with four possible exceptions: the constraints are not binding, there are externalities, the cost of government administration is reduced, and resources are redistributed among persons so that someone's welfare is increased. The following discussion is limited to considering the effect of specific regulations on the ability of financial institutions to meet consumers' demands

---

24. See, for example, Black (1975) and Knight (1975).
25. It should be noted that before the prohibition of interest payments on demand deposits (in 1933), banks generally paid interest only on large account balances and generally did not charge for individual services rendered.

efficiently. In general, we do not consider the welfare effects of these regulations on individuals (in part because we believe these to be unimportant).

Government regulations on financial intermediaries may be grouped as follows: (1) licensing, (2) price control, (3) credit allocation, and (4) supervision. Each is discussed in turn.

First, unlike most other enterprises, financial intermediaries generally cannot be established without permission from some regulatory agency. In addition, bank-type financial institutions require regulatory permission to expand via branching, a method that is prohibited or restricted by many states, with expansion across state lines being generally prohibited. Financial intermediaries also are prohibited or restricted from offering specific financial commodities and services.[26] Licensing regulations also may prevent financial intermediaries from organizing production of financial commodities and services in efficient ways. Restrictions on the intermediaries' ability to jointly produce and offer their output at locations of their choosing necessarily increases the transactions costs (including inconvenience costs) that some consumers must bear.

Second, control over the prices received and paid by financial intermediaries are imposed by the states and the federal government. State-imposed usury laws place ceilings on the amounts that intermediaries can receive on loans.[27] As is the case for price controls generally, interest rate restrictions tend to misallocate resources. When they are effective, usury laws result in restricted availability of riskier and operationally more costly loans as financial intermediaries shift their funds to loans whose net yields are within legal limits. Since the ceilings are stated as rates per dollar and rarely are changed, inflation increases the effectiveness of the ceilings as the premium for inflation increases to the point where loans are not as profitable as other investments. Larger business loans are made in preference to smaller loans since, generally, larger loans require lower operating expenses per dollar loaned. Tie-in arrangements, such as compensating balances, are used which effectively increase the rate of interest charged. Smaller consumer loans are not offered, except as "loss leaders" (Benston, 1975; Bowsher, 1975). If the ceilings become sufficiently restrictive, consumers cease using the services of regulated financial intermediaries and, where the law permits, direct loans and other forms of disintermediation take their place. The net result seems to be a decline in welfare.

---

26. For example, only commercial banks can offer demand deposits. Thrift institutions cannot offer non–real estate related commercial loans. Consumer cash loans (except for real estate–related and student loans) cannot be offered by thrift institutions in most states. Commercial banks cannot make equity investments or offer equity investment services to consumers.

27. See Bowsher (1975), pp. 20–21, for a table that summarizes the usury rates state by state.

Ceilings on deposit payments similarily have dysfunctional effects. The argument that prohibiting interest payments on demand deposits is necessary to keep banks from making risky loans in an effort to offset the interest expense has been shown to be false (Benston, 1964). Rather the prohibition has the effect of a government-administered oligopolistic cartel price enforcement. Ceilings on the rates paid on time and savings deposits also have the effect of raising transactions costs, as financial intermediaries and consumers attempt to evade the restrictions. Premiums and promotions are less valuable to consumers than their cash equivalents and disintermediation is generally more costly than intermediation. However, the cost to consumers of disintermediation may exceed the benefits (which appears to be the case for holders of smaller savings accounts).[28] The effect, then, of ceilings on the prices financial intermediaries may charge and pay for funds is to increase transactions costs (borne by the intermediaries and consumers) and misallocate resources.[29]

The third form of government regulation, control or credit allocation, takes at least four forms: (1) mortgage lending is encouraged by a variety of subsidies, (2) loans made to finance purchases of securities are discouraged by margin requirements that call for relatively large amounts of collateral, (3) small consumer cash loans are limited by state-imposed limitations on maturities and interest rate ceilings, and (4) mandatory credit allocation to groups and areas which presumably have been discriminated against have been proposed. Other controls have been attempted in the past, such as "moral suasion" by the Federal Reserve to discourage banks from making foreign and other undesirable loans and wartime controls on consumer loans and mortgages.[30]

Although there is doubt that subsidies on mortgage loans actually increase the stock of housing (Jaffee, 1975; Meltzer, 1974), there seems little doubt that controls reduce some forms of lending by financial intermediaries. In the short run, such controls as margin requirements for loans to purchase securities can

---

28. See Pyle (1974) for an estimate of the opportunity losses incurred by savers from interest rate regulation.

29. The ceilings have been defended as necessary for the continued viability of specialized thrift institutions and beneficial to deserving groups (such as the housing industry, in the belief that the intermediaries' reduced cost of funds necessarily will be passed on to mortgages and that an interest rate differential in favor of thrift institutions will favor allocation of credit to mortgage loans). Even assuming that savers who find it too costly to disintermediate should (and do) support home builders and buyers, the effectiveness of this form of subsidy has been questioned by a large number of studies (see Meltzer, 1974; and Jaffee, 1971). Since this argument explicitly assumes intermediaries associate sources and uses of funds, it is highly doubtful that this rationale is valid. The continued viability of financial intermediaries who are required by regulations to concentrate on mortgage loans and savings and time deposits, though, is in question as continued inflation increases the effectiveness of interest rate ceilings.

30. We also should mention that non–interest bearing required reserves in effect allocate resources from users of deposits to the federal government.

reduce the amount of funds allocated for this purpose. But, as Mayer (1975) concludes after an extensive review of the literature and analysis of credit allocation schemes: "credit allocation is not an efficient system. The shifts in the distribution of credit which it tries to bring about are of doubtful value, and, in any case, credit allocation would be ineffective in the long run. But this would not prevent it from imposing substantial costs on the economy" (p. 91).[31]

Efforts of authorities to force or encourage financial intermediaries to lend specific groups or in specific areas also have been proposed.[32] It is possible that these efforts will succeed, particularly if the institutions have not been making loans as a consequence of misinformation or prejudice. However, if past experience is a guide, the net effect is likely to be the imposition of additional transactions costs with little effect on the allocation of credit.

Finally, financial intermediaries have almost always been subjected to rather close supervision by governmental authorities. This supervision takes the form of detailed reporting requirements (i.e., quarterly call reports by banks, monthly reports by savings and loan associations, annual statutory reports by life insurance companies, etc.) and (for bank-type intermediaries) direct examination. Several reasons explain this type of supervision: (1) the public-facility nature of most intermediaries, wherein the general public believes or is encouraged to believe that funds deposited in a financial intermediary are "safe"; (2) the fact that the assets held by financial intermediaries can be misappropriated relatively easily if controls are not maintained; (3) the externalities that are believed to exist, wherein the failure of one intermediary affects others (bank runs) and the economy in general; and (4) deposits are insured by government agencies (FDIC, FSLIC, NCUA).[33]

One important effect of close supervision is increased transactions costs. The supervised financial intermediaries must bear the direct cost of assessments and examination fees. They also absorb the costs of meeting the examiners' and supervisors' requests for data and the opportunity cost of complying with their orders. In equilibrium, these costs are borne by the purchasers of their output. However, the benefits from examination should be deducted from the costs. The principal benefit is the savings by consumers of the information and insurance costs that they otherwise would have to bear were the FDIC, FSLIC, and NCUA not examining the institutions and insuring deposits and shares. These cost savings would appear to be relatively greater for holders of small deposits, since much of the cost

---

31. Also see Benston (1975) for an example of the effect of state-imposed restrictions on driving almost all of the consumer finance companies in Maine out of business.

32. These proposals include mandatory mortgage loans in sections of a city presumably discriminated against (anti–redlining), loans to black-owned businesses, loans to women, and so on.

33. These reasons are analyzed in Benston (1973) and, with the exception of the last reason, are found generally not to be valid.

of information about the operations of an institution is fixed with respect to the amount deposited. Borrowers, on the other hand, have much less interest in the safety of their creditors.

## Conclusions on Government Regulation and Financial Intermediation

Government regulation increases the transactions costs of financial intermediation principally by restricting financial intermediaries from operating as efficiently as they otherwise would. Licensing restrictions increase the costs. Obviously, these restrictions increase the transactions costs of financial intermediation. Furthermore there appear to be few offsetting benefits for consumers, other than some reduction in information costs derived from the knowledge that the regulatory authorities can punish a poorly or fraudulently run intermediary by removing its license or refusing it permission to expand. Controls on interest payments and charges, mandatory credit policies, and close supervision also result in higher transactions costs and asset misallocations. Only examination and deposit insurance appear to reduce some information and insurance costs that consumers otherwise would incur.

On the other hand, government regulations may benefit existing financial institutions at the expense of consumers and of would-be competitors. This conclusion would be consistent with the capture hypothesis of regulation.

However, a mitigating factor should be mentioned. There is considerable contemporary evidence that financial institutions, acting in their own self-interest, have and are breaking down the regulatory barriers. The prohibition of interest payments on demand deposits is violated by "free" checking and, most recently, by negotiable orders of withdrawal accounts and other demand deposit-like systems offered by thrift institutions. Automatic shifts between checking and savings deposits in commercial banks and the establishment and growth of money management funds also are examples of institutional methods of effectively paying interest on demand deposits. Place-of-business funds transfer terminals, located in food and other stores by savings and loan associations, are permitting them to offer demand deposit-like services at remote locations in unit banking areas. Approval of these systems by the Federal Home Loan Bank Board in January 1974 led to the Comptroller of the Currency's approval in December 1974 of similar customer-bank-communication-terminals. These, in turn, are forcing a number of state authorities in unit banking states to approve their use by state banks.[34] Thus, the higher opportunity value of deposits appears to have made the same

---

34. See Lovati (1975) for a review of these developments.

existing electronics technology economically feasible. The regulatory barriers are being breached. But of course, the price paid by consumers is greater than had the barriers not initially existed.

## VI. Conclusions

In this essay we have tried to show that the analysis of transactions costs is central to the theory of financial intermediation. Financial intermediaries produce financial commodities which can be used to effect consumers' intertemporal, intratemporal and state-determined consumption decisions. Changes in technology and in consumer-borne transactions costs alter the types of financial commodities produced, the way in which they are packaged, and the institutions that produce and sell them to consumers. Furthermore, government regulation essentially restricts financial intermediaries from changing the specific commodities they produce to meet changes in technology and consumer tastes. We believe a more complete analysis would show the relationship between specific types of transactions costs and the type of financial intermediary and financial commodity that should arise to reduce these costs. We feel that this approach represents an appropriate direction for future analysis.

### REFERENCES

Bell, Frederick W. and Murphy, Neil B., *Costs in Commercial Banking: A Quantitative Analysis of Bank Behavior and Its Relations to Bank Regulation*, Research Report No. 41, Boston: Federal Reserve Bank of Boston, 1968.

Benston, George J., "Interest Payments on Demand Deposits and Bank Investment Behavior," *Journal of Political Economy*, 72, October 1964, pp. 431–49.

Benston, George J., "Economies of Scale and Marginal Costs in Banking Operations," *National Banking Review*, June 2, 1965, pp. 507–49.

Benston, George J., "Cost of Operations and Economies of Scale in Savings and Loan Associations," in *Study of the Savings and Loan Industry*, Federal Home Loan Bank Board, Washington: U.S. Government Printing Office, 1970, pp. 971–1209.

Benston, George J., "Savings Banking and the Public Interest," *Journal of Money, Credit and Banking*, 4, February 1972 (Part II), pp. 131–226.

Benston, George J., "Bank Examination," *Bulletin*, New York University, Institute of Finance, Nos. 89–90, May 1973, p. 73.

Benston, George J., "The Costs to Consumer Finance Companies of Extending Consumer Credit," in *Technical Studies Volume II*, National Commission on Consumer Finance, U.S. Government Printing Office, Washington: 1974, pp. 1–158.

Benston, George J., "State Controls on Consumer Finance Company Loans: The Case of Maturity Regulation in Maine," in *Government Credit Allocation: Where Do We Go from Here?* Institute for Contemporary Studies, San Francisco, and the Center for Research in Government Policy of the Graduate School of Management, University of Rochester, New York, 1975, pp. 181–208.

Black, Fischer, "Bank Funds Management in an Efficient Market," *Journal of Financial Economics*, 2, December 1975, pp. 323–39.

Black, Fischer and Scholes, Myron, "The Pricing of Options and Corporate Liabilities," *Journal of Political Economy*, 81, May–June 1973, pp. 637–59.

Bowsher, Norman N., "Usury Laws: Harmful When Effective," *Review*, Federal Reserve Bank of St. Louis, 56, August 1974, pp. 16–23.

Brunner, Karl and Meltzer, Allan H., "The Uses of Money: Money in the Theory of an Exchange Economy," *American Economic Review*, 61, December 1971, pp. 784–805.

Cagen, Phillip, *Determinants and Effects of Changes in the Stock of Money*, New York, 1965.

Feige, Edgar L. and Parkin, Michael, "The Optimal Quantity of Money, Bonds, Commodity Inventories, and Capital," *American Economic Review*, 62, June 1971, pp. 335–49.

Friedman, Milton and Schwartz, Anna J., *A Monetary History of the United States, 1867–1960*, Princeton, 1963.

Halpern, Paul J. and Mathewson, G. Frank, "Economies of Scale in Financial Institutions: A General Model Applied to Insurance," *Journal of Monetary Economics*, 1, 1975, pp. 203–20.

Hamada, Robert, "Investment Decision with a General Equilibrium Mean-Variance Approach," *Quarterly Journal of Economics*, 85, November 1971, pp. 667–83.

Hyman, David, "A Behavioral Model for Financial Intermediation," *Economic and Business Bulletin*, Vol. 24, Spring–Summer 1972.

Jaffee, Dwight M., *Credit Rationing and the Commercial Loan Market*, New York: John Wiley and Sons, 1971.

Jaffee, Dwight M., "Housing Finance and Mortgage Market Policy," in *Government Credit Allocation: Where Do We Go from Here?* Institute for Contemporary Studies, San Francisco, and the Center for Research in Government Policy and Business of the Graduate School of Management, University of Rochester, New York, 1975, pp. 93–122.

Jensen, Michael and Meckling, William, "Theory of the Firm: Managerial Behavior, Agency Costs, and Ownership Structure," Working Paper, Graduate School of Management, University of Rochester, New York.

Kardouche, George K., *The Competition for Savings*, New York: Conference Board, 1969.

Karni, Edi, "The Value of Time and the Demand for Money," *Journal of Money, Credit and Banking*, 6:1, February 1974, pp. 45–64.

Klein, Michael, "A Theory of the Banking Firm," *Journal of Money, Credit and Banking*, 3:2 (Part 1), May 1971.

Knight, Robert E., "Customer Profitability Analysis, Part II: Analysis Methods at Major Banks," *Monthly Review*, Federal Reserve Bank of Kansas City, October 1975, pp. 11–23.

Long, John, "Comment on the Pricing of Corporate Debt: The Risk Structure of Interest Rates," *Journal of Finance*, 29, May 1974.

Longbrake, William A. and Haslem, John A., "Productive Efficiency in Commercial Banking: The Effects of Size and Legal Form of Organization on the Cost of Producing Demand Deposit Services," *Journal of Money, Credit and Banking*, 7, August 1975, pp. 317–30.

Lovati, Jean M., "The Changing Competition between Commercial Banks and Thrift Institutions for Deposits," *Review*, Federal Reserve Bank of St. Louis, July 1975, pp. 2–8.

Mayer, Thomas, "Credit Allocation: A Critical View," in *Government Credit Allocation: Where Do We Go from Here?* Institute for Contemporary Studies, San Francisco, and the Center for Research in Government Policy of the Graduate School of Management, University of Rochester, New York, 1975, pp. 39–92.

Melitz, Jacques and Pardue, Morris, "The Demand and Supply of Commercial Bank Loans," *Journal of Money, Credit and Banking*, 5:2, May 1973, pp. 669–92.

Meltzer, Allan H., "Credit Availability and Economic Decisions: Some Evidence from the Mortgage and Housing Markets," *Journal of Finance*, 29:3, June 1974, pp. 763–77.

Pesek, Borris P., "Bank's Supply Function and the Equilibrium Quantity of Money," *Canadian Journal of Economics*, 3:3, August 1970, pp. 357–83.

Pierce, James L., "Commercial Bank Liquidity," *Federal Reserve Bulletin*, 52, August 1966, pp. 1093–101.

Pyle, David H., "Descriptive Theories of Financial Institutions," *Journal of Financial and Quantitative Analysis*, December 1972, pp. 2009–29.

Pyle, David H., "The Losses on Savings Deposits from Interest Rate Regulation," *Bell Journal of Economics and Management Science*, 5:2, Autumn 1974, pp. 614–22.

Savings, Thomas R., "Transactions Costs and the Demand for Money," *American Economic Review*, 61, June 1971, pp. 407–20.

Smith, Clifford, "Option Pricing: A Review," *Journal of Financial Economics*, 3, January/March 1976.

Towey, Richard E., "Money Creation and the Theory of the Banking Firm," *Journal of Finance*, 39, March 1974, pp. 57–72.

Zabel, Edward, "Consumer Choice, Portfolio Decisions, and Transactions Costs," *Econometrica*, 41, March 1973, pp. 321–35.

# 12

# The Impact of Maturity Regulation on High Interest Rate Lenders and Borrowers

## I. Borrowing Controls and Consumer Welfare

Perhaps because of the continuing influence of the Old Testament, Aristotle, and medieval Christianity,[1] many people and governments do not regard interest simply as a price paid for a good or service. Although few people today believe that charging interest for the use of money is immoral, our laws and regulations reflect the still-held belief that people *ought* not to pay more than a given rate of interest and *ought* not to borrow without restrictions. As a consequence, state usury and small loan laws restrict the amount that can be charged and the maximum amount that can be loaned to individuals.

Limitations on the time over which a "high rate" lender (consumer finance company) may extend loans to a consumer is the most recent regulation imposed by those who wish to protect consumers from presumably rapacious lenders. These "consumer advocates" believe that many consumer finance companies, which are permitted to charge rates averaging about 24 percent, deliberately keep their clients in debt continuously. Richard Poulos, Federal Referee in Bankruptcy for the Southern District of Maine and perhaps the most forceful proponent of legislation restricting the period of indebtedness to small loan companies, puts the argument as follows:

---

Research for this essay was supported by the National Commission on Consumer Finance. Additional support was provided by the Institute for Humane Studies. Thanks are due to Neil Murphy, James Kershner, and Dan Sullivan of the University of Maine, who supervised and conducted the survey of borrowers; Richard Poulos and Gerald Cope, who provided background documents; the finance companies and the State of Maine Banking Department, who generously provided data; and Kim Benston and Joe Safier, who aided in research. Of course, they are not responsible for and may not agree with the essay.

1. See Taeusch (1942).

High interest has always plagued civilization. Most regulation has concentrated on controlling the *rate* of interest by setting maximum statutory limits. But this is not enough. Any problems about interest must be resolved by also considering (1) the *amount* of the loan and (2) the length of *time* for which it was granted. And the effectiveness of whatever restrictions may exist as far as these two factors are concerned must be tested against their possible evasion by the device of *renewals*.

Loans for short terms, even at high rates of interest, are not overly burdensome for most poor persons. The cost to meet some monetary emergency by a loan of one or two years is not exorbitant. But no one, let alone a low income person, can long endure (1) high rates of interest (2) on relatively large amounts of indebtedness (3) over long periods of time, from 3–8 years or more....

Renewals soon convert short term loans into long term obligations thereby subjecting the debtor to economic slavery. This has the effect of diverting large amounts of money from a debtor's limited income merely for the purpose of paying interest, thus hampering him from meeting the basic necessities of life for himself and his family. His financial strength is sapped to a point where any common hazard of life such as illness, loss of employment, divorce, etc., inevitably leads to a personal financial catastrophe compelling him to seek relief from welfare agencies or, ultimately, from the bankruptcy court. (Undated, pp. 24–25)

In large measure because of the efforts of Mr. Poulos and other "consumer advocates," the state of Maine adopted a law in 1967 which reduces the maximum interest rate that finance companies could charge to 8 percent on any loan balance remaining unpaid after 36 months. While this legislation probably benefited and may have been supported by the finance companies' competitors (commercial banks, credit unions, loan sharks, etc.), the principal proponents appear motivated primarily by a desire to help consumers. Whether or not the law served this purpose is the subject of the analysis which follows. The situation in Maine provides us with a valuable "laboratory experiment" from which the effects of such restrictive legislation can be measured and evaluated before it is extended to other jurisdictions.

The analysis is presented in four additional sections. The next section describes the effect on finance companies in Maine of the law which limited small loan maturities to 36 months. Hypotheses about the reasons for the dramatic decline in finance company offices and assets and the effect of this decline on consumers are delineated in the balance of the section. Tests of the hypothesis are developed and reported in sections III and IV. Section III analyzes hypotheses concerning the effect of the restrictive legislation on finance company operations, while section IV investigates its impact on the availability of consumer credit. Section V presents data to test hypotheses about the characteristics of long-term borrowers, those whom the legislation is designed to protect. The study and findings are summarized in the last section.

## II. Hypotheses on the Effect of "Limiting" Small Loan Maturities to 36 Months

### Conditions Obtaining before and after the Law

Maine's 8 percent limitation on the interest consumer finance companies can charge on loan balances unpaid after 36 months has been very strictly applied. The maturity of a loan is dated from its inception; extensions, rewritings, and additional cash advances are not considered new loans. Nor can the effects of the "limitation" be avoided by splitting loans, since this practice previously was (and still is) prohibited. The consequences attending the law have been considerable.

At the time the law was passed (1967), 116 offices (licenses) were operated by 28 finance companies in the state (as of June 30). In 1965, 111 offices had been operated by 27 companies. By June 1972 the number had decreased to 24 offices operated by 9 companies and by June 1975 the number had decreased further to 14 offices operated by 6 companies. By 1977 all consumer finance companies will have closed. As figure 12.1 shows, the reduction in offices and companies occurred primarily since 1969, the year in which the legislation affected the companies' loan portfolios and the year in which most companies realized that they were unlikely to succeed in getting the "36 month limitation" repealed or modified. Similarly, the dollar amount of loans outstanding fell from $31.0 million in December 1967 to $10.8 million in December 1971. (Later data are not available.)

### Proponents' Hypotheses

While proponents of the law did not expect the dramatic decline experienced, they consider the situation a net benefit for consumers.[2] These consumer advocates believe that the finance companies had been making exorbitant and immoral profits and view their departure as proof that they are not satisfied with normal returns. As they see it, the "36 month limitation" reduces the finance companies' revenues by preventing them from "exploiting" consumers: no longer can they entice consumers into renewing loans or compound more than 60 days unpaid interest in contravention of law.[3]

---

2. Quotations and sources of the viewpoints summarized are given in Benston (1974b).
3. The law permits lenders to add no more than 60 days unpaid interest to the principal on which additional interest is compounded. A "renewal" creates a new loan to which another 60 days unpaid interest can be added to principal.

Some supporters of the law also believe that national companies pulled out of Maine to "teach the state a lesson" and show other states that restrictive legislation means losing the small loan companies. They argue that the national companies find forgoing "normal" profits a price well worth paying to administer this lesson. However, the data presented in figure 12.1 refute this hypothesis. The decline in the number of national and local companies and their offices was about the same. Indeed, local companies appear to have ceased operations sooner.

A somewhat different "business" explanation for the decline in the number of finance companies is that the companies simply closed some of their offices to achieve economies of scale. As a consequence, it is argued, larger companies could operate at lower costs and thus "live" with the new legislation.

In any event, the consumer advocates believe that consumers were not seriously inconvenienced by the decline in finance company lending. Quite the contrary,

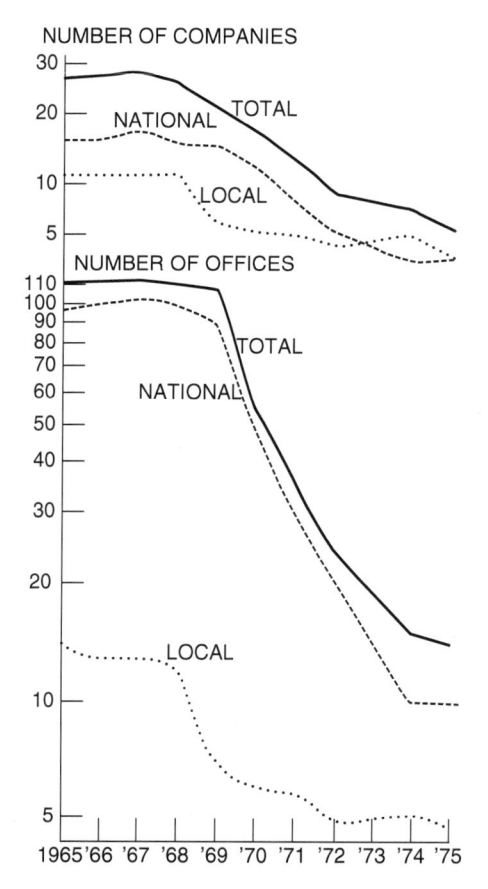

FIGURE 12.1 Number and Total, National and Local Companies and Offices Operating in Maine, as of June 20, 1965 through 1972 (1973 data not available)

they view the increase in credit union loans from $166 million in December 1967 to $225 million in December 1971 as evidence that borrowers were being served effectively by lower rate lenders and that, consequently, they benefited from the legislation.

## Opponents' Hypotheses

Opponents of the legislation believe that the virtual elimination of consumer finance companies is due primarily to the negative effect of the "36 month limitation" on ordinary operating expenses and revenue. The law not only effectively prohibits them from making loans with maturities longer than 36 months (since the 8 percent they are permitted to charge is about the same rate at which they obtain the funds loaned, leaving nothing for operating expenses and losses); it also makes renewals past this limit very unprofitable. This prohibition, the companies claim, does not allow them to serve regular customers or extend the term of a loan on which a borrower is unable to make scheduled payments.[4] Consequently, the small loan company cannot renew or extend loans, but must limit its operations to making one-time loans.[5]

The companies deny the consumer advocates' belief that they should be able to make normally profitable one-time loans with maturities of less than 36 months. Operating expenses are higher under such restrictions, they claim. Lending to a present borrower is much less expensive than lending to a new customer: the credit check required is much less extensive, the interview need not be as long, and, most important, the risk is less since the present customer's payment record is known. The cost of acquiring customers also increases if lending to present customers is made prohibitively unprofitable. In addition, the law creates much higher collection costs and loan losses. When a customer cannot make his payments, the usual practice is to reduce the size of the payments and extend the term of the loan. With this practice made unprofitable, the companies must formally declare the loan in default and obtain a court judgment, a more expensive procedure for both companies and customers.

Finally, opponents of the law question the claim that consumers are served better when one source of supply, finance companies, is eliminated as a competitor for consumers' trade. While some borrowers may be served better by

---

4. As one company vice president puts it in correspondence with the author: "Each time the borrower refinances his loan with the lender, the term of the loan becomes shorter and the monthly payment larger than the payment on the previous loan. Eventually, because of the 36 month limitation that dates from the initial loan, the term of the loan becomes so short and the payment so large that the lender can no longer serve the borrower's needs since he is unable to make the big payment each month."

5. While data on the percentage of loans made to present customers are not reported to the Bank Commissioner in Maine, data from large companies and from other states indicate that about 62 percent of the number of loans made are renewals (with and without cash added), about 27 percent are made to new borrowers, and 11 percent to former borrowers.

commercial banks and credit unions, others may not be able to borrow from legal lenders at all.

## Summary of Hypotheses

In summary, the following hypotheses are proposed by proponents and opponents of the "36 month limitation."

### Proponents

1. Finance companies were making abnormal and immoral returns before the penalty on maturities over 36 months was imposed, and now they are not satisfied with normal returns.
2. Abnormal, immoral revenue was generated by tempting consumers into making improvident loans which they couldn't repay and had to renew.
3. National companies suspended operations to "teach Maine and other states a lesson" (this hypothesis is rejected by figure 12.1).
4. Economies of scale, rather than the adverse effects of the law, led the companies to close and consolidate offices.
5. In any event, consumers were benefited, not hurt, because they were able to obtain loans at credit unions and other lower rate lenders.

### Opponents

1. The 8 percent maximum rate on balances outstanding more than 36 months decreases average gross yields intolerably.
2. Renewals are no longer profitable, and new customers require higher acquisition and operating expenses.
3. Since extensions of loans to borrowers in default is very costly when the balance earns only 8 percent gross, companies are forced to attempt to collect these loans rather than "work with" the customer.
4. Consumers are worse off when an important source of credit is no longer available.

In large measure, then, the alternative positions are based (1) on assumptions about the loan companies' revenue, expenses, and return on capital, and (2) on the effects of the drastic decline in finance company lending on consumers. To put these viewpoints into perspective and render them testable, a descriptive model is presented in section III of the revenue and costs that a profit-maximizing lender faces when deciding whether or not to grant a loan. With this model, the effect of the maturity and other restrictions on the lender's decision-making function can be shown. With the important parameters of the model estimated, a test of the alternative hypotheses about loan company behavior can be made. Hypotheses on the availability of credit to consumers are considered in section IV.

## III. Tests of Hypotheses on Finance Company Revenue and Costs

### Revenue and Costs from Small Loans

In deciding the level of its loan portfolio in a particular location or state, and whether or not to grant a loan to a specific individual, a consumer finance company must estimate the net cash flow that will be generated. With respect to the individual borrower, the company faces a certain outflow of the net cash loaned, the operations cost of processing the required papers, an uncertain inflow of payments, and the additional operations cost of processing the payments. Simply accepting payments and making bookkeeping entries is a small part of the expense of serving a customer. The type of customer who borrows from finance companies requires more personal time and resource-consuming attention than customers who borrow from commercial banks or credit unions. This is part of the product he purchases. Were this attention not given, the probability of nonpayment would increase.

As with investments generally, there is an optimal level of resources for "servicing" loans. At some point, the present value of greater expected amounts of payments is exceeded by the present value of additional expenditures on servicing. In general, if the expected net present value is not positive, the company will not make the loan. And where the state enforces a ceiling on the amount of interest and fees that can be charged, neither the company nor the borrower has the option of increasing the gross amount of cash inflow.

Nevertheless, a loan may be made to a borrower for whom an initial loan appears unprofitable (negative expected net cash flow) if the company expects a profitable long-term relationship with him. Several factors lead to this expectation. First, the operations cost of extending a second or additional loan may be less than the cost of a new loan because the company already has established records for the borrower. Second, the company obtains information about the probability of repayment and the cost of servicing in the course of lending, information purchased at the cost of a negative expected present value cash flow from the first loan. However, this may be a profitable investment if the company is able to reduce its expected losses and the "excessive" operations cost of dealing with initially "unprofitable" customers by granting small first loans from which it determines the best prospects for larger second loans. Finally, although a company might find loans under a given dollar size unprofitable (since gross income is determined by a ceiling rate per dollar while operating costs are primarily a function not of the dollar amount loaned but of servicing the customer), it might be willing to make these loans as "loss leaders." If, in the company's experience, first-time borrowers tend to make larger successive loans that are profitable, it would be willing to make individually unprofitable first loans. By making the customer a first loan, the company expects a high proportion of customers to borrow from it again because satisfaction with the service and/or inertia keeps them from changing to other lenders, even lower cost lenders such as commercial banks or credit unions.

However, before these complex possibilities are structured and specified, the direct effect of the law on revenue is analyzed.

## Effect of the "36 Month Limitation" on Revenue

Reduction of revenue is an obvious effect of the law restricting gross interest yields to 8 percent on balances outstanding more than 36 months. The law, in effect, reduces the ceiling rate on loans to a weighted average of loans outstanding less and more than 36 months. The magnitude of this effect can be determined by calculating the average gross yield ($A$) on loans of different maturities, with the following formula:[6]

$$(1+A)^{p+u} = (1+P)^p (1+U)^u, \quad (12.1)$$

$P$ = profitable (higher) rate allowed up to 36 months,
$U$ = unprofitable (8 percent) rate allowed after 36 months,
$p$ = number of periods remaining at rate $P$,
$u$ = number of subsequent periods at rate $U$.

Solving equation (12.1) for $A$ yields

$$A = [(1+P)^p (1+U)^u]^{1/p+u} - 1. \quad (12.2)$$

Values for $A$ show one extreme effect of the law, since it is the average gross yield on funds outstanding over the entire period, $p + u$. The average gross yield also can be calculated on the assumption that a loan is repaid in equal periodic amounts. In this event, $A$ is calculated from equation (12.3):

$$\frac{(1+A)^{p+u} A}{(1+A)^{p+u} - 1} = \frac{(1+P)^p (1+U)^u}{\sum_{l=0}^{u-1}(1+U)^l + (1+U)^u \sum_{j=0}^{p-1}(1+P)^j}. \quad (12.3)$$

Table 12.1, part A shows the average rate, $A$, on funds not repaid until the end of the period $p + u$ of various combinations of years over which a loan earns profitable

---

6. I am indebted to Marshall Freimer for discussions that clarified and simplified the following analysis.

TABLE 12.1 Average Gross Yields Assuming Profitable Yields (P) of 30 and 24 percent and Unprofitable Yield (U) of 8 Percent, over Combinations of Three-Year Periods

| Years ($u$) at Unprofitable Yield ($U$) of 8 Percent | Years ($p$) at Profitable Yield ($P$) of 30 Percent ||| Years ($p$) at Profitable Yield ($P$) of 24 Percent |||
|---|---|---|---|---|---|---|
| | 3 | 2 | 1 | 3 | 2 | 1 |
| (A) Loan unpaid over entire period | | | | | | |
| 1 | 24 | 22 | 19 | 20 | 18 | 16 |
| 2 | 21 | 19 | 15 | 17 | 16 | 13 |
| 3 | 19 | 16 | 13 | 16 | 14 | 12 |
| (B) Loan repaid in equal periodic installments | | | | | | |
| 1 | 28 | 26 | 23 | 23 | 21 | 19 |
| 2 | 26 | 24 | 19 | 21 | 19 | 16 |
| 3 | 24 | 22 | 17 | 20 | 18 | 14 |

gross yields, $P$, of 30 and 24 percent and an unprofitable gross yield, $U$, of 8 percent. Part B of table 12.1 shows the average rate, $A$, on a loan repaid in equal installments over the period, $p+u$. Thus a finance company can expect a loan made for three years at 24 percent, but outstanding for an additional one, two, or three years will earn an average yield of 20 percent, 17 percent, and 16 percent. If this loan is repaid in equal installments over a four-, five-, or six-year period, the average gross yield is 23, 21, and 20 percent. Considering the likelihood that only a fraction of a loan with a greater than three-year maturity will be outstanding when the lower 8 percent ceiling applies and that some original loans made will be repaid entirely within three years, the postlaw average gross yields are of a magnitude imposed in some other states and higher than the rates charged by banks. Thus, while the lower gross yields might explain a reduction in the number and riskiness of loans made, it does not appear to be the primary explanation of the demise of the industry. Consequently, I now turn to an analysis of their operating costs.

## Operating Cost Analysis

Operating cost data as reported to the Maine Bank Commissioner were gathered for each year 1960 through 1971.[7] A cost model was estimated, based on an extensive consideration of the finance company operations presented in another paper (Benston, 1974a). The primary output variable is the number of loans serviced,

---

7. After extensive checking (that proved time-consuming, frustrating, and necessary), some of the data had to be rejected for obvious deficiencies in reporting. In particular, a company's first full year of operation and last year of operation were discarded as unrepresentative of normal operating conditions. A description of the sample is presented in Benston (1974b, table 3).

approximated by the average number outstanding during the year. Other variables are included to account for cost differences among firms that are not related to the primary output. A multiplicative cost function is assumed (from which log-linear regression were run) as follows:

$$OC = b_0 NLO^{b_1}(NLM/O)^{b_2}(NLL/M)^{b_3}DEL60+^{b_4}(NLO/OF)^{b_5}LOCAL^{b_6}u, \qquad (12.4)$$

$OC$ = operating costs per year (default losses, interest, and income taxes not included),

$NLO$ = average number of loans outstanding [(number year beginning + number year end)/2],

$NLM/O$ = number of loans made per year to number outstanding ($NLO$),

$NLL/M$ = number of large (over $1,000) loans made to the total number made × 100 + 1 (1 is added because some companies did not make large loans in this event log [($NLL/M$) + 1] = 0).

$DEL60+$ = dollars of loans delinquent 60 days or more per dollar of loans outstanding × 100,

$NLO/OF$ = $NLO$ per office,

$LOCAL$ = 10 if the company is local, 1 if it is national,

$u$ = error term, where log $u$ has mean equal to 0 and is distributed independently across units.

"Output" is measured by $NLO$; $NLM/O$ measures the rate of growth of a company; $NLL/M$ is an output homogeneity measure which extensive testing of a much larger amount of branch data from three major companies (Benston, 1974a) showed to be the only meaningful distinction of loan size; $DEL60+$ measures the additional costs of handling delinquencies; $NLO/OF$ measures the economies of scale related to office size rather than company size; and $LOCAL$ measures differences in reported operating costs between local companies that tend to be owner-run and national companies that allocate central company overhead to their Maine operations. Unfortunately, data on loans to new, present, and former borrowers are not reported to the state, nor could these data be acquired from a sufficient number of companies.

The cost of servicing a small loan was estimated with multiple regression analysis after all variables were transformed to common logarithms. Regressions were computed for each year individually, 1960 through 1971. Table 12.2 gives the regression coefficients and $t$-values computed for each year.[8] Notable in the

---

8. The regressions were tested for conformance with homoskedisticity, linearity, and independence as follows: the data were ordered by the principal independent variable, $NLO$; the residuals were plotted and Durbin-Watson statistics and first-order serial correlation coefficients were computed. These tests indicated the desired conformance.

TABLE 12.2 Determinants of Total Operating Expenses Regression Coefficients (t-values). Dependent Variable: Total Expenses before Income Taxes, Interest, and Losses[a]

| Year | NLO | NLM/O | NLL/M | DEL60+ | NLO/OF | LOCAL | CONST |
|---|---|---|---|---|---|---|---|
| 1960 | 1.18 | 0.65 | 0.020 | −0.11 | 0.26 | 0.22 | 0.30 |
|  | (8.59) | (1.04) | (1.24) | (0.67) | (1.37) | (1.80) | (1.60) |
| 1961 | 1.16 | [b] | 0.070 | 0.12 | 0.38 | 0.17 | 0.60 |
|  | (11.46) |  | (0.83) | (1.13) | (3.12) | (1.97) | (0.65) |
| 1962 | 1.22 | 0.03 | 0.061 | 0.60 | −0.02 | 0.22 | [b] |
|  | (12.71) | (2.39) | (6.35) | (4.53) | (0.12) | (2.14) |  |
| 1963 | 1.10 | 0.74 | 0.044 |  | 0.27 | 0.22 | [b] |
|  | (8.90) | (2.07) | (4.44) | (3.39) | (1.76) | (1.98) |  |
| 1964 | 1.15 | [b] | 0.035 | 0.16 | 0.24 | 0.30 | 0.20 |
|  | (4.22) |  | (1.99) | (0.85) | (0.72) | (1.28) | (0.66) |
| 1965 | 1.30 | 1.30 | 0.067 | 0.23 | −0.20 | 0.43 | 0.38 |
|  | (9.29) | (4.11) | (5.55) | (1.18) | (0.99) | (3.69) | (2.15) |
| 1966 | 1.29 | 0.21 | 0.037 | 0.33 | [b] | 0.36 | 0.23 |
|  | (13.14) | (0.74) | (2.12) | (1.48) |  | (2.38) | (0.82) |
| 1967 | 1.28 | 0.52 | 0.077 | 0.15 | −0.09 | 0.39 | 0.15 |
|  | (8.88) | (1.96) | (4.35) | (1.00) | (0.40) | (2.70) | (0.70) |
| 1968 | 1.10 | 0.46 | 0.041 | −0.05 | 0.49 | [b] | 0.10 |
|  | (17.45) | (1.33) | (2.42) | (0.60) | (4.07) |  | (0.31) |
| 1969 | 1.07 | 0.20 | 0.050 | −0.19 | 0.42 | 0.13 | 0.16 |
|  | (7.73) | (1.22) | (1.59) | (1.39) | (1.68) | (0.82) | (0.90) |
| 1970 | 1.19 | [b] | 0.055 | −0.04 | 0.09 | 0.45 | 0.50 |
|  | (4.55) |  | (1.14) | (0.16) | (0.19) | (1.35) | (1.60) |
| 1971 | 1.06 | −0.20 | 0.016 | −0.057 | 0.057 | 0.027 | 1.47 |
|  | (8.47) | (1.29) | (0.71) | (0.63) | (0.32) | (0.26) | (4.13) |

[a] $R^2$ for any year's regression is no less than .96. Variables were converted to common logarithms for regressions.
[b] F-value too small for inclusion.

table are the positive (though not large) coefficients for large loans (NLL/M), positive (though not consistently significant) coefficients for local versus national companies (LOCAL), and generally insignificant coefficients for the size of office (NLO/OF).

## Economies of Scale Hypothesis

The coefficients estimated contradict the hypothesis that consumer finance companies reduced the number of offices to achieve economies of scale. First, the average size of office did not increase over the period: the geometric mean number of loans per office were 367 in 1960, 246 in 1964, 278 in 1967, and 269 in 1970. Second, the insignificant coefficients of the size of office variable (NLO/OF) and the consistently greater than unity (though not statistically significantly greater) coefficients of the scale variable (NL) are contrary to the "economies of scale" hypothesis.[9]

## Tests of the Hypothesis that the Maturity Limitation Makes "Normal" Operations Unprofitable

Competing hypotheses about profitability of "normal" operations were tested by estimating the annual cost of making and servicing a loan compared to the revenue produced by the loan, given the legal ceiling rates. While it may seem that the maximum legal ceiling rate in Maine of 36 percent before 1967 and 30 percent thereafter on small loans is high, the data indicate that operating costs were even higher.

Average (and marginal, since these are almost the same) costs of making and servicing loans under $1000 were calculated from the coefficients presented in table 12.2 and the underlying data. The estimates, presented in table 12.3, show generally increasing average costs per loan over the period. From 1960 through 1963 costs averaged about $56 a loan. From 1964 through 1967, when the "36 month limitation" was enacted, they were about $70 a loan. For 1968 through 1970 per

TABLE 12.3 Average Annual Operating Cost per Loan under $1,000 (Income Taxes, Interest, and Default Losses not Included) Assessed at Geometric Means[a]

| Year | All Variables Included | Only Variables Significant at .05 Level Included Amount | Variables |
|---|---|---|---|
| 1960 | 55.72 | 53.15 | NLO, NLO/OF |
| 1961 | 54.73 | 53.44 | NLO, NLO/OF, LOCAL |
| 1962 | 62.89 | 62.92 | NLO, LOCAL, NLM/OF, LL/NLM, DEL60+ |
| 1963 | 62.81 | 62.08 | NLO, LOCAL, NLM/OF, LL/NLM, DEL60+ |
| 1964 | 66.48 | 64.63 | NLO, LOCAL, LL/NLM |
| 1965 | 76.79 | 72.46 | NLO, LOCAL, LL/NLM, NLM/O |
| 1966 | 75.11 | 71.44 | NLO, LOCAL, LL/NLM |
| 1967 | 66.68 | 65.14 | NLO, LL/NLM, NLO/OF |
| 1968 | 96.25 | 96.55 | NLO, LL/NLM, NLO/OF |
| 1969 | 78.23 | 75.97 | NLO, NLO/OF |
| 1970 | 82.08 | 73.54 | NLO, NLO/OF |
| 1971 | 105.32 | 68.33 | NLO, CONST |

[a]All variables evaluated at geometric mean values against coefficients given in table 12.2, with $LL/NLM$ set equal to 1 (log $LL/NLM = 0$). Since operating $\overline{cost = OC} = b_0 NLO^{b_1} (NLM/O)^{b_2} (NLL/M)^{b_3}$, etc., setting $NLL/M$ to 1, average cost = $OC/NLO = b_0 \overline{NLO}^{b_1-1} \overline{(NLM/O)}^{b_2}$ etc., where bars denote geometric means. Marginal costs can be calculated by multiplying average cost by $b_1$. Since $b_1$ is not significantly different from 1, these calculations are not presented.

9. Since all the data are in logarithms, the coefficients measure elasticities directly. For example, the 1960 coefficient of 1.18 indicates that a 10 percent increase in the number of loans outstanding would on the average result in an 11.8 percent increase in operating costs.

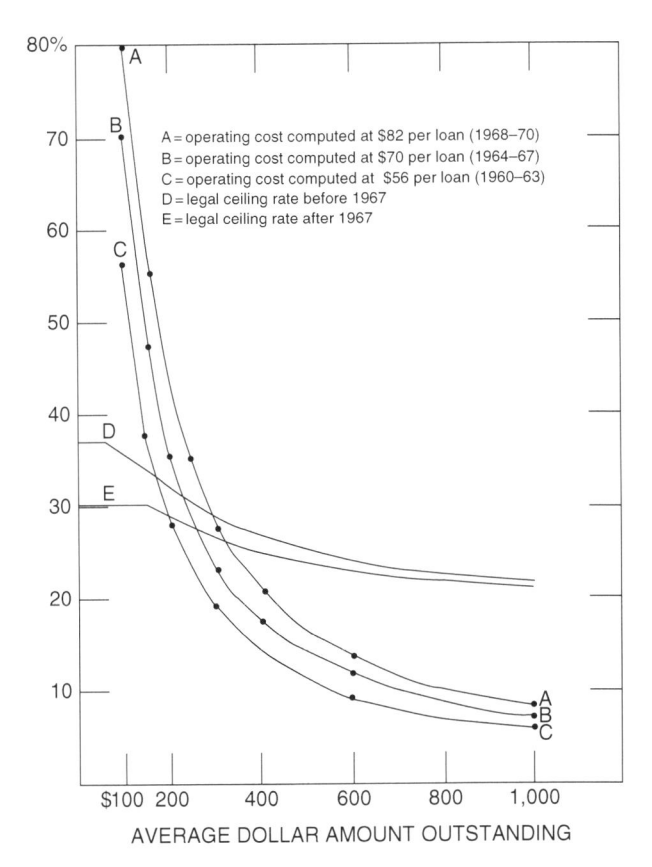

FIGURE 12.2 Average Operating Costs and Legal Ceiling Rates per Dollar of Loans

loan costs averaged about $82.[10] In part, the increasing costs mirror changes in the price level. However, the ceiling rates under which the companies operate were not changed to reflect changes in nominal costs. Rather, in 1967, the annual ceiling rate on loans with initial amounts of under $150 was reduced from 36 to 30 percent. Figure 12.2 shows average annual operating costs expressed as a percentage of dollars of loans outstanding, together with Maine's ceiling rates in effect before and after the 1967 law change. It seems clear that even under the higher rates allowed before 1967, loans under $150 probably were not profitable (recall that default losses and interest are not included in the average costs). With the lower ceiling rates the finance companies do not appear able to cover operating costs and interest for loans under about $500. Why, then, do they make these loans?

---

10. It is interesting to note that operating costs per loan in 1968, 1969, and 1970, estimated from data from 124 national companies, averaged $72 (Benston, 1974a).

The reason finance companies make apparently unprofitable loans (except when the negative contribution margin becomes too great) is suggested by the description of loan company operations presented above. Unprofitable small loans may be made when the company expects that a portion of these customers will renew these loans for larger amounts, primarily by borrowing again before the loan matures. Also, the loan company is able to assess the risk of lending larger amounts by first lending smaller sums. Thus, an initially unprofitable loan may result in a later profitable relationship. As is indicated by the model, the present value of the expected net cash flow from the customer is expected to be positive.

This explanation is consistent with the data. The 1967 reduction in rate ceilings for loans under $150 made these *very* unprofitable. The number of under $100 loans made dropped from 13 and 14 percent of total loans made in 1966 and 1967 to 7 and 3 percent of the total in 1968 and 1969 (Benston, 1974b, fig. 3). But companies still found loans of $100 to $300 worth making. Until 1969, the number of loans made of this size did not change greatly. However, the "36 month limitation," which became operationally effective in 1969, deprived them of the opportunity to engage a customer in a profitable long-term relationship. The effect on the average size of loans made by four major finance companies (from whom data could be obtained), shown in figure 12.3, also is consistent with the implications of the analysis. Loans made to new and former borrowers were consistently smaller than those made to present borrowers. Average amounts for all three types of loans increased over time as inflation reduced the real amount of funds borrowed and as increasing operating and money costs made smaller loans less profitable to the finance companies. In 1969, when the "36 month limitation" became effective (and the particular companies whose data are

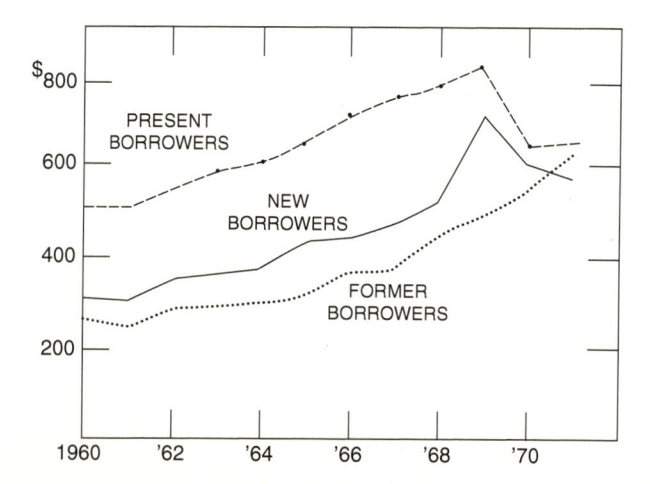

FIGURE 12.3 Average Size of Loans Made to New, Present and Former Borrowers in Maine, 1960–1971 (means of averages at three major finance companies)

reported realized that the law would not be repealed), the average size of loans made to new borrowers increased sharply from $482 in 1967 and $528 in 1968 to $712 in 1969. In comparison, the average size of loans made to present borrowers was $758 in 1967, $778 in 1968 and $822 in 1969. As figure 12.3 shows, by 1970 and 1971 size of loans made to new, present, and former borrowers averaged about the same.

## Costs of Lending to New versus Present Customers

The numbers or amounts of loans made to present borrowers are not reported to the Maine authorities. However, comparative differences in the cost of lending to new and former borrowers versus present borrowers were measured in a study of the branch operations of one small and three major consumer finance companies. The methodology and data used, and detailed findings derived, are reported in Benston (1974a). In that study, data from approximately 2,600 branches for each of the three years were analyzed. Regressions of direct cash operating expenses (total direct branch expenses not including occupancy, advertising, losses, and interest) were run for each year of each company on output (the average number of loans serviced), cost homogeneity variables (percent of loans made to new borrowers, percent of large [over $1,000] loans made, percent of other than personal loans made, relative factor prices in the county, and whether or not the branch was in a suburb), and market structure and legal variables (concentration ratios, state laws on entry restrictions, and creditors' remedies). The elasticities estimated indicate that an increase in the percentage of loans made to new borrowers from, say, 25 to 30 percent, and an offsetting decrease in the percentage made to present borrowers might result in a 1.6 to 3.2 percent increase in total branch costs for one company, a 0.4 to 1.5 increase for the second, as much as a 4.9 percent increase for the third, and no significant difference for the fourth. The data on former borrowers are not consistent: two companies' data show operating costs to be lower the higher the percentage of former borrowers, while two reveal higher costs. However, the coefficients estimated are not statistically significant.

It appears, then, that new borrowers are served at not much higher cost than present or former borrowers, so that even if a finance company made 54 rather than 27 percent of its loans to new customers, its operating costs might increase by only 10 percent. Consequently, it does not appear that a law restricting lending to new customers would increase operating costs sufficiently to "explain" the demise of the small loan companies in Maine.

## Collection Costs and Losses

The effect of the "36 month limitation" on collection costs and losses can be illustrated by considering the monthly payments schedule for a loan that provides the borrower with about $600. At the present ceiling annual simple interest equivalent rate of 26 percent, the monthly payment for a 12-month loan is $58, for a 24-month loan $32, and for a 30-month loan $28.[11] For about an $800 loan, the rate is a bit more than 24 percent and the monthly repayments are $80 for a 12-month loan, $44 for a 24-month loan, and $36 for a 30-month loan. The take-home family income of the average small loan borrower in Maine is between $475 and $550 a month.[12] While the borrower normally can make the required payments, a small disaster, such as illness or job layoff, might make it difficult for him to keep up to date. The loan companies recognize the possibility and usually "work with" the borrower by allowing him to extend his payments, often lending him additional funds to "tide him over." Possibly because of this practice, the lost rate actually experienced had been relatively low. Measured as charge-offs or increases to allowances for bad debts less recoveries divided by average dollars of loans outstanding, the net loss rate experienced by Maine consumer finance companies averaged 2.22 percent from 1960 through 1967. (The low was 1.87 in 1962 and the high 2.62 in 1967.)

The lower gross yields allowed by the "36 month limitation" apparently changed the trade-off between higher operating expenses and lower default costs. In 1968 the net loss rate increased to 3.25 percent, in 1969 to 4.10 percent, in 1970 to 7.66 percent, and in 1971 (the last year for which data are available) to 8.41 percent. The companies apparently could not require repayment within 36 months without incurring additional losses.

Thus, the analyses support the hypothesis that the "36 month limitation" made customary operations by finance companies unprofitable. It appears that (1) the impossibility of extending loans, when the borrower is unable to pay on time with consequent increase in defaults and reduction in revenue from which operating and other costs could be paid, and (2) the impossibility of maintaining a long-term customer relationship were important factors in the decision of finance companies to cease operations in Maine, though the additional cost of lending to new compared to present customers did not appear important. This hypothesis is tested further with an analysis of the companies' profitability before and after the restrictive legislation was effective.

## Profitability of Finance Companies

Those who urged passage of the "36 month limitation" and the reduction in ceiling rates argue that the companies could easily withstand the lower revenue. As Governor Kenneth Curtis said in 1969: "Indeed, our small loan regulating laws

---

11. The actual proceeds are adjusted up or down to make the monthly payments equal, even dollar amounts.
12. Source: Interviews with finance company executives and analysis of survey data presented in section V.

are, and they remain, favorable to small loan concerns." To provide a test of this contention, the annual yield on assets was computed for each finance company whose data are given above for the years 1960 through 1971. Because the data do not permit an unambiguous measure of yield, two rates were computed: (1) net small loan business operating income before income taxes and interest as a percent of average loans outstanding;[13] and (2) net total operating income from all sources before income taxes and interest expense as a percentage of average assets "used and useful," which includes working capital, furniture and fixtures, and so on, in addition to loans receivable. While the returns on equity would have been preferable numbers, the data (particularly those of national companies and unincorporated local companies) do not allow meaningful measures.

The data were disaggregated because some critics believe that national finance companies shift profits from life, accident, and disability insurance to an affiliated or owned insurance company to understate the income data reported to the bank commissioner. Mean percentage rates of return on assets are given for local and national companies, for the companies grouped according to asset size (under and over $1 million), and for all companies. Figure 12.4 presents these data graphically.

Without some standard of comparison, one can only draw definitive conclusions about the data that show a negative rate of return. Nevertheless, unless the reports are in error, it is clear that the net income before income tax and interest expense of most finance companies in Maine after 1969 (when the 1967 law began to take effect) was inadequate to support continued operations. For all companies, small loan operating income, as a percentage of average outstanding loans, dropped from 10.8 percent in 1960 to 6.0 percent in 1967, to 4.6 percent in 1969, and then to 1.7 percent and 0.08 percent in 1970 and 1971. The reduction was similar for total net operating income, for local and national, small, medium, and large companies.

Turning (with less certainty) to the period before the law, it appears that finance companies' return on assets was reasonably good, considering that they are relatively highly leveraged. However, even before the 1967 law was enacted, their yields were trending downward, as figure 12.4 graphically shows. In part, the reduced percentages are explained by the increasing operating costs shown in table 12.3. Average costs per loan increased from $55.72 in 1960 to $66.68 in 1967. Interest on the funds they borrowed also increased over the period,[14] but the maximum rates companies could charge did not increase. It appears, then, that their rapid exodus from the state was a result of decreasing returns due primarily to the "36 month

---

13. Income taxes are omitted because they need not reflect current operations and because they are often allocated arbitrarily by national companies. Interest also is often allocated arbitrarily by national companies and is largely a function of the type of financing (debt versus equity, primarily) used.

14. The annual average rate of finance company paper placed directly, three to six months, from 1960 through 1971 was 3.54 (1960), 2.68, 3.07, 3.40, 3.83, 4.27 (1965), 5.42, 4.89, 5.69, 7.16, 7.23 (1970), and 4.91 (*Federal Reserve Bulletin*, various issues).

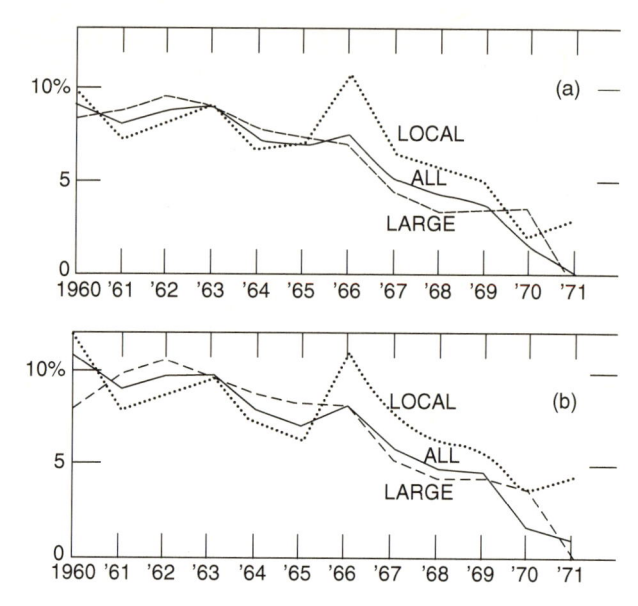

FIGURE 12.4 Net Income before Income Taxes and Interest Expense; All Local and Large (Assets over $1 million) Companies (Benston [1974a, tables 6 and 7]). (a) Small loan net income as percentage of average loans outstanding; (b) total net income as percentage of average assets "used and useful."

limitation" and secondarily to the reduction in the rate ceiling and maximum loan size. These factors were compounded by greater bad debt losses, largely due also to the "36 month limitation."

## IV. The Effect of the Decline in Finance Companies' Lending on the Availability of Credit to Consumers

### Description of Data

A large sample of borrowers was interviewed to determine directly the effect of the reduction in finance company lending on their customers.[15] In November and

---

15. An analysis was made of the supply and demand of consumer loans outstanding in Maine at consumer finance companies, industrial banks, federal and state credit unions, commercial banks, and mutual savings banks at each year-end, 1965 through 1967. The demand coefficients estimated were used to predict the amount of loans demanded in 1968 through 1971. Though the results are not conclusive, the amount of loans supplied appear to be significantly (though not radically) less than the amounts demanded. See Benston (1974b) for details.

December 1971, four major consumer finance companies which were shrinking and/or discontinuing their operations in Maine were asked to supply the names, telephone numbers, addresses, and other information on former or present customers who had wanted to take out or increase loans during the previous four months, but whose requests were refused because the company was not extending or making loans. In all cases, these were people to whom the companies would have been pleased to lend had they not decided to reduce or eliminate their operations in Maine. Names, addresses, and telephone numbers of 771 borrowers were received from the companies.

All borrowers for whom valid telephone numbers could be found were contacted.[16] In all, 436 persons were contacted at this stage of the survey. The telephone interviews proved very satisfactory, in part because the interviewers were very good at establishing rapport. The principal interviewer was a graduate student at the University of Maine who was familiar with much of the state. After some experimentation, he developed the technique of conducting an apparently unstructured conversation of from four to six minutes, during which he avoided leading the borrowers to answers, yet managed to get replies to most of the questions. When an interviewee wouldn't give information until specific questions were asked and then seemed to be answering to please or get rid of the interviewer, the interview was marked "refused to respond." Most in this group include people who simply wouldn't speak to the interviewer. Of the 436 people contacted, 58 (13.3 percent) refused to answer and 378 (86.6 percent) gave the requested information. The interviewers believe that they received valid answers to their questions, with one exception, the question "What percentage amount of loan was outstanding when you attempted to renew your loan?" Many interviewees gave vague replies which indicated that they either really did not know the amount or did not understand the question.

The 436 borrowers contacted represent 56.6 percent of the sample. It would be potentially misleading to assume that the persons not contacted are like those contacted; the absence of locatable telephone numbers might be an indication that inability to borrow additionally from the finance companies put them in a particularly difficult financial situation. Consequently, a subsample of 82 (24.2 percent) of the 335 borrowers not contacted was selected. (The subsample comprised all borrowers in several towns.) The last known home and work addresses of these borrowers was obtained, from which *all* were located (eventually) and interviewed, although this proved quite time-consuming. Thus a control against the 235 persons not contacted was established.

---

16. Initially, borrowers were sent a letter that informed them of the study and that they would be contacted by telephone, assuring them that they would not be sold anything, that the information gathered would be kept confidential, and that the study might benefit them. The letters appeared to be ignored completely. Consequently this procedure was abandoned.

The principal question the borrowers were asked was whether or not they had obtained elsewhere the funds for which they had gone to the finance companies. To ascertain which characteristics were associated with ability or inability to get funds, data on the borrowers were obtained from the finance companies, as follows: occupation, weekly gross salary, age, marital status, number of dependents, number of years the borrower was continuously in debt to the finance company, and the number of previous loans with the finance company.[17]

The data were used first to determine whether or not the 460 borrowers contacted (67.2 percent) are representative of the entire sample of 771. Chi-square statistics were computed from two-way comparisons of the samples. The chi-square statistics show no significant differences (at the 5 percent level) in any of the characteristics measured between the people who answered the initial telephone survey (A) and those who refused (R), between the A group and those who were contacted by field interviews (C), and between the C group and those not contacted (N). Only those who answered the initial survey (A) and those not contacted (N) showed significant differences. The most striking differences are: those not contacted (N) include a slightly higher percentage of unskilled and much higher percentage of professional workers, they earn somewhat less on average, a higher percentage of them are single, and they have fewer dependents than the A group.[18] Of greatest interest for this study is the fact that the groups do not differ much in number of years in debt or number of previous loans. Consequently, it is concluded that the 460 borrowers interviewed, on which the balance of this section is based, represent well the entire sample of 771.

## Ability to Borrow and Source of Funds of Individuals Surveyed

Table 12.4 shows that close to half the borrowers obtained funds (O) from other sources and half did not obtain new funds (NO). This table also shows that of those people who were able to borrow, most wanted the money to consolidate debts (54.5 O versus 48.9 percent NO) or buy a used car (19.5 O versus 12.7 NO). Among people who did *not* obtain funds, the percentage wanting to purchase furniture and household items was highest (10.0 NO versus 5.6 percent O). People who wanted to borrow for "socially acceptable purposes," that is, to pay medical bills, make home improvements, or pay school expenses, were about evenly divided, O versus NO. There seems no evidence that those who did not obtain funds wanted the money for obviously "less worthy" purposes.

---

17. The price at which loans were obtained was not asked, since all finance companies charge the legal maximum.

18. See Benston (1974b, tables 10, 11, and 13) for details.

TABLE 12.4 Primary Reason for Original Borrowing: Obtained (O) and Not Obtained (NO) New Funds

| Percentages | O | NO |
|---|---|---|
| Consolidate debts | 54.5 | 48.9 |
| Used car | 19.5 | 12.7 |
| Medical bills | 7.4 | 8.7 |
| Furniture and household items | 5.6 | 10.0 |
| Home improvements | 5.2 | 4.8 |
| School-related expenses | 2.6 | 3.5 |
| Miscellaneous | 5.2 | 11.4 |
|  | 100.0 | 100.0 |
| Number of borrowers | 231 | 229 |
| Chi-square | 12.78 | |
| (at 5 percent level, 6 degrees of freedom = 12.60) | | |

Each of the seven characteristics reviewed above, plus the percent of loan unpaid at the time the borrower wanted additional funds, and reason for borrowing, were examined to determine what distinguished those who obtained funds (O) from those who did not (NO). This examination and the chi-square statistics computed revealed that the only significant difference between the O and the NO former finance company customers is the "reason for borrowing" (see table 12.4).[19] Thus (contrary to expectations), the explanation of why some people did and some did not obtain funds is not discernible from the data collected. The interviewers were unable to say whether the people who did not borrow tried to borrow but were refused, could not find another institution in their area from which to borrow (such as a credit union), gave up trying after being told that the finance company would not advance them funds ("if they wouldn't lend to me, who would?"), or bought more goods on credit but did not consider this "borrowing."

Those who obtained funds were queried about the source. Most (39.8 percent) shifted their debt to another finance company, which shows that the "36 month limitation" was not entirely effective. Banks provided loans to 32.9 percent, 20.8 percent borrowed from a credit union, and 6.5 percent from other sources. None said they borrowed from an unlicensed lender.

---

19. The chi-square statistics for the other characteristics are reported in Benston (1974b). None is significant at the 5 percent level. Eisenbeis and Murphy (1974) subjected these data to a multivariate analysis. They also added variables for "sex" and "ethnic" factors (French surname) to test for the possibility of discrimination. They concluded "the multivariate analysis of successful and unsuccessful borrowers in this study supports Benston's work. That is, in terms of the characteristics that were available and which are typically used in credit scoring models, there does not seem to be a systematic relationship between denials and the measures reflecting credit worthiness."

Those who did not obtain funds took one of three actions. Most continued to pay regularly (77.3 percent). Only one person (0.4 percent) declared bankruptcy. The balance missed some payments but were paying off or had paid off the loan (22.3 percent).[20]

In summary, these data support the tentative conclusion that other lenders did not completely replace the loans that would have been made by the finance companies. More specifically, the interviews indicate that half of the former "good" finance company customers did not obtain the funds they wanted and 40 percent of those who did obtain funds got them from another finance company.[21] Unfortunately, nothing is known about the source (if any) of funds for people who would have been first-time borrowers from finance companies.

Of course, some "consumer advocates" argue that most of the former long-term finance company customers were now "out of the companies' clutches" because they couldn't or didn't borrow additional funds or borrowed from another source. The characteristics of these debtors whom these consumer advocates want to protect are analyzed next.

## V. Long- and Short-Term Borrowers: Characteristics and Relationship with Bankruptcy

An important motivation (among "consumer advocates" at least) behind the enactment of the "36 month limitation" is the belief that long-term borrowers need protection from the finance companies and from themselves. In-depth psychological, economic, and sociological studies of long-term borrowers would be desirable to determine whether the legislation is, in fact, wanted by and helpful to them. Unfortunately, such studies are not only very expensive to make, but difficult to interpret. However, the economic and other measurable characteristics of long-term borrowers can be compared to those of shorter term borrowers to determine what characterizes those people who are presumed to need protection. Data on the sample of borrowers described above are used for this analysis.

---

20. The interviewees also were asked how they felt about not having been able to borrow from their customary finance company. Seventy-five percent of those who obtained funds and 55 percent of those who did not felt "better off." A detailed analysis of the data is given in Benston (1974b).

21. Some interviewees indicated that some finance companies evaded the law by means of a simple subterfuge. The borrowers were told to pay off their loan with a check that would not be deposited until they had obtained another loan at another (suggested) finance company. Data on aggregate finance company loans indicate that this practice was not widespread (see Benston, 1974b, fig. 6).

## Characteristics of Long- and Short-Term Borrowers

In percentage terms, the finance company customers surveyed on whom additional data were available (383 observations) were previously in debt to the company the following number of years: 1 year, 13 percent; 2 to 4 years, 42 percent; 5 to 8 years, 20 percent; 9 to 12 years, 16 percent; and 13+ years, 10 percent. With respect to number of loans previously held, the percentages are: 1, 23 percent; 2 to 4, 34 percent; 5 to 8, 21 percent; and 9 +, 21 percent. Thus, most of these people were in debt continuously to finance companies for much longer than the 36 months the law allows.

Tables were prepared and chi-square statistics computed to determine differences in the characteristics of long- and short-term borrowers.[22] Years of previous indebtedness and number of previous loans were compared with their occupation, salary, age, marital status, number of dependents, reason for wanting original loans, ability to obtain funds, and reaction to not being able to borrow from their customary finance company. Only "age" revealed a chi-square statistic significant at the 5 percent level. Not surprisingly, a high proportion of borrowers (relative to their number in the sample) who were previously in debt only 1 year or who had only one previous loan were under 34 years of age. And among borrowers in debt 13 or more years or with nine or more previous loans, most were in the 45 to 64 age bracket. The number of previous loans and years in debt of the other age groups were in approximate proportion to their distribution in the sample.

Although the chi-square statistics indicate no other "significant" differences in the other characteristics, examination of the tables (presented in Benston, 1974b) reveals some interesting facts. Long-term borrowers (those continuously in debt for 9 or more years = CD, or those who had nine or more previous loans = PL) tend to be skilled workers (CD and PL), people who make $200 or more per week (PL), between 45 and 64 years of age (CD and PL), people with no dependents (CD and PL), and borrowers who wanted the money to consolidate debts (PL). The long-term borrowers appear *not* to be professional workers (CD), people making less than $80 a week (PL), and those under 34 years of age (CD and PL). Very-long-term debtors (those in debt continuously for 13 or more years) include *fewer* than expected borrowers with three or more dependents and those who wanted money for medical bills, furniture, and home improvements. Short-term debtors (those continuously in debt for less than four years = CD, or with one previous loan = PL) tend to be unskilled workers (CD and PL), people earning less than $80 a week (PL), those under 24 (CD) or 34 (PL), married borrowers (CD and PL), people with five or more dependents (CD and PL), and those whose primary reason for

---

22. These tables and analyses are presented in Benston (1974b).

borrowing was to pay medical bills (*CD* and *PL*). Further, short-term borrowers appear *not* to be skilled, semi-skilled workers, or white-collar workers (*CD* and *PL*), to make over $161 a week (*PL*), to be between 45 and 64 years of age (*CD* and *PL*), to be unmarried people, or to have one or no dependents (*CD* and *PL*).

In my opinion, the portrait of the long-term borrower that emerges from the data reviewed is not consistent with the view that they are a homogeneous group who are ill-equipped to handle their financial affairs. Rather their occupations, salaries, marital status, number of dependents, and stated reasons for borrowing show that they are diverse. Only age is significantly (and obviously) related to previous indebtedness. Further, the data suggest that the relationship between borrowers' characteristics and whether they are short- or long-term debtors is consistent with the view of borrowers as rational consumers whose debts reflect their economic and family positions and need for credit. As a further test of whether long-term indebtedness is "bad" for consumers and/or society, the relationship between such borrowing and bankruptcies is considered next.

## Long-Term Borrowing and Bankruptcy

Concern over the number of personal bankruptcies filed in Maine was an important reason for the enactment of the "36 month limitation." In a speech supporting the legislation on April 5, 1967, State Senator Peter Mills said:

> The real question, however, is why do people become so indebted that they cannot meet their monthly payments and, therefore, are compelled to file bankruptcy. The main reason for this is the:
> 
> (a) high *cost* of credit,
> (b) on unreasonable *large indebtedness*,
> (c) for *long periods of time*.

The Federal Referee in Bankruptcy for the Southern District of Maine, Richard Poulos (who strenuously and effectively supported the restrictive legislation), also considered long-term indebtedness an important cause of bankruptcies,[23] perhaps because he comes in direct and frequent contact with those who declare bankruptcy and with their creditors.

Aside from the important philosophical (and empirical) question of whether bankruptcy is detrimental to consumer welfare, the preliminary question to be answered is whether long-term indebtedness is associated with (or a causal factor of) bankruptcies. Some data on this question were gathered by Referee Poulos from

---

23. See last sentence of quote above.

TABLE 12.5 Number of Times Loan Was Previously Rewritten at a Large Finance Company

| Number of Rewrites | Cases in Bankruptcy Number | Cases in Bankruptcy Percentage | Good Customers Number | Good Customers Percentage |
|---|---|---|---|---|
| 0 | 2 | 2.2 | 0 | 0.0 |
| 1 | 59 | 65.6 | 17 | 14.0 |
| 2 | 13 | 14.4 | 18 | 14.9 |
| 3 | 2 | 2.2 | 11 | 9.1 |
| 4 | 1 | 1.1 | 4 | 3.3 |
| 5 | 3 | 3.3 | 9 | 7.4 |
| 6 | 1 | 1.1 | 6 | 5.0 |
| 7 | 1 | 1.1 | 4 | 3.3 |
| 8 | 1 | 1.1 | 6 | 5.0 |
| 9 | 1 | 1.1 | 3 | 2.5 |
| 10 | 1 | 1.1 | 7 | 5.8 |
| 11 | 2 | 2.2 | 1 | 0.8 |
| 12+ | 3 | 3.3 | 35 | 28.9 |
|  | 90 | 99.8 | 121 | 100.0 |
| No information | 261 | 290.0 | 116 | 95.9 |
|  | 351 |  | 237 |  |

351 bankruptcy cases on file as of June 13, 1972, in which a particular finance company was the principal creditor. Poulos's staff analyzed the available files and determined the number of times the loan in question had previously been rewritten (with or without an additional cash advance). This determination could be made for 90 of these loans. Table 12.5 gives the number and percentage of the rewrites of this total compared to similar data, from the same company, of borrowers who were included in the sample above. It is clear from table 12.5 that the people who declared bankruptcy had renewed their loans far less often than those who were considered good customers by the finance company and who, when credit was cut off, did not declare bankruptcy. Thus, the available data runs contrary to the belief that such long-term indebtedness is a causal factor of bankruptcy. Rather, as several studies have shown, bankruptcy appears related to harsh wage garnishments and unexpected costly medical problems, job losses, and marriage failures.[24]

## VI. Summary and Conclusions

This study analyzes legal restrictions on the length of time during which people may borrow from relatively high interest rate lenders—finance companies. The

---

24. See Stanley and Girth (1971) and Shuchman and Jantscher (1972).

arguments for and against such legislation are based, in large measure, on alternative hypotheses about the operations of finance companies, on the effect of the law on the availability of credit, and on the desire to protect long-term borrowers. An opportunity to test these hypotheses occurred when Maine passed legislation in 1967 that imposed on finance companies a ceiling rate of 8 percent simple interest on loan balances outstanding for more than 36 months.

There were 28 finance companies in Maine just before the legislation was enacted, and they had 116 offices. By June 30, 1972, the total had dropped to nine companies and 24 offices. Loan dollars outstanding declined from $31.0 to $10.8 million. The companies' gross earnings were affected, but the major effect was on their operating costs. Empirical analysis of finance company operations shows that the cost of processing loans makes those under about $300 to $400 unprofitable. Since first-time borrowers tend to borrow such small amounts, the companies count on the larger, profitable loans taken when customers renew or add to their initial loans. In addition, finance companies depend on loan extensions to allow a borrower who is "in trouble" to pay out his debt. These factors explain why finance companies cannot operate profitably with the "36 month limitation" in force. The data analyzed also show that finance companies do not experience economies of scale, did not consolidate their operations, and probably ceased operations because their rates of return declined to the point where no other course was sensible. Thus, the data analyzed are inconsistent with the "consumer advocates" hypotheses 1, 2, 3, and 4 given in section II. The data also are inconsistent with the finance companies' hypotheses 1 and 2, but support their hypothesis 3. The major finding, though, was not suggested by the proponents of the legislation. It appears that the major effect of the legislation is that it restricts finance companies from engaging in profitable long-term borrower relationships in which unprofitable first-time loans serve as "loss leaders."

Individual borrowers were interviewed to determine the effect of the finance companies' radical decline in lending. The sample consisted of 518 former finance company borrowers who wanted to borrow additionally from the companies in 1970 but were turned away because the companies were closing their operations. Half of these "good" customers did not obtain funds elsewhere. Forty percent of those who did obtain funds borrowed from other finance companies. All of those who did obtain funds paid off their loans, some with difficulty. An analysis of the characteristics (occupation, salary, age, dependents, etc.) of those who did and did not obtain funds revealed no significant differences. Thus the data do not support the belief of the "consumer advocates" who claimed borrowers were served without the finance companies, since only half those who wanted to borrow and to whom the finance companies would have loaned obtained the desired funds.

The occupations, and so on, of long-term debtors were compared to those of short-term debtors to determine what characterizes the people whom the legislation was designed to protect. Not surprisingly, "age" is the only significantly different (at the 5 percent level) factor—long-term debtors are middle aged, short-term debtors are young. However, the systematic (though not statistically significant) differences associated with short- and long-term indebtedness are consistent with the view that long-term indebtedness is a function of the usual demands and resources of consumers. Finally, the hypothesis that long-term indebtedness with finance companies leads to bankruptcy was tested and rejected.

The conclusion of this analysis is that legislation that restricts the term of finance company loans to consumers drives these lenders out of the market and hence limits the availability of funds to consumers. This limitation appears unjustified and unfair to consumers who would prefer the services offered by finance companies or who have no other legal alternative.

## REFERENCES

Benston, G.J., 1974a, The costs to consumer finance companies of extending consumer credit, in: National Commission on Consumer Finance, Technical studies II (U.S. Government Printing Office. Washington, D.C.), 1–158.

Benston, G.J., 1974b, An analysis of Maine's "36 month limitation" on finance company small loans, in: National Commission on Consumer Finance, Technical studies II (U.S. Government Printing Office, Washington, D.C.), 1–63 (pages are renumbered).

Eisenbeis, R. and N.B. Murphy, 1974, Interest rate ceilings and consumer credit rationing: A multivariate analysis of a survey of borrowers, *Southern Journal of Economics* 41, 115–23.

Poulos, R.E., undated, Proposed revisions for the treatment of uncontrovertable claims, in Ch. XIII proceedings, unpublished paper.

Shuchman, P. and G.R. Jantscher, 1972, Effects of the federal minimum exemption from wage garnishments on non-business bankruptcy rates, *Commerical Law Journal* 77, 360–63.

Stanley, D.T. and M. Girth, 1971, *Bankruptcy: Problem, process, reform* (Brookings Institution, Washington, D.C.).

Taeusch, C.F., 1942, The concept of "usury": The history of an idea, *Journal of the History of Ideas* 3, 291–318.

# 13

# Risk on Consumer Finance Company Personal Loans

## I. Introduction

The losses incurred by consumer finance companies are considerably greater than those experienced by other lenders of consumer cash installment loans: in 1970, for example, losses net of recoveries as a percentage of outstanding loans averaged 1.80 for consumer finance companies, 0.63 for commercial banks, and 0.26 for federal credit unions. In addition, finance companies incur considerably greater operating expenses than do the other consumer lenders: average direct branch office operating expense, less occupancy cost, per loan at finance companies is estimated to be $38 compared to $24 at commercial banks.[1] Much of these amounts are expended to prevent borrowers from becoming delinquent and to keep delinquencies from becoming losses.

Because it was recognized that legal lenders would not make funds available to high-risk borrowers at the usury ceiling rates, all states except Arkansas have adopted small loan laws that permit licensed lenders to make installment loans to consumers at higher rates. These higher rate ceilings presumably are designed to permit most borrowers to obtain funds at rates that reflect lenders' costs, including the cost of risk (nonrepayment). Where the ceilings are not sufficiently high, lenders might refuse to lend to higher risk borrowers. Several studies find this expected result. A positive, significant correlation is reported between gross income and loan losses, these variables being assumed to be proxies for legal ceiling rates and risk incurred. Shay (1967, 1970), Goudzwaard (1968), and Kawaja (1969, 1971) using 1964 statewide data, find positive correlations between loan losses and gross

---

The study was supported by the National Commission on Consumer Finance. Thanks also are due to Dr. Lees Booth of the National Consumer Finance Association and to a major consumer finance company (who prefers not to be identified) for providing the data used.

1. Benston (1977b). Data are for 1970 for finance companies and 1965 adjusted to 1970 prices for commerical banks.

income (both as percentages of average outstandings). Zwick (1967) also finds this relationship using data from 48 finance companies. However Goudzwaard (1969, 1970) questions these findings. He analyzed the demographic and financial characteristics of samples of individual borrowers from companies in three pairs of cities, wherein a city in a low interest ceiling state was paired with a city in a high interest ceiling state. He reports no significant difference among the borrowers, which appears to contradict the other findings.[2]

The present study supplements and expands the scope of the research reported in these papers. Data from 124 finance companies are analyzed to determine the variables associated with losses, net of recoveries, in each of three years. Estimates of the amount of net losses incurred by size of loan and the effect of scale economies are provided. The effects of state laws that restrict entry and creditors' legal remedies are measured. In addition, since these data (and data previously analyzed) relate charge-offs and recoveries of loans made in previous years to loans made or outstanding in a current year, the net losses incurred on loans made by a large finance company were traced back to the loan amounts originally advanced.

## II. Theory

Conceptually, losses on loans are a function of the risk incurred in serving specific borrowers, the resources expended to reduce loan losses and laws that restrict or enhance the lender's ability to collect amounts due. Obviously a lender will tend to expend resources to avoid making loans to borrowers from whom the net present value of expected cash flows (including servicing costs) is negative.[3] Lenders also monitor loans outstanding to increase the probability that the amounts due will be repaid. At the margin, a dollar spent on screening borrowers and monitoring loans should be equated with the present value of the revenue expected.

State usury laws (that limit the amount that can be charged) reduce the lender's expected cash inflow from borrowers and hence increase the benefit to the lenders from screening out high-risk borrowers. (However where lenders operate in noncompetitive markets, interest rate ceilings may increase the amount of funds loaned to some borrowers.[4]) Laws that restrict creditors' collection practices

---

2. Greer (1973, p. 93) questions the validity of Goudzwaard's findings because the characteristics of average rather than marginal borrowers are compared. Greer also studied the question with second quarter 1971 data on the statewide loan rejection rates of three major finance companies in 48 states (1973, pp. 95–101). He found a significant negative correlation between rejection rates and interest rate ceilings. However, he coded Arkansas, which has a very low 10 percent usury law and hence no finance companies, as a 100 percent rejection rate. The negative correlation may be due to this extreme outlier.

3. Portfolio effects may enter the calculation where the covariance of cash flows between a specific loan or type of loan and the portfolio of loans held affects the lenders' cost of capital. See Avio (1974) for a formal analysis.

4. See Goudzwaard (1968), Shay (1970), and Greer (1974) for illustrations.

(such as the prohibition of wage garnishments) might increase the costs of collecting loans and hence increase the benefits from avoiding high risks and from monitoring present borrowers. Since it is neither efficient nor possible for lenders to expend sufficient screening and monitoring costs to eliminate all loan losses, the risks they accept and losses they incur should be a positive function of the interest ceiling rate, ceteris paribus. However, lenders in states that restrict their ability to collect bad debts should experience lower loan losses, ceteris paribus, as a consequence of activities to screen out loans that would be more difficult to collect.

Given the impact of state laws, lenders' loan losses are a function of the proclivity of the borrowers residing in the lenders' market to repay their debts and the lenders' operating efficiency. One measure of the borrowers' willingness to repay debts is the degree to which the personal bankruptcy laws are used. Within these constraints, lenders attempt to assess the probability that a specific borrower will repay his or her loan when due with credit scoring, judgment, credit investigations, and past experience with the borrower. Once a loan is made, the probability of nonrepayment is maintained or reduced by such means as personal contact with the borrower. The cost of these activities may be subject to economies of scale. Regulatory considerations also direct attention to this factor. Many states have enacted restrictions on entry (convenience and advantage clauses) in the expectation that fewer, larger lenders can achieve lower costs and hence operate profitably under lower interest rate ceilings, ceteris paribus. (A more direct means of the effect of these entry restrictions on losses also is included in the analysis.)

Given the estimated risk and cost of lending, finance companies either can reject an applicant or vary the amount loaned. The relationship between the loan amounts and losses is important to measure because state interest ceiling rates are given in these terms. No provision is made in the state small loan laws for differential ceilings for borrowers with different characteristics (unless size of loan is considered a sufficient proxy). However, lenders may choose to accept greater risk on loan amounts where the differential between the ceiling rate determined revenue and marginal cost (contribution margin) is greater.

To summarize, loan losses are considered to be a function of the loan amount, scale economies, borrowers' willingness to repay debt, and state laws that impose interest ceiling rates, restrict creditors' collection remedies, and restrict entry. A description of the data used for this analysis follows.

## III. Data from 124 Consumer Finance Companies

Data collected by the National Consumer Finance Association (NCFA) from its member companies were analyzed.[5] Since 1961, the NCFA has asked its members

---

5. Zwick (1967) used data from this source from 48 companies for his study.

for annual balance sheet, income statement, and operations data. These data for the years 1968, 1969, and 1970 were analyzed. Consistency and other checks of each company's data within each year and across years were made. As a consequence, a number of errors were found and corrected. However, 19 companies (13 percent) had to be omitted because the errors and inconsistencies could not be corrected or reconciled, because the companies were only peripherally in the direct personal small loan business, or because reports for all three years could not be obtained.[6] This left 124 companies in the sample. Most of these companies operate in one state, some over regions, and a few nationwide. None have offices in Arkansas (which does not have a small loan statute).

As of December 31, 1972, the sample companies in the aggregate held $5,564 million of direct personal installment loans.[7] They range in size (in 1970) from $0.09 million in direct personal loans and 120 accounts outstanding to $1,283.6 million in loans and 1,657,900 accounts. The geometric mean dollar and number of loans outstanding are $1.3 million and 2,600 loans. Few of these companies are entirely in the small loan business. Less than half the portfolios (receivables) of 10 percent of the sample are direct personal loans. Most companies, though, are primarily small loan lenders: 56 percent have over 90 percent of their receivables in direct personal loans.

Losses net of recoveries average 9 percent of the companies' pretax total expenses. (The cost of borrowed funds averages 26 percent and operating expenses, 65 percent of total expenses.) Net losses include amounts charged off plus additional increases to loss reserves less recoveries. Since the net loss amounts booked in a particular year are related imperfectly to the loans processed during that year, the data for the three years, 1968, 1969, and 1970, also were averaged to partially offset this limitation.

As is discussed above, net losses[8] are considered to be a function of the operations of consumer finance companies and of the laws of the states in which they operate. Additional (homogeneity) variables are included to account for differences among companies that might affect the amount of net losses recorded. The following explanatory variables, then, were included in the analysis (all 1968 and 1969 dollar amounts were adjusted to 1970 prices by the GNP deflator).

Company operations:

NLS = number of (direct personal) loans serviced, a simple average of beginning and end of year numbers. NLS measures the scale of a

---

6. Zwick (1967) does not state how or whether he determined the accuracy of his numbers.

7. Data on total direct cash lending by consumer finance companies were not published by the Federal Reserve Board for the years analyzed. In 1964, when such data were published, Zwick (1967) states that his NCFA sample of 48 companies held 93 percent of the outstanding consumer finance company installment credit (p. 60).

8. Net losses as a percentage of average dollars of loans outstanding also was used as a dependent variable. The coefficients estimated are very similar in signs and magnitudes to those reported below.

company's operations since it is the principal measure of output.[9] Since the dependent variable is undeflated for company size, there should be a very significant relationship between it and NLS.

NLS/OF = number of loans serviced per office (NLS divided by the number of offices). This variable measures the economies of scale of a plant.

AVLM = average size of (direct personal) loans made, the total dollars loaned divided by the number of loans made. AVLM ranges from $322 to $1,118 (average over the three years' data). (This variable was used, rather than the amount of loans outstanding, because the graduated interest rate ceilings are stated in terms of initial loan amounts.)

NLM/S = number of loans made per loan serviced (NLS). The greater this variable, the greater the relative growth of the company. The coefficient of the variable also measures the differential effect on losses of making compared to servicing loans, since NLS is included in the regression equation.

Homogeneity variables:

P/R90+ = 10 if direct personal loans as a percentage of total receivables is over 90 percent, 1 otherwise (see next variable for explanation).[10]

P/R50− = 10 if the amount of direct personal loans as a percentage of total receivables is less than 50 percent, 1 otherwise. Losses on other loans could not be excluded. This and the preceding variable are included to adjust the data for these costs. Dummy variables were used because the relationship between net losses and the percentage of other receivables need not be linear (or log-linear). Analysis of the sample dictated the "natural" break points (90 and 50 percent) that are used. The percentages for each company can vary from year to year. On the average, P/R90+ = 10 for 56 percent of the sample and P/R50− = 10 for 10 percent. The coefficient of P/R90+ should be negative and that of P/R50− positive, since companies with more other loans have greater losses, given a scale of operations based on the number of direct personal loans only (NLS).

NCORP = 10 if the company is not a corporation, 1 if it is not (8 percent of the sample are noncorporations). This variable is included to account for the possibility that corporate policies on recording losses differ from those of companies whose owners are directly taxed.

---

9. See Benston (1977a, 1977b) for more complete discussions.
10. Since the data are transformed to common logarithms in the regressions, the dummy variables are log 10 = 1, log 1 = 0.

State usury laws and entry restrictions (47 states: Hawaii, Alaska, and Arkansas are excluded):

- IRC = interest rate ceiling on small loans in the state, in percentages. IRC is an average of APRs taken at $100 intervals up to $1,500 or the legal maximum size, if lower. A weighted average of state IRCs was constructed for regional and national companies.
- ENTVR = 10 if entry into the state is very restricted, 1 otherwise (23 states).
- ENTNR = 10 if entry into the state is not restricted, 1 otherwise (12 states). Where companies operate in more than one state, the condition that predominated was used. For national companies, both variables were coded 1 (moderately restricted entry is assumed).[11]

State restrictions on creditor's legal remedies:[12]

- WAR = 10 if wage assignment is restricted or prohibited (so that the debtor cannot agree to allow the creditor, at his or her option without the necessity of obtaining a court order, to require that the debtor's employer to assign-garnishee his or her wages to the creditor), 1 otherwise (WAR = 10 for 31 states)
- HDCR = 10 if the holder in due course defense is restricted or prohibited (so that the creditor cannot maintain that, as a holder in due course of the debtor's note, his or her claim cannot be offset by the debtor's defense that the goods or services purchased, for which the note was assigned, are defective, etc.), 1 otherwise (HDCR = 10 for five states).
- GARR = 10 if garnishment of wages is restricted or prohibited (so that a creditor cannot obtain a court order that requires the debtor's employer to assign the debtor's wages to the creditor), 1 otherwise (GARR = 10 for 11 states).
- CJR = 10 if confession of judgment is restricted or prohibited (so that the creditor cannot ask the debtor to confess his/her acquiescence to a judgment in advance should the loan be defaulted, thus saving the creditor the cost of obtaining a judgment from a court), 1 otherwise (CJR = 10 for 36 states).

Proclivity to repay; bankruptcy law usage:[13]

---

11. Though the small loan laws of all but six states have "convenience and advantage" clauses that limit the granting of licenses to operate loan offices, many states do not enforce these clauses restrictively. The senior officers of four nationwide or multiregional finance companies were asked, in interviews, to rate each state's administration of the clause as very restrictive, moderately restrictive, or nonrestrictive. The degree of agreement was almost complete.

12. These variables are due to a state-by-state analysis by Alan Feldman, a lawyer on the staff of the National Commission on Consumer Finance. Where companies operate in more than one state, the predominant condition was used. National companies were assigned 1 = no restriction.

13. Weighted averages were used for companies that operate in more than one state; national averages were used for national companies.

BANK/P = number of nonbusiness (straight) bankruptcies per 100,000 population in a state. With a straight bankruptcy, a debtor is discharged of all his or her debts (save certain nondischargeable obligations and those incurred by fraud) and loses most of his or her assets. (The allowable asset exemptions vary widely among states.)

XIII/B = the number of Chapter 13 (wage earners') bankruptcies as a percentage of total nonbusiness bankruptcies in a state. In a Chapter 13 bankruptcy, the court-appointed Referee in Bankruptcy acts as a consolidator of debts and collection agency. The debtor keeps his or her assets, but must pay off his or her obligations to the extent the Referee deems feasible over a period of three years, after which the debtor is discharged from bankruptcy and the remaining obligations are canceled.

## IV. Findings: Analysis of Finance Company Data

One-stage least squares regressions were computed, there being no reason to specify simultaneous equations. The variables were converted to (common) logarithms because previous analyses indicated that this form provided the required statistical properties for deriving inferences from the coefficients.[14] Table 13.1 gives the coefficients, standard errors, and *t* values estimated for 1968, 1969, 1970, and an average of the data (the basic data were averaged before the variables were constructed). The coefficients of the different samples generally are insignificantly different from each other. The exception is the 1970 data, where several significant coefficients, notably NLS, AVLM, and IRC differ in magnitude from those of the other years' data. A recheck of the data did not reveal the reason for the difference. Consequently, the analysis of the findings and the implications drawn therefrom are based primarily on the 1968, 1969, and average coefficients.

### Economies of Scale and Restrictions on Entry

The coefficients of the output variable, NLS, are uniformly greater than one, significantly so in two of the three years and in the average. However, the measured diseconomies of scale are not great: a 100 percent increase in company output indicates an average increase in losses of 108.5 percent (all other variables, including NLS/OF, held constant). Some economies of scale are indicated on the office level (which is the more relevant measure for the restrictions on entry argument).

---

14. See Benston (1977a, 1977b) and references therein.

TABLE 13.1 Losses Net of Recoveries (124 consumer finance companies)
Regression Coefficients (first line), Standard Errors (in parentheses), t Values (third line)

|  | AVG | 1970 | 1969 | 1968 |
|---|---|---|---|---|
| **Company operations** | | | | |
| NLS (number of loans serviced) | 1.085* <br> (0.038) <br> 28.763 | 1.128** <br> (0.043) <br> 26.492 | 1.067 <br> (0.040) <br> 26.539 | 1.129** <br> (0.040) <br> 28.024 |
| NLS/OF (number of loans serviced per office) | −0.157 <br> (0.123) <br> −1.275 | −0.192 <br> (0.138) <br> −1.394 | −0.224* <br> (0.133) <br> −1.689 | −0.260* <br> (0.131) <br> −1.980 |
| AVLM (average size of loans made) | 1.088** <br> (0.260) <br> 4.190 | 0.580* <br> (0.270) <br> 2.145 | 1.063* <br> (0.287) <br> 3.699 | 1.135** <br> (0.278) <br> 4.087 |
| NLM/S (number of loans made/number serviced) | 0.363 <br> (0.363) <br> 1.000 | −0.070 <br> (0.374) <br> −0.187 | 0.332 <br> (0.346) <br> 0.961 | 0.540 <br> (0.354) <br> 1.525 |
| **Homogeneity** | | | | |
| P/R90+ (over 90 percent personal loans) | −0.129* <br> (0.064) <br> −2.020 | −0.141* <br> (0.065) <br> −2.166 | −0.208** <br> (0.065) <br> −3.190 | −0.080 <br> (0.070) <br> −1.147 |
| P/R50− (less than 50 percent personal loans) | 0.353** <br> (0.098) <br> 3.613 | 0.289** <br> (0.110) <br> 2.640 | 0.191* <br> (0.100) <br> 1.903 | 0.307** <br> (0.097) <br> 3.166 |
| NCORP (noncorporation) | −0.095 <br> (0.101) <br> −0.942 | −0.062 <br> (0.118) <br> −0.526 | 0.014 <br> (0.101) <br> 0.141 | (a) |
| **State usury law and entry restrictions** | | | | |
| IRC (mean interest rate ceiling) | 0.860 <br> (0.566) <br> 1.518 | 0.353 <br> (0.679) <br> 0.520 | 0.720 <br> (0.711) <br> 1.013 | 1.703** <br> (0.611) <br> 2.785 |
| ENTNR (entry not restricted) | 0.112 <br> (0.114) <br> 0.988 | 0.147 <br> (0.133) <br> 1.099 | −0.022 <br> (0.126) <br> −0.178 | 0.141 <br> (0.107) <br> 1.316 |
| ENTVR (entry very restricted) | 0.049 <br> (0.074) <br> 0.659 | 0.110 <br> (0.087) <br> 1.262 | −0.036 <br> (0.080) <br> −0.448 | 0.100 <br> (0.082) <br> 1.209 |
| **Restrictions on creditors' legal remedies** | | | | |
| WAR (wage assignments restricted) | 0.007 <br> (0.070) <br> 0.106 | 0.036 <br> (0.083) <br> 0.435 | 0.040 <br> (0.076) <br> 0.518 | 0.041 <br> (0.071) <br> 0.588 |
| HDCR (holder in due course restricted) | 1.000 <br> (1.000) <br> 1.000 | 0.074 <br> (0.139) <br> 0.530 | 0.043 <br> (0.134) <br> 0.324 | 0.029 <br> (0.145) <br> 0.198 |
| GARR (garnishment of wage restricted) | −0.127 <br> (0.100) <br> −1.275 | −0.211* <br> (0.111) <br> −1.904 | −0.086 <br> (0.119) <br> −0.729 | −0.152* <br> (0.085) <br> −1.789 |
| CJR (confession of judgment restricted) | −0.044 <br> (0.062) <br> −0.707 | −0.060 <br> (0.072) <br> −0.840 | −0.037 <br> (0.071) <br> −0.525 | 0.056 <br> (0.072) <br> 0.782 |

*(continued)*

TABLE 13.1 Continued

|  | AVG | 1970 | 1969 | 1968 |
|---|---|---|---|---|
| Proclivity to repay | | | | |
| BANK/P (straight bankruptcy/ population) | −0.075 (0.100) −0.753 | −0.113 (0.122) −0.925 | −0.081 (0.116) −0.699 | [a] |
| XIII/B (Chapter 13 bankruptcy per straight bankruptcy) | 0.043 (0.072) 0.598 | 0.017 (0.084) 0.196 | 0.117 (0.083) 1.409 | 0.036 (0.080) 0.447 |
| CONSTANT | −6.018** (1.248) −4.822 | −3.855* (1.403) −2.748 | −5.462** (1.471) −3.714 | −7.501** (1.345) −5.576 |
| $R^2$ | .954 | .941 | .945 | .944 |

[a]Too insignificant to enter equation.
**$t$ values over 2.358 (one-tail) indicate significance at the 1 percent level.
*$t$ values over 1.658 (one-tail) indicate significance at the 5 percent level (for NLS, significance is measured from one rather than zero).

A doubling of the number of accounts serviced per office (NLS/OF) (with no change in NLS) indicates an average decrease in losses on only 7.8 percent (but more for the individual years). The coefficients measured are significant at the .05 levels for two years and at about the .10 level for one year and the average.[15] The negative coefficient of NLS/OF could measure either greater efficiency of controlling loan losses or greater selectivity in accepting risks.

The variable that measures directly the effect of entry restrictions, ENTVR, has coefficients that are positive, weakly significant (.10 level or above) for the average, 1968, and 1970, and negative with almost no significance for 1969. However, the coefficients of variables that measures no restrictions in entry (ENTNR) are very similar in magnitudes and signs to the restricted entry variable, ENTVR. This fact plus the inconsistency of signs among samples and the weak or nonsignificance of the coefficients leads to the conclusion that restrictions on entry do not measurably affect loan losses incurred.

## Interest Rate Ceiling and Risk

The coefficients of the interest rate ceiling variable (IRC) are uniformly positive, but are not consistently significant or close in magnitude. The positive coefficients

---

15. Since the state usury laws, entry restrictions, restrictions on creditors' legal remedies, and proclivity to repay variables may be imperfectly related to the operations of individual companies, the regressions were rerun with these variables omitted. The coefficients estimated for NLS are almost unchanged and those for NLS/OF are almost the same as those reported, with the exception of the 1970 data. The coefficient and $t$ value in this sample are −0.097 and −0.839.

indicate that companies operating in states that permit them to charge higher rates of interest incur greater losses (and hence may be assumed willing to accept more risky borrowers). Though the $t$ statistics give one only limited confidence in the levels measured, they reveal an elasticity of losses with respect to interest ceiling rates of close to one (except for 1970), which implies that higher ceilings benefit riskier borrowers at least in that lenders appear willing to make loans to them. Lenders also benefit, since ceteris paribus, a given percentage increase in revenue is much greater in amount than the same percentage increase in losses. (However, their collections cost also may be higher.)

## Restrictions on Creditors' Legal Remedies

Three of the creditors' remedies are insignificantly related to losses. The signs of WAR and HDCR are uniformly positive, though the $t$ values are less than 0.6 in only one instance. The coefficients of CJR are negative in three regressions and positive in one, and the $t$ values are less than 0.8. Only GARR has coefficients with $t$ values greater than 1.3 (except for 1969). The coefficients also are consistently negative. Thus it appears that states' restrictions on creditors' legal remedies either had no effect on their losses or, in the case of garnishments of wages (GARR), had a possible negative effect.

The magnitudes of the coefficients of GARR indicate that the losses incurred are lower by from 38 to 18 percent (5 percent on the average) in states where wage garnishments are restricted or prohibited. While the not significant $t$ values do not give one much confidence in these numbers, it does appear reasonable to conclude that the restrictions did reduce losses (and presumably risk) incurred, perhaps to the detriment of more risky borrowers.

## Proclivity to Repay: Use of Bankruptcy Proceedings

The coefficients of the straight bankruptcy variable (BANK/P) are negative but insignificant ($t < 0.9$) for all samples. The coefficients of the Chapter 13 (wage earners') variables (XIII/B) are also uniformly insignificant but are positive. This somewhat unexpected finding indicates that the losses incurred by consumer finance companies are dependent more on the companies' ability to screen and work with borrowers than on the borrowers' proclivity to use the bankruptcy laws to avoid repaying their debts.

## Losses and the Size of Loans Made

The amount of net losses per loan and per dollar of loan were calculated at several levels of the average size of loans made (AVLM), with variables that measure the scale of operations (NLS and NLS/OF), interest rate ceiling (IRC), and proclivity

TABLE 13.2 Annual Losses Net of Recoveries per Loan and per Hundred Dollars of Loan Made at Selected Loan Sizes (Other Variables at Geometric Means or Selected Values[a])

|  | Average Loan Size (AVLM) | | |
| --- | --- | --- | --- |
|  | $300 | $600 | $900 |
| Per loan |  |  |  |
| AVG | 3.71 | 5.75 | 8.94 |
| 1970 | 3.75 | 5.60 | 7.08 |
| 1969 | 3.23 | 6.74 | 10.38 |
| 1968 | 3.24 | 7.11 | 11.27 |
| Per hundred dollars of loan made |  |  |  |
| AVG | 1.43 | 1.30 | 1.19 |
| 1970 | 0.90 | 0.96 | 0.99 |
| 1969 | 1.25 | 0.93 | 0.79 |
| 1968 | 1.08 | 1.12 | 1.15 |

[a] For all years: NLS = 2500; NLS/OF = 650; P/R90+ = 10; P/R50−, NCORP, ENTVR = 1; ENTNR, WAR, HDCR, GARR, and CJR = 10. All other variables are at their geometric mean values of their year.

to pay (BANK/P and XIII/B) held constant at their geometric mean values. The homogeneity and state law variables were set equal to 10 (in logs) so that the numbers calculated refer to a corporation with receivables that are 90 percent or more in consumer direct personal loans and that does business in a state where creditors' legal remedies and entry are not restricted.

Table 13.2 gives the amount of net losses per loan and per $100 of loans made at loan sizes of $300, $600, and $900. (Recall that average AVLM is the average loan size made by a company.) Average net losses per loan increase with the average size of loan made from $2.71 for $300 loans to $8.94 for $900 loans ("average" regression). Per dollar of loans made, net losses decline slightly, from 1.43 percent for $300 loans to 1.19 percent for $900 loans ("average" regression). By way of contrast, the average net losses per dollar of loans *outstanding* for the companies sampled, unadjusted for other factors, are 1.80 percent in 1970, 1.82 percent in 1969, 1.72 percent in 1968, and 1.81 percent for the three-year average.

## Losses and Operating Expenses

It was postulated that lenders may trade off greater expenditures of screening out high risks and of monitoring loans for losses incurred. This possibility was tested for by regressing operating expenses (expenses other than interest, losses, advertising, and income taxes) on losses net of recoveries as a percentage of average loan amounts outstanding (the dependent variable of the regressions given above) plus the independent variables described above and listed in table 13.1 (all variables in common logarithms). The coefficients (and $t$ values) of this variable for each regression are as follows: average = 0.039 (0.968); 1970 = 0.038 (0.939); 1969 = 0.087 (2.282); 1968 = too insignificant to enter regression. Thus the coefficients are generally positive but insignificant. Both findings are inconsistent with the hypotheses that operating expenses and net losses are substitutes.[16]

## V. Loss Rates Associated Directly with Loans Made

A possibly important shortcoming of the finance company data analyzed above is the lack of direct association between the losses recorded and the loans made or outstanding in a particular year. Another data limitation is the use of the range of average loans made by companies to stand for the size distribution of loans, when the average may not be a sufficient statistic. These limitations are recognized by Fiedler (1971) is his comprehensive compilation of credit statistics, when he identified "large gaps in our statistical arsenal" as including "the almost complete absence of credit experience data tied back to the original dates the loans were made" (p. 7).

A study of loan losses experienced by a major regional consumer finance company at all of its branch offices in eight states was undertaken to overcome these limitations. All of the loan amounts written off (net of amounts recovered) from January 1, 1968, through June 30, 1971, were recorded, along with the date and amount of each loan at the time it was written.[17] (Loans made to present customers were recorded, in effect, as if they were new loans, even if the loan was a rewrite with no cash advance, on the assumption that in granting the loan the manager was putting that amount of funds at risk at that time.) This period was chosen because the company believed that by June 1970 and June 1971 virtually all loans made in 1968 and 1969 would be charged off, collected, or rewritten. The cumulated net charge-offs were summed according to the amount of the loan when made (as defined above), grouped into five size of loan groups: $0–300, $301–600, $601–1,000, $1,001–1,500, and $1,500+. The net losses on loans made in 1968 and 1969 were divided by the dollar amounts of all loans made in 1968 and 1969 in their respective groups to determine the loss rate by size of loan made.

Table 13.3 presents the results of these computations. The replication of the study provides an indication of the validity of the numbers and the stability of the loss rates. Only in Louisiana (and in a few instances, Missouri and Texas) do the loss rates by size of loan made differ very much between years.

---

16. This finding is consistent with the results obtained from a study of the branch office operations of four finance companies (2,500 observations in each year, 1968, 1969, and 1970). Direct operating expenses (which exclude allocated central office expenses) were regressed on output, homogeneity, and market structure variables, including dollars of delinquencies (60 days and over) as a percentage of average outstandings. The coefficients computed generally are insignificant and small in magnitude. See Benston (1977b), table 2.

17. The data were checked for errors of classification. In five instances where the errors could not be corrected, the branches were removed from the study.

TABLE 13.3 Loss Rate Experience by Size of Loan Made of a Major Finance Company in Eight States Mean Rates and Standard Errors (in parentheses)

|  | Florida 1968 | Florida 1969 | Georgia 1968 | Georgia 1969 | Indiana 1968 | Indiana 1969 | Illinois 1968 | Illinois 1969 | Louisiana 1968 | Louisiana 1969 | Michigan 1968 | Michigan 1969 | Missouri 1968 | Missouri 1969 | Texas 1968 | Texas 1969 |
|---|---|---|---|---|---|---|---|---|---|---|---|---|---|---|---|---|
| $0 –300 | 1.94 (1.30) | 2.07 (1.72) | 2.50 (2.44) | 2.91* (1.47) | 3.85* (2.00) | 4.10* (2.40) | 2.64 (1.65) | 2.20 (1.81) | 6.46 (4.18) | 4.82* (2.58) | 2.60* (1.32) | 2.67* (1.40) | 1.77 (1.51) | 2.35* (1.28) | 2.81 (2.14) | 2.71 (2.02) |
| 301 –600 | 1.85* (0.89) | 1.81** (0.84) | 3.76* (1.61) | 4.03* (1.95) | 3.18* (1.60) | 3.39 (2.12) | 2.27 (1.46) | 2.05 (1.24) | 2.98* (1.55) | 2.44* (1.35) | 2.77** (0.90) | 2.35* (1.30) | 2.88 (1.88) | 2.73 (2.33) | 4.21* (2.21) | 3.30 (2.28) |
| 601 –1,000 | | | 2.58* (1.03) | 3.32* (1.76) | 2.58* (1.21) | 2.13* (1.20) | 1.75 (1.16) | 1.64* (0.93) | 6.02* (3.43) | 4.88* (2.75) | 1.96* (0.66) | 1.72* (0.71) | 3.11 (1.95) | 2.77 (2.10) | 3.97 (2.48) | 3.07* (1.72) |
| 1,001 –1,500 | | | 3.33 (2.03) | 3.23* (1.51) | | | 2.13 (1.72) | 2.24 (1.41) | 15.13 (10.55) | 8.05 (10.12) | | | 2.99 (1.90) | 4.17 (3.18) | 2.11 (1.45) | 2.21 (1.63) |
| 1,500 + | | | 2.92 (1.84) | 3.42 (2.30) | | | 1.59 (1.53) | 1.22 (0.79) | 13.54* (6.97) | 11.10 (9.18) | | | 2.67* (1.32) | 3.18 (2.96) | 4.32 (3.80) | 3.04 (3.02) |
| F statistic | 0.14 | 0.80 | 1.39 | 0.72 | 4.21* | 7.04** | 2.94* | 3.11* | 10.75** | 3.98** | 5.22** | 4.91** | 1.41 | 1.37 | 5.30* | .12** |
| $0 –1,000 | 1.90 (1.10) | 1.93 (1.33) | 2.78* (1.22) | 3.51* (1.49) | 3.19* (1.69) | 3.20 (2.11) | 1.89 (1.17) | 1.72 (0.92) | 4.97* (2.46) | 3.38* (1.79) | 2.44* (1.05) | 2.25* (1.23) | 2.56 (1.77) | 2.52 (2.01) | 3.71* (1.88) | 3.02 (1.82) |
| 1,001 + | | | 2.97* (1.59) | 3.06** (1.10) | | | 1.30 (1.03) | 1.13 (0.77) | 12.74 (7.77) | 7.61 (6.67) | | | 2.32 (1.56) | 3.08 (2.64) | 2.06 (1.49) | 1.78 (1.30) |
| F statistic | | | 0.12 | 0.81 | | | 5.03* | 8.39** | 16.28** | 6.65* | | | 0.17 | 0.49 | 16.49** | 10.31* |
| State mean | 1.90 (1.10) | 1.93 (1.33) | 3.01* (1.65) | 3.38* (1.77) | 3.19* (1.69) | 3.20 (2.11) | 2.11 (1.48) | 1.88 (1.34) | 8.52 (7.59) | 5.92 (6.49) | 2.44* (1.05) | 2.24* (1.23) | 2.70 (1.78) | 3.09 (2.44) | 3.44 (2.49) | 2.89 (2.10) |
| Number of observations (branches) | 46 | 45 | 14 | 14 | 28 | 28 | 47 | 46 | 18 | 16 | 29 | 29 | 17 | 19 | 40 | 41 |

*Significant at .05 level
**Significant at .01 level

The loss rates measured in this study are considerably greater than those found for the 124 finance companies. Excluding Louisiana (of which more below), the average loss rate per dollar of loan made experienced by the company is 2.67 percent, compared to the average for the 124 companies of 1.28 percent. The company's data also show some significant differences among loan sizes. The $F$ statistics given in table 13.3 are significant for Indiana, Illinois, Michigan, and (in 1968) Texas. However, differences within the states are not uniform. Higher loss rates are shown for smaller loans in Michigan and Indiana; Illinois's and Texas's loss rates are uneven over ascending loan size groups. The very high rates for loans over $1,000 dominate the Louisiana data. With respect to the dichotomy between loans less and greater than $1,000, the smaller loans have higher loss rates in Illinois and Texas while the reverse is true for Louisiana. These results together with the magnitudes of the differences lead to the conclusion that size of loan is not consistently associated with rates of loss among the eight states sampled.

The loan loss rates among states differ considerably. If the finance company accepted greater risks in states where the ceiling rate is higher, there could be a positive association between the rate ceiling and the loss rate, ceteris paribus. There are too few observations to support a comprehensive analysis. A partial analysis was conducted with a plot of the average loss rates experienced for each loan size group in a state against that state's ceiling rate for loans of that size. The plot (not reproduced because of space limitations) reveals that, with Louisiana omitted, there is no significant correlation of loss rates and interest rate ceilings within loan size groups.[18]

Since the loan size groups chosen may be too narrow, the average loss rate in each state was computed and compared with the average interest rate charged in each state.[19] The interest charges and loss rates are positively, though rather imperfectly, correlated.[20] The Spearman rank correlation coefficient is 0.536, which is not significant. However, if Florida, which shows the lowest loss rates and the sixth highest interest charge rate, is omitted from the sample, the Spearman rank correlation coefficient is 0.750, which is significant at the 5 percent level. And if Louisiana is omitted, the rank correlation is 0.600.

This limited study, then, provides but weak or no support to the hypothesis that higher interest rate ceilings result in higher losses, ceteris paribus, with the exception of Louisiana. Here the hypothesis is strongly accepted. The company whose data are presented stated that the high losses they experienced are the result of their having consciously accepted greater risks to take advantage of the higher rates they were permitted to charge.

---

18. The (insignificant) correlation coefficient is −0.028 with Louisiana omitted and 0.298 (significant at the .06 level with Louisiana included).
19. The average interest rate charged is taken from Schober and Shay (1973), table 16-1.
20. The table giving the data is omitted due to space limitations.

A comparison of each state's loss rate with the state's restrictions on creditors' legal remedies reveals an imperfect, though slightly positive relationship. Thus, there is no support for the hypothesis that restrictions on the remedies results in the lender's incurring less risk, as measured by lower loss rates.

## VI. Summary and Conclusions

The loan loss experience (net of recoveries) of 124 consumer finance companies in each of three years reveals results that are consistent with the findings of previous studies: net losses are positively, though not strongly significantly, associated with the average ceiling rates in the states in which the companies operate. The coefficients measured indicate an elasticity of net losses with respect to the interest rate ceilings of 0.86 (on average), which is consistent with the hypothesis that higher interest rate ceilings result in lenders accepting more risks but in earning even greater revenues, ceteris paribus. The data from the 124 companies also show diseconomies of scale on the company level but some economies of scale on the office (plant) level. However, restrictions on entry when measured directly tend, if anything, to increase net losses. The relative use of bankruptcy proceedings by individuals in a state do not appear to affect losses. Restrictions on creditors' legal remedies also are generally unrelated to net losses, with the exception of garnishment of wages (GARR). Lower net losses appear to be experienced in states where garnishments are restricted or prohibited.

The data reveal that, ceteris paribus, net losses average about $1.30 per $100 of loan made with little variation according to the size of loan. Since the size of loan made variable is a company-wide average and since the net losses booked are not directly related to the loans made, a detailed study of one company's experience in eight states was undertaken. This study confirms the conclusion that net losses per dollar of loan are not consistently related to the size of loan made. However, the amount of net losses measured per dollar of loans made is more than twice the level measured for the 124 company study that used average size of loans made. The individual company study does not find a relationship between interest rate ceilings and net losses per dollar of loan made with the exception of one state (Louisiana) where there is no effective ceiling on loans over $300. Since operating costs (which excludes interest) are not essentially related to the amount loaned,[21] this finding, on the whole, is inconsistent with the hypothesis that finance companies tend to advance to risky borrowers those loan amounts on which the contribution margin is greatest. Rather it appears that they react to interest rate ceilings by raising or lowering the overall level of risk incurred while lending to each borrower the amount that they expect he or she can repay at the overall level of risk assumed.

21. See Benston (1977a).

Thus, the findings derived from the data from 124 companies, while consistent with previous studies, indicate a weaker relationship between net losses and interest rate ceilings. The individual company study findings are consistent with those reported by Goudzwaard (1969) (who also used individual company loan office data, though in a univariate analysis) with the exception of the results for the high ceiling rate state, Louisiana.

One tentative conclusion that might be drawn from these findings is that the acceptance of risk by consumer finance companies, while a positive function of the level of state interest rate ceilings, is only partially measured by the amount of net losses incurred, ceteris paribus. Though the loss rates experienced by the companies are several times those experienced by lower rate lenders, the magnitudes of the differentials are much less than the differences in interest rates received. However, the companies' operating costs are much higher than those of low-rate lenders. Thus it seems plausible to hypothesize that the risk assumed by finance companies also is a positive function of the monitoring costs they incur. (Screening costs may be positively or negatively related to the degree of risk accepted depending on the risk inherent in the population screened.) The question that remains unanswered is whether these higher operating costs plus higher net losses offset the higher interest charged so that finance companies earn a "normal" profit, one comparable to that earned by low-rate lenders. Or, do finance companies who operate in high interest rate ceiling states accept somewhat greater risks but still earn extranormal profits because they are able to take advantage of consumers' insensitivity to interest rates? Answers to these questions are considered in another essay.

REFERENCES

Kenneth L. Avio. "On the Effect of Statutory Interest Rate Ceilings," *Journal of Finance*, 29 (December 1974), pp. 1383–95.

George J. Benston. "Graduated Interest Rate Ceilings and Operation Costs by Size of Small Consumer Cash Loans," *Journal of Finance*, 32 (September 1977a).

George J. Bentson. "Rate Ceiling Implications of the Cost Structure of Consumer Finance Companies," *Journal of Finance*, 32 (December 1977b).

Edgar R. Fiedler. *Measures of Credit Risk and Experience*, New York: National Bureau of Economic Research, 1971.

Maurice B. Goudzwaard. "Price Ceilings and Credit Rationing," *Journal of Finance*, 23 (March 1968), pp. 177–85.

Maurice B. Goudzwaard. "Consumer Credit Charges and Credit Availability," *Southern Economic Journal*, 35 (January 1969), pp. 214–23.

Maurice B. Goudzwaard. "Discussion," *Journal of Finance*, 25 (May 1970), pp. 526–28.

Douglas F. Greer. "An Econometric Analysis of the Personal Loan Credit Market," in *An Econometric Analysis of Consumer Credit Markets in the United States*, eds. Douglas F. Greer and Robert P. Shay, Technical Studies Volume IV, The National Commission on Consumer Finance, Washington, D.C.: U.S. Government Printing Office, 1973.

Douglas F. Greer. "Rate Ceiling, Market Structure, and the Supply of Finance Company Personal Loans," *Journal of Finance*, 29 (December 1974), pp. 1363–82.

Michael Kawaja. "The Economic Effects of Regulation," *Southern Economic Journal*, 35 (January 1969), pp. 231–38.

Michael Kawaja. *Regulation of the Consumer Finance Industry: A Case Study of Rate Ceilings and Loan Line Limits in New York State*, New York: Columbia University Press, 1971.

Milton W. Schober and Robert P. Shay. *State and Regional Estimates of the Price and Volume of the Major Types of Consumer Installment Credit in Mid 1971*, Technical Study III, National Commission Consumer Finance, Washington, D.C.: U.S. Government Printing Office, 1973.

Robert P. Shay. "State Regulation and the Provision of Small Loans," in *The Consumer Finance Industry: Its Costs and Regulation*, eds. John M. Chapman and Robert P. Shay, New York: Columbia University Press, 1967, chapter 4.

Robert P. Shay. "Factors Affecting Price, Volume and Credit Risk in the Consumer Finance Industry." *Journal of Finance*, 25 (May 1970), pp. 503–15.

Jack Zwick. "A Cross-Section Study of Industry Costs and Earnings," in *The Consumer Finance Industry: Its Costs and Regulation*, eds. John M. Chapman and Robert P. Shay, New York: Columbia University Press, 1967, chapter 3.

# 14

# Rate Ceiling Implications of the Cost Structure of Consumer Finance Companies

THE CEILING RATES OF INTEREST PERMITTED BY STATE small loan laws for consumer cash loans are inversely dependent on the size of loan: that is, loans under $300 may bear 36 percent interest while lenders can charge no more than 15 percent on amounts over $1,000. The ceiling rate schedules are based, in large measure, on an assumed relationship between lending costs (including interest and risk) and loan size, a relationship about which little is known. Restrictions on entry imposed by many states are based, in part, on assumed economies of scale. This study presents measurements of these costs and scale economies derived from a statistical analysis of the records of some 2,500 branches of three consumer finance companies in each of three years, supplemented by a similar study of data from 124 finance companies. Average and marginal costs and economies of scale are calculated. The analysis indicates that the size-of-loan method of stating ceiling rates is inappropriate. Though a considerably improved method is suggested, any cost-based ceilings are not likely to be very close to "optimal."

## I. Introduction

State regulation of the rates charged by consumer finance companies to borrowers is related to the historical, social, moral, and ethical concerns about interest charges for money.[1] Hence the usury laws. A modification was provided by the

---

This paper was supported by the National Commission on Consumer Finance. Thanks are due to consumer finance companies for providing data and advice (though not direction), to Tom Woodford for programming and Joe Safier, Kim Benston and others for research assistance.

1. A more extensive discussion of the history of governmental regulation of loan rates may be found in Kawaja (1971), chapter 2, and references cited therein.

Uniform Small Loan Law, drafted in 1916, which allowed rates of up to 3.5 percent a month for loans under $300. Prior to its complete or partial adoption by state legislatures, the state usury statutes (which generally limited annual interest rates to 6 or 8 percent) made lending small amounts to individuals economically impossible. As a consequence, small loans were available only from loan sharks and, in limited amounts, from fraternal or charitable organizations.

Since 1916, small loan laws have been adopted by all states except Arkansas (and the District of Columbia), under which lenders must obtain a license to make loans (usually less than a specified size) at higher than the legal rates. Though the laws differ among states, they similarly specify maximum rates that are higher for smaller loans. For example, the most common version of a new model law called the Uniform Consumer Credit Code (UCCC), adopted by some 7 to 11 states (depending on how loosely one defines "version"), permits 36 percent interest a year on the first $300 of loans, 21 percent on the balance between $301 and $1,000, and 15 percent on amounts over $1,000, with an average rate of not less than 18 percent. The laws of many states also restrict the number of licensees (finance company offices) that can be operated, in part because of a belief that economies of scale permit larger offices to process loans at lower costs which, in turn, makes lower rate ceilings less restrictive of credit availability.

Any effective ceiling, of course, results in the denial of service to some borrowers.[2] The legislative history of small loan laws (which provide exceptions to the general usury statutes), though, indicates the desire to permit legal lenders to provide credit at rates that reflect the costs of lending to "credit-worthy" borrowers.[3] These appear to be defined operationally as consumers to whom finance companies will lend at rates that will cover costs (defined more explicitly in section II) and (not very high) losses and permit a "reasonable" return on invested capital.[4] The inverse relationship between the ceiling rates and the dollar size of

---

2. See Greer (1974) and references cited therein for analysis of the effect of interest rate ceilings on credit availability.

3. The Sixth Draft of the Uniform Small Loan Law (1935) introduced graduated rate ceilings. Kawaja (1971) observes: "The graduated rate was designed to equalize the profitability of large and small loans" (p. 29).

4. In deciding whether or not to make a loan, a company must expect that the present value of receipts (the interest portion of which is governed by the interest rate ceiling) exceeds the present value of expenditures (which include operating costs that are incurred as a consequence of the loan), discounted at the rate of capital (which as Avio, 1974, shows may be a function of repayment risk and the covariance of returns among loans). A "loss" loan might be made if offsetting profitable future loans are expected and the present value of the entire relationship is positive, or if the company believes that some loss loans should be made for ethical or political reasons. See Benston (1976a) for an analysis of the former situation.

loans is based on an assumption that lenders' costs, and so on, are similarly related, so that lenders will be willing to make loans over the amount spectrum permitted by the law.[5]

Given the legislative conclusion that ceiling rates on small loans are desirable, it is necessary to estimate the specific relationship between lenders' costs and the size of loans.[6] Alternatively, if costs are primarily a function of other variables, another basis for stating interest rate ceilings should be considered that might be more consonant with legislative intent. Knowledge about the cost structure of consumer finance companies also is required to determine whether the effect on costs of economies of scale, if they exist, are sufficient to justify restrictions on the licensing of lenders.[7]

## II. The Small Loan Cost Function

The small loan lender is seen as facing an essentially exogenously determined demand function for loans, under the constraints of state-imposed ceiling rates and laws governing collection practices. Essentially, transactions costs limit the extent of the market. A consumer finance company typically does not lend to borrowers who work or live far from it because otherwise the cost of monitoring the loan would be too great. Borrowers typically do not attempt to borrow at loan offices that require them to incur extensive travel cost. The lender thus faces customers whose numbers are limited by the geographical extent of the market in which the lender has been given a license by the state to operate and whose characteristics (such as propensity to repay debt) are a "given" to the lender. The amounts and maturities that these customers wish to borrow, however, may be influenced by the lender, who either may refuse them loans they want and/or "entice" them into taking loans in amounts determined by the lender.

The costs of making and securing small loans (or any loan) may be usefully delineated into (1) the cost of money—the opportunity cost of lending funds to borrowers, (2) the cost of risk—losses net of recoveries, and (3) operations costs—salaries, occupancy, supplies, and so on. The cost of money (holding risk

---

5. See Johnson (1967) for a discussion of the issues involved in the regulation of consumer loans and lenders.

6. Two published studies measure costs with respect to the size of loans: Zwick (1967) and Nagata (1973). The available data and the methodology used limit severely their usefulness for present purposes. (Nagata's findings are discussed further below.)

7. In all except six states, an application for a license to operate under the small loan laws must show that the prospective loan office serves the public's "convenience." A major reason (other than maintaining monopolies for established lenders) for limiting the number of small loan companies and offices is the belief that the industry is subject to economies of scale. See Sartoris [1971] for a complete review and analysis of the convenience and advantage clause.

constant) clearly is linearly proportional to the amount of funds outstanding. Therefore, no further analysis is required.[8] The cost of risk need not be linearly or proportionally related to the amount loaned. Risk also may be a function of operating costs expended, since more extensive credit checks and monitoring of delinquent loans can be traded off for lower defaults and higher collections. However, the amount of net losses incurred need not have the same functional relationship to the amounts of loans made or outstanding as have operation costs. Therefore, these two elements of the small loan cost function are best analyzed separately.

Field study of the operations of small loan companies (and other lenders) has led me to the following simplified two-step decision process. The companies tend first to set a level of expected risk, which is a function of the ceiling rates in the state, the cost of collecting delinquent loans (a function, in large part, of state laws and the propensity of customers to repay their obligations).[9] Then they determine the level of monitoring necessary to hold actual losses to the expected amount.[10] Setting the level of risk requires information about the potential risk of lending to a specific borrower. This information may be obtained from two sources. For a present or former borrower, the lender's previous experience is reviewed. Secondarily, the customer is reinterviewed and information (such as salary, type of job, previous credit experience, assets, etc.) is updated, checked (probably with a credit bureau) and analyzed (possibly with a credit scoring model). If he is a new borrower, only the interview, and so on, are available. Therefore, the company tends initially to offer a smaller loan than it later may offer when experience shows the customer to be "good."[11] The cost of gathering this information thus is related more to whether the customer is a new, present, or former borrower than to the size of the loan.

---

8. The cost of funds is the lender's cost of capital (debt and equity), which is a function of its portfolio of loans and other business. The size distribution, maturity structure, and riskiness of the loan portfolio is determined by exogenous demand and the profit maximizing decisions described below. I assume that these decisions are made independently of the effect they may have on the lender's cost of capital, since I believe that this indeed is what is done. However, see Avio (1974) for a formal analysis.

9. Losses do not appear to be a function of the size of loans made, which indicates that lenders tend to make that size of loan that is consistent with a preferred level of risk. However, losses are positively related to the level of legal interest rate ceilings. (See Benston, 1977a).

10. Of course, lenders equate the marginal cost of monitoring with the marginal revenue (saving) from reduced losses. However, their experience appears to indicate that the probability of a loan becoming uncollectable primarily is a function of the customer served and economic conditions, unless monitoring is insufficient. Then losses increase such that a trade-off between less monitoring and more losses is not profitable.

11. The size of initial loans averages two-thirds that of loans to present borrowers (Benston, 1976a).

With the risk decision made, lenders incur operating costs to the point where, given expected losses and the cost of funds, marginal costs are equated with marginal revenue and profits (or more correctly, shareholders' wealth) is maximized. Marginal revenue is determined by the legal rate ceiling and the size of loans made. Since the level of risk and the operating costs incurred to cope with it are primarily a function of exogenous factors (state laws, population characteristics, number of new customers, etc.), the decision about what level of operating costs to incur is predominantly a function of the level and type of output expected. When the cost of funds changes (and the ceiling rate on loans does not change), lenders react by changing the riskiness, size, and number of loans they are willing to make to (or push on) borrowers, given the operating cost of making and servicing loans. Of course, the borrowers need not borrow more than they wish. Therefore, borrowers' demand and the lender's costs determine the size composition, and so on, of loans made. Since the lender's cost of funds is readily available from market data and since the level of risk accepted is primarily a function of the ceiling rate permitted on loans, state laws, and population characteristics,[12] attention is directed toward estimates of the functional relationship between operating costs and the size of loans.

## Analysis of Operating Costs

Operating costs may be expressed functionally as:[13]

$$C = f(Q, T, D, O, P, M), \qquad (14.1)$$

where

$C$ = operating costs,
$Q$ = quantity of (personal loans) output,
$T$ = type of customer served,
$D$ = delinquency and collection activities,
$O$ = other non-personal loan activities,
$P$ = relative factor prices for inputs,
$M$ = market factors and laws that affect operating costs.

The nature and measurement of each of these factors is discussed next.

---

12. Benston (1977a).
13. A description and analysis of the operations of finance companies upon which this choice of variables is based may be found in Benston (1974).

*C, operating costs,* include salaries, supplies, rent, and so on—in short, all of the recorded annual expenses except interest, bad debts and recoveries, income taxes, and the imputed cost of capital. It is necessary that recorded expenses measure well the opportunity cost of producing output in the period in which output is recorded. Such is the case for the annual costs of consumer finance companies.[14] The most important single expense is labor: salaries account for some 58 percent of total operating costs and 38 percent of total expenses (including losses and interest) before taxes. Since the industry is not unionized and since labor turnover averages about 80 percent a year, currently recorded labor costs are a good measure of opportunity costs. Almost all consumer finance companies rent their branch offices; hence the major nonopportunity accounting cost, depreciation, is of relatively small importance.

*Q, quantity of output,* can be measured by the number of loans made, the number serviced or by the dollar amounts loaned. Of the alternatives, most cost-related operations appear associated with making and servicing loans, as such. Therefore, the number of loans made and serviced (per year) are considered the primary output variables. The dollar size of loans (which is an important variable for policy considerations since legal rate structures are predominantly a function of loan amounts) also may be important if larger loans require more careful checking of credit and greater concern should the borrower become delinquent. However, given the rather limited range of loan amounts made by consumer finance companies (most states limit loans to under $2,000), there is no reason to believe that the size of loans serviced (outstanding) affects operating costs.

*T, the type of customer served,* affects operating costs to the extent that the cost of recording, processing, and collecting a loan differ by customer. Many characteristics of customers might be considered. However, the only one on which data generally are recorded is whether or not a loan is made to a new, former, or present borrower. Lending to new customers probably is more expensive than lending to former customers for whom the company has previous applications and lending experience. Present customers may be the least expensive to lend to, unless a new or additional loan is made because of the customer's inability to maintain payments, in which event time consuming financial counseling may be required.

*D, delinquency and collection activities,* generally are undertaken by the same personnel who make and service loans. In addition, companies may trade off effort on delinquencies for losses on uncollectable accounts. Since loan losses are not included in operating expenses but the salaries and other expenses of delinquency

---

14. Analysis for periods of less than one year is likely to introduce serious measurement problems. Consumer finance companies face seasonal fluctuations. Nevertheless, they charge many expenses on an annual accrued basis and rarely release personnel simply because of a temporary decline in output. For these reasons, the usefulness of Nagata's (1973) study of monthly data is limited.

control are included, it is necessary to include "delinquencies" in the analysis as an independent variable.[15]

*O, other nonpersonal loan activities*, must be accounted for as an independent variable since there is no direct way to separate operating expenses due to these other operations.[16] The most important of these other activities is sales financing, that is, lending to individuals through merchandisers to finance purchases, usually of consumer durables.

*P, relative input factor prices*, must also be accounted for. Annual operating costs may differ among branches because the prices paid for labor, occupancy, supplies, and so on, are a function of prices in a location. Since labor averages 58 percent of total expenses and since other expenses in an area probably are highly correlated with salaries, the wage level in a branch's area is used as an index. Specifically, the index ($P$) is average wages per employee paid by consumer finance companies and related financial enterprises (commercial banks, mutual savings banks, and savings and loan associations) in the county in which a branch is located.[17] Differences in purchasing power among years also must be accounted for the coefficients calculated to be comparable. For this purpose, the gross national product deflator is used to adjust 1969 and 1968 prices to 1970 equivalents. Thus all prices are given in terms of 1970 purchasing power.

*M, market factors and laws*, that may affect consumer finance company operations include the following: (a) state laws that restrict creditors' legal remedies (in particular laws that (1) restrict or prohibit wage assignments, (2) garnishment of wages, (3) confession of judgment, and (4) holder in due course defenses)[18]; (b) restriction of entry as a consequence of enforced convenience and advantages clauses in the state small loan laws[19]; and (c) the extent of competition (as measured by the ratios of the number of consumer finance company offices to total banking offices in a county).

---

15. State laws on collection remedies which may affect operating costs are considered with $M$, market factors.

16. Though some states require a separation of expenses by type of business, the allocations reported essentially are arbitrary.

17. These data are published for the four types of financial institutions by the U.S. Commerce Department (various years) for states and counties where there are at least three companies. The data are taken from the first quarter FICA (social security) returns.

18. Special studies were conducted to determine the extent to which the laws were enforced in each state. See Benston (1976c). These variables were entered into the regressions in dummy variable form.

19. These clauses (see note 2) are enforced differentially, such that entry is considered (in 1970) very restrictive in 23 states, moderately restrictive in 8 states, and easy in the remainder, including the 6 states without this clause. See Benston (1976c) for the source of this evaluation and list of the states. Arkansas, Alaska, and Hawaii are excluded.

## III. The Data

Detailed analysis of costs, by size of loan and scale of operations in particular, can be made only with data derived from branch office operations. Counts of the numbers and dollar amounts of loans made and serviced of different size are not available from a sufficiently large number of companies to provide an adequate number of observations for statistical analysis. Cost data on the branch operations of individual companies also are likely to be recorded more consistently than those recorded by many companies. Another advantage of branch data is that they relate to operations limited to a specific area for which observations on factor prices and market conditions can be relatively accurately measured.

For this study, detailed branch operations data were provided by three finance companies for the years 1968, 1969, and 1970.[20] Two are major companies which operate in most states. The third is a very large company that operates in about 20 states. (The description of the companies is deliberately vague to protect their identities.) Two of these companies could provide data for all three years, and one for two of the three years. For each of the two years in which all three companies were represented, the operations of about 2,500 branches were analyzed.

Only those branches in operation two years or longer are analyzed, to exclude one-time start-up costs. The same branches are included in each of the three years analyzed (1968, 1969, and 1970) to ensure that differences between years are not due to sample variations. Expenses not directly incurred by a branch (home office and other allocated expenses) were not included. Annual direct operating expense data were disaggregated into salaries (excluding fringe benefits but including bonuses), occupancy (rent, heat, light, janitorial services), telephone and telegraph, and other. Considerable effort was expended to ascertain that the companies reported data consistently (with respect to branches, years, and each other) and without error.

Operating data (independent variables) collected for each branch and year to specify the cost function (14.1) include the following.

Output ($Q$):

$NLM_i$ = number of personal loans made for each of 15 loan-size categories (where $i = 1, 2,..., 15$) (dollar amounts also were collected for accuracy checks),[21]

---

20. Data were provided by two additional medium-sized companies. One of these had to be dropped because it was uncooperative in checking and correcting data that appeared incorrect, perhaps because of some management changes that the company was experiencing at the time. The other company included allocated home office expenses by mistake, an error that was not caught until it was too late to rerun the data.

21. The dollar size categories are 0–100, 101–200,..., 701–800, 801–1000, 1001–1500, 1501–2000,..., 2501–3000, 3001–4000, 4001+.

NLS = average number of (total) personal loans serviced (average of 12 month-end outstandings) (DLS, the dollar amounts also were collected for accuracy checks).

Type of Customer Served ($T$): number (and dollars, net of discount), of personal loans made to

NLMNB = new borrowers,
NLMPB = present borrowers,
NLMFB = former borrowers.

Delinquency ($D$):

DELA60 = dollar amount of loans delinquent 60 days or more, average of month-end balances.[22]

Other nonpersonal loan activities ($O$):

NSCM = number of other loans made, predominantly sales finance contracts (dollar amounts also were collected for accuracy checks),
NSCS = average number of other loans serviced, predominantly sales finance contracts (average of 12 month-end outstandings) (dollar amounts also were collected for accuracy checks).

Factor prices ($P$) and market factors ($M$) were measured as indicated above (section II). In addition, the location of each branch as suburban or urban was included as a variable.

## IV. Estimation of the Cost Function

As the discussion in section II indicates, the output of consumer finance companies essentially is demand determined. Hence a single equation model in which each observation represents a point at which a local demand curve intersects with a long-run supply curve is appropriate. Long-run costs (more than short-run) also are relevant to interest rate regulation.

Previous studies of the operating costs of financial intermediaries concluded that the number of loans serviced per period is the best measure of output.[23] However, since the rate ceiling schedules imposed by state small loan laws are stated in terms of dollars of loans made, the relationship between

---

22. Field interview revealed that only delinquencies stated in terms of 60 or 90 days past due could be provided consistently by the companies.
23. See Benston (1972) for a review of these studies.

operating cost and loan sizes was analyzed. As indicated above, the number of loans made for each of 15 loan-size categories ($NLM_i$) was collected. A model was specified that included these data as output variables (Benston, 1977b). The coefficients of $NLM_i$ estimated are statistically insignificant and/or inconsistent and economically unbelievable. Few are significantly different from zero at the .05 level, many are smaller than their standard errors, and their magnitudes and signs change inconsistently over an ascending range of loan size categories. Further, the coefficients for the same variables differ markedly in magnitude, significance and, in some instances, even in sign among the samples: coefficients do not agree between years of the same company and between companies in the same year. These findings obtained for alternative groupings of $NLM_i$. Only the coefficients of number of the loans made over $1,000 are, generally, significant, consistent, and meaningful.[24] Consequently, except for these "large" loans, the sizes of loans made were determined to be not meaningful.

In accordance with the rationale presented in previous studies, a multiplicative functional relationship between the variables is specified. Among other advantages, it yields nonlinear cost functions and direct estimates of economies of scale.

The following set of regressions was computed, where each observation is a finance company branch, for each year, 1968, 1969, and 1970:

$$C_d = a Q_i^{\pi d_i} H_j^{\pi h_j} M_k^{\pi m_k} U, \qquad (14.2)$$

where

$C_d$ = Cost: Salaries ($d = 1$), total direct expenses less occupancy ($d = 2$), total direct expenses ($d = 3$) or contribution margin per dollar ($d = 4$),
$Q_i$ = quantity (level) and type of output ($i = 1,..., 4$),
$H_j$ = output homogeneity variables that adjust for differences in the output between branches (including differences in factor prices) ($j = 1,..., 5$),
$M_k$ = market structure variables that measure differences in costs associated with differences in market conditions and state laws ($k = 1,..., 6$),
$U$ = unspecified variables.

The determinants (independent variables) are as follows:[25]

---

24. A complete explanation of the regressions computed and the coefficients estimated therefrom are given in Benston (1977b).
25. Because the function is multiplicative and to reduce collinearity, a number of the variables are transformed to ratios, as indicated.

$Q_i$:     NLS = number of (personal) loans serviced (average of 12 month-end number of loans outstanding).[26]

NB/NLM = number of (personal) loans made to new borrowers as a percentage of the total number of (personal) loans made.[27]

FB/NLM = number of (personal) loans made to former borrowers as a percentage of the total number of (personal) loans made.[27]

LL/NLM = number of large (over $1,000) (personal) loans made as a percentage of the total number of (personal) loans made plus 1.0.[28]

$H_j$:    SC/NLS = number of sales finance contract loans serviced as a percentage of the number of (personal) loans serviced plus 1.0.[28]

NLM/S = number of (personal) loans made (NLM) as a ratio of the number serviced (NLS).

DEL60+ = delinquency rate, measured as the average dollars of (personal) loans delinquent 60 days or more (DELA60) as a percentage of the average dollars of (personal) loans outstanding at month-end.

SUBURB = 10 if branch is located in a suburb or rural area, 1 if branch is located in an urban area (log 10 = 1, log 1 = 0).

FACTPR = relative factor prices measured by the average wages paid per employee by finance companies, commercial and mutual savings banks and savings and loan associations in the county in which the branch is located.

$M_k$: dummy variables for entry restricted by convenience and advantage laws and for the four restrictions of creditors' legal remedies (10 = restricted, 1 = not restricted since log 10 = 1, log 1 = 0); the degree of competition is measured by the ratio of the number of consumer finance company offices to the total number of banking offices in the county.[29]

$U$: error term, where log $U$ has mean = 0 and is distributed independently across units.

---

26. The number of loans made (NLM) was tested as an alternative measure of output. The $R$ squares computed (observations and other variables the same) were, on average, 4 percentage points lower than when NLS was used. This result is the same as that found in a study of savings and loan costs, which are better explained by the number of mortgages serviced than the number made (Benston, 1970, pp. 704–5). However, the effect of differences in NLM is accounted for with a homogeneity variable, NLM/S. This variable also measures the effect on costs of a more rapidly growing branch.

27. The number of loans made to present borrowers is omitted to avoid overidentification. Thus the coefficients of NB/NLM and FB/NLM measure the cost of loans made to new or former borrowers relative to the cost of loans made to present borrowers.

28. Some branches do not make loans greater than $1,000 or sales finance contract loans. Since the variables are transformed to logarithms, 1 is added to these variables for all branches so that a logarithm can be taken (log 1 = 0, log 0 is not defined).

29. The coefficients of these variables are not presented to save space; consequently they are not described in detail. See Benston (1976c) for a further discussion.

TABLE 14.1 Geometric Means of Antilogarithms of Output and Homogeneity Variables Standard Errors (in parentheses) Expressed as Percentage Increases of the Means

| | \multicolumn{7}{c}{Company and Year} | | | | | | |
|---|---|---|---|---|---|---|---|---|
| | \multicolumn{3}{c}{A} | \multicolumn{2}{c}{B} | \multicolumn{3}{c}{C} | | | |
| Variable | 1970 | 1969 | 1968 | 1970 | 1969 | 1970 | 1969 | 1968 |
| NLS | 1,170 | 1,210 | 1,200 | 1,080 | 1,060 | 1,080 | 1,060 | 1,060 |
| | (64%) | (66%) | (69%) | (62%) | (67%) | (49%) | (42%) | (44%) |
| NB/NLS | 25.0 | 25.0 | 25.5 | 23.2 | 23.4 | 24.9 | 24.3 | 23.2 |
| | (40%) | (43%) | (41%) | (48%) | (57%) | (33%) | (34%) | (37%) |
| FB/NLS | 10.6 | 10.1 | 10.4 | 11.5 | 11.3 | 11.7 | 12.5 | 11.4 |
| | (27%) | (29%) | (29%) | (32%) | (35%) | (26%) | (24%) | (25%) |
| LL/NLS | 9.0 | 8.3 | NA | 15.9 | NA | 5.7 | 5.1 | 4.4 |
| | (186%) | (182%) | | (311%) | | (352%) | (317%) | (278%) |
| SC/NLS | 18.0 | 16.0 | 12.2 | 21.4 | 23.0 | 2.5 | 2.1 | NA |
| | (137%) | (151%) | (181%) | (230%) | (242%) | (224%) | (163%) | |
| NLM/S | 1.35 | 1.14 | 1.11 | 1.38 | 1.28 | 1.26 | 1.19 | 1.03 |
| | (20%) | (19%) | (15%) | (22%) | (30%) | (44%) | (23%) | (19%) |

NA = Data not available.

The geometric means and standard deviations expressed as percentages of the means of the important output and homogeneity variables are presented in table 14.1. To protect the anonymity of the companies, the columns are identified by letters for companies (A, B, C).

Separate regressions were computed for each year for each company.[30] These provide replications of the model and an important check on the meaningfulness of the coefficients estimated. Regressions were computed with salaries, total direct expenses less occupancy, and total direct expenses as dependent variables as a check on the consistency of the data between companies and years and among branches of a company and to determine whether the functional relationship of cost to output, and so on, differed for different constructs of costs.

Regressions also were computed with contribution margin per dollar as a dependent variable. This variable, measured as total branch income less total direct expenses as a percentage of the average dollar amount of personal loans

---

30. The multiplicative form was converted to linear form for multiple regression analysis by transforming all variables to common logarithms.

outstanding, allows one to consider further the impact of economies of scale and other factors on consumer finance company profitability.

The regressions were tested for conformity with the statistical requirements of homoskedasticity. The data for each regression were ordered by the major independent variable, log NLS, and divided into quintiles.[31] The standard deviations of each quintile were computed and subjected to Bartlett's test for homogeneity. The residuals were also plotted. The tests (statistical and visual) of the residuals for Companies A and C showed them to conform to the homoskedasticity requirements of the regression model. They also indicated that the log-linear form of the major output and scale variables, log NLS, fits the data best. However, the tests indicated some curvilinearity (though only slight heteroskedasticity) with respect to Company B's regressions. The last two quintiles had positive mean residuals, indicating that the larger branches were subject to some decreasing economies of scale. An additional variable, the square of log NLS was introduced, but it proved colinear with log NLS. Therefore, the regressions as given by equation (14.4) were computed, although it should be noted that for Company B, the coefficients probably underestimate the larger branches' costs by approximately 6 to 8 percent.

As measured by the $R^2$'s, the expense models fit the data very well; the smallest and median $R^2$'s of the total direct expense regressions are .758 and .858, of the total less occupancy regressions are .804 and .805, and of the salaries regressions are .759 and .857. However the $R^2$'s of the contribution margin regressions are much lower; the low is .087 and the median .240. Therefore, I believe that meaningful conclusions can be drawn from the coefficients computed with the expense regressions, at least. To conserve space, only the coefficients computed for total direct costs (table 14.2) and contribution margin per dollar of loans (table 14.3) as the dependent variables are presented. The coefficients computed for the other costs constraints are very similar in magnitude and statistical significance.[32] The coefficients of the market structure variables ($M_k$) also are not shown, since their impact is not discussed in this essay.[33]

Conclusions derived from these coefficients about economies of scale and the other determinants of operating expense are drawn next, followed by estimates of the average and marginal cost per loan serviced.

---

31. Where the number of observations was not divisible by 5 without a remainder, the "extra" observations were omitted by random selection.

32. See tables 4, 6, 7, 8, and 9 in Benston (1972).

33. The regressions also were computed with the market structure variables omitted. These omissions had little effect on the major output variable, NLS, though the other variables were changed somewhat. See Benston (1972). The impact of state laws that restrict entry and creditors' collection practices are the subject of another paper, Benston (1976c).

TABLE 14.2 Total Direct Operating Expenses All Variables, Regression Coefficients (first line), Standard Errors (in parentheses), t Value (third line) (all variables are in common logarithms)

|  | Company and Year ||||||||
|  | A ||| B || C |||
|  | 1970 | 1969 | 1968 | 1970 | 1969 | 1970 | 1969 | 1968 |
|---|---|---|---|---|---|---|---|---|
| OUTPUT NLS | 0.797 | 0.819 | 0.818 | 0.767 | 0.743 | 0.708 | 0.627 | 0.627 |
|  | (0.011) | (0.010) | (0.010) | (0.010) | (0.010) | (0.021) | (0.025) | (0.032) |
|  | 72.724 | 84.115 | 85.895 | 77.064 | 75.174 | 33.106 | 24.838 | 19.462 |
| NB/NLM | 0.043 | 0.053 | 0.085 | 0.019 | 0.069 | b | 0.054 | 0.051 |
|  | (0.022) | (0.018) | (0.018) | (0.013) | (0.013) |  | (0.034) | (0.040) |
|  | 1.969 | 2.993 | 4.672 | 1.443 | 5.411 |  | 1.582 | 1.285 |
| FB/NLM | −0.037 | −0.038 | −0.003 | −0.037 | −0.032 | 0.084 | 0.089 | 0.067 |
|  | (0.022) | (0.019) | (0.020) | (0.015) | (0.016) | (0.031) | (0.040) | (0.047) |
|  | −1.679 | −2.013 | −0.134 | −2.457 | −2.059 | 2.703 | 2.193 | 1.440 |
| LL/NLM | 0.015 | 0.022 | a | 0.013 | a | 0.031 | 0.017 | −0.011 |
|  | (0.006) | (0.005) |  | (0.003) |  | (0.020) | (0.023) | (0.029) |
|  | 2.487 | 4.124 |  | 3.799 |  | 1.515 | 0.716 | −0.367 |
| CONST. | 1.176 | 1.220 | 1.772 | 1.462 | 1.691 | 2.166 | 2.284 | 2.268 |
|  | (0.128) | (0.113) | (0.077) | (0.118) | (0.123) | (0.205) | (0.247) | (0.302) |
|  | 9.204 | 10.824 | 22.956 | 12.355 | 13.754 | 10.565 | 9.249 | 7.502 |
| HOMOGENEITY SC/NLS | 0.068 | 0.043 | 0.033 | 0.097 | 0.091 | 0.024 | 0.015 | a |
|  | (0.007) | (0.006) | (0.005) | (0.005) | (0.005) | (0.005) | (0.008) |  |
|  | 9.947 | 7.575 | 6.290 | 19.176 | 18.655 | 4.495 | 1.952 |  |
| NLM/S | 0.017 | −0.012 | 0.010 | −0.067 | −0.034 | 0.056 | 0.052 | 0.011 |
|  | (0.028) | (0.029) | (0.028) | (0.022) | (0.018) | (0.026) | (0.050) | (0.072) |
|  | 0.608 | −0.548 | 0.354 | −2.978 | −1.911 | 2.158 | 1.051 | 0.148 |
| DEL60+ | 0.012 | b | −0.009 | 0.012 | 0.017 | b | 0.015 | −0.004 |
|  | (0.012) |  | (0.011) | (0.007) | (0.007) |  | (0.017) | (0.024) |
|  | 1.008 |  | −0.786 | 1.678 | 2.509 |  | 0.887 | −0.149 |
| SUBURB | −0.009 | −0.010 | −0.013 | −0.016 | −0.016 | −0.009 | −0.013 | −0.010 |
|  | (0.005) | (0.004) | (0.004) | (0.004) | (0.004) | (0.007) | (0.008) | (0.009) |
|  | −1.924 | −2.354 | −2.849 | −4.168 | −3.881 | −1.260 | −1.648 | −1.034 |
| FACTPR | 0.323 | 0.290 | 0.088 | 0.220 | 0.137 | 0.042 | 0.097 | 0.134 |
|  | (0.042) | (0.037) | (0.020) | (0.036) | (0.037) | (0.059) | (0.070) | (0.089) |
|  | 7.691 | 7.892 | 4.278 | 6.082 | 3.689 | 0.714 | 1.394 | 1.511 |
| $R^2$ | .878 | .900 | .901 | .872 | .868 | .883 | .827 | .775 |

[a] Data not available or company did not make such loans.
[b] Coefficient too insignificant for inclusion.
t Value greater than 2.807 (one-tail) or 2.576 (two-tail) indicates significance at the 1 percent level.
t Value greater than 2.241 (one-tail) or 1.960 (two-tail) indicates significance at the 5 percent level.

TABLE 14.3 Contribution Margin as a Percentage of Average Dollars of Loans Outstanding, Regression Coefficients (first line), Standard Errors (in parentheses) t Value (third line) (all variables are in common logarithms)

|  | \multicolumn{8}{c}{Company and Year} |
|  | \multicolumn{3}{c}{A} | \multicolumn{2}{c}{B} | \multicolumn{3}{c}{C} |
|  | 1970 | 1969 | 1968 | 1970 | 1969 | 1970 | 1969 | 1968 |
|---|---|---|---|---|---|---|---|---|
| OUTPUT NLS | 0.061 | 0.073 | 0.090 | 0.061 | 0.146 | 0.039 | 0.037 | 0.087 |
|  | (0.011) | (0.010) | (0.010) | (0.013) | (0.016) | (0.055) | (0.052) | (0.041) |
|  | 5.415 | 7.189 | 9.215 | 4.804 | 9.357 | 0.708 | 0.710 | 2.127 |
| NB/NLM | −0.075 | −0.016 | −0.059 | −0.004 | −0.075 | 0.144 | [b] | −0.018 |
|  | (0.022) | (0.019) | (0.019) | (0.018) | (0.020) | (0.068) |  | (0.050) |
|  | −3.410 | −0.864 | −3.188 | −0.211 | −3.761 | 2.112 |  | −0.356 |
| FB/NLM | 0.109 | 0.192 | 0.191 | −0.017 | −0.118 | 0.073 | 0.333 | 0.170 |
|  | (0.023) | (0.020) | (0.020) | (0.020) | (0.024) | (0.084) | (0.081) | (0.059) |
|  | 4.762 | 9.592 | 9.362 | −0.837 | −4.847 | 0.868 | 4.115 | 2.889 |
| LL/NLM | −0.012 | −0.048 | [a] | −0.018 | [a] | −0.045 | −0.084 | −0.150 |
|  | (0.006) | (0.006) |  | (0.004) |  | (0.052) | (0.047) | (0.036) |
|  | −1.944 | −8.494 |  | −4.044 |  | −0.869 | −1.801 | −4.131 |
| CONST. | 0.593 | 1.369 | 0.942 | 0.915 | 1.118 | 1.252 | 0.210 | 0.446 |
|  | (0.133) | (0.122) | (0.079) | (0.152) | (0.197) | (0.538) | (0.496) | (0.382) |
|  | 4.452 | 11.198 | 11.870 | 6.037 | 5.681 | 2.328 | 0.422 | 1.168 |
| HOMOGENEITY SC/NLS | 0.059 | 0.063 | 0.032 | 0.031 | 0.056 | 0.011 | [b] | [a] |
|  | (0.007) | (0.006) | (0.005) | (0.006) | (0.008) | (0.014) |  |  |
|  | 8.214 | 10.528 | 5.925 | 4.845 | 7.158 | 0.805 |  |  |
| NLM/S | −0.371 | −0.111 | −0.325 | −0.118 | 0.357 | 0.121 | 0.051 | −0.238 |
|  | (0.028) | (0.030) | (0.029) | (0.030) | (0.024) | (0.070) | (0.101) | (0.091) |
|  | −13.033 | −3.651 | −11.326 | −3.872 | 15.003 | 1.730 | 0.502 | −2.616 |
| DEL60+ | [b] | −0.038 | 0.023 | −0.010 | −0.032 | 0.023 | 0.035 | −0.012 |
|  |  | (0.011) | (0.011) | (0.010) | (0.011) | (0.050) | (0.033) | (0.031) |
|  |  | −3.288 | 2.019 | −1.008 | −2.962 | 0.458 | 1.053 | −0.376 |
| SUBURB | [b] | 0.003 | 0.003 | [b] | 0.028 | 0.010 | 0.010 | 0.013 |
|  |  | (0.005) | (0.005) |  | (0.006) | (0.017) | (0.016) | (0.012) |
|  |  | 0.557 | 0.739 |  | 4.428 | 0.586 | 0.606 | 1.092 |
| FACTPR | 0.118 | −0.172 | −0.061 | 0.021 | −0.110 | 0.074 | 0.111 | 0.161 |
|  | (0.044) | (0.040) | (0.021) | (0.048) | (0.060) | (0.154) | (0.144) | (0.112) |
|  | 2.694 | −4.326 | −2.888 | 0.440 | −1.843 | 0.480 | 0.770 | 1.435 |
| $R^2$ | .302 | .378 | .288 | .140 | .323 | .437 | .459 | .564 |

[a] Data not available or company did not make such loans.
[b] Coefficient too insignificant for inclusion.
$t$ Value greater than 2.807 (one-tail) or 2.576 (two-tail) indicates significance at the 1 percent level.
$t$ Value greater than 2.241 (one-tail) or 1.960 (two-tail) indicates significance at the 5 percent level.

## V. Description of the Findings

### Economies of Scale

Since the relationship between cost and output is log-linear, the coefficients of the output variable, the average number of loans serviced (log NLS), provide a direct measure of economies of scale (elasticity)—the percentage change in costs associated with a percentage change in output.[34] In all of the regressions, the *t* values of the NLS coefficients are no less than 19 for Company *C* and 72 for Companies *A* and *B*. Also, the elasticities for different years of the same company are very similar. Thus the coefficients of NLS appear to be consistent measures of the underlying elasticities.[35]

All of the elasticities computed are significantly less than 1.0, indicating economies of scale. For total direct expenses (table 14.2), total less occupancy, and salaries (not shown) the elasticities averaged over the years are 0.81, 0.91, and 0.90 for Company *A*; 0.76, 0.83, and 0.83 for Company *B*; and 0.68, 0.75, and 0.71 for Company *C*. Thus, the elasticities indicate fairly substantial economies of scale; averaging over Companies *A*, *B*, and *C*, the elasticities of output (NLS) with respect to total expense, total less occupancy, and salaries are 0.87, 0.81, and 0.71.[36]

I believe that a major reason for the economies of scale is the relatively small size of the offices operated by the companies, a result of which is discontinuities in the use of personnel. About 1,100 loans are serviced by the average office (see table 14.1). Some 10 percent of the offices of two companies and 6 percent of the other serve as few as 600 customers while more than 2,100 customers are served by about 10 percent of the offices of one company, 6 percent of another, and 2 percent of the third. In comparison, commercial banks, whose direct installment loans cost function shows much smaller economies of scale (the elasticity of NLS is 0.967) serve many more customers.[37] For example, the average $25 million bank studied services 6,500 loans, a $75 million bank 20,000 loans, and a $120 million bank 31,300 loans.[38] The size of office measured by the number of employees also is small. The average number of employees per office (and the standard deviation) is 6.4 (3.3) for one company, 4.7 (2.1) for another, and 6.0 (1.5) for the third.

---

34. For example, the coefficient of log NLS for total direct operating expenses of .797 measured for Company *A*, 1970 (table 14.2) means that a doubling of the number of loans serviced is associated with an increase in cost of 79.7 percent, ceteris paribus.

35. The coefficients were virtually unchanged when insignificant variables were omitted from the regressions.

36. Nagata (1973, p. 1332), who analyzed data from 45 branches of a company within a state with a similar model reports an elasticity of 0.77 for total direct expenses.

37. Bell and Murphy (1968), p. 49.

38. Ibid., table XIII-2, p. 225, 1965 data.

The greater economies of scale indicated by the smaller coefficients of the salaries regression is consistent with the belief that there are discontinuities in the use of personnel.

Although larger offices appear subject to economies of scale, the effect on the contribution margin is not great, though positive (table 14.3). The coefficients of log NLS are significant for Companies A and B, averaging 0.07 for A and 0.11 for B. They are insignificant and average 0.05 for Company C. It appears, then, that larger offices are more profitable, though not overwhelmingly so.

## Type of Borrower (NL/NLM and FB/NLM)

Two variables measure the effect on operating cost of lending to new, present, and former borrowers; the percentage of the total number of loans made to new borrowers, NB/NLM, and the percentage of the number made to former borrowers, FB/NLM.[39] The average (geometric mean) percentages of loans made to new and former borrowers are given in table 14.1. The percentages for each company and years are remarkably similar; about 25 percent of the loans are made to new borrowers, 11 percent to former borrowers, and the balance, 64 percent, to present borrowers. However, as the standard errors show, there is considerable variation among offices.

The signs of the coefficients of NB/NLM indicate that new borrowers are most costly to serve and are less profitable per dollar of loans outstanding than are present or former borrowers. However, the coefficients are not consistently statistically significant and differ considerably in magnitude. The magnitudes also are rather small; on the average a 20 percent increase in the percentage of loans made to new borrowers, say from 25 to 30 percent of the number of loans made, and an offsetting decrease in the percentage made to present borrowers, might result in a 1.2 percent increase in cost for Company A and a 0.9 percent increase for Company B.

The coefficients of FB/NLM generally are negative in the expense regressions of Companies A and B and positive for Company C. The coefficients in the contribution margin regressions are inconsistent. Thus it is difficult to interpret these data. Perhaps some companies may make loans only to "good" former customers and others may not be as choosy. Or the findings may be due to errors in classification of customers, where present customers are not reliably distinguished from former customers.

## Large Loans (LL/NLM)

The percentage (of the number) of large loans (loans of $1,000 or more, net of interest) to the total number of loans made was included as a variable because the

---

39. The percentage of loans made to present borrowers is determined by NB/NLM and FB/NLM, since the percentages must add to 100.0.

analysis of the relationship between loan size and cost discussed above indicated that only this size loan appeared to affect costs differentially. These loans amount to about 9 percent of Company *A*'s loans made, 16 percent of Company *B*'s loans, and 5 percent of Company *C*'s loans (see table 14.1). The coefficients of LL/NLM generally are significant for Companies *A* and *B* but insignificant for Company *C*. These findings may be due to the relative number of large loans made by each company, if those who make fewer large loans do so more as a by-product of small loan lending than as a separate, though related, business. In any event, this magnitude of the coefficients for Companies *A* and *B* is rather small (0.01 to 0.02); it indicates that a doubling of the percentage of large loans made (the total made held constant) might result in a 1 or 2 percent increase in operating costs. However, the contribution margin regressions (table 14.3) show negative coefficients for LL/NLM, indicating that large loans are relatively less profitable than smaller loans.

### Other Business: Sales Finance Contracts (SC/NLS)

As expected, the greater the percentage number of sales finance contract loans serviced to personal cash loans serviced, the greater the operating costs. The companies vary widely in the proportion of the "other" business to their primary output, NLS. The geometric mean of SC/NLS ranges from 12.2 in 1968 to 18.0 in 1970 for Company *A*, and averages 22.2 for Company *B* and 2.3 for Company *C* (table 14.1). The coefficients of SC/NLS also vary considerably, though all are positive and significant except for Company *C*'s 1968 regression. (The effect on costs of possible interaction between sales finance contract loans and personal loans is discussed below.)

### Number of Loans Made Relative to the Number Serviced (NLM/S)

As table 14.1 shows, the companies made about 20 percent more loans than they serviced.[40] Over the three-year period, the mean ratio increased.[41] Since the denominator of the variable, NLS, is included in the equations as a variable, the coefficient of NLM/S measures the effect on costs of making loans, holding constant the number of loans serviced. The inconsistently signed, insignificant

---

40. Since the number of loans serviced is an average of 12 month-end numbers, a loan made at mid-year is counted as a half-loan serviced.

41. This change need not indicate greater total growth for the companies if smaller branches grew relatively more than larger branches.

coefficients found for the total expense regressions (and the other cost regulations not shown) indicate that operating costs are not a function of the number of loans made, given the number of loans serviced.

The contribution margin percentage regressions are not as easily explained. Strongly significant negative coefficients are found for Company $A$, a negative (1970) and a positive (1969) coefficient for Company $B$, and insignificant coefficients for Company $C$. Furthermore, the magnitudes of the coefficients among years and companies differ widely. These conflicting findings are difficult to interpret. Were it not the case that the data were very carefully checked, errors in the numbers would be a plausible explanation. Rather, I believe that other factors peculiar to offices of a company and a year are reflected in the variables. As a consequence, they may not measure what they were expected to measure with respect to the contribution margin percentages.

### Location (SUBURB)

For all the the cost regressions, the uniformly negative coefficients of this variable indicate that operating costs are lower for suburban offices than for urban locations, all other things equal. (However, the relationship is not significant for Company $C$.) Although a variable that measures differences in county wage rates (FACTPR) is included in the regressions, SUBURB may measure additionally lower factor prices in suburbs compared to urban areas in the same county. But it seems more likely that this variable measures differences in the cost of services to urban and suburban customers. In any event, the reciprocal of the antilogarithms of the coefficients of SUBURB measure the percentage difference in costs of suburban compared to urban offices, ceteris paribus. The coefficients average about 0.01, which indicates that the costs of offices in suburban locations are about 98 percent of those of urban offices. Thus, while the lower costs are significant for Companies $A$ and $B$, they are not great. With respect to the contribution margin per dollar of loans outstanding, the coefficients of SUBURB are quite insignificant (with the exception of Company $B$'s 1969 data) and of very small magnitude. It appears, then, that urban branches are not much more expensive to operate than suburban ones and, in any event, are not less profitable.

## VI. Calculation of Costs

### Average and Marginal Annual Operating Costs per Loan Serviced

The average and marginal costs of servicing a loan for a year may differ among companies for three important reasons. First, the companies operate in different environments, facing different factor prices, different state laws on creditors' remedies, and so on. Second, they have a different proportion of loans to new, present, and former borrowers, different amounts of other business conducted in the same office, and so on. Third, their costs may differ because of variations in efficiency, scale of operation, centralization of management, and so on. The effects of the first two groups of factors are analyzed above. To determine the effect on costs of differences in scale and efficiency (as well as to test the assumption that the companies report costs equivalently), it is necessary to eliminate or otherwise account for the effect of the other factors on costs. The procedure described next was used to achieve this purpose.

As is discussed above, costs were computed from the following regression:

$$C_d = a\text{NLS}^{q_1}(\text{LL/NLM}+1.0)^{q_2}(\text{SC/NLS}+1.0)^{h_i}Z_z^{\pi b_s}, \qquad (14.3)$$

where the variables are as described above and Z stands for all other variables in equation (14.3). The effect on operating cost of sales finance contracts and large loans is removed by setting SC/NLS and LL/NLS equal to zero (no sales finance contracts or large loans). Other factors that differ among companies also are standardized by setting them equal to the following values (before logarithms): NB/NLM = 25.0 (percent); FB/NLM = 10.0 (percent); NLM/S = 1.2; DEL60+ = 3.0 (percent); FACTPR = 1,500; and SUBURB = 1.0 (urban branch assumed).[42]

Since the coefficients of the market factor variables were generally not statistically significant but were relatively large in magnitude and occasionally different in sign among companies and, for the same company, across years, the average and marginal costs presented are calculated from regressions computed without these variables. The difference, though, between the numbers computed from regressions including and excluding the market variables is in general less than 10 percent. Thus the average and marginal costs computed are for an urban branch that does not make large loans or purchase sales finance contracts,[43] with the other homogeneity and market factor variables the same across firms and years. Average cost per loan serviced then = C/NLS = $a\text{NLS}^{q_1-1}\overline{Z}_z^{\pi b_z}$ and marginal cost = $\partial C/\partial \text{NLS}$ = $aq_1\text{NLS}^{q_1-1}\overline{Z}_z^{\pi b_z}$, where $\overline{Z}_z$ are the other variables specified as described.

Table 14.4 presents the average (panel A) and marginal (panel B) total (annual) direct cost per loan separately for each company and year. The amounts were computed at five levels of NLS since the measured economies of scale (the coefficient of NLS is less than 1.0) result in lower costs per loan

---

42. With the exception of SUBURB, the values are the geometric means of the data rounded to even numbers.
43. The interrelationship between servicing personal loans and sales finance contracts may not be entirely eliminated, as is discussed further below.

TABLE 14.4 Average and Marginal Annual Total Direct Expense per Small Loan Serviced, All Other Variables Held Constant at Predetermined Values

| Company and Year | Level of Average Number of Loans Serviced per Year ||||| 
| --- | --- | --- | --- | --- | --- |
| | 300 | 500 | 1000 | 1500 | 200 |
| A. Average cost | | | | | |
| A1970 | 54.36 | 49.06 | 42.70 | 39.36 | 37.15 |
| A1969 | 56.99 | 51.95 | 45.82 | 42.58 | 40.42 |
| A1968 | 59.33 | 54.17 | 47.88 | 44.55 | 42.33 |
| B1970 | 43.56 | 38.71 | 33.00 | 30.06 | 28.13 |
| B1969 | 47.01 | 41.29 | 34.63 | 31.24 | 29.04 |
| C1970 | 69.02 | 59.56 | 48.77 | 43.39 | 39.93 |
| C1969 | 82.07 | 67.77 | 52.27 | 44.91 | 40.32 |
| C1968 | 85.84 | 71.14 | 55.15 | 47.52 | 42.75 |
| B. Marginal cost | | | | | |
| A1970 | 43.46 | 39.22 | 34.13 | 31.47 | 29.70 |
| A1969 | 46.67 | 42.54 | 37.53 | 34.87 | 33.10 |
| A1968 | 48.77 | 44.53 | 39.36 | 36.62 | 34.80 |
| B1970 | 33.52 | 29.79 | 25.39 | 23.13 | 21.65 |
| B1969 | 35.08 | 30.81 | 25.84 | 23.31 | 21.67 |
| C1970 | 49.11 | 42.38 | 34.70 | 30.87 | 28.41 |
| C1969 | 51.33 | 42.38 | 32.69 | 28.09 | 25.21 |
| C1968 | 54.30 | 45.00 | 34.88 | 30.06 | 27.04 |

at higher numbers of loans serviced.[44] Figures 14.1 and 14.2 present the data graphically.

Several observations can be drawn from the tables and figures. First, the amounts for the same company for each year are very similar. However, some trend in costs over time seems to have occurred. (Recall that the dollar amounts were adjusted for general price level changes to 1970 prices.) In general, 1970 costs per loan serviced are lower than those for 1969 which, in turn, are lower than those for 1968. The second general observation is that Company B's total expenses are uniformly lower than those of the other companies. One reason may be that they charge their branches with fewer costs than do the other companies. However, salary costs (not presented) are fairly uniformly charged to branches by the companies and Company B's salaries per loan (average and marginal) are lower by about the same proportion as their other expenses per loan are lower. Therefore,

---

44. Average (and marginal) costs also were computed with the statistically insignificant (at .05 level) variables omitted. The amounts differed from those given in table 14.4 by less than $2.00 per loan in all but a few cases. See Benston (1974), tables 14 and 17. Average and marginal salary and total expenses less occupancy costs also were computed. See Benston (1974), tables 15, 16, 18, and 19 and figures 10, 11, 13, and 14.

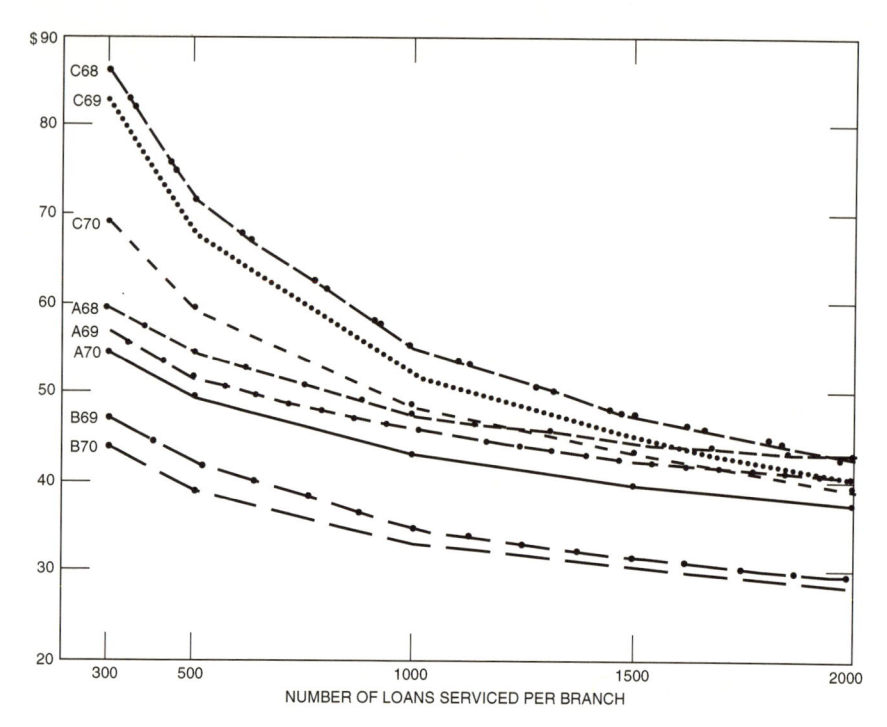

FIGURE 14.1 Average Annual Total Direct Expenses per Loan Serviced at Branch Offices of Three Major Finance Companies (A, B, C) Output and Homogeneity Variables 1968, 1969 and 1970

I believe that while differences in accounting procedures no doubt exist and were not completely overcome, Company B's lower costs may be due to another factor.

It was mentioned above that the average size of finance company offices is rather small—for the three major companies, the geometric mean office has six employees and services 1,100 loans. This small size results, I believe, in discontinuities in the use of personnel and other inputs. As table 14.1 shows, Company B has a larger percentage of sales finance contracts to personal loans. Further, the coefficients of this variable (SC/NLS) are one and a half to two times as large as the coefficients computed for the other companies. Hence, when the estimated cost of servicing sales finance contracts is subtracted (by setting SC/NLS to zero), Company B's costs per personal loan are less than those of the other companies. If this explanation is correct, finance companies should consider the cost saving potential of diversification.

## Overhead

The costs, estimated above, of servicing (and making) consumer loans exclude the supervisory, legal, and other services provided by the "home offices" of the

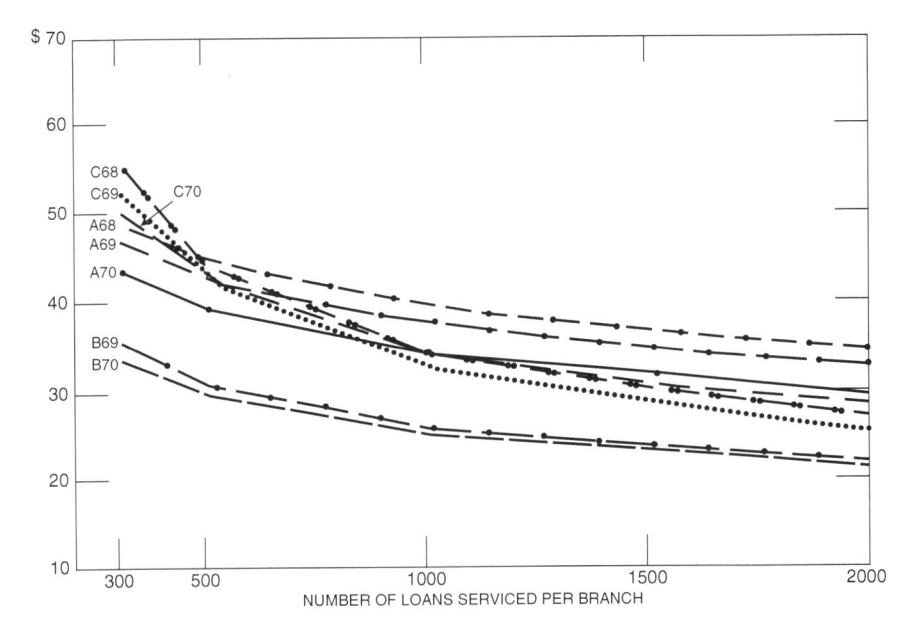

FIGURE 14.2 Marginal Annual Total Direct Expenses per Loan Serviced at Branch Offices of Three Major Finance Companies (A, B, C) Output and Homogeneity Variables 1968, 1969 and 1970

companies. Although there is no conceptual way to allocate meaningfully these costs to the branches and, thence, to individual loans, they should not be omitted from the cost estimates presented.

Annual overhead expenses (which exclude interest, charge-offs and recoveries, and federal income taxes) were collected from Companies $A$, $B$, and $C$ for as many years as they believed the data were meaningful or available. Companies $A$ and $B$ supplied data for 1960 through 1971; Company $C$'s data cover 1961 through 1971. Because inflation characterized the period, the dollar amounts were adjusted to 1970 prices with the GNP deflator. A "model" was developed to analyze overhead as a function of the number of direct cash loans serviced (outstanding), the number of loans per branch, the number of branches opened, and the number closed.[45] Various forms of the functional relationships were tried.

---

45. The model estimated is $OH = A^{b_1} \cdot B^{b_2} \cdot C^{b_3} \cdot \text{NLS}^{b_4 A + b_5 B + b_6 C} \cdot (\text{NLS}/\text{NB})^{b_7} \cdot (\text{NB})^{b_8} \cdot (\text{NBO}/\text{NB})^{b_9} \cdot (\text{NBC}/\text{NB})^{b_{10}} \cdot ((\text{SC}/\text{NLS}) \cdot 100.0 + 1.0)^{b_{11}}$ where NLS = year end number of loans outstanding, NB = number of branches at year end, NBO = number of branches opened during year, NBC = number of branches closed during year, SC = number of sales finance contract loans at year end, and $A$, $B$ and $C$ are dummy variables where $A$ = 10 for Company $A$, 1 otherwise, and so on.

In a statistical sense, they were successful—the residuals behaved "properly," the coefficients of all variables except the percentage of the number of sales finance contracts to the number of direct cash loans serviced had $t$ values greater than 3.0. When the means of the variables were "plugged in" the cost per loan was "sensible" (indeed, the estimates are very similar to those given below). However, when other values (within the range of the data) were "plugged in," the numbers generated were ridiculous. Therefore, it was concluded that the "sophisticated" analysis was not meaningful.

Overhead per loan, then, is estimated simply by dividing the annual overhead amounts, excluding and including advertising, by the number of direct cash loans outstanding for each company plus a weighted number of sales finance loans serviced. These "other" loans were weighted by the ratio of the average coefficients of SC/NLS to NLS to adjust them for their relative importance (with respect to costs).

Table 14.5 presents the average annual overhead per loan (in 1970 prices). These amounts are rather stable over the time period, particularly for Company B and (excepting 1971) for Company C.[46] The amounts calculated for each year, 1968, 1969, and 1970, therefore, are used as the estimates of average overhead per loan.

Total average operating expenses per loan are taken to be the sum of the overhead (including and excluding advertising) incurred in each year (table 14.5) plus

TABLE 14.5 Average Annual Overhead per Loan (in 1970 prices)

|  | Including Advertising ||| Excluding Advertising |||
| --- | --- | --- | --- | --- | --- | --- |
|  | Co. A | Co. B | Co. C | Co. A | Co. B | Co. C |
| 1971 | 22.69 | 20.21 | 18.05 | 18.92 | 15.67 | 16.05 |
| 1970 | 23.26 | 19.88 | 15.24 | 19.50 | 15.01 | 13.53 |
| 1969 | 23.00 | 21.24 | 15.84 | 16.64 | 15.62 | 13.94 |
| 1968 | 20.53 | 21.24 | 15.85 | 15.37 | 15.20 | 12.83 |
| 1967 | 19.66 | 20.99 | 14.52 | 14.31 | 14.76 | 13.00 |
| 1966 | 17.99 | 20.80 | 14.73 | 12.46 | 14.04 | 12.59 |
| 1965 | 17.65 | 22.42 | 14.18 | 12.13 | 14.57 | 12.05 |
| 1964 | 17.51 | 22.46 | 13.68 | 12.11 | 13.95 | 11.30 |
| 1963 | 15.21 | 22.37 | 13.00 | 9.80 | 14.10 | 10.12 |
| 1962 | 14.73 | 22.81 | 11.91 | 9.68 | 14.26 | 9.73 |
| 1961 | 14.21 | 24.60 | 11.43 | 9.10 | 16.02 |  |
| 1960 | 15.16 | 21.85 |  | 10.00 | 14.47 |  |
| Average | 18.47 | 21.74 | 14.40 | 13.34 | 14.81 | 12.51 |

46. The inclusion of the number of sales finance contract loans changed the average overhead amount but little, since the weights reduced the number greatly.

TABLE 14.6 Total Annual Operating Expense per Loan and per Hundred Dollars of Loan Balances Outstanding (1970 data), Three Major Finance Companies at Branches Servicing 1,000 Loans[a]

|  | Including Advertising ||| Excluding Advertising |||
| --- | --- | --- | --- | --- | --- | --- |
|  | Co. A | Co. B | Co. C | Co. A | Co. B | Co. C |
| A. Per loan |  |  |  |  |  |  |
| 1970 | $65.96 | $52.88 | $64.01 | $62.20 | $48.01 | $62.30 |
| 1969 | 68.82 | 55.87 | 68.11 | 62.46 | 50.25 | 66.21 |
| 1968 | 68.41 |  | 71.00 | 63.25 |  | 67.98 |
| B. 1970 total as percentages of average loan balances outstanding[b] ||||||
| $ 50 | 132% | 106% | 128% | 124% | 96% | 124% |
| 100 | 66 | 53 | 64 | 62 | 48 | 62 |
| 150 | 44 | 36 | 44 | 42 | 32 | 42 |
| 300 | 22 | 18 | 22 | 21 | 16 | 31 |
| 500 | 13 | 11 | 13 | 12 | 10 | 12 |
| 1000 | 7 | 5 | 3 | 6 | 5 | 6 |

[a] Sources: table 14.5 and table 14.4, panel A.
[b] The initial amount of a one-year loan is approximately twice the average amount outstanding.

direct total operating expenses at a branch that services 1,000 loans (table 14.4, panel A). These amounts are given in table 14.6, panel A. In 1970, total costs per loan, excluding advertising, averaged $66 for Company A, $53 for Company B, and $64 for Company C. Other estimates derived in another study from company-wide data[47] for a $600 loan (about the average size) is $72, a figure not too different than those estimated from the branch data.

## Operating Costs per Dollar of Loan

State legal rate ceilings are stated in terms of the dollar amounts of loans; hence the cost data per loan should be similarly stated. The analysis indicates that operating costs are not a function of the dollar size of loans made (other than loans over $1,000). Consequently, the costs as percentages of loan amounts simply are the amounts presented in table 14.6, panel A, divided by varying dollar amounts. The quotients are given in table 14.6, panel B, for 1970 operating costs. Figure 14.3 charts the hyperbola calculated from this exercise. In addition to these branch-derived data, amounts calculated from an analysis of the operating costs of 124 companies[48] also are charted in figure 14.3. The latter curve is not a hyperbola

47. Benston (1976b).
48. Ibid.

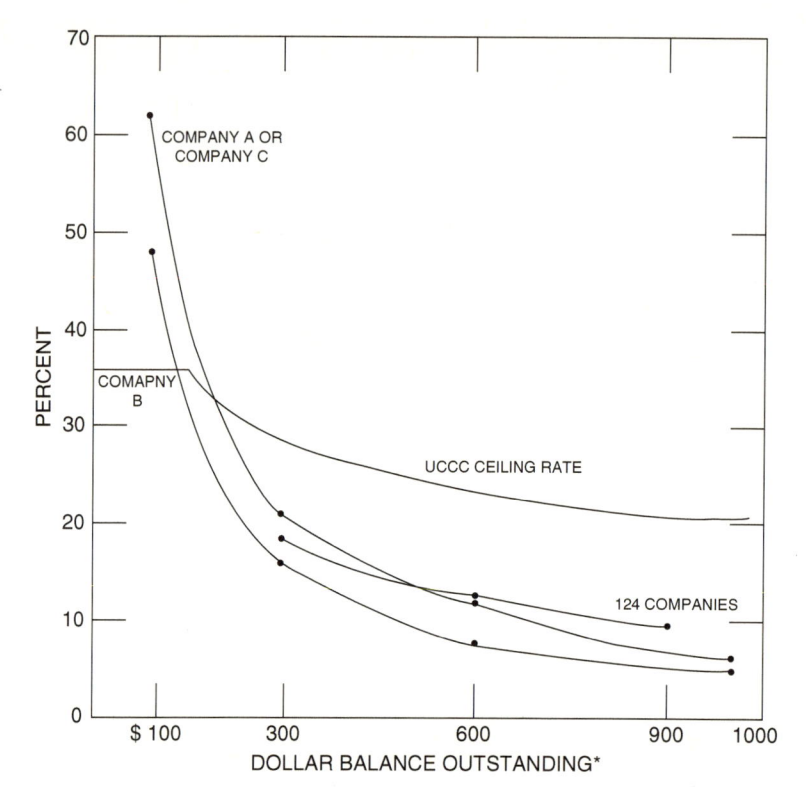

FIGURE 14.3 Average Annual Total Operating Cost (Excluding Advertising, Losses and Taxes) as a Percentage of the Dollar Amount of Loan Balances Outstanding at Branch Offices of Three Major Finance Companies and 124 Companies, 1970 Data

because the size of loans is a significant variable in the company-wide regressions (in part because large loans are not excluded from the data). Nevertheless, the amounts per loan and per dollar of loans are quite similar to those calculated for the three companies. The UCCC ceiling rate also is charted in figure 14.3.

## VII. Policy Implications of the Findings

The two principal policy considerations discussed in section I to which this study of finance company cost function pertains are (1) economies of scale and (2) interest rate ceilings.

The fairly large economies of scale measured on the office level indicate that larger offices could serve borrowers at a lower operations cost. It would seem, then, that these findings (together with the lack of significance of the variables that measured restrictions or ease of entry[49]) would argue for restrictive "convenience and advantage" laws, on the assumption that the companies would pass the savings on to their customers.[50] One way of assuring this, some state regulators argue, is to prohibit the companies from charging customers more than a ceiling rate which would be set relatively low.

It is important to note that, though the elasticities computed indicate substantial economies of scale, it is the dollar magnitudes per loan that are the figures of interest to consumers. The average branch services 1,000 loans a year. Were branches to service 1,500 loans rather than 500 loans a year, average operating costs per loan might decrease (on average) by $10 a loan for Companies A and B and $21 a loan for Company C. Were a branch to service 2,000 rather than 1,000 loans a year, average operating costs might be $5 a loan less at companies A and B and $11 a loan less at company C. These are the maximum estimated amounts by which the consumer might benefit were restrictive licensing effective in increasing the size of loan company offices.

In addition, regulators should realize that, were the number of licensees restricted, the borrowers' travel and waiting costs and the quality of service they would receive probably would be adversely affected. These costs are not included in the estimates presented above. I believe them to be greater than the operations savings that could be achieved, since otherwise I expect that some company would find it profitable to offer people larger offices and lower prices.[51] Admittedly, though, this judgment is subjective.

With respect to costs per loan, the study reports amounts that, by bank standards, are quite high. The average direct branch operating expense, less occupancy expense per loan (at a branch servicing 1,000 loans a year), computed for the three companies studied ranges from $28 to $49. In contrast, the average direct cost per consumer loan estimated at commercial banks in 1965, in 1970 prices, is about $24.[52] Some might argue that these data show simply that consumer finance companies are inefficient. This explanation, no doubt true for some companies, is unlikely to be valid generally.

---

49. Not presented herein. See Benston (1976c).

50. The positive coefficients of output (NLS) in the contribution margin regressions (table 14.3) are consistent with the conclusion that the companies did not pass all "savings" from economies of scale to their customers. However, the coefficients are not large and the $R$ squares of the regressions are low.

51. It also is important to point out that the finance companies probably couldn't expand the size of their offices without losing a very important product that borrowers apparently want to purchase. Because an average office has five employees, it can be run with a minimum of bureaucracy. Consequently, the manager can provide borrowers with direct, fast, flexible, confidential, personal service. I believe that the value of this service to borrowers, and therefore to companies, explains why some companies have not established large offices.

52. Bell and Murphy (1968). It should be noted, however, that this figure is a weighted average of *all* consumer loans serviced by a commercial bank, which includes indirect as well as direct loans.

The costs per loan are based on the branch operations of three large companies. In a separate sample of 124 companies, very similar costs per loan were estimated.[53] This analysis also was replicated with three years' data. It is doubtful if all of these companies are inefficient. Surely it would pay most companies to be efficient, since the amounts they fail to save are lost by their owners. Rather, the higher costs of consumer finance companies are due to the nature of their operations and the types of persons with whom they deal. Knowing customers individually, and working with them when they miss payments, and so on, is expensive, but no doubt cheaper than accepting losses or engaging in court action to collect past due accounts.

Because operating costs are, on the whole, invariant with respect to the amount of the loan (though not to the number of loans serviced), costs expressed as a rate per dollar appear very high for small loans. Figure 14.3 shows this relationship. The curve plotted therein should be raised uniformly by amounts that cover the cost of risk and the cost of money. The cost of risk (as detailed in another paper—Benston, 1977a) was found not to be a function of the size of loan.[54] It averages from 2 to 3 percent of the initial loan amount.[55] Interest cost might be estimated as a weighted average of debt and equity costs. If the borrowing rate is 7 percent (the rate in 1970), the before-tax return on equity is 20 percent, and the percentage of equity to assets 26 percent, the average cost of funds is 10 percent. Thus if all factor costs are to be "covered" (roughly) and the 1970 total operating costs (including advertising) of Companies A and C of $65 per loan are "typical," the ceiling rate on a one-year loan, expressed as an equivalent annual rate on the balance outstanding, would have to be about 144 percent on loans with an initial amount of $100 ($50 outstanding on average) and 14 percent on additional amounts outstanding.[56]

However, it is potentially misleading to state costs (and the legal ceiling rate) as a percentage of dollars outstanding for small loans as one does for large loans, such as mortgages. For large loans, the operations costs of processing the paperwork and dealing with the customer is small relative to the cost of funds. But for small loans, operations costs per loan are relatively high. Consequently, for small loans the amount required to cover costs appears unconscionably high (144 percent for $100 loan). Therefore, it would be better to state the rates in two parts: $65 to service a loan for a year plus 14 percent of loan balances outstanding.

---

53. Benston (1976b).

54. The company's assessment of risk appears to determine the amount which it is willing to extend to a borrower, given the ceiling rate permitted by the state. There is little evidence of a trade-off between risk and the rate charged or of portfolio balancing as suggested by Avio (1974).

55. The rate of charge-offs net of recoveries as a percentage of average receivables is reported by major lenders as from 1.5 to 2 percent.

56. $65 for operating expenses + risk at 2% of the initial amount = $67/$50 average amount outstanding = 134% + 10% cost of funds = 144%. Additional amounts require only additional risk (2% on initial amount or 4% on average amount outstanding) + cost of funds (10%) = 14%.

In addition, as the current inflation has shown, ceiling rates should not be fixed, but should be tied to a market interest rate that reflects the inflation cost of money. The rate at which consumer finance companies can lend necessarily is a direct function of the rate at which they can borrow, which in turn is a function of the expected rate of inflation. The rate per dollar allowed, therefore, should be a function of the borrowing rate (say, the finance company or commercial paper rates published in the *Federal Reserve Bulletin*) and the service charge allowed should be adjusted to reflect changes in the general purchasing power of the dollar. As it now stands, the ceiling rates allowed to consumer finance companies put them in an almost impossible position. For example, due to inflation, a loan made for $300 in 1964 is equivalent to a $416 loan made in 1974.[57] The UCCC ceiling rate averages 36 percent per annum on an initial $300 loan and about 32 percent per annum on an initial $416 loan. In effect inflation has lowered the legal ceiling rate on small loans. Yet the finance company paper rate increased to 8.53 percent in 1974 (November), compared to 3.83 percent in 1964 and the cost of labor, and so on, also has increased.

This effective reduction in ceiling rates tends, in part, to reduce the profitability of consumer finance companies. The primary effect, though, is a decrease in the availability of funds to consumers from this source. In the aggregate, the percentage of installment loans held by finance companies declined from 50 percent in 1965 to 39 percent in 1974.[58] More directly, the ceiling rate reduction makes smaller loans unprofitable and, consequently, makes these loans unavailable to consumers. Household Finance, for example, reports a steady decline in the percentage of loans made for amounts under $250 from 3.7 percent of the total made in 1965 to 1.0 percent in 1972 (the latest year reported).[59] Loans under $500 declined from 16.9 percent in 1965 to 5.3 percent in 1972. On the other hand, loans of $2,000 and more increased from 9.3 percent in 1965 to 33.8 percent in 1972 and loans over $1,000 increased from 36.8 percent in 1965 to 73.8 percent in 1972. This change in the distribution of loans by size is not surprising. Figure 14.3 (plus losses and interests of about 14 percent) shows that loans with balances outstanding of about $400 (initial amount of about $800) are not profitable in the long run. Though finance companies may offer loans in these amounts (or less) in the long run as "loss leaders,"[60] and in the short run because marginal costs are about $8 a loan less than average costs, it is apparent that they will not

---

57. Adjusted by the Consumer Price Index.
58. Source: *Federal Reserve Bulletin*, November 1974, pp. 47–48.
59. Source: Household Finance Corporation (1973). (The 1973 report does not provide these data.)
60. For a model of why finance companies make such loans and an empirical analysis of the effect of a state law that prevented finance companies from renewing loans see Benston (1976a).

continue to do so as ceiling rates decline and operating and interest costs increase. Thus the states may be returning some consumers to the pre-1916 situation when legal loans were not available.

In addition, the ceiling rate structures enacted by most states encourage lenders to "push" larger loans on borrowers than the borrowers might wish, since the largest loan that a borrower can repay is the most profitable. Since interest rate ceilings were designed primarily to prevent this type of expected behavior (which nevertheless, may not occur, since borrowers need not accept more funds than they wish), this built-in incentive to lenders seems perverse.

Aside from these considerations, the study shows that no ceiling rate structure, even the one suggested, can be optimal in the sense that it reflects operating, borrowing and risk costs. The study shows that costs vary from company to company and over time. In addition, costs differ depending on whether a company lends to new or present borrowers, conducts other business in the same office, or is located in a high- or low-factor cost area. It is almost impossible for a state regulatory agency to estimate these costs with any accuracy. Hence, although the structure of interest rates suggested above is preferable to the present static procedure, based entirely on dollar amounts, I should emphasize that cost-determined regulation of interest rates and charges is hardly exact either, as this study shows.

## REFERENCES

Kenneth L. Avio. "On the Effects of Statutory Interest Rate Ceilings," *Journal of Finance*, 29, December 1974, 1383–95.

Frederick Bell and Neil J. Murphy. *Costs in Commercial Banking*, Research Report No. 41, Federal Reserve Bank of Boston (Boston, Mass., 1968).

George J. Benston. "Cost of Operations and Economies of Scale in Savings and Loan Associations," research paper in *Study of the Savings and Loan Industry*, directed by Irwin Friend, Federal Home Loan Bank Board, U.S. Government Printing Office, Washington, D.C., 1970; 677–761.

George J. Benston. "Economies of Scale of Financial Institutions," *Journal of Money, Credit and Banking*, 4, May 1972, 312–41.

George J. Benston. "The Costs to Consumer Finance Companies of Extending Consumer Credit," the National Commission on Consumer Finance, Technical Studies, Volume II, U.S. Government Printing Office, Washington, D.C., 1974.

George J. Benston. "The Impact of Maturity Regulations on High Interest Rate Lenders and Borrowers," *Journal of Financial Economics*, 1976a.

George J. Benston. "Costs of Operations and Economies of Scale of Consumer Finance Companies," unpublished paper, 1976b.

George J. Benston. "The Cost and Effect of Legal Restrictions on the Operations of Consumer Finance Companies," unpublished paper, 1976c.

George J. Benston. "Risk on Consumer Cash Loans," *Journal of Finance*, May 1977a.

George J. Benston. "Graduated Interest Rate Ceilings and Operating Costs by Size of Small Consumer Cash Loans," *Journal of Finance*, July 1977b.

Douglas F. Greer. "Rate Ceilings, Market Structure, and the Supply of Finance Company Personal Loans," *Journal of Finance*, 29, December 1974, 1363–82.

Household Finance Corporation. *1972 Annual Report to Shareholders*, Chicago, 1973.

Robert W. Johnson. "Regulation of Finance Charges on Consumer Installment Credit," *Michigan Law Review*, 66, November 1967, 81–114.

Michael Kawaja. *Regulation of the Consumer Finance Industry: A Case Study of Rate Ceilings and Loan Size Limits in New York State*, Studies in Consumer Credit No. 3, Graduate School of Business, Columbia University, New York, 1971.

Ernest Nagata. "The Cost Structure of Consumer Finance Small-Loan Operations," *Journal of Finance*, 28, December 1973, 1327–37.

William L. Sartoris. "The Convenience and Advantage Clause in Small-Loan Legislation—Pro and Con," *Business Lawyer*, 27, November 1971, 349–60.

U.S. Department of Commerce. *County Business Patterns*, U.S. Government Printing Office, Washington, D.C., various years.

Jack Zwick. "A Cross-Section Study of Industry Costs and Savings," in *The Consumer Finance Industry: Its Costs and Regulation*, John M. Chapman and Robert P. Shay, eds., Columbia University Press, New York, 1967, 55–86.

# 15

# The Self-Serving Management Hypothesis

## Some Evidence

### Managerial Motivations to Act Contrary to Shareholder Interests

That corporate managers, like other humans, tend to act in self-serving ways is hardly an original insight. This truism was applied to large corporations with diversely held shares by Berle and Means (1934). Since managers rarely own more than a very small fraction of the shares, Berle and Means postulated that this separation of ownership and control gives rise to the problem of professional managers maximizing their own welfare at the expense of shareholders. Kaysen (1960) and Gordon (1961) specified that the managers' personal goals of security, power, prestige, advancement, and personal income take precedence over corporate profits. Baumol (1962, 1967) particularized the hypothesis by specifying sales maximization as a major managerial goal. Marris (1964) developed the hypothesis more completely, presenting behavioral evidence showing that managers' pecuniary and nonpecuniary rewards are positively related to the growth rate of their companies.

Reid (1968) extended the hypothesis to mergers. Analyzing data from 478 firms over the period 1951–61, he found merger activity positively related to sales, assets, and employee growth more than to the growth in market price per share and profits. He concludes: "Mergers appear to contribute more to size maximization than to profitability; thus they tend to serve managers' interests and goals,

---

Michael Jensen, Clifford Smith, and Jerold Zimmerman made valuable comments. Itzhak Swary helped with the data collection.

independent of those of stockholders" (Reid, 1968, p. 4). Mueller (1980) drew a similar conclusion from studies of mergers in seven countries. He summarizes these findings as follows:

> the rather consistent lack of evidence that mergers led to or were expected to lead to significant increases in profits is inconsistent with all the neo-classical theories of mergers. Some form of managerial motive for mergers—as, say, in the pursuit of growth—is left as a sort of residual explanation for why mergers might take place. (Mueller, 1980, pp. 313–14)

Conglomerate mergers, in particular, have been viewed as generally inconsistent with the neoclassical hypothesis that mergers are undertaken to benefit shareholders, since they do not appear to promise clear economic benefits. Unlike horizontal mergers that offer the prospect of economies of scale in manufacturing and distribution, and vertical mergers that might be undertaken to achieve production or monitoring efficiencies, conglomerates seem to some observers to be creatures of their senior managers' preferences for running large organizations.[1] This belief was supported by the dismal stock market performance of many conglomerates that followed grandiose claims by CEOs about their ability to achieve great gains from combining seemingly diverse enterprises. For example, Harold Geneen, then chairman and president of perhaps the most famous conglomerate, International Telephone & Telegraph Corporation (ITT), asserted that from 1960 to 1965 his company had "developed the ability through management skill, routines, and techniques to set and progressively meet higher competitive standards and achieve them in practically every line and product we have undertaken."[2] The drop in the share prices of ITT from 1970 through 1974 of 62.5 percent (compared to a decline in the New York Stock Exchange [NYSE] Index of 30 percent) led some observers to question both the ability and incentives of the conglomerates' senior managers.

## Refutations of the Hypothesis

The sales maximization version of the self-serving management hypothesis was refuted by Lewellen and Huntsman (1970) and Masson (1971). The authors of both papers gathered data from proxy statements on corporate managers' *total* compensation (cash salaries, bonuses, and indirect, deferred and contingent stock

---

1. See Mueller (1969) for a statement of this hypothesis and Benston (1980, ch. 2) for a description of the benefits shareholders derive from mergers.
2. Quoted by Salter and Weinhold (1978, p. 170).

option, retirement, and other compensation arrangements). They report that the managers' total compensation is much more highly related to their companies' stock price and (for Lewellen and Huntsman) earnings performance than to sales.[3]

The merger-for-the-benefit-of-managers (but not shareholders) version of the hypothesis has been questioned on three grounds. One is that the performance of the acquiring company was not correctly measured, since it is based on accounting profits, which often provide poor measures of economic performance.[4] Second, in comparing pre- and postmerger profits, the studies did not account for changes unrelated to the merger.[5] Third, studies that measure the effect of mergers on shareholder wealth by examining changes in share prices at and around the time the tender offers and mergers were announced (event studies) show that shareholders of the acquiring firms are more likely than not to have gained from mergers. Jensen and Ruback (1983, p. 22) summarize these findings as follows:[6]

> The reported positive returns to *successful bidders* in *tender offers* and the generally negative returns to *unsuccessful bidders* in both *mergers* and *tender*

---

3. Lewellen and Huntsman (1970, p. 711) examined "the cross-sectional relationships between executive compensation and company performance at three-year intervals, beginning with 1942 and ending with 1963" for 50 of the 94 largest *Fortune* 500 companies. They concluded: "Because the results of the study persistently indicate that both reported profits and equity market values are substantially more important in the determination of executive compensation than are sales—indeed, sales seem to be quite irrelevant—the clear inference is that there is a greater incentive for management to shape its decision rules in a manner consonant with shareholder interests than to seek the alternative goal of revenue maximization" (Lewellen and Huntsman, 1970, pp. 718–19). Masson (1971) sampled 39 electronics, aerospace, and chemical companies for the years 1947–66. He found that the executives' compensation was more a function of changes in the market values of their firms than of changes in the firms' sales or earnings per share. Indeed, Masson (1971, p. 1285) finds that "there *may* be a tendency for firms to pay their executives not to emphasize sales or profits performance at the expense of stock market performance, from which it follows that executives *may* derive utility value from current sales and profits figures" (emphasis in original). He also examined the relationship between the companies' stock market performance from 1948–50 through 1963–65 and the relative amount of their executives' compensation that was based on changes in sales, earnings per share, and stock performance (as derived from his previous analysis). Masson (1971, pp. 1289–90) reports that "the conclusions are that stock-oriented executive incentives are better able to benefit the stockholder than profit incentives or sales incentives," since he finds that sales and profit-related compensation are negatively related to company performance.

4. See Mueller (1977) for a survey of the accounting-based studies.

5. For example, Winslow (1973) compared the pre- and postmerger profit rates of return on assets of 28 firms acquired during 1964–68 by four major conglomerates. Finding that the profit rates declined, he concluded that the conglomerates were poorly managed. Conn (1976) compared these rates of return with those of firms in similar industries and of the manufacturing sector over the same time period. He concludes that "declining conditions in the industries of acquired firms and the manufacturing sector account for the poor performance of the acquired firms, not ineffective management" (Conn, 1976, p. 1172).

6. See Benston (1980, pp. 37–45) for a review of six of these studies.

*offers* are consistent with the hypothesis that mergers are positive net present value projects. The measurement of returns to bidders in mergers is difficult, and perhaps because of this the results are mixed. The evidence suggests, however, that returns to *successful bidding* firms in *mergers* are zero. (emphasis in original)

The inconclusive findings for acquiring firms' shareholders in mergers may reflect the prior impounding in share prices of the market's expectation that the acquiring firms will be engaging in profitable merger activity, as Schipper and Thompson's (1983) evidence suggests. The findings also may reflect the consequences of a competitive market for acquired companies, such that the owners of these properties get all the gains.

## Support for the Hypothesis

Despite the evidence to the contrary, the hypothesis that the managers of diversely held corporations often act contrary to the interests of their shareholders still appears to be widely held. One reason seems to be the apparent lack of relationship between the remuneration of top corporate officers and the performance of their firms. This view was given considerable exposure in a *Fortune* article (Loomis, 1982) in which the return in 1981 on the stockholders' equity of 140 large companies was compared to the remuneration (salary plus bonuses) paid to their chief executives. The charts presented show little relationship between these two variables. Loomis (1982, p. 42) concludes:

> In the upper reaches of corporate America, the market frequently does not seem to work. In a totally rational world, top executives would get paid handsomely for first-class performance, and would lose out when they flopped. But to an extraordinary extent, those who flop still get paid handsomely.

Reid (1976) similarly studied data from an earlier period on 11 conglomerates that the Federal Trade Commission (FTC) had identified as being "merger-active." The shareholders of these companies experienced an average percentage decline in the value of their shares of 66.9 percent over the five years 1970–74 (compared to a 30 percent decline in the NYSE index). The least decline was 37.4 percent (General Telephone & Electric) and the greatest was 93.6 percent (Litton Industries) (see Reid, 1976, table 6.4, p. 97). He states:

> While the stockholders of the conglomerates were generally experiencing a much higher than average shrinkage in the market value of their holdings the total compensation of the officers and directors was increasing. For the 11 merger-active conglomerates identified by the Federal Trade

Commission, officer and director compensation increased from $28 million in 1970 to over $34 million in 1973. In only 1 of the 11 firms was there a decline in officer and director compensation, and this resulted from a substantial thinning of the ranks. (Reid, 1976, p. 98)

Lev (1983, p. 15) cites studies showing "positive market reaction to spin-offs and leveraged buy-outs" in deciding that "we are justified in doubting, if not actually rejecting, the value maximization explanation of managerial behavior in mergers—the argument that mergers are done to maximize stockholders' wealth." These studies plus his review of event studies showing what he describes as "mostly negative market consequences around and after acquisitions" leads him to conclude:

> if...I were forced to make a choice among the various hypotheses about motives for mergers & acquisitions, I would lean away from the value-maximizing hypothesis and towards the managerial preferences explanation...What we seem to be witnessing in the rise of conglomerate firms is mostly "expansion" or "growth for growth's sake." And this of course is consistent with all those managerial motives of power, prestige, empire-building, etc., which come with managing larger firms.

Of course, growth by merger need not be contrary to the interests of shareholders. The shareholder-benefit motivation for mergers is questioned only when share prices do not seem to reflect the presumed benefit, or, more tellingly, when the conglomerates' share prices decline. Moreover, such ex post results are consistent with the hypothesis that the CEOs made the best (or at least unbiased) decisions at the time for their shareholders by acquiring companies, but unpredictable subsequent events caused the losses. An alternative, the self-serving management hypothesis, is that the CEOs acted opportunistically, overestimating the benefits from acquisitions because they could thus increase the size of their domains, and hence, their pecuniary and nonpecuniary rewards.

## A Test of the Self-Serving Management Hypothesis

The hypothesis is tested by examining the personal financial gains and losses achieved and absorbed by the senior managers of the major conglomerates, most (perhaps all) of which engaged in extensive merger activity. If the self-serving management hypothesis were correct, these managers would have taken actions that tended to increase their personal well-being even when shareholders' wealth decreased. The managers' well-being could be expressed in the change in their financial wealth and in the security of their positions. The numbers used by Reid (1976) and Loomis (1982) are insufficient for this test, since the compensation of these managers is not limited to their salaries and bonuses. Rather, as Lewellen and Huntsman (1970) and Masson (1971) point out, the executives' compensation includes such benefits as stock options.[7]

Importantly, the researchers who studied the behavior of conglomerates (as well as those who generally studied management-controlled versus owner-controlled firms, with the notable exception of Lewellen, 1971) did not include a material part of the senior executives' rewards and penalties from their decision-making positions in their companies—the executives' personal holdings of the companies' shares.[8] These shares in the companies they manage provide the executives with the same sort of gains and losses that are experienced by their shareholders. They are a means by which the executives bond themselves to the companies. Furthermore, it would be misleading to identify a company as "manager controlled" only when the managers control at least 10 percent of the company's shares (a metric used by many researchers interested in owner versus management controlled firms), with the implication that the managers have no motivationally meaningful interest in the company. This metric is misleading since a very small percentage of a large publicly traded company is a lot of money, making it very unlikely that a manager could own as much as 5 percent of his or her company. For executives (as for other people) the determining variable is the amount of the executive's total wealth invested in the companies they manage. Therefore, the executives' wealth changes resulting from their stock ownership should be included with their other compensation.

In addition, should the managers make decisions that turn out to be harmful to shareholders, they could lose their jobs. The hypothesis that the top managers of conglomerates where share prices decreased significantly left their companies more frequently than did the managers of the other conglomerates studied is tested below.

Conglomerates were chosen because much concern is with this form of enterprise. The particular sample examined here was taken from an article by Salter and Weinhold (1978) to focus on controversial firms. They critically reviewed the performance in 1967, 1973, 1975, and 1977 of 36 diversified manufacturers identified by the FTC in 1969 as representative of companies pursuing strategies of diversification by merger and not classifiable in standard industrial categories. To

---

7. See Smith and Watts (1982) for a description and discussion of such benefits.
8. Lewellen and Huntsman (1970) and Lewellen (1968) do not mention the executive's share holdings. Masson (1971) states that he estimated compensation as did Lewellen (1968). His only mention of stock holdings is the following: "Stock options are calculated on a present-value basis net of opportunity cost of exercise of option, and stock value is estimated on the change in present value of price change and dividends accrued each year" (Masson, 1971, p. 1283).

be included, a company had to meet four conditions: (1) assets of $250 million or more, (2) 50 percent or more of its total sales derived from manufactured products, (3) less than 50 percent of its total sales from one industry, and (4) three or more product lines. The 36 companies include all except two of those analyzed by Reid (1976). General Telephone and Electric and General American Transportation were omitted, perhaps because they did not meet the product diversification criteria.[9]

The subjects of this study are managers who also were directors of their companies. Their positions gave them decision-making power over the major activities (including mergers) of their firms.[10] Their annual salaries and bonuses, retirement benefits, stock options, and share holdings were obtained from company proxy statements. The data were gathered for the years 1967 through 1977 for the 36 companies covered by the Salter and Weinhold (1978) article. Unfortunately, proxy statements could not be obtained for all companies and years over this period. Missing data reduced the sample to 29 conglomerates for the six years 1970–75.[11]

The conglomerates studied had from two to five officer-directors. The total stock gains and losses plus salary and other remuneration of each officer-director were summed and averaged for each company (since the CEO is assumed to share major decisions with his fellow officer-directors). Thus each observation is the monetary rewards of the average officer-director in each of the 29 conglomerates.

The annual rewards of the average officer-director of each of the 29 companies were measured as described next, after which three potentially important shortcomings of the measurements are discussed.

*Remuneration.* The amounts include salary, profit sharing, and bonuses and an additional 20 percent for fringe benefits. The proxy statements often did not give the amount of retirement and other fringe benefits consistently. Those that did averaged around 20 percent. Hence, this percentage was added to the salary amounts for all officer-directors in lieu of fringe benefits. Though this percentage is arbitrary, it is preferable to eliminating fringe benefits or including them inconsistently. In any event, as the tables presented below show, reasonable alternative percentages would have no effect on the findings.

---

9. The percentage decline in share prices of these companies over the years considered by Reid (1976) were less than the mean of his data. Hence their exclusion would not appear to bias the present study against Reid's hypothesis.

10. Lewellen (1971) used the same type of managers for his study.

11. The seven companies from the Salter-Weinhold list omitted are GAF, W.R. Grace, ICI, NL Industries, Ogden, and Studebaker-Worthington. The included companies are Avco, Bangor Punta, Bendix, Boise Cascade, City Investing, Colt Industries, FMC, General Tire, Gulf & Western, ITT, Walter Kidde, Koppers, LTV, Litton, Martin Marietta, 3M, Norton Simon, Rapid-American, SCM, Signal, Singer, Sperry Rand, TRW, Teledyne, Tenneco, Textron, U.S. Industries, White Consolidated, and Whittaker.

*Change in value of stock options.* Number of options held at the beginning and end of the year divided by two, valued at the change in price per share of the company (adjusted for stock dividends and splits) from the beginning to the end of the year. When the average exercise price of the option was less than the year-end price, the option was valued at zero. Though it would have been preferable to have valued the options with the option pricing model, the required data were not available;[12] in any event, as the tables show, the findings are unlikely to change appreciably.

*Change in value of share holdings.* Number of shares held at the beginning and end of the year divided by two, valued at the price per share at the beginning of the year times the annual yield per share.[13] The yield is the annual geometric mean of monthly returns (including dividends), measured with CRSP file data. The final dollar amounts for each year were converted to 1975 dollars with the gross national product implicit price deflator so that the annual amounts would be comparable.

Three potentially important biases from the measurements employed should be mentioned. One is the before- rather than after-tax measurement of the managers' financial rewards. As a consequence, remuneration is overstated more than is gains from stock options and share holdings, since the stock gains are taxed at a lower capital gains rate. Capital losses are not generally overstated, however, since capital loss tax deductions were limited to capital gains plus $3,000. Therefore, the before-tax numbers used in this study bias the conclusions in favor of the self-serving management hypothesis.

Second, the present value of expected remuneration changes was not added to the annual salary, bonus, and fringe benefits amounts, though this would be consistent with the "annual change in wealth" approach of this study. This limitation only affects the salary component of remuneration, since bonuses tend to be determined for each year independently. Murphy (1985) finds that top managers' bonuses average 32 percent of their total salary plus bonuses. The remaining bias works against the self-serving management hypothesis.

Third, Murphy (1985) and Coughlan and Schmidt (1985) show that the managers' current remuneration is related to their companies' current year's stock performance. Therefore, the managers' total remuneration amount overstates the

---

12. The measure used is incorrect, for two reasons. (1) By Jensen's inequality, the value of a portfolio of options with different exercise prices is greater than the value of options on the same number of shares at the average exercise price. (2) The derivative of the option value with respect to the stock price is greater than zero but less than one. See Smith (1976, p. 25).

13. This measure understates the gains to officer-directors if they are able to take advantage of inside information. The gains and losses accruing to officer-directors also were measured as net of market-wide changes with the capital asset pricing model using monthly CRSP data and the Treasury bill rate as the risk-free rate. The findings are almost the same as those reported below.

extent to which they are assumed to be rewarded for their self-serving behavior, because it contains a portion that is related to changes in shareholder wealth.

## Findings

The shareholders of the 29 conglomerates studied experienced considerable variation in returns over the years 1970 through 1975. As shown on the last line of table 15.1, annual returns of between −10 percent and +10 percent occurred for only 13.2 percent of the observations (an annual return for a company). Returns of less than −30 percent and more than +30 percent were found for 25.3 percent and 20.1 percent of the observations. Table 15.2, which shows the returns for each year, provides more disaggregated data. As table 15.2 shows, the shareholders of the following number of companies experienced negative returns of at least 30 percent a year over the six-year period: 14, 1, 2, 14, 13, and 0. Over this period, annual gains of more than 30 percent were experienced by the shareholders of 1, 10, 3, 1, 0, and 20 companies.

Tables 15.1 and 15.2 and figure 15.1 relate the top executives' pretax changes in wealth from stock holding, stock options, and remuneration to the returns to shareholders. The data are aggregated into five groups of returns (less than −30 percent, −30 to −10 percent, −10 to +10 percent, +10 to +30 percent, and more than +30 percent). The average executive's remuneration (over all companies for the six years, taken from table 15.2) was $174,000 per year (1975 dollars). As tables 15.1 and 15.2 and figure 15.1 show, there was little relationship between the remuneration and the returns on the conglomerates' shares. The standard deviations (shown in parentheses in table 15.2) are relatively small. These data, taken alone, are consistent with Reid's (1976) and Loomis's (1982) conclusion that company performance and top executives' remuneration are unrelated.

Importantly, however, the tables and chart show that remuneration was a relatively small portion of the executives' company-related changes in wealth.[14] Rather, changes in the market values of the shares the executives' owned in their companies (and, to a considerably lesser degree, stock options) overwhelmed their remuneration.

Table 15.1 shows that the pretax remuneration of the average executive exceeded the absolute value of his pretax change in wealth from shares only for companies with stock returns of from −10 percent to +10 percent. In years when

---

14. The sum of the amounts shown in the tables for "stock holding" plus "stock option" may not exactly equal "stock total," and this amount plus "remuneration" may not exactly equal "total wealth change," because the amounts shown are the means of each variable for each officer-director. Thus the totals are the means of the amounts that each officer-director got, rather than the sums of the means.

TABLE 15.1 Annual Wealth Changes of Average Conglomerate Officer-Director Related to Annual Returns on Their Companies' Shares, 1970–75, Amounts Averaged over Companies and Years (thousands of 1975 dollars)

| Source of Average Officer-Director's Change in Wealth | Returns | | | | |
| --- | --- | --- | --- | --- | --- |
| | Less than −30% | −30% to −10% | −10% to +10% | +10% to +30% | More than +30% |
| Stock holding | −1,139 | −357 | −25 | 213 | 1,027 |
| Stock option | −72 | −18 | 1 | 14 | 28 |
| Stock total | −895 | −325 | −24 | 227 | 1,040 |
| Remuneration | 173 | 169 | 170 | 158 | 201 |
| Total wealth change | −1,040 | −206 | 146 | 385 | 1,241 |
| Number of observations | 44 | 32 | 23 | 40 | 35 |
| % of total number of obs. | 25.3 | 18.4 | 13.2 | 23.0 | 20.1 |

*Source*: Table 15.2.

TABLE 15.2 Annual Wealth Changes of Average Conglomerate Officer-Director Related to the Annual Returns on Their Companies' Shares, 1970–75, Means and Standard Deviations in Parentheses (thousands of 1975 dollars)

| Source of Average Officer-Director's Change in Wealth | Returns | | | | |
| --- | --- | --- | --- | --- | --- |
| | Less than −30% | −30% to −10% | −10% to +10% | +10% to +30% | More than +30% |
| *1970* | | | | | |
| Stock holding | −1,392 | −95 | −150 | 373 | 497 |
| | (1,495) | (94) | (156) | (370) | (0) |
| Stock option | −67 | −9 | 1 | 2 | 101 |
| | (107) | (13) | (7) | (2) | (0) |
| Stock total | −1,459 | −105 | −149 | 375 | 598 |
| | (1,524) | (105) | (160) | (369) | (0) |
| Remuneration | 131 | 127 | 134 | 121 | 77 |
| | (45) | (49) | (52) | (14) | (0) |
| Total wealth change | −1,328 | 23 | −15 | 496 | 675 |
| | (1,521) | (71) | (121) | (368) | (0) |
| Number of companies | 14 | 5 | 6 | 3 | 1 |
| *1971* | | | | | |
| Stock holding | −2,098 | −302 | −69 | 150 | 965 |
| | (0) | (288) | (97) | (124) | (857) |
| Stock option | −207 | −51 | −0 | 26 | 15 |
| | (0) | (51) | (0) | (46) | (31) |
| Stock total | −2,368 | −353 | −69 | 176 | 980 |
| | (0) | (339) | (97) | (150) | (851) |
| Remuneration | 182 | 140 | 163 | 114 | 158 |
| | (0) | (10) | (12) | (59) | (32) |
| Total wealth change | −2,186 | −213 | 94 | 290 | 1,138 |
| | (0) | (329) | (85) | (203) | (845) |

(*continued*)

TABLE 15.2 Continued

| Source of Average Officer-Director's Change in Wealth | Returns |  |  |  |  |
|---|---|---|---|---|---|
|  | Less than −30% | −30% to −10% | −10% to +10% | +10% to +30% | More than +30% |
| Number of companies | 1 | 2 | 3 | 13 | 10 |
| *1972* | | | | | |
| Stock holding | −3,026 | −387 | 78 | 326 | 942 |
|  | (2,401) | (285) | (159) | (359) | (516) |
| Stock option | 0 (0) | −3 | 6 | 13 | 23 |
|  |  | (7) | (40) | (19) | (32) |
| Stock total | −3,026 | −390 | 84 | 339 | 965 |
|  | (2,401) | (283) | (175) | (360) | (547) |
| Remuneration | 163 | 145 | 171 | 159 | 155 |
|  | (4) | (34) | (98) | (33) | (58) |
| Total wealth change | −2,863 | −245 | 255 | 498 | 1,120 |
|  | (2,405) | (281) | (242) | (384) | (596) |
| Number of companies | 2 | 6 | 8 | 10 | 3 |
| *1973* | | | | | |
| Stock holding | −820 | −482 | −60 | 91 | 4,202 |
|  | (709) | (416) | (82) | (57) | (0) |
| Stock option | −83 | −45 | −15 | 11 | 0 |
|  | (143) | (105) | (18) | (10) | (0) |
| Stock total | −903 | −527 | −75 | 102 | 4,202 |
|  | (748) | (463) | (100) | (49) | (0) |
| Remuneration | 188 | 173 | 198 | 162 | 243 |
|  | (96) | (26) | (3) | (11) | (0) |
| Total wealth change | −715 | −354 | 123 | 264 | 4,445 |
|  | (694) | (443) | (103) | (60) | (0) |
| Number of companies | 14 | 9 | 2 | 3 | 1 |
| *1974* | | | | | |
| Stock holding | −847 | −407 | 1 | 80 | — |
|  | (1,649) | (348) | (9) | (55) |  |
| Stock option | −67 | 0 | −2 | 2 | — |
|  | (187) | (0) | (3) | (3) |  |
| Stock total | −914 | −407 | −1 | 82 | — |
|  | (1,652) | (348) | (12) | (56) |  |
| Remuneration | 204 | 212 | 187 | 203 | — |
|  | (97) | (52) | (37) | (13) |  |
| Total wealth change | −710 | −195 | 186 | 285 | — |
|  | (1,615) | (335) | (42) | (63) |  |
| Number of companies | 13 | 9 | 3 | 4 | 0 |
| *1975* | | | | | |
| Stock holding | — | −21 | 22 | 231 | 938 |
|  |  | (0) | (0) | (177) | (1,601) |
| Stock option | — | 0 | 0 | 5 | 38 |
|  |  | (0) | (0) | (11) | (115) |
| Stock total | — | −21 | 22 | 236 | 976 |
|  |  | (0) | (0) | (177) | (1,694) |
| Remuneration | — | 156 | 296 | 224 | 237 |
|  |  | (0) | (0) | (28) | (98) |
| Total wealth change | — | 135 | 318 | 460 | 1,213 |
|  |  | (0) | (0) | (201) | (1,735) |
| Number of companies | 0 | 1 | 1 | 7 | 20 |

THE SELF-SERVING MANAGEMENT HYPOTHESIS 363

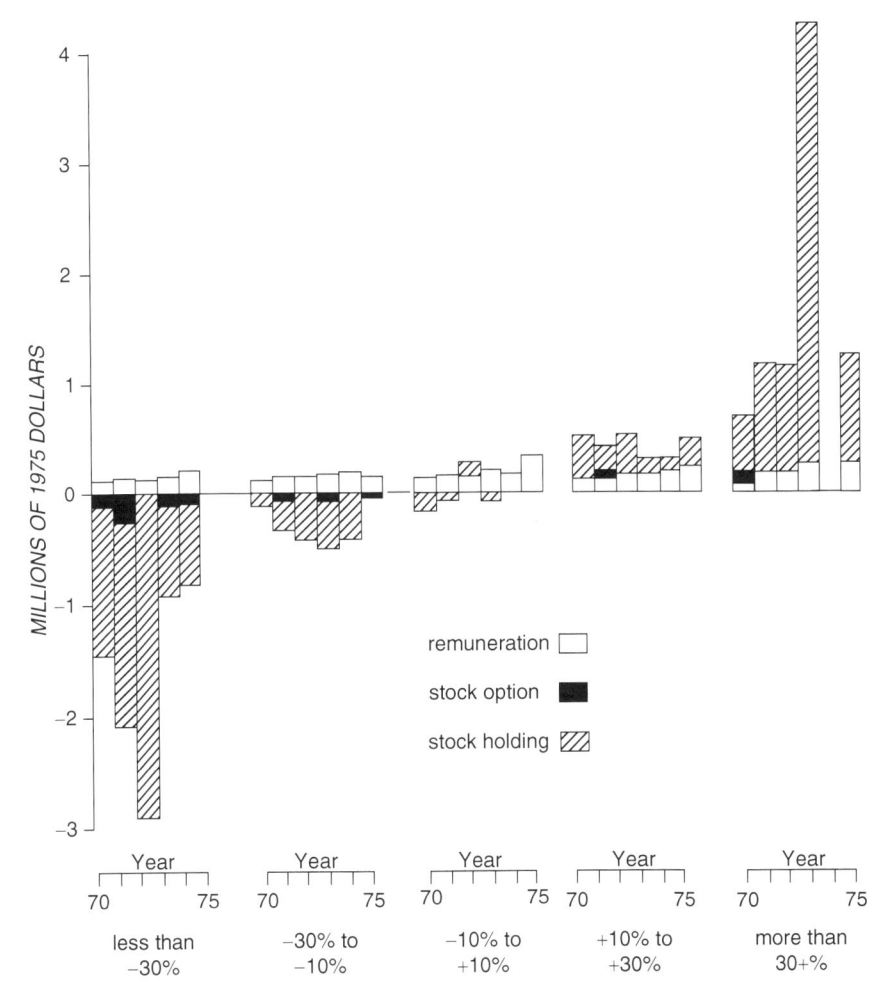

FIGURE 15.1 Annual Wealth Changes of Average Conglomerate Officer-Director Related to Annual Returns on Their Companies Shares by Year, 1970–1975 (in 1975 dollars)

his company's shares returned shareholders from −30 percent to −10 percent, the average top manager of a conglomerate lost 2.22 times his remuneration (stock total/remuneration). Those managing companies with returns of from +10 percent to +30 percent made 1.44 times their remuneration. At the extreme returns of less than −30 percent and more than +30 percent, the average officer-director lost or gained 5.17 times his remuneration. These data are consistent with those reported by Lewellen (1971). His study of officer-directors of 80 companies over the years 1940 through 1963 found that: "When those dividends and [capital] gains are added to the stock-related compensation of executives, the resulting totals run anywhere from three to five times the value of the corresponding fixed-dollar rewards from salary, cash bonuses, pensions, and similar items" (Lewellen, 1971, p. 11).

There also is considerable variability in the share-related amounts within years and among years, as is indicated by the standard deviations in table 15.2. A more precise indication of the range of the executives' annual changes in wealth due to their ownership of their companies' shares and options is provided by table 15.3. As the table shows, the means and ranges are considerable. In 1974 the senior executives in one company lost an average of $6,176,000 and in 1975 those in another gained an average of $7,559,000 (both amounts in 1975 dollars). Few of the average officer-directors of conglomerates where share returns decreased by more than 10 percent failed to lose more than their remuneration, and all gained several times their remuneration when share returns increased by more than 10 percent.

TABLE 15.3 Total Change in Wealth of Average Conglomerate Officer-Director Related to the Annual Returns on Their Companies' Shares, 1970–75, Means, Maximums, and Minimums (thousands of 1975 dollars)

| Returns | Total Change in Wealth Per Officer-Director ||||||
|---|---|---|---|---|---|---|
| | 1970 | 1971 | 1972 | 1973 | 1974 | 1975 |
| *Less than −30%* | | | | | | |
| Mean | −1,328 | −2,186 | −2,863 | −715 | 710 | — |
| Minimum | −5,555 | −2,186 | −5,268 | −2,602 | −6,176 | — |
| Maximum | −53 | −2,186 | −458 | 12 | 72 | — |
| Number of companies | 14 | 1 | 2 | 14 | 13 | 0 |
| *−30% to −10%* | | | | | | |
| Mean | 23 | −213 | −245 | −354 | −195 | 135 |
| Minimum | −81 | −542 | −690 | −1,023 | −746 | 135 |
| Maximum | 101 | 116 | 75 | 115 | 164 | 135 |
| Number of companies | 5 | 2 | 6 | 9 | 9 | 1 |
| *−10% to +10%* | | | | | | |
| Mean | −15 | 94 | 255 | 123 | 186 | 318 |
| Minimum | −245 | −25 | 51 | 20 | 156 | 318 |
| Maximum | 137 | 169 | 676 | 226 | 245 | 318 |
| Number of companies | 6 | 3 | 8 | 2 | 3 | 1 |
| *+10% to +30%* | | | | | | |
| Mean | 496 | 290 | 497 | 263 | 285 | 461 |
| Minimum | 171 | 113 | 138 | 219 | 194 | 208 |
| Maximum | 1,011 | 803 | 1,485 | 349 | 352 | 844 |
| Number of companies | 3 | 13 | 10 | 3 | 4 | 7 |
| *+30% and over* | | | | | | |
| Mean | 675 | 1,138 | 1,120 | 4,445 | — | 1,213 |
| Minimum | 675 | 263 | 468 | 4,445 | — | 144 |
| Maximum | 675 | 3,268 | 1,909 | 4,445 | — | 7,559 |
| Number of companies | 1 | 10 | 3 | 1 | 0 | 20 |

TABLE 15.4 Share Returns (Three-Year Geometric Average) of Conglomerates Where an Officer-Director Terminated Employment Compared to Conglomerates Where There Was no Change

| Year | Officer-Director Left Position No. | Mean[a] | Other Conglomerates No. | Mean | Difference between Means | Significance Level of Difference[c] |
|---|---|---|---|---|---|---|
| 1970 | 6 | −17.9 (13.3)[b] | 23 | −13.7 (17.4) | −4.2 | 30% |
| 1971 | 12 | −16.9 (12.9) | 17 | −11.9 (11.6) | −5.0 | 16 |
| 1972 | 7 | 6.2 (12.1) | 22 | −5.0 (17.1) | 11.2 | 7 |
| 1973 | 7 | −10.9 (13.1) | 22 | −1.2 (16.7) | −9.7 | 9 |
| 1974 | 4 | −17.1 (16.2) | 25 | −20.2 (14.0) | 3.1 | 36 |
| 1975 | 10 | −15.0 (21.9) | 19 | −3.7 (14.5) | −11.3 | 6 |

[a] Mean = geometric mean of year and previous two years.
[b] Standard deviation.
[c] One-tail $t$-test; all variances are not significantly different at 0.05 level.

Thus, though some large values affect the averages reported, the findings reported apply generally to the top managers studied.

The additional hypothesis tested is whether the officer-directors of the conglomerates lost more than monetary wealth as a consequence of the poor performance of their companies. Did they also tend to lose their jobs? Unfortunately, the hypothesis cannot be tested directly, since top executives rarely are publicly fired. The test employed compares the geometric average share price returns of the year an officer-director left his company and the two previous years with similarly measured returns for the other conglomerates.[15] A finding that officer-directors left after their shareholders experienced significantly greater losses than those experienced by the shareholders of conglomerates where the top executives did not leave is consistent with the hypothesis.

As shown in table 15.4, in four of the six years 1970–75, the mean share returns of the conglomerates where an officer-director left were negative and lower than

---

15. The choice of the particular three-year geometric average employed was made before the data were analyzed. Though another period (e.g., the same year, the prior year, or an average of the two) might have yielded a "better" fit, this would have been ex post hypothesis "testing" or, if accounted for, would have used up too many degrees of freedom. It also should be noted that the test is subject to noise since some officer-directors probably left their jobs for reasons not related to the poor performance of their firms, for example, better positions, and voluntary retirement.

the returns on the shares of the other conglomerates. Two of these differences (1973 and 1975) are significant at the .09 level or lower (one-tail test). For the two years where the difference in returns is positive (1972 and 1974), one difference is statistically significant at the .07 level, and the other is insignificant and very small.[16]

## Implications for the Hypothesis

The data show that the officer-directors of 29 major conglomerates, including most of those described as "merger prone," gained and lost personal wealth as their companies' shareholders gained and lost. Though individually they did not own more than small percentages of the total shares outstanding, the amounts they owned yielded annual gains and losses that swamped their remuneration. The average officer-director's remuneration averaged $174,000 (in 1975 pretax dollars) and did not vary much among companies with widely differing share returns. But his annual share-determined gains were $1,040,000 (1975 pretax dollars) in a year when his company's share prices and dividends increased by more than 30 percent. The average top manager of a company with share returns that decreased by more than 30 percent lost $1,139,000 in that year. It should be noted that, though these amounts might not represent the total annual income of the managers from all sources, the amounts derived from owning their companies' shares are large, particularly compared to their remuneration. Thus, whether or not the managers made wise decisions, they tended to gain and lose along with their shareholders. These results are inconsistent with the self-serving management hypothesis that ascribes mergers and other corporate actions to the top managers' desire to benefit themselves at the expense of their shareholders.

The generally positive relationship between the officer-directors leaving their firms and the poor stock market performance of the firms also is inconsistent with the self-serving hypothesis that managers tend to make decisions that benefit themselves, even though they expect that the result might be harmful to shareholders. One cannot know whether or not the top managers studied considered, ex ante, the possibility that they might lose their positions as well as much of their personal wealth were they to make decisions that turned out poorly for shareholders. But the data show that this tended to occur, a result that is consistent with that reported by Coughlan and Schmidt (1985).

Consequently, the data analyzed are inconsistent with the self-serving management hypothesis, unless one subscribes to a rather peculiar version of this

---

16. Because the years over which returns are measured overlap, the annual samples are not independent and could not be pooled.

hypothesis—that is, that such is the desire to govern huge groups that a manager is willing to take a monetary loss for this psychic gain. The data do not speak directly to the hypothesis that managers act so as to benefit their shareholders, but are not inconsistent with it. If the merger and other decisions made by the officer-directors of the conglomerates studied were ex ante harmful to shareholders, those top managers also hurt themselves.

With respect to the universal nature of these findings, it should be noted that the data analyzed are derived from very large conglomerates. Since these corporations are not representative of corporations generally, the findings should not be generalized without further study. (However, see Lewellen [1971] and Murphy [1985] for confirming evidence.) The reader also should note that the findings apply to the average officer-director. The decisions of individual top managers should be analyzed with respect to their individual stock holdings. This analysis could relate the merger and other decisions of the managers to the changes in their wealth derived from remuneration compared to changes in the value of their investment in company shares.

## Implications for Agency Theory

The data presented above indicate that the officer-directors of large corporations with diversely held shares studied tend to own a sufficiently large amount of shares in their companies to give them a considerable incentive to make decisions that tend to increase the market value of those shares.[17] For these top managers, stock options and annual remuneration are not nearly as important as determinants of changes in their wealth. It appears, therefore, that stock ownership is an important means by which the managers are induced or bonded to act in the interest of shareholders. This method of dealing with the agency problem has the advantage of tying the financial interests of senior officers who are likely to be close to retirement age directly to the shareholders' gains and losses.

The hypothesis that company stock holdings serve to overcome the principal-agent problem could be tested further by examining the officer-directors' total portfolios and holdings of their corporations' shares before and after they leave their corporate posts. Are the officer-directors' portfolios as undiversified as they appear? (They could be *very* wealthy.) Did they diversify their share holdings after they left their corporations? Positive answers would be consistent with the agency hypothesis.

It also would be interesting to learn how the officer-directors got their corporate shares. If the top managers came up through the ranks, it is likely that they

---

17. I am indebted to Jerold Zimmerman for discussions that led to this extension of the essay.

obtained their holdings through the exercise of stock options. Are people who make it to the top those who have shown their concern for the shareholders by exercising the options and holding the shares? Were those who came from other corporations given phantom stock or stock options or did they have the resources to purchase shares directly? If they purchased the shares, did this result in their holding undiversified portfolios? If they held undiversified portfolios, were they compensated for the risk with higher remuneration and/or with greater opportunities to use inside information? Positive answers to these questions would be consistent with share holdings being a preferred way of dealing with agency problems.

## REFERENCES

Baumol, William J., 1962, On the theory of the expansion of the firm, *American Economic Review* 52, 1078–87.

Baumol, William J., 1967, *Business behavior, value and growth*, Rev. ed. (Harcourt, Brace & World, New York). First ed., 1959 (Macmillan, New York).

Benston, George J., 1980, *Conglomerate mergers: Causes, consequences, and remedies* (American Enterprise Institute, Washington, D.C.).

Berle, Adolf and Gardiner Means, 1934, *The modern corporation and private property* (Macmillan, New York).

Conn, Robert L., 1976, Acquired firm performance after conglomerate merger, *Southern Economic Journal* 43, 1170–73.

Coughlan, Anne T. and Ronald M. Schmidt, 1985, Executive compensation, management turnover, and firm performance: An empirical investigation, *Journal of Accounting and Economics* 7.

Gordon, Robert, 1961, *Business leadership in the large corporation* (University of California Press, Berkeley).

Jensen, Michael C. and Richard S. Ruback, 1983, The market for corporate control: The scientific evidence, *Journal of Financial Economics* 11, 5–50.

Kaysen, Carl, 1960, The corporation: How much power? What scope? in: Edward S. Mason, ed., *The corporation in modern society* (Harvard University Press, Cambridge, Mass.), 85–105.

Lev, Baruch, 1983, Observations on the merger phenomenon and a review of the evidence, *Midland Corporate Finance Journal* 1, 6–16.

Lewellen, Wilbur G., 1968, *Executive compensation in large industrial corporations* (National Bureau of Economic Research, New York).

Lewellen, Wilbur G., 1971, *The ownership income of management* (National Bureau of Economic Research, New York).

Lewellen, Wilbur G. and Blaine Huntsman, 1970, Managerial pay and corporate performance, *American Economic Review* 60, 710–20.

Loomis, Carol J., 1982, The madness of executive compensation, *Fortune Magazine*, July 12, 42–52.

Marris, Robin, 1964, *The economic theory of managerial capitalism* (Free Press, Glencoe, Ill.).

Masson, Robert Tempest, 1971, Executive motivations, earnings, and consequent equity performance, *Journal of Political Economy* 79, 1278–92.

Mueller, Dennis C., 1969, A theory of conglomerate mergers, *Quarterly Journal of Economics* 83, 643–59.

Mueller, Dennis C., 1977, The effects of conglomerate mergers: A survey of the empirical evidence, *Journal of Banking and Finance* 1, 315–34.

Mueller, Dennis C., 1980, A cross-national comparison of results, in: Dennis C. Mueller, ed., *The determinants and effects of mergers: An international comparison* (Oelgeschlager, Gunn & Hain, Cambridge, Mass.), 299–314.

Murphy, Kevin J., 1985, Corporate performance and managerial remuneration, *Journal of Accounting and Economics* 7.

Reid, Samuel R., 1968, *Mergers, managers and the economy* (McGraw-Hill, New York).

Reid, Samuel R., 1976, *The new industrial order: Concentration, regulations and public policy* (McGraw-Hill, New York).

Salter, Malcolm S. and Wolf A. Weinhold, 1978, Diversification via acquisition: Creating value, *Harvard Business Review*, July–Aug., 166–76.

Schipper, Katherine and Rex Thompson, 1983, Evidence on the capitalized value of merger activity for acquiring firms, *Journal of Financial Economics* 11, 85–119.

Smith, Clifford W. Jr., 1976, Option pricing: A review, *Journal of Financial Economics* 3, 3–51.

Smith, Clifford W. Jr. and Ross L. Watts, 1982, Incentive and tax effects of executive compensation plans, *Australian Journal of Management* 7, 139–57.

Winslow, John F., 1973, *Conglomerates unlimited: The failure of regulation* (Indiana University Press, Bloomington).

# 16

# Why Effective Spreads on NASDAQ Were Higher than on the New York Stock Exchange in the 1990s

WITH ROBERT A. WOOD

## I. Introduction, Hypotheses, and Overview

In the 1990s the NASDAQ stock market was subjected to severe adverse publicity. By the mid-1990s the greater increase in spreads on NASDAQ than on the New York Stock Exchange (NYSE) at the beginning of the decade was noted and criticized. Christie and Huang (1993) found that quoted spreads decreased substantially on 51 stocks that moved in 1990 from NASDAQ to the NYSE or Amex, as did Barclay (1997) for 472 stocks that moved from NASDAQ between 1983 and 1992. Christie and Schultz (1994) then reported that in 1991 NASDAQ market makers, but not NYSE traders, "avoided" quoting prices in odd eighths on 70 of the 100 actively traded NASDAQ stocks they sampled. They concluded that even-eighths quoting is evidence of "implicit collusion" that resulted in wider spreads. Christie, Harris, and Schultz (1994) found that spreads on four of the five most heavily traded of the 70 NASDAQ stocks dropped on May 27, 1994, the day after the Christie–Schultz findings were publicized. These studies led to investigations

---

We thank Marshall Blume and Jim Rosenfeld for helpful suggestions on the present draft and Sunil Wahal for suggestions on earlier drafts that substantially improved the presentation. We also are indebted to the Reviewers of this journal for very helpful criticisms, comments and suggestions and to the editor, Wayne Ferson, for allowing us to deal with and take advantage of their concerns and suggestions.

by the Department of Justice (DOJ, 1996) and the Securities and Exchange Commission (SEC, 1996), including examination of tape-recorded conversations among traders employed by NASDAQ market makers. The recordings revealed that some traders berated and threatened traders at other firms who offered quotations that "broke the spread" and asked other traders to put in quotations that would establish a desired price. These clearly illegal (under the antitrust statutes) acts and the evidence from the academic research and DOJ/SEC investigations were followed by a class-action lawsuit resulting in a December 1997 $925 million settlement, as well as SEC fines and changes in NASDAQ operating procedures instituted in January 1997.[1]

Christie and Schultz (1994) also spawned several conferences and academic studies. Among these, Huang and Stoll (1996) (HS),[2] Bessembinder and Kaufman (1997) (BK), and Keim and Madhavan (1997), using 1994 or earlier data, document higher NASDAQ effective spreads (the absolute difference between a transactions price and the midpoint of the prevailing best bid/offer).[3] Although these spreads were not adjusted for commissions and other trading costs, it was generally accepted that for some reason trading on NASDAQ was more costly to investors.[4] Christie and Schultz (1995, p. 199) believe that "brokerage firms making markets in NASDAQ stocks...implicitly colluded to maintain profits at supracompetitive levels." Barclay's (1997) supports this conclusion, based on his finding that spreads on NASDAQ stocks quoted on even eighths, but not those quoted on mixed eighths, dropped when they moved to the New York or American stock exchanges, thereby presumably escaping the collusion. HS, Godek (1996), Dutta and Madhaven (1997), and Kandel and Marx (1999) propose that preferencing and payment for order flow (wherein some NASDAQ market makers pay retail brokers for sending them trades and promise to match the best prices quoted) reduce NASDAQ market makers' incentives and ability to compete vigorously. BK accept both Christie-Schultz's collusion explanation and preferencing as possible reasons for higher NASDAQ spreads. However, they find no support for Christie-Harris-Schultz's (1994) drop-in-spreads conclusion when the sample is

---

1. We were not involved in the lawsuit and do not know why the parties settled. Attempts to fix prices (whether successful or not) are per se violations of law that can subject defendants to treble damages.

2. They review earlier literature and conclude: "Despite this volume of research, the difference in execution costs between NASDAQ and the NYSE has not been clearly established" (p. 317).

3. Kothare and Laux (1995) examined only NASDAQ quoted spreads in the month of October in 1984, 1988, and 1992. They find a substantial increase over this period, and state (p. 42): "Our main finding is that, even controlling for other factors that influence spreads, spreads are positively associated with the extent of institutional trading activity."

4. Chan and Lakonishok (1997) adjusted trades by 33 large investment management firms for commissions and found that the differences were related to the size of firm traded, rather than the market. However, they caution that their findings do not necessarily apply to retail trades.

extended to 300 stocks. In addition, Grossman, Miller, Fischel, Cone, and Ross (1997, pp. 45–50), in a more extensive study of the sample used by Christie and Schultz (1994) and of a larger sample of stocks, similarly find no support for the Christie-Harris-Schultz conclusion. Furthermore, shares of one of the four (Microsoft) experienced a two-for-one split a few days earlier and the drop in its spread is consistent with the split. Thus, the Christie-Harris-Schultz finding is based on 3 of the 70 Christie-Schultz even-eighths quoted stocks. Benston (2007) replicated and extended Barclay's (1997) study and finds that the greater decline in spreads on even-eighths quoted stocks was due 21 of 362 (3.1 percent) thinly traded stocks with quoted spreads over 1.50 on which NASDAQ market makers faced informed-trade risk not present on NYSE/Amex. Furthermore, there is no difference in the spread decline after the Christie-Schultz results were publicized.

We suggest an alternative hypothesis that contributes to an understanding of the higher NASDAQ spreads in the 1990s—day trading primarily over its small order execution system (SOES). In June 1988 NASDAQ changed SOES from an e-mail inquiry system to an order entry system in response to the criticism the traders were unable to submit orders during the October 1987 market crash. Trades made through SOES had to be honored automatically and instantly by market makers at quoted prices for up to 1,000 shares with up to five repetitions. Making SOES mandatory had a dramatic impact on NASDAQ. Day traders began using the SOES system to purchase (sell) and quickly sell (purchase) stocks with stale quotes—quotes that individual market makers failed to change coincident with market shifts when their attention was diverted to other stocks. Consequently, market makers drastically reduced the number of stocks covered by their individual dealers and implemented costly software and systems to minimize stale quotes. We hypothesize that because market makers could not know which stocks might be "hit" by day traders and to compensate for the additional costs they incurred, as shown analytically by Glosten and Milgrom (1985) and Copeland and Galai (1983), they raised offer prices and lowered bids on all the stocks they followed, thereby widening quoted spreads. Whether or not as a result market makers made higher than competitive net profits is not our concern here; rather, we offer an explanation as to why spreads on NASDAQ compared to the NYSE increased in the 1990s.

Several observers have rejected the "SOES day trade" hypothesis. Indeed, firms that promoted day trading claimed that it was beneficial, because it offered individual traders an opportunity to effect transactions efficiently, which resulted in more effective price determination (e.g., Houtkin, 1995). Kothare and Laux (1995, p. 44) dismiss day trading on SOES as an explanation for the increase in NASDAQ spreads among the three months they examined in 1984, 1988, and 1992, because "at the time of this writing, SOES accounts for only 2% of total NASDAQ volume." HS (p. 348) similarly dismiss day trading as an explanation for higher NASDAQ spreads, in part because "SOES trades account for only a small fraction of NASDAQ volume." Yet by the mid-1990s the Electronic Traders Association, which represented 26 SOES dealers (not all such dealers were members) who catered to day traders, called "SOES bandits," claimed that day trades generated 20 percent of NASDAQ trades.[5] HS and BK additionally dismiss SOES day trading, because they find that NASDAQ market makers but not NYSE traders appear to have achieved positive realized spreads, from which they conclude that NASDAQ trades do not contain more adverse information costs than NYSE trades. In contrast to the realized spread metric employed by HS and BK, which measures costs to liquidity suppliers in an accounting sense, we calculate the opportunity gains and losses to estimate the effect of SOES day trading on spreads rather than on the dealers' accounting net profits. We also disaggregate the data by trade size to separate the effects of trades made by SOES day traders from those of other traders. Furthermore, because HS and BK studied only two years, 1991 and 1994, with relatively few observations (175 and 300 NASDAQ–NYSE pairs), their view was somewhat limited. In contrast, we present and analyze data over 13 years, 1987–99, years that span both NASDAQ's SOES day trading experience and substantial changes in NASDAQ and NYSE spreads, from which we conclude that trading by SOES bandits are an important reason for the increase in relative effective spreads on NASDAQ but not on the NYSE.

Figure 16.1 shows relative effective (half) spreads (RES) on NASDAQ and NYSE trades, measured as the absolute difference between a transaction price and the midpoint of best bid and offer (BBO) in effect five seconds before the transaction divided by the transaction price. RES are computed daily from trade-weighted transactions and averaged (equally weighted) monthly from January 2, 1987 (the earliest date for which we have data), through December 31, 1999. We calculate this metric for all actively traded stocks on NASDAQ and the NYSE, where "active" is defined as having at least five trades per trading day (9:30 A.M.–4:00 P.M.) for at least 10 days per month and a price per share of at least $10, but not more than $80.[6] We include only the days with five trades or more per day.[7] As robustness

---

5. See Byrne (1997). Gene Finn, National Association of Securities Dealers (NASD) chief economist at the time, confirms this estimate.

6. To screen out extreme errors in the data not otherwise caught, we require an intraday variance of the midpoints of the inside quotes (best bids and offers, or BBO) that is less than 4.0, which reduced the sample by 0.001 percent. In addition, extreme values of prices and quotes were filtered, removing less than 0.001 percent of the observations. A maximum price of $80 excludes high-tech and dot-com NASDAQ stocks that were subject to extreme volatility and severely widened spreads during the bubble period of the late 1990s.

7. The NASDAQ (NYSE) sample includes an average of 1,370 (1,743) stocks per month. The January 1987 NASDAQ (NYSE) sample size of 757 (1,471) stocks declines through late 1988 and then increases gradually to 1,718 (2,000) stocks in December 1999. Through 1989, the ratio of NASDAQ to NYSE stocks ranges between 0.3 and 0.5 (14 percent are at 0.3); thereafter, the ratio ranges between 0.7 and 1.0 (7 percent are at 0.7). Data are missing for the NYSE and/or NASDAQ for April, May, and August 1987, April and July 1988, and November and December 1989. Data sources: 1987–92 data were provided by ISSM; 1993–99 data were obtained from the NYSE TAQ database.

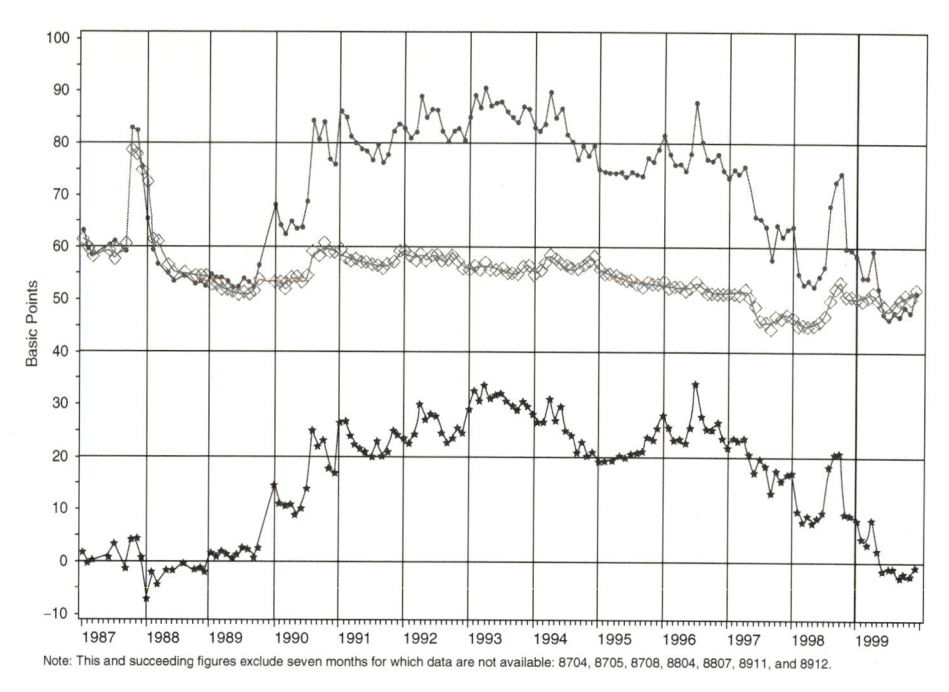

FIGURE 16.1 NASDAQ and NYSE Relative Effective Spreads (RES), 1987–99 NASDAQ RES = (●), NYSE RES + 18.4 basis points = (◊), adjusted NASDAQ less NYSE RES = (★)

checks, we also calculated and graphed RES using observations with at least 10 trades a day (based on the possibility that day traders concentrated on actively traded stocks), medians instead of means, only stocks that traded throughout the period (202 on NASDAQ and 627 on the NYSE), only stocks with trades of 1,000 shares or less, 2,000 shares or less, and so on by thousands through 5,000 shares or less, and all shares traded. Further, we formed matched portfolios in each month with a linear programming model that minimizes the Euclidean distance measures between NYSE and NASDAQ stocks, discussed further in section VII. In each case the resulting figures very closely mirror those shown in figure 16.1.

The use of RES rather than effective spreads accounts for changes in price levels during the 13 years studied and which Wood and McInnish (1992) find is responsible for 80 percent of the variation in spreads. We examined changes in the ratio of the average price per share of NASDAQ to NYSE stocks to determine if differences in RES on these markets changed as a result of changes in the denominator rather than the numerator. The ratio is almost unchanged over the period. Other differences, though, are important. NASDAQ stocks tend to be riskier, not as liquid, and more subject to inventory costs because they are held, bought, and sold by dealers rather than transacted through brokers. Further, during our sample period stocks traded net (principal) for institutional trades on NASDAQ, while institutional orders traded on the NYSE with commissions (agency) as an additional charge. Consequently, spreads on NASDAQ tend to be wider than those on the NYSE. To compensate (in part) for these factors, we calculate the difference between the average RES for NASDAQ minus the average RES for NYSE over the "base" period, January 1987 through May 1988 (prior to the start of mandatory SOES trading), excluding the three 1987 market-crash months, October, November, and December. We add the difference, 18.4 basis points, to the NYSE RES values to approximate comparability between the NASDAQ and NYSE metrics over our entire sample period. When the three market-crash months were included, the difference is 18.2 basis points. We recognize that over the 11.5 years to which we apply the scaling factor to equalize the two venues, there were numerous changes in market mechanisms, some unique to each market center and some affecting both. Yet comparison of the two markets over an extended period is inherently interesting and the topic addressed we feel is vitally important for understanding the NASDAQ market in the 1990s. Nevertheless we must interpret our finding cautiously, considering our comparison method.

Figure 16.1 reveals the shock to RES values resulting from the market crash of October 1987. Note that the NASDAQ and adjusted NYSE RES closely track one another, including the market-crash months. Focusing on the NASDAQ less adjusted NYSE metric, beginning in late 1989 we observe a surge that peaks in early 1993. The NASDAQ RES in early 1993 exceeds the market crash peak. Thereafter the difference declines steadily, with some acceleration in the decline following publication of Christie and Schultz's (1994) findings on May 26, 1994, through December 1994. Then the difference increases through 1996, and subsequently declines somewhat erratically back to zero in June 1999 as the NASDAQ and NYSE RES converge. Thus, we see that a powerful economic force increased the RES of NASDAQ relative to that of the NYSE over a 10-year period, from August 1989 through November 1999.

What economic force could have caused this large and long-lasting difference? And what caused the RES to revert to their pre-August 1989 difference? Consider, first, the collusion hypothesis.[8] If the difference between NASDAQ and NYSE RES were the result of collusion, there should be some explanation as to why it began in mid-1989 and did not end until mid-1999. There is no doubt that the Christie and Schultz (1994) and Christie, Harris, and Schultz (1994) papers, the DOJ/SEC

---

8. A fairly large number of papers have been written and published debating the collusion hypothesis. See, for example, papers published in volume 45 (1997) of the *Journal of Financial Economics* (which tend to support the hypothesis) and papers noted in Grossman et al. (1997), which reject it. We do not and cannot adequately review the arguments and evidence here. Rather, we only raise questions relating to the differences shown in our figure 16.1.

(1996) investigations, the class-action lawsuit, and SEC fines had a very strong impact on NASDAQ market makers. NASDAQ trading practices were scrutinized, changed, and closely monitored. It does not seem feasible that collusion could have persisted in this environment after 1994. Yet in 1995 and 1996 the gap between the NASDAQ and NYSE RES widened, even though a number of factors put downward pressure on RES. First, systems designed to eliminate stale quotes increased in effectiveness over time. Second, the Manning court rulings in 1994/95 gave public limit orders priority over dealer quotes. Third, increasingly dealers who wished to display customer limit orders would do so on Instinet (or other ECNs as they became available) where they could not be subject to SOES day trading (referred to as "being SOESed" by NASDAQ market makers).[9] Hence, executions against these ECN quotes were often inside the Level II BBO (which did not include ECN quotes), thereby depressing RES. Fourth, the "brake-light" effect, resulting from the DOJ/SEC investigations into collusion, may have depressed RES. Thus, in the face of these downward pressures and despite exposure of the alleged collusion, NASDAQ RES increased in 1995 and 1996.

In January 1997 NASDAQ implemented Order Handling Rules (OHR) that required the public display of limit orders that bettered dealer quotes (with some exceptions). Further, dealers were not permitted to post different quotes to Instinet and NASDAQ Level II. Also, brokers were able to hit multiple quotes simultaneously through SelectNet, replicating the SOES bandits use of the "monster button." In addition, the Actual Size Rule, which reduced the minimum depth that market makers had to post for quotes from 1,000 to 100 shares, was implemented in three stages—100 stocks in January and February 1997, an additional 100 stocks in October 1997, and all remaining stocks in July 1998. NASDAQ RES declined somewhat erratically throughout this period, and by mid-1999 the NASDAQ-less-adjusted-NYSE RES returned to zero. By this point in time the NASDAQ rules had been modified to the point the SOES day traders had essentially no advantages over other traders and SOES banditry gradually ceased.

If there were "even-eighths tacit collusion" among market makers, it may have resulted from a reaction to the costs imposed on them by SOES day traders, wherein market makers compensated by rounding quotations in their favor to even eighths. Or, as Finn has suggested (in conversation), market makers could have reduced the option value of stale quotes exercised against them by widening the contra side of their quotes. Since an unwritten NASDAQ rule specified that if a dealer's own quote was greater than five-eighths they could only change their quote by one-fourths, even-eighth quoting could be due to widened own-spreads.

---

9. According to Gene Finn, dealers' quotes represented 95 percent of all ECN quotes in the 1994–96 period, with the remainder coming from buy-side funds.

While it is possible that this may have widened spreads beyond the noncollusive amount resulting from SOES day trading pressure, it is unlikely that the additional amount would have been large, considering the levels of the NASDAQ/NYSE RES gap in the years before the May 26, 1994, publication of Christie and Schultz's (1994) even-eighths findings and the gap in 1996, well after publicity about those findings and the DOJ and SEC investigations of collusion, as well as the class-action lawsuit. Also note that the NASDAQ market had existed for years with no evidence or charge of collusion, and that there is no evidence or charge of collusion for NYSE stocks, although for the most part broker/dealers had both NYSE and NASDAQ trading desks.

Finally, we are not aware of any paper or investigation that explains why collusion among NASDAQ market makers would have begun around mid-1989. We do not claim that there was no collusion, as the tapes of traders' conversations indicate at least an attempt by some to affect prices. Our concern is with the assertion that pervasiveness of collusion was the primary reason for the increase in NASDAQ relative to NYSE RES. It appears that some economic pressure other than collusion was responsible for the relationship shown by figure 16.1.

Although the preferencing and payment-for-order-flow hypothesis could be responsible in part for higher NASDAQ spreads, it does not appear to be responsible for the pattern shown in figure 16.1. The practice of directing institutional order flow flourished before 1987, with the relaxation in 1986 of Section 28E of the Securities Exchange Act, which governs soft-dollar arrangements. In June 1990 the SEC, in a letter ruling, decreed that directed principal trades generating soft dollars were not covered by the "safe harbor" provisions of Employee Retirement Income Security Act (ERISA) (1984), and that pension fund managers had to prove that any directed trade obtained best execution. With respect to retail trades, before October 1991 a market maker who agreed to be preferenced for a particular stock had to accept orders from any dealer or order entry firm without pre-notification for up to 1,000 shares. After that date, market makers could be preferenced only with their permission. None of these changes are noticeably related to the pattern shown in figure 16.1. From discussions with practitioners and regulators, including NASD's chief economist (Gene Finn) during this period, we are not aware of any other changes in soft dollars or preferencing that could produce the results observed in figure 16.1. Further, both preferencing and payment-for-order flow affected both NASDAQ and NYSE stocks, so if these factors were influencing NASDAQ stocks we would expect to see similar influences with NYSE stocks, which is not the case.

We turn now to the SOES day-trading explanation, which we show is consistent with the differences between NASDAQ and NYSE RES over the 13-year period. We describe SOES history and day trading in section II, which drives our division of the 13 years studied into the seven periods specified. In section III we present data on the extent of SOES day trading. Based on this analysis and following other researchers and practitioners (e.g., Battalio, Hatch, and Jennings, 1997; Harris and Schultz, 1997, 1998; Houtkin, 1995), we use trades of the maximum amount eligible for SOES—1,000, 500, or 100 shares—as our initial, preliminary measure of SOES day trades. In section IV, we calculate liquidity supplier's losses and gains to informed SOES day traders and other traders. We calculate this metric for six trade sizes, five that are eligible for trading through SOES and one that is not (which serves as a control). The metric is examined during the periods before SOES became mandatory and after it was phased out, as well as for NYSE transactions. Adjusting for trades at the maximum trade size that were not made through SOES, we find informed-trade losses ascribed to SOES day trades average at least 21 basis points on 1,000-share trades, and 15 basis points on 500-share trades and 21 basis points on 100-share trades when these were the SOES maximum trade size. In contrast, we estimate that market makers obtained additional gains of 17, 7, and 10 basis points on 100-, 101–499-, and 500-share trades (when not the SOES maximum size). We believe these gains are due to market makers' actions to reduce informed trade losses to SOES day traders and related operating costs. During this time, there were very small and statistically insignificant increases in informed trade costs on NYSE stocks of zero to two basis points.

We also find that market makers compensated for informed-trade losses to SOES day traders, as well as the costs of substantially reduced coverage by individual market makers and system enhancements to reduce stale quotes, by increasing quoted sale and decreasing quoted buy prices, thereby widening spreads. In section V we present relative effective spreads (RES) for each of the six trade sizes and find that the RES increased much more for the smaller trade sizes. Thus, investors who used the smaller trade sizes, who on the whole were unable to trade within the BBO, incurred substantially greater actual transactions costs.

In section VI we compare changes in the percentage of volume at the maximum SOES trade size (our proxy for SOES day trades) and the percentage of stocks quoted on even eighths (the Christie-Schultz proxy for tacit collusion among NASDAQ market makers) with the difference in RES on NASDAQ and NYSE stocks over the 13 years studied. These data are consistent with the SOES day-trade and inconsistent with the even-eighths tacit-collusion hypotheses. Section VII applies robustness checks wherein prior results are verified. Section VIII states our conclusions and the implications of our study for contemporary issues.

## II. Description of SOES History and Day Trading

In this section we provide background regarding SOES to inform the analyses that follow. In response to brokers not answering telephones during the market crash on October 19, 1987, the NASD, under pressure from the SEC, formed a blue-ribbon committee of market makers from leading broker/dealers. This committee recommended that quotes by all market makers should be executable automatically for NASDAQ Level II market orders of up to 1,000 shares submitted over the already developed but voluntary SOES. The SEC approved this change on June 9, 1988. Since market makers were required to honor up to five repetitions, they were required to fill orders aggregating as much as 5,000 shares at the best posted quote. (If the market for a stock was crossed or locked—the ask less than or equal to the bid—restrictions were removed and unlimited orders could be submitted over SOES.) This requirement contrasts sharply with the 100-share minimum order size imposed on NYSE specialists. Finally, on the surface SOES may seem similar to the NYSE DOT system, but DOT machines are only issued to brokerage firms and the specialist has 15 seconds to consider market orders.

Soon after SOES was made mandatory, some dealers began picking off market makers whose quotes became momentarily stale on the NASDAQ quotation system. The NASD attempted to stop this use of the system by adopting a rule change (approved by the SEC on December 14, 1988) prohibiting members from entering orders through SOES on their own accounts or on behalf of a professional trading account, which is defined as any account in which five or more "day trades" by an individual trader or firm were executed through SOES during any trading day or where a professional pattern in SOES is exhibited. However, SOES day traders could avoid this restriction by executing one side of a trade outside of SOES and by trading from several ostensibly separate accounts. A "professional pattern" also proved difficult to establish.[10] From conversations with NASDAQ economists, market makers, and observations of data presented later (see figure 16.2), we determined that SOES day trading did not become really active and widespread until after June 1990. We term the months 8/88 through 6/90 the "Adjustment" period.[11]

SOES day trading "took off" largely through the efforts of two NASDAQ market makers, Datek and All-Tech (especially All-Tech's CEO, Harvey Houtkin, who calls himself the "original SOES bandit"; Houtkin, 1995). These firms recruited individual traders, now known as SOES day traders (or activists or bandits) and provided them with NASDAQ Level II terminals and software that would permit them to use the SOES system to pick off stale quotes. SOES day traders adopted a variety of strategies over time, including identifying the onset of buy/sell programs

---

10. In 1993 the U.S. Court of Appeals for Washington, D.C. formally voided the rule, because it was vague and did not apply to telephone orders for quoted stocks.

11. Data for July 1988 are not available. The analysis is not changed appreciably if the "Adjustment" period were included in the following period we delineate.

380  FINANCE

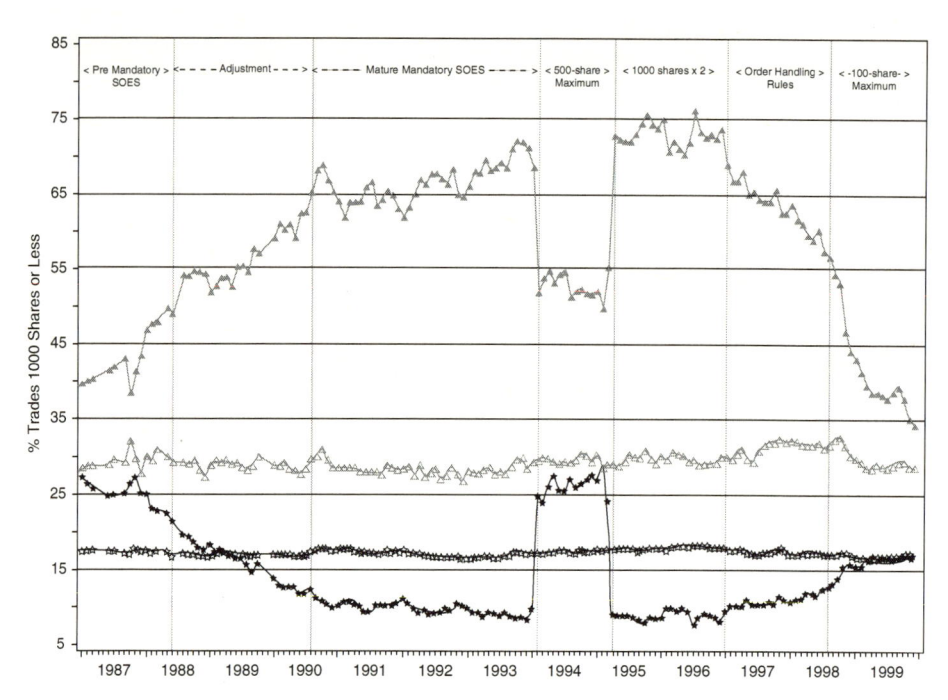

FIGURE 16.2 500- and 1000-Share Dollar Volume as a Percentage of Total Dollar Volume of 1000 Shares or Less for NASDAQ and NYSE 500-Share NASDAQ Dollar Volume = (★), 1000 NASDAQ = (▲), 500 NYSE = (☆), 1000 NYSE = (∆)

by institutional investors, stepping in front of these programs by absorbing the available liquidity, and then resupplying the liquidity at a short-term profit.[12] For example, 15 market makers might quote the same best offer price on a stock, and a major broker (which generally deals in substantial size transactions) begins a buy program for a client with the intent of obtaining a large number of shares at or near that price. Upon observing the broker acquiring liquidity from one or two market makers, SOES day traders instantly buy the shares offered by the remaining market makers through SOES (referred to as "hitting the monster button," a

---

12. See Houtkin (1995, ch. 8) and Harris and Schultz (1998) for descriptions of SOES trading techniques. Also see Battalio, Hatch, and Jennings (1997, table 1) for a case study of trades in Apple Computer common stock during a 10-minute period that illustrates SOES day trading. At 11:26 on June 20, 1995, between 14 and 15 market makers quoted an ask price of $46.625. Within the next minute, with the exception of one broker, the ask increased to $46.750. This broker was hit with 12 1,000-share buy orders. Before the ask quote leveled off at $46.875, four more 1,000-share buy orders were placed.

procedure denied to brokers by NASD rule that required a broker to approach market makers serially). The bandits then offer the shares to the acquiring broker (who must obtain the shares to fulfill an order) at higher prices, often through SelectNet (Harris and Schultz, 1998). Thus, the initial market maker incurred an opportunity cost, having sold the stock at too low a price. Harris and Schultz (1998, p. 45) also report that "although SOES day traders are prohibited from selling short through SOES...[they] circumvent this restriction by purchasing 1,000 shares of each stock that they would like to sell short. These shares are placed in the bandit's hedge account. When the bandit believes that a stock will be moving down in the short-term, he uses SOES to sell shares from his hedge account." (Note that this process results in higher informed trading costs to market makers.) We term this period, 7/90–1/94 (after which the rules changed), "Mature Mandatory SOES." Although in the mid-1990s market makers adopted software and decreased the number of stocks their traders followed, these procedures were not sufficient to contain the increasing number of day traders who also adopted software to identify stale quotes and institutional trading programs. The procedures did, though, increase market makers' operating costs.

The NASD convinced the SEC to experiment by reducing temporarily the maximum SOES trade size from 1,000 to 500 shares and from five to two the maximum number of times a market maker must honor an order before changing a quote. These rules were in effect from January 31, 1994, through March 26, 1995, when the SEC ended its prior temporary ruling. We call this the "500-share Maximum" period. After that date, the maximum trade size of 1,000 shares was restored, but the number of orders that had to be filled before a quote could be changed remained at two. We call this the "1,000 Shares × 2" period.

In January 1997 the SEC mandated several Order Handling Rule (OHR) changes in NASDAQ operations that were applied to selected stocks in 22 waves, beginning on January 16 and ending on October 13, 1997.[13] Market makers were permitted to reduce their own quoted number of shares from 1,000 to 100 for the 50 stocks in the January 16 wave and 50 stocks in the February 10 wave. Barclay, Christie, Harris, Kandel, and Schultz (1999) and Weston (2000) study these first two waves and find that spreads declined substantially. They say that the lower spreads were not due to a reduction in the cost of informed SOES trades. In October 1997, the rule was applied to an additional

13. SEC Release No. 34-37619A, File No. S7-30-95, Order Execution Obligations, Final Rules 17 CFR Part 240. The change also requires that better customer limit orders be reflected in the public quote (unless the customer specifically does not agree), the Excess Spread Rule (which dictates the maximum difference between bid and ask quotes) was relaxed, and market makers were permitted to quote stocks in sixteenths after June 1997. See Barclay et al. (1999) and Weston (2000) for a more detailed description and analyses.

100 stocks, and in July 1998 to all NMS stocks.[14] To examine the effects of these changes, we divide the years 1997–99 into two periods, the "Order Handling Rules" period, 1/97–7/98, and the "100-share Maximum" period, 8/98–12/99. During and, especially, after this period, trading through ECNs increased greatly and decimalization was introduced in 2000. Hence, we do not extend our analysis beyond 1999.

To summarize, based on the development of SOES described in this section, we divide the 13 years analyzed into seven periods: "Pre-mandatory SOES" (1/87–5/88); "Adjustment" (8/88–7/90), when SOES developed and the NASD attempted unsuccessfully to restrict its use; "Mature Mandatory SOES" (8/90–1/94); "500-share Maximum" (2/94–3/95), when the SEC allowed NASDAQ to reduce the maximum trade size from five repetitions of 1,000 shares to two repetitions of 500 shares; "1,000 shares × 2" (4/95–12/96), when the maximum trade size but not the number of repetitions was restored; "Order Handling Rules" (1/97–7/98), when these were introduced; and "100-share Maximum" (8/98–12/99), when pursuant to the Actual Size Rule market makers were allowed to reduce their own quoted depth to 100 shares on their quotes. (Customer limit orders posted by dealers for their customers would reflect their actual size.) With this background we are prepared to examine the impact of SOES day trading on NASDAQ.

## III. The Extent of SOES Day Trading

As noted above, SOES was limited initially to 1,000-share trades. Thus, we will confine our analysis to 1,000 shares and below, using 1,001–5,000-share (1–5K) trades as a comparison. However, as also noted above, SOES day trading strategies morphed over time in response to regulatory pressure and evolving profitable opportunities. In particular, day traders increasingly used the NASDAQ SelectNet system and phone orders in the early 1990s, both to enter into positions and to unwind them as well in quantities that might differ from 1,000 shares per trade. So the validity of using 1–5K trades as a benchmark weakens over time.

We *initially* measure SOES day trades as trades made at the maximum quantity that can be transmitted through SOES—1,000 shares, except during the 500-share maximum, when the maximum was 500 shares, and the period

---

14. However, if customer limit orders offered more or asked less than the market maker, the sum of customer limit orders for the number of shares offered at that price are posted, pursuant to the Actual Size Rule. See SEC Release No. 34-40139; File No. SR-NASD-97-26.

8/98–12/99, when market makers were permitted to quote as few as 100 shares.[15] We recognize that the maximum SOES trade size is an imperfect measure of SOES trades made by day traders. This metric both understates and overstates SOES day trading. It understates SOES day trading, because day traders can trade different quantities. They also can unwind their positions with trades of any size and not necessarily through SOES, as their goal is to end the day with no inventory. The metric overstates SOES day trading, because all 1,000-share trades (and 500- and 100-share trades when these were the maximum) are not made by SOES day traders or even through SOES. This is especially true following the SEC requirement in 1991 that the NASDAQ SOES 1,000-share quote minimum be extended to SelectNet and phone orders. Our base period, January 1987–May 1988, is somewhat contaminated since we are told by equity-trading professionals that day traders picked off stale quotes before SOES was made mandatory.

Figure 16.2 shows the percentages of the dollar volumes of 1,000- and 500-share trades to the dollar volumes on all NMS trades of SOES-eligible trades (1,000 shares or less), averaged over months, January 1987 through December 1999. In this and succeeding figures, vertical lines identify the end of each of the seven periods of SOES history that we delineate. Similar data for NYSE trades offer a contrast. From the onset of our data we observe that NASDAQ 1,000-share trades are 10 percentage points higher than the NYSE percentage and climbing, suggesting that day traders may have been picking off stale market maker quotes even before SOES was made mandatory in June 1988. By the end of the "Adjustment" period, the percentage of 1,000-share trades increased to 63 percent and the percentage of 500-share trades decreased to 12 percent. Over the "Mature Mandatory SOES" period, 1,000-share trades averaged 67 percent and 500-share trades averaged 10 percent. During the February 1994 through March 1995 "500-share Maximum" period the dollar-volume percentages for 1,000-share trades declined sharply to an average of 53 percent, while the percentage of 500-share trades increased to 26 percent, an almost exactly offsetting movement of 17 percentage points. It is important to note that the percentage of NASDAQ 1,000-share trades still remained quite high relative to that of the NYSE, which likely reveals that many day traders continued to employ or even increase their use of SelectNet and phone orders to place 1,000-share trades. Hence, even with the reduction of SOES pressure on market makers with the

---

15. Houtkin (1995, p. 39) states, after describing the reduction of the maximum trade size to 500 shares at the time he was writing: "1,000 shares has proven to be a more optimally sized order [than a smaller order]." Our discussions with market makers additionally support our assumption that SOES bandits trade the maximum number of shares per order. Harris and Schultz (1997) and Battalio, Hatch, and Jennings (1997) also use this metric. Harris and Schultz (1998, p. 40), who study individual SOES day trades, state: "Trades are for 1000 shares because that is the maximum size allowed in SOES."

500-share maximum, the net pressure on market makers was not substantially reduced. This important fact was apparently missed in the studies of the "500-share Maximum" period conducted by and for the SEC, which found that spreads did not decrease substantially even with the halving of mandatory SOES size. Consequently, the SEC determined that SOES day trading was not the cause of earlier observed widened NASDAQ spreads, the "experiment" should be discontinued, and the maximum SOES trade size should be returned to 1,000 shares. After the resumption to the 1,000-share maximum, the percentages returned close to their previous levels. From January 1997 through December 1999, the percentage of 1,000-share volume declined almost continuously to 34 percent, a bit below the percentage before SOES was made mandatory, thereby reflecting the impact of the rule changes and the resultant relative reduction in SOES day trading. Although the dollar amount of 1,000-share trades actually increased slightly (to 112 percent of the December 1996 level), the dollar amounts of the smaller trade sizes increased substantially, thereby decreasing the dollar-volume percentage of 1,000-share trades.

In contrast, over the same 13-year period, the dollar-volume percentages of NYSE 1,000- and 500-share trades to the total volume of all trades of 1,000 shares or less were virtually unchanged at between 27 and 33 percent for 1,000-share trades and 17 and 18 percent for 500-share trades. Considering that many traders, particularly institutional investors who trade 1,000-share lots, act in both markets with a common objective, it appears that the patterns shown in figure 16.2 are endogenous to NASDAQ, rather than the result of exogenous events that affect trades in stock markets generally.

We next estimate the extent to which SOES day trading has imposed costs on market makers and other liquidity suppliers in the form of informed-trade opportunity costs. For comparison we calculate this metric for non-SOES trades and for NYSE trades. We separate the effects of SOES day trades and other trades with a simple formula (described in section IV).

## IV. Informed-Trade Losses Due to SOES Day Trading

### Concepts, Measurement, and Previous Studies

As noted above, NASDAQ market makers incur an opportunity loss when they sell a stock at time $t$ for less than they would have received had they sold it at time $t + \tau$ or when they pay more for a stock at time $t$ than they would have paid had they bought the stock later, at time $t + \tau$. They gain from the reverse sequence—selling stock at a lower price than a later possible purchase and buying at a higher price than a later sale.[16] We term these "informed-trade" losses and gains, on the assumption that one side or the other has superior information or ability.

Harris and Schultz (1997) examine transactions from a sample of 20 NASDAQ stocks with the greatest market capitalization at year-end 1993 over the period November 1, 1993, through March 31, 1994. Defining SOES day trades as "clusters...of three or more consecutive trades [at the same quoted price] of the maximum allowable size under the prevailing SOES rules, 'they find' that in the twenty minutes after 1000- [or 500-] share clustered buying [or selling] begins, the bid [or ask] price of the stock increases [or decreases] by about $0.18 on average" (ibid., p. 137). No significant change was found for other trade sizes. Harris and Schultz (1997, p. 165) interpret this finding as "[indicating] that SOES trades have greater information content than other trades." They also state that their results "confirm that SOES bandits and other traders submit clusters of orders that trade ahead of short-term price changes" (ibid., p. 158). Battalio, Hatch, and Jennings (1997) report a similar trading pattern. Thus, these findings indicate that SOES day traders impose informed-trade opportunity costs on market makers.

HS (1996) study 1991 data for 175 pairs of NASDAQ and NYSE stocks with a procedure that yields opposite results. They calculate the market makers' "realized half-spread" as the increase or decrease in the price at which a stock is purchased or sold (identified as such with the Lee and Ready, 1991, algorithm, which we also use) and its price (not identified as a purchase or sale) five or thirty minutes later. They find: "For all trades at the bid, the realized half-spread averages 15.3 cents...[and] for all trades at the ask, the realized half spread averages 13.6 cents" (ibid., p. 328). These results are essentially the same for the 5- and 30-minute intervals and for each of the three trade sizes specified (<1,000 shares, 1,000 < 10,000 shares, and 10,000+ shares). Similar calculations reveal much smaller, insignificant amounts for a matched sample of NYSE stocks. Based on these findings, HS "reject the theory that higher execution costs on NASDAQ are the result of an inability of dealers to cope with adverse information and SOES bandits" (ibid.). BK similarly measure realized half-spreads for a paired sample of 300 NASDAQ and 300 NYSE stocks in 1994. They divide this sample into small trades (less than $10,000), medium trades ($10,000 through $199,000),

---

16. We did not employ the procedure used by Barclay and Hendershott (2004) (which is due to Lin, Sanger, and Booth, 1995, who cite other papers from which the method is derived) of regressing the change in quote on the effective spread to calculate a coefficient that measures the proportion of the spread due to adverse selection costs, as we believe it is not applicable to the situation we study. Day traders take advantage of stale quotes, wherein the BBO has changed but some market makers have failed to change quickly enough. Also, our method of sectioning trades into relatively small divisions allows us to control differences in transactions costs (which Lin et al., 1995, find are a function of trade size) and inventory costs are small (given the short time spans considered herein and as found by other studies).

and large trades (over $200,000). They also report higher realized half-spreads for NASDAQ than for NYSE stocks (where higher amounts indicate greater costs to investors and gains to NASDAQ market makers and NYSE specialists, floor traders, and limit orders), although their numbers are 24.9 basis points for NASDAQ and 12.5 basis points for NYSE transactions. Based on this finding, they conclude that "the wider quoted and effective spreads on NASDAQ cannot be attributed to greater adverse information costs on NASDAQ" (ibid., p. 300).[17]

The conflicting and inconsistent findings reported by Harris and Schultz (1997), HS, and BK could be due to the different samples or time periods studied or to the way they measure informed trades (which they call adverse selection).[18] Unlike the realized spread measure employed by HS and BK, we measure the opportunity gain or loss to liquidity suppliers. We ask: "if liquidity suppliers had been able to wait 300 seconds before executing a buy or sell, would they have gained or lost as a result of having waited?" We measure this opportunity cost by comparing a buy/sell initiated trade with a subsequent buy/sell initiated trade 300 seconds later. In contrast, HS and BK compare each trade, identified as buy- or sell-initiated, with a subsequent trade at least 30 minutes later that can be either buy- or sell-initiated—in effect comparing the initial transaction with the subsequent spread midpoint.[19]

Realized spreads measure the cost incurred by market makers assuming that they unwind their position randomly at the bid or the ask. Our intent, though, is not to measure the change in dealer net profits from mandatory SOES. We are unable to fully measure all dealer costs since major components, such as the costs of drastically reduced coverage by individual market makers and the cost of software and systems to minimize stale quotes, are not observable. Thus, we focus directly on the information content of trades, rather than on realized spreads and dealer profits. We do not claim that NASDAQ dealers did not make potentially large profits, perhaps as a result of collusion or payment for order flow. We simply argue that SOES, both directly and indirectly, caused effective spreads to widen above and beyond the impact of other factors.

In addition, HS and BK do not distinguish among trades made by SOES bandits and those made by other traders. We separate the data into six trade sizes,

---

17. Foucault, Röell, and Sandås (2003) present a model of SOES bandit behavior and empirical estimates of their effect on spreads based on December 1996 data. We believe that their model is incorrectly specified, in large measure because they do not consider bandits' payoffs from picking off stale quotes and their use of the "monster button." Among other shortcomings, they do not consider the effect of ECNs in December 1996. Furthermore, they assume that the effect of SOES banditry is reflected both immediately and only on the spreads of the individual stocks they trade. As we point out, market makers could not know which stocks would be subject to SOES day trades and hence had incentives to offer quotes that reflected the cost imposed on them by that otherwise unpriced option.

18. Neither Harris and Schultz (1997) nor BK contrast their findings with those of HS.

19. We examined lengths greater than 300 seconds but found that greater lengths provided similar results while 300 seconds increased our sample size.

which allows us to isolate and test hypotheses about the possible effect of SOES day trading.

## Per Trade Basis Point Opportunity Losses or Gains to NASDAQ Market Makers (and Other Traders) from Informed Trades, Not Yet Adjusted for Other-Than-SOES Day Trades or Offset by Larger Effective Spreads

We use the Lee and Ready (1991) algorithm to identify each transaction at time $t$ in stock $i$ by a market maker as a buy or sell.[20] The opportunity loss or gain on the transaction is measured by the change in the price of the next purchase if the initial transaction is a purchase or sale if the initial transaction is a sale that occurs at least five minutes later, at $t + \tau$, within the same day.[21] Consequently, we exclude trades that occur in the last five minutes of the trading day, and trades during a day that are not followed by a trade on the same side of the spread. The liquidity provider suffers an opportunity loss when, for a sale, $P_{it+\tau} - P_{it} > 0$ or, for a purchase, $P_{it+\tau} - P_{it} < 0$, and gains when the reverse occurs. To account for differences at a point in time and changes over time of the prices of the stocks traded, we divide the opportunity loses or gains for each transaction by $P_{it}$, to obtain the percentage loss or gain (in basis points).

As noted earlier, to provide adequate tests of the hypotheses, we disaggregate the NASDAQ and NYSE data into five trade sizes that can be transacted through SOES—100, 101–499, 500, 501–999, and 1,000 shares—and one trade size that cannot be transacted through SOES 1,001–5,000 (1–5K) shares. The informed-trade (opportunity) loss or gain is assigned to a trade size according to the number of shares of the first transaction ($P_{it}$). The observations are stock days. Within a day,

---

20. Ellis, Michaely, and O'Hara (2000) compare the accuracy of this quote procedure with a tick rule, the Lee and Ready (LR) (1991) combined tick rule for trades at the BBO midpoint and quote rule for other trades, and their alternative of using the quote rule for trades executed at the quote and the tick rule for all other trades. Using a sample where the direction of the trade is known, they find that their alternative is more accurate for transactions other than at quotes (61 percent versus 55 percent). However, they find almost no difference in accuracy using the LR rule for trades of 5,000 shares or less. (They do not present such data for their quote-tick alternative.) Hence, although their alternative might be more accurate than the quote rule we employ, we believe that there is no bias among the trade sizes we examine, which is central to our investigation. Misidentification of purchases or sales bias our measure of market makers' informed trade costs downward, as illustrated earlier, thereby understating their costs of trades by SOES bandits.

21. To the extent that market makers do not report trades in the exact order they are effected, there can be sequencing error. However, this is mitigated by our using a five-minute delay. HS used both 5- and 30-minute delays and BK used both 30-minute and 1-day delays, with similar results. Furthermore, there is no reason to believe that this problem imparts a bias, as there was no change in practice or association with a given trade size of which we are aware over the period studied.

for each trade size, we average the calculated informed-trade basis points; for trade sizes that cover a range (e.g., 101–499 shares), the dollar volumes of each transaction weight the basis points. The gains or losses are not further weighted, yielding informed-trade basis points on the average stock on the average day. If we did not do this, the very high volume stocks would dominate the findings.

Figure 16.3 shows liquidity supplier's (opportunity) gains and losses per trade in basis points from informed and uninformed trades for the average stock on an average trading day in a month, January 1987 through December 1999, for each of the six trade sizes. Before June 1988, when SOES was made mandatory (excluding the 1987 "market crash" months of October, November, and December), market makers had informed-trade losses on 500- and 1,000-share trades (denoted by stars and triangles), each averaging 16 basis points (17 if the market-crash months were included). Apparently, informed traders used both trade sizes, as these often were the quoted amounts posted by market makers. After SOES was made mandatory, the percentage of informed-trade losses on 500-share trades declined until they became an average gain of three basis points in the "Mature Mandatory SOES" period, 8/90–1/94. The relative volume of 500-share trades declined simi-

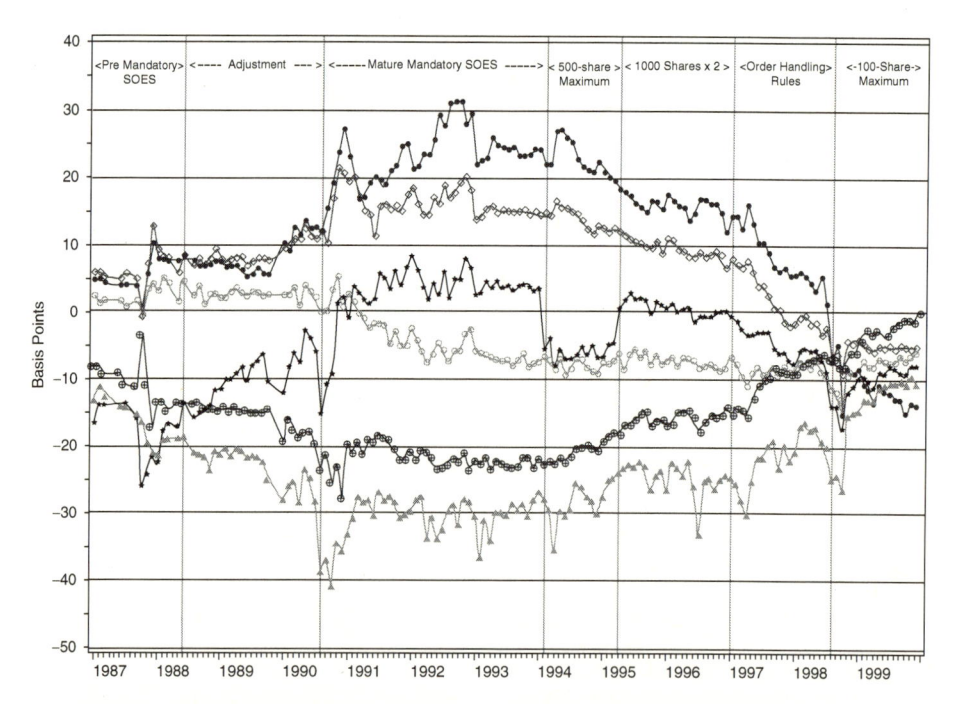

FIGURE 16.3  Monthly Average Gains (Losses) per Trade to NASDAQ Market Makers from Informed Trades, in Basis Points 100 Share Trades = (●), 101–499 = (◊), 500 = (★), 501–999 = (○), 1000 = (▲), 1–5 K = (⊕)

larly, as shown in figure 16.2. Informed-trade losses on 1,000-share trades, which include both SOES day trades and other transactions, increased to 31 basis points, on average, in the "Mature Mandatory SOES" period.

When the maximum SOES trade size was reduced to 500 shares during the "500-share Maximum" period, market makers' informed-trade losses on 1,000-share trades declined by an average of 2.5 basis points, while those on 500-share trades increased by 8.7 basis points. We interpret these continuing, though somewhat lower, average informed-trade losses on 1,000-share trades when 500 shares was the SOES maximum as showing that some SOES day traders successfully shifted their trades to SelectNet and telephone orders. They took advantage of NASDAQ's requirement (beginning in 1991) that market makers must fulfill quotations for at least 1,000 shares from those sources (per interview with Gene Finn, then chief economist for NASD). Harris and Schultz (1997, p. 139) also state: "brokerage firms who specialize in trading for SOES bandits generally allow customers access to [SelectNet and Instinet] through their trading desk." Following restoration of the maximum trade size to 1,000 shares, in the "1,000 Shares × 2" period average informed-trade losses on 500-share trades decreased by 7 basis points to a 1 basis point gain, while average losses on 1,000-share trades continued to become somewhat smaller. Over the next two periods, market makers experienced increased losses on 500-share trades and smaller losses on 1,000-share trades. After July 1998, when SOES was limited to 100-share trades, informed trade losses on 1,000-share trades were fairly close to the amount in the Pre-Mandatory SOES period, 1/87–5/88.

In contrast, market makers experienced similar informed-trade gains from 100-share and 101–499-share trades (denoted by solid circles and diamonds) through mid-1998, when 100 shares became the SOES maximum for all stocks. (Note that except for 500-share trades when these were the maximum, after the "Pre-mandatory SOES" period the patterns for trades of less than 1,000-share trades are similar.) These gains were about 8 basis points through mid-1990, then about 14 basis points through mid-1994, after which the gains decreased. However, after market makers were allowed to reduce the number of shares quoted to 100 on some stocks after 1996 and on all stocks after July 1998 informed-trade gains on 100-share trades became losses—14 basis points by December 1999.

Trades of 1–5K shares (denoted by crosses within circles), which cannot be made through SOES, provide a control. Market makers suffered informed-trade losses on the 1–5K-share trades averaging 11 basis points before SOES was made mandatory (excluding the market crash months), gradually increasing to about 16 basis points through March/April 1997, and then decreasing to 2 basis points by December 1999. Thus, 1,000-share trades and 500-share trades during the 500-share maximum appear to have imposed substantially greater informed-trade losses (or gains) on market makers than other trade sizes. In our calculations of the amounts of these increases due to SOES day traders (presented shortly), we take into account the changes in informed-trade losses from 1–5K-share trades.

The data are summarized in table 16.1, panel A, which presents the percentage-of-share-price gains (losses) per trade in basis points for each of the six trade sizes, averaged over the seven periods that describe states of SOES history. With very few exceptions (noted in panel D of the table), these amounts are significantly different from zero at the .01 level or lower. Over the 77 months when day trading through SOES was most prevalent (8/90–12/96), market makers had informed-trade losses on 1,000-share trades averaging (over all months) 29 basis points, compared to average informed-trade losses on 1–5K-share trades of 20 basis points. Market makers had informed-trade gains averaging 21 and 14 basis points on 100- and 101–499-share trades, and almost no gains or losses on 500-share trades (excluding the period when 500 shares was the maximum SOES-eligible trade size) and losses of 5 basis points 501–999-share trades. (The averages are lower by one to two basis points if the "Adjustment" period months were included.) Also shown are the percentages of 1,000-share trades to all trades of 1,000 shares or less (1,000 sh. % of all <=1,000).

## Comparison with NYSE Trades

Similarly computed informed trade gains and losses for NYSE liquidity providers over the same period and for the same trade sizes as the NASDAQ trades can serve as an indicator of the extent to which the informed trade gains and losses experienced on NASDAQ are due to time-dependent factors that affect stock trading generally or the trades through SOES, which are unique to NASDAQ.[22] The data, presented in panel C of table 16.1, indicate relatively small mean informed trade losses to specialists, floor traders, and limit orders for all trade sizes and all periods, all significantly different from zero at the .01 level. (Since the Pre-mandatory-SOES base period is subtracted, the $t$ test provides a measure of significant difference from that period.) This finding might be due to specialists, who are required to stabilize prices by moving against the market or (more likely) to losses incurred on limit orders, which offer other investors options similar to those offered by NASDAQ market makers to informed traders (e.g., SOES day traders).

---

22. We understand that NYSE specialists sometimes list (report) as a single trade several individual trades that cleared at the same price. To the extent that this occurs, the NYSE trade sizes are incorrect. We understand that this practice did not change over the 13 years studied. Indeed, as shown in figure 16.2, the proportion of NYSE 500- and 1,000-share trades was almost unchanged over the period studies. Table 16.1 shows almost unchanged NYSE adverse selection losses by trade size over the period. Thus, either this practice does not affect the NYSE data much or, if it did, does not affect our findings.

TABLE 16.1 Opportunity Gains (Losses) per Trade to NASDAQ Market Makers from Informed Trades on the Average Stock on the Average Day, in Basis Points by Size of Trade Averaged over Pre- and Postmandatory SOES Periods, January 1987–December 1999

|  |  | SOES-Eligible Trade Sizes (number of shares per trade) |  |  |  |  | 1,000 sh. % | SOES ineligible |
|---|---|---|---|---|---|---|---|---|
| Periods | No. Months* | 100 | 101–499 | 500 | 501–999 | 1,000 | of all ≤1,000 | 1–5K |
| *A. NASDAQ* |  |  |  |  |  |  |  |  |
| Pre-mandatory SOES (1/87–5/88) | 10** | 6 | 6 | (16) | 2 | (16) | 41% | (11) |
| Adjustment (8/88–7/90) | 22 | 8 | 9 | (9) | 3 | (23) | 53% | (16) |
| Mature Mandatory SOES (8/90–1/94) | 42 | 23 | 16 | 3 | (4) | (31) | 61% | (22) |
| 500-share Maximum (2/94–3/95) | 14 | 23 | 14 | (6) | (8) | (28) | 52% | (21) |
| 1,000 shares × 2 (4/95–12/96) | 21 | 16 | 10 | 1 | (7) | (25) | 67% | (16) |
| Order Handling Rules (1/97–7/98) | 19 | 8 | 2 | (5) | (8) | (21) | 60% | (10) |
| 100-share Maximum (8/98–12/99) | 17 | (11) | (5) | (10) | (8) | (14) | 44% | (4) |
| Average 8/90–12/96 (note 2) |  | 21 | 14 | 1 | (6) | (29) | 61% | (20) |
| *B. NYSE* |  |  |  |  |  |  |  |  |
| Pre-mandatory SOES (1/87–5/88) | 10** | 0 | (3) | (6) | (5) | (6) | 29% | (6) |
| Adjustment (8/88–7/90) | 22 | (0) | (2) | (6) | (4) | (5) | 29% | (6) |
| Mature Mandatory SOES (8/90–1/94) | 42 | (1) | (3) | (7) | (5) | (6) | 28% | (7) |
| 500-share Maximum (2/94–3/95) | 14 | (1) | (2) | (6) | (4) | (5) | 30% | (6) |
| 1,000 shares × 2 (4/95–12/96) | 21 | (1) | (2) | (5) | (4) | (5) | 30% | (5) |
| Order Handling Rules (1/97–7/98) | 19 | (1) | (2) | (5) | (3) | (5) | 31% | (4) |
| 100-share Maximum (8/98–12/99) | 17 | (2) | (2) | (6) | (3) | (5) | 30% | (4) |

|  | No. Months* | 100 | 101–499 | 500 | 501–999 | 1,000 Other | Day Trades | 1–5 K |
|---|---|---|---|---|---|---|---|---|
| *C. NASDAQ mandatory-SOES periods less pre-mandatory period means (note 2) less similar NYSE change* |  |  |  |  |  |  |  |  |
| Adjustment (8/88–6/90) | 22 | 3 | 2 | 6 | (0) | (5) | (17) | (5) |
| Mature Mandatory SOES (8/90–1/94) | 42 | 18 | 10 | 19 | (6) | (10) | (23) | (10) |
| 500-share Maximum (2/94–3/95) | 14 | 18 | 7 | 0 | (10) | (10) | (24) | (10) |
| 500-share day trades |  |  |  |  |  |  | (18) |  |

*(continued)*

TABLE 16.1 Continued

| Periods | No. Months* | SOES-Eligible Trade Sizes (number of shares per trade) ||||| 1,000 sh. % of all <=1,000 | SOES ineligible 1–5K |
| | | 100 | 101–499 | 500 | 501–999 | 1,000 | | |
|---|---|---|---|---|---|---|---|---|
| 1,000 shares × 2 (4/95–12/96) | 21 | 12 | 3 | (3) | (11) | (5) | (15) | (5) |
| Order Handling Rules (1/97–7/98) | 19 | 4 | (6) | (9) | (13) | (1) | (19) | (1) |
| 100-share Maximum (8/98–12/99) | 17 | 0 | (12) | (14) | (12) | 6 | | 6 |
| 100-share day trades | | | | | | | (14) | |
| Average 8/90–12/96 [note 2] | 77 | 17 | 7 | 10 | (8) | (9) | (21) | (9) |

D. *Statistical significance of means at the .01 level or lower*

Panel A: significantly different from zero, all means except:
"Order Handling Rules" period: 101–499 shares (.08 level)

Significantly different from "Pre-mandatory SOES" period means, all means except:
"Adjustment" period: 501–999 shares (.09 level)
"Order Handling Rules" period-100 shares (.02 level) and 1–5K shares (.09 level)
"100-share Maximum" period: 1000 shares (.27 level)

Panel B: significantly different from zero, all means

Significantly different from "Pre-mandatory SOES" period means, all means except:
"Adjustment" period: 1,000 and 1–5K shares
"Mature Mandatory SOES" period: 101–499 shares (.04 level); 500 and 501–999 shares

Panel B: significantly different from zero, all means
"500-share Maximum" period: 1,000 shares (.06 level); 1–5 K shares
"100-share Maximum" period: 500 shares (.03 level)
Panel C: significantly different from zero, all means except:
"Adjustment" period: 501–999 shares
"Order Handling Rules" period: 1–5K shares
"100-share Maximum" period: 1,000 shares

This table shows the opportunity gains (losses) to market makers ascribed to informed trades by SOES day traders and others, grouped according to trade size. The observations include stocks for which there are at least five trades in a day and trades at least five minutes later on the same side of the BBO, aggregated daily for each stock. The observations (stock days) are averaged over months and the months are averaged over periods that describe stages of SOES history. Panels A and B show the informed-trade losses (gains) for each of the periods (and the percentages of 1,000-share trades to total trades of 1,000 shares or less) for the NASDAQ and NYSE samples. Panel C reduces the NASDAQ amounts to those ascribed to mandatory SOES trading by subtracting the averages of informed-trade gains (losses) in the pre-mandatory SOES period from those in the following periods and also subtracting the change from the "Pre-mandatory SOES" period in informed-trade gains (losses) on the same-trade-size NYSE stocks, except for 500-share trades and 100-share trades when these were the SOES maximum trade size, rather than to trades of the same size when the size was the SOES maximum, are calculated with formula (1a) described in the text, using "1,000 sh.% of all b = 1,000" given in panel A to estimate the percentage of 1,000-share trades made by SOES day traders. The amounts for other-than day trades ($IT_o$) are described in note 1. Panel D indicates the statistical significance of the means presented in panels A, B, and C

*Data for 4/87, 5/87, 8/87, 4/88, 7/88, 11/89, and 12/89 are not available.
**Excluding the 1987 market crash months of October, November, and December.

Note 1: Basis points for other-than day trades ($IT_o$) for 1,000 share trades are basis points for 1–5 K trades; for 500-share and 100-share trades when these were the SOES-maximum trade size, amount in previous period plus the change in 101–499-share trades from its previous period amount adjusted for the change in those periods of NYSE amounts for 500- or 100-share trades.

Note 2: Weighted by number of months; in panel B, excludes 500- and 100-share day trades listed with 100-share trades.

Indeed, Harris and Hasbrouck (1996, table 7), who measure the ex post order performance of NYSE completely filled limit orders using a procedure similar to the one we employ, find uniformly negative performance at a time (November 1990–January 1991) when the market generally was rising.[23] In our NYSE sample, the ranges of the mean number of negative basis points over the seven SOES periods for each trade size are: 100-share trades, 1–2; 101–499-share trades, 2–3; 500-share trades, 5–7, 501–999-share trades, 4–5, 1,000- and 1–5K-share trades, 3–6. The changes in the means from period to period are either zero or one basis point and the maximum cumulative change is two basis points. None of the changes are significant. Thus, the NYSE data are consistent with the hypothesis that SOES substantially affected informed trade gains and losses on NASDAQ and inconsistent with there having been a market-wide change in informed trading.

## Adjustment for NASDAQ Informed Trades by Other-Than-SOES Day Traders

We employ two procedures for adjusting the NASDAQ data for trades by other-than-SOES day traders from which we can separate losses from SOES day traders and other traders who make 1,000-, 500-, and 100-share trades, when these were the maximum SOES trade size: (1) deduction of informed-trade losses and gains in each trade size in the period before SOES was made mandatory, adjusted for contemporaneous changes in NYSE trades, and (2) calculations based on changes in the percentages of 1,000-, 500-, and 100-shares when these became and later no longer were the SOES maximum trade sizes.

As shown in figure 16.3 and panel A of table 16.1, market makers experienced informed-trade losses and gains before SOES was made mandatory in June 1988. After the SOES maximum trade size was reduced to 100 shares, largely after July 1998, the levels of informed trade losses and gains generally returned to or toward these pre-mandatory SOES levels (particularly for 1,000-share trades), except for 100-share trades which then became the SOES maximum trade size. Consequently, we estimate net mandatory-SOES-related informed-trade costs and gains ($NIT$) on NASDAQ ($N$) for each trade size ($s$) in a mandatory-SOES period ($p$), $NIT_{Nsp}$, as follows. We start with the NASDAQ informed-trade basis points ($IT_{Nsp}$) and subtract the average basis points in the base "Pre-mandatory-SOES" period

---

23. Battalio, Greene, Hatch, and Jennings (2002) also measure the performance of limit orders in October–November 1990 and find small positive returns. However, they state: "the order pairs likely to be included in our performance measure are those associated with small positive returns. Thus our economic performance measure, by examining only order pairs with exactly one order filing, is likely to differ from the negative performance of Harris and Hasbrouck (1996) and SEC (1997) that include all filled orders" (ibid., note 16, p. 178).

(excluding the 1987 market crash months, which only slightly affects the numbers) ($IT_{Nsb}$). The difference, ($IT_{Nsp} - IT_{Nsb}$), is the increase or decrease over the base. To account for changes due to other factors that occurred in the same period, we next subtract the comparable NYSE change ($IT_{Ysp} - IT_{Ysb}$). Thus, $NIT_{Nsp} = IT_{Nsp} - IT_{Nsb} - (IT_{Ysp} - IT_{Ysb})$. Panel C of table 16.1 presents these differences.

The net informed-trade basis points include trades by both SOES day traders and other traders of 1,000 shares and, at times, 500 and 100 shares. We estimated the net informed-trade basis points on SOES day trades for each mandatory-SOES period by noting that the amounts that we calculate ($NIT_{Nsp}$) are weighted averages of SOES day trades ($NIT_{DT}$) and other informed trades ($NIT_O$), where $P_{DT}$ equals the percentage of the dollar volume of day trades to the dollar volume of total trades of the same share size:

$$NIT_{Nsp} = NIT_{DT} * P_{DT} + NIT_O * (1 - P_{DT}), \text{ or} \qquad (16.1)$$

$$NIT_{DT} = 1/P_{DT} * (NIT_{Nsp} - NIT_O) + NIT_O. \qquad (16.1a)$$

For 1,000-share trades we determined $P_{DT}$ by deducting the percentage of 1,000-share trades in the "Pre-mandatory-SOES" period from the percentage in each subsequent period (shown in the second column from the right in panel A of table 16.1 labeled "1,000 sh. % of all <= 1,000") and dividing the difference by that percentage to obtain an estimate of the percentage increase due to SOES day trading. $P_{DT}$, thus calculated, is 23.6 percent in the "Adjustment" period, 33.3 percent in the "Mature Mandatory SOES" period, 21.7 percent in the "500-share Maximum" period, 39.0 percent in the "1,000 Shares × 2" period, 32.1 percent in the "Order Handling Rules" period, and 6.5 percent in the "100-share Maximum" period. These percentages tend to overestimate the proportion of SOES day trading to the extent that some of the proportional increase was in other 1,000-share trades. In particular, it might seem strange that when the maximum SOES trade size was reduced to 500 shares, the percentage of 1,000-share trades declined by 9.1 percentage points to 52 percent rather than to 41 percent, the percentage before SOES was made mandatory. As described earlier (discussion of figure 16.3), the bandits could effect 1,000-share trades through venues other than SOES (e.g., SelectNet and telephone). Note, though, that lower $P_{DT}$ would result in higher day-trade informed-trade losses. $IT_O$ is assumed to be equal to the NYSE-adjusted change on 1–5K-share trades of the same stocks. (Since $NIT_{Nsp}$ is given, lower assumed values for $NIT_O$ would yield higher values of $NIT_{DT}$.) Our calculation of informed-trade losses on day trades ($NIT_{DT}$) is shown in panel C of table 16.1. These average informed-trade losses (which tend to be understated) range over the periods between 15 and 24 basis points and average 21 basis points over the 77 active-SOES months, 8/90–12/96 (20 basis points if the "Adjustment" period was included).

For 500-share trades, when this was the maximum SOES trade size (2/94–3/95), the dollar volume of 500-share trades to the total dollar volume of trades of 1,000 shares or less increased by 10.4 percentage points (from 19.1 to 29.6 percent of the total), apparently due to SOES day trading. Thus, assuming that just previously there were no 500-share day trades, during the "500-share Maximum" period $P_{DT}$ equals 54.5 percent. During this period, informed-trade losses on 500-share trades increased by nine basis points, from a positive three to negative six basis points. We assumed that $NIT_O$ is the same as the basis points in the previous period plus the NYSE-adjusted (negative) change in 101–499-share trades from its previous period basis points, from which we calculated average informed trade losses of 16 basis points. During this period we also calculate average informed-trade losses for 1,000-share trades of 26 basis points, which is consistent with some day traders having shifted to SelectNet and telephone orders, as discussed earlier.

We used the same procedure to calculate informed-trade losses to SOES day traders who use 100-share trades in the "100-share Maximum" period. We calculated that $P_{DT}$ is 116.2 percent. For $NIT_O$ we use the previous period amount, 3 basis points plus the NYSE-adjusted (negative) change in 101–499-share trades, from which we calculated informed-trade losses ($NIT_{DT}$) of 14 basis points.

Market makers, though, obtained additional informed-trade gains from trades of 100, 101–499, and 500 shares (except when this was the maximum SOES size). We suggest that these gains are associated with SOES day trading, because they are due to market makers' efforts to reduce informed-trade losses by updating quotes more rapidly, in part by having traders follow fewer stocks. We next measure the extent to which market makers acted to offset these increases in informed-trade and other related trading costs (e.g., labor and equipment expense), thereby increasing effective spreads.[24]

## V. The Effect of SOES Day Trades on Relative Effective Spreads

### Measurement of RES

As noted earlier, market makers might react to higher informed-trade costs imposed by SOES day traders by increasing selling prices and decreasing buying prices for stock. We analyze the extent to which this occurred with relative effective spreads (RES). The effect on RES of the number of shares traded is accounted for by grouping the data into the six trade-size groups analyzed earlier. Within each trade size group, the RES for each stock for each trading day are averages of the

---

24. We acknowledge the following limitations of the above analysis: (1) misclassification of buys and sells by the Lee-Ready algorithm and (2) the increasing posting of limit orders on Instinet (and later their competitors) by buy-side traders attracted to earning the widened spread with patient trading. Both factors will, to a degree, distort this analysis.

RES on each trade; for the trade sizes that include a range (e.g., 101–499 shares), we weight the transactions by the number of shares traded. The observations are "stock-days." The monthly data for NASDAQ stocks are presented in figure 16.4. RES on NYSE stocks are similar among the six trade sizes, with RES on 1,000-share trades about eight basis points lower through 1991, after which the difference gradually declines to about three basis points, as shown in table 16.2, panel B. Over the 13 years studied, the NYSE RES follow the pattern shown in figure 16.1.

### RES by Size of Trade

Figure 16.4 and table 16.2 extend and confirm the analysis of RES shown in figure 16.1 by trade size. We estimated the effect of SOES day trading on NASDAQ RES with the same procedure used for informed trades, as described in section IV. That is, we calculated the additional RES in the post-mandatory SOES periods by subtracting from the RES in each period the RES in the pre-mandatory SOES base period adjusted for the comparable NYSE change in RES, and then calculated the RES due to SOES day trades with equation (16.1a), where RES is substituted for informed trades (IT).

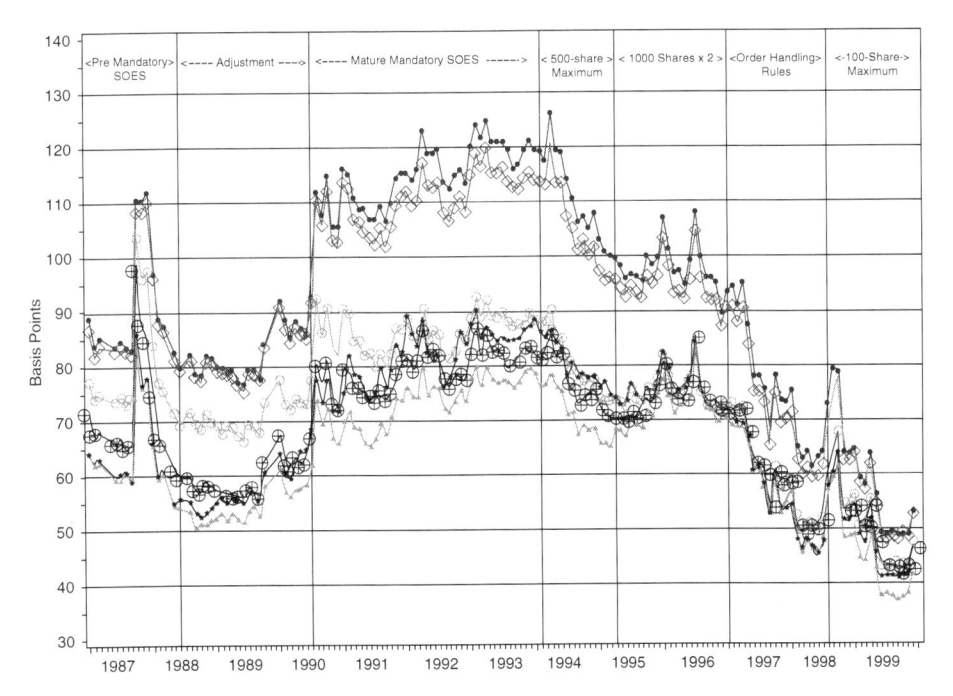

FIGURE 16.4 Relative Effective Spreads (RES) by Trade Size 100 Share Trades = (●), 101–499 = (◊), 500 = (★), 501–999 = (○), 1,000 = (▲), 1–5K = (⊕)

TABLE 16.2 Relative Effective Spreads (RES), Transactions on NASDAQ and the NYSE by size of trade averaged over pre- and post-mandatory SOES periods, January 1987–December 1999

| Periods | No. Months | SOES-Eligible Trade Sizes (Number of Shares per Trade) ||||||| SOES ineligible 1–5 K |
| | | 100 | 101–499 | 500 | 501–999 | 1,000 | |
|---|---|---|---|---|---|---|---|
| *A. NASDAQ* | | | | | | | |
| Pre-mandatory SOES (1/87–5/88) | 10** | 86 | 85 | 61 | 76 | 61 | 68 |
| Adjustment (8/88–7/90) | 22 | 82 | 82 | 58 | 71 | 55 | 60 |
| Mature Mandatory SOES (8/90–1/94) | 42 | 115 | 111 | 82 | 86 | 74 | 79 |
| 500-share Maximum (2/94–3/95) | 14 | 111 | 106 | 80 | 80 | 71 | 77 |
| 1,000 shares × 2 (4/95–12/96) | 21 | 98 | 95 | 76 | 75 | 72 | 74 |
| Order Handling Rules (1/97–7/98) | 19 | 76 | 73 | 57 | 60 | 57 | 60 |
| 100-share Maximum (8/98–12/99) | 17 | 59 | 58 | 49 | 52 | 46 | 51 |
| Average 7/90–12/96 (note 1) | 77 | 110 | 105 | 80 | 82 | 73 | 78 |
| *B. NYSE* | | | | | | | |
| Pre-mandatory SOES (1/87–5/88) | 10** | 39 | 40 | 41 | 40 | 31 | 40 |
| Adjustment (8/88–7/90) | 22 | 36 | 36 | 36 | 34 | 27 | 32 |
| Mature Mandatory SOES (8/90–1/94) | 42 | 37 | 37 | 37 | 36 | 30 | 36 |
| 500-share Maximum (2/94–3/95) | 14 | 33 | 34 | 34 | 33 | 28 | 35 |
| 1,000 shares × 2 (4/95–12/96) | 21 | 29 | 30 | 30 | 30 | 26 | 32 |
| Order Handling Rules (1/97–7/98) | 19 | 23 | 24 | 24 | 24 | 21 | 26 |
| 100-share Maximum (8/98–12/99) | 17 | 24 | 25 | 26 | 26 | 23 | 30 |
| Average 7/90–12/96 (note 1) | 77 | 34 | 34 | 35 | 34 | 28 | 35 |

C. NASDAQ less adjusted NYSE (NASDAQ less NYSE in the "Pre-Mandatory SOES" period)

| | | | | | | | |
|---|---|---|---|---|---|---|---|
| Pre-mandatory SOES: NASDAQ less NYSE | 10** | 47 | 45 | 20 | 35 | 29 | 27 |
| Adjustment (8/88–7/90) | 22 | (1) | 1 | 2 | 2 | (1) | (7) | 1 |
| Mature Mandatory SOES (8/90–1/94) | 42 | 31 | 29 | 24 | 15 | 15 | 13 | 16 |
| 500-share Maximum (2/94–3/95) | 14 | 31 | 27 | 26 | 12 | 14 | 10 | 15 |
| 500-share day trades | | | | | | | 28 | |
| 1,000 shares × 2 (4/95–12/96) | 21 | 22 | 20 | 25 | 10 | 17 | 20 | 15 |
| Order Handling Rules (1/97–7/98) | 19 | 6 | 4 | 13 | 1 | 7 | 8 | 6 |
| 100-share Maximum (8/98–12/99) | 17 | (12) | (12) | 3 | (9) | (7) | | (6) |
| 100-share day trades | | | | | | | (10) | |
| Average 7/90–12/96 (note 1) | 77 | 29 | 26 | 25 | 13 | 15 | 14 | 15 |

This table shows the RES accruing to market makers from SOES day traders and others, grouped according to trade size. For each transaction the RES are calculated as twice the absolute difference between the transaction price and the midpoint of the best bid and offer (BBO), divided by the midpoint price, in basis points, and are aggregated daily for each stock. The observations (stock days) are averaged over months, which are averaged over periods that describe stages in SOES history. Panels A and B show the RES on NASDAQ and NYSE trades. Panel C presents, for each period during which SOES was mandatory and trade size, the RES on NASDAQ stocks less the adjusted RES on NYSE stocks (RES plus the difference between the NASDAQ and NYSE RES in the "Pre-mandatory SOES" period). Panel C provides an estimate of the additional changes in RES associated with SOES, using equation (16.1a) as described in the text and in table 16.1.

All means are statistically significantly different from zero at least at the .01 level, except panel C. Adjustment: 100, 101–499, 500 (5 percent level), 1,000 (9 percent level), 1–5K. Order Handling Rules: 101–499 (5 percent level), 501–999. 100-share Maximum: 500.

*Data for 4/87, 5/87, 8/87, 4/88, 7/88, 11/89, and 12/89 are not available.

**Excluding the 1987 market crash months of October, November, and December.

Note 1: Weighted by number of months; in panel B, excludes 500- and 100-share day trades listed with 100-share trades.

In the "Pre-mandatory SOES" period RES are ordered by trade size with the exception of 500- and 1,000-share trades, which have the lowest RES. This lends credence to the NASD's assertion that some stale quotes were being picked off before SOES became mandatory. In the "Mature Mandatory SOES" period we see the dramatic increase in 100 and 101–499 RES accompanied by substantial increases in the other trade sizes. As SOES day trading increased through mid-1990 (see figure 16.2), market makers increased their quoted offers and decreased their quoted bids, thereby increasing RES on shares traded at the quote, apparently to compensate for the informed trade losses and trading costs imposed by SOES day traders.

We ascribe the negative RES calculated for the "100-share Maximum" period primarily to the Order Handling Rules that became effective during 1997. The switch from 1/8th to 1/16th tick size in July 1997, accompanied by the elimination of the Excess Spread Rule, also contributed to the decline in RES.

Note that RES on 1,000-share trades did not increase as did RES on the smaller trade sizes, despite the higher informed trade and operating costs imposed on NASDAQ market makers. We believe this is due to two factors. One is that SOES day traders were able to obtain shares at quoted prices before the market makers could change the quotes, which is their essential strategy; this reduced their RES. The other factor is that they could bargain for prices within the quotes when laying off their inventory, similar to negotiations effect by other traders in large numbers of shares, as is shown next.

## Trading inside the Spread

In the "Pre-mandatory SOES" period the percentage of trading inside the spread on NASDAQ was under 5 percent with a brief exception during the crash period (see figure 16.5). Apparently traders were for the most part satisfied with trading at the spread. Then in mid-1989 the widening of spreads was accompanied by a rapid increase in trading inside the spread, ordered by trade size. We ascribe this change as due to market makers giving preferential pricing to known institutional customers that were not SOESing them.

The percentage of larger-size (1K and 1–5K) trades inside the BBO increased, as shown in figure 16.5, from about 5 percent in mid-1989 to 22 and 27 percent in early 1994. Over this period, the percentages also increased for smaller trade sizes. These increases explain the approximate stability of RES through about March 1996 for trades of 500 shares and larger, and through March 1994 for trades under 500 shares, and the subsequent declines in RES through 1998. In the 77-month active SOES period, 7/90–12/96, NASDAQ RES averaged 77 and 110 basis points for 100- and 101–499-share trades, and between 73 and 80 basis points for the other trade sizes. In contrast, over this period, NYSE RES averaged 28 basis points for 1,000-share trades and 34–35 basis points for the other trade sizes. The percentage

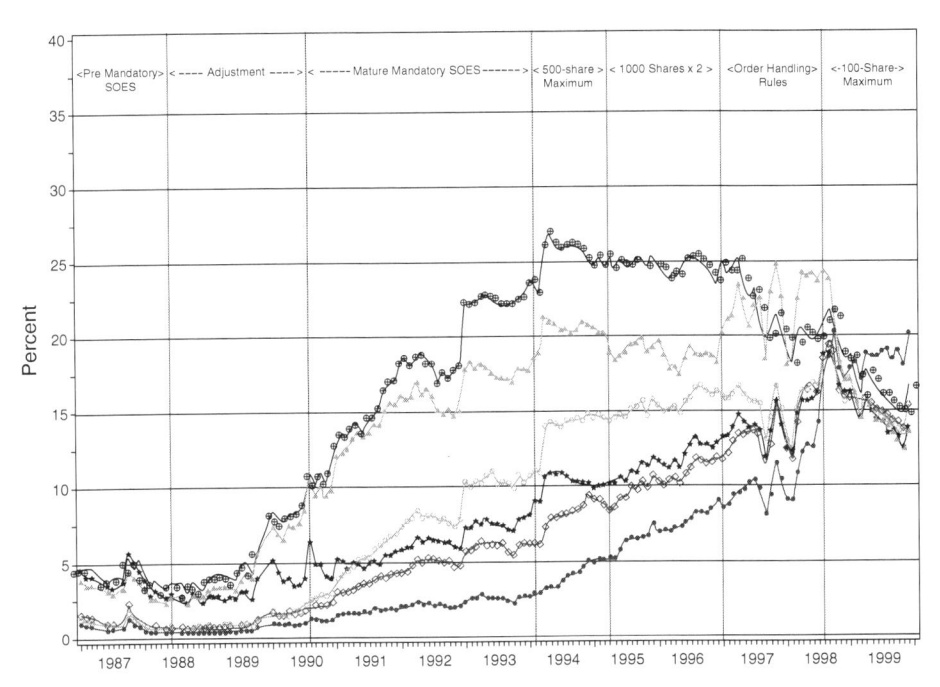

FIGURE 16.5 Percentage of NASDAQ Dollar Volume Traded Inside the BBO by Trade Size
100 Share Trades = (●), 101–499 = (◇), 500 = (★), 501–999 = (○), 1000 = (▲),
1–5K = (⊗)

of NASDAQ trades inside the BBO, though, continued to increase only for trades of 500 and fewer shares. By year-end 1999, NASDAQ RES were both lower and closer to each other than before SOES was made mandatory, and the percentages traded inside the BBO were similar at about 15 percent. A notable exception is the increase in the percentage of 100-share trades inside the BBO after this became the maximum SOES trade size.

In June 1989 Instinet became anonymous. Then dealers who wished to display their customers' limit orders could do so without being subject to the one-fourth unwritten quote-change rule and without being SOESed. Hence, two markets developed—NASDAQ Level II and Instinet (and other ECNs as they developed). Increasingly institutional trading migrated to ECNs, as reflected in the widening gap between 100–499-share RES and the remainder. Since access to ECNs was by invitation only, retail business and SOES dealers (for the most part) were excluded from ECNs. Hence, both spreads and prices were much more favorable on Instinet. Consequently its volume soared and competition was attracted with the formation of additional ECNs. Thus all of our metrics are increasingly skewed by ECN trading, which we are unable to distinguish from NASDAQ dealer trading.

## The Extent to Which Estimated Costs Imposed by Day Traders Explain the Increase in NASDAQ over NYSE RES

As shown in figure 16.3 and table 16.1, we estimate that SOES day traders imposed costs on market makers. These additional costs, taken alone, only partially explain the higher RES shown in figure 16.1, since we estimate that SOES day trades comprise less than a quarter of the volume of trades of 1,000 shares or less (see table 16.1 panel 3). However, the opportunity cost of "informed" day trades is only part of the cost imposed on market makers by day traders. Faced with having to offer day traders a free option to take out or sell up to 5,000 shares at a quoted price before it could be changed, market makers reduced the number of companies each trader followed and invested in equipment that provide earlier warnings of interests in stocks followed. It also may be that market makers took advantage of their jointly experienced SOES day trades and increased selling prices and decreased buying prices more than necessary to offset costs imposed by day traders. Or, we may have underestimated the informed trade costs imposed by day traders.

Of course, some other factor not studied here or elsewhere may have played a role. As noted above, the possibilities suggested by other researchers are implicit collusion, preferencing, and payment for order flow. As also noted above, preferencing and payment for order flow do not fit the data pattern as there were no corresponding changes in these practices. If collusion were the prime mover, why were so many large traders permitted to trade inside the widened spreads? Consequently, we believe that the most likely cause of the dramatic increase in trading inside the spread coincident with mandatory SOES is pressure from SOES bandits which widened spreads, but trading inside the spread which was granted to known institutional traders.[25] The analysis of changes in the percentage of stocks quoted on even-eighths over the period studied, presented next, provides additional support for this explanation.

## VI. Comparison with the Percentage of Even-Eighths

We examined the extent to which changes in SOES day trading and even-eighths quotations track changes in the difference in NASDAQ and NYSE RES over the 13 years studied in figure 16.6. For SOES day trades we used the volume of trades at the SOES maximum size to total trades of 1,000 shares or less (denoted by triangles). We followed the Christie-Schultz (1994) rule for determining the percentage of even-eighths quotes. If 75 percent of the time-weighted BBOs in a month

---

25. Further, as previously noted many ECN trades would occur inside the NASDAQ Level II quote.

# EFFECTIVE SPREADS ON NASDAQ AND THE NYSE IN THE 1990S

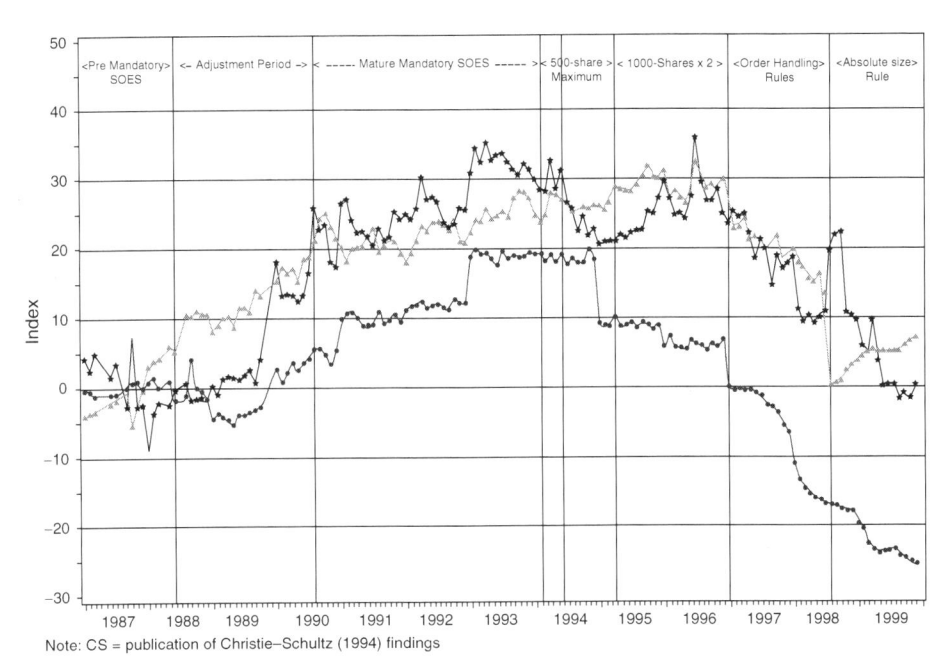

FIGURE 16.6 Differences in Relative Effective Spreads (RES) on NASDAQ and NYSE, Percentages of Volume at Maximum SOES Trade Size to Total Dollar Volume of 1000 Shares or Less, and Percentage of Stocks Quoted on Even Eighths, Monthly, 1987–99 All Normalized by Dividing by Averages over 1/87–6/88 NYSE–NASDAQ RES = (★), SOES Maximum = (▲), % Even Eighths = (●)

were both at even eighths, we classified the stock as "even-eighth."[26] Stocks quoted with an odd-sixteenth spread are less than 1 percent of the sample in all months prior to July 1997 and are but 4 percent in December 1997. However, in January 1998 this percentage is 13 percent, and it increases monotonically to 26 percent in December 1999.

To facilitate comparison, we normalized the data to equal about zero initially by dividing the monthly data by their averages over the "Pre-mandatory-SOES" period (1/87–6/88). For the even-eighths sample the average is 51.3; thus, before SOES was made mandatory, half the actively traded stocks on NASDAQ were quoted on even eighths. If "avoidance" of odd-eighths quotes by market makers were a valid measure of collusion, it would appear that there was no collusion on NASDAQ before mid-1988.

---

26. We also computed the even-eighth percentages by restricting the sample to stocks with at least 10 trades a day in 10 days of a month. This restriction increases the percentage of even-eighth quoted stocks by about two percentage points.

Figure 16.6 shows a fairly close movement of all three series through 1994, with some important differences. The correlation coefficients of the RES Difference are 83 percent for the SOES Maximum Percentage and 65 percent for the Percentage Even Eighths. The SOES Maximum Percentage leads RES during the "Adjustment Period," while Percentage Even Eighths lags RES during this period and through most of the "Mature mandatory SOES" period. Interestingly, the percentage of even-eighths stocks increases through December 1992 and then plateaus through December 1994, before decreasing. Thus, there is almost no change in the percentage after publication of the Christie-Schultz findings on May 26, 1994.[27] Thereafter, the SOES Maximum Percentage tracks the RES very closely, with the exception of the "Actual Size Rule" period. (With these data from this period excluded, the correlation coefficient increases to 86 percent.) This appears to result from our having to assume that in the previous "Order Handling Rules" period the SOES maximum trade size was 1,000 shares for all stocks and the quoted depth then dropped to 100 shares, even though the decline in the SOES maximum was gradual. In contrast, after 1994 the percentage of even-eighths stocks declines much more than the RES. One reason for the decline is that we included only even-eighth-quoted stocks as "evens," although with the adoption of sixteenths in 1997 one might consider a two-sixteenth-quoted stock an even.

It appears that, in response to the informed-trade costs imposed by SOES day traders, NASDAQ market makers tended to round up or down their offers and bids, apparently to even numbers. As a result, the percentage of stocks quoted on even eighths increased. As market makers gained more experience with day trades and monitored stocks more closely by following fewer issues, they were able to be selective and more precise, particularly with respect to stocks for which there was much competition. Consequently, we believe, the percentage of even-eighths-quoted stocks declined, but relative effective spreads did not decline until SOES was effectively phased out.

## VII. Robustness Checks

In order to test the robustness of our findings we conduct several further tests. While our sample generation procedure creates the largest possible sample size of both NASDAQ and NYSE stocks, individual stocks may drop in and out of the sample set month by month. Furthermore our adjustment of the NYSE RES to match that of NASDAQ during the base period may not adequate control for difference in NYSE and NASDAQ stocks over our entire test interval. To address these concerns we consider several different sample sets of portfolios and replicate our tests.

---

27. We examined the even-eighth percentage of a subsample of stocks that bridged 1994 and 1995 and found a similar sharp decrease from December 1994 to January 1995.

First, we form matched pairs of NASDAQ and NYSE stocks in each of our sample months using four Euclidean distance measures:

$$D_{i,j,k} = \frac{(Q_{i,j} - Y_{i,k})^2}{(Q_{i,j} + Y_{i,k})/2},$$

where $D_{i,j,k}$ measures the Euclidian distance between NASDAQ stock $Q_j$ and NYSE stock $Y_k$ for $i$ = price, share volume traded, volatility, and market cap. Then each of the four distance measures are normalized by subtracting their median value and dividing by their interquartile range (assuming that we have contaminated and nonnormal distributions) within each month. These metrics are then combined into an aggregate distance measure by

$$\overline{D}_{j,k} = (2*D_{1,j,k} + D_{2,j,k} + D_{3,j,k} + D_{4,j,k})/4,$$

with a double weight given to the price distance, since McInish and Wood (1992) find that price is the most important spread determinant. The optimal combination of matched pairs that minimize the aggregate Euclidian distance within each sample month is found with the following linear programming model.

Minimize

$$\sum_j \sum_k f_{j,k} \overline{D}_{j,k}, j = 1,\ldots, \text{NASDAQ stocks}, k = 1,\ldots, \text{NYSE stocks}$$

subject to

$$\sum_k f_{j,k} \leq 1 \pm \Delta, k = 1,\ldots, \text{NYSE stocks},$$

$$\sum_j f_{j,k} \leq 1 \pm \Delta, j = 1,\ldots, \text{NASDAQ stocks},$$

$$\sum_j f_{j,k} \geq 0.30*(\{\#\text{NASDAQSTOCKS}\}) \pm \Delta,$$

where $f_{jk}$ is the LP solution variable that will have a value of 1 if the $j$th NASDAQ stock is paired with the $k$th NYSE stock and 0 otherwise.[28] The $\Delta$ has a value of 0.1 percent of each of the right-hand-side values, which allows the LP to attain feasibility. The first two constraints limit each NYSE and NASDAQ stock to entering at most once in the solution, while the third constraint forces 30 percent of the NASDAQ stocks into the solution—a level selected to generate a sufficiently large sample with the best possible matches between NASDAQ and NYSE stocks.[29] The advantage of forming matched pairs in this manner is that

---

28. The solution values, which are bounded between 0 and 1, will naturally gravitate to 0 or 1 since this LP is an assignment problem. The few positive solution values that are less than one are rounded to 0 or 1.

29. As more matches are required of the LP, the quality of each successive match will deteriorate.

all possible combinations are examined simultaneously in deriving the optimal set of matched pairs.

Figure 16.1 recast with these matched pairs using trades with share volumes of 1,000 and less is shown in figure 16.7. As can be seen the result is quite similar to that shown in figure 16.1.

We also calculated and graphed RES using observations with at least 10 trades a day (based on the possibility that day traders concentrated on actively traded stocks), medians instead of means, only stocks that traded throughout the period (202 on NASDAQ and 627 on the NYSE), only trades of 1,000 shares or less, 2,000 shares or less, and so on by thousands through 5,000 shares or less, and finally all shares traded. In each case patterns quite similar to figure 16.1 result.[30]

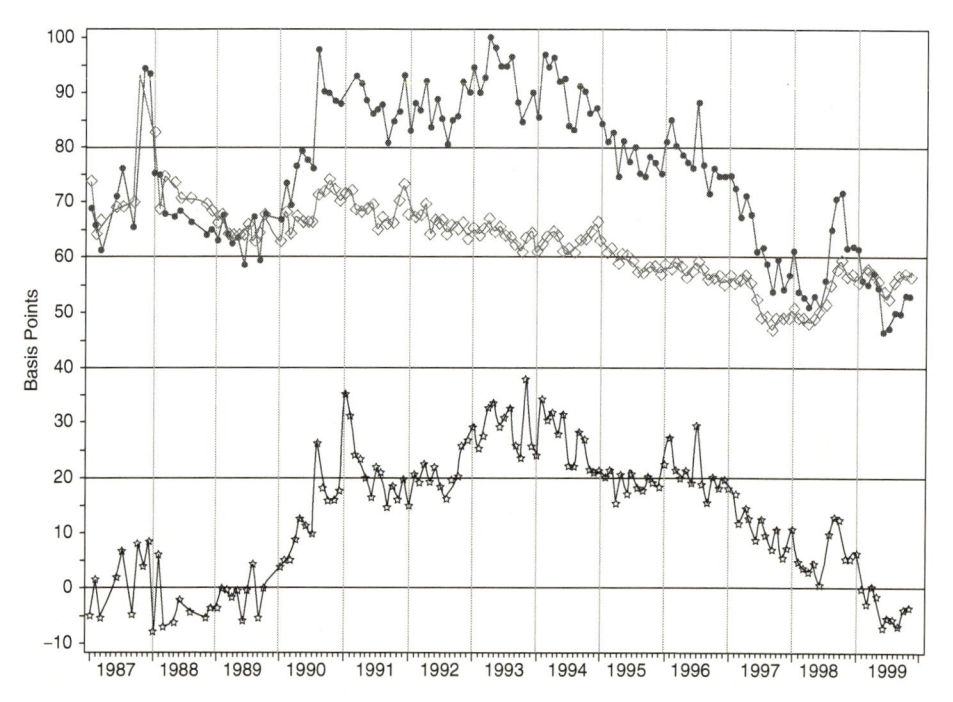

FIGURE 16.7 NASDAQ and NYSE RES for All Trades 1000 Shares and Less, 1987–99, 30% NASDAQ Match with NYSE NASDAQ RES = (●), NYSE RES + 20.82 Basis Points = (◊), Adjusted NASDAQ Less NYSE RES = (☆)

30. These results will be provided upon request.

## VIII. Conclusions

We find a remarkable pattern of RES on NASDAQ compared to NYSE stocks. From January through August 1989, RES on NASDAQ (plus 18.4 basis points) and the NYSE moved in very close concert. The difference then increased through the mid-1990s, and then decreased, until by year-end 1999 it returned to its pre-August 1987 level. We consider the two hypotheses that were advanced to explain this phenomenon, at least through 1994—"collusion" among NASDAQ market makers to widen spreads and "preferencing and payment for order flow," which reduces competition, thereby widening spreads. Evidence is presented that is inconsistent with these hypotheses. We posit an alternative hypothesis that SOES day trading on NASDAQ was at least an important cause of the divergence in NASDAQ/NYSE trading costs. This hypothesis is subjected to five tests: the introduction of mandated SOES in June 1988, the change in the SOES maximum trade size from 1,000 to 500 shares in January 1994 and then back again in March 1995, and the gradual and then the complete reduction of the SOES maximum trade size to 100 shares after 1996. From the changes in volume of these and other trade sizes, we compute increases in informed trade costs incurred by NASDAQ market that appear due to SOES day traders and the changes in trades within the BBO quotes and relative effective spreads that we believe resulted therefrom. These findings are contrasted with similar measurements of stocks traded on the NYSE, which did not have a mandatory SOES. The tests provide results that are consistent with the hypothesis that day trading, primarily through NASDAQ's mandatory SOES, was largely responsible for the higher NASDAQ spreads. We also find that the SOES system that was designed to benefit small traders actually hurt them, as they bore the brunt of the higher spreads.

Prior empirical studies employ from one month to one year of data. Of necessity such studies must assume an immediate correlation between SOES bandit trading and spreads, which presumes that market makers can anticipate such trading and adjust spreads accordingly. Our discussions with practitioners reveal that market makers could not anticipate such events. Furthermore, SOES banditry began slowly with the onset of mandatory SOES and continued through most of the 1990s, being mitigated with the Order Handling Rules that began with a phased introduction in June 1997, and the subsequent Absolute Size Rule. Thus, in our view only a sample window that covers the entire time period can capture the impact of SOES banditry.

Given the differences between NASDAQ and the NYSE—stock characteristics, market mechanisms, institutions trading net on NASDAQ and with commissions on the NYSE—we gross up NYSE RES to match those of the NASDAQ sample in our base period, January 1987–May 1988. Then we maintain the same scaling factor for the remaining 9.5 years. A series of changes—some affecting just one market while others affect both—weaken this relationship over time. These include the rapid growth of ECNs on NASDAQ (which resulted from the pressure from SOES banditry), the tick size reduction to teenies in 1997, rule changes on both markets, and the impact of the DOJ NASD prosecution. Yet we take comfort from robustness checks and the convergence of NASDAQ and NYSE RES in 1999 after the introduction of NASDAQ rule changes implemented to mitigate the influences of the bandits.

The blue-ribbon committee that recommend automatic execution of trades submitted over the SOES electronic network included senior market makers who had grown up in the dealer environment and who had little comprehension of the potential impact of electronic trading on this environment. They (and the SEC) failed to recognize the impact on dealer costs of traders being able to pick off stale quotes electronically with automatic executions. This failure spawned an enormous growth in SOES day traders who ultimately executed 20 percent of NASDAQ trades and who greatly increased NASDAQ trading costs over a decade. Furthermore, institutional traders, as well as market makers seeking to avoid interacting with day traders, fueled the growth of ECNs—SOES day traders did not have access to ECNs. Thus, mandatory SOES executions not only affected spreads on NASDAQ in the 1990s, but continue to play out today, as ECNs have come to dominate trading in NASDAQ stocks. An important lesson from the SOES "experiment" is that traders can and will take advantage of a system that offers them the opportunity to profit from its weaknesses.

While we have focused primarily on the impact of SOES bandits on widened spreads and the resultant increased cost of trading, it is worth noting that a substantial cost was imposed on pension and mutual fund holders through front running institutional order flow. Specifically, bandits would identify the onset of institutional buy/selling, acquire existing liquidity and offer it back at worse prices, thereby increasing costs of the money funds. Hence the irony of mandatory SOES is that it not only hurt the intended beneficiaries, small investors (as shown in figure 16.3), but fund holders also paid a dear price.

## REFERENCES

Barclay, Michael J., 1997. Bid-ask spreads and the avoidance of odd-eighth quotes on NASDAQ: an examination of exchange listings. *Journal of Financial Economics* 45, 35–60.

Barclay, Michael J., Christie, William G., Harris, Jeffrey H., Kandel, Eugene, Schultz, Paul H., 1999. The costs of trading NASDAQ issues: the impact of limit orders and ECN quotes. *Journal of Finance* 54, 1–34.

Barclay, Michael J., Hendershott, Terrance, 2004. Liquidity externalities and adverse selection: evidence from trading after hours. *Journal of Finance* 59, 681–710.

Battalio, Robert, Greene, Jason, Hatch, Brian, Jennings, Robert, 2002. Does the limit order routing decision matter? *Review of Financial Studies* 15, 159–94.

Battalio, Robert H., Hatch, Brian, Jennings, Robert, 1997. SOES trading and market volatility. *Journal of Financial and Quantitative Analysis* 32, 225–38.

Benston, George J., 2007. Did NASDAQ market makers successfully collude to increase spreads? A reexamination of evidence from stocks that move from NASDAQ to the New York or American stock exchanges. Financial Markets Group, London School of Economics, Special Paper 170, January, at http://fmg.lse.ac.uk or SSRN.

Bessembinder, Hendrik, Kaufman, Herbert M., 1997. A comparison of trade execution costs for NYSE and NASDAQ-listed stocks. *Journal of Financial and Quantitative Analysis* 32, 287–310.

Byrne, John A., 1997. The power and politics of SOES. *Traders Magazine*, April.

Chan, K.C., Lakonishok, C.L., 1997. Institutional equity trading costs: NYSE versus NASDAQ. *Journal of Finance* 713–35.

Christie, William G., Harris, Jeffrey H., Schultz, Paul H., 1994. Why did NASDAQ market makers stop avoiding odd-eighths quotes? *Journal of Finance* 49, 1841–60.

Christie, William G., Huang, Roger D., 1993. Market structures and liquidity: a transactions data study of exchange listings. *Journal of Financial Intermediation* 3, 300–326.

Christie, William G., Schultz, Paul S., 1994. Why do NASDAQ market makers avoid odd-eighths quotes? *Journal of Finance* 49, 1813–40.

Christie, William G., Schultz, Paul S., 1995. Did NASDAQ market makers implicitly collude? *Journal of Economic Perspectives* 9, 199–208.

Copeland, Thomas E., Galai, Dan, 1983. Information effects on the bid-ask spread. *Journal of Finance* 38, 1457–69.

Department of Justice (DOJ), 1996. Competition impact statement, *United States of America, Plaintiff v. 25 named NASD securities firms* (Mays Gorey Jr. Attorney for Plaintiff United States of America), July 17.

Dutta, Prajit K., Madhaven, Ananth, 1997. Competition and collusion in dealer markets. *Journal of Finance* 52, 245–76.

Ellis, Katrina, Michaely, Roni, O'Hara, Maurine, 2000. The accuracy of trade classification rules: evidence from NASDAQ. *Journal of Financial and Quantitative Analysis* 35, 529–51.

Foucault, Thierry, Röell, Ailsa, Sandås, Patrik, 2003. Market making with costly monitoring: an analysis of the SOES controversy. *Review of Financial Studies* 16, 345–84.

Glosten, Lawrence R., Milgrom, Paul R., 1985. Bid, ask and transaction prices in a specialist market with heterogeneously informed traders. *Journal of Financial Economics* 14, 71–100.

Godek, Paul E., 1996. Why NASDAQ market makers avoid odd-eighths quotes. *Journal of Financial Economics* 41, 465–74.

Grossman, Sanford J., Miller, Merton H., Fischel, Daniel R., Cone, Kenneth R., Ross, David J., 1997. Clustering and competition in asset markets. *Journal of Law and Economics* 40, 23–60.

Harris, Jeffrey H., Schultz, Paul M., 1997. The importance of firm quotes and rapid executions: evidence from the January 1994 SOES rules change. *Journal of Financial Economics* 45, 135–66.

Harris, Jeffrey H., Schultz, Paul M., 1998. The trading profits of SOES bandits. *Journal of Financial Economics* 50, 39–62.

Harris, Lawrence, Hasbrouck, Joel, 1996. Market vs. limit orders: the SuperDOT evidence on order submission strategy. *Journal of Financial and Quantitative Analysis* 31, 213.

Houtkin, Harvey, 1995. *The SOES Bandit's Guide: Day Trading in the 21st Century.*

Huang, Roger, Stoll, Hans, 1996. Dealer versus auction markets: a paired comparison of execution on NASDAQ and the NYSE. *Journal of Financial Economics* 41, 313–57.

Kandel, Eugene, Marx, Leslie M., 1999. Payment for order flow on NASDAQ. *Journal of Finance* 54, 35–66.

Keim, Donald B., Madhavan, Ananth, 1997. Transactions costs and investment style: an inter-exchange analysis of institutional equity trades. *Journal of Financial Economics* 46, 265–92.

Kothare, Meeta, Laux, Paul A., 1995. Trading costs and the trading systems for NASDAQ stocks. *Financial Analysts Journal* 42–53 (March–April).

Lee, Charles, Ready, Mark, 1991. Inferring trade direction from intraday data. *Journal of Finance* 46, 733–46.

Lin, Ji-Chai, Sanger, Gary, Booth, G. Geoffrey, 1995. Trade size and components of the bid-ask spread. *Review of Financial Studies* 8, 1153–83.

McInish, Thomas, Wood, Robert, 1992. An analysis of intraday pattern in bid/ask spreads for NYSE stocks. *Journal of Finance* 47, 753–64.

Securities and Exchange Commission, 1996. Report pursuant to section 21(a) of the Securities Exchange Act of 1934 regarding the NASD and the NASDAQ Market.

Weston, James P., 2000. Competition on the NASDAQ and the impact of recent market reforms. *Journal of Finance* 55, 2565–98.

Wood, Robert A., McInnish, Thomas H., 1992. An analysis of intraday pattern in bid/ask spreads for NYSE stocks. *Journal of Finance* 47, 753–64.

# *Index*

Note: Page numbers followed by *f* and *t* denote figures and tables, respectively.

Ability to borrow
   primary reason for original borrowing, 297*t*
   survey on individuals, 296–98
Accounting data, 28, 35, 36
   and expectations of, 30–33
   and stock prices, 26
Accounting disclosure requirements, SEC
   corporate financial statements, content of, 179
   data on usefulness of, 179
   disclosure on securities market, 177–84
   goals of, 167, 172
   investors of financial statements, 172–77
   justification of Securities Act, 167–68
   semiannual financial reports, forms, 172
   value of, examination, 165
Accounting for derivative instruments, and hedging activities, 219
Accounting for derivative, problems of, 199–200
Accounting profession, impact of SEC, 184
   accounting practices and principles, 186–87
   auditing practices, changes in, 185
   independence, 185–86
   public accountants, independence of, 185–86

Accounting requirements, impact on firm's behavior, 195
Accounting Series Release (ASR)
   codification of, 99
   cost specification, 101
   disclosure philosophy, 67–68, 188
   firms' asses, replacement value of, 203
Accounting standards
   contents and format of, 222–28
   issue on format in, 218
   major driver of complexity in, 222
   need for true-and-fair override in, 229
   traditional revenue/expense model, 227–28
Accounting statements, information disclosure
   economic situation of corporations, reflection on, 77
   financial variables, definition of, 75
   information content of, 73–77
   investors' expectations, impact on, 74
   models used for reporting, 74
   returns to sophisticated users of, 77–78
   usefulness of, 77, 93
   value of, 93
Accounting to derivatives, application to
   advantages and disadvantages of, 210–12
   CPAs, role of, 212–13

Accounting to derivatives (*continued*)
  derivatives held as hedges, 209
  derivatives held for trading and investment, 208
  for derivatives risk, 213
Accruals, assets and liabilities valuations, 205
Active public regulatory agency
  adaptive, to specific disclosure, 103–5
  expertise and public interest orientation, 107–8
  improving the quality of data, 109
  less discriminatory in securities statutes, 106–7
  protecting investors and preventing fraudulence, 109–12
  SEC, advantages of, 103
  securities statutes and regulations, professional implementation of, 105–6
  uniformity in data disclosure, 108–9
Active stock trading, definition of, 373
Actual Size Rule, 382$n$14, 404
  impact on market makers, 382
  implementation stages of, 376
Adjustment for data for trades in NASDAQ, 394–96
Adjustment period, 379, 404
  percentage of 1,000-share trades in, 383
  SOES day trading, 379
Adoption by the United States Financial Reporting System of a Principles-Based Accounting System, 217
Agency theory, implications for, 367–68
AICPA Code of Professional Conduct, 216
  Auditing Standards Board of, 217$n$3
  Rule 203, fair representation in accounting, 216
All-inclusive net income, reported financial accounting data, 173
Alternative valuations of, 128$n$20
  and financial accounting statements, 130$t$
American Accounting Association (AAA), 222
  Financial Accounting Standards Committee, 222
American Council of Life Insurance (ACLI), 122

American Institute of Certified Accountants (AICPA), 99, 172, 192
  Code of Professional Conduct, 216, 217$n$3
Annual wealth changes, of average conglomerate Officer-director, 361$t$, 361–62$t$
Anticipated exposures, hedging, 197
Asset/liability accounting model, 218
  content and format of, 223–26
  fair value measurement in, 225
  measurement and recognition of revenue and expenses in, 223
  problems with, 224
Assets and liabilities exchange, valuation of, 205
Assets holding, 259
  motivation for, 259
  transaction cost, impact of, 262
Average (algebraic mean) residuals, 84
Average and marginal costs, loan serviced, 339–40, 341$t$, 341$n$44
Average monthly residuals in subperiods, 85$t$
Azurix, Enron subsidiary, 152

Balance sheet
  appraisals and goodwill, 186
  in asset/liability accounting model, 223
Balance sheet numbers, for accounting derivatives application, 210
Bankruptcy filing by borrowers
  data on, 301$t$
  reasons for, 300
Bankruptcy law usage, 313
Basic functions and rules, accounting
  conservatism and realization, 206–8
  control and valuation, 203–5
  income and expense recognition, 205–6
Bayesian approach, 21$n$26
Best bid and offer (BBO), trading, 373, 376, 378
  growth of larger size trading in, 400
Bid-asked price per share, determinants of, 246–48
Bid-asked spreads, determinants of, 245
Blue-ribbon committee, market markers, 379, 408
Blue sky legislation, 188

Brake-light effect, DOJ/SEC investigations, 376
Branch operations data, analysis of operations cost of loan, 328–29
Bright-line definition of control, accounting, 220, 225, 235, 237

Calculation of costs per loan serviced, 339–45, 348
Capital asset pricing model (CAPM), 250–51, 255, 260
Cash dividends, 26, 27
   adjustments of, 28–30
   and changes in stock prices, 173
Cash flow, reported financial accounting data, 173
Cash flow and fair-value-determined net income, of Enron
   prepays, 158
   sales to SPEs, 159
   share trusts, 159–60
Ceiling rates, reduction in, 292–94
Center for Research in Security Prices (CRSP), 35
Certified public accountants (CPA)
   documentation, need for, 213
   in financial information disclosure, 70
   and NYSE corporations, audit of, 68
   role of, 212
Changes in dividends, 28
Coefficients of
   location (SUBURB), 339
   new borrower, number of loans made (NLM), 337
Collection costs and losses, 36 month limitations, 291–92
Collusion hypothesis
   spreads on NASDAQ and NYSE, differences in, 375–76, 407
Commercial enterprises, private debt placements, 182
Committee on Accounting Procedures (CAP), AICPA, 232
Common stock investment versus direct placement investment breakdown of respondents, 123t
Common stock questionnaire, 122
Common stock price, 28

Communication industry, private debt placements, 182, 184
Compustat, 36, 39, 74, 75, 76
Concept-based standards, 222
Conglomerate mergers, 353
Conglomerates, share returns of, 365t
Conservatism, accounting concept, 206–7
Conservative accounting bias, SEC, 181
Consumer advocates, regulations on loans, 278
Consumer finance companies cost structure, rate ceiling implications of
   cost calculation of, 339–42
   cost function, estimation of, 329–35
   data on, 328–29
   economies of scale, 336–37
   location of, 339
   number of loans to number serviced, 338–39
   operating costs, analysis of, 325–26
   operating costs per dollar of loan, 345–46
   overhead, 342–45
   policy implications, 346–50
   sales finance contract, 338
   small loan cost function, 323–25
   type of borrower, 337
   type of loans, 337–38
Consumer finance company personal loans
   creditors' legal remedies, restrictions on, 313
   data analysis, 310
   data from finance companies, 306–10
   interest rate ceiling, 312–13
   legal restrictions on, 305, 312, 318
   loss rates with loan made, 315–18
   operating expenses, 314–15
   proclivity to repay, 313
   restrictions on entry, 310–12
   risks on, 304–5
   size of loans, 313–14
   theory of, 305–6
Consumer finance company, 283
Consumer welfare, detrimental effects of bankruptcy on, 300
Consumer's demands
   for financial commodities, transactions costs, 262–63

# INDEX

Consumer's demands (*continued*)
　intertemporal consumption, transactions costs, impact of, 260–61
Contents and format, accounting standards, 222–28
　asset/liability accounting model, 223–26
　revenue/expense approach, 226–28
　true-and-fair override, 228–31
Corporate financial disclosure
　public (U.S.) and private (U.K.) regulations, 97–98
Corporate financial disclosure, regulations of, 98–101
　application of U.K. Companies Act, 98–99, 99–100
　application of U.S. Securities Act, 98
Corporate officers
　and remuneration, 354
Cost-accounting records, 10–11
Cost analysis
　commonly used methods, 4–5
Cost behavior, 3–4
　general problem of, 4–7
　illustration of, 21–22
　multiple regression analysis of, 7–10
　regression equation, functional form of, 19–20
　requirements of, 10–18
Cost decision problems, types of
　one-time problem, 7
　recurring decision problems, 6
Cost estimation, 7
Cost function, estimation of, 329–35
Cost of production, financial commodities, 266
Cost of risk
　in lending, 304
　small loan cost function, 323–24, 325
Cost recording implications of, 10–11
　correlations among the explanatory (independent) variables, 15–17
　cost-related factors, specifications of, 12
　distribution of the nonspecified factors (disturbances), 17–18
　errors of measurement, 13–15
　number of time periods, 11
　range of observations, 12
　time period length of, 11
Cost reduction, financial intermediation, 258–59

Cost-related factors, specifications of, 12
Costs as assets, income recognition, 206
Cost saving potential, diversification of finance companies, 342
Cost variance, 18$n$23
Credit allocation, financial intermediaries, 270, 271
Creditor's legal remedies, 309
　legal restrictions on, 313, 318
Credit to consumers, decline in, 294–98
Critical event and matching, income and expense recognition of, 205–6
Currency-price hedging
　aspects of, 195–96
　evidence on, 199
　frequency distribution of disclosures, data, 198$t$
Current financial reporting requirements, FASB' proposal on revision of, 200–202
Current value accounting, 116
Customer-bank-communication-terminals, 273

Data format and type in financial disclosure, 108
Day trading, SOES, 377
　effects of, 385–87
　extent of, 382–84, 387
　growth of, 379
　hitting the monster button procedure in, 380
　impact on spreads, 373
　informed-trade losses due to, 384–87
Dealer and stakeholders' relationship, 247–48
Debt financing, 120
Define GAAP, 127, 128, 131, 135
Delinquency and collection activities, 326–27
Demand deposits
　demands for, 261
　prohibition of interest payments on, 273
Demand for Alternative Accounting Measurements (DAAM), 116–17
　criticisms of, 118
　and scale of investment operations, 129–31
　shortcomings, survey of, 117–18

of stock investment officers, 125–28
and years of experience, 131–35
Department of Justice
  investigations on NASDAQ market makers, 371, 376
Department of Trade (DT), U.K., 98, 100
Derivatives accounting
  accounting problems, 191
  application to accounting for, 209–13
  FASB's accounting approaches, scope of, 199, 201
  financial reporting of, 189–92
  future contracts, 197
  impact on firms' ability, 191
  losses related to, 189
Difference in loan loss rates, 317
Differences in scale and efficiency, effect on costs of, 340
Direct costing, in cost analysis, 4
Direct expenses per loan serviced, annual average of, 342t
Directing institutional order flow, 377
Direct placement, 119
  questionnaire, 122
  and stock investment officers' DAAM, 125–28
Disclosure and nondisclosure groups, algebraic differences, 83
Disclosure corporations
  cumulative residual of, 87f
  distributions of residuals, data, 86f
Disclosure of fair values, accounting for derivative, 199–200
Disclosure on securities market, impact on accounting profession, 184–87
  direct placements, 180
  new securities markets, 177–79
  SEC's Accounting Regulations, 180–84
Disclosure requirements, Securities Exchange Act, 66–68
  form and content, financial statements, 67
Disclosure statute, 66, 84, 93, 165, 188. See also Securities Exchange Act of 1934
Disclosure to stockholders, 108
Distributions of residuals, nondisclosure corporations, 86f
Diversification
  of finance companies, 342

of financial commodities, 268
Documentation in accounting, CPAs, 213
Double-entry bookkeeping, accounting, 227
Dynergy, 156

Economies of scale, 306, 310, 336–37, 346
  personal contact with the borrower, 306
Economies of scale hypothesis, 288
Elasticity
  computation of, 336
  economies of scale, 347
Electric, gas, and water industry, private debt placements, 184
Electronic communication network (ECN) quotes
  execution of, 376, 401
  growth of, 408
Electronic Traders Association, SOES dealers, 372–73
Emerging Issues Task Force (EITF), 192, 229
Employee Retirement Income Security Act (ERISA), 377
Energy production facilities, of Enron, 149–50
Enron and fair-value accounting
  Braveheart partnership with Blockbuster, 154–55
  broadband services of, 153–54
  cash flows, 158–60
  Dabhol, other projects, and Azurix, 151–53
  debts as price risk liability, 158
  derivatives trading, 155–56
  energy contracts, 148–49
  energy management contracts, 153
  energy production Facilities, 149–50
  "merchant" investments, 150–51
Enron Broadband Services (EBS), 153–54
Enron Capital and Trade Resources (ECT), 149
Enron Energy Services (EES) contracts
  accounting cover-ups, 153
  gas contracts, 149
  presumed profitability validation of, 161
Even-eighths tacit collusion, 378
  causes of, 376–77

Examining the accounting reports, shareholders' right of, 166
Expertise and public interest orientation, SEC, 107–8
External accountants, professional judgment of derivatives accounting, 211–12
Extractive industry, private debt placements, 182

Fair game in stock market, concept of, 93, 94
Fair-value accounting, 146
  actual market prices, number on, 147
  adoption and use of, 148–56
  and auditors' validation of, 160–62
  cash flow and net income, 158–60
  hierarchy levels in, 146
  and management compensations and expenses, 156–58
Fair-value hierarchy, 147
Fair-value measurements, FASB, 218, 237
False accounting, risks on, 219
FAS 133, 159, 219
FASB. *See* Financial Accounting Standards Board (FASB)
Federal Home Loan Bank Board, 34
Federal Trade Commission (FTC), 355
Finance and real estate industry, private debt placements, 182
Finance companies
  credit to consumers, availability of, 294–98
  decline of, 280
  impact of 36 month limitation on, 289*f*
  profitability of, 292–94
  revenue and costs, 283–94
Finance company cost function, principal policy considerations, 346–50
Financial accounting, general functions of, 203–4
Financial Accounting Standards Board (FASB), 99, 146
  accounting standards' format convergence, 218
  asset/liability approach, 218
  CPAs, scope of, 211–12
  fair-value measurements, 218
  impact of "concept-based" standards on, 222
  key features of, 193
  principles-based standard setting, 218
  as proponents of principles-based standards, 219–20
  proposed solutions, accounting for derivatives, 199
  reporting requirements of, 190
  rules-based standards, development of, 219
  standard setting strategy of, 216
Financial Accounting Standards Board (FASB) proposal, derivatives
  advantages of, 200–201
  constrains on firms in using derivatives, 202
  hedge accounting elimination of, 200–202
  scope of, 200–202
  supplementary disclosure of "fair values", 199–200
Financial accounting statement
  alternative statement for, 125–26*t*
Financial assets and liabilities
  fair price estimation, proposal to, 202–3
Financial commodities
  demand for, 260–62
  lending and borrowings, conflicts, 264–65
  market price of, 263
  production of, 263–68
  specialization of, 268
Financial commodities' production, 267
Financial data available to investors, SEC, 109
Financial disclosure
  disclosure requirements. *See* Disclosure requirements, Securities Exchange Act
  investors' relevance, 172–73
  regulatory structures of, 99
Financial disclosure mandate, in U.S. and U.K., 102
Financial disclosure regulation, cost of
  learning and following regulation, 101
  in U.S. and U.K., 101–3
Financial information disclosure, stock markets
  benefits of, 69
  CPA, role of, 70
  effectiveness of, hypotheses, 81–82

fairness, concept of, information
    disclosure, 69
financial statements, form and content
    of, 67
    marginal costs of, 68
    published financial statements, impact
        of, 71
    sales and cost of goods sold, data on, 71t
    speed and accuracy in, 72
Financial intermediation
    analysis of, basic problems, 259
    demand for commodities, 260
    forms of, 258
Financial Reporting Council, U.K., 232
    umbrella body for accounting and audit
        regulator, 232
Financial reporting of currency derivatives
    study of annual reports, 195–99
    survey of firms, 194–95
Financial statement content, accounting
    impact of true-and-fair override on, 218
Financial statements
    misleading effects of, 180
    mutual funds, performance of, 175–77
500-share maximum period, trade size,
    381, 389, 395
Five-year forecast model, 34, 47–51t
Fixed costs, definition of, 9n9
Fixed-variable method, of cost analysis,
    4–5
Footnote disclosure, for accounting
    derivatives application, 210–11
Forecasted transactions, hedging of, 201
Form 9K, for semiannual report, 172
Former borrower (FB), 337
*Fortune* 500 companies, 354n3
Fraud and misleading data in financial
    disclosure, SEC, 109
Fraud, information disclosure of, 69–72
    lack of evidence on, 70
    stock prices, manipulated information, 71

GAAP. *See* Generally accepted accounting
    principles (GAAP)
Gains and losses, offset, 202
Gaps in NASDAQ/NYSE, RES, 377
Garnishments of wages (GARR), 309, 311t,
    313, 318
Gas Bank, 149

Generally accepted accounting principles
    (GAAP), 123, 124–25, 208, 237, 238
    inclusion of a true-and-fair override in,
        recommendations, 238
    override in codification of, 228
    rules-based approach in U.S., 237
    specification of, 217
Geometrically distributed lags model, 34,
    52–54t
Government regulation, financial
    intermediaries, 269–73
    impacts on financial institutions, 270
    types of, 270, 273
Great Depression period, 66, 78, 84

Hedge accounting, elimination of, 200–202
Hedge accounting rules, and FASB, 190
    and AICPA papers, 193t
    application of, 192
    industrial classification data, 196t
    reporting requirements, criticism on,
        192–94
    restrictive nature of, 191
Hedges, derivatives as, 209–10
    matching procedure, application of, 209
    realized gains and losses on, 209
Heteroskedasticity, 18n23
Higher interest rate ceilings and higher
    losses, association between, 317
High interest, lenders and borrowers,
    maximum statutory limits on, 278
High-risk borrowers
    loans by legal lenders to, 304
    screening of, 305
Historical-cost accounting data, 204
Hitting the monster button procedure, day
    trading, 381, 386n17
Holding risk (HR), 249
Homogeneity variables, net losses, 307
Homoskedasticity, 18n23, 28, 332–33
100-share maximum period, 396, 404

Income recognition, 206
Income statement, for accounting
    derivatives application, 210
Income statement, of Enron, 156t
Individual borrowers, 302
Individual companies, residual variance
    of, 88t

Individual security and general market condition, 29–30
Inflation, impact on legal ceiling rates, 349
Informed-trade losses on market makers, 389
  500-share maximum period, 389
  100-share maximum period, 396
Informed-trade opportunity costs, on market makers, 385, 391–92t, 402
Insider risk (IR), 249, 251
Institute of Chartered Accountants in England and Wales, 108
Intangible assets, treatment of, 207
Interest rate ceiling
  coefficients of, 312
  and net losses, association between, 319
  and risk, 312–13
Interest rate ceilings, consumer finance companies, 329, 346, 349
  cost-determined regulation of, 350
  cost structure, implications of, 321
  state regulations, 321
Interest rate risk, 267
Interim reports, 33
International Accounting Standards Board (IASB)
  bold print identification of principles, 230
  fair value measurements, priority to, 224
  format of accounting standards, convergence, 218, 232
  true-and fair override use of, 236
International Financial Reporting Interpretations Committee, 230
International Financial Reporting Standards (IFRS), 218, 230, 232, 235–37
  approaches in U.S. and U.K., 235
  limitations on true-and-fair overrides, 232, 236
International Telephone & Telegraph Corporation (ITT), 353
Intertemporal consumption, and transaction cost, 260–61
Interview approach, for accounting data, 24–25
Intratemporal consumption, and transactions cost, 261–62
Inventory amount, and transfer of shares, 246

Inventory carrying costs, 246–47
Investigations on NASDAQ market makers, 371, 376
Investment analyst firms, function of, 166
Investment subsidiaries, of Enron, 160
Investment type and experience, 137
Investment-type independent variable, 136
Investors, trading information, 221
Investors and speculators, information and rational decision of, 72–73
  financial data users, returns to, 77–78
  financial statements and prices, 73–77
Investors' confidence in the market, 90–93
Investors' legal actions against public accountants, 169–70
Investors of financial statements, to SEC requirements, 172–73
  performance of mutual funds, 175–77
  reported financial accounting data ad stock prices, 173–75

Jensen's inequality, 359n12

Landell v. Lybrand, 70
Large loans (LL/NLM)
  coefficients of, 337–38
  operating cost of, 348
Lawsuits risks, on false accounting, 219
Lenders and borrowers, 277
  borrowing control and consumer welfare, 277–79
  financial company, revenue and costs of, 283–84
  limiting small loan maturities, 279–83
  maturity regulation on high interest rate, impact of, 277
Lending and borrowing, financial commodities
  conflict of interests, 264–65
  information costs, specialized expertise, 266
Length of time in borrowing, legal restrictions on, 301
Level 3 fair-value accounting, of Enron, 148
License restrictions, finance companies, 322, 347
Licensing, financial intermediaries, 270, 273

Life insurance company investment officers
  comparison group, 120–21
  nonpublic information, availability, use, and cost of, 119–20
  questionnaire for, 123–24
  size and sophistication, 118–19
Life insurance corporation
  development study of, 121–22
  inference of, 142–44
  limitations of study, 144
Limited liability companies, requirements of, 98
Listed companies, stock exchanges disclosure requirements of, 79
Loan
  demands for, 262
  operating costs per dollar, 345–46, 346t
Loan collection practices, legal restrictions on, 305
Loan losses
  and loan serviced, association between, 315–18
  and operating expenses, 314–15
  and size of loans made, 313–14
Loan portfolio, riskiness of, 324n8
Loans, lending and borrowing
  amount of, 278
  length of time for, 278
  restrictions on, 277
Loan size and interest rate ceilings, inverse relationship of, 322–23
Location (SUBURB), operating costs, 339
London Stock Exchange
  advantages of, 106
  authority of, 100
  interest orientations of, 107
  risk reduction aspect, 113
Long-term borrowers
  characteristics of, 299–300
  relationship with bankruptcy, 298–301
Long-term indebtedness
  bankruptcy, 300, 301t
  impact on finance companies, 303
Losses, related to derivatives, 189
Loss leaders
  and finance companies, 349
  and loans, 284
"Loss" loan, 322n4

Loss or gain in transaction, NASDAQ and NYSE trading, 387, 388, 388f

Machine hours, 16, 16n22
Maine Bank Commissioner, 285
Making and securing small loans
  cost of, 323
  elements of, 323–24
Management compensation, in Enron, 156–58
Manager controlled company, 357
Mandated disclosure and hedge accounting issues, 192–94
Mandatory-SOES periods
  classifications in, 395
  impact on NASDAQ spreads, 408
Manipulation
  disclosure of, 69–72
  by managers, derivatives accounting, 211–12
Manning court rulings, public limit orders, priority of, 376
Manufacturing industry, private debt placements, 182
Mariner Energy, Houston, 151
Market factor variables, coefficients of, 340
Market factors and laws, 327
Market index, dispersion of, 80
Market makers
  blue-ribbon committee of, 379, 408
  financial intermediation, 259
  informed-trade opportunity costs, 385
  role in NASDAQ spreads, 372
  SOES day trading, 379
"Market" model, 250
Market price data, 35
Market price of stock
  and accounting data, 30–33
Market prices, 120, 147
Market risk, regression results, 252t
Market values, embedded derivatives of, 201
Mark-to-fair-value accounting, of Enron, 149, 158
Martingale hypothesis, in stock market, 92
Mature mandatory SOES period, 395
  mandatory-SOES period, day trades on, 395
  RES, growth of, 400

## INDEX

Maturity limitation on loans, 288–91
  impact on normal operations, 289f
Maturity regulation on high interest rate, impact of, 277
Maximum trade size reduction, 394
Merchant investments, of Enron, 150–51
Merger diversification of, 357–58
Merger-for-the-benefit-of-managers (but not shareholders) version, 354
Merger prone conglomerates, 366
Mergers
  activity of, 352–53
  conglomerate mergers, 353
Misrepresentation and fraud, accounting, 167–68, 170
  corporate financial statements, 167
*Moody's Manuals*
  New York Stock Exchange (NYSE), trading statements, 171t
  stockholders' statistics, 249
Multiple regression analysis of, 3–4, 7–10
  contributive factors and costs, 8
  objection to, 3
  requirements of, 10–11
Multiple regression, in cost-causing factor, 5–6
  applicability, 6
  criticisms of, 5
Multivariate analysis, for alternative financial accounting measurement, 136–42
Mutual funds and securities, comparative study, 77–78
Mutual funds' performance, analysis of, 175–77, 187

NASDAQ SelectNet system, day trading, 382
NASDAQ spreads, 371, 386
  documentation on, 371
  investigations on, 371
  market makers' role in, 372
NASDAQ stocks
  impact of SOES day trading on, 382, 397f, 398f
  informed trade gains and losses for, 390–94
  nature of, 374
  RES of, 375, 397f, 398f, 406f, 407

National Consumer Finance Association (NCFA), 307
National Stock Summary, 249, 251
"Net income" constructs, 39
Net losses, 307n8
  function of the operations, finance companies, 307
  per loan and per dollar of loan, 313–14, 314t
Net losses per dollar of loan and loan size, association between, 318
Net operating income, reported financial accounting data, 173
Net sales, reported financial accounting data, 173
Net securities issues, as percentage of expenditures, 179f
New borrower, 337
New securities market, impact of disclosure, 177–79
  redemption, new security issues net of, 178t
New versus present customers, cost of lending, 291
New York Stock Exchange (NYSE), 35, 68, 245
  delisting of Corporations, gross income disclosure, 90
  liquidity, informed trade gains and losses for, 390
  listings of, 89
  quarterly reporting requirements in, 74
  riskiness and stock price changes on, 94
No forecast model, 34, 40–41t, 41–42t
Nonconstant variance, 18n23
Nondisclosure corporations, cumulative residual of, 87f
Nonpayment of loan, 283
Nonpersonal loan activities, 327
Nonrepayment of loans, 304, 306
Nonspecified factors (disturbances), distribution of, 17–18
  independence from explanatory variables, 17–18
  normal distribution of the disturbances, 15–16
  serial correlation of the disturbances, 17
  variance of the disturbances, 15
Number of loans made (NLM)

coefficients of, 330, 331
new borrower, coefficients, 337
Number of loans serviced (NLS), 311, 338n40
NYSE. *See* New York Stock Exchange (NYSE)

Objectives-oriented standards, accounting, 221
  characteristics of, 221–22
  SEC reports of, 222–23, 228
Operating cost analysis, 285–87
Operating cost of lending
  impact on finance companies, 302
  new versus present customers, 291
  small loans, 286, 288t
Operating costs, 326
Operations costs
  analysis of, 325–27
  customer type, 326
  sales finance contracts (SC/NLS), 338
  small loan cost function, 323–24, 325
Opportunity cost of lending funds, small loan cost function, 323–24
Order Handling Rules (OHR)
  public display of limit orders, 376
  SEC mandate, 376, 381–82
Order handling rules period, 395, 404
Output measurement of, consumer finance companies, 329, 332t
Output variable, coefficients in economies of scale (elasticity), 336
Overcapitalization, 168
Overhead expenses
  of Enron, 157
  of finance companies, 342–45
  functional relationships, various forms of, 343, 344t, 345t
Over-the-counter market (OTC), 202, 245

Partial regression coefficient, and annual accounting data, 55
Patterns for trades, 389
Percentage of even-eighths, 402–4
Perfect market, financial intermediation, 259–60
Periodic reporting process, in U.S. and UK, 101
Personal bankruptcies filed in Maine, 300

Phantom equity, compensation of, 149
Policy Implications, finance company cost function, 346–50
Portfolio risk, stock market corporations, 82t
Portfolio size, 137–39
Post-SEC period
  flow of new issues, 179
  information disclosure of, 94
  observations on regressions, 80
Preferencing and payment-for-order-flow hypothesis
  NASDAQ spreads, 377, 402, 407
Pre–Great Depression period, business abuses, 93
Pre-Mandatory SOES period
  informed trade losses in, 389, 394
  ordering RES, 400
Pre-SEC period
  corporate financial disclosure in, 170–72
  disclosure firms, outlier percentage of, 91
  fraud in financial reporting, evidence on, 187
  regressions, observations on, 80
  suit against public accountants in, 169
Present borrower, 337
Pretax loss booking, in EBS, 154
Prevention of fraud and misleading data, 109–11
Previous ratio forecast model, 34
Price control, financial intermediaries, 270
Pricing, of financial commodities and services, 269
Principal stock exchanges, 78–79
Principles-based accounting standards
  case for, 219–22
  concept-oriented standard, 222
  object-oriented standards, 221–22
  proponents of, 219–20
  in U.K., 232–35
Private debt placements, 182
Private placement market rankings, corporate debt
  direct debt placements, data on, 183t
  ratios of, 181–84
Private regulatory agency, U.K., 104
Proclivity to repay loans, 313

Production, of financial commodities
  costs of, 265–67
    general considerations for, 263–65
    labor and capital goods in, 265
    specialization and diversification in, 267–68
Professional accountancy bodies, U.K., 100
Professional experience and DAAM, 131–35
Professional expertise, in financial
    disclosure, 107–8
Professional judgment, of public
    accountants, 214
Public accountants' independence, SEC
    definition of, 186
Public Company Accounting Oversight
    Board, 217
"Public good" nature of accounting
    information, 117
Public offering, 120
Published accounting data
  cash dividends, 26
  empirical method, 25
  method of investigation, 24–26
  model description, 27
Published financial data, information
    disclosure
  economic situation of corporations,
    reflection on, 77
  financial variables, definition of, 75
  information content of, 73–77
  investors' expectations, impact on, 74
  models used for reporting, 74
  returns to sophisticated users of, 77–78
  usefulness of, 77, 93

Quality
  of the financial data, SEC
  of output, 326
Questionnaire, for life insurance company
    investment officers, 123–24
Questionnaire approach, for accounting
    data, 24–25

Railroads industry, private debt
    placements, 184
Rate ceiling and the loss rate, association
    between, 317
Rate ceilings, interest, 329, 346, 349
Real estate investment trust companies, 267
Realization, accounting concept, 208

Reduction in lending, effect of, 294–96
  analysis on, 294$n$15
Reduction of revenue, gross interest yields,
    284
Regression, computation of, 16–17, 21–22
Regression coefficients
  computations of, 332–33, 332$t$, 334$t$
  total operating expenses, 287$t$
Regression equation, functional form of,
    19–20
Relative Effective Spreads (RES), 374$f$
  changes in price levels, stock trading, 374
  effect of SOES day trades on, 396–402
  impact of brake-light effect on, 376
  measurement of, 396–97
  of NASDAQ and NYSE, 375
  on NYSE stocks, 375, 397
  RES difference, 404
  shock to, 374$f$
Relative input factor prices, 327
Remuneration, 358
Reported financial accounting data
  and stock prices, 173–75, 173$n$24
  usefulness to investors, evaluation of, 174
Reported income, SEC reports
  relevance to investors, 172–73, 174
Reports, financial accounting of
    derivatives, 214
Required disclosure, hypotheses about
  avoided disclosure, 81
  in benefits, 81–82
  imposing cost, 81
  not disclosing of, 81
  not imposing sufficient cost, 82
Residual market prices, in stock market,
    86, 92
Restrictions in licensing, financial
    intermediaries, 273
Restrictions on entry, impact on loan
    losses, 312
Restrictions on finance companies, state
    legislations, role of, 350
Return on security and market,
    relationship of, 250
Revenue and costs from small loans,
    283–84
Risk
  measures of, 251
  and spread, relationship of, 249

Risk, derivatives
  accounting for, 213
  hedges, scope of, 214
Riskiness of securities, impact of SEC on, 94
Risks and higher interest rate ceilings, association between, 318
Rules-based approach, U.S. accounting standards, 216, 217
  reasons for, 219
  criticism on, 220
Rules versus principles debate, accounting standards, 218

Safe harbor provisions
  of Employee Retirement Income Security Act (ERISA), 377
Safe harbor, accounting practices, 211
Sales finance contracts (SC/NLS), 338
Sarbanes-Oxley Act of 2002, 162, 217
SAS 57, 161
SAS 69, amendment to, 216, 217n3
Scale hypothesis, economies of, 287–88
Scale of investment operations
  and DAAM, relationship of, 129–31
Scale of operation, differences in operating costs per loan serviced, 340
Securities Act of 1933, 97, 119, 165
  corporate financial disclosure, 170–72
  corporate financial statements, misinterpretations and fraudulence in, 167–68
  investors' legal action against public accountants, 169–70
Securities and Exchange Commission (SEC), 97, 112, 189
  accountants' liabilities in reporting data, 109
  adaptability of, 104
  complexity of, impact, 108
  and Enron, 149
  financial disclosure mandate, 97
  function of, 114
  funding for, 112
  investigations on NASDAQ market makers, 371, 376
  public interest orientation of, 107
  registration of, 120
  regulatory responsibilities of, 99–100, 105
  securities statutes, application of, 106
Securities and Exchange Commission (SEC), 2003 reports, 217
  conclusions and suggestions on, 237–39
  investigation on Enron, 217n5
  on objectives-oriented standards, 222–23
  as proponents of principles-based standards, 219–20
  Section 108(d), instructions to SEC, 217
Securities Exchange Act of 1934, 66, 97, 165
  disclosure requirements of, 67–68
  fraudulence and manipulation of, 69–72
  investors and speculators, rational decisions of, 72–78
  investors' confidence in market, 90–93
  losses by stockholders, 89–90
  on NYSE securities, 78–89
  rationale underlying legislation of, 68–69
  reason for enactment of, 90
Securities Exchange Act, Section 28E, relaxation of
  directing institutional order flow, impact on, 377
Securities fraud, stock markets in U.S., 110
Securities statutes and regulation, SEC
  application of, less discriminatory aspect, 106
  professional implementation of, 105
Securities statutes and regulations, professional implementation of, 105–6
Securities, dependent and independent variables distribution of, 252t
Security prices, rate of change of, 29
Self-serving management hypothesis
  findings of, 360–66
  implications for, 366–67
  managerial motivations of, 352–53
  merger-for-the-benefit-of-managers (but not shareholders) version, 354
  refutations of, 353–55
  support for, 355–56
  test for, 356–60
Shareholders' interest, and managerial motivations of, 352–53
Share holdings, change in value of, 359

Sharpe Markowitz market model, 94
Short-term borrowers
　characteristics of, 299–300
　relationship with bankruptcy, 298–301
Size of trade, by RES, 397–400
Smaller CPA firms. impact on SEC, 186
Small investors, under SEC, 111
Small loan companies, period of indebtedness to, 277
Small loan cost function, 323
Small loan laws, 304
Small loan maturities, 36 month limitations, 284
　effect of, 284–85
　finance companies, profitability of, 302
　opponents of, 281–82
　proponents of, 279–81, 282
　reason for enactment of, 300
Small loan maturities, limitations of
　conditions obtaining before and after, 279
　opponents' hypotheses, 281–82
　proponents' hypotheses, 279–81
Small Order Execution System (SOES) day trading
　changes in, 372
　description of, 378–82
　development period, classifications, 382
　effects of, 396–402
　extent of, 382–84
　history of, 378–82
　hypothesis in, 372
　impact on NASDAQ spreads, 386
　informed-trade losses 384–87
　maximum percentage, 404
　small traders in, 407
SOES banditry, 373, 376, 386n17, 407–8
　impact on small traders and fund holders, 407, 408
　NASDAQ spreads by, 372
"Sophisticated" investors, 117
Sources of fund, 267
　survey on individuals, 296–98
Specialized expertise, lending and borrowing, 266
Spread and explanatory variables, empirical findings of, 252–54
Spreads on NASDAQ and NYSE, 372, 374f
　adjustment for NASDAQ informed trades, 394–96
　comparison of NASDAQ with NYSE, 390–94
　comparison with percentage of even-eighths, 402–4
　informed losses of day trading, 384–87
　point opportunity, losses or gain, 387–90
　reasons for differences in, 371–78, 407–8
　robustness checks, 404–6
　SOES day trading, effects of, 396–402
　SOES day trading, extent of, 382–84
　SOES description and day trading, 378–82
Standard economic theory
　specification of variables, 248–49
　variables of, 248
Standard Securities Corporation, 35
Standard setters in accounting, 219
State laws on consumer finance company
　effects of, 305
　on creditor's legal remedies, 309
　usury laws, 305
Statement of Financial Accounting Standards (SFAS), 146
　derivative disclosure issues, 190
　*Fair-Value Measurements*, 146, 147
　reporting requirements, criticism on, 192–94
　SFAS 19, 203
　SFAS 52, 190, 192, 193t, 197, 209
　SFAS 80, 192, 193t
　SFAS 114, 199n7
　SFAS 115, 207, 208
　SFAS 119, 190, 199, 210
Statement of Principles for Financial Reporting
　about Accounting Standards Board's conceptual framework, 232
State regulations on interest rates, 321, 322
　license restrictions, finance companies, 322, 350
State usury laws and entry restrictions, 309
Stockholders, losses by, 89–90
Stockholders' rights
　examining the accounting reports, 166
　filing suit against public accountants, ability of, 169, 188
Stock options
　calculation of, 357n8
　change in value of, 359

Stock ownership, 367
Stock total, 360*n*14
Stock versus mutual investment breakdown of respondents, 123*t*
Straight bankruptcy variable, 313
Sufficient information, accounting disclosure requirements, SEC
 implication of, 166
 relevance to investors, 172–73, 174, 177, 187
Supervision, financial intermediaries
 government regulations on, 270, 272
 impact on transaction cost, 272–73
 types of, 272
Supplement GAAP, 127, 128, 131*n*21, 135
Systematic risk (SR), 251

Three-year forecast model, 34, 46–47*t*
Thrift institutions, bankruptcy, 267
Time frame for reporting
 forms, semiannual financial reports, 172
Total asset size, 136
Total change, of average conglomerate Officer-director, 364*t*
Trading and investment, derivatives, 208
 current-value accounting, importance of, 208
 fair value pricing in, 209
Trading inside the spread, 400–401, 402
Traditional revenue/expense model, accounting, 218
 content and format of, 226–28
 description of, 226
 reason for preference of, 238
Transactions cost
 and demand for financial commodities, 262–63
 and intertemporal consumption, 260–61
 and intratemporal consumption, 261–62
Transactions cost approach, financial intermediation, 257
 demand for, 259–60
 government regulation of, 269–74
 pricing of financial commodities and services, 269
 production of, 263–65
True-and-fair override, 228–31
 approach of IFRS on, 235–37

 content and format of, 228–31
 independent auditors' responsibility in, 238
 professional responsibility for accountants in, 218
 about SEC Reports' rejection of, 228
 standard setting strategy, 216
 U.K. experience with, 231–35
 use of, 218
Type of borrower, 337, 348
Type of consumer served, 326

U.K. accounting standards, 232–35
U.K. Companies Acts, 1948, 97
 disclosure requirements under, 97
 regulatory responsibilities of, 99
U.K. Companies Acts, 1967, 97
U.K. experience, with true-and-fair override, 231–35
U.K. Financial Reporting Standard (FRS), 231
*Ultramares Corp. v. Touche, Niven and Co.*, 70
Underwriting, in debt financing, 120
Unexpected financial accounting data, reporting, 174
Uniform Consumer Credit Code (UCCC), 322
Uniform small loan law, 322
Unit banking, 273
Unprofitable loans, of finance companies, 290
Unsystematic risk (UR), 250, 251
 coefficient of, 254
 regression results, 253*t*
Urgent Issues Task Force in U.K., 232
U.S. accounting standards, 216
 asset and liability accounting model, 223–26
 contents and format of, 222–23
 international financial reporting standard, 235–37
 principles-based standard, case for, 219–22
 reasons for rules-based, 219
 revenue/expense approach, 226–28
 rules-based approach, 216
 true-and-fair override, 228–35
U.S. disclosure regulations, 101

U.S. Federal Securities Acts, 97–98
U.S. GAAP. *See* Generally accepted accounting principles (GAAP)
U.S. Public Companies Accounting Oversight Board, 239

Usury ceiling rates, interest, 304, 305
Usury laws, 270, 305, 309, 312*n*15, 321

Watered stock, 168
Watergate revelations, impact on SEC, 99